Hallesche Schriften zur Betriebswirtschaft

Band 37

Diese Schriftenreihe soll als Forum für wissenschaftliche Arbeiten der neugegründeten und 1993 wiedereröffneten Wirtschaftswissenschaftlichen Fakultät der Martin-Luther-Universität Halle-Wittenberg auf dem Gebiet der Betriebswirtschaftslehre dienen. Die zahlreichen betriebswirtschaftlichen Professuren wollen mit der Herausgabe dieser Halleschen Schriften zur Betriebswirtschaft das breite Spektrum ihrer wissenschaftlichen Arbeitsgebiete dokumentieren. Die Publikationen umfassen insbesondere betriebswirtschaftliche Dissertationen und sonstige ausgewählte wissenschaftliche Arbeiten der Halleschen Fakultätsmitglieder.

Weitere Bände in der Reihe http://www.springer.com/series/12217

Sven Hentschel

The Taxation of Permanent Establishments

A Critical Analysis of the Authorised OECD Approach and Its Implementation in German Tax Law under Specific Consideration of the Challenges Imposed to the PE Concept by the Digitalisation of the Economy

Springer Gabler

Sven Hentschel
Martin-Luther-University Halle-Wittenberg
Halle (Saale), Germany

Dissertation, Martin-Luther-University Halle-Wittenberg, 2020

ISSN 2628-2100 ISSN 2628-2119 (electronic)
Hallesche Schriften zur Betriebswirtschaft
ISBN 978-3-658-33999-9 ISBN 978-3-658-34000-1 (eBook)
https://doi.org/10.1007/978-3-658-34000-1

Responsible Editor: Marija Kojic
This Springer Gabler imprint is published by the registered company Springer Fachmedien Wiesbaden GmbH part of Springer Nature.
The registered company address is: Abraham-Lincoln-Str. 46, 65189 Wiesbaden, Germany

Foreword

The rules governing the taxation of Permanent Establishments (PE) date back to the early days of tax treaties—a time where businesses were organised locally in close reach to their customers. Although the PE rules are a fundamental part of the existing international tax system they are beset by a multitude of conceptual difficulties and practical problems increasingly giving rise to disputes. Against this backdrop, the OECD carried out intensive work throughout the past decades to address some of the core issues. The implementation of the Authorised OECD Approach (AOA) in Article 7 OECD Model Tax Convention in 2010, which brought the taxation of PEs closer in line with the taxation of subsidiaries, can certainly be regarded as a significant achievement. Other significant changes to the PE rules resulted from the OECD/G20's Base Erosion and Profit Shifting (BEPS) Project. Especially, BEPS Action 7, focusing on the prevention of the artificial avoidance of the PE status, and BEPS Actions 8–10, focusing on the alignment of transfer pricing outcomes with value creation, can be regarded as substantial milestones in this context. Another set of challenges to the PE rules, which have historically been built on the notion of a 'brick and mortar' economy, arises from the ongoing digitalisation of the economy. Possible reform proposals to address these challenges are currently discussed under Pillar One as part of Action 1 of the OECD/G20's BEPS project.

The doctoral thesis of Dr. Sven Hentschel has analysed the current rules governing the taxation of PEs under specific consideration of the challenges imposed to these rules by the digitalisation of the economy. To do so, Dr. Hentschel followed a two-step approach. In the first step, the current rules governing the taxation of PEs, as implemented in the OECD Model Tax Convention and German domestic tax law, were analysed and deviations between the approaches were identified. Furthermore, changes influencing the rules as a result of the BEPS Project were outlined and analysed. In a second step, the focus was shifted to the digitalisation of the economy and its impact on the PE rules. The special merit of this part consists in the assessment of the Pillar One reform proposal of the OECD/G20 Inclusive Framework on BEPS which was assessed against overarching tax principles that have traditionally guided the development of taxation systems. Moreover, recommendations for further work on Pillar One are provided by Dr. Hentschel.

The doctoral thesis of Dr. Sven Hentschel is a diversified and highly innovative work that meets both methodical as well as tax law requirements. His primary academic achievement is the examination of a highly complex area of international taxation in its ramifications, to point out regulatory deficits and to provide valuable recommendations to further develop the international corporate tax system. Against this background, Mr. Hentschel's doctoral thesis is a major contribution that is not only of particular relevance for international research in this field, but also for tax practitioners and national governments as well as supranational organisations dealing with this issue. Therefore, I strongly recommend the doctoral thesis of Dr. Sven Hentschel to this audience.

Halle (Saale) Prof. Dr. Gerhard Kraft
March 2021

Acknowledgements

This doctoral thesis was written while I was working at the Chair of Business Taxation led by Prof. Dr. Gerhard Kraft at the Martin-Luther-University Halle-Wittenberg. It was accepted by the Faculty of Law, Economics and Business of the Martin-Luther-University Halle-Wittenberg in 2020. The print version of this thesis was updated to the legal status of March 2021.

It is my sincere pleasure to thank all those who supported me during the preparation of this doctoral thesis. First and foremost, I am indebted to my thesis supervisor, Prof. Dr. Gerhard Kraft, whose inspiring lectures not only sparked my interest in international taxation, but who also actively encouraged me to join his chair and pursue my academic path. His professional guidance, constant support and the trust he put in me enabled me to pursue my research interests in the best possible way. I owe him my deep gratitude for being my academic as well as personal mentor. Moreover, I wish to thank Prof. Dr. Dr. h.c. Ralf Michael Ebeling for providing the second assessment of my doctoral thesis and Prof. Dr. Claudia Becker, Prof. Dr. Christian Bierwirth and Prof. Dr. Wolf-Heimo Grieben for their participation in the examination committee.

I sincerely thank my current and former colleagues at the chair Katja Poley, Uta Preil, Christin Haberkorn, Prof. Dr. Diana Beck and Prof. Dr. Till Moser for their constant support and the excellent research atmosphere and team spirit we shared. Furthermore, I would like to thank Gary Rüsch, Dr. Christian Heider, Dr. Marcel Herbort, Prof. Dr. Daniela Hess and Prof. Dr. Martin Dombrowski not only for the many fruitful and pleasant conversations we had throughout our research time, but also for the enjoyable moments we were able to share at various seminars and conferences.

Finally and most importantly, I wish to thank the most important people in my life, my parents Petra Hentschel and Helfried Hentschel as well as my brother René Hentschel for their constant and incredible support, encouragement and unconditional love. Words cannot express how grateful I am for everything they have done for me. I proudly dedicate this doctoral thesis to them.

Halle (Saale) Sven Hentschel
March 2021

Contents

Abbreviations

AICPA	Association of International Certified Professional Accountants
AmtshilfeRLUmsG	Amtshilferichtlinie-Umsetzungsgesetz (Mutual Assistance Directive Implementation Act)
AOA	Authorised OECD Approach
Art.	Article
BB	Betriebs-Berater (periodical, Germany)
BEAT	Base Erosion and Anti-Abuse Tax
BEPS	Base Erosion and Profit Shifting
BFH	Bundesfinanzhof (German Federal Tax Court)
BFHE	Amtliche Sammlung der Entscheidungen des Bundesfinanzhofs (rulings of the German Federal Tax Court, an official compendium)
BFH/NV	Sammlung amtlich nicht veröffentlichter Entscheidungen des Bundesfinanzhofs (periodical, compendium of rulings of the German Federal Tax Court not published officially)
BFuP	Betriebswirtschaftliche Forschung und Praxis (periodical, Germany)
BGBl.	Bundesgesetzblatt (German Federal Law Gazette)
BGH	Bundesgerichtshof (German Federal Court)
BIFD	Bulletin for International Fiscal Documentation (periodical, Netherlands)
BIT	Bulletin for International Taxation (periodical, Netherlands)
BMF	Bundesministerium der Finanzen (Federal Ministry of Finance)

BR-Drucks.	Bundesrats-Drucksachen (Gazette of the German Bundesrat, an unofficial compendium)
BsGaV	Betriebsstättengewinnaufteilungsverordnung (Ordinance on the Allocation of Profits of Permanent Establishments)
BStBl.	Bundessteuerblatt (German Federal Tax Gazette)
BVerfG	Bundesverfassungsgericht (German Federal Constitutional Court)
CbC	Country-by-Country
CFC	Controlled Foreign Company
CITA	Corporate Income Tax Act
CCCTB	Common Consolidated Corporate Tax Base
Comm.	Commentary
CP	Content Provider
CTA	Covered Tax Agreement
CTJ	Canadian Tax Journal (periodical, Canada)
CUP	comparable uncontrolled price
DB	Der Betrieb (periodical, Germany)
DE	Deutsch (German)
DEMPE	development, enhancement, maintenance, protection and exploitation
DLJ	Duke Law Journal (periodical, US)
DPT	Diverted Profit Tax
DStZ	Deutsche Steuer-Zeitung (periodical, Germany)
DTA	Double Tax Agreement
EBIT	Earnings Before Interest and Taxes
EBITDA	Earnings Before Interest, Taxes, Depreciation and Amortisation
EC	European Commission
ECJ	European Court of Justice
e-commerce	electronic commerce
Ed.	Editor
Edn.	Edition
Eds.	Editors
e.g.	for example
EGAO	Einführungsgesetz zur Abgabenordnung (Introductory Act to the German Fiscal Code)
EN	English
ET	European Taxation (periodical, Netherlands)
ETRA	External Tax Relations Act

EU	European Union
EU TPD	European Union Transfer Pricing Documentation
FA	FinanzArchiv (periodical, Germany)
FCG	Fiscal Code of Germany
FCTO	Federal Central Tax Office
F/W/B/S	Flick/Wassermeyer/Baumhoff/Schönfeld
FR	FinanzRundschau (periodical, Germany)
FTR	Florida Tax Review (periodical, US)
GAAP	Generally Accepted Accounting Principles
GAufzV	Ordinance on the Documentation of Profit Allocations
GBL	German Basic Law
GCC	German Commercial Code
GFC	German Fiscal Code
GloBE	Global Anti-Base Erosion
GILTI	Global Intangible Low-Taxed Income
GST	Goods and Services Tax
HBR	Harvard Business Review
H/K/G/R	Haun/Kahle/Goebel/Reiser
i.a.	inter alia
i.e.	id est
ICT	Information and Communication Technology
IFA	International Fiscal Association
IFRS	International Financial Reporting Standards
IFST	Institut Finanzen und Steuern
ISP	Internet Service Provider
ISR	Internationale SteuerRundschau (periodical, Germany)
IStR	Internationales Steuerrecht (periodical, Germany)
ITA	Income Tax Act
ITJ	International Tax Journal (periodical, US)
ITPJ	International Transfer Pricing Journal (periodical, Netherlands)
IWB	Internationale Wirtschafts-Briefe (periodical, Germany)
JbFSt	Jahrbuch der Fachanwälte für Steuerrecht
lit.	letter
LPIB	Law and Politics in International Business (periodical, US)
MCAA	Multilateral Competent Authority Agreement
MLI	Multilateral Instrument
no./nos.	number(s)
NTJ	National Tax Journal (periodical, US)

NWB	Neue Wirtschafts-Briefe
OECD	Organization for Economic Co-operation and Development
OECD MC	OECD Model Tax Convention
OECD MC Comm	OECD Commentary on the OECD Model Tax Convention
OFD	Oberfinanzdirektion (Regional Tax Office)
p./pp.	page(s)
para./paras.	paragraph(s)
PBT	Profit Before Tax
PE	Permanent Establishment
PF	Public Finance Public Finance (periodical, US)
PIStB	Praxis Internationale Steuerberatung (periodical, Germany)
PSM	Profit Split Method
R&D	Research&Development
RIW	Recht der Internationalen Wirtschaft (periodical, Germany)
Sec	Section
SCA	Stock Corporation Act
SMJ	Strategic Management Journal
StB	Der Steuerberater (periodical, Germany)
StuB	Steuern und Bilanzen (periodical, Germany)
StuW	Steuer und Wirtschaft (periodical, Germany)
SWI	Steuer und Wirtschaft International (law review, Austria)
TFDE	Task Force on the Digital Economy
TLR	Tax Law Review (periodical, US)
TNI	Tax Notes International (periodical, US)
TNTF	Tax Notes Today Federal (periodical, US)
TNMM	Transactional net margin method
TP Guidelines	Transfer Pricing Guidelines for Multinational Enterprises and Tax Administrations
TPI	Transfer Pricing International
TPITP	Tax Planning International Transfer Pricing
TPSM	Transactional Profit Split Method
TTA	Trade Tax Act
UN	United Nations
UN MC	United Nations Model Tax Convention
UPE	Ultimate Parent Entity
VAT	Value Added Tax
VCLT	Vienna Convention on the Law of Treaties
vol.	volume
vs.	versus

VWG BsGa	Verwaltungsgrundsätze Betriebsstättengewinnaufteilung (Administrative Principles on the Allocation of Profits of Permanent Establishments)
W/A/D	Wassermeyer/Andresen/Ditz
W/K/S/D	Wassermeyer/Kaeser/Schwenke/Drüen
WiSt	Wirtschaftswissenschaftliches Studium (periodical, Germany)
WTJ	World Tax Journal (periodical, Netherlands)
ZEW	Zentrum für Europäische Wirtschaftsforschung GmbH

List of Figures

A. Introduction

C. Fundamentals of the Taxation of Permanent Establishments

D. The Attribution of Profits to Permanent Establishments

E. Digitalisation of the Economy and Its Implications for the PE Concept

F. Adapting the International Corporate Tax System to the Digitalisation of the Economy

List of Tables

E. Digitalisation of the Economy and Its Implications for the PE Concept

F. Adapting the International Corporate Tax System to the Digitalisation of the Economy

Annex

A. Introduction

I. Context

Where an enterprise carries out business activities beyond a purely domestic setting, potentially more than one jurisdiction may have a legitimate claim to tax the profits derived from those activities. Taking fiscal sovereignty as a given, it emerges to be a crucial and perhaps one of the most important elements of the international tax system that all legitimate participating jurisdictions are entitled to claim their fair share of taxable income from cross-border business activities.[1] Put another way, fair conditions must be determined, under which the respective jurisdictions have a right of taxation.[2] In this context, it is desirable that effective and internationally accepted jurisdictional rules are established, not only to prevent an overlapping of tax jurisdiction with possible harmful effects on inter-nation equity and tax neutrality,[3] but also to prevent enterprises from base erosion and profit shifting (hereinafter: BEPS), e.g. through discretionary transfer pricing activities.[4]

Since the early days of tax treaties, there has been a general consensus that business profits derived by an enterprise are taxable solely by the country of residence (i.e. the country where the corporate headquarter is physically located), unless the enterprise is considered to have a sufficient level of economic activity

[1] Cf. *Richman*, Taxation of Foreign Investment Income, 15; *Graetz/Hear*, DLJ 1997, 1021 (1033); *Jacobs/Spengel/Schäfer*, Intertax 2004, 268 (270).

[2] Cf. *Bird*, Shaping a New International Tax Order, BIFD 1988, 292 (297).

[3] Cf. detailed on the tax principles of inter-nation equity and tax neutrality chapter B.II.2 and chapter B.III of this thesis.

[4] Cf. *Musgrave*, Public Finance 1972, 394 (395 et seq.).

S. Hentschel, *The Taxation of Permanent Establishments*, Hallesche Schriften zur Betriebswirtschaft 37, https://doi.org/10.1007/978-3-658-34000-1_1

in the country of source (i.e. the country where the business activities take place) to justify taxation in that country.[5] This sufficient level of economic activity is also referred to as the 'nexus' rule, which is met if the non-resident enterprise operates in the source country through a permanent establishment (hereinafter: PE) that can broadly be described as a fixed place of business.[6] In other words, the source country can in principle only tax profits of a non-resident enterprise if that enterprise carries on business activities in the source country through a PE, but only those profits which are attributable to the PE.[7]

The internationally agreed rule underlying profit allocation to a PE is the arm's length principle as implemented in Article 7 of the OECD Model Tax Convention (hereinafter: OECD MC).[8] Historical practice has developed a number of alternative approaches with regard to the interpretation of this Article, which has created substantial problems of double taxation and double non-taxation.[9] These approaches can generally be grouped into the 'Relevant Business Activity' approach and the 'Functionally Separate Entity' approach.[10] The lack of a common interpretation has led the Committee on Fiscal Affairs to work on a more consistent interpretation and application of the rules implemented in Article 7 OECD MC.[11] As a result of that work, the 'Functionally Separate Entity' approach was adopted

[5]Cf. *Ditz*, in: Schönfeld/Ditz (Eds.), DBA-Kommentar, Art. 7 (2008), para. 2. Critical regarding the source and residence concept under the conditions of modern global economies cf. *Schön*, WTJ 2009, 67 (67 et seqq.).

[6]For an overview of the history of the PE concept see *Skaar*, Permanent Establishment—Erosion of a Tax Treaty Principle, 75 et seqq. as well as chapter C.I. of this thesis. For the definition of the term PE as implemented in Article 5 OECD MC see chapter C.IV of this thesis.

[7]Apart from this general attribution rule, certain categories of business profits may be subject to taxation in the source country even in the absence of a PE established in the source country, e.g. income derived from immovable property (Article 6 OECD MC) and the respective capital gains derived from the sale of immovable property (Article 13 OECD MC). Separate distribution rules also apply for dividends (Article 10), interests (Article 11 OECD MC) and royalties (Article 12 OECD MC) that may be subject to withholding tax in the source country even if no PE is established it that country.

[8]This rule is also implemented in the UN Model Tax Convention (hereinafter: UN MC). Nevertheless, since Double Tax Agreements concluded by Germany mostly follow the regulatory proposals of the OECD MC the following explanations will focus on the provisions as implemented in the OECD MC.

[9]Cf. OECD, PE Report 2008, Preface, para. 3.

[10]Cf. OECD, PE Report 2008, Part I, para. 8.

[11]Cf. OECD, PE Report 2008, Part I, para. 3.

as the 'Authorised OECD Approach' (hereinafter: AOA) and considered as the preferred interpretation of Article 7 OECD MC.[12]

Since the early days of tax treaties, there has been a general consensus that business profits derived by an enterprise are taxable solely by the country of residence (i.e. the country where the corporate headquarter is physically located), unless the enterprise is considered to have a sufficient level of economic activity in the country of source (i.e. the country where the business activities take place) to justify taxation in that country[13] In this context, it is of particular importance to identify the significant people functions, as the attribution of assets and risks (and ultimately also the attribution of profits) to the PE should be based on these functions.[14] The AOA was fully implemented in the OECD MC through a revised version of Article 7 OECD MC in 2010. In Germany, the AOA was implemented in Section 1(5) of the External Tax Relations Act (hereinafter: ETRA) through the Mutual Assistance Directive Implementation Act applicable for fiscal years starting after 31 December 2012.[15] The corresponding ordinance on the application of the arm's length principle to PEs under Section 1(5) ETRA, the so-called 'Ordinance on the Allocation of Profits of Permanent Establishments'[16] (hereinafter: BsGaV), was issued by the Federal Ministry of Finance on 17 October 2014.

It follows that physical presence is the central element of both a) the PE threshold as the nexus determining the circumstances in which a non-residence enterprise is deemed to engage in a sufficient degree of economic activity in the source country to justify taxation by that jurisdiction, and b) the attribution of profits to the PE on the basis of the arm's length principle, which focuses mainly on the functions performed by the people and the assets used.[17] However, with the growth of information and communication technology (hereinafter: ICT) that has accompanied the digitalisation of the economy in recent decades, physical presence became less relevant for enterprises to make profits in a cross-border context.[18] ICT has changed business models and enabled enterprises to carry out

---

[12]Cf. OECD, PE Report 2008, Part I, para. 9.

[13]Cf. OECD, PE Report 2008, Part I, para. 13.

[14]Cf. OECD, PE Report 2010, Part I, paras. 15 et seq.

[15]Mutual Assistance Directive Implementation Act, 26 June 2013, BGBl. I 2013, 1809. See on the temporal scope of application Section 21(20) sentence 3 ETRA.

[16]BsGaV, 13 Oct. 2014, BGBl. I 2014, 1603.

[17]Cf. OECD, BEPS Action 1: Interim Report 2018, para. 378.

[18]For an overview of the evolution of ICT see OECD, BEPS Action 1: Final Report 2015, paras. 64 et seqq.

business activities in a country other than the country of residence without giving rise to a PE.[19] Furthermore, the integration of national economies and markets has increased significantly in recent decades, making it easier for multinational enterprises (hereinafter: MNEs) to engage in tax planning strategies that can lead to BEPS and thus tax losses for governments.[20] These developments revealed weaknesses of the international tax framework. Therefore, at its meeting in Los Cabos from 18–19 June 2012, the G20 demanded action and tasked the OECD with developing an action plan to find solutions to prevent BEPS.[21]

The BEPS Action Plan contains 15 action points and aims to 'ensure the coherence of corporate income taxation at the international level'[22]. The results of the BEPS Action Plan were presented by the OECD on 5 October 2015.[23] Various action points of the BEPS Action Plan contain changes that are relevant for the taxation of PEs. In this context, not only have changes been agreed to the PE definition to address techniques used to inappropriately circumvent a tax nexus in the source country, but changes have also been developed that affect the attribution of profits to the PE aiming to realign the place where profits of an enterprise are taxed with the place where real economic activities take place and where value is created.[24] In particular, BEPS Action 7,[25] which focuses on preventing the artificial avoidance of the PE status, and BEPS Actions 8–10,[26] which focuses on aligning of transfer pricing outcomes with value creation, can be regarded as significant milestones in this context.

However, most of the key challenges posed by highly digitalised enterprises remain largely unaddressed by the BEPS measures. As business activities become less dependent on actual physical presence of property and people, the effectiveness of the reinforced principles and even the whole PE concept built on the notion of a 'brick and mortar' economy, is challenged.[27] As a consequence, a growing stock of literature argues that the current taxation rules no longer meet

[19]For an overview of new business models brought about by ICT see OECD, BEPS Action 1: Final Report 2015, paras. 109 et seqq.

[20]Cf. OECD, Action Plan on Base Erosion and Profit Shifting 2013, p. 7.

[21]Cf. G20, Leaders Declaration, Los Cabos, 18–19 June 2012, para. 48.

[22]OECD, Action Plan on Base Erosion and Profit Shifting 2013, p. 13.

[23]For an overview of the BEPS Actions cf. OECD, BEPS Project—Explanatory Statement, p. 13 et seqq.

[24]Cf. OECD, BEPS Action 1: Interim Report 2018, para. 379.

[25]Cf. OECD, BEPS Action 7: Final Report 2015.

[26]Cf. OECD, BEPS Actions 8–10: Final Report 2015.

[27]Cf. *Kofler/Mayr/Schlager*, ET 2017, 523 (526).

the requirements of today's digitalised world,[28] 'where businesses rely heavily on hard-to-value intangibles, data and automation, which facilitate online trading across borders with no physical presence'[29]. The business models operated by Google and Facebook, e.g., benefit from the data of their users who reside in different countries. Nevertheless, in many cases neither a physical PE is established nor needed by these enterprises in the market country[30] where the ultimate customers/users, from whom the enterprise exploits user-generated content and data, reside.[31] But even if a PE is established in the market country, the mechanism of the AOA mostly results in the situation that only a very small amount of the enterprise's profits can be attributed to the market country.

These challenges arising from the digitalisation of the economy have been dealt with by BEPS Action 1. While the Final Report on BEPS Action 1,[32] published in 2015, and the Interim Report on the tax challenges arising from digitalisation,[33] published in 2018, merely analysed potential tax policy alternatives to address broader direct tax challenges raised by the digitalisation of the economy but did not present any concrete solutions, the OECD/G20 Inclusive Framework on BEPS (hereinafter: Inclusive Framework) continued its intensive work on these issues to develop a long-term solution.

In a Policy Note[34], approved by the Inclusive Framework on 23 January 2019, concrete proposals framed within two complementary pillars were proposed. Under the first pillar, new rules on the allocation of taxing rights (nexus) and on profit allocation are reviewed.[35] Under the second pillar, referred to as the Global Anti-Base Erosion (hereinafter: GloBE) proposal, remaining BEPS issues are focused on.[36] Since the publication of this document, the work under Pillar One has significantly gained momentum with the publication of two public

---

[28] See, e.g., *Brauner*, Intertax 2018, 462 (462); *Petruzzi/Buriak*, TNI 90 (2018), 91 (92); *Kemmeren*, EC Tax Review 2018, 72 (73); *Kofler/Mayr/Schlager*, ET 2017, 523 (526); de *Wilde*, Intertax 2018, 466 (466).

[29] EC, 21 Sep. 2017, COM(2017) 547 final, p. 2.

[30] In the following, a distinction is made between the market country as destination country tapping the consumer side of the market and the market country as source country in case a presence beyond the supply of goods and services is established by the taxpayer, see for this distinction also *Schön*, BIT 2018, 278 (288).

[31] Cf. *Schön*, BIT 2018, 278 (278).

[32] OECD, BEPS Action 1: Final Report 2015.

[33] OECD, BEPS Action 1: Interim Report 2018.

[34] OECD, BEPS Action 1: Policy Note 2019.

[35] Cf. OECD, BEPS Action 1: Policy Note 2019, p. 1

[36] Cf. OECD, BEPS Action 1: Policy Note 2019, p. 2.

consultation documents released on 13 February 2019[37] and 9 October 2019[38]. While the first public consultation document outlines three different proposals that would all require changes to the existing nexus, as well as profit allocation rules, the second document aims to combine the significant commonalities of the three proposals in a so-called 'Unified Approach'. The fundamental architecture of the approach suggested in the second public consultation document, the so-called 'Secretariat Proposal for a "Unified Approach" under Pillar One', was approved by the Inclusive Framework on 29–30 January 2020.[39] This new approach aims, i.a., to reallocate taxing rights in favour of market jurisdictions by creating a new nexus rule that does not depend on physical presence in the market jurisdiction and goes beyond the arm's length principle.[40]

The outbreak of the COVID-19 pandemic in 2020 and political disagreement among the members of the Inclusive Framework slowed down the work on BEPS Action 1. Therefore, the initial intention to produce a final report by the end of 2020 could not be met.[41] Rather, in July 2020 the G20 mandated the Inclusive Framework to produce reports on the Blueprints of Pillar One (hereinafter: Pillar One Blueprint) and Pillar Two (hereinafter: Pillar Two Blueprint) by the G20 Finance Ministers meeting in October 2020.[42] These reports together with the Cover Statement were published on 12 October 2020.[43] As emphasised in the Cover Statement, the Inclusive Framework aims at bringing the work on both Pillars to a successful conclusion by mid-2021.[44]

---

[37] OECD, BEPS Action 1: Public Consultation Document 2019.

[38] OECD, BEPS Action 1: Secretariat Proposal for a Unified Approach 2019.

[39] Cf. OECD, BEPS Action 1: Statement on the Two-Pillar Approach 2020.

[40] Cf. OECD, BEPS Action 1: Statement on the Two-Pillar Approach 2020, Annex 1, para. 10.

[41] For the timeline cf. OECD, BEPS Action 1: Statement on the Two-Pillar Approach 2020, Annex 1, para. 4.

[42] Cf. OECD, BEPS Action 1: Report on Pillar One Blueprint 2020, p. 4.

[43] For the Report on Pillar One Blueprint cf. OECD, BEPS Action 1: Report on Pillar One Blueprint 2020. For the Report on Pillar Two Blueprint cf. OECD, BEPS Action 1: Report on Pillar Two Blueprint 2020. For the Cover Statement by the Inclusive Framework on the Reports on the Blueprints of Pillar One and Pillar Two cf. OECD, BEPS Action 1: Cover Statement on the Blueprints 2020.

[44] Cf. OECD, BEPS Action 1: Cover Statement on the Blueprints 2020, para. 9.

II. Objectives and Research Approach

The main objective of this thesis is to analyse the current rules governing the taxation of PEs as implemented in the OECD MC and German national tax law and to evaluate whether these rules can be considered suitable to meet the challenges arising from the digitalisation of the economy.

To do so, this thesis follows a two-step approach. First, the two essential elements of the PE concept are analysed: a) the PE threshold as implemented in Article 5 OECD MC and Section 12 GTC, and b) the rules governing the attribution of profits to the PE as implemented in Article 7 OECD MC 2017 and Section 1(5) ETRA in conjunction with the BsGaV. Despite the general uniform framework, areas where deviations between the OECD approach and the German approach exist are identified and analysed.

Throughout the analysis, changes influencing the PE threshold as well as the profit attribution rules as a result of the BEPS Actions are examined and critically evaluated. From my understanding, such an in-depth analysis, which brings together the examined aspects relevant in the PE context, is not yet to be found in the academic literature. The current state-of-the-art research literature focuses either on weaknesses of the conceptual approach of the AOA[45] or on the deviations that exist between the OECD and the German approach with regard to the PE threshold and the attribution of profits to PEs.[46] In particular, an in-depth analysis that explicitly elaborates the effects of the relevant BEPS Action points and their influence for the PE threshold as well as the profit attribution rules cannot yet be found in the academic literature.[47]

---

[45] See i.a. *Collier/Vella*, WTJ 2019, 159 (159 et seqq.); *Mödinger*, Internationale Erfolgs- und Vermögensabgrenzung zwischen Stammhaus und Betriebsstätte nach der Neufassung des Art. 7 OECD MC, 127 et seqq.; *Margerie*, Gewinnermittlung und Gewinnabgrenzung bei Betriebsstätten, 186 et seqq.; *Heyd*, Internationale Gewinnabgrenzung bei der Geschäftstätigkeit über Betriebsstättenstrukturen, 61 et seqq.

[46] See i.a. *Froitzheim*, Steuerliche Selbstständigkeitsfiktion der Betriebsstätte, 290 et seqq.; *Delarber*, Steuerliche Einflüsse auf die grenzüberschreitende Betriebsstättenbesteuerung, 7 et seqq. Also commentary literature deals with these deviations. For deviations that exist regarding the PE threshold see, e.g., *Puls*, in: W/A/D (Eds.), Betriebsstätten-Handbuch, paras. 2.1 et seqq.; *Wassermeyer/Kaeser*, in: W/K/S/D (Eds.), Doppelbesteuerung, Art. 5 MA, paras. 8 et seqq.; *Hruschka*, in: Schönfeld/Ditz (Eds.), DBA-Kommentar, Art. 5 (2014), paras. 34 et seqq. For deviations that exist regarding the profit attribution rules see, e.g., *Andresen*, in: W/A/D (Eds.), Betriebsstätten-Handbuch, paras. 5.1 et seqq.; *Kraft*, in: Kraft (Ed.), AStG—Kommentar, § 1 AStG, paras. 660 et seqq.

[47] Existing literature either deal with this issue rather shortly, see i.a. *Böhmer*, in: W/A/D (Eds.), Betriebsstätten-Handbuch, paras. 14.138 et seqq.; *Collier/Vella*, WTJ 2019, 159 (174

Second, the digitalisation of the economy has not only put pressure on the PE threshold, which generally requires a certain level of physical presence in the source country, but also on the approach for profit attribution to the PE, which, broadly speaking, does not allow for the attribution of profits to the PE if no significant people functions are carried out by the PE. Against this background, difficulties arising from the digitalisation of the economy are elaborated and put in more precise terms with regard to their influence on the PE concept. The analysis is supported by case studies that reflect the challenges these business models impose to the PE concept.

Based on these findings, the work carried out by the Inclusive Framework to develop a long-term solution to the broader tax challenges arising from the digitalisation of the economy is analysed. In this context, the fundamental architecture of the Pillar One Blueprint, as approved by the Inclusive Framework on 8–9 October 2020, is analysed and assessed against widely accepted overarching principles of tax policy. The overall objective of this part is to analyse whether the Pillar One approach may prove suitable to overcome the shortcomings of the PE concept arising from challenges imposed by the digitalisation of the economy. While previous OECD proposals to address the challenges that arise from the digitalisation of the economy have already been subject of extensive debate,[48] academic literature assessing the Pillar One Blueprint, as approved by the Inclusive Framework on 8–9 October 2020, under the overarching principles of tax policy presented in chapter B cannot be found in literature to the extent presented in this thesis.[49]

---

et seqq.); *Petruzzi/Peng*, TPI 168 (168 et seqq.), or focus on the overall impact of the individual BEPS action points for the international tax framework, see, e.g., for BEPS-Action 7: *Andresen*, in: Kofler/Schnitger (Eds.), BEPS-Handbuch, chapter H, and for BEPS-Actions 8–10: *Jerabek/Kofler/Kroppen/Rasch*, in: Kofler/Schnitger (Eds.), BEPS-Handbuch, chapter I.

[48] See i.a. *Schön*, Intertax 2019, 1003 (1003 et seqq.); *Pistone/Nogueira/Andrade*, ITAXS 2019, Issue 2, 1 (1 et seqq.); *Pinto*, CTJ 2017, 291 (331); *Benz/Böhmer*, DB 2018, 1233 (1233 et seqq.); *Blum*, BIT 2015, 314 (314 et seqq.); *Kofler/Mayr/Schlager*, ET 2017, 523 (523 et seqq.).

[49] *Förster/Greil/Hilse* evaluate the former version of the Pillar One Blueprint, the Secretariat Proposal for a Unified Approach, under the principles of effectiveness, neutrality, efficiency and resilience, see *Förster/Greil/Hilse*, ITPJ 2020, 3 (3 et seqq.). Also, the Business at OECD Tax Committee provides some very brief comments regarding the appropriateness of the Secretariat Proposal for a Unified Approach with respect to the Ottawa Taxation Framework principles, see Business at OECD, Comments on Secretariat Proposal, para. 13.

Due to the high degree of complexity of this research topic, certain limitations must be made. First, since Double Tax Agreements (hereinafter: DTAs) concluded by Germany mostly follow the regulatory proposals of the OECD MC,[50] the explanations refer to the OECD MC as it reads on 21 November 2017, unless otherwise indicated. Reference to the UN MC is only made in cases where it proves suitable for the issue elaborated. The focus on the OECD MC 2017 allows for an in-depth analysis of the deviations that exist between the provisions of the OECD MC 2017 and German tax law dealing with the taxation of PEs.[51]

The second limitation relates to the use of the overarching tax principles presented in chapter B of this thesis. While these principles would certainly also be suitable to analyse the current rules governing the taxation of PEs, such an in-depth analysis of the profit allocation rules as implemented in Article 7 OECD MC under similar tax principles has already been carried out by *Mödinger*[52] and is therefore not part of this thesis. Only where it appears necessary due to significant non-compatibility with the overarching tax principles, some reflections are expressed throughout the analysis. However, for the purpose of this thesis, the overarching tax principles as presented in chapter B are mainly used to assess the proposed fundamental architecture of the Pillar One Blueprint, which may form the basis for corporate tax reform.

The last limitation relates to the discussion on adopting the international tax system to the digitalisation of the economy (chapter F). While the Inclusive Framework currently follows two complementary pillars within the discussion on BEPS Action 1, as outlined above, the assessment conducted in this thesis focuses on Pillar One due to its significance and interplay with the PE rules. Also, other approaches on how to reshape the current international tax rules to cope with the tax challenges arising from the digitalisation of the economy proposed

---

[50] Cf. also BMF, 22 Aug. 2013, IV B 2—S 1301/13/10009.

[51] For difficulties that arise in the case that the provision governing the attribution of profits to the PE of the tax treaty between Germany and another treaty partner is not based on the latest version of the OECD MC see chapter D.II.4 of this thesis.

[52] See in more detail *Mödinger*, Internationale Erfolgs- und Vermögensabgrenzung zwischen Stammhaus und Betriebsstätte nach der Neufassung des Art. 7 OECD-MA.

by academic scholars[53] and supranational institutions[54] are all insightful and have their own rational. However, these approaches are outside the scope of this thesis.

III. Structure

The thesis is divided into seven chapters. An overview of the structure can be found in Figure 1 at the end of this subchapter. After the introduction (chapter A), general, widely accepted overarching tax principles that have traditionally guided the development of taxation systems are presented and put in more precise terms

[53]E.g. suggestions on amending the PE threshold: *Collin/Colin* arguing that the collection of data via regular and systematic monitoring of users in a country should in itself create a taxable presence in that country, cf. *Collin/Colin*, Task Force on Taxation of the Digital Economy, pp. 114 et seqq.; *Hongler/Pistone* suggesting a new PE nexus based on physical presence that consists of four main requirements or elements: (1) digital services, (2) user threshold, (3) a certain time threshold and (4) a *de minimis* revenue threshold, cf. *Hongler/Pistone*, Blueprints for a New PE Nexus, IBFD Working Paper 2015, pp. 22 et seqq. Moreover, suggestions for the development of specific transfer pricing guidelines for the digital economy were made, cf. i.a. *Olbert/Spengel*, WTJ 2017, 3 (33 et seqq.). Also, suggestions for the introduction of a withholding tax for digital transactions were presented, i.a. *Brauner/Báez*, Withholding Taxes in the Service of BEPS Action 1, IBFD Working Paper 2015, pp. 4 et seqq.; *Báez/Brauner*, Taxing the Digital Economy Post BEPS … Seriously, University of Florida Levin College of Law Research Paper No. 19–16, pp. 7 et seqq. For an overview and evaluation of the different proposal cf. *Pfister*, Die Besteuerung der digitalen Wirtschaft, 178 et seqq. Furthermore, *Förster/Greil/Hilse* propose a 'kind of amount A system' in which consolidated profits are considered as the result of value-creating elements, which are then allocated to the different countries in proportion to their respective contributions to value creation as well as modifications to Amount B and C, see in more detail for the concept *Förster/Greil/Hils,* ITPJ 2020, 3 (12 et seqq.). *Schön* proposes a concept of 'digital investment' that would allow market jurisdictions to claim a larger share of the overall tax revenue. Under this concept, taxing rights are not allocated based on sales, but rather on the invested capital in a particular market for the purpose of accessing a specific customer base, see in more detail for the concept *Schön*, BIT 2018, 278 (288 et seqq.). Another approach presented by *Devereux/Auerbach/Keen/Oosterhuis/Schön/Vella* is the 'residual profit allocation by income' approach, in which the right to tax routine profits is allocated to the country where functions and activities take place and the right to tax residual profits to the market country where sales are made to third parties, see in more detail for the concept *Devereux/Auerbach/Keen/Oosterhuis/Schön/Vella*, Residual profit allocation by income, Working Paper 2019.

[54]E.g. the European Union proposed the introduction of a Digital Service Tax at EU level at a rate of 3% on gross revenue from digital services as an interim measure and a long-term approach for taxing revenues derived from a significant digital presence. For the Significant Digital Presence proposal cf. EC, 21 Mar. 2018, COM(2018) 147 final. For the Digital Service Tax proposal see EC, 21 Mar. 2018, COM(2018) 148 final. After the EU's finance ministers

with regard to the subject under investigation (chapter B). These principles are used for assessing the proposed fundamental architecture of the reform proposal presented under Pillar One, which may form the basis for corporate tax reform.

In chapter C, fundamental aspects of the taxation of PEs are presented. These aspects include a brief overview of the historical development of the PE concept (chapter C.I), the rationale and justification underlying the PE concept (chapter C.II) as well as the examination of the elements of the PE definition as set out in Section 12 GFC (chapter C.III) and Article 5 OECD MC (chapter C.IV). In this context, similarities and differences between the German and the OECD approach are outlined and discussed. Furthermore, modifications resulting from the BEPS Actions are analysed.

In chapter D, the focus is shifted to the attribution of profits to PEs. The analysis undertaken is twofold. First, the emphasis is put on the attribution of profits to PEs under tax treaty law (chapter D.I). Therefore, some general explanations on the attribution of profits in the PE context are given (chapter D.I.1–chapter D.I.3), before the AOA, as implemented in Article 7 OECD MC, is analysed in further detail (chapter D.I.4). In this context, changes in profit attribution for PEs resulting from BEPS Actions 8–10 are elaborated and critically assessed. The BEPS project also resulted in a revision of the documentation requirements that are of relevance in the PE context. More precisely, BEPS Action 13 resulted in a complete rewrite of chapter V of the Transfer Pricing Guidelines for Multinational Enterprises and Tax Administrations (hereinafter: TP Guidelines) that shall be applied by analogy in the PE context. The new documentation requirements that provide for a three-tiered approach to transfer pricing documentation consisting of a master file, a local file and a CbC Report are described and critically evaluated (chapter D.I.5).

Second, the concept of the AOA as implemented in Section 1(5) ETRA and the BsGaV is introduced and critically analysed (chapter D.II.1–chapter D.II.3). Even though the German approach follows the two-step approach of the AOA as developed by the OECD, several deviations exist, mostly resulting from an unequal treatment of inbound and outbound PEs. These deviations are identified and resulting risks of double taxation are elaborated in-depth. However, double taxation may also result from the fact that most German tax treaties currently in

failed to agree on the proposals due to opposition from countries like Denmark, Finland, Ireland and Sweden on 12 Mar. 2019, the EU abandoned the proposal of the Digital Service Tax and emphasised that it would rather focus on the broader international tax discussions that are underway at the level of the OECD. Only if progress was not made in the course of 2020 by the OECD, the EU would then revisit the issue, cf. Council of the European Union, 12 Mar. 2019, Outcome of the Council Meeting, p. 6.

force are not yet based on Article 7 OECD MC 2017, which means that the AOA is not necessarily the governing principle for profit attribution to PEs in these treaties. To mitigate the risk of double taxation, Germany has enacted an 'escape clause' in Section 1(5) sentence 8 ETRA. Before taking a closer look at the escape clause and the requirements for its application, the analysis first examines the current German tax treaty network and develops a taxonomy of treaties, which proves necessary to examine whether the escape clause of Section 1(5) sentence 8 ETRA can be applied with regard to each of the identified categories (chapter D.II.4).

The last subchapter attempts to provide an overview of the documentation and reporting requirements the taxpayer must comply with in the PE context (chapter D.II.5). Throughout the analysis, a particular focus is placed on the changes to national documentation and reporting requirements as a result of BEPS Action 13. In this regard, the question is examined as to whether the revised national documentation and reporting requirements represent meaningful tools for standardising transfer pricing documentation requirements on an international level.

Based on the results derived from the previous chapters, in chapterE the focus is shifted to the digitalisation of the economy and its impact on the PE concept. First, tax challenges arising from the digitalisation of the economy are illustrated (chapter E.I). Second, to evaluate the effectiveness of the BEPS measures in addressing the tax challenges imposed by the digitalisation of the economy, a brief overview of the different measures is provided (chapter E.II). Thereby, the discussion is restricted to the outcomes of BEPS Action 7, BEPS Actions 8–10 and BEPS Action 3 due to its significance for the digital sector. Based on these findings, the appropriateness of the presented measures on meeting the tax challenges raised by the digitalisation of the economy is discussed and then, in a third step, illustrated with the help of two case studies (chapter E.III). Fourth, the underlying problem of the digitalisation of the economy for the corporate tax system and how countries cope with this problem unilaterally are discussed (chapter E.IV).

A possible approach on how to address the tax challenges arising from the digitalisation of the economy as outlined in the Pillar One Blueprint is analysed in chapter F. To do so, the outline of the fundamental architecture of Pillar One is described in a first step (chapter F.II) and then, in a second step, assessed against the overarching principles of tax policy (chapter F.III). In a last step, recommendations are presented on how certain aspects of the approach can be improved to be more compatible with the overarching principles of tax policy (chapter F.IV).

The thesis concludes with a summary of the main results (chapter G).

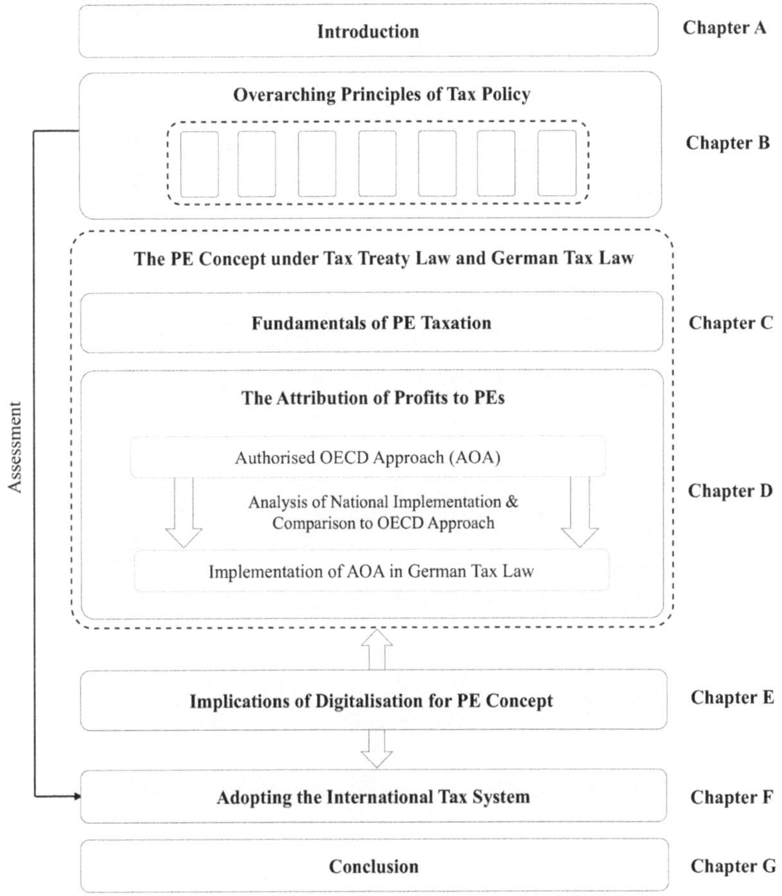

Figure 1 Structure of this Thesis (Source: Own illustration)

B. Overarching Principles of Tax Policy

I. Preliminary Remarks

There are several widely accepted overarching principles of tax policy that have traditionally guided the development of tax systems. These principles include equity, neutrality, efficiency, certainty and simplicity, effectiveness and fairness as well as flexibility.[1] In preparation for the Ottawa Ministerial Conference on Electronic Commerce in 1998, the Committee on Fiscal Affairs of the OECD adopted the report: 'Electronic Commerce: Taxation Framework Conditions' (hereinafter: Ottawa report) which drew the conclusion that the aforementioned tax principles[2] should not only be applicable in relation to conventional commerce but also in

[1] Cf. i.a. *Richman*, Taxation of Foreign Investment Income, 5 et seqq.; *Musgrave*, United States Taxation of Foreign Investment Income, 71 et seqq.; *Musgrave/Musgrave*, in: Bird/Head (Eds.), Modern Fiscal Issues, 63 et seqq.; *Vogel*, Intertax 1988, 310 (310 et seqq.); *Vogel*, Intertax 1988, 393 (393 et seqq.); *Schön*, WTJ 2009, 67 (71 et seqq.); *Pinto*, E-Commerce and Source-Based Income Taxation, 17 et seqq.; *Pinto*, BIT 2006, 266 (266 et seqq.); *De Wilde*, Intertax 2010, 281 (285 et seqq.); *Graetz*, TLR 2001, 261 (297 et seqq.); *Kaufman*, Law and Policy in International Business 1998, 145 (145 et seqq.); *Li*, CTJ 2002, 823 (823 et seqq.); *Bärsch*, Taxation of Hybrid Financial Instruments, 43 et seqq.; *Mödinger*, Internationale Erfolgs- und Vermögensabgrenzung zwischen Stammhaus und Betriebsstätte nach der Neufassung des Art. 7 OECD-MA, 49 et seqq.; *Jacobs/Spengel/Schäfer*, Intertax 2003, 214 (217 et seqq.); OECD, BEPS Action 1: Final Report 2015, paras. 10 et seqq.

[2] The report 'Electronic Commerce: Taxation Framework Conditions' published in 1998 did not contain the principle 'equity'.

S. Hentschel, *The Taxation of Permanent Establishments*, Hallesche Schriften zur Betriebswirtschaft 37, https://doi.org/10.1007/978-3-658-34000-1_2

relation to electronic commerce (hereinafter: e-commerce).[3] Even though the principle of 'equity' was not explicitly mentioned in the Ottawa report, the importance of this principle for the design of tax policy was emphasised in the Final Report on BEPS Action 1 dealing with the tax challenges raised by the digital economy.[4] The Final Report on BEPS Action 1 also underlines that, despite the fact that at the time these tax principles emerged many of the business models that challenge the current taxation rules did not exist, these principles continue to be relevant, also in the digital economy.[5]

Therefore, for the purpose of this analysis, these overarching principles of tax policy represent a useful theoretical framework against which the suggested reform proposals to the international corporate taxation rules, strongly rooted in fundamental features such as the PE concept and the arm's length principle, can be assessed against. In the following, each of the overarching principles of tax policy will be explained in further detail and put in more precise terms with regard to its significance for the reform proposal currently suggested under Pillar One.

II. Equity

1. Dimensions of Equity

According to *Vogel*, the term 'equity' cannot be defined.[6] Neither is it possible to prove or disprove that something is equitable in the same way as this can be done with regard to empirical facts.[7] Rather, equity is an interpretative concept that bridges the moral and the legal world.[8] Therefore, unfolding what equity demands for the design of taxation rules is no easy undertaking.

---

[3]Cf. OECD, Electronic Commerce: Taxation Framework Conditions 1998, para. 9. Since the publication of the report, these principles are referred to as the Ottawa Taxation Framework Conditions, cf. OECD, Taxation and Electronic Commerce 2001, p. 3. Detailed for the applicability of these principles in order to justify source-based taxation in an e-commerce environment see *Pinto*, E-Commerce and Source-Based Income Taxation, 17 et seqq.

[4]Cf. OECD, BEPS Action 1: Final Report 2015, para. 10.

[5]Cf. OECD, BEPS Action 1: Final Report 2015, para. 10.

[6]Cf. *Vogel*, Intertax 1988, 393 (393).

[7]Cf. *Vogel*, Intertax 1988, 393 (393).

[8]Cf. *Vogel*, Intertax 1988, 393 (393).

Traditional theory has put forward two dimensions of equity that can be distinguished: inter-nation equity and inter-taxpayer equity.[9] In the following, both dimensions shall be explained in further detail.

2. Inter-Nation Equity

a. Fundamental Concept

Taken fiscal sovereignty as given, it appears to be an essential and maybe one of the most important elements in the current international tax system that all legitimate participating jurisdictions are able to claim their fair share of taxable income from cross-border business activities.[10] Even though sharing taxable income is effectively a 'zero-sum game' for the participating jurisdictions as one jurisdiction's gain means another jurisdiction's loss,[11] for an investor who realises income from cross-border business activities the question arises to what degree the foreign jurisdiction where the business activities are carried out is entitled to levy taxes on the income generated.[12] Put another way, fair conditions have to be determined, under which the relevant jurisdictions shall have a right to tax.[13] If jurisdictions share different opinions about the origin and, thus, the taxation of the income, the risk of double taxation exists. Therefore, the principle of inter-nation equity seeks an equitable allocation of taxing rights among jurisdictions to ensure that each jurisdiction receives an appropriate share of tax revenues from cross-border transactions.[14]

---

[9]The first to distinguish equity considerations with respect to individual equity and inter-nations equity was *Peggy Musgrave* (formerly: *Richman*), cf. *Richman*, Taxation of Foreign Investment Income, 11 et seqq. She broadened the work of *Richard Musgrave* (*Musgrave*, Criteria for Foreign Tax Credit, 83) who distinguished the two aspects of tax neutrality and equity for the problem of worldwide vs. source taxation, cf. *Vogel*, Intertax 1988, 216 (216). Detailed on inter-nation equity considerations see also *Musgrave/Musgrave*, in: Bird/Head (Eds.), Modern Fiscal Issues, 63 et seqq.

[10]Cf. *Richman*, Taxation of Foreign Investment Income, 15; *Graetz/Hear*, DLJ 1997, 1021 (1033); *Jacobs/Spengel/Schäfer*, Intertax 2004, 268 (270).

[11]Cf. *Li*, CTJ 2002, 823 (827).

[12]Cf. *Musgrave/Musgrave*, in: Bird/Head (Eds.), Modern Fiscal Issues, 68.

[13]Cf. *Bird*, Shaping a New International Tax Order, BIFD 1988, 292 (297).

[14]The principle of inter-nation equity is attributed to *Peggy Musgrave* (formerly: *Richman*), cf. *Richman*, Taxation of Foreign Investment Income, 15 et seq.; *Musgrave*, Public Finance 1972, 394 (394 et seqq.); *Musgrave*, in: McLure (Ed.), The State Corporation Income Tax, 228 (228 et seqq.); *Musgrave*, in: Cnossen (Ed.), Tax Coordination in the European Community, 202 et seqq.; *Musgrave*, in: Cnossen (Ed.), Taxing Capital Income in the European Union,

Throughout history, scholars have disagreed over the appropriate policy framework which meets the requirement of inter-nation equity best.[15] A right to tax income from cross-border transactions can either be based on residence or on source.[16] Whereas the concept of residence acknowledges the right of a jurisdiction to tax all profits of its residence earned worldwide, the concept of source acknowledges the right of a jurisdiction to tax all profits that arise within its geographical borders.[17] A solid legitimation for the allocation of jurisdictional claims between the source and the residence country can be derived from the principle of 'economic allegiance'.[18] This principle implies that the jurisdiction that provides the benefits to support the income realisation of the enterprise, e.g. public infrastructure or government services, is entitled to tax the corresponding profits.[19] Thus, the income allocation should be based on each jurisdiction's share in the income generating activities of the business entities.[20] However, due to the fact that income-generating activities are usually carried out in both jurisdictions, this theory or principle can be invoked by both the residence country and the source country.[21] Moreover, the principle of economic allegiance would require the identification and operationalisation of different levels of intensity, which, as

---

46 et seqq.; see also *Vogel*, Intertax 1988, 393 (398 et seq.); *Jacobs/Spengel/Schäfer*, Intertax 2004, 268 (270 et seq.); OECD, BEPS Action 1: Final Report 2015, para. 12.

[15] See i.a. *Musgrave/Musgrave*, in: Bird/Head (Eds.), Modern Fiscal Issues, 68; *Musgrave*, Brooklyn Journal of International Law, 1335 (1356); *Graetz*, TLR 2001, 261 (297 et seqq.); *Zuber*, Anknüpfungsmerkmale und Reichweite der internationalen Besteuerung, 110.

[16] Cf. *Schäfer*, International Company Taxation in the Era of Information and Communication Technologies, 31.

[17] Cf. *Musgrave*, in: Cnossen (Ed.), Taxing Capital Income in the European Union, 47.

[18] Cf. *Jacobs/Spengel/Schäfer*, Intertax 2004, 268 (270 et seqq.); *Vogel*, Intertax 1988, 393 (398); *Zuber*, Anknüpfungsmerkmale und Reichweite der internationalen Besteuerung, 108 et seq.; *Graetz*, TLR 2001, 261 (297, note 146). According to Sec. 3(1) GFC, taxes are cash benefits that do not require a return by the state. Therefore, the principle of economic allegiance can only be utilised for the tax law when perceived as benefit principle, cf. *Hey*, in: Tipke/Lang (Eds.), Steuerrecht, Sec. 3 para. 44. For further analysis of the relationship between the principle of economic allegiance and the benefit theory cf. *Kaufman*, Law and Policy in International Business 1998, 145 (198 et seqq.).

[19] Cf. *Waltrich*, Cross-Border Taxation of Permanent Establishments, 186 et seqq.; *Jacobs/Spengel/Schäfer*, Intertax 2004, 268 (270)

[20] Cf. *Jacobs/Spengel/Schäfer*, Intertax 2004, 268 (270); *Musgrave*, Public Finance 1972, 394 (400); *Musgrave/Musgrave*, in: Bird/Head (Eds.), Modern Fiscal Issues, 82; *Schäfer*, International Company Taxation in the Era of Information and Communication Technologies, 37; *Lehner/Reimer*, IStR 2005, 542 (542).

[21] Cf. *Schön*, BIT 2018, 278 (287); *Bärsch*, Taxation of Hybrid Financial Instruments, 57. A detailed analysis of the benefit theory and its applicability in order to justify residence as

Schön rightly argues, 'can hardly be measured by any straightforward qualitative standard'[22]. Against this background, it becomes evident that, while the principle of economic allegiance can be utilised to justify a tax claim by the involved jurisdictions, it does neither prove suitable to measure the precise contributions of the participating jurisdictions where business activities are carried out, nor does it prove suitable for the allocation of an equitable share of tax revenues.[23]

To determine the profit-generating activity and thus the profits' source, two economic concepts exist: the 'supply approach' and the 'supply-demand approach'.[24] According to the supply approach, as the name indicates, the source of income is located where the factor services which generate this income operate.[25] Thus, income can only be generated through the use of production factors. Consequently, the consumer market of the produced goods and services does not represent a factor that contributes to the added value of the company according to this approach.[26]

Under the supply-demand approach, the market value is created through the interaction of supply and demand.[27] Therefore, the tax base is to be shared between the jurisdiction where 'value' is added and the jurisdiction where the product is used.[28] This approach implies that the product's value also depends on the utility level it has for the consumer and consequently influences the amount of income that can be generated with the products. It is argued that consumers do not only consider production costs when determining their marginal price for the relevant good but also the subjective gain of utility.[29] Consequently, both the jurisdiction where value is added as well as the jurisdiction which provides the consumer market should be entitled to tax.[30]

---

well as source-based taxation in an e-commerce environment see *Pinto*, E-Commerce and Source-Based Income Taxation, 17 et seqq.

[22] *Schön*, BIT 2018, 278 (287).

[23] Cf. *Hey*, IWB 2004, 2003 (2007 et seqq.); *Richman*, Taxation of Foreign Investment Income, 16; *Schön*, WTJ 2009, 67 (75 et seq.); *Schön*, BIT 2018, 278 (287); *Schäfer*, International Company Taxation in the Era of Information and Communication Technologies, 80.

[24] The economic concepts are attributed to Peggy Musgrave: *Musgrave*, United States Taxation of Foreign Investment Income, 233 et seq.

[25] Cf. *Musgrave*, United States Taxation of Foreign Investment Income, 234; also *Jacobs/Spengel/Schäfer*, Intertax 2004, 268 (270).

[26] Cf. *Jacobs/Spengel/Schäfer*, Intertax 2004, 268 (270).

[27] Cf. *Musgrave*, in: McLure (Ed.), The State Corporation Income Tax, 228 (234).

[28] Cf. *Musgrave*, in: McLure (Ed.), The State Corporation Income Tax, 228 (234).

[29] Cf. *Musgrave*, in: McLure, (Ed.), The State Corporation Income Tax, 228 (234); *Oestreicher*, Konzern-Gewinnabgrenzung, 179; *Schäfer*, International Company Taxation in the Era of Information and Communication Technologies, 80.

[30] Cf. *Musgrave*, in: McLure (Ed.), The State Corporation Income Tax, 228 (234).

b. Significance for the Subject under Investigation

The question of whether the entitlement to tax should be based on the supply approach or the supply-demand approach is controversial and a key element in the current discussion of the Inclusive Framework under Pillar One. More precisely, it is questionable whether the market country in its role as a destination country should be entitled additional taxing rights over the income of non-resident enterprises. According to *Musgrave*, 'there seems to be no straightforward economic basis for choosing between the two'[31]. An evaluation of the two approaches rather 'depends on how entitlements are viewed'[32]. This evaluation by *Musgrave*, even though published more than three decades ago, is still valid.

Under current international tax law, the provision of a consumer market is not a criterion that entitles a jurisdiction to levy corporate taxes on the income earned in a country.[33] Rather, until an enterprise of one state carries on business activities to the extent that a PE is constituted in another state in which it is not a resident, it should not be regarded to participate in the economic life of that state to the extent that it falls within the taxing jurisdiction of that other state.[34] The contribution by the country of demand (i.e. the market country in its role as a destination country) is rather covered by indirect taxes such as Value Added Tax (hereinafter: VAT) and Goods and Services Tax (hereinafter: GST).[35]

However, in the 'digital age', so it is argued, enterprises are able to be economically present in a market country and generate a substantial amount of profits in this country without the need to establish a physical presence in the market country.[36] Since the PE concept is predominantly rooted in physical presence requirements, this development challenges the market jurisdictions' ability to tax the corresponding profits which were generated within its borders.[37] Against this background, it must be analysed whether the reform proposals currently discussed under Pillar One proposing to create a new taxing right and new profit allocation rules appear to be suitable in order to overcome the shortcomings of the current

---

[31] Cf. *Musgrave,* in: McLure (Ed.), The State Corporation Income Tax, 228 (234).

[32] Cf. *Musgrave,* in: McLure (Ed.), The State Corporation Income Tax, 228 (234).

[33] Cf. *Schreiber*, StuW 2004, 212 (212); cf. also *Schäfer,* International Company Taxation in the Era of Information and Communication Technologies, 81.

[34] Cf. OECD MC Commentary 2017, Art. 5, para. 132.

[35] Cf. *Andersson*, BIT 2018, 684 (686); *Schön*, BIT 2018, 278 (285 et seq.); *Schön*, Intertax 2019, 1003 (1010). See in more detail for an overview of VAT/GST treatment of digital services OECD, BEPS Action 1: Interim Report 2018, paras. 291 et seqq.

[36] See in more detail OECD, BEPS Action 1: Interim Report 2018, paras. 131 et seqq.

[37] See in more detail chapter E of this thesis.

international tax rules and may lead to a more equitable allocation of taxing rights among jurisdictions.

3. Inter-Taxpayer Equity

a. Fundamental Concept

Apart from inter-nation equity, also inter-taxpayer equity must be considered when evaluating taxation rules. A basic perception, common to most economically advanced and democratically governed countries, is that recipients of equal income should also be treated equally as taxpayers.[38] Therefore, so *Musgrave*, 'all residents and citizens of a certain country [...] should be taxed by that country at rates equal for all those receiving equal income from whatever source, be it domestic or foreign'[39].

Against this background, criteria must be identified that can be used for an equal distribution of taxes among taxpayers. Traditional theory put forward the 'ability-to-pay principle' which demands an equal treatment of taxpayers according to their economic capacity.[40] In this context, net income has been considered and widely used as the suitable yardstick by which the ability-to-pay is

---

[38]Cf. *Richman*, Taxation of Foreign Investment Income, 11.

[39]*Richman*, Taxation of Foreign Investment Income, 11 et seq.

[40]The ability-to-pay principle is attributed to *Adam Smith* who introduced this principle as a yardstick in order to achieve equality of taxation, cf. *Smith*, An Inquiry Into the Nature and Causes of the Wealth of the Nations, 1976, 825. For further details on the ability-to-pay principle cf. *Hey*, in: Tipke/Lang (Eds.), Steuerrecht, Sec. 3, paras. 40 et seqq.; *Birk*, Das Leistungsfähigkeitsprinzip als Maßstab der Steuernormen, 1 et seqq.; *Musgrave/Musgrave*, Public Finance in Theory and Practice, 223 et seqq.; *Vogel*, in: Kirchhof/Offenhaus/Schöberle (Eds.), Steuerrecht, 367 et seqq.; *Tipke*, Die Steuerrechtsordnung, 2000, 323 et seqq.; *Tipke*, StuW 1988, 262 (262 et seqq.); *Lang*, StuW 1990, 331 (331 et seqq.); *Kirchhof*, StuW 2011, 365 (365 et seqq.); *Kirchhof*, StuW 1985, 319 (319 et seqq.); *Kirchhof*, StuW 1984, 297 (297 et seqq.); *Schön*, StuW 2012, 213 (213 et seqq.); *Birk*, StuW 2000, 328 (328 et seqq.); *Birk*, StuW 1983, 293 (293 et seqq.); *Schneider*, StuW 1984, 356 (356 et seqq.); *Biergans/Wasmer*, FR 1985, 57 (57 et seqq.); *Franz*, StuW 1988, 17 (17 et seqq.); *Kempny*, StuW 2011, 377 (377 et seqq.); *Beiser*, StuW 2005, 295 (295 et seqq.); *Schaumburg/Schaumburg*, StuW 2013, 61 (61 et seqq.). Other concepts discussed in literature that may be used for an equal distribution of taxes among taxpayers are the 'poll tax principle' and the 'benefit principle'. While the poll tax principle calling for an equal tax burden for all taxpayers in order to finance public expenditure has been criticised for disregarding individual circumstances of the taxpayers, the benefit principle demanding an allocation of the tax burden in proportion to the benefits the taxpayers receive from government services raises practical difficulties of implementation, cf. *Tipke*, Die Steuerrechtsordnung, 2000, 475 et seqq. Implementation difficulties arise,

measured.[41] Even though the ability-to-pay principle is more readily applied to individual taxpayers, it can also be applied to corporations due to the fact that taxation at the corporate level essentially influences the income flowing to the shareholder.[42]

In this context, the term 'ability-to-pay' refers to the earnings of a taxable entity.[43] A distinction is usually made between horizontal and vertical equity.[44] Horizontal equity suggests that taxpayers in similar circumstances face a similar tax burden.[45] In order to ensure vertical equity, it is required that taxpayers in better circumstances face a respectively larger part of the tax burden.[46] Although the ability-to-pay principle is criticised for being too vague and susceptible to ideological and political fallacies, it is the most widely used economic concept to define equity among taxpayers and therefore has a major impact on tax policy throughout the world.[47]

---

for example, with regard to the definition of the benefits. The benefits may refer to the willingness to pay for public services and goods, the costs associated with the public services and goods or the utility level associated with the consumption of the services and goods, cf. *Müller*, Verwirklichung von Gerechtigkeit und Entscheidungsneutralität in den Einkommen- und Körperschaftsteuersystemen der EU-Mitgliedstaaten, 7 et seq.; *Wendt*, A Common Tax Base for Multinational Enterprises in the European Union, 33. Therefore it is difficult to apply the benefit principle to many categories of public contributions, cf. *Frebel*, Erfolgsaufteilung und -besteuerung im internationalen Konzern, 36. Another difficulty is that it is not possible to exclude public goods, nor is an exclusion always desirable, cf. also *Wendt*, A Common Tax Base for Multinational Enterprises in the European Union, 33. Due to these difficulties, it is argued that both principles are not appropriate for an equal distribution of the tax burden among taxpayers, *Tipke*, Die Steuerrechtsordnung, 2000, 475 et seqq.

[41] Cf. i.a. *Bärsch*, Taxation of Hybrid Financial Instruments, 54; *Fleming/Peroni/Shay*, FTR 2001, 299 (309).

[42] Cf. *Musgrave*, Brooklyn Journal of International Law 2001, 1335 (1335 et seqq.); *Graetz*, TLR 2001, 261 (295 et seqq.); *Hey*, Harmonisierung der Unternehmensbesteuerung in Europa, 119.

[43] Cf. *Jacobs/Spengel/Schäfer*, Intertax 2003, 214 (219).

[44] Cf. *Musgrave/Musgrave*, Public Finance in Theory and Practice, 223 et seqq.; *Vogel*, in: Kirchhof/Offenhaus/Schöberle (Eds.), Steuerrecht, 367 et seqq.; *De Wilde*, Sharing the Pie, 45; *Kleineidam* in: Kleineidam (Ed.), Unternehmenspolitik und internationale Besteuerung, 691 (694); *Kleineidam*, in: Klein/Stihl/Wassermeyer (Eds.), Unternehmen—Steuern: Festschrift für Hans Flick zum 70. Geburtstag, 857 (862 et seq.).

[45] Cf. *Musgrave/Musgrave*, Public Finance in Theory and Practice, 223.

[46] Cf. *Musgrave/Musgrave*, Public Finance in Theory and Practice, 223.

[47] Cf. *Schön*, WTJ 2009, 67 (pp. 71 et seq.). In some countries it is traced back to the constitution and therefore rendered immune for new legislative tendencies, cf. *Schön*, WTJ 2009, 67 (72).

Nonetheless, it is questionable how the ability-to-pay principle can be utilised in order to ensure equity among taxpayers, especially in an international context.[48] As pointed out by *Musgrave,* in an international context all income needs to be considered, 'be it domestic or foreign'[49] because the source where the income is derived from does not influence the ability-to-pay of an individual.[50] Therefore, the ability-to-pay of a taxpayer cannot be limited by political or geographical borders; rather it needs to be connected with a worldwide taxation of income.[51] However, this view poses problems because, as *Schön* argues, worldwide taxation requires to include the global income of a taxpayer in a literal sense.[52] More precisely, taxpayers need to be enabled to set off profits and losses from various sources.[53] In an international context, where at least two different jurisdictions are involved, these circumstances can be considered best by the country of residence, where a close relationship to the taxpayer is presumed and the collection of the required information of the taxpayer might be easier to administrate.[54] If the ability-to-pay principle is interpreted according to the valuation of the country of residence, it implies that a taxable entity can only have one single ability-to-pay.[55]

Contrary to this approach, the ability-to-pay principle could be interpreted according to the valuation of the source country. Such an interpretation assumes that the economic ability-to-pay is split up into two parts: the ability-to-pay of the country of residence and the one of the source country.[56] This territorially defined view of the ability-to-pay rests upon the assumption that the ability-to-pay of the taxable entity differs contingent on the diverse economic conditions that exist in

---

[48]Even though the origin of the ability-to-pay principle is rooted in domestic tax law it can be extended to cross-border transactions, cf. *Schön*, WTJ 2009, 67 (71 et seq.); *Bärsch*, Taxation of Hybrid Financial Instruments, 54; *Jacobs/Spengel/Schäfer*, Intertax 2003, 214 (219).

[49]*Richman*, Taxation of Foreign Investment Income, 12.

[50]Cf. *Musgrave/Musgrave*, in: Bird/Head (Eds.), Modern Fiscal Issues, 68 et seq.

[51]Cf. *Schön*, WTJ 2009, 67 (72); *Ault/Bradford*, in: Razin/Slemrod (Eds.), Taxation in the Global Economy, 11 (22); *Fleming/Peroni/Shay*, FTR 2001, 299 (301 et seq.); *Fleming/Peroni/Shay*, JATTA 2008, 35 (59 et seq.); *Graetz/Hear*, DLJ 1997, 1021 (1034 et seq.); *Green*, CLR 1993–1994, 18 (29 et seqq., 70 et seq.); *McLure*, in: Canadian Tax Foundation, World Tax Conference, 6:1 (6:3). Critical on this issue *Vogel*, Intertax 1988, 310 (310); *Vogel*, Intertax 1988, 393 (393); Vogel, Intertax 1988, 216 (216 et seqq.).

[52]Cf. *Schön*, WTJ 2009, 67 (72).

[53]Cf. *Schön*, WTJ 2009, 67 (72); *Homburg*, Allgemeine Steuerlehre, 292 et seq.; *Spengel*, Internationale Unternehmensbesteuerung in der Europäischen Union, 320.

[54]Cf. *Schön*, WTJ 2009, 67 (72).

[55]Cf. *Jacobs/Spengel/Schäfer*, Intertax 2003, 214 (219).

[56]Cf. *Jacobs/Spengel/Schäfer*, Intertax 2003, 214 (219); *Bärsch*, Taxation of Hybrid Financial Instruments, 55.

the various jurisdictions concerned.[57] However, since the ability-to-pay principle solely focuses on the earnings of the taxpayer, regardless of whether the earnings flow from the country of source or the country of residence, a territorially defined ability-to-pay principle cannot be maintained.[58]

Even though the above analysis illustrates that the ability-to-pay principle may be well equipped to support residence taxation of worldwide income,[59] in taxation practice, the source country continues to levy tax on income which is economically connected with its territory.[60] Thus, the implementation of allocation rules between the different jurisdictions is essential to avoid overtaxation (mainly caused by double taxation) and undertaxation (mainly caused by non-taxation) of income derived by the taxpayer. However, as pointed out by *Schön*, the ability-to-pay principle only helps to define the cake by providing 'a common framework for all involved countries when it comes to the definition of the income as such, i.e. the measurement of the tax basis which is to be separated between the involved countries'[61], but it does not help to slice it.[62] Consequently, a common understanding of the term 'income' is essential in the first place which can then be allocated to the different jurisdictions.[63] In this regard, the ability-to-pay principle requires that allocation rules should be designed in a way that overtaxation as well as undertaxation of this income is avoided.[64]

b. Significance for the Subject under Investigation

With regard to any new nexus and profit allocation rules that are currently developed under Pillar One as an answer to the tax challenges arising from the digitalisation of the economy, it is essential that these rules aim to avoid overtaxation as well as undertaxation of income derived by the taxpayer. This requires that these new rules are clearly defined and provide for a framework that can be

---

[57] Cf. *Jacobs/Spengel/Schäfer*, Intertax 2003, 214 (219).

[58] Cf. *Homburg*, Allgemeine Steuerlehre, 292; *Musgrave/Musgrave*, in: Bird/Head (Eds.), Modern Fiscal Issues, 68 et seq.; *Jacobs/Spengel/Schäfer*, Intertax 2003, 214 (219); *Schön*, WTJ 2009, 67 (73). Different view: *Schaumburg*, Internationales Steuerrecht, para. 6.58.

[59] Cf. *Schön*, WTJ 2009, 67 (73).

[60] Cf. *Schön*, WTJ 2009, 67 (73); *Avi-Yonah*, International Tax as International Law, 12; *Green*, The Future of Sourced-Based Taxation of the Income of Multinational Enterprises, 31 et seqq.

[61] *Schön*, WTJ 2009, 67 (73).

[62] Cf. *Schön*, WTJ 2009, 67 (73). Detailed for the definition of income see *Brauner*, TLR 2003, 259 (267 et seqq.).

[63] Cf. *Schön*, WTJ 2009, 67 (73).

[64] Cf. *Schön*, WTJ 2009, 67 (73).

implemented into the national tax law of the participating jurisdictions in a consistent manner. Moreover, the rules shall be designed so that possibilities for tax planning are avoided.

Furthermore, as the principle of inter-taxpayer equity also demands that taxpayers in similar circumstances should bear a similar tax burden,[65] it is of significance that arbitrary cut-off points with regard to the application of the new rules as well as unjustifiable ring-fencing of certain business models are avoided. Nevertheless, as the following subchapter illustrates, the later consideration may also be derived from the principle of neutrality.

III. Neutrality

1. Fundamental Concept

The concept of tax neutrality is a major objective of tax policy and is related to the process of decision-making of economic actors.[66] As such, the concept comes in many different forms. From an economic point of view, the idea of tax neutrality is that a tax or a particular tax provision ought not to affect the economic decision of a rational investor to act in a specific manner.[67] This call for a framework that is not distorted by tax considerations rests on the assumption that efficiency will be highest if all income-producing factors are distributed solely by a market mechanism, without taxation law interfering.[68]

In the context of tax policy, this theoretical concept implies that tax provisions shall not induce the taxpayer to make any adjustments to the use of resources. Such tax-induced adjustments could lead to inefficiencies and welfare losses, e.g. 'dead-weight losses' through an excess burden of taxation.[69] In this sense, tax neutrality also entails that tax systems should minimise discrimination with regard to particular economic choices.[70] This implies that the same tax principles should

---

[65]Cf. OECD, BEPS Action 1: Final Report 2015, para. 11.

[66]Cf. *Auerbach,* in: Auerbach/Feldstein (Eds.), Handbook of Public Economics, 61 (61 et seq.); *Spengel,* Internationale Unternehmensbesteuerung in der Europäischen Union, 233; *Elschen/Hüchtebrock,* FA 1983, 253 (253); *Wellisch,* Jahrbücher für Nationalökonomie und Statistik 2003, 332 (334); *Wagner,* StuW 1992, 2 (3 et seqq.); *Schön,* BIT 2015, 271 (272); *Elschen,* StuW 1991, 99 (99 et seqq.).

[67]Cf. *Schön,* BIT 2015, 271 (272).

[68]Cf. *Li,* CTJ 2002, 823 (828); *Jacobs/Spengel/Schäfer,* Intertax 2003, 214 (217).

[69]Cf. *Schön,* BIT 2015, 271 (272); *Elschen/Hüchtebrock,* FA 1983, 253 (253 et seqq.); *Zuber,* Anknüpfungsmerkmale und Reichweite der internationalen Besteuerung, 48 et seqq.

[70]Cf. OECD, BEPS Action 1: Final Report 2015, para. 10.

apply to different forms of businesses. However, it also entails that specific features that cause distortion and that may otherwise undermine a neutral application of the tax principles must be addressed accordingly.[71]

The concept of tax neutrality should also prevail in open economies. Therefore, when looking at the concept of neutrality from an international context, it requires that cross-border transactions of multinational investors are treated neutral within the framework of national tax systems.[72] In other words, the pattern of taxation shall not affect the taxpayer's decision to carry on business activities within its country or abroad.[73] Such decisions shall rather be determined by other considerations, e.g. the geographical advantages the relevant countries can provide.[74] The ideal state of this concept would be a world with fully harmonised tax rates and tax provisions which would prevent discriminatory and competitive tax treatments of business and investment decisions.[75] Such harmonised tax rates and tax provisions would result in a world where business and investment decisions can be made irrespective of the source of income or the location of residence.[76] However, in practice, such a state is no real option.[77] First of all, it would require a worldwide consensus of governments with regard to double taxation conventions and second, a full harmonisation of domestic tax law of the respective jurisdictions, insofar as it is relevant to international tax situations, would be required.[78] Apparently, such considerations have little in common with the current international tax law.

---

[71] Cf. OECD, BEPS Action 1: Final Report 2015, para. 10.

[72] Cf. *Jacobs/Spengel/Schäfer*, Intertax 2003, 214 (217); *Spengel*, Internationale Unternehmensbesteuerung in der Europäischen Union, 224; *Schreiber*, Besteuerung der Unternehmen, 577.

[73] Cf. *Musgrave,* United States Taxation of Foreign Investment Income, 109.

[74] Cf. *Schön*, WTJ 2009, 67 (78).

[75] Cf. *Schön*, WTJ 2009, 67 (78); *Brauner*, TLR 2003, 259 (291 et seq.).

[76] Cf. *Musgrave,* United States Taxation of Foreign Investment Income, 109; *Schön*, WTJ 2009, 67 (72).

[77] See in more detail *Roin*, Journal of Legal Studies 2002, 61 (61 et seqq.).

[78] Cf. *Schön*, WTJ 2009, 67 (78).

Taken the differences in international tax law as given, the concept of neutrality can only be achieved according to the valuation of one jurisdiction.[79] In this context, traditional theory has put forward different concepts, namely capital export neutrality, capital import neutrality as well as capital ownership neutrality.[80]

2. Capital Export Neutrality

The concept of capital export neutrality is based on the residence principle and is therefore favoured by many economists as a requirement for worldwide economic efficiency.[81] The basic idea of this concept is that an investor in a given jurisdiction shall face the same tax burden, regardless whether his investment is made domestically or in a foreign jurisdiction.[82] Put another way, taxes should not cause investors to favour either foreign or domestic investments.[83] Capital export neutrality may be attained in different ways. The easiest way in terms of administrability is that the country of residence taxes the worldwide income of the investor in accordance with the tax rules applicable in the country of residence, while the country of source entirely waives its competence to tax income that is connected with its territory.[84] Capital export neutrality may also be attained with

---

[79] Cf. *Jacobs/Spengel/Schäfer*, Intertax 2003, 214 (217); *Spengel*, Internationale Unternehmensbesteuerung in der Europäischen Union, 230 et seqq.; *Zuber*, Anknüpfungsmerkmale und Reichweite der internationalen Besteuerung, 115 et seqq. Critical towards these concepts *Brown*, FTR 2011, 565 (600 et seqq.).

[80] Cf. *Musgrave*, Criteria for Foreign Tax Credit, 83 (83 et seqq.). *Richard Musgrave* seems to have been the first who distinguished between capital export and capital import neutrality, cf. *Vogel*, Intertax 1988, 310 (311); also *Musgrave*, United States Taxation of Foreign Investment Income, 119; *Ault/Bradford*, in: Razin/Slemrod (Eds.), Taxation in the Global Economy, 11 (22); EC, 23 Oct. 2001, COM(2001) 582 final, 27. For a detailed overview of the concepts of capital export neutrality and capital import neutrality with regard to economic welfare and the taxation of foreign income see US Department of the Treasury, A Policy Study, 23 et seqq.

[81] Cf. US Department of the Treasury, A Policy Study, 23 et seqq.; *Li*, CTJ 2002, 823 (828).

[82] Cf. EC, 23 Oct. 2001, COM(2001) 582 final, 27; *Li*, CTJ 2002, 823 (828).

[83] Cf. *Musgrave/Musgrave*, in: Bird/Head (Eds.), Modern Fiscal Issues, 63 (69); *McLure*, CESifo Forum 2000, 10 (11).

[84] Cf. *Griffith/Hines/Sørensen*, in: Mirrlees et al. (Eds.) Dimensions of Tax Design: The Mirrlees Review, 914 (926); *Schön*, WTJ 2009, 67 (79); *Vogel*, Intertax 1988, 310 (311); *Jacobs/Spengel/Schäfer*, Intertax 2003, 214 (217).

source country taxation as long as the country of residence offers an unlimited tax credit for the tax paid in the source country.[85]

3. Capital Import Neutrality

The alternative concept of capital import neutrality is based on the source principle and is often favoured by business representatives because it promotes competitive neutrality with regard to the country where the investment is carried out.[86] The basic idea of this concept is that all investments in a given jurisdiction shall be subject to the same overall tax rate, no matter whether the investment is made by a domestic or a foreign investor. Consequently, an investor's tax burden does not depend on his residency.[87] Capital import neutrality requires that residence countries and source countries apply uniform source rules when determining the income to tax and exempt, respectively.[88] Most commonly, capital import neutrality is attained if the income generated within a jurisdiction is exclusively subject to taxation in the source country and consequently exempt from taxation in the country of residence (source-only taxation).[89]

---

[85]Cf. *Schön*, WTJ 2009, 67 (79). However, since numerous jurisdictions limit the granted tax credit to the level of taxation that would occur domestically, capital export neutrality is missed when the tax rate of the source country exceeds the tax rate of the country of residence or when other limitations prevent a full tax credit (e.g. per-item limitations; per-country limitations), cf. *Kahle*, StuW 2005, 61 (62); *Schön*, WTJ 2009, 67 (79).

[86]Cf. *Musgrave*, Criteria for Foreign Tax Credit, 84 et seqq.; *Vogel*, Intertax 1988, 310 (311); *Li*, CTJ 2002, 823 (828). Although the concept of capital import neutrality ensures that foreign investors do not suffer a competitive disadvantage with regard to the overall tax burden compared to domestic investors, some disadvantages can be identified, cf. *Jacobs*, Internationale Unternehmensbesteuerung, 23. One of these disadvantages is the increased incentive of tax planning with the help of transfer pricing. If foreign income is exempt from taxation in the country of residence, investors and companies from that residency could lower their overall tax-burden by transferring certain parts of the company or specific functions and its related chances and risks from high to low tax jurisdictions, *Jacobs*, Internationale Unternehmensbesteuerung, 23 et. seq. This, however, would cause distortions of taxpayers' decisions with regard to the location of investment and thus violates the concept of decision neutrality, cf. *Wendt*, A Common Tax Base for Multinational Enterprises in the European Union, 46.

[87]Cf. *Jacobs/Spengel/Schäfer*, Intertax 2003, 214 (218).

[88]Cf. *Brown*, FTR 2011, 565 (601 et seqq.).

[89]Cf. *Griffith/Hines/Sørensen*, in: Mirrlees et al. (Eds.) Dimensions of Tax Design: The Mirrlees Review, 914 (926); *Jacobs/Spengel/Schäfer*, Intertax 2003, 214 (218).

4. Capital Ownership Neutrality

Another concept that has been put forward by *Desai* and *Hines* in recent years is the concept of capital ownership neutrality.[90] They point out that assets developed by multinationals, e.g. through R&D, or marketing are often highly specific and the productivity of such assets may depend highly on who owns and controls them.[91] Against this background, it is important that tax rules do not distort cross-border ownership patterns.[92] Capital shall rather be transferred to the jurisdiction where it can be utilised most efficiently. That is the case if it is impossible to increase output through the trade of capital ownership among investors.[93] This does not necessarily require that capital is equally productive in the hands of all investors but that each investor acquires the assets that guarantee the highest pre-tax return and hence the highest after-tax return since taxes should not influence decisions of cross-border investment.[94] Consequently, the investor who is willing to pay the highest price on a pre-tax basis is automatically the (most productive) owner of the asset.[95] This concept implies as well that a change of the capital owner must be possible without a corresponding realisation of unrealised gains.[96]

Capital Ownership Neutrality is attained either if the income generated within a jurisdiction is exclusively subject to taxation in the source country and consequently exempt from taxation in the country of residence (source-only taxation) or if the country of residence taxes the worldwide income of the investor in accordance with the tax rules applicable in the country of residence while the country of source entirely waives its competence to tax income that is connected with its territory (residence-only taxation).[97]

---

[90] Cf. *Desai/Hines*, NTJ 2003, 487 (487).

[91] Cf. *Griffith/Hines/Sørensen,* in: Mirrlees et al. (Eds.) Dimensions of Tax Design: The Mirrlees Review, 914 (953).

[92] Cf. *Desai/Hines*, Economic Foundations of International Tax Rules, 24.

[93] Cf. *Desai/Hines*, NTJ 2003, 487 (495).

[94] Cf. *Griffith/Hines/Sørensen,* in: Mirrlees et al. (Eds.), Dimensions of Tax Design: The Mirrlees Review, 914 (953).

[95] Cf. *Desai/Hines*, NTJ 2003, 487 (495); cf. also *Waltrich*, Cross-Border Taxation of Permanent Establishments, 185.

[96] Cf. *Kraft/Gebhardt*, FR 2012, 403 (403 et seqq.); *Gebhardt*, Deutsches Tax Treaty Overriding, 109; *Moser*, Die Hinzurechnungsbesteuerung nach den §§ 7–14 AStG und die Besteuerung ausländischer Familienstiftungen nach § 15 AStG, 17.

[97] Cf. *Schön*, WTJ 2009, 67 (81).

5. Significance for the Subject under Investigation

All concepts discussed provide tax neutrality in different ways and are somehow idealistic concepts, requiring that cross-border business activities are only taxed once either in the country of residence or in the country of source.[98] However, the fundamental goal of the concept of tax neutrality aiming to minimise discrimination with regard to particular economic choices is of significance for the subject under investigation in different ways.

The concept implies that the decision with regard to the kind of business activities carried on should, in principle, be independent of tax consequences. This point proves of particular relevance with regard to the approach currently discussed unter Pillar One aiming to introduce a new nexus apart from the traditional PE concept as well as new profit allocation rules. Since the OECD emphasises that digital technology is adopted across the economy and is therefore increasingly the economy itself,[99] the concept of tax neutrality requires that any new rules that may be developed do not only affect specific enterprises or business models. Put differently, rather than 'ring-fencing', any new taxation rules considered should be applicable to all enterprises and business activities, no matter what kind of business model is carried on by the enterprise.

Furthermore, the principle of neutrality also requires that tax rules shall not influence decisions of enterprises to grow beyond certain revenue or profit margin thresholds. Therefore, and this is again of particular relevance for the reform proposals currently discussed unter Pillar One, in order to prove neutral any new taxation rules suggested should not put forward arbitrary and unjustifiable quantitative thresholds that may influence business decisions.

IV. Efficiency

1. Fundamental Concept

Another well-recognised principle for the design of tax rules is efficiency. In general, efficient tax rules are those which minimise both compliance costs for taxpayers as well as administration costs for the relevant tax authorities.[100]

[98] Cf. *Bärsch*, Taxation of Hybrid Financial Instruments, 52.

[99] Cf. OECD, BEPS Action 1: Final Report 2015, para. 115.

[100] Cf. OECD, Electronic Commerce: Taxation Framework Conditions 1998, para. 9; *Graetz*, TLR 2001, 261 (310). From the perspective of the society, both compliance as well as administration costs are social costs due to diverting resources which could have been used for

Compliance costs incur directly at the level of the taxpayer when following their tax-related obligations.[101] With regard to cross-border transactions, such costs arise due to the various requirements imposed by the respective jurisdictions where business activities are carried on, e.g. the need to calculate different tax bases as a result of different profit allocation rules, the preparation of transfer pricing documentation such as a local file, a master file and a CbC Report or the need to consider and comply with deviating administrative procedures in the respective jurisdictions.[102] Moreover, costs incurred by entrusting third parties such as tax specialists in order to comply with their tax related obligations are regarded as compliance costs.[103]

Administration costs, in contrast, arise to tax authorities who are obliged to establish and operate a comprehensive and functioning tax system.[104] Such costs incur due to, e.g., the implementation of control mechanisms to avoid the abuse of tax law, the need to employ tax experts to carry out mutual agreement procedures and arbitration proceedings or the verification of transfer prices.[105]

Administration costs and compliance costs are interrelated.[106] On the one hand, the level of administration costs depends on the taxpayers' will to arrange their tax affairs in a way that suits the tax authorities. Some taxpayers, especially those engaged in cross-border activities, might be willing to spend considerable resources to engage tax experts in order to avoid or mitigate their tax burden

---

more productive purposes and are therefore to be avoided, cf. *Graetz*, TLR 2001, 261 (310); *Bärsch*, Taxation of Hybrid Financial Instruments, 69.

[101] Cf. *Shaw/Slemrod/Whiting,* in: Mirrlees et al. (Eds.), Dimensions of Tax Design: The Mirrlees Review, 1100 (1106). For an overview of the development of compliance costs measured with regard to the time in hours spent to prepare the tax return see *Collier/Kari/Ropponen/Simmler/Todtenhaupt*, Dissecting the EU's Recent Anti-Tax Avoidance Measures, EconPol Policy Report, Sept. 2018, 21 et seqq.

[102] Cf. *Wagner*, BFuP 2005, 528 (529 et seq.); *Wagner*, StuW 2005, 93 (94 et seq.); *Tresch*, Public Finance: A Normative Theory, 172; *Bärsch*, Taxation of Hybrid Financial Instruments, 70.

[103] Cf. *Shaw/Slemrod/Whiting,* in: Mirrlees et al. (Eds.), Dimensions of Tax Design: The Mirrless Review, 1100 (1106); *Bärsch*, Taxation of Hybrid Financial Instruments, 70.

[104] Cf. *Shaw/Slemrod/Whiting,* in: Mirrlees et al. (Eds.), Dimensions of Tax Design: The Mirrless Review, 1100 (1106); *Tresch*, Public Finance: A Normative Theory, 171; *Bärsch*, Taxation of Hybrid Financial Instruments, 70.

[105] Cf. *Jacobs/Spengel/Schäfer*, Intertax 2004, 268 (271); *Weisbach*, The University of Chicago Law Review 1999, 860 (871); *Bärsch*, Taxation of Hybrid Financial Instruments, 70.

[106] Cf. *Tresch*, Public Finance: A Normative Theory, 172; *Waltrich*, Cross-Border Taxation of Permanent Establishments, 188.

through tax planning and tax avoidance strategies.[107] In response, tax authorities consider it worthwhile to expend resources to limit the damage of such behaviour for the overall society.[108] On the other hand, the level of compliance costs also depends on administrative procedures and requirements. Changes in the tax law, e.g., especially if those changes increase the complexity of the law code, usually result in higher compliance costs for the taxpayer.[109] If the compliance costs exceed an acceptable level for the taxpayer, negative effects on international trade and investment may occur, regardless of the actual tax burden itself.[110]

2. Significance for the Subject under Investigation

With regard to the subject under investigation, any changes to the international corporate tax system must also be evaluated from an efficiency point of view. Especially, if existing international tax rules are not replaced but rather complemented, as currently suggested under Pillar One, it must not only be assessed whether such additional rules are appropriate to address the tax challenges arising from the digitalisation of the economy but also at what costs such additional rules are introduced. Any additional measures must be both administrable for the tax authorities and executable under reasonable efforts for the taxpayer.

V. Certainty and Simplicity

1. Fundamental Concept

The principle of certainty and simplicity demands that tax rules ought to be clear and simple to understand, so that taxpayers understand their obligations and entitlements.[111] *Adam Smith* already emphasised in 1776, when he talked about the

[107] Cf. *Guyton/Hare/Stavrianos/Toder*, NTJ 2003, 673 (675); *Schön*, Intertax 2019, 1003 (1007).

[108] Cf. *Shaw/Slemrod/Whiting*, in: Mirrlees et al. (Eds.), Dimensions of Tax Design: The Mirrless Review, 1100 (1106).

[109] Cf. *Bärsch*, Taxation of Hybrid Financial Instruments, 70 et seq.; *Guyton/Hare/Stavrianos/Toder*, NTJ 2003, 673 (675); *Waltrich*, Cross-Border Taxation of Permanent Establishments, 189.

[110] Cf. *Bennett/Dunahoo*, Intertax 2005, 51 (53).

[111] Cf. *Hey*, in: Tipke/Lang (Eds.), Steuerrecht, Sec. 3, para. 243; *Lang*, StuW 2011, 144 (151); *Schäfer*, International Company Taxation in the Era of Information and Communication

four principles of an economically efficient taxation,[112] that 'the time of payment, the manner of payment, the quantity to be paid, ought all to be clear and plain to the contributor, and to every other person'[113].

This does not imply that legal provisions have to be designed in the sense that even non-specialised taxpayers are able to calculate their tax liability *ex ante.*[114] Such simplifications seem practically utopian.[115] However, it can be demanded that legal provisions are designed in a way that taxpayers can anticipate the tax consequences in advance of a transaction.[116] In this regard, a distinction can be made between the determinedness of tax provisions and the clarity of tax provisions.[117] The requirement of determinedness, on the one side, addresses the use of vague and indeterminate legal terms that leave room for various interpretations and leeway in the taxable event.[118] On the other side, the requirement of clarity is concerned with the relation of the provisions to one another.[119] Especially, legal provisions that suffer from unsurpassed complexity, e.g. through the use of a 'rule/exception/counter-exception/exception of the counter-exception'-structure could cause that tax rules do not comply with the requirement of certainty and simplicity.[120] While the use of vague and indeterminate legal terms are mostly used purposefully in order to leave the legal provision open for further developments, regulations that fail to comply with the requirement of determinedness are usually not intended and rather a result of poor legislation.[121]

Technologies, 81; OECD, BEPS Action 1: Final Report 2015, para. 10; OECD, E-Commerce: Transfer Pricing and Business Profits Taxation, p. 91, para. 66.

[112]The four principles Smith talked about were: 'equality of taxation', 'certainty of taxation', 'convenience of payment' and 'economy in collection', cf. *Smith*: An Inquiry Into the Nature and Causes of the Wealth of the Nations, 1976, 825 et seqq.

[113]*Smith*, An Inquiry Into the Nature and Causes of the Wealth of the Nations, 1976, 825, para. 4.

[114]Cf. *Lang*, StuW 2011, 144 (151); *Ditz*, Internationale Gewinnabgrenzung bei Betriebsstätten, 103 et seqq.

[115]Cf. *Ditz*, Internationale Gewinnabgrenzung bei Betriebsstätten, 103.

[116]Cf. OECD, BEPS Action 1: Final Report 2015, para. 10.

[117]This distinction is made by the German Federal Constitutional Court, cf. e.g. BVerfG, 9 Apr. 2003, 1 BvL 1/01, BVerfGE 108, 52; cf. also *Hey*, in: Tipke/Lang (Eds.), Steuerrecht, Sec. 3, para. 244; *Waldhoff/Grefrath*, IStR 2013, 477 (478 et seqq.).

[118]Cf. *Hey*, in: Tipke/Lang (Eds.), Steuerrecht, Sec. 3, para. 244.

[119]Cf. *Hey*, in: Tipke/Lang (Eds.), Steuerrecht, Sec. 3, para. 244.

[120]Cf. *Hey*, in: Tipke/Lang (Eds.), Steuerrecht, Sec. 3, para. 244.

[121]Cf. *Hey*, in: Tipke/Lang (Eds.), Steuerrecht, Sec. 3, para. 244.

The requirement of certainty also relates to the stability of the tax system and the tax practices in a country.[122] In order to promote certainty, tax rules and tax practices should be stable over time. Frequent chances of tax rules and their interpretation make it hard for taxpayers to foresee and calculate their tax burden which could result in a negative or a delaying impact on investment decisions.[123]

Both principles are not only closely related to each other, i.e. the more complex tax rules are, the greater the likelihood that the principle of certainty is compromised,[124] but they are also interrelated to other principles of taxation such as the principle of efficiency and equity.[125] Regarding the interrelation of simplicity and certainty to the efficiency of tax rules, it can be said that tax rules that are simple and certain usually reduce both compliance costs for taxpayers and administration costs for the relevant tax authorities. This can be explained by the observation that simple and certain tax rules usually do not provide tax avoidance opportunities, unintentional tax arbitrage or international preferential tax regimes.[126] Such activities may trigger deadweight losses for the economy and should therefore be avoided.[127] However, a higher degree of simplicity might also lead to a lower level of equity as complex tax statutes and tax procedures are usually implemented in order to promote thoughts of equity.[128]

2. Significance for the Subject under Investigation

In order to be able to anticipate the tax consequences of taxpayers' business activities in advance it is key that any new taxing rights and profit allocation rules

---

[122] Cf. EC, 23 Oct. 2001, COM(2001) 582 final, 28.

[123] Cf. EC, 23 Oct. 2001, COM(2001) 582 final, 28. A report of the IMF/OECD for the G20 Finance Ministers on tax certainty identifies further reasons for tax uncertainty which includes the following: increased internationalisation of business activities and emergence and spread of new business models, fragmented and unilateral policy decisions, heightened concern with aggressive tax planning, specific court decisions or updates to international tax rules, cf. IMF/OECD, Report on tax certainty 2017, p. 5. The report also outlines practical tools to enhance tax certainty, cf. IMF/OECD, Report on tax certainty 2017, p. 6.

[124] Cf. AICPA, Guiding principles of good tax policy, p. 7.

[125] Cf. *Graetz*, TLR 2001, 261 (310 et seq.).

[126] Cf. EC, 23 Oct. 2001, COM(2001) 582 final, 28.

[127] Cf. OECD, BEPS Action 1: Final Report 2015, para. 10.

[128] Cf. EC, 23 Oct. 2001, COM(2001) 582 final, 28; *Waltrich*, Cross-Border Taxation of Permanent Establishments, 190; *Slemrod*, in: Aaron/Gale (Eds.), Economic Effects of Fundamental Tax Reform, 355 (357).

developed, as currently discussed under Pillar One, are precise and insofar leave no room for various interpretations and leeway. Especially, the use of vague and indeterminate legal terms should be avoided in order to promote the principle of certainty and simplicity.

In this regard, it is also fundamental that any taxation rules developed must precisely define all relevant conditions under which taxable income is to arise in a given jurisdiction.[129] Furthermore, in order to enhance certainty, the new approach should not provide for the use of several different alternatives, as such new rules must also be implemented into the national taxation law of the various countries. While such alternative solutions would certainly enhance flexibility and acceptance among countries, they would most likely also lead to differences in implementation which in turn may cause double taxation.

VI. Effectiveness and Fairness

1. Fundamental Concept

The principle of effectiveness and fairness comprises three important characteristics of taxation rules. First, they ought to produce the right amount of tax at the right time.[130] Second, they should minimise the potential for tax evasion and avoidance strategies while at the same time keep counteracting measures proportionate to the respective risks involved.[131] This also implies that both double taxation and double non-taxation shall be avoided. Third, taxation rules should be enforceable in order to prove effective in practice.[132] In this context, it is evident that taxation rules that cannot be enforced in practice can neither prove effective nor fair since they are not capable to achieve its basic objective.[133] Enforceability directly interrelates with simplicity, since tax rules that are simple and easy to understand can also be enforced more easily.[134]

---

[129] Cf. *Förster/Greil/Hilse*, ITPJ 2020, 3 (5).

[130] Cf. OECD, Electronic Commerce: Taxation Framework Conditions 1998, para. 9; OECD, BEPS Action 1: Final Report 2015, para. 10.

[131] Cf. OECD, Electronic Commerce: Taxation Framework Conditions 1998, para. 9; OECD, BEPS Action 1: Final Report 2015, para. 10.

[132] Cf. OECD, BEPS Action 1: Final Report 2015, para. 10.

[133] Cf. *Jacobs/Spengel/Schäfer*, Intertax 2013, 214 (221).

[134] Cf. *Bärsch*, Taxation of Hybrid Financial Instruments, 74.

2. Significance for the Subject under Investigation

Taxation rights for corporate profits are considered to produce the right amount of tax at the right time if they are aligned with the jurisdiction in which those corporate profits are deemed to arise.[135] Against this background, it needs to be analysed whether the new nexus as well as profit allocation rules currently being developed under Pillar One appear suitable to meet this policy objective, especially taking into account the challenges arising to the PE rules through the digitalisation of the economy. In this context, it is also to be analysed whether these new rules are designed in a way that they avoid the potential for double taxation as well as non-double taxation and reduce the potential for tax evasion and avoidance.

Additionally, it is key that any new taxation rights developed are designed in a way that they can be implemented by all members of the Inclusive Framework requiring that the new taxation rules meet the basic legal requirements of the participating jurisdictions.[136] Moreover, within the European Union, compliance of the new taxation rules with the fundamental freedoms is required.[137]

Furthermore, when assessing effectiveness and fairness, it appears to be of importance that the new taxing right also proves enforceable in practice, i.a. these new rules should be designed in a way that they prove implementable by all members of the Inclusive Framework, i.e. not only by developed countries but also by developing and emerging countries.[138]

VII. Flexibility

1. Fundamental Concept

The criterion of flexibility calls for a tax framework that is flexible and dynamic enough in order to accommodate commercial and technological developments, taking into account that such developments are often difficult to predict.[139] While structural features of tax rules should certainly prove durable in a changing policy

[135] Cf. *Förster/Greil/Hilse*, ITPJ 2020, 3 (4).

[136] Cf. *Förster/Greil/Hilse*, ITPJ 2020, 3 (5).

[137] Cf. *Förster/Greil/Hilse*, ITPJ 2020, 3 (5); *Junkers*, IStR 2019, 850 (851).

[138] Cf. OECD, BEPS Action 1: Final Report 2015, para. 10.

[139] Cf. OECD, Electronic Commerce: Taxation Framework Conditions 1998, para. 9; OECD, BEPS Action 1: Final Report 2015, para. 10.

context and insofar provide certainty for the taxpayer, tax rules should further allow governments to respond as needed not only to meet revenue needs, but also to keep pace with new developments, may it be through the emergence of new business models, changes in business practices or other changes induced through technological or commercial development.[140] Insofar, taxation rules should be capable of adoption if certain aspects of the taxation rules need to be revisited.[141]

The degree of flexibility may cause tension with other taxation principles such as the principle of stability as well as certainty and simplicity.[142] While flexibility may be obtained through the use of vague and indeterminate legal terms in order to leave tax rules open for further developments, it must be considered that flexibility received in this way may only be bought at the expense of certainty and simplicity. Furthermore, quick changes to the tax rules may also affect their stability.[143] Hence, trade-offs could result when trying to achieve the principle of flexibility.

2. Significance for the Subject under Investigation

The digitalisation of the economy has brought about new business models that do not require a physical presence in the market country to generate substantial revenues in this country. This development challenges the ability of the market jurisdiction to tax the corresponding profits generated within its borders.[144] Against this background, it is necessary to analysed whether the new rules currently being developed under Pillar One prove flexible enough not only to address the current challenges brought about to the corporate taxation rules, but also to accommodate future commercial and technological developments.

---

[140] Cf. OECD, BEPS Action 1: Final Report 2015, para. 10.

[141] Cf. OECD, Are the Current Treaty Rules for Taxing Business Profits Appropriate for E-Commerce? Final Report 2004, para. 88.

[142] Cf. HM Revenue & Customs, Corporate Tax Reform, p. 11, *Bärsch*, Taxation of Hybrid Financial Instruments, 73; *Neumark*, Grundsätze gerechter und ökonomisch rationaler Steuerpolitik, 54 et seq., 283 et seqq.

[143] Cf. HM Revenue & Customs, Corporate Tax Reform, p. 11.

[144] Cf. *Spinosa/Chand*, Intertax 2018, 476 (479); *Hadzhieva*, Impact of Digitalisation on International Tax Matters, p. 10; OECD, BEPS Action 1: Interim Report 2018, para. 379.

C. Fundamentals of the Taxation of Permanent Establishments

I. Historical Development of the PE Concept

1. Origins of the PE Concept

The origins of the PE concept trace back to Prussia.[1] Initially, the term 'Betriebsstätte'[2] was used in a non-tax-oriented context in the Industrial Code of Prussia[3] as early as 1845 and was later adopted in the business legislation of the German Empire.[4] In this context, the term denoted the space used for the conduct of a business activity.[5] PE as a concept for tax purposes emerged as the need of preventing double taxation among different Prussian municipalities grew in the middle of the 19th century.[6] More precisely, the model for municipality regulation suggested that a 'trade with a fixed place of business'[7] should only be taxed in the respective municipality where it is located, regardless of whether the owner

[1]Cf. *Skaar*, Permanent Establishment—Erosion of a Tax Treaty Principle, 76.

[2]EN: Permanent Establishment.

[3]Industrial Code of Prussia, 17 Jan. 1845, Sec. 26, see Prussian statute book 41 (1845).

[4]Cf. *Kolck*, Der Betriebsstättenbegriff im nationalen und internationalen Steuerrecht, 15; *Skaar*, Permanent Establishment—Erosion of a Tax Treaty Principle, 76.

[5]Cf. *Kolck*, Der Betriebsstättenbegriff im nationalen und internationalen Steuerrecht, 11, note 9 with further references; *Skaar*, Permanent Establishment—Erosion of a Tax Treaty Principle, 76; *Sokolov*, in: Brugger/Plansky (Eds.), Permanent Establishments in International and EU Tax Law, 13 (15).

[6]Cf. *Skaar*, Permanent Establishment—Erosion of a Tax Treaty Principle, 76.

[7]DE: Stehendes Gewerbe.

S. Hentschel, *The Taxation of Permanent Establishments*, Hallesche Schriften zur Betriebswirtschaft 37, https://doi.org/10.1007/978-3-658-34000-1_3

of the business lives in another municipality.[8] The first PE definition comparable to today's German terminology can be found in the German Double Taxation Act of 1909[9] which intended to eliminate double taxation among German states.[10]

2. Adoption of the PE Concept in International Tax Treaties

The first contemporary international tax treaty that contained fundamental elements of a PE definition was the 1899 convention[11] entered into by Austria-Hungary and Prussia.[12] Its pivotal concept, which was born out of the necessity to settle the conflict between residence state and source state taxation and insofar homogenise the tax-treatment applicable to cross-border business transactions, was defined as follows:

> 'The term "business establishment" includes branch establishments, factories, depots, offices, places where purchases and sales are effected and other business facilities by which the owner, partner, manager, or other permanent representative carries on his business activities.'[13]

This convention, which provides an early attempt to define the basic rule for the taxation of business profits by other means than a mere list of examples, clearly

---

[8]Cf. *Skaar*, Permanent Establishment—Erosion of a Tax Treaty Principle, 76 et seq.; also *Kroppen*, IWB 2005, 727 (728).

[9]German Double Taxation Act, 22 Mar. 1909, RGBl. 1909, 332.

[10]Cf. *Skaar*, Permanent Establishment—Erosion of a Tax Treaty Principle, 78. A PE was defined in Art. 3(2) of the German Double Taxation Act of 1909 as follows: 'Betriebsstätte im Sinne dieses Gesetzes ist jede feste örtliche Anlage oder Einrichtung, die der Ausübung des Betriebs eines stehenden Gewerbes dient. Außer dem Hauptsitz eines Betriebes gelten hiernach als Betriebsstätten: Zweigniederlassungen, Fabrikationsstätten, Ein- und Verkaufsstellen, Niederlagen, Kontore und sonstige zur Ausübung des Gewerbes durch den Unternehmer selbst, dessen Geschäftsteilhaber, Prokuristen oder andere ständige Vertreter unterhaltene Geschäftseinrichtungen.'.

[11]DTA, Prussia/Austria-Hungary, 21 June 1899; cf. *League of Nations*, Double Taxation and Fiscal Evasion, Collection of International Agreements 1928, Vol. 1, 249.

[12]Cf. *Skaar*, Permanent Establishment—Erosion of a Tax Treaty Principle, 79.

[13]Translation by *Peter Rohn*, Director of the University of Washington Treaty Research Center, cf. *Williams*, Fundamentals of Permanent Establishments, 3. The original German wording is as follows: 'Als Betriebsstätten gelten Zweigniederlassungen, Fabrikationsstätten, Niederlagen, Comptoire, Ein- oder Verkaufsstellen und sonstige Geschäftseinrichtungen zur Ausübung des stehenden Gewerbes durch den Unternehmer selbst, Geschäftsinhaber, Prokuristen oder andere ständige Vertreter', Art. 2(1) sentence 2 DTA, Prussia/Austria-Hungary, 21 June 1899.

favours source state taxation and became the model for a number of DTAs in order to determine whether or not a particular kind of income shall be taxed in the country where it originates.[14]

The post-World War I developments proceeded along the original German lines and were marked by initiatives of newly-founded international organisations aiming to end the negative effects of international double taxation on international business and trade which were felt even stronger due to the high post war taxes.[15] This work led to the first Draft of a Bilateral Convention for the Prevention of Double Taxation by the League of Nations in 1927.[16] Article 5 of this convention determines that the taxation of business profits was allocated to the source state if the enterprise operated through a PE in that state. Instead of providing a general definition of the term PE, Article 5(2) of the draft convention rather provided a list of examples which was phrased as follows:

> 'The real centres of management, affiliated companies, branches, factories, agencies, warehouses, offices, depots, shall be regarded as permanent establishments. The fact that an undertaking has business dealings with a foreign country through a *bona fide* agent of independent status (broker, commission agent, etc.) shall not be held to mean that the undertaking in question has a permanent establishment in that country.'[17]

In this regard, it is noteworthy that in addition to branches also 'affiliated companies' which comprises subsidiaries were included in the PE concept.[18] Compared to tax treaties concluded before 1927, where the inclusion of affiliated companies was not usual, this draft legislation allows for source state taxation to a greater extent.[19]

---

[14]Cf. *Reimer,* in: Reimer/Rust (Eds.), Klaus Vogel on Double Taxation Conventions, Art. 5, para. 2; *Skaar*, Permanent Establishment—Erosion of a Tax Treaty Principle, 80; *Kroppen*, IWB 2005, 727 (728).

[15]Cf. *Williams*, Fundamentals of Permanent Establishments, 3; *Skaar*, Permanent Establishment—Erosion of a Tax Treaty Principle, 81 et seqq.

[16]Cf. League of Nations, 12 Apr. 1927, Double Taxation and Tax Evasion—Report.

[17]League of Nations, 12 Apr. 1927, Double Taxation and Tax Evasion—Report, p. 11. This 1927 Draft Convention appears to be the first report of the Fiscal Committee of the League of Nations where the German term 'Betriebsstätte' is translated as 'permanent establishment' rather than 'business establishment' as done before, cf. *Skaar*, Permanent Establishment—Erosion of a Tax Treaty Principle, 87, note 91.

[18]Cf. *Skaar*, Permanent Establishment—Erosion of a Tax Treaty Principle, 87; *Kroppen*, IWB 2005, 727 (728).

[19]Cf. *Skaar*, Permanent Establishment—Erosion of a Tax Treaty Principle, 87 et seq.

The 1940 s were marked by a controversial discussion between advocates that supported broad source state taxation (Mexico Draft of 1943)[20] and advocates that were in favour of broad residence state taxation (London Draft of 1946)[21].[22] While the Mexican model introduced a system in which the PE was only an example, not a decisive criterion for the taxation of business profits in the source state and was therefore supported by capital importing countries, the London model returned to the need of a PE as a condition for source state taxation of business profits and was consequently supported by capital exporting countries.[23] Neither the Mexican model nor the London model has succeeded in establishing a general definition of the basic rule of the PE.[24]

3. The Emergence of the OECD Model Tax Convention

Where the work on developing a system for the avoidance of double taxation had left off by the League of Nations, the Organisation for European Economic Cooperation (hereinafter: OEEC) and its successor, the OECD, continued.[25] In 1963, the Committee on Fiscal Affairs, which was formed in 1956, submitted a summary report to which the complete OECD MC and an official commentary (hereinafter: OECD MC Commentary) were appended.[26] The appearance of the PE concept in Article 5 OECD MC in 1963 and the slightly modified version in 1977 marked the beginning of a new era in international taxation.[27] Most of the changes in the definition of the PE during that time strengthened residence state taxation and therefore narrowed down the scope of taxation in the source state.[28]

---

[20] Cf. League of Nations, Mexico Draft 1943.

[21] Cf. League of Nations, London Draft 1943.

[22] Cf. *Kroppen*, IWB 2005, 727 (728).

[23] Cf. *Skaar*, Permanent Establishment—Erosion of a Tax Treaty Principle, 92 et seq.; *Lüdicke*, Überlegungen zur deutschen DBA Politik, 115; *Esterer*, in: Beck'sche Steuerkommentare et al. (Eds.), Doppelbesteuerung, 137 (137).

[24] Cf. OECD MC Commentary 2017, Introduction, para. 4; *Skaar*, Permanent Establishment—Erosion of a Tax Treaty Principle, 95.

[25] Cf. *Uckmar*, in: Amatucci (Ed.), Double Taxation Conventions, 161 (162).

[26] Cf. *Uckmar*, in: Amatucci (Ed.), Double Taxation Conventions, 161 (162 et seq.).

[27] Cf. *Kroppen*, IWB 2005, 727 (728); *Skaar*, Permanent Establishment—Erosion of a Tax Treaty Principle, 100; *Sokolov*, in: Brugger/Plansky (Eds.), Permanent Establishments in International and EU Tax Law, 13 (28).

[28] Cf. *Sokolov*, in: Brugger/Plansky (Eds.), Permanent Establishments in International and EU Tax Law, 13 (28).

Since 1977, the pressure to update Article 5 OECD MC and the corresponding OECD MC Commentary to the fundamentally changing, global circumstances has increased significantly and not only stopped the trend to narrow the nexus for taxation in the source state but rather reversed this trend.[29] Several updates to Article 5 OECD MC and the OECD Commentary to Article 5 resulted in a constant reduction of the PE threshold allowing source state taxation to a greater extent. This development is reflected, e.g., by the discussion on the optional extension of the PE threshold by a so-called service PE as well as the so-called 'painter-example' in the OECD MC.[30]

4. The BEPS Project and Its Implications for the PE Concept

Further changes to the PE concept were introduced as a result of the BEPS project which was initiated at the meeting of the G20 in Los Cabos from 18–19 June 2012.[31] At this meeting, the G20 demanded action against the trend of base erosion and profit shifting initiated through MNEs which engage in tax planning strategies ultimately resulting in revenue losses for governments.[32] The BEPS Action Plan contains 15 action points and aims to 'ensure the coherence of corporate income taxation at the international level'[33].

The results of the BEPS Action Plan were presented by the OECD on 5 October 2015.[34] Several action points of the BEPS Action Plan contain changes that are relevant for the taxation of PEs. Especially, BEPS Action 7 aiming to prevent the artificial avoidance of the PE status through, e.g., the use of commissionaire arrangements and specific activity exemptions used to inappropriately avoid a tax nexus in the source state resulted in changes to Article 5 OECD MC and the corresponding OECD MC Commentary.[35] These changes continued the trend to

[29] Cf. *Sokolov*, in: Brugger/Plansky (Eds.), Permanent Establishments in International and EU Tax Law, 13 (26 et seq.); *Kroppen*, IWB 2005, 727 (728); *Esterer*, in: Beck'sche Steuerkommentare et al. (Eds.), Doppelbesteuerung, 137 (137 et seqq.).

[30] For the optional extension of the PE threshold by a Service PE cf. OECD MC Commentary 2017, Art. 5, para. 155. For the painter example cf. OECD MC Commentary 2017, Art. 5, para. 17.

[31] G20, Leaders Declaration, Los Cabos, 18–19 June 2012, para. 48.

[32] Cf. OECD, Action Plan on Base Erosion and Profit Shifting 2013, p. 13.

[33] OECD, Action Plan on Base Erosion and Profit Shifting 2013, pp. 13 et seqq.

[34] OECD, BEPS Project—Explanatory Statement.

[35] See in more detail OECD, BEPS Action 7: Final Report 2015.

widen the PE threshold in order to strengthen taxation of the source state.[36] Also other BEPS Actions either have a direct or an indirect effect on the taxation of PEs. Especially, BEPS Action 1 dealing with the tax challenges raised by the digital economy,[37] BEPS Action 3 aiming to strengthen Controlled Foreign Company (hereinafter: CFC) rules,[38] BEPS Action 6 dealing with the prevention of tax treaty abuse,[39] BEPS Actions 8–10 focusing on the alignment of transfer pricing outcomes with value creation,[40] BEPS Action 13[41] containing changes to transfer pricing documentation as well as BEPS Action 15 introducing the Multilateral Instrument (hereinafter: MLI).[42] Throughout the analysis, the changes resulting from these action points will be elaborated in further detail.

Figure 1 provides an overview of the BEPS project and classifies the different BEPS Actions around three main pillars:

II. Rationale and Justification Underlying the PE Concept

Despite its significance and long-standing history, the PE concept as implemented in the OECD MC is only a recommended format which does not have legal biding force, neither at international nor at national level.[43] Nevertheless, OECD member countries largely use the OECD MC as a basis when concluding or revising their bilateral DTAs.[44]

If implemented in the respective bilateral DTAs of the contracting states, the PE concept functions as a threshold for determining whether a particular type of income arising in a state of which the taxpayer is not a resident may or may not be taxed in the state where it originates.[45] According to Article 7(1) OECD MC, the source state can generally only tax business profits of a non-resident enterprise if this enterprise carries on business activities in the source state through a PE.

[36] Cf. also *Wassermeyer/Kaeser*, in: W/K/S/D (Eds.), Doppelbesteuerung, Art. 5 MA, para. 1.

[37] See in more detail OECD, BEPS Action 1: Final Report 2015.

[38] See in more detail OECD, BEPS Action 3: Final Report 2015.

[39] See in more detail OECD, BEPS Action 6: Final Report 2015.

[40] See in more detail OECD, BEPS Actions 8–10: Final Report 2015.

[41] See in more detail OECD, BEPS Action 13: Final Report 2015.

[42] See in more detail OECD, BEPS Action 15: Final Report 2015.

[43] Cf. *Uckmar*, in: Amatucci (Ed.), Double Taxation Conventions, 161 (162 et seq.).

[44] Cf. OECD MC Commentary 2017, Introduction, para. 13.

[45] Cf. OECD MC Commentary 2017, Art. 7, para. 1; *Reimer*, in: Reimer/Rust (Eds.), Klaus Vogel on Double Taxation Conventions, Art. 5, para. 2.

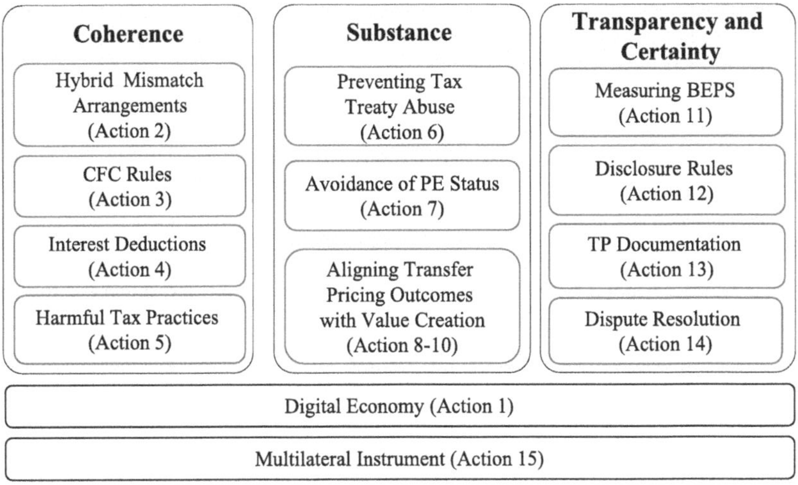

Figure 1 Overview of the BEPS Project (Source: Own illustration based on OECD, Launch of the 2015 Final Reports, slide 8)

Put differently, until an enterprise of one state carries on business activities to the extent that a PE is constituted in another state in which it is not a resident, it should not be regarded to participate in the economic life of that state to the extent that it falls within the taxing jurisdiction of that other state.[46] Insofar, the PE concept reconciles requirements of inter-nation equity and fairness by assigning tax revenue to the source state and maintaining efficiency and simplicity by establishing a minimum threshold in order to avoid unconditional source-based taxation if the contact of the taxpayer to the source country is only peripheral or occasional.[47]

Commonly, three aspects are put forward in order to justify the PE concept. First, from a historical point of view, the original idea behind the PE concept was that it could be understood as an expression of 'economic allegiance' to the source state, requiring anyone obtaining substantial benefits from an economic community to reimburse this community for the benefits obtained in form of taxes.[48] Put differently, it is argued that the source states right to tax profits that

[46]Cf. OECD MC Commentary 2017, Art. 5, para. 132.

[47]Cf. *Reimer*, in: Reimer/Rust (Eds.), Klaus Vogel on Double Taxation Conventions, Art. 5, para. 3.

[48]Cf. *Pinto*, E-Commerce and Source-Based Income Taxation, 78.

can be attributed to the PE should be regarded as a compensation for the source states efforts to create, safeguard and maintain good economic conditions such as public infrastructure or government services for the foreign investors.[49]

Second, the PE concept aims to provide neutrality between different forms of a secondary establishment that are available to foreign investors, i.e. a PE and a foreign subsidiary.[50] Put another way, by attributing the profits generated by a PE to the source state, the PE is put on equal footing with a resident entrepreneur.[51]

Third, practical justifications are put forward. By establishing a minimum threshold and thereby restricting taxation by the source state to cases where a certain level of economic activity in the source state is exceeded,[52] the PE threshold aims to reduce both compliance costs for taxpayers as well as administration costs for the relevant tax authorities.[53] Thought in this way, the PE threshold can be viewed as representing a workable balance or compromise between the needs of businesses that operate in a cross-border context and tax administrations.[54]

Nevertheless, in particular the idea of compensation requires new justification or must be reconsidered, as it originates from the former DTAs between industrialised countries and can therefore only be transferred to a limited extent to today's globalised service society.[55] This is particularly evident in the attempt to transfer the traditional understanding of the PE concept to the taxation of the digitalised economy.[56]

---

[49] Cf. *Vogel*, in: Vogel (Ed.), Grundfragen des Internationalen Steuerrechts, 3 (27 et seq.); *Reimer*, in: Reimer/Schmid/Orell (Eds.), Permanent Establishments, Part 1 [B], para. 37.

[50] Cf. *Reimer*, in: Reimer/Schmid/Orell (Eds.), Permanent Establishments, Part 1 [B], para. 40; *Kahle/Kindich*, in: Lübbehüsen/Kahle (Eds.), Brennpunkte der Besteuerung von Betriebsstätten, para. 2.15. See in more detail with regard to the equal treatment of PEs and resident enterprises *Kulcsár*, in: Gutiérrez/Perdelwitz (Eds.), Taxation of Business Profits in the 21st Century, 231 (231 et seqq.).

[51] Cf. *Reimer*, in: Reimer/Rust (Eds.), Klaus Vogel on Double Taxation Conventions, Art. 5, para. 3; *Reimer*, in: Reimer/Schmid/Orell (Eds.), Permanent Establishments, Part 1 [B], para. 40.

[52] Cf. *Wassermeyer/Kaeser*, in: W/K/S/D (Eds.), Doppelbesteuerung, Art. 5 MA, para. 1.

[53] Cf. *Reimer*, in: Reimer/Rust (Eds.), Klaus Vogel on Double Taxation Conventions, Art. 5, para. 3; *Reimer*, in: Reimer/Schmid/Orell (Eds.), Permanent Establishments, Part 1 [B], para. 40.

[54] Cf. *Pinto*, E-Commerce and Source-Based Income Taxation, 79.

[55] Cf. *Kahle/Kindich*, in: Lübbehüsen/Kahle (Eds.), Brennpunkte der Besteuerung von Betriebsstätten, para. 2.16.

[56] See in more detail chapter E of this thesis.

In light of the above, it became evident that the PE concept can be construed as a sourcing rule and a threshold.[57] A sourcing rule, because the PE concept determines that profits which are attributable to a PE located in a treaty state are deemed to arise from sources that are located in that treaty state and a threshold because the PE sets a limit as to when an enterprise resident in a treaty state can be taxed in the other treaty state.[58] Nevertheless, treaty law can only define the limits of the taxation rights of a source state but cannot constitute national taxing rights itself.[59] In other words, the extent to which a treaty state levies taxes—within the boundaries established by the DTA—is exclusively determined by its own domestic law.[60] Consequently, both, domestic law and treaty law have their own purpose and provide their own definitions with regard to the respective terms used in order to suit their objectives. Therefore, in the following the definition of the PE concept as implemented in German domestic tax law as well as tax treaty law will be analysed in further detail.

III. PE Definition under German Tax Law

1. Conceptual Foundation

In German tax law, the definition of the PE is implemented in Section 12 GFC (hereinafter: German Fiscal Code). Accordingly, a PE is defined as a fixed place of business or facility that serves the business of an enterprise.[61] This national definition is important both in connection with a PE established in Germany (inbound scenario) as well as when establishing a PE abroad (outbound scenario). However, the legal consequences vary depending on whether the PE is established in Germany or abroad.[62]

On the one hand, the degree of economic or jurisdictional connection determines the limited tax liability of a non-resident investor in Germany (inbound

[57] Cf. *Skaar*, Permanent Establishment—Erosion of a Tax Treaty Principle, 10 et seqq.

[58] Cf. *Ceballos*, in: Brugger/Plansky (Eds.), Permanent Establishments in International and EU Tax Law, 59 (62).

[59] Cf. *Kaeser*, in: W/K/S/D (Eds.), Doppelbesteuerung, Art. 7 MA (2010), para. 690; *Kraft*, in: Kraft (Ed.), Außensteuergesetz—Kommentar, § 1, para. 610; *Debatin*, insert to DStR 23/1992, 1 (2); *Kessler/Huck*, StuW 2005, 193 (203).

[60] Cf. *Vogel/Rust*, in: Reimer/Rust (Eds.), Klaus Vogel on Double Taxation Conventions, Introduction, paras. 52 et seqq.

[61] Cf. Sec. 12 sentence 1 GFC.

[62] Cf. *Ditz*, Internationale Gewinnabgrenzung bei Betriebsstätten, 10.

scenario).[63] According to Section 1(4) and Section 49(1) no. 2(a) of the German Income Tax Act (hereinafter: ITA) in conjunction with Section 2 no. 1 and Section 7 and 8(1) of the German Corporate Income Tax Act (hereinafter: CITA), a limited tax liability in Germany is triggered if a non-resident enterprise carries out business activities through a PE as defined in Section 12 GFC or through a domestic permanent agent as defined in Section 13 GFC.[64] Insofar, the PE serves as a decisive factor for establishing limited tax liability of a foreign enterprise in Germany.[65] Additionally, the income attributable to the PE is also subject to trade tax pursuant to Section 2(1) sentence 3 and Section 2(6) of the German Trade Tax Act (hereinafter: TTA).[66]

On the other hand, the PE threshold limits the worldwide income tax principle (Section 2(1) German ITA) for enterprises which are resident in Germany, and which are therefore subject to unlimited tax liability in Germany. More precisely, the existence of a PE outside of Germany established by an enterprise resident in Germany (outbound scenario) leads to a relief for the taxes paid in that country in form of a tax credit in Germany according to Section 34c German ITA. In this regard, the PE threshold serves as a connecting factor for foreign income as defined in Section 34d sentence 1 no. 2 lit. a) German ITA.[67] Correspondingly, for trade tax purposes the profits earned by the enterprise resident in Germany are reduced by the income attributable to the foreign PEs according to Section 9 no. 3 TTA.

As outlined, the PE definition under Section 12 GFC serves, *inter alia*,[68] to differentiate domestic respectively foreign source income from non-domestic respectively non-foreign source income.[69] Therefore, a profound understanding of the term is of significance. The general definition as set out in Section 12 sentence 1 GFC attempts to point out the essential characteristics of a PE, namely:

---

[63]Cf. *Endres/Spengel*, International Company Taxation and Tax Planning, § 8.03[A], 309.

[64]See in this context BFH, 28 July 1993, I R 15/93, BStBl. II 1994, 148.

[65]Cf. *Koenig*, in: Koenig (Ed.), AO, § 12 AO, para. 1.

[66]Cf. *Ditz*, Internationale Gewinnabgrenzung bei Betriebsstätten, 10 et seq.; *Kahle/Kindich*, in: Lübbehüsen/Kahle (Eds.), Brennpunkte der Besteuerung von Betriebsstätten, para. 2.5.

[67]Cf. *Kahle/Kindich*, in: Lübbehüsen/Kahle (Eds.), Brennpunkte der Besteuerung von Betriebsstätten, para. 2.6.

[68]For a detailed overview of the relevance of the PE definition under Sec. 12 GFC for other German Tax Acts see *Koenig*, in: Koenig (Ed.), AO, § 12 AO, para. 1; *Drüen*, in: Tipke/Kruse (Eds.), AO/FGO, § 12 AO, para. 3.

[69]Cf. Sec. 34d and 49 German ITA.

- the existence of a place of business or facility;
- the fixed nature of that place of business or facility; and
- an activity carried out by the fixed place of business or facility that serves the business of the enterprise.

In addition to this general definition, Section 12(2) GFC provides a positive non-exhaustive list of examples which are deemed to give rise to a PE. In particular, the following examples shall be considered to constitute a PE:[70]

1. the place of business management;
2. branches;
3. offices;
4. factories or workshops;
5. warehouses;
6. purchasing offices or sales outlets;
7. mines, quarries or other stationary, moving or floating facilities for the exploitation of natural resources;
8. building sites or constructions or installation projects, including those moving or floating, where a) an individual building site or construction or installation project, or b) one of several coexistent building sites or constructions or installation projects, or c) a number of immediately successive building sites or constructions or installation projects last(s) more than six months.

In the following, the essential characteristics of the PE definition, which have been concretised by the highest German court jurisdiction in a hardly manageable casuistry of individual cases, will be elaborated in further detail.

2. Essential Characteristics of a PE under Section 12 GFC

a. Place of Business or Facility

(1) Physical Presence

The term 'place of business or facility' generally requires a physical presence of the enterprise in the source country.[71] In order to be physically present in the source country every tangible asset or every bundling of tangible assets that could

---

[70]Translation provided by the Language Service of the Federal Ministry of Finance.

[71]Cf. *Endres/Spengel*, International Company Taxation and Tax Planning, § 8.03[A], 310.

serve as a basis to carry on a business activities is considered sufficient.[72] The specific use of that place for carrying on the enterprise's business is not necessary.[73] The requirements for a physical presence are rather broadly and can include premises (i.a. buildings, rooms), defined or definable areas (i.a. warehouse, depot) and facilities (i.a. factories, company branch, workshops, machines[74], mining plants[75], pipelines[76], satellite reception systems[77], advertising pillars[78]).[79] Facilities can be considered as a subtype of a place of business which implies that a precise distinction to a place of business may prove challenging in some cases[80].[81] A lack of definable structural demarcation[82] or a lack of an independent functionality[83] does not preclude the qualification as a place of business or facility.

(2) Right of Disposal

Another requirement for a PE to be established is the existence of a formal or other right to use the place of business or facility.[84] Even though the wording

---

[72]Cf. BFH, 3 Feb. 1993, I R 80–81/91, BStBl. II 1993, 462; BFH, 30 Oct. 1996, II R 12/92, BStBl. II 1997, 12; BFH, 17 Sept. 2003, I R 12/02, BStBl. II 2004, 396.

[73]Cf. *Endres/Spengel*, International Company Taxation and Tax Planning, § 8.03[A], 310.

[74]Cf. BFH, 5 Oct. 1965, I B 387/62 U, BStBl. III 1965, 668.

[75]Cf. RFH, 20 Feb. 1935, I A 218/34, RStBl. 1935, 572.

[76]Cf. BFH, 30 Oct. 1996, II R 12/92, BStBl. II 1997, 12.

[77]Cf. BFH, 25 May 2000, III R 20/97, BStBl. II 2001, 365.

[78]Cf. BFH, 6 Aug. 1958, II 251/57 U, BStBl. III 1958, 379.

[79]Cf. *Kahle/Kindich*, in: Lübbehüsen/Kahle (Eds.), Brennpunkte der Besteuerung von Betriebsstätten, para. 2.22; *Heinsen*, in: Looks/Heinsen (Eds.), Betriebsstättenbesteuerung, para. 141.

[80]Cf. BFH, 3 Feb. 1993, I R 80–81/91, BStBl. II 1993, 462.

[81]Cf. *Wassermeyer/Kaeser*, in: W/K/S/D (Eds.), Doppelbesteuerung, Art. 5 MA, para. 31; *Drüen*, in: Tipke/Kruse (Eds.), AO/FGO, § 12 AO, para. 4; *Musil*, in: Hübschmann/Hepp/Spitaler (Eds.), AO/FGO, § 12 AO, para. 8; *Koenig*, in: Koenig (Ed.), AO, § 12 AO, para. 6; *Frotscher*, in: Schwarz/Pahlke (Eds.), AO/FGO, § 12 AO, para. 8.

[82]Cf. BFH, 8 Mar. 1988, VIII R 270/81, BFH/NV 1988, 735.

[83]Cf. BFH, 30 Oct. 1996, II R 12/92, BStBl. II 1997, 12.

[84]Cf. BFH, 10 May 1961, IV 155/60 U, BStBl. III 1961, 317. Detailed in this regard *Kahle/Kindich*, in: Lübbehüsen/Kahle (Eds.), Brennpunkte der Besteuerung von Betriebsstätten, para. 2.32; *Reiser/Cortez*, IStR 2013, 6 (6 et seq.); *Kahle/Ziegler*, DStZ 2009, 834 (837); *Heinsen*, in: Looks/Heinsen (Eds.), Betriebsstättenbesteuerung, para. 143.

of Section 12 GFC does not directly reveal this aspect, it was introduced by the German Federal Tax Court's predecessor, the 'Reichsfinanzhof'.[85]

Although the existence of a formal or other right to use the place of business or facility does not necessarily presuppose ownership rights of the place of business or facility,[86] an exclusive and sustained right of use which cannot be deprived or restricted without substantial efforts is required.[87] In other words, 'it is sufficient that the enterprise's de facto situation is such that it has a certain place of business at its disposal'[88]. Whether the authority to dispose is granted against payment or free of charge is not decisive in this regard.[89] A formal contract that grands the right of use is not necessary.[90]

Moreover, rented[91] or leased[92] places are deemed to be adequate to possess a certain degree of disposal over the place of business or facility.[93] However, the mere use of facilities which are open to the public or temporary access rights[94] are not sufficient as to regard a place of business or facility at the disposal of the enterprise.[95]

b. Fixed Nature

The notion of 'fixed' consists of a geographical and a temporal component. Both components are interconnected and complement each other[96], i.e. the lesser the geographical nexus, the more decisive the temporal component and vice versa.[97]

---

[85]Cf. RFH, 4 Mar. 1927, B I 27, RStBl. 1927, 112; RFH, 19 Dec. 1934, VI A 230/34, RStBl. 1935, 490.

[86]Cf. BFH, 30 Jan. 1974, I R 87/72, BStBl. II 1974, 327.

[87]Cf. BFH, 14 July 2004, I R 106/03, BFH/NV 2005, 154; BFH, 4 June 2008, I R 30/07, BStBl. II 2008, 922; BFH, 18 Mar. 2009, III R 2/06, BFH/NV 2009, 1457. See also *Endres/Spengel*, International Company Taxation and Tax Planning, § 8.03[A], 310; *Heinsen,* in: Looks/Heinsen (Eds.), Betriebsstättenbesteuerung, para. 143.

[88]*Lüdicke*, Bulletin—Tax Treaty Monitor 2004, 190 (190).

[89]Cf. BFH, 3 Feb. 1993, I R 80/91, BStBl. II 1993, 462; BFH, 23 May 2002, III R 8/00, BStBl. II 2002, 513.

[90]Cf. BFH, 10 May 1961, IV 155/60 U, BStBl. III 1961, 317.

[91]Cf. BFH, 30 Jan. 1974, I R 87/72, BStBl. II, 1974, 327.

[92]Cf. BFH, 28 Oct. 1977, III R 77/75, BStBl. II 1978, 116.

[93]Cf. *Heinsen,* in: Looks/Heinsen (Eds.), Betriebsstättenbesteuerung, para. 143.

[94]Cf. BFH, 19 Mar. 1981, IV R 49/77, BStBl. II 1981, 583.

[95]Cf. *Endres/Spengel*, International Company Taxation and Tax Planning, § 8.03[A], 310.

[96]Cf. BFH, 19 Sept. 2003, I R 12/02, BStBl. II 2004, 396.

[97]Cf. *Loschelder*, in: Weber-Grellet (Ed.), EStG—Einkommensteuergesetz—Kommentar, § 49 EStG, para. 23.

The geographical nexus requires that the place of business or the facility is located within the boundaries of the source country.[98] The term 'fixed' does not imply that the PE must be physically attached to the ground.[99] Therefore, also movable property such as mobile stalls can qualify as a fixed place of business or facility if the same location is used regularly.[100] Constantly changing parking and drop-off points, such as those used in the taxi industry, do usually not qualify as fixed for the purpose of the geographical nexus.[101] Furthermore, motor trucks, ships or aircrafts do usually not qualify as a PE since they lack the requirement of a fixed nexus in the source country.[102] However, each fixed place of business or facility needs to be considered on a case-by-case basis.[103]

The temporal component implies that a certain degree of permanence beyond the purely temporary is required. In this regard, the question on how much time is required in order to qualify as a fixed place of business or facility is crucial. Even though the German law does not define any specific minimum period for the fixed nature of a PE,[104] the German Federal Tax Court and the Federal Ministry of Finance typify that the business activity shall be carried out for a minimum period of six months.[105] In this context, it is the actual and not the intended duration that is decisive.[106] However, as stated by the German Federal Tax Court, the six months period can only be regarded as a point of reference, not as a fixed threshold.[107] Therefore, the prevailing view in literature[108] suggests that the evaluation of the fixed nature of the place of business or facility should be decided

[98]Cf. *Endres/Spengel*, International Company Taxation and Tax Planning, § 8.03[A], 311.

[99]Cf. *Koenig*, in Koenig (Ed.), AO, § 12, para. 9; *Endres/Spengel*, International Company Taxation and Tax Planning, § 8.03[A], 311.

[100]Cf. BFH, 13 Sept. 2000, X R 174/96, BStBl. II 2001, 734.

[101]Cf. BFH, 18 Oct. 1962, IV 319/60 U, BStBl. III 1963, 38.

[102]Cf. *Heinsen,* in: Looks/Heinsen (Eds.), Betriebsstättenbesteuerung, para. 141.

[103]Cf. *Endres/Spengel*, International Company Taxation and Tax Planning, § 8.03[A], 311.

[104]A minimum requirement for the existence of a PE only exists for building sites, constructions or installation project, cf. Sec. 12. S. 2 No. 8 GFC.

[105]Cf. BFH, 30 Oct. 1973, I R 50/71, BStBl. II 1974, 107; BFH, 19 May 1993, I R 80/92, BStBl. II 1993, 655; BMF, 24 Dec. 1999, IV B 4—S 1300—111/99, BStBl. I 1999, 1076, paras. 1.1.1.1 and 1.2.1.1.

[106]Cf. *Heinsen,* in: Looks/Heinsen (Eds.), Betriebsstättenbesteuerung, para. 142; *Endres/Spengel*, International Company Taxation and Tax Planning, § 8.03[A], 310.

[107]Cf. BFH, 17 Sept. 2003, I R 12/02, BStBl. II 2004, 396.

[108]Cf. *Drüen,* in: Tipke/Kruse (Eds.), AO/FGO, § 12 AO, paras. 10, 21; *Mössner,* in: Kirchhof/Lehner/Raupach/Rodi (Eds.), Staaten und Steuern, 945 (954); *Lampert,* in: Mössner et al. (Eds.), Steuerrecht international tätiger Unternehmen, para. 2.109; *Musil,* in:

contingent upon the individual circumstances of each case. Nevertheless, as decided by the German Federal Tax Court, a place of business cannot be regarded as fixed if it lasts merely three months or less in the source country.[109] Also recurrent activities that last only for a short period of time (less than six months) but are repeated periodically, lack to have a certain degree of permanence.[110]

c. Serving the Business of the Enterprise

(1) General Elements

If there is a fixed place of business or facility within the meaning of Section 12 GFC, another requirement for the existence of a PE is that this fixed place of business or facility serves the business of the enterprise.[111] According to the German Federal Tax Court, a fixed place of business or facility serves the business of the enterprise if it is used a) directly, and b) for a certain period of time in order to carry on business activities of the enterprise.[112] In this respect, it is of no significance whether the activity is a core business activity or of ancillary nature.[113] A ruling of the German Federal Tax Court regarding automated 'noise measurement stations' of an airport operator illustrates that even a fixed place of business or facility where activities are carried on that merely serve regulatory requirements (noise measurement) are sufficient in order to serve the business of the enterprise for the purpose of Section 12 GFC.[114]

However, a fixed place of business or facility that serves the business purpose of the enterprise only indirectly does not constitute a PE.[115] Under this premise, social facilities, such as fitness facilities, changing rooms and recreation homes

---

Hübschmann/Hepp/Spitaler (Eds.), AO/FGO, § 12 AO, para. 15; *Möller*, StuB 2005, 350 (351).

[109]Cf. BFH, 28 Aug. 1986, V R 20/79, BStBl. II 1987, 162.

[110]Cf. BFH, 17 Sep. 2003, I R 12/02, BStBl. II 2004, 396. In that case the German Federal Tax Court argued that a stall at a Christmas market that is run by an enterprise for a period of four weeks each year does not constitute a PE due to a lack of the permanent reference to a certain spot of the earth's surface, see also *Hilbert/Engel*, Intertax 2012, 462 (468 et seq.).

[111]Cf. BFH, 30 Oct. 1996, II R 12/92, BStBl. II 1997, 12.

[112]Cf. BFH, 17 Aug. 1966, IV R 172/66, BStBl. II 1966, 548; BFH, 10 Feb. 1988, VIII R 159/84, BStBl. II 1988, 653.

[113]Cf. BFH, 8 Dec. 1971, I R 3/69, BStBl. II 1972, 289; BFH, 3 Feb. 1993, I R 80–81/91, BStBl. II 1993, 462.

[114]Cf. BFH, 16 Dec. 2009, I R 56/08, BStBl. II 2010, 492.

[115]Cf. BFH, 10 Feb. 1988, VIII R 159/84, BStBl. II 1988, 653.

that only serve social needs of the employees, do not directly serve the business purpose and therefore do not constitute a PE.[116]

Nevertheless, whether a fixed place of business or facility serves the business of the enterprise depends on the individual circumstances of each case.[117] Therefore, comparable fixed places of business or facilities can lead to different assessments with regard to the question whether or not a PE is established in the respective case.[118]

(2) Presence of Personnel

In this regard, it seems worth discussing whether a fixed place of business or facility can serve the business purpose of the enterprise without the presence of human beings. With reference to the German Federal Tax Court and its famous 'pipeline-verdict'[119], the presence of personnel is, in principle, not required.[120] According to this verdict, a pipeline running underground through German territory is already considered sufficient to establish a PE, despite the fact that no personnel is employed in Germany and the sole purpose of the pipeline is the passive transit of oil.[121] Although this verdict was discussed controversial,[122] the prevailing view supports the finding of the German Federal Tax Court.

Consequently, also fully automated facilities where artificial intelligence promotes the substitution of manpower with autonomous systems are deemed to satisfy the existence of a PE if the fixed place of business or facility serves the business purpose of the enterprise.[123] Difficulties that arise with regard to the profit attribution to such PEs are discussed in detail in chapter D.II.3.b.(1)(c).

---

[116]Cf. *Koenig*, in: Koenig (Ed.), AO, § 12 AO, para. 19; also *Kahle/Kindich*, in: Lübbehüsen/Kahle (Eds.), Brennpunkte der Besteuerung von Betriebsstätten, para. 2.42.

[117]Cf. *Drüen*, in: Tipke/Kruse (Eds.), AO/FGO, § 12 AO, para. 19; *Bernütz*, IStR 1997, 353 (356); *Hutter/Schmidt*, IStR 2000, 650 (653); *Arndt/Fetzer*, BB 2001, 1175 (1176). Critical *Portner*, IStR 1998, 553 (554 et seq.); *Portner*, IStR 1999, 641 (643); *Wassermeyer*, in: Drenseck/Seer (Eds.), Festschrift Kruse, 589 (591 et seq.).

[118]Cf. *Ditz*, Internationale Gewinnabgrenzung bei Betriebsstätten, 17.

[119]Cf. BFH, 30 Oct. 1996, II R 12/92, BStBl. II 1997, 12.

[120]Cf. BFH, 30 Oct. 1996, II R 12/92, BStBl. II 1997, 12. Also *Ditz*, Internationale Gewinnabgrenzung bei Betriebsstätten, 17 et seq.; *Endres/Spengel*, International Company Taxation and Tax Planning, § 8.03[A], 310.

[121]Cf. BFH, 30 Oct. 1996, II R 12/92, BStBl. II 1997, 12.

[122]Advocates of the conclusion that a PE can be triggered without the presence of personnel cf. *Bernütz*, IStR 1997, 353 (356); *Hutter/Schmidt*, IStR 2000, 650 (653); *Arndt/Fetzer*, BB 2001, 1175 (1176). Critical *Portner*, IStR 1998, 553 (554); *Portner*, IStR 1999, 641 (643); *Hidien/Rodenhäuser*, DStZ 2007, 689 (693).

[123]Cf. BFH, 30 Oct. 1996, II R 12/92, BStBl. II 1997, 12.

3. Positive List Indicating a PE

Section 12 sentence 2 GFC sets forth a non-exhaustive list of examples which are deemed to give rise to a PE. In this regard, it is controversial whether a) this list of PEs can only be seen as *prima facie*[124] PEs, given that each of the examples can only be considered a PE if they meet the common features laid down in Section 12 sentence 1 GFC, or b) Section 12 sentence 2 GFC can be understood as a stand-alone list of PE examples that trigger a PE in an *a priori* fashion.[125] While the later interpretation would ultimately lead to a fictitious extension of the PE definition of Section 12 sentence 1 GFC, the first interpretation would consider the positive list of business activities merely as an illustrative list of examples.

Even though it is argued that the employment of the phrase 'in particular' in the wording of Section 12 sentence 2 GFC is indicative for the fact that the positive list of business activities laid down in Section 12 sentence 2 GFC can only be regarded as a non-exhaustive illustrative list of PE examples, the German Federal Tax Court[126] and the Federal Ministry of Finance[127] consider the examples listed in Section 12 sentence 2 GFC as a stand-alone list of PE examples that triggers a PE in an a priori fashion even if the features laid down in Section 12 sentence 1 GFC are not met.[128] Although the interpretation of Section 12 sentence 2 GFC as a stand-alone list of PE examples that triggers a PE in an a priori fashion extends the PE definition and therefore ultimately leads to an expansion of the number

---

[124]See in more detail for the phrases *prima facie* and *a priori Pijl*, Intertax 2005, 189 (191 et seqq.).

[125]Advocates of consideration a): i.a. *Jacobs*, Internationale Unternehmensbesteuerung, 305; *Roth*, in: Herrmann/Heuer/Raupach (Eds.), EStG, KStG: Kommentar, § 49 EStG, para. 205; *Kumpf*, Besteuerung inländischer Betriebstätten von Steuerausländern, 36. Advocates of consideration b): i.a. BMF, 24 Dec. 1999, IV B 4—S 1300—111/99, BStBl. I 1999, 1076; BFH, 28 July 1993, I R 15/93, BStBl. II 1994, 148 et seqq.; BFH, 21 Apr. 1999, I R 99/97, BStBl. II 1999, 694 et seqq.; *Koenig*, in: Koenig (Ed.), AO, § 12 AO, para. 23; *Drüen*, in: Tipke/Kruse (Eds.), AO/FGO, § 12 AO, para. 23; *Heinsen*, in: Looks/Heinsen (Eds.), Betriebsstättenbesteuerung, para. 143.

[126]Cf. BFH, 28 July 1993, I R 15/93, BStBl. II 1994, 148.

[127]Cf. BMF, 24 Dec. 1999, IV B 4—S 1300—111/99, BStBl. I 1999, 1076, para. 1.1.1.1.

[128]Agreeing *Musil*, in: Hübschmann/Hepp/Spitaler (Eds.), AO/FGO, § 12, para. 25; *Puls*, in: W/A/D (Eds.), Betriebsstätten-Handbuch, para. 2.145. Cf. in more detail with regard to building sites or constructions or installation projects *Storck*, Ausländische Betriebsstätten im Ertrag- und Vermögensteuerrecht, 169.

of PEs, the view by the German Federal Tax Court and the Federal Ministry of Finance is also supported in literature[129].

However, for practical purposes, the consequences of the disagreement between advocates of consideration a) and b) seem rather limited since most of the examples listed in Section 12 sentence 2 GFC comply with the common features of a PE set forth in Section 12 sentence 1 GFC anyway.[130]

4. Special PE Cases

a. Building Sites or Constructions or Installation Projects

Pursuant to Section 12 sentence 2 no. 8 GFC, building sites or constructions or installation projects constitute a PE, where an individual, one of several or a number of immediately successive building sites or constructions or installation projects last for a period of more than six months. From a practical point of view, such PEs can be regarded as the most important example out of the non-exhaustive list set forth in Section 12 sentence 2 GFC.[131] In contrast to most other PEs, building sites or constructions or installation projects are from the outset only established for a certain period of time and then closed after its purpose is achieved.[132] Consequently, in literature such PEs are considered as 'fictitious' PEs.[133] Since they do not need to meet the common features laid down in Section 12 sentence 1 GFC in order to constitute a PE, Section 12 sentence 2 no. 8 GFC can be regarded as an extension of the PE definition of Section 12 sentence 1 GFC.[134]

Due to the mere temporary nature of building sites or constructions or installation projects, its existence as a PE is contingent upon a certain minimum

---

129 Cf. i.a. *Koenig,* in: Koenig (Ed.), AO, § 12 AO, para. 23; *Drüen,* in: Tipke/Kruse (Eds.), AO/FGO, § 12 AO, para. 23; *Heinsen,* in: Looks/Heinsen (Eds.), Betriebsstättenbesteuerung, para. 143.

130 Cf. *Kahle/Ziegler*, DStZ 2009, 834 (839); *Kahle/Kindich,* in: Lübbehüsen/Kahle (Eds.), Brennpunkte der Besteuerung von Betriebsstätten, para. 2.51; *Scheffler*, Internationale betriebswirtschaftliche Steuerlehre, 257.

131 Cf. *Kahle/Kindich*, in: Lübbehüsen/Kahle (Eds.), Brennpunkte der Besteuerung von Betriebsstätten, para. 2.63. *Lampert* points out that such PEs are of high relevance from a practical point of view, cf. *Lampert,* in: Mössner et al. (Eds.), Steuerrecht international tätiger Unternehmen, para. 2.126.

132 Cf. *Puls*, in: W/A/D (Eds.), Betriebsstätten-Handbuch, para. 2.145; *Görl*, in: Vogel/Lehner (Eds.), DBA-Kommentar, Art. 5, para. 62.

133 Cf. *Merkert*, DB 1968, 1238 (1238); *Schmitz*, Kommentar zum Internationalen Steuerrecht der Bundesrepublik Deutschland, 255.

134 Cf. *Wuermli*, in: Beck'sche Steuerkommentare et al. (Eds.), Doppelbesteuerung, 171 (175).

duration.[135] The implementation of a temporal threshold with regard to such sites and projects is internationally common and is supported by most scholars,[136] since it establishes a fixed criterion when to regard such sites and projects in the source country as a PE. However, the specific threshold chosen by the German legislator of six months must be criticised. Both, the OECD MC[137] and the UN MC[138] refer to a minimum time threshold of twelve months in order for building sites or constructions or installation projects to constitute a PE. The twelve-months threshold can typically be found in DTAs between Germany and industrialised countries; the six-month threshold, on the contrary, mostly in DTAs between Germany and developing countries.[139] However, such deviations create substantial inconsistencies and difficulties in triangular cases, ranging from the non-consideration of losses to double non-taxation.[140]

b. Server PE

Even though the question as to whether a fully automated server may constitute a PE has been discussed for quite some time,[141] the significance of this issue

---

[135] Cf. *Puls*, in: W/A/D (Eds.), Betriebsstätten-Handbuch, para. 2.145.

[136] Cf. *Puls*, in: W/A/D (Eds.), Betriebsstätten-Handbuch, para. 2.144; *Delarber*, Steuerliche Einflüsse auf die grenzüberschreitende Betriebsstättenbesteuerung, 36. *Rehfeld* also argues that a time threshold in this context was implemented in order to minimise administrative procedures, cf. *Rehfeld*, in: Gosch/Kroppen/Grotherr/Kraft (Eds.), DBA-Kommentar, Art. 5 OECD-MA, para. 93.

[137] Cf. Art. 5(3) OECD MC.

[138] Cf. Art. 5(3) lit. a UN MC.

[139] Cf. *Heinsen,* in: Looks/Heinsen (Eds.), Betriebsstättenbesteuerung, para. 217.

[140] Cf. *Reimer*, in: Reimer/Rust (Eds.), Klaus Vogel on Double Taxation Conventions, Art. 5, para. 244.

[141] Cf. for the discussion *Lampert,* in: Mössner et al. (Eds.), Steuerrecht international tätiger Unternehmen, paras. 2.151 et seqq.; *Pinkernell*, Internationale Steuergestaltung im Electronic Commerce, 27 et seqq.; *Thile/König*, IWB 2018, 1 (1 et seqq.); *Kahle/Baschnagel/Kindich*, FR 2016, 193 (193 et seqq.); *Bendlinger*, Die Betriebsstätte in der Praxis des internationalen Steuerrechts, 135 et seqq.; *Monsenego*, ITPJ 2014, 247 (247 et seqq.); *Bal*, BIT 2012, 335 (335 et seqq.); *Findeis/Eickmann*, DStZ 2008, 139 (139 et seqq.); *Jacobs*, Internationale Unternehmensbesteuerung, 336 et seqq.; *Puls*, Die Betriebsstätte im Abgaben- und Abkommensrecht, 43 et seqq.; *Kahle/Ziegler*, DStZ 2009, 834 (834); *Knödler*, Besteuerung von Ertrag und Umsatz im Electronic Commerce, 119 et seqq.; OECD, Are the Current Treaty Rules for Taxing Business Profits Appropriate for E-Commerce? Final Report 2004; *Kaminski/Strunk*, IWB 2002, 947 (947 et seqq.); *Hahn*, SWI 2002, 17 (17 et seqq.); *Peter*, Fortentwicklung des Betriebsstättenprinzips, 153 et seqq.; *Pinkernell/Ditz*, FR 2001, 1193 (1194 et seqq.); *Strunk*, IWB 2001, 151 (151 et seqq.); *Steimel*, IStR 2000, 490 (490 et seqq.); *Kessler/Peter*, BB 2000, 1545 (1545 et seqq.); *Arndt/Fetzer*, BB 2001, 1175 (1175 et seqq.); *Geurts*, Intertax

increased over time as ICT has led to an economy that heavily relies on widely accessible and efficient online communication networks and services, software as well as hardware.[142] According to Section 12 GFC a PE requires a fixed place of business or facility that serves the business of an enterprise. As discussed earlier, the presence of personnel is not a requirement for the existence of a PE.[143] Therefore, also fully automated servers can serve the business of an enterprise and may therefore constitute a PE if the other requirements of the PE definition, as set forth in Section 12 GFC, are met.

First of all, a server only constitutes a PE if the requirement of being fixed is met. In this respect, a distinction must be made between the tangible component (actual server hardware) and the non-tangible components (software and data which is stored on or used by the hardware).[144] While the actual server hardware may constitute a fixed place of business and thus could be considered a PE in the country where it is situated, the software and data which is stored on or used by the server hardware does not qualify as a fixed place of business. As discussed above, the term 'fixed' does not imply that the server must be physically attached to the ground.[145] Rather, it is required that the server is not moved over a specific period of time. As pointed out earlier, the German Federal Tax Court and the Federal Ministry of Finance typify a minimum period of six months which can only be regarded as a point of reference, not as a fixed threshold.[146] It follows that servers that are wired at a particular site and remain at that location for a minimum period of six months can be regarded to be of a fixed nature and may therefore constitute a PE if the other requirements are met.[147]

Another important requirement in this context is that the server is at the disposal of the enterprise. In this regard, another distinction must be made between the enterprise that operates the server (Internet Service Provider [hereinafter: ISP])

2000, 173 (173 et seqq.); *Gummert/Trapp*, MMR 1998, 350 (350 et seqq.); *Eicker/Scheifele*, IWB 1999, 377 (377 et seqq.); *Holler/Heerspink*, BB 1998, 771 (771 et seqq.); *Strunk*, BB 1998, 1824 (1824); *Wichmann*, in: Fischer/Strunk (Eds.), Steuerliche Aspekte des Electronic Commerce, 65 (73 et seqq.).

[142]For an overview of the role of servers within the different layers of ICT cf. OECD, BEPS Action 1: Final Report 2015, paras. 99 et seqq.

[143]Cf. BFH, 30 Oct. 1996, II R 12/92, BStBl. II 1997, 12.

[144]Cf. OECD MC Commentary 2017, Art. 5, para. 123.

[145]Cf. *Koenig*, in Koenig (Ed.), AO, § 12, para. 9; *Endres/Spengel*, International Company Taxation and Tax Planning, § 8.03[A], 311.

[146]Cf. BFH, 17 Sept. 2003, I R 12/02, BStBl. II 2004, 396.

[147]Cf. *Kahle/Kindich*, in: Lübbehüsen/Kahle (Eds.), Brennpunkte der Besteuerung von Betriebsstätten, para. 2.176.

and the enterprise that carries on business through the server (Content Provider [hereinafter: CP]). Commonly, both enterprises are not the same which raises the question whether the server is at the disposal of the ISP and/or the CP. In many cases a server of an ISP is used by many different CPs (e.g. provision of web hosting services for different enterprises on the same server of a domestic ISP).[148] In these cases, the server is usually not exclusively used by one specific CP and therefore not at the disposal of the CP. Consequently, the server may only constitute a PE for the ISP and not for the CP.[149]

Nevertheless, a server may be at the disposal of the CP in two cases. First, if the server is owned and operated by the CP.[150] Second, if the server is owned by the ISP but exclusively used by the CP that has disposal over the server ('dedicated server').[151] The latter case requires the CP to have knowledge or at least access to the knowledge of where his server racks are located.[152] Actual physical access to the server, which may be part of a large server farm, is not required.[153] Nevertheless, in order for the CP to have disposal over the server it is indispensable that the CP has the exclusive control of the 'micro-physical structures' through which data is being processed and stored.[154] Therefore, new developments like 'clouds' (virtual server) usually do not constitute a PE for the CP since the CP does not have control of the underlying cloud infrastructure (unless in the first case where the server is owned and operated by the CP).[155] Rather, the CP has only access to a virtual server which is available to everyone who has access to

---

[148] Cf. *Pinkernell*, Internationale Steuergestaltung im Electronic Commerce, 31; *Thiele/König*, IWB 2018, 376 (380).

[149] Cf. *Pinkernell*, Internationale Steuergestaltung im Electronic Commerce, 31.

[150] Cf. *Kahle/Ziegler*, DStZ 2009, 834 (841); *Pinkernell*, Internationale Steuergestaltung im Electronic Commerce, 30.

[151] Cf. *Lampert*, in: Mössner et al. (Eds.), Steuerrecht international tätiger Unternehmen, para. 2.154; *Pinkernell*, Internationale Steuergestaltung im Electronic Commerce, 30.

[152] Cf. *Reimer*, in: Reimer/Schmid/Orell (Eds.), Permanent Establishments, Part 2 [J], para. 486.

[153] Cf. *Reimer*, in: Reimer/Schmid/Orell (Eds.), Permanent Establishments, Part 2 [J], paras. 484 et seq.; *Findeis/Eickmann*, DStZ 2008, 139 (143). For a different view see *Thiele/König* arguing that physical access to the server is required, cf. *Thiele/König*, IWB 2018, 376 (379 et seq.).

[154] Cf. *Reimer*, in: Reimer/Schmid/Orell (Eds.), Permanent Establishments, Part 2 [J], para. 485.

[155] For the same conclusion that clouds cannot constitute a PE for the CP, cf. *Thiele/König*, IWB 2018, 376 (378); *Pinkernell*, Internationale Steuergestaltung im Electronic Commerce, 32; *Bal*, BIT 2012, 335 (336). For an overview of the term cloud computing cf. OECD, BEPS Action 1: Final Report, paras. 140 et seqq. For an overview of the most common examples of

the cloud.[156] The situation is different for the ISP that provides the hardware (i.e. the host-computer at the server farm).[157] This host-computer may constitute a PE for the ISP.[158]

Lastly, in order to constitute a PE according to Section 12 GFC the server must serve the business of the enterprise.[159] Whether the server carries out a core business activity or rather an activity of ancillary nature (e.g. provision of communication links, advertising of services or goods, supplying information, gathering market data for the enterprise and relying information through a mirror server for efficiency and security purposes) does not matter in this context.[160]

c. Service PE

As elaborated above, one of the criteria for a PE to be established is the existence of a fixed place of business that is at the disposal of the enterprise, i.e. the enterprise has an exclusive and sustained right to use the fixed place of business or facility which cannot be deprived or restricted without substantial efforts. This requirement proves problematic in cases of cross-border provision of services. According to the German Federal Tax Court, the mere act of doing business in the premises of the contracting party is not sufficient in order to constitute a PE for the enterprise within the meaning of Section 12 GFC due to a lack of disposal over that premises.[161] Also circumstances where the business activity is carried

---

cloud computing service models (i.e. infrastructure-as-a-service [IaaS], platform-as-a-service [PaaS] and software-as-a-service [SaaS]) cf. OECD, BEPS Action 1: Final Report, para. 143.

[156]Cf. OECD, BEPS Action 1: Final Report, para. 141; *Lampert,* in: Mössner et al. (Eds.), Steuerrecht international tätiger Unternehmen, para. 2.155. In general, resources to which customers have access to are not stored on one single server or computer. Rather, they are stored on a network of computers that may allocate the user's data and software to other servers if such a location is best in order to satisfy the demand efficiently, cf. OECD, BEPS Action 1: Final Report, para. 141.

[157]Cf. *Lampert,* in: Mössner et al. (Eds.), Steuerrecht international tätiger Unternehmen, para. 2.155.

[158]Cf. *Kahle/Baschnagel/Kindich,* FR 2016, 193 (196); *Lampert,* in: Mössner et al. (Eds.), Steuerrecht international tätiger Unternehmen, para. 2.155; *Pinkernell,* Internationale Steuergestaltung im Electronic Commerce, 32.

[159]Cf. BFH, 30 Oct. 1996, II R 12/92, BStBl. II 1997, 12.

[160]Cf. BFH, 8 Dec. 1971, I R 3/69, BStBl. II 1972, 289; BFH, 3 Feb. 1993, I R 80–81/91, BStBl. II 1993, 462.

[161]Cf. BFH, 4 June 2008, I R 30/07, BStBl. II 2008, 922.

on over several years in the premises of the contracting party cannot be regarded sufficient for this place of business to constitute a PE for the enterprise if no disposal of the enterprise over the premises exists.[162]

Since the concept of the Service PE, as known from the OECD MC Commentary,[163] contradicts the traditional German PE concept, which requires a fixed place of business and a certain degree of disposal, Germany does regularly not make use of its taxing right if such a Service PE is established according to the respective DTA in Germany.[164]

5. Permanent Representative

Apart from the PE concept, German domestic tax law provides another concept which entitles the source country to tax business activities carried out without the need to establish a fixed place of business at source: the concept of the permanent representative.[165] Section 13 GFC defines a permanent representative as a 'person who conducts the business of an enterprise in a sustained manner and, in doing so, is subject to its instructions'[166]. Whether this person is a commissionaire or agent (independent representative) or an employee of the enterprise (dependent representative) does not make a difference, provided that they habitually act in the business interest of the enterprise and are bound by instructions.[167] Section 13 sentence 2 GFC points out that especially persons who a) conclude or broker contracts or solicit orders, or b) maintain a stock of goods or merchandise and make deliveries from this stock shall constitute a permanent representative as long as they act on behalf of the enterprise in a sustained manner.

The provision dealing with the permanent representative aims at closing potential gaps that would otherwise occur in cases where the representative does not

[162]Cf. BFH, 4 June 2008, I R 30/07, BStBl. II 2008, 922.

[163]Cf. OECD MC Commentary 2017, Art. 5, paras. 14 et seqq., para. 155. See in more detail for the concept of the Service PE under tax treaty law chapter C.IV.6.d of this thesis.

[164]Cf. *Endres/Freiling*, PIStB 2012, 189 (190); *Kahle/Kindich*, in: Lübbehüsen/Kahle (Eds.), Brennpunkte der Besteuerung von Betriebsstätten, para. 2.200. See in this context also the order of the OFD Karlsruhe, 16 Sep. 2014, S 130.1/316-St 222, IStR 2015, 887.

[165]For an overview of the legal development of the permanent representative in German tax law, cf. *Lampert,* in: Mössner et al. (Eds.), Steuerrecht international tätiger Unternehmen, paras. 2.156 et seqq.

[166]Translation provided by the Language Service of the Federal Ministry of Finance.

[167]Cf. *Endres/Spengel*, International Company Taxation and Tax Planning, § 8.03[A], 313.

carry on activities through a fixed place of business.[168] On the contrary, in cases where the requirements of a PE are fulfilled, e.g. by an agent who carries out his work in another state through an office (fixed place of business), the question of whether or not an Agent PE is established is of no significance since that office constitutes a PE for the enterprise according to Section 12 GFC.[169]

The distinction between a PE and a permanent representative is decisive for levying German trade tax. As elaborated above, Section 2(1) sentence 3 of the German TTA determines that trade tax is levied on commercial business activities which are carried out through a PE in Germany. Accordingly, the German trade tax is based on the PE concept and does not include the permanent representative. Therefore, even though a foreign enterprise which carries out business through a permanent representative in Germany triggers non-resident tax liability in its own right pursuant to Section 13 GFC in conjunction with Section 49(1) no. 2 lit. a ITA, the foreign enterprise is not subject to trade tax.[170]

IV. PE Definition under Tax Treaty Law

1. Conceptual Foundations of Tax Treaty Law

a. Relation of Tax Treaty Law and German Domestic Law

As pointed out above, DTAs are international agreements that intend to eliminate double taxation.[171] The creation and the consequences of DTAs are determined by the rules contained in the Vienna Convention on the Law of Treaties of 23 May 1969 (hereinafter: VCLT)[172]. Hereafter, a DTA comes into existence upon the declaration of consent by the respective treaty states.[173] In Germany, a declaration of consent is in general made by the Federal President[174] and implemented in the ordinary legislative procedure by Parliament in the form of a federal law

[168] Cf. *Puls*, in: W/A/D (Eds.), Betriebsstätten-Handbuch, para. 2.204; *Kumpf*, Besteuerung inländischer Betriebsstätten von Steuerausländern, 48.

[169] Cf. *Endres/Spengel*, International Company Taxation and Tax Planning, § 8.03[A], 313; *Wassermeyer/Kaeser*, in: W/K/S/D (Eds.), Doppelbesteuerung, Art. 5 MA, para. 192.

[170] Cf. *Wassermeyer/Kaeser*, in: W/K/S/D (Eds.), Doppelbesteuerung, Art. 5 MA, para. 191b.

[171] Cf. *Debatin*, DB 1989, 1692 (1692 et seqq.).

[172] UN, Vienna Convention on the Law of Treaties, Treaty Series 1155 (1969), 331.

[173] Cf. *Vogel/Rust*, in: Reimer/Rust (Eds.), Klaus Vogel on Double Taxation Conventions, Introduction, para. 41.

[174] Cf. Art. 59(1) German Basis Law.

according to Article 59(2) of the German Basic Law (hereinafter: GBL).[175] Even though Article 59(2) GBL provides that international tax treaties have the same rank as statutory federal law,[176] Section 2(1) GFC determines that DTAs shall take precedence over tax legislation insofar as they have become directly applicable domestic law.[177] However, due to the fact that Section 2 GFC is a provision of statutory federal law itself, it cannot eliminate the legal circumstance that the provision of Article 59(2) GBL leads to the legal consequence that DTAs have the same rank as statutory federal law and do not rank above it.[178] Consequently, the ordered primacy of international treaty law by Section 2 GFC cannot be interpreted in a way that international treaty law is always superior to statutory federal law (*lex superior derogate legi inferiori*).[179] A ruling by the Federal Constitution Court clarifies that legislation is not barred from enacting statutes even if those contravene international treaty law within the meaning of Article 59(2) GBL (*treaty override*).[180] This follows from the principle of democracy, which requires that later legislation (*lex posterior derogate legi priori*) may revoke all legal acts of previous legislation.[181] A different result cannot be derived from the principle of the Constitution's openness to international law.[182] Even though this principle is

---

[175] After the implementation legislation is signed by the Federal President, it is promulgated in the Federal Law Gazette (BGBl.). For further details cf. *Vogel/Rust*, in: Reimer/Rust (Eds.), Klaus Vogel on Double Taxation Conventions, Introduction, para. 40.

[176] An exception applies in case an 'opening clause' of the GBL applies, that is if an international treaty falls within the scope of a more specific constitutional provision dealing with the relationship between international law and domestic law and accords a different rank to the international treaties (particularly Art. 23–25 GBL), cf. BVerfG, 15 Dec. 2015, 2 BvL 1/12, BVerfGE 141,1.

[177] Cf. *Koenig*, in Koenig (Ed.), AO, § 2 AO, para. 13; *Ditz*, Internationale Gewinnabgrenzung bei Betriebsstätten, 21; *Bron*, IStR 2007, 431 (432); *Drüen*, in: Tipke/Kruse (Eds.), AO/FGO, § 2 AO, para. 1; *Heger*, SWI 2011, 95 (98); *Oellerich*, in: Beermann/Gosch (Eds.), AO/FGO, § 2 AO, para. 73.

[178] Cf. *Koenig*, in Koenig (Ed.), AO, § 2 paras. 13, 17; *Ditz*, Internationale Gewinnabgrenzung bei Betriebsstätten, 22; *Wassermeyer*, StuW 1990, 404 (411).

[179] Cf. *Koenig*, in Koenig (Ed.), AO, § 2 AO, para. 13.

[180] Cf. BVerfG, 15 Dec. 2015, 2 BvL 1/12, BVerfGE 141, 1, para. 49. Detailed for the relation of treaty law and German national law *Schönfeld/Häck*, in: Schönfeld/Ditz (Eds.), DBA-Kommentar, Systematik, paras. 179 et seqq.

[181] Cf. BVerfG, 15 Dec. 2015, 2 BvL 1/12, BVerfGE 141, 1, paras. 33, 50.

[182] Cf. BVerfG, 15 Dec. 2015, 2 BvL 1/12, BVerfGE 141, 1, para. 33.

of constitutional rank, it does not entail a strict constitutional duty to obey the entire rules of international law.[183]

However, domestic law and treaty law are two mutually independent legal spheres.[184] While DTAs establish an independent mechanism in order to avoid double taxation by restricting tax claims where overlapping claims by the respective treaty states are expected, and therefore draw 'boundaries' on domestic taxation, the extent to which a treaty state levies taxes—within the boundaries established by the DTA—is exclusively determined by its own domestic law.[185] Consequently, both, domestic law and treaty law have their own purpose and provide their own definitions with regard to the respective terms used in order to suit their objectives.

b. Objective of the PE Definition under Treaty Law

In light of the above, the definition of the PE in treaty law and in German national law pursues different objectives and therefore needs to be strictly distinguished.[186] While the PE definition under Section 12 GFC serves to differentiate domestic respectively foreign source income from non-domestic respectively non-foreign source income,[187] the PE definition in Article 5 OECD MC serves to streamline and homogenise the different fiscal interests of the treaty states by providing a uniform interpretation of what should give rise to a PE in the respective treaty states.[188] According to Article 31(1) VCLT, '[a] treaty shall be interpreted in good faith in accordance with the ordinary meaning to be given to the terms of the treaty in their context and in the light of its object and purpose'. Even though the PE definition of Article 5 OECD MC was significantly influenced by German Law,[189] recourse to the PE definition of Section 12 GFC is formally inadmissible.[190] Such

[183]Cf. BVerfG, 15 Dec. 2015, 2 BvL 1/12, BVerfGE 141, 1, para. 33; cf. also The Federal Constitutional Court, Press Release of 12 Feb. 2016, No. 9/2016.

[184]Cf. BFH, 15 June 1973, III R 118/70, BStBl. II 1973, 810; BFH, 21 Aug. 1985, I R 63/80, BStBl. II 1986, 4; BFH, 27 Jan. 1988, I R 241/83, BStBl. II 1988, 574; BFH, 17 Nov. 1999, I R 7 /99, BStBl. II 2000, 605.

[185]Cf. *Vogel/Rust*, in: Reimer/Rust (Eds.), Klaus Vogel on Double Taxation Conventions, Introduction, paras. 52 et seqq.

[186]Cf. BFH, 28 June 1972, I R 35/70, BStBl. II 1972, 785.

[187]Cf. Sec. 34d and 49 German ITA.

[188]Cf. *Wassermeyer/Kaeser*, in: W/K/S/D (Eds.), Doppelbesteuerung, Art. 5 MA, para. 8; *Puls*, in: W/A/D (Eds.), Betriebsstätten-Handbuch, para. 2.1; *Ceballos*, in: Brugger/Plansky (Eds.), Permanent Establishments in International and EU Tax Law, 59 (61).

[189]See in more detail chapter C.I.1 of this thesis.

[190]Cf. *Wassermeyer/Kaeser*, in: W/K/S/D (Eds.), Doppelbesteuerung, Art. 5, para. 8.

recourse would only be admissible according to Article 3(2) OECD MC[191] if the respective treaty does not provide a definition of the PE.[192] Nevertheless, recourse to German national law and the rulings of the German Federal Tax Court are possible with regard to the interpretation of terms which are not defined in the respective tax treaties, such as the term 'fixed place of business' or the adequate degree of disposal.[193] This, however, leads to different tax assessments of the same case in the treaty states and therefore causes 'qualification conflicts'.[194] In order to achieve a common understanding of the respective provisions and the terms used in the provision between the treaty partners, the OECD introduced the OECD MC Commentary, which must be accorded due importance.[195]

c. Relevance of the OECD MC Commentary[196]

(1) Rational and Use

For each Article of the OECD MC, the Committee of Fiscal Affairs provides a detailed Commentary. Even though not legally binding, the OECD MC Commentary intents to interpret the respective provisions of the Convention. As pointed out by the OECD, the worldwide recognition of the provisions of the OECD MC and their incorporation into various tax treaties have helped to make the Commentaries on the provisions of the OECD MC a widely accepted guide for the interpretation and application of the provisions of tax treaties.[197] The OECD further elaborates that '[a]s the Commentaries have been drafted and agreed upon by the experts appointed to the Committee on Fiscal Affairs by the Governments

[191] Cf. in more detail for the provision of Art. 3 para. 2 OECD MC *Leisner-Egensperger*, IStR 2014, 10 (10 et seqq.); *Pohl*, in: Schönfeld/Ditz (Eds.), DBA-Kommentar, Art. 3, para. 74; *Lang*, IWB 2011, 281 (281 et seqq.).

[192] Cf. *Hruschka*, in: Schönfeld/Ditz (Eds.), DBA-Kommentar, Art. 5 (2014), para. 1; *Görl*, in: Vogel/Lehner (Eds.), DBA-Kommentar, Art. 5, para. 8.

[193] Cf. *Hruschka*, in: Schönfeld/Ditz (Eds.), DBA-Kommentar, Art. 5 (2014), para. 1; *Görl*, in: Vogel/Lehner (Eds.), DBA-Kommentar, Art. 5, para. 8; *Kahle/Kindich*, in: Lübbehüsen/Kahle (Eds.), Brennpunkte der Besteuerung von Betriebsstätten, para. 2.86; *Waltrich*, Cross-Border Taxation of Permanent Establishments, 54.

[194] See in more detail on qualification conflicts *Beck*, Qualifikationskonflikte im Internationalen Steuerrecht.

[195] Cf. *Wassermeyer*, in: W/K/S/D (Eds.), Doppelbesteuerung, Vor Art. 1 MA, para. 34.

[196] The following chapter was already published in a slightly modified version and was incorporated into this thesis with the consent of the co-authors (© 2018 IBFD. Originally published as S. Hentschel, G. Kraft & T. Moser, Permanent-Establishment Taxation in Germany in the Post-AOA-Implementation Era: A Primer on Exceptions and Problem Areas in 58 Eur. Taxn. 2/3, Journals IBFD, 73 (75 et seq.). Reproduced with permission.).

[197] Cf. OECD MC Commentary 2017, Introduction, para. 15.

of Member countries, they are of special importance in the development of international fiscal law'[198]. Also, Articles 31 and 32 of the VCLT supports the use of Commentaries as an aid to the interpretation of tax treaties. Even though the Commentaries on the Articles are not designed to be annexed to the actual treaties between the respective states, which are binding international instruments unlike the Commentary on the OECD MC, they can serve as valuable assistance, not only with regard to the interpretation and application of the treaties but also for the settlement of any disputes between the treaty states.[199] As pointed out by *Vogel/Rust*, the Commentaries on the Articles serve not only the tax administrations of the treaty states which routinely consult the Commentaries when interpreting bilateral tax treaties and the taxpayers in conducting and planning their business and investments but also play a key part in the judge's deliberations in reaching their decision.[200]

(2) Relations with Previous Versions

Different views exist, however, with regard to the question of whether a change in the Commentary may affect the interpretation of a tax treaty that was concluded before the Commentary was published (static versus dynamic approach).[201] As in 2017 a number of changes were made to Article 5 OECD MC and its respective Commentary, this question is of particular importance with regard to the interpretation of the PE definition in the various tax treaties.

In the view of the Committee of Fiscal Affairs, changes and additions to the Commentaries are, in general, applicable to the interpretation of tax treaties concluded before their adoption because such amendments reflect the consensus of the OECD member countries with regard to the proper interpretation of existing provisions.[202] Accordingly, tax treaties shall be interpreted dynamically in light of the latest Commentary. However, amendments to the Articles of the OECD MC and changes to the OECD MC Commentary that are a direct result of these amendments are not relevant to the application or interpretation of previously

---

[198] OECD MC Commentary 2017, Introduction, para. 29.

[199] Cf. *Vogel/Rust*, in: Reimer/Rust (Eds.), Klaus Vogel on Double Taxation Conventions, Introduction, para. 29.

[200] Cf. *Vogel/Rust*, in: Reimer/Rust (Eds.), Klaus Vogel on Double Taxation Conventions, Introduction, paras. 29.1 et seqq.

[201] Cf. *Gosch*, IStR 2015, 709 (709 et seq.); *Hemmelrath/Kepper*, IStR 2013, 37 (39 et seq.); *Kraft/Dombrowski*, IWB 2015, 87 (88 et seq.); *Kahle/Kindich*, in: Lübbehüsen/Kahle (Eds.), Brennpunkte der Besteuerung von Betriebsstätten, paras. 4.97 et seqq.; *Lang/Brugger*, Australian Tax Forum 2008, 95 (98 et seq.).

[202] Cf. OECD MC Commentary 2017 Introduction, para. 35; *Förster*, IStR 2007, 398 (398).

concluded tax treaties if the provisions of these treaties are different in substance from the amended Articles.[203]

The German Federal Tax Court, however, does not share this view and follows a static approach.[204] Under a static approach, the interpretation of a tax treaty can only be based on the Commentary as it was phrased at the time the tax treaty was negotiated.[205] Consequently, changes to the Commentary cannot automatically affect tax treaties retroactively. The most compelling argument for this approach is related to the concept of separation of powers. Under this principle, it would be highly questionable if representatives of the executive branch were, at the OECD level, able to change the meaning of certain provisions of tax treaties that were implemented as a result of a national legislative procedure.[206]

2. Structure of Article 5 OECD MC

Article 5(1) OECD MC provides the fundamental definition of the PE term. Accordingly, a PE is defined as 'a fixed place of business through which the business of an enterprise is wholly or partly carried on'.

This general definition attempts to point out the essential characteristics of a PE, which are:

- the existence of a place of business;
- the fixed nature of that place of business; and
- the carrying on of the business of the enterprise through this fixed place of business.

In addition to this general definition, Article 5(2) OECD MC provides a positive non-exhaustive list of examples which are deemed to give rise to a PE similar to Section 12 sentence 2 GFC. In particular, the following examples are considered to constitute a PE:

a) a place of management;
b) a branch;

---

[203] Cf. OECD MC Commentary 2017, Introduction, para. 35.

[204] Cf. BFH, 25 May 2011, I R 95/10, BFHE 234, 63; BFH, 9 Feb. 2011, I R 54/10, BStBl. II 2012, 106.

[205] Cf. BFH, 25 May 2011, I R 95/10, BFHE 234, 63; BFH, 9 Feb. 2011, I R 54/10, BStBl. II 2012, 106.

[206] Cf. *Lang*, ÖStZ 2006, 203 (210).

c) an office;
d) a factory;
e) a workshop; and
f) a mine, an oil or gas well, a quarry or any other place of extraction of natural resources.

Paragraph 3 provides explicitly that building sites, constructions or installation projects constitute a PE only if they last more than twelve months.

Paragraph 4 contains a negative catalogue of business activities of, in general, an auxiliary or preparatory character which do not constitute a PE, even if these activities are carried on through a fixed place of business.

Paragraph 5 and paragraph 6 give guidance to the specific type of the 'Agent PE'. While paragraph 5 stipulates the conditions under which an enterprise should be treated as having a PE at source in respect of activities of a person acting for it, paragraph 6 deals with exceptions for agents of independent status.[207]

Paragraph 7 clarifies that in circumstances where a company which is a resident of a contracting state controls or is controlled by a company which is a resident of the other contracting state, or which carries on business through a PE or otherwise in that other state, shall not lead to the conclusion that each company constitutes a PE of the other.[208]

Paragraph 8 explains the circumstances under which a person or enterprise is closely related to an enterprise.

The above structure of Article 5 OECD MC reveals that certain similarities to Article 12 GFC can be identified, especially with regard to the essential characteristics of the PE definition. However, despite these similarities their interpretation might differ. In the following, the PE definition as implemented in Article 5 OECD and concretised by the OECD MC Commentary will be discussed. In this context, deviations between the OECD and the German approach will be elaborated and changes to the PE definition induced through BEPS Action 7 will be discussed.

[207] Cf. *Reimer*, in: Reimer/Rust (Eds.), Klaus Vogel on Double Taxation Conventions, Introduction, para. 29. For a detailed analysis of the Agent PE cf. *Dombrowski*, Betriebsstättenbesteuerung vor und nach Umsetzung des AOA, 204 et seqq.

[208] As expressed by *Reimer*, this provision has only declaratory meaning and can be regarded as legally superfluous, cf. *Reimer*, in: Reimer/Rust (Eds.), Klaus Vogel on Double Taxation Conventions, Art. 5, para. 370.

3. Essential Characteristics of a PE under Article 5 OECD-MC

a. Place of Business

(1) Physical Presence

Pursuant to the OECD MC Commentary, the term 'place of business' covers any premises, installations or facilities used for carrying on the business of the enterprise, irrespective of the fact whether or not they are used exclusively for that purpose.[209] A place of business may also exist if no premises are required or available for carrying on the enterprise's business and the enterprise simply has a certain amount of space at its disposal.[210] According to the German Federal Ministry of Finance, the term 'place of business' used in the OECD MC corresponds content-related to the term 'place of business or facility' used in Section 12 GFC.[211] The fact that facilities are not explicitly mentioned in the definition of the PE term in Article 5(1) OECD MC can be regarded irrelevant with respect to the interpretation of the term since the OECD MC Commentary considers facilities as a subtype of a place of business.[212]

(2) Right of Disposal

Even though not explicitly mentioned in Article 5 OECD MC,[213] the traditional interpretation of a PE as set forth in the OECD MC Commentary requires that the place of business must be at the disposal of the taxpayer.[214] In this regard, the term 'disposal' means the authority to use the place of business directly.[215] Similar to the German approach, it is immaterial whether the premises, installations

---

[209] Cf. OECD MC Commentary 2017, Art. 5, para. 10.

[210] Cf. OECD MC Commentary 2017, Art. 5, para. 10.

[211] Cf. BMF, 24 Dec. 1999, IV B 4—S 1300—111/99, para 1.2.1.1.

[212] Cf. OECD MC Commentary 2017, Art. 5, para. 10.

[213] According to *Reimer*, this requirement follows from the term 'through' as used in Art. 5(1) OECD MC, cf. *Reimer*, in: Reimer/Rust (Eds.), Klaus Vogel on Double Taxation Conventions, Art. 5, para. 102; also *Kroppen*, IWB 2005, 727 (731 et seq.); *Kumpf*, in: Haarmann (Ed.), Die beschränkte Steuerpflicht, 27 (35). Critical in this regard *Wassermeyer/Kaeser*, in: W/K/S/D (Eds.), Doppelbesteuerung, Art. 5 MA, para. 42.

[214] Cf. OECD MC Commentary 2017, Art. 5, para. 10.

[215] Cf. *Reimer*, in: Reimer/Rust (Eds.), Klaus Vogel on Double Taxation Conventions, Art. 5, para. 103.

or facilities are owned or rented by or are otherwise at the disposal of the enterprise.[216] Consequently, the place of business may also be situated in the business facilities of another enterprise.[217]

However, in contrast to the German approach, the requirements for the affirmation of the right of disposal were significantly reduced by the OECD.[218] As a consequence, no formal or other right to use the place of business is required; thus, the effective use is sufficient.[219] Therefore, a PE could for example also exist where an enterprise illegally occupies a specific location where it carries on its business.[220] Furthermore, according to the OECD MC Commentary, the mere performance of business activities at a specific location that belongs to another enterprise on a continuous basis during an extended period of time can also constitute a PE.[221] In this context, the so-called 'painter-example' in the OECD MC Commentary illustrates that the mere presence of a painter who spends three days a week for a period of two years in a large office building of its main client, constitutes a PE of that painter (Service PE)[222].[223] Even though Germany has officially rejected the interpretation of the 'painter example' as illustrated in paragraph 17 of the OECD MC Commentary 2017 on Article 5,[224] this example outlines that, according to the OECD, a PE might even be triggered through the mere use of the place of business. However, the position of the OECD is disputed by the prevailing view in literature which holds that the described circumstances

[216] Cf. OECD MC Commentary 2017, Art. 5, para. 10.

[217] Cf. OECD MC Commentary 2017, Art. 5, para. 10.

[218] Cf. *Haase*, in Haase (Ed.), Außensteuergesetz/Doppelbesteuerungsabkommen, Art. 5 OECD MC, para. 70; *Delarber*, Steuerliche Einflüsse auf die grenzüberschreitende Betriebsstättenbesteuerung, 94.

[219] Cf. OECD MC Commentary 2017, Art. 5, para. 10.

[220] Cf. OECD MC Commentary 2017, Art. 5, para. 11.

[221] Cf. OECD MC Commentary 2017, Art. 5, para. 12.

[222] See in more detail for the service PE chapter C.IV.6.d of this thesis.

[223] Cf. OECD MC Commentary 2017, Art. 5, para. 17; also *Nitikman*, CTJ 2009, 213 (213 et seqq.); *Ditz/Quilitzsch*, FR 2012, 493 (495). See in more detail with regard to the Service PE *Haase/Dorn*, IWB 2011, 721 (722); *Bendlinger*, IStR 2009, 521 (523); *Wassermeyer/Kaeser*, in: W/K/S/D (Eds.), Doppelbesteuerung, Art. 5 MA, paras. 259 et seqq.

[224] Germany regards the painter example as inconsistent with the principles stated in Art. 5 para. 12 first sentence OECD MC Commentary 2017, thus not giving rise to a PE under Art. 5 (1) OECD MC, cf. para. 178 OECD MC Commentary 2017. For DTAs that were concluded before 2003, the German Federal Tax Court does not follow the approach of the OECD, cf. BFH, 24 July 2004, I R 106/03, BFH/NV 2005, 154; BFH, 4 June 2008, I R 30/07, BStBl. II 2008, 922.

do neither meet the criteria of the right of disposal nor constitute a fixed place of business under German or under treaty law.[225]

b. Fixed Nature

According to Article 5(1) OECD MC, the place of business must be of a 'fixed' nature. In line with the German view, the notion of 'fixed' consists of a geographic and a temporal component.[226]

With regard to the geographic component, the OECD states that there has to be a certain link between the place of business and a specific geographic point.[227] However, this does not mean that the place of business has to be fixed to the soil and consequently rigidly unmovable during the entire course of the performance of the respective business activity.[228] It is sufficient that the equipment constituting the place of business remains on a particular site. While a gold mine for example clearly constitutes a fixed place of business, even though business activities may move from one location to another,[229] a satellite in geostationary orbit cannot be regarded as a fixed place of business due to a lack of permanent connection to the ground.[230]

Apart from the geographical component, a certain degree of permanency is required.[231] While the place of business may not constitute a PE if it is of a purely temporary nature, an explicit time limit is not mentioned in Article 5 OECD MC. Only with regard to building sites, construction or installation projects dealt with in Article 5(3) OECD MC, a minimum period of twelve months—which is different from the six months threshold of Section 12 sentence 2 no. 8 GFC—is required. For all other PEs, the OECD MC Commentary argues for a time period of six months.[232] However, this time period should not be interpreted as a fixed

---

[225] Cf. *Wang/Schreiber,* in Reimer/Schmid/Orell (Eds.), Permanent Establishments, § 8.03 [D], para. 52; *Delarber*, Steuerliche Einflüsse auf die grenzüberschreitende Betriebsstättenbesteuerung, 95. Further with regard to the Service PE cf. *Ditz/Quilitzsch*, FR 2012, 493 (494); *Kaeser*, IStR 2012, 674 (676); *Grotherr/Endert*, in: Lüdicke/Mössner/Hummel (Eds.), Das Steuerrecht der Unternehmen, 157 (161).

[226] Cf. detailed *Schaffner*, How Fixed Is a Permanent Establishment, 117 et seqq.

[227] Cf. OECD MC Commentary 2017, Art. 5, para. 21.

[228] Cf. OECD MC Commentary 2017, Art. 5, para. 21.

[229] Cf. OECD MC Commentary 2017, Art. 5, para. 23.

[230] Cf. OECD MC Commentary 2017, Art. 5, para. 27.

[231] Cf. OECD MC Commentary 2017, Art. 5, para. 28. For a detailed analysis with regard to the temporal component cf. *Perdelwitz*, in: Gutiérrez/Perdelwitz (Eds.), Taxation of Business Profits in the 21st Century, 27 (27 et seqq.).

[232] Cf. OECD MC Commentary 2017, Art. 5, para. 28.

limit but rather as a guideline that allows tolerance in both directions.[233] In contrast to the German approach, a place of business may also constitute a PE even though it only exists for a very short period of time, if the nature of the business is such that it will only be carried on for a such a short period.[234] Furthermore, recurrent activities, i.e. activities which last for a relatively short time but are repeated regularly, should be considered permanent, even if the individual periods in which the business activity is carried out are shorter than six months.[235]

c. Carrying on Business of the Enterprise

(1) General Elements

While the domestic PE definition in Section 12 GFC requires a fixed place of business or facility that 'serves' the business of an enterprise, Article 5(1) OECD MC demands a fixed place of business 'through which' the business of an enterprise is wholly or partly carried on. Even though the German Federal Ministry of Finance is of the opinion that the different expressions shall be interpreted in the same way,[236] it is argued that the activity threshold under domestic law to be lower than under Article 5(1) OECD MC.[237] Also, the German Federal Court of Justice (BGH) dealt with this difference between Art. 5 OECD MC and Section 12 GFC and concluded that Art. 5 OECD MC contains a narrower interpretation of the PE definition, since it requires that the business activity of an enterprise is wholly or partly carried on 'through' the fixed place of business.[238]

However, the OECD MC Commentary argues that the words 'through which' must be given a wide meaning so as it can be applied to any situation where

---

[233] Cf. *Hilbert/Engel*, Intertax 2012, 462 (468).

[234] Cf. OECD MC Commentary 2017, Art. 5, para. 28 sentence 2. Germany reserves its position concerning the scope and limits of application of guidance in para. 28 sentence 2 and paras. 29, 30 OECD MC Commentary 2017 and takes the view that in order to permit the assumption of a fixed place of business, a certain minimum period of presence during the year concerned is required in order to meet the necessary degree of permanency, irrespective of the recurrent or other nature of an activity, cf. OECD MC Commentary 2017, Art. 5, para. 179.

[235] Cf. BFH, 17 Sep. 2003, I R 12/02, BStBl. II 2004, 396; OECD MC Commentary 2017, Art. 5, para. 179.

[236] Cf. BMF, 24 Dec. 1999, IV B 4—S 1300—111/99, BStBl. I 1999, 1076, para. 1.2.1.1.

[237] Cf. *Wassermeyer/Kaeser*, in: W/K/S/D (Eds.), Doppelbesteuerung, Art. 5 MA, para. 10; *Schnitger/Bildstein*, Ubg 2008, 444 (447); *Musil*, in: Hübschmann/Hepp/Spitaler (Eds.), AO/FGO, § 12 AO, para. 47a; *Pinkernell*, Internationale Steuergestaltung im Electronic Commerce, 94 et seq.

[238] Cf. BGH, 24 Oct. 1988, 3 StR 533/87, HFR 1990, 150.

business activities are carried on at a location that is at the disposal of the enterprise for that purpose.[239] In this respect, the type of business of the enterprise is irrelevant as long as it serves the enterprise's overall purpose.[240] Consequently, the business activity does not need to be of a productive character.[241]

Nevertheless, the ruling of the German Federal Tax Court[242] with regard to the operation of an automated 'noise measurement station' constituting a PE for the airport operator, illustrates that Section 12 sentence 1 GFC is wider than Article 5(1) OECD MC.[243] This is due to the fact that the ruling of the German Federal Tax Court illustrated that even activities carried out at a fixed place of business that merely serve regulatory requirements (noise measurement) are regarded as sufficient for the fixed place of business to serve the business of an enterprise.[244]

(2) Presence of Human Beings

With regard to the question whether or not the presence of human beings is necessary in order to constitute a PE under Article 5 OECD MC, different views exist. Especially the expression 'carried on' used by Article 5(1) OECD MC is weighted as a factor that makes the presence of personnel acting on behalf of the enterprise necessary.[245] Even though there is no specific reference to human interventions in Article 5(1) OECD MC, it has been argued that paragraph 6 of the Commentary to Article 5 OECD MC, specifically the phrase 'carrying on of the business of the enterprise through this fixed place of business [...] means usually that persons who, in one way or another, are dependent on the enterprise (personnel) conduct the business of the enterprise'[246], implies that the presence

---

239 Cf. OECD MC Commentary 2017, Art. 5, para. 20.

240 Cf. *Ceballos*, in: Brugger/Plansky (Eds.), Permanent Establishments in International and EU Tax Law, 59 (67).

241 Cf. OECD MC Commentary 2017, Art. 5, para. 35. In line with the German approach, social facilities, such as fitness facilities, changing rooms and recreation homes that only serve social needs of the employees do not directly serve the business purpose and therefore do not constitute a PE, cf. *Ceballos*, in: Brugger/Plansky (Eds.), Permanent Establishments in International and EU Tax Law, 59 (67).

242 BFH, 16 Dec. 2009, I R 56/08, BStBl. II 2010, 492.

243 Cf. *Pinkernell*, Internationale Steuergestaltung im Electronic Commerce, 94 et seq.

244 Cf. *Pinkernell*, Internationale Steuergestaltung im Electronic Commerce, 95.

245 Cf. *Wassermeyer/Kaeser*, in: W/K/S/D (Eds.), Doppelbesteuerung, Art. 5 MA, para. 10; *Buciek*, DStZ 2003, 139 (142).

246 Cf. OECD MC Commentary 2017, Art. 5, para. 6.

of human beings to be a requirement for a PE to exist.[247] Also, paragraph 39 of the Commentary to Article 5 OECD MC supports the view that the presence of human beings is necessary by stating that '[i]n most cases, the business of an enterprise is carried on by entrepreneur or persons who are in a paid-employment relationship with the enterprise (personnel)'. The same conclusion can be drawn from paragraph 41 of the Commentary to Article 5 OECD MC, which states that even in cases where the business of the enterprise is carried on mainly through fully automatic equipment, a minimum level of human interaction through 'setting up, operating, controlling and maintaining such equipment'[248] is required.

However, the jurisprudence of the German Federal Tax Court indicates that the presence of human beings is not required, and this not only within the meaning of Section 12 GFC, but also for treaty purposes.[249] A clarification of the OECD with regard to the application of the PE definition in e-commerce points in the same direction. Hereafter, human interventions are not a requirement for a PE to exist.[250] However, according to the OECD, changes to the OECD Commentary are not deemed necessary since paragraph 6 and paragraph 39 of the Commentary to Article 5 OECD MC are still accurate and do not support the conclusion that the presence of human beings is a requirement.[251] Also, paragraph 127 of the Commentary to Article 5 OECD MC argues that '[t]he presence of personnel is not necessary to consider that an enterprise wholly or partly carries on its business at a location when no personnel are in fact required to carry on its business at a location'. This conclusion shall not only apply to e-commerce but also to activities in which equipment operates automatically.[252]

[247]Cf. OECD Committee on Fiscal Affairs, Clarifications on the Application of the Permanent Establishment definition in E-Commerce, paras. 10 et seqq. See for the discussion *Buciek*, DStZ 2003, 139 (142 et seq.); *Wassermeyer/Kaeser*, in: W/K/S/D (Eds.), Doppelbesteuerung, Art. 5 MA, paras. 33, 33a; *Portner*, Ertragssteuerliche Aspekte des E-Commerce, 33 et seqq.; *Pinkernell*, Internationale Steuergestaltung im Electronic Commerce, 90 et seq.

[248]OECD MC Commentary 2017, Art. 5, para. 41.

[249]Cf. BFH, 30 Oct. 1996, II R 12/92, BStBl. II 1997, 12.

[250]Cf. OECD Committee on Fiscal Affairs, Clarifications on the Application of the Permanent Establishment Definition in E-Commerce, paras. 12 et seqq.

[251]Cf. OECD Committee on Fiscal Affairs, Clarifications on the Application of the Permanent Establishment Definition in E-Commerce, 2000, paras. 12 et seqq.

[252]OECD MC Commentary 2017, Art. 5, para. 127.

In light of the above, it must therefore be assumed that the presence of human beings is not a necessary requirement for a PE to exist according to Article 5 OECD MC, irrespective of the business activity carried on through the PE.[253]

4. Positive List Indicating a PE

Similar to Section 12 sentence 2 GFC, Article 5(2) OECD MC sets forth a list of examples of places of business that could give rise to a PE. The phrase 'includes especially' employed by the wording of Article 5(2) OECD MC indicates that this list cannot be regarded as exhaustive.[254] Rather, the list is merely an illustration of *prima facie* PEs that give rise to a PE only if the requirements laid down in Article 5(1) OECD MC are met.[255]

Therefore, unlike Section 12 sentence 2 GFC, the examples listed in Article 5(2) OECD MC cannot be regarded as a stand-alone list of PE examples that give rise to a PE in a priori fashion and consequently do not extend the scope of the PE's concept beyond the definition laid down in Article 5(1) OECD MC.[256] This result is not only explicitly stated in paragraph 45 of the Commentary to Article 5 OECD MC but can also be derived from the historical interpretation.[257] While the pre-1977 version of the OECD MC listed building sites, constructions or assembled projects[258] in Article 5(2) lit. g, the 1977 version and the following

---

[253]Cf. *Heinsen*, in: Looks/Heinsen (Eds.), Betriebsstättenbesteuerung, para. 189; *Puls*, in: W/A/D (Eds.), Betriebsstätten-Handbuch, para. 2.97; *Ceballos*, in: Brugger/Plansky (Eds.), Permanent Establishments in International and EU Tax Law, 59 (68); *Ditz*, Internationale Gewinnabgrenzung bei Betriebsstätten, 32 et seqq.; *Delarber*, Steuerliche Einflüsse auf die grenzüberschreitende Betriebsstättenbesteuerung, 91 et seq.; *Pinkernell*, Internationale Steuergestaltung im Electronic Commerce, 90 et seq.

[254]Cf. OECD MC Commentary 2017, Art. 5, para. 45.

[255]Cf. OECD MC Commentary 2017, Art. 5, para. 45.

[256]Cf. *Heinsen*, in: Looks/Heinsen (Eds.), Betriebsstättenbesteuerung, para. 206; *Görl*, in: Vogel/Lehner (Eds.), DBA-Kommentar, Art. 5, para. 37; *Reimer*, in: Reimer/Rust (Eds.), Klaus Vogel on Double Taxation Conventions, Art. 5, para. 160; *Hruschka*, in: Schönfeld/Ditz (Eds.), DBA-Kommentar, Art. 5 (2014), para. 87; *Wassermeyer/Kaeser*, in: W/K/S/D (Eds.), Doppelbesteuerung, Art. 5 MA, para. 61; *Delarber*, Steuerliche Einflüsse auf die grenzüberschreitende Betriebsstättenbesteuerung, 100.

[257]Cf. *Reimer*, in: Reimer/Rust (Eds.), Klaus Vogel on Double Taxation Conventions, Art. 5, para. 160; *Kahle/Kindich*, in: Lübbehüsen/Kahle (Eds.), Brennpunkte der Besteuerung von Betriebsstätten, para. 2.93.

[258]The term 'assembled projects' was replaced in the 1977 version of the OECD MC by 'installation projects'.

allocated this category of PEs into (a separate) paragraph 3. This change has untied building sites, constructions or installation projects from the requirements laid down in Article 5(1) OECD MC.[259] Besides the desire to exclude building sites, constructions or installation projects more clearly from constituting a PE if they last twelve months or less, the amendment also aimed at widening the spectrum of such projects.[260]

Even though this view renders the list of examples set out in Article 5(2) OECD MC to a mere illustration of places of business that only constitute a PE if the requirements of Article 5(1) OECD MC are met, this interpretation is in line with the overwhelming country practice.[261] The consequences of the fact that Germany follows a different approach in Section 12 GFC seem to be rather limited in practice, since most of the PEs listed in Section 12 sentence 2 OECD MC comply with the requirements of the PE definition of Section 12 sentence 1 OECD MC anyway.[262]

5. Preparatory or Auxiliary Activities

a. Conceptual Approach

Article 5(4) OECD MC plays an essential role for international business as it includes a list of exceptions according to which a PE is deemed not to exist, even though the business activity is carried on through a fixed place of business.[263] Article 5(4) OECD MC is *lex specialis* in relation to Article 5(1), (2) and (3) OECD MC.[264] Accordingly, although the general elements of the PE definition

---

[259] Cf. *Reimer*, in: Reimer/Rust (Eds.), Klaus Vogel on Double Taxation Conventions, Art. 5, para. 176; *Kahle/Kindich*, in: Lübbehüsen/Kahle (Eds.), Brennpunkte der Besteuerung von Betriebsstätten, para. 2.93.

[260] Cf. *Reimer*, in: Reimer/Rust (Eds.), Klaus Vogel on Double Taxation Conventions, Art. 5, paras. 178 et seqq.

[261] Cf. *Sasseville/Skaar*, in: IFA, CDFI 2009, Volume 94a, 17 (31 et seq.).

[262] Cf. with regard to the German approach *Kahle/Ziegler*, DStZ 2009, 834 (839); *Kahle/Kindich*, in: Lübbehüsen/Kahle (Eds.), Brennpunkte der Besteuerung von Betriebsstätten, para. 2.51; *Scheffler*, Internationale betriebswirtschaftliche Steuerlehre, 257.

[263] Cf. OECD, BEPS Action 7: Final Report 2015, p. 28, para. 10.

[264] Cf. BFH, 23 Jan. 1985, I R 292/81, BStBl. II 1985, 417; *Görl*, in: Vogel/Lehner (Eds.), DBA-Kommentar, Art. 5, para. 86; *Delarber*, Steuerliche Einflüsse auf die grenzüberschreitende Betriebsstättenbesteuerung, 114. *Wassermeyer/Kaeser* point out that it can be argued whether all exceptions listed in Art. 5(4) OECD MC would actually meet the requirements set out in Art. 5(1) OECD MC, cf. *Wassermeyer/Kaeser*, in: W/K/S/D (Eds.), Doppelbesteuerung, Art. 5 MA, para. 151.

laid down in Article 5(1) OECD MC are met, the business activities listed cannot be regarded sufficient in order to constitute a PE.[265] In other words, the exceptions listed in Article 5(4) OECD MC restrict the scope of the PE definition contained in Article 5(1) OECD MC and exclude from its scope a number of fixed places of business.

As put forward in the OECD MC Commentary 2017, preparatory or auxiliary activities may very well contribute to the productivity of an enterprise.[266] However, as such activities are in general so far from an actual profit realisation, efficiency reasons, especially administrative feasibility, may justify not to allow source taxation if only activities of a preparatory or auxiliary nature are carried out in the source state by the non-resident enterprise.[267]

b. Changes through the BEPS Project

At the time the list of exceptions to the definition of a PE was first introduced, the activities covered therein were generally considered to be activities of a preparatory or auxiliary character.[268] However, since then the business world has undergone significant changes in the way how business is conducted.[269] Hence, activities previously considered being of a merely preparatory or auxiliary character may in today's business environment correspond to core business activities.[270] In order to ensure that each of the exceptions included in Article 5(4) OECD MC is restricted to activities that are otherwise of a preparatory or auxiliary character, this paragraph was modified as a result of BEPS Action 7. The changes are indicated in the following:[271]

'Notwithstanding the preceding provisions of this Article, the term "permanent establishment" shall be deemed not to include:

a) the use of facilities solely for the purpose of storage, display or delivery of goods or merchandise belonging to the enterprise;

---

[265] Cf. OECD MC Commentary 2017, Art. 5, para. 58.

[266] Cf. OECD MC Commentary 2017, Art. 5, para. 58.

[267] Cf. OECD MC Commentary 2017, Art. 5, para. 58.

[268] Cf. OECD, BEPS Action 7: Final Report 2015, p. 10.

[269] For an overview of the evolution of ICT and its impact on the economy cf. OECD, BEPS Action 1: Final Report 2015, paras. 64 et seqq.

[270] Cf. OECD, BEPS Action 7: Final Report 2015, p. 10; *Schoppe/Popat*, BB 2016, 1113 (1113).

[271] Additions to the existing provision appear in bold and deletions are marked through strikethroughs.

b) the maintenance of a stock of goods or merchandise belonging to the enterprise solely for the purpose of storage, display or delivery;
c) the maintenance of a stock of goods or merchandise belonging to the enterprise solely for the purpose of processing by another enterprise;
d) the maintenance of a fixed place of business solely for the purpose of purchasing goods or merchandise or of collecting information, for the enterprise;
e) the maintenance of a fixed place of business solely for the purpose of carrying on, for the enterprise, any other activity ~~of a preparatory or auxiliary character;~~
f) the maintenance of a fixed place of business solely for any combination of activities mentioned in subparagraphs a) to e), ~~provided that the overall activity of the fixed place of business resulting from this combination is of a preparatory or auxiliary character,~~

provided that such activity or, in the case of subparagraph f), the overall activity of the fixed place of business, is of a preparatory or auxiliary character.'

The changes result in the fact that activities listed in subparagraphs a) to d) are only excluded from the PE exemption if they are preparatory or auxiliary in character.[272] The amendments ensure that it will not be possible that a business's core activities inappropriately benefit from the stated exception for preparatory and auxiliary activities.[273] Consequently, also warehouse activities or activities carried out in a fixed place of business for the purpose of purchasing of goods or merchandise or of collecting information may now constitute a PE unless the enterprise can prove that such activities are merely preparatory or auxiliary in character.[274]

Furthermore, BEPS concerns arise from a technique that is usually referred to as the fragmentation of contracts. In order to prevent such techniques, a new paragraph 4.1 was introduced in Article 5 OECD MC. This provision aims to clarify that it shall not be possible to avoid triggering the PE threshold by the fragmentation of a cohesive operating business into small business operations just for the sake of arguing that each part is engaged only in activities that are preparatory or auxiliary in nature, captured by the list of exceptions.[275] This new provision can be regarded as a rational consequence of the choice to restrict the scope of Article

[272]Cf. *Kraft/Hentschel/Apler*, Ubg 2017, 318 (321).

[273]Cf. *Saint-Amans/Russo*, BIT 2016, 236 (238).

[274]For a detailed analysis of the significance of the changes for warehouse activities cf. *Kraft/Hentschel/Apler*, Ubg 2017, 318 (318 et seqq.). See also in this regard *Bendlinger*, TPI 2018, 53 (53 et seqq.); *Storck/Mechtler*, in: Lang/Pistone/Rust/Schuch/Staringer (Eds.), Base Erosion and Profit Shifting, 51 (53 et seqq.).

[275]Cf. OECD, BEPS Action 7: Final Report 2015, p. 10.

5(4) OECD MC to activities that are preparatory or auxiliary in nature since, in the absence of such a rule, it would be fairly easy to segregate activities by using closely related enterprises which would go beyond the respective threshold when taken together.[276]

c. Deviations of German National Law from OECD Approach

German national law does not provide for a provision that is similar to Article 5(4) OECD MC.[277] Rather, activities that are carried on through a fixed place of business and that are of a preparatory or auxiliary character can still trigger a PE under German national law.[278] The difference between Section 12 GTC and Article 5 OECD MC can be justified with the fact that Article 5 OECD MC requires a fixed place of business *through* which the business of an enterprise is wholly or partly carried on, while Section 12 GFC considers it sufficient that the fixed place of business or facility *serves* the business of an enterprise.[279] As discussed above, in order for a fixed place of business or facility to serve the business of the enterprise it is sufficient that the place of business or facility supports the enterprise's purpose.[280] In this respect, any direct usefulness of the fixed place of business or facility for an activity carried on in there justifies such a place to constitute a PE.[281]

[276] Cf. OECD, BEPS Action 7: Final Report 2015, p. 39, para. 15. See in more detail with regard to the anti-fragmentation clause *Schuch*, SWI 2017, 654 (654 et seqq.).

[277] Cf. *Rehfeld*, in: Gosch/Kroppen/Grotherr/Kraft (Eds.), DBA-Kommentar, Art. 5 OECD-MA, para. 106; *Hruschka*, in: Schönfeld/Ditz (Eds.), DBA-Kommentar, Art. 5 (2014), para. 131.

[278] Cf. *Wassermeyer*, in: Drenseck/Seer (Eds.), Festschrift für Heinrich Wilhelm Kruse zum 70. Geburtstag, 589 (592).

[279] Cf. *Hruschka*, in: Schönfeld/Ditz (Eds.), DBA-Kommentar, Art. 5 (2014), para. 131; *Delarber*, Steuerliche Einflüsse auf die grenzüberschreitende Betriebsstättenbesteuerung, 119. See in more detail for the difference between the phrases 'through' and 'serves' chapter C.IV.3.c.(1) of this thesis.

[280] Cf. BFH, 30 Oct. 1996, II R 12/92, BStBl. II 1997, 12.

[281] Cf. BFH, 30 Oct. 1996, II R 12/92, BStBl. II 1997, 12.

6. Special PE Cases

a. Building Sites or Constructions or Installation Projects

(1) Conceptual Approach

Building sites or constructions or installation projects are not part of the positive list of Article 5(2) OECD MC indicating a PE. Rather, they are dealt with in a separate paragraph 3 of Article 5 OECD MC. Besides the construction of buildings, the term 'building site or construction or installation project' also covers the construction of roads, bridges or cabals as well as the renovation of such projects.[282]

Whether or not a building site or construction or installation projects constitute a PE is contingent upon the time period they last for. As explicitly phrased in Article 5(3) OECD MC, such projects only constitute a PE if they last more than twelve months. Projects, which do not meet the twelve months threshold do not of itself constitute a PE, even in the case that it contains an installation, e.g. a workshop or an office within the meaning of Article 5(2) OECD MC, associated with the construction activity.[283]

In order for such projects to constitute a PE, there is no need that the requirements of the basic PE laid down in Article 5(1) OECD MC, such as a fixed place of business or a certain degree of disposal, are met.[284] However, the phrase 'only' indicates that building sites or construction or installation projects do not constitute a PE if they last less than twelve months, even if the requirements laid down in Article 5(1) OECD MC are met.[285] These findings illustrate that Article 5(3) OECD MC does not only extend the definition of the PE as laid down in Article 5(1) OECD MC but is at the same time *lex specialis* to Article 5(1) OECD MC and therefore restricts its application.[286]

---

[282] Cf. OECD MC Commentary 2017, Art. 5, para. 50.

[283] Cf. OECD MC Commentary 2017, Art. 5, para. 49.

[284] Cf. *Heinsen,* in: Looks/Heinsen (Eds.), Betriebsstättenbesteuerung, para. 215; *Wassermeyer/Kaeser*, in: W/K/S/D (Eds.), Doppelbesteuerung, Art. 5 MA, para. 95.

[285] Cf. *Gassner*, in: Gassner/Lang/Lechner (Eds.), Die Betriebsstätte im Recht der Doppelbesteuerungsabkommen, 57 (60); *Puls*, in: W/A/D (Eds.), Betriebsstätten-Handbuch, paras. 2.146 et seq.; *Delarber*, Steuerliche Einflüsse auf die grenzüberschreitende Betriebsstättenbesteuerung, 102.

[286] Cf. *Wassermeyer/Kaeser*, in: W/K/S/D (Eds.), Doppelbesteuerung, Art. 5 MA, paras. 91 et seqq.

As explicitly mentioned in the OECD Commentary, the twelve-month threshold applies to each individual project or site.[287] In this regard, the time previously spend on other projects or sites that are totally unconnected should not be considered. Furthermore, a building site should be regarded as a single unit, even if a) it is based on several contracts, e.g. in order to escape the twelve-months threshold, or b) the orders have been placed by several persons, provided that this building site forms a coherent geographical and commercial whole.[288]

(2) Changes through the BEPS Project

BEPS Action 7 identified several tax planning strategies as a tool for the artificial avoidance of the PE status in the source state.[289] One of these strategies seeks to circumvent the twelve-month threshold through the practice of splitting up contracts into several parts, while each of these contracts covers a period of less than twelve months and is attributed to different companies owned by the same group.[290]

In order to address concerns in this regard, the OECD provides two possible solutions. The first solution can be found in the Report on BEPS Action 6: 'Preventing the Granting of Treaty Benefits in Inappropriate Circumstances' which suggests the application of the Principle Purpose Test (PPT).[291] The PPT can be regarded as a more general anti-abuse rule which is based on the principle purpose of the arrangement.[292] If the principle purpose of the arrangement is to obtain treaty benefits, then such benefits will be denied unless it is established that granting such benefits is in accordance with the purpose and object of the provision of the treaty.[293]

The second solution can be applied by countries that do not want to introduce a general anti-abuse rule. Therefore, paragraph 52 of the OECD MC Commentary

---

[287] Cf. OECD MC Commentary 2017, Art. 5, para. 51. Cf. in more detail for the time threshold *Rehfeld*, in: Gosch/Kroppen/Grotherr/Kraft (Eds.), DBA-Kommentar, Art. 5 OECD-MA, paras. 93 et seqq.; *Hruschka*, in: Schönfeld/Ditz (Eds.), DBA-Kommentar, Art. 5 (2014), paras. 124 et seqq.; *Puls*, in: W/A/D (Eds.), Betriebsstätten-Handbuch, paras. 2.171 et seqq.

[288] Cf. OECD MC Commentary 2017, Art. 5, para. 51.

[289] For an overview cf. OECD, BEPS Action 7: Final Report 2015, p. 9 et seqq.

[290] Cf. OECD, BEPS Action 7: Final Report 2015, p. 42, para. 16; OECD, BEPS Action 6: Final Report 2015, p. 69, para. 29.

[291] Cf. OECD, BEPS Action 6: Final Report 2015, p. 69, para. 29.

[292] Cf. OECD, BEPS Action 6: Final Report 2015, p. 9. See in more detail with regard to the PPT *Kuźniacki*, WTJ 2018, 233 (233 et seqq.).

[293] Cf. OECD, BEPS Action 6: Final Report 2015, p. 9.

2017 offers countries an option of a specific anti-abuse rule that can be implemented in the respective DTAs. According to this "anti-split provision", activities performed over periods that last more than 30 days should be aggregated in order to determine whether the 12-month threshold has been exceeded.[294] In this regard, also activities that are carried out by closely related enterprises should be aggregated.[295] These different periods are then added together to determine whether they constitute a PE.[296]

(3) Deviations of German National Law from OECD Approach

By derogation from the German approach, which provides that building sites or constructions or installation projects are part of the non-exhaustive positive list of Section 12 sentence 2 GFC, such sites and projects are dealt with in a separate paragraph 3 of Article 5 OECD MC. Accordingly, building sites or constructions or installation projects are not part of the positive list of Article 5(2) OECD MC indicating a PE.

The most significant difference between the German and the OECD approach is the temporal requirement according to which building sites or constructions or installation projects shall constitute a PE. While Section 12 sentence 2 no. 8 GFC provides that building sites or construction or installation projects constitute a PE only if they last more than six months, Article 5(3) OECD MC refers to a period of twelve months. This finding suggests that differences with regard to the temporal threshold can also be identified in the respective DTAs between Germany and other states.[297] While the 12-month threshold can be detected typically in DTAs with industrialised countries, the 6-month threshold can mostly be found in DTAs between Germany and developing countries.[298] However, such deviations create substantial inconsistencies and difficulties in triangular cases, ranging from the non-consideration of losses to double non-taxation.[299]

---

[294] Cf. OECD MC Commentary 2017, Art. 5, para. 52.

[295] Cf. OECD MC Commentary 2017, Art. 5, para. 52.

[296] Cf. OECD MC Commentary 2017, Art. 5, para. 52.

[297] For an overview of the different time thresholds in DTAs between Germany and selected states cf. *Delarber*, Steuerliche Einflüsse auf die grenzüberschreitende Betriebsstättenbesteuerung, 105.

[298] Cf. *Heinsen*, in: Looks/Heinsen (Eds.), Betriebsstättenbesteuerung, para. 217.

[299] Cf. *Reimer*, in: Reimer/Rust (Eds.), Klaus Vogel on Double Taxation Conventions, Art. 5, para. 244.

b. Server PE

(1) Conceptual Approach

As examined in the context of Article 12 GFC, the question as to whether a server may be regarded to constitute a PE has been discussed quite intensively.[300] This question is also of great significance in the context of Article 5 OECD MC since treaty law aims to streamline and homogenise the different fiscal interests of the contracting treaty states.[301] Detailed clarification in this regard is provided by the Commentary on Article 5 OECD MC.[302]

According to Article 5(1) OECD MC a PE requires a fixed place of business through which the business of an enterprise is wholly or partly carried on. As pointed out above, the presence of personnel is not a requirement for the existence of a PE.[303] Therefore, also an automated server operated by an enterprise at a particular location may constitute a PE. However, as examined in the context of Section 12 GFC, a distinction between physical computer equipment (hardware) and software and data which is stored on or used by this hardware must also be made for the purpose of Article 5 OECD MC.[304] Whether these components constitute a PE is to be determined by examining the general requirements for

[300] Cf. for the discussion *Lampert*, in: Mössner et al. (Eds.), Steuerrecht international tätiger Unternehmen, paras. 2.151 et seqq.; *Pinkernell*, Internationale Steuergestaltung im Electronic Commerce, 27 et seqq.; *Thile/König*, IWB 2018, 1 (1 et seqq.); *Kahle/Baschnagel/Kindich*, FR 2016, 193 (193 et seqq.); *Bendlinger*, Die Betriebsstätte in der Praxis des internationalen Steuerrechts, 135 et seqq.; *Monsenego*, ITPJ 2014, 247 (247 et seqq.); *Bal*, BIT 2012, 335 (335 et seqq.); *Findeis/Eickmann*, DStZ 2008, 139 (139 et seqq.); *Jacobs*, Internationale Unternehmensbesteuerung, 336 et seqq.; *Puls*, Die Betriebsstätte im Abgaben- und Abkommensrecht, 43 et seqq.; *Kahle/Ziegler*, DStZ 2009, 834 (834); *Knödler*, Besteuerung von Ertrag und Umsatz im Electronic Commerce, 119 et seqq.; OECD, Are the Current Treaty Rules for Taxing Business Profits Appropriate for E-Commerce? Final Report 2004; *Kaminski/Strunk*, IWB 2002, 947 (947 et seqq.); *Hahn*, SWI 2002, 17 (17 et seqq.); *Peter*, Fortentwicklung des Betriebsstättenprinzips, 153 et seqq.; *Pinkernell/Ditz*, FR 2001, 1193 (1194 et seqq.); *Strunk*, IWB 2001, 151 (151 et seqq.); *Steimel*, IStR 2000, 490 (490 et seqq.); *Kessler/Peter*, BB 2000, 1545 (1545 et seqq.); *Arndt/Fetzer*, BB 2001, 1175 (1175 et seqq.); *Geurts*, Intertax 2000, 173 (173 et seqq.); *Gummert/Trapp*, MMR 1998, 350 (350 et seqq.); *Eicker/Scheifele*, IWB 1999, 377 (377 et seqq.); *Holler/Heerspink*, BB 1998, 771 (771 et seqq.); *Strunk*, BB 1998, 1824 (1824); *Wichmann*, in: Fischer/Strunk (Eds.), Steuerliche Aspekte des Electronic Commerce, 65 (73 et seqq.).

[301] Cf. *Wassermeyer/Kaeser*, in: W/K/S/D (Eds.), Doppelbesteuerung, Art. 5 MA, para. 8.

[302] Cf. OECD MC Commentary 2017, Art. 5, paras. 123 et seqq.

[303] Cf. OECD MC Commentary 2017, Art. 5, para. 127.

[304] Cf. OECD MC Commentary 2017, Art. 5, para. 123.

the existence of a PE according to Article 5 OECD MC (i.e. fixed place of business [physical presence and right of disposal] as well as carrying on the business through that fixed place).[305]

While a website (i.e. a combination of electronic data and software) does not constitute tangible property and therefore does not have a location that may constitute a fixed place of business,[306] the actual hardware (i.e. the server on which the website is stored) may constitute such a fixed place of business and thus could be considered a PE in the country where it is situated.[307] In this context, it is not important whether the server could potentially be moved but rather whether the server is actually moved.[308] It follows that servers which are mobile and which are connected to the internet from different locations do not constitute a PE.[309] However, most servers are wired at a particular (mostly cooled) site and remain at that location not only temporary and may therefore constitute a PE.[310] Temporary in this context means a time period of less than six months.[311]

If the geographical and temporal component is met, the central question is whether the server is at the disposal of the enterprise. As already examined in the context of Article 12 GFC, a distinction between the ISP and the CP, which are commonly not the same, is also necessary for the purpose of Article 5 OECD MC. In most cases the server may only constitute a PE for the ISP that operates

---

305 Cf. OECD MC Commentary 2017, Art. 5, paras. 123 et seqq.

306 This assessment of the OECD MC Commentary is not shared by some member states of the OECD as well as emerging economies, cf. OECD MC Commentary 2017, Art. 5, paras. 176 et seqq. Chile and Greece for example do not adhere to the principles as well as India due to fear that the interpretation of the OECD MC Commentary pushes back their right to tax at source too far, cf. *Pinkernell*, Internationale Steuergestaltung im Electronic Commerce, 88. The Indian tax administration even accessed that websites shall constitute a PE. However, the Kolkata Income Tax Appellate Tribunal did not approve that assessment, *Pinkernell*, Internationale Steuergestaltung im Electronic Commerce, note 268.

307 Cf. OECD MC Commentary 2017, Art. 5, para. 123.

308 Cf. OECD MC Commentary 2017, Art. 5, para. 125.

309 Cf. *Lampert*, in: Mössner et al. (Eds.), Steuerrecht international tätiger Unternehmen, para. 2.154.

310 Cf. *Kahle/Kindich*, in: Lübbehüsen/Kahle (Eds.), Brennpunkte der Besteuerung von Betriebsstätten, para. 2.176.

311 For general considerations regarding the temporal threshold for the existence of a PE within the meaning of Article 5 OECD MC cf. OECD MC Commentary 2017, Art. 5, para. 28 and chapter C.IV.3.b of this thesis. For a discussion of the temporal threshold in the server context see *Andresen* arguing that for reasons of consistency the same temporal threshold should be applied as used for building sites or constructions or installation projects in the respective DTA, cf. *Andresen*, in: W/A/D (Eds.), Betriebsstätten-Handbuch, para. 11.23.

the server since the server is usually not owned and not at the disposal of the CP.[312] In regard to this matter, the OECD MC Commentary concludes that even if a contract between the ISP and the CP may be set up in a way that the fees payed to the ISP are contingent upon the amount of disk space used to store the software and data, such contracts do usually not lead to the situation that the server is at the disposal of the CP.[313] The mere control of the data (virtual control) is insufficient.[314] However, as put forward by the OECD MC Commentary, a server may be at the disposal of the CP if the server is owned (or leased) and operated by the CP.[315] This assessment is in line with the distinction between a dedicated server and the provision of hosting services as used in the context of Article 12 GFC.[316]

With respect to the requirement that the business of the enterprise must be carried on wholly or partly through that fixed place (i.e. at the location where the enterprise has a server at its disposal), it is concluded in the OECD MC Commentary that this requirement shall be examined on a case-by-case basis.[317] As already emphasised, the presence of human beings is not required in that context as long as the business activity can be carried out without personnel.[318]

Nevertheless, even if the general requirements for the existence of a PE are met, Article 5(4) OECD MC must be considered. In accordance, no PE is deemed to exist (neither for the CP nor for the ISP) if the activities carried on through the server are merely of a preparatory or auxiliary character.[319]The Commentary on Article 5 OECD MC lists five activities in the area of e-commerce that are generally regarded as preparatory or auxiliary, namely the provision of communication links, advertising of services or goods, supplying information, gathering market data for the enterprise and relaying information through a mirror server for efficiency and security purposes.[320] Whether the activities carried on through

[312]Cf. *Wassermeyer/Kaeser*, in: W/K/S/D (Eds.), Doppelbesteuerung, Art. 5 MA, para. 33a.

[313]Cf. OECD MC Commentary 2017, Art. 5, para. 124.

[314]Cf. *Reimer*, in: Reimer/Schmid/Orell (Eds.), Permanent Establishments, Part 2 [J], para. 482.

[315]Cf. OECD MC Commentary 2017, Art. 5, para. 124.

[316]Cf. *Pinkernell*, Internationale Steuergestaltung im Electronic Commerce, 89.

[317]Cf. OECD MC Commentary 2017, Art. 5, para. 126.

[318]See in more detail chapter C.IV.3.c.(2) of this thesis.

[319]Cf. OECD MC Commentary 2017, Art. 5, para. 128.

[320]Cf. OECD MC Commentary 2017, Art. 5, para. 128.

the server are merely preparatory or auxiliary or core business activities depends on the nature of the business performed at that location.[321]

In this context, two exceptions apply. In case functions listed under Article 5(4) OECD MC form in itself a significant part of the business activity of the entire enterprise (exception 1), or in the case other core functions of the enterprise are carried on through that server (exception 2), a PE is deemed to exist.[322] A typical example for exception 1 is an ISP that operates its own servers in order to provide services to customers.[323] As argued by *Pinkernell*, this example can be applied to all enterprises that provide hardware based and mostly automated commercial services (e.g. cloud computing).[324] In order to illustrate exception 2, the OECD MC Commentary uses the example of an 'e-tailer', i.e. an enterprise that sells products through the internet.[325] Even though the enterprise may operate a server, it is not in the business of operating such servers. The mere fact that is does so (e.g. for the purpose of hosting a website which may be used for advertising, providing information to potential customers or displaying a catalogue of products) is not sufficient in order to determine a Server PE for the enterprise at a given location.[326] However, certain core functions that are related to the sale of the e-tailer such as the conclusion of contracts with customers, the processing of payments and the 'delivery' of the products via download, which are performed automatically through the server, shall not be considered to be preparatory or auxiliary for that enterprise.[327] More broadly, it can be concluded that every dedicated server that meets the requirements of Article 5(1) OECD MC and that autonomously handles online transactions (i.e. performs the aforementioned core business activities) can be regarded to constitute a Server PE.[328] This is especially the case for e-tailers, enterprises that perform advertising for third parties, enterprises that operate virtual market places, auction platforms, app stores streaming services and online data bases.[329]

---

[321]Cf. OECD MC Commentary 2017, Art. 5, para. 130.

[322]Cf. OECD MC Commentary 2017, Art. 5, para. 129.

[323]Cf. OECD MC Commentary 2017, Art. 5, para. 130.

[324]Cf. *Pinkernell*, Internationale Steuergestaltung im Electronic Commerce, 92 et seq.

[325]Cf. OECD MC Commentary 2017, Art. 5, para. 130.

[326]Cf. OECD MC Commentary 2017, Art. 5, para. 130.

[327]Cf. OECD MC Commentary 2017, Art. 5, para. 130.

[328]Cf. *Pinkernell*, Internationale Steuergestaltung im Electronic Commerce, 93; *Andresen*, in: W/A/D (Eds.), Betriebsstätten-Handbuch, para. 11.23.

[329]Cf. *Pinkernell*, Internationale Steuergestaltung im Electronic Commerce, 93. However, this view is not shared by all OECD member countries. The United Kingdom for example

In contrast, a server that is involved in an offline transaction carried out online (e.g. an online retail shop as operated by Amazon where the products are displayed online and the contract with customers and the payment is concluded online, however the delivery of the physical product is done offline via parcel) may not be sufficient to constitute a PE.[330] Such a server can also not be regarded as an independent agent within the meaning of Article 5(5) OECD MC since a server is not itself a 'person' as defined in Article 3 OECD MC that is a requirement for Article 5(5) OECD MC.[331]

(2) Changes through the BEPS Project

Within the BEPS project, two action points can be identified that deal with the PE term in more detail, namely BEPS Action 1 and BEPS Action 7.

More specifically, BEPS Action 1 analysis several new policy alternatives to address broader direct tax challenges raised by the digitalisation of the economy. Among these alternatives, there is also a new nexus based on the concept of a significant economic presence based on technology and other automated tools.[332] However, none of the options discussed were recommended by the OECD in the Final Report on BEPS Action 1. Consequently, BEPS Action 1 did not result in a change of Article 5 OECD MC. Rather, the OECD emphasised that certain aspects of the broader direct tax challenges that are raised by the digitalisation of the economy will be mitigated once the other BEPS measures are implemented.[333]

One of these other measures is BEPS Action 7 focusing on the prevention of the artificial avoidance of the PE status. As examined above, BEPS Action 7 led to

---

takes the view that a server that is used by an e-tailer, either together with websites or alone, cannot as such constitute a PE, cf. OECD MC Commentary 2017, Art. 5. para. 176.

[330] Cf. for the discussion *Pinkernell*, Internationale Steuergestaltung im Electronic Commerce, 93 et seq.

[331] Cf. *Andresen*, in: W/A/D (Eds.), Betriebsstätten-Handbuch, para. 5.19.

[332] Cf. OECD, BEPS Action 1: Final Report 2015, paras. 277 et seqq. See in more detail for the option of a significant economic presence and its implications in the area of electronic commerce *Kahle/Baschnagel/Kindich*, FR 2016, 193 (197 et seq.). The other two alternatives discussed were a withholding tax on certain types of digital transactions and an equalisation levy. For discussion on withholding tax cf. OECD, BEPS Action 1: Final Report 2015, paras. 292 et seqq. For discussion on equalisation levy cf. OECD, BEPS Action 1: Final Report 2015, paras. 302 et seqq.

[333] Cf. OECD, BEPS Action 1: Final Report 2015, para. 357.

a modification of Article 5(4), (5) and (6) OECD MC and the corresponding Commentary. However, these modifications do not directly influence the determination whether or not a server may constitute a PE for the taxpayer.[334]

(3) Deviations of German National Law from OECD Approach

When it comes to the assessment of whether a server may constitute a PE, the German and the OECD approach can be regarded as rather aligned. For the purpose of both, Section 12 GFC as well as Article 5 OECD MC, the general requirements for the existence of a PE must be met by a server in order to constitute a PE for the enterprise.

However, one significant deviation exists that relates to the activities carried on by the server. While the OECD MC Commentary determinates that no PE shall be considered to exist where the activities carried on through a server are restricted to preparatory or auxiliary activities covered by Article 5(4) OECD MC,[335] no such differentiation between different kinds of activities is made in the context of Section 12 GFC. Rather, the activities performed by the server are of no significance in order to determine whether a PE is deemed to exist under Article 12 GFC. Consequently, also activities listed by the OECD MC Commentary that are to be regarded as preparatory or auxiliary activities and generally do not trigger a PE for the enterprise under Article 5 OECD MC (e.g. the provision of communication links, advertising of services or goods, supplying information, gathering market data for the enterprise and relying information through a mirror server for efficiency and security purposes),[336] may trigger a PE in the context of Section 12 GFC if the other general requirements for the existence of a PE are met.

c. Agent PEs

(1) Conceptual Approach

Agent PEs are dealt with under Article 5(5) and (6) OECD MC. While Article 5(5) OECD MC stipulates the conditions under which an enterprise is deemed to have a PE in respect of any activity of a person acting for it (dependent agent), Article 5(6) OECD MC covers an exception for independent agents.

For the purpose of Article 5(5) OECD MC, an activity of a person constitutes an Agent PE if the following conditions are met:

---

[334] Cf. *Thiele/König*, IWB 2018, 376 (382). For same conclusion but a more detailed analysis cf. *Kahle/Baschnagel/Kindich*, FR 2016, 193 (199).

[335] Cf. OECD MC Commentary 2017, Art. 5 para. 128. For exceptions see OECD MC Commentary 2017, Art. 5 paras. 129 et seq.

[336] Cf. OECD MC Commentary 2017, Art. 5, para. 128.

- a person acts in one contracting state on behalf of the enterprise of the other contracting state;
- thereby, that person habitually concludes contracts or plays the principal role that leads to the conclusion of contracts;
- that person concludes the contracts without material modifications by the enterprise who this person is working for;
- that person's activities are not limited to activities listed in Article 5(4) OECD MC; and
- that person does not act as an independent agent who falls under Article 5(6) OECD MC.[337]

Since an agent may be completely mobile within the territory of the source state, Article 5(5) OECD MC does not require a fixed geographical link to a specific situs as a compulsory feature of the Agent PE.[338] However, the legal consequences between a regular PE and an Agent PE do not differ. Consequently, all Articles of the OECD MC which refer to the existence of a PE also apply to Agent PEs.[339] An agent acting on behalf of an enterprise can also constitute several PEs for that enterprise in different states if the respective conditions are met in each state.[340]

Article 5(6) OECD MC needs to be read in conjunction with Article 5(5) OECD MC that provides a counter-exception for the Agent PE in case of an independent agent.[341] The distinction between a dependent and an independent agent gives rise to great uncertainty and leads to divergent applications by the respective states.[342] According to the OECD MC Commentary 2017, the question

---

[337] Cf. OECD MC Commentary 2017, Art. 5, para. 84.

[338] Cf. *Reimer*, in: Reimer/Rust (Eds.), Klaus Vogel on Double Taxation Conventions, Art. 5, para. 310; *Rehfeld*, in: Gosch/Kroppen/Grotherr/Kraft (Eds.), DBA-Kommentar, Art. 5 OECD-MA, para. 132; *Hruschka*, in: Schönfeld/Ditz (Eds.), DBA-Kommentar, Art. 5 (2014), para.165; *Feuerstein*, in: Brugger/Plansky (Eds.), Permanent Establishments in International and EU Tax Law, 105 (108).

[339] Cf. *Reimer*, in: Reimer/Rust (Eds.), Klaus Vogel on Double Taxation Conventions, Art. 5, para. 311.

[340] Cf. *Rehfeld*, in: Gosch/Kroppen/Grotherr/Kraft (Eds.), DBA-Kommentar, Art. 5 OECD-MA, para. 132.

[341] Cf. detailed *Puls*, in: W/A/D (Eds.), Betriebsstätten-Handbuch, paras. 2.204 et seqq.; also *Rehfeld*, in: Gosch/Kroppen/Grotherr/Kraft (Eds.), DBA-Kommentar, Art. 5 OECD-MA, para. 132.

[342] Cf. *Reimer*, in: Reimer/Rust (Eds.), Klaus Vogel on Double Taxation Conventions, Art. 5, para. 310. According to the Committee on Fiscal Affairs, especially Commissionaire arrangements have been a key preoccupation for the respective tax administrations, cf.

whether or not an agent is considered to be independent of the enterprise depends on the degree of obligations which the agent has towards the enterprise.[343] An agent cannot be regarded as independent if he is subject to comprehensive control or to detailed instructions by the enterprise.[344] In this regard, it is also fundamental to determine whether the entrepreneurial risk is borne by the agent (e.g. by being remunerated on the basis of a contingent fee instead of a fixed basis) or by the enterprise the agent represents.[345] These challenges illustrate that the determination has to be made on a case-by-case basis.

(2) Changes through the BEPS Project

As a result of BEPS Action 7 both Article 5(5) and Article 5(6) OECD MC and the corresponding Commentary were modified significantly.[346] These modifications are aimed at tightening the requirements of the Agent PE and consequently lead to a widening of the definition of the Agency-PE.[347] The modifications especially address commissionaire arrangements and similar strategies that seek to avoid the application of Article 5(5) OECD MC. The Final Report on BEPS Action 7 points out the following strategies used in order to prevent the application of Article 5(5) OECD MC:

- contracts are substantially negotiated in a state but not concluded in that state due to the fact that they are authorised or finalised abroad;
- a person habitually exercises an authority to conclude contracts and therefore triggering the exception of Article 5(5) OECD MC, even though this person is closely related to the foreign enterprise.[348]

OECD, BEPS Action 7: Final Report 2015, p. 10; *Heinsen,* in: Looks/Heinsen (Eds.), Betriebsstättenbesteuerung, para. 248.

[343] Cf. OECD MC Commentary 2017, Art. 5, para. 104.

[344] Cf. OECD MC Commentary 2017, Art. 5, para. 104.

[345] Cf. OECD MC Commentary 2017, Art. 5, para. 104.

[346] Detailed for the modification cf. *Kroppen,* in: Lüdicke/Mellinghoff/Rödder (Eds.), Festschrift für Dietmar Gosch, 221 (221 et seqq.); *Wagemann,* IWB 2016, 14 (15 et seqq.); *Bendlinger*, TPI 2018, 53 (53 et seqq.); *Storck/Petruzzi,* in: Lang/Pistone/Rust/Schuch/Staringer (Eds.), Base Erosion and Profit Shifting, 83 (94 et seqq.).

[347] Cf. *Puls,* in: W/A/D (Eds.), Betriebsstätten-Handbuch, para. 2.207. Cf. also in this regard *Schmidt-Heß,* IStR 2016, 165 (165 et seq.); *Schoppe/Reichel,* BB 2016, 1245 (1245 et seqq.); *Meyer-Sandberg/Hecht,* in: Lübbehüsen/Kahle (Eds.), Brennpunkte der Besteuerung von Betriebsstätten, 3.129.

[348] Cf. OECD, BEPS Action 7: Final Report 2015, pp. 9 et seq.

In order to prevent enterprises from using such strategies that avoid the establishment of an Agent PE, the requirements of the Agent PE in Article 5(5) OECD MC were tightened through BEPS Action 7. The changes to Article 5(5) OECD MC are indicated in the following:[349]

> '5. Notwithstanding the provisions of paragraphs 1 and 2 **but subject to the provisions of paragraph 6**, where a person ~~other than an agent of an independent status to whom paragraph 6 applies~~ is acting **in a Contracting State** on behalf of an enterprise and ~~has, and habitually exercises, in a Contracting State, an authority to conclude contracts,~~ **in doing so, habitually concludes contracts, or habitually plays the principal role leading to the conclusion of contracts that are routinely concluded without material modification by the enterprise, and these contracts are**
>
> **a)** in the name of the enterprise, **or**
>
> **b) for the transfer of the ownership of, or for the granting of the right to use,**
>
> **property owned by that enterprise or that the enterprise has the right to use, or**
>
> **c) for the provision of services by that enterprise,**
>
> that enterprise shall be deemed to have a permanent establishment in that State in respect of any activities which that person undertakes for the enterprise, unless the activities of such person are limited to those mentioned in paragraph 4 which, if exercised through a fixed place of business (other than a fixed place of business to which paragraph 4.1 would apply), would not make this fixed place of business a permanent establishment under the provisions of that paragraph.'

Accordingly, in order to establish an Agent PE, there is no need that a person acting in a contracting state on behalf of the enterprise holds the authority to conclude contracts. The new approach considers it sufficient that this person plays the principal role leading to the conclusion of contracts which are afterwards routinely concluded without material modifications by the enterprise.[350] In other words, a pure 'economic power of representation' by an agent is sufficient in order to constitute an Agent PE.[351]

---

[349] Additions to the existing provision appear in bold and deletions are marked through strikethroughs.

[350] Cf. Art. 5(5) OECD MC 2017.

[351] Cf. *Puls*, in: W/A/D (Eds.), Betriebsstätten-Handbuch, para. 2.207. Detailed for the modifications to Article 5(5) OECD MC see *Andresen*, in: Kofler/Schnitger (Eds.), BEPS-Handbuch, Chapter H, paras. 22 et seqq.

Furthermore, changes to Article 5(6) OECD MC were made through BEPS Action 7. The changes to Article 5(6) OECD MC are indicated in the following:[352]

> '6. ~~An enterprise shall not be deemed to have a permanent establishment in a Contracting State merely because it carries on business in that State through a broker, general commission agent or any other agent of an independent status, provided that such persons are acting in the ordinary course of the business.~~ Paragraph 5 shall not apply where the person acting in a Contracting State on behalf of an enterprise of the other Contracting State carries on business in the first-mentioned State as an independent agent and acts for the enterprise in the ordinary course of that business. Where, however, a person acts exclusively or almost exclusively on behalf of one or more enterprises to which it is closely related, that person shall not be considered to be an independent agent within the meaning of this paragraph with respect to any such enterprise.'

Additionally, Article 5(8) OECD MC was newly implemented in the OECD MC 2017 clarifying the circumstance under which a person is closely related to an enterprise in this regard. Article 5(8) OECD MC is worded as follows:

> '8. For the purposes of this Article, a person or enterprise is closely related to an enterprise if, based on all the relevant facts and circumstances, one has control of the other or both are under the control of the same persons or enterprises. In any case, a person or enterprise shall be considered to be closely related to an enterprise if one possesses directly or indirectly more than 50 per cent of the beneficial interest in the other (or, in the case of a company, more than 50 per cent of the aggregate vote and value of the company's shares or of the beneficial equity interest in the company) or if another person or enterprise possesses directly or indirectly more than 50 per cent of the beneficial interest (or, in the case of a company, more than 50 per cent of the aggregate vote and value of the company's shares or of the beneficial equity interest in the company) in the person and the enterprise or in the two enterprises.'

The modifications introduced through BEPS Action 7 provide that a person cannot be considered to constitute an independent agent if he acts exclusively or almost exclusively for one or more enterprises where he is closely related to.[353] Consequently, an independent status of an agent is very unlikely if the activities of that agent are performed entirely or almost entirely on behalf of only one enterprise or a group of enterprises characterised by the fact that they are closely related to

[352]Deletions to the existing provision are marked through strikethroughs.

[353]Cf. OECD MC Commentary 2017, Art. 5, para. 111.

each other.[354] The respective modifications result in the effect that the measures of proof for an independent agent were increased substantially.[355]

From a business perspective, the respective modifications are viewed critically due to the fact that they are contrary to the aims of increased legal certainty and predictability.[356] This new approach enables tax authorities to extent their taxing rights, since this approach makes it possible to tax (sales-related) activities of an agent which are conducted without (civil) authorisation.[357] In this respect, it is to be feared that the Agent PE might be used by tax authorities in order to defend national fiscal interests.[358]

(3) Deviations of German National Law from OECD Approach

In contrast to Article 5(5) and Article 5(6) OECD MC, neither a dependent nor an independent agent constitutes a PE under German tax law.[359] Nevertheless, according to Section 13 GFC in conjunction with Section 49(1) no. 2 lit. a ITA, a 'permanent representative' triggers non-resident tax liability in its own right, entirely separated from the PE matter.[360] The fact that the OECD MC does not distinguish between an agent and a PE and rather includes the definition of

[354] Cf. OECD MC Commentary 2017, Art. 5, para. 111.

[355] Cf. *Heinsen,* in: Looks/Heinsen (Eds.), Betriebsstättenbesteuerung, para. 247. Detailed for the modifications to Article 5(5) OECD MC see *Andresen,* in: Kofler/Schnitger (Eds.), BEPS-Handbuch, Chapter H paras. 35 et seqq.

[356] Cf. *Wassermeyer*, SWI 2010, 505 (506 et seq.); *Puls*, in: W/A/D (Eds.), Betriebsstätten-Handbuch, para. 2.207. Critical also *Meyer-Sandberg/Hecht*, in: Lübbehüsen/Kahle (Eds.), Brennpunkte der Besteuerung von Betriebsstätten, 3.129.

[357] Cf. *Puls*, in: W/A/D (Eds.), Betriebsstätten-Handbuch, para. 2.207.

[358] Cf. *Puls*, in: W/A/D (Eds.), Betriebsstätten-Handbuch, para. 2.207. As suggested by *Haarmann*, solutions for BEPS shall rather be searched for in the area of transfer pricing, cf. *Haarmann*, in: Beck'sche Steuerkommentare et al. (Eds.), Doppelbesteuerung, 161 (169); see also *Meyer-Sandberg/Hecht*, in: Lübbehüsen/Kahle (Eds.), Brennpunkte der Besteuerung von Betriebsstätten, 3.129.

[359] Cf. *Wang/Schreiber*, in: Reimer/Schmid/Orell (Eds.), Permanent Establishments, § 8.03 [D], para. 57. However, in this regard it should be noted that in case no agreement between Germany and another State for the avoidance of double taxation and the prevention of fiscal evasion with respect to taxes on income and on capital which deals with the taxation of the foreign enterprise is in place, the German Federal Ministry of Finance follows the differentiation between a dependent and an independent agent similar to the provisions of Art. 5(5) OECD MC and Art. 5(6) OECD MC, cf. R 49.1 of the German Income Tax Guidelines.

[360] See in more detail chapter C.III.5 of this thesis.

an agent within Article 5 OECD MC—probably for reasons of simplification—must be criticised since such a simplification cannot be regarded adequate for the concept of the permanent representative as an alternative form of a PE.[361]

Similar to the OECD approach, the business activity of the permanent representative within the meaning of Section 13 GFC has to be carried on in a sustained manner. However, in contrast to Article 5(5) OECD MC, the activities carried out by the permanent representative can be of any kind (e.g. also business management activities such as giving instructions or the delivery of goods)[362] and do not need to lead to the conclusion of contracts.[363] This implies that the activities carried out by the permanent representative can also be limited to mere preparatory or auxiliary activities.[364] Consequently, in contrast to the OECD approach, also mere representatives who only carry on preparatory or auxiliary activities constitute a permanent representative pursuant to Section 13 GFC.

Given the analysis above, it can be concluded that despite the latest changes to Article 5(5) and Article 5(6) OECD MC and the corresponding Commentary through the adoption of BEPS Action 7 which resulted in a widening of the Agent PE definition in the OECD MC, Section 13 GFC still has a broader scope than the Agent PE concept under Article 5(5) and Article 5(6) OECD MC.[365]

d. Service PE

For many decades, a consensus among OECD member countries existed that the provision of services carried on within the source state by a non-resident taxpayer shall not constitute a PE in itself under Article 5(1) OECD MC.[366] However, in 2003, the OECD inserted four different examples in the OECD MC Commentary

---

[361] Cf. *Puls*, in: W/A/D (Eds.), Betriebsstätten-Handbuch, para. 2.205. Critical with regard to the establishment of a fictitious PE of an agent also *Wassermeyer/Kaeser*, in: W/K/S/D (Eds.), Doppelbesteuerung, Art. 5 MA, para. 193.

[362] See in more detail in this regard *Hruschka*, in: Schönfeld/Ditz (Eds.), DBA-Kommentar, Art. 5 (2014), para. 159.

[363] Cf. *Hruschka*, in: Schönfeld/Ditz (Eds.), DBA-Kommentar, Art. 5 (2014), para. 159.

[364] Cf. *Hruschka*, in: Schönfeld/Ditz (Eds.), DBA-Kommentar, Art. 5 (2014), para. 149. On the contrary, the OECD approach requires that the person's activities are not limited to activities listed in Art. 5(4) OECD MC, cf. OECD MC Commentary 2017, Art. 5, para. 84.

[365] See also *Hruschka*, in: Schönfeld/Ditz (Eds.), DBA-Kommentar, Art. 5 (2014), para. 149. Also arguing for a broader scope of Section 13 GFC before the latest changes to Art. 5(5) and Art. 5(6) OECD MC and the corresponding Commentary through the adoption of BEPS Action 7 *Waltrich*, Cross-Border Taxation of Permanent Establishments, 55; *Koenig*, in: Koenig (Ed.), AO, § 12, para. 9.

[366] Cf. *Reimer*, in: Reimer/Rust (Eds.), Klaus Vogel on Double Taxation Conventions, Art. 5, para. 398.

in order to illustrate cases when the provision of services shall constitute or shall not constitute a PE.[367] Especially, the fourth example[368] of a painter who spends three days a week for a period of two years in a large office building of its main client and the conclusion drawn from the OECD that a PE of that painter exists in the described case invoked a long-lasting dispute.[369]

In 2008, the OECD updated the OECD MC Commentary which brought about a substantial broadening of the PE notion.[370] Among other clarifications with regard to the Service PE, the Committee of Fiscal Affairs offers an optional extension of the PE threshold in Article 5 para. 155 of the OECD MC Commentary, which may be implemented by member countries that wish to do so. Accordingly, a Service PE shall exist if employees or other personnel of the enterprise provide services in the other contracting state, but only if the duration of their activity exceeds 183 days on an aggregated level during a twelve-month period and more than 50 percent of the gross revenue attributable to active business activities of the enterprise during the period of presence are derived from the services performed in that state.[371] In such cases a fixed place of business is not necessary in order to constitute a PE.[372] The concept of the Service PE is implemented in the German DTAs with China[373], Liberia[374], Philippines[375], South Africa[376],

---

[367] Cf. OECD MC Commentary 2017, Art. 5, paras. 14 et seqq.

[368] Cf. OECD MC Commentary 2017, Art. 5, para. 17.

[369] As explicitly expressed in para. 178 of the Commentary on Art. 5 OECD MC, Germany does not agree with the interpretation of the painter example. Also, the German Federal Tax Court found that a PE can basically not be found by the usage of the facilities of the client, cf. BFH, 24 July 2004, I R 106/03, BFH/NV 2005, 154; BFH, 4 June 2008, I R 30/07, BStBl. II 2008, 922.

[370] Cf. *Reimer*, in: Reimer/Rust (Eds.), Klaus Vogel on Double Taxation Conventions, Art. 5, paras. 405 et seq.

[371] Cf. OECD MC Commentary 2017, Art. 5, para. 156.

[372] Cf. *Wang/Schreiber*, in: Reimer/Schmid/Orell (Eds.), Permanent Establishments, § 8.03 [D], para. 53.

[373] Art. 5(3) lit. b DTA, Federal Republic of Germany- People's Republic of China, 28 Mar. 2014, BGBl. II 2015, 1647.

[374] Art. 5(7) DTA, Federal Republic of Germany-Republic of Liberia, 25 Nov. 1970, BGBl. II 1973, 1285.

[375] Art. 5(3) lit. b DTA, Federal Republic of Germany-Republic of Philippines, 9 Sept. 2013, BGBl. II 2014, 822.

[376] Art. 5(3) lit. b DTA, Federal Republic of Germany-Republic of South Africa, 9 Aug. 2008, has not yet entered into force.

Australia[377] and Turkey[378].[379] Since the concept of the Service PE contradicts the traditional German PE concept, which requires a fixed place of business and a certain degree of disposal, Germany does regularly not make use of its taxing right if such a Service PE is established in Germany.[380]

7. Implementation of BEPS Action 7 Outcomes via MLI

a. Purpose of the MLI

Since the final reports published by the OECD are not legally binding,[381] effecting the changes to the PE definition on treaty level requires amendments to the respective bilateral tax treaties.[382] In order to facilitate this process, an 'ad hoc Group'[383] has developed the report on 'Multilateral Convention to Implement Tax Treaty Related Measures to Prevent Base Erosion and Profit Shifting'[384], also referred to as the report on the 'Multilateral Instrument' (hereinafter: MLI). Together with the Explanatory Statement[385], the MLI was adopted on 24 November 2016.[386] The MLI aims to streamline the implementation of treaty related BEPS measures by allowing countries to quickly amend their bilateral tax treaty

---

[377] Art. 5(8) DTA, Federal Republic of Germany-Commonwealth of Australia, 12 Nov. 2015, BGBl. II 2016, 1114.

[378] Art. 5(3) lit. b DTA, Federal Republic of Germany-Republic of Turkey, 19 Sept. 2011, BGBl. II 2012, 526.

[379] Cf. *Wassermeyer/Kaeser*, in: W/K/S/D (Eds.), Doppelbesteuerung, Art. 5 MA, paras. 259 et seqq.; *Wang/Schreiber,* in: Reimer/Schmid/Orell (Eds.), Permanent Establishments, § 8.03 [D], para. 53; *Heinsen,* in: Looks/Heinsen (Eds.), Betriebsstättenbesteuerung, para. 203.

[380] Cf. *Endres/Freiling*, PIStB 2012, 189 (190); *Kahle/Kindich,* in: Lübbehüsen/Kahle (Eds.), Brennpunkte der Besteuerung von Betriebsstätten, para. 2.200.

[381] Cf. *Fehling/Kampermann*, IStR 2017, 638 (638).

[382] Cf. *Schönfeld/Häck*, in: Schönfeld/Ditz (Eds.), DBA-Kommentar, Systematik, para. 86.

[383] Cf. in more detail for the objective and participants of the ad hoc Group OECD, BEPS Action 15: Final Report 2015, p. 11. For further explanations with regard to the ad hoc Group cf. *Benz/Böhmer*, ISR 2017, 27 (28); *Bendlinger*, SWI 2017, 2 (2 et seq.).

[384] Cf. OECD, BEPS Action 15: Final Report 2015.

[385] Cf. OECD, Explanatory Statement to the Multilateral Convention to Implement Tax Treaty Related Measures to Prevent Base Erosion and Profit Shifting (hereinafter: Explanatory Statement to the Multilateral Convention).

[386] Cf. OECD, BEPS Progress Report 2017, p. 13.

network without the need to implement the respective changes on a treaty-by-treaty basis.[387] In contrast to an amending protocol to an existing tax treaty which would directly amend the text of the tax agreement, the MLI applies alongside the existing tax treaties and thus modifies their application to implement the BEPS measures.[388]

In the context of BEPS-Action 7, the MLI can be regarded as the route envisaged for transposing the outcomes of the report.[389] More specifically, part IV of the MLI deals with strategies that are designed to avoid the PE status and contains the following Articles:

- Article 12 MLI: Artificial Avoidance of Permanent Establishment Status through Commissionaire Arrangements;
- Article 13 MLI: Artificial Avoidance of Permanent Establishment Status through the Specific Activity Exception;
- Article 14 MLI: Splitting-up of Contracts; and
- Article 15 MLI: Definition of a Person Closely Related to an Enterprise.[390]

In this regard, it is important to note that there is no obligation for a jurisdiction to sign the MLI, even if that jurisdiction is a participant of the ad hoc Group.[391] However, in case a jurisdiction decides to sign the MLI, the instrument requires the Signatory to commit himself to a core set of provisions[392] as part of the MLI, but also grands the possibility to opt in, opt out or choose between alternative

[387]Cf. OECD, BEPS Progress Report 2017, p. 13. With regard to practical implications of the MLI cf. *Haase*, IWB 2017, 16 (17). For reflections on the MLI with respect to fiscally transparent entities cf. *Nikolakakis/Austry/Jones/Baker/Blessing/Danon/Goradia/Hattingh/Inoue/Luedicke/Maisto/Miyatake/van Raad/Vann/Wiman*, BTR, 295 (295 et seqq.).

[388]Cf. OECD, Explanatory Statement to the Multilateral Convention, para. 13. See in more detail with regard to the interpretation of the MLI *Lang*, SWI 2017, 11 (11 et seqq.); *Baker*, BTR 2017, 281 (281).

[389]Cf. *De Wilde*, Intertax 2017, 556 (556).

[390]For an overview of Art. 12–15 MLI cf. *Grotherr*, Ubg 2017, 188 (194).

[391]Cf. *Schönfeld/Häck*, in: Schönfeld/Ditz (Eds.), DBA-Kommentar, Systematik, para. 89.

[392]The core set of provisions are the following: Art. 6 (Purpose of a Covered Tax Agreement), Art. 7 (Prevention of Treaty Abuse), Art. 16 (Mutual Agreement Procedure) and Art. 17 (Corresponding Adjustments). In this regard, it shall be noted that despite the fact that Art. 17 is not a minimum standard in a strict sense, it contains the obligation of transposition of the recommendation (best practices) of the underlying BEPS Action Point 14 (Making Dispute Resolution Mechanism More Effective), cf. *Gradl/Kiesewetter*, IStR 2018, 1 (3, note 25).

provisions with respect to other issues covered by the MLI.[393] Consequently, the approach chosen leaves considerable scope for jurisdictions to structure their tax treaty policies according to their individual needs.[394] Nevertheless, the MLI is not an à la carte instrument that permits jurisdictions to make choices on a treaty-by-treaty basis when deciding how they want the MLI to modify and affect their tax treaty network.[395] Rather, jurisdictions are required to express how they want to modify their 'Covered Tax Agreements'[396] (hereinafter: CTAs) by the MLI before signature and have to apply these modifications to all of their CTAs or at least with respect to a subset of their CTAs.[397]

Subsequent modifications to the bilateral tax treaties that are covered by the MLI are explicitly permitted according to Article 30 MLI. Additionally, Article 37 MLI gives the respective jurisdictions the option to withdraw from the MLI by means of a notification addressed to the OECD. Apart from this, German national legislation is not barred from enacting statutes that contravene amendments implemented through the MLI ('treaty override').[398] This finding follows from the principle of democracy which requires that later legislation be able to revoke any legal acts of previous legislation (*lex posterior derogate legi priori*).[399]

b. Implementation Process of the MLI

The transposition of treaty-related BEPS measures into tax treaties requires contracting states to undertake a complicated process of signature, ratification and implementation.[400] Jurisdictions have been able to sign up to the MLI since 1 January 2017. On 7 June 2017, a first high-level signing ceremony took place

[393] Cf. OECD, BEPS Action 15: Final Report 2015, p. 19, para. 16. See in more detail on the flexibility provided by the MLI OECD, Explanatory Statement to the Multilateral Convention, para. 14; cf. also *Grotherr*, Ubg 2017, 125 (127).

[394] Cf. OECD, Explanatory Statement to the Multilateral Convention, para. 14; *Böhmer*, in: W/A/D (Eds.), Betriebsstätten-Handbuch, para. 14.135; *De Wilde*, Intertax 2017, 556 (558).

[395] Cf. OECD, Frequently Asked Questions on the Multilateral Instrument (MLI), p. 4, question 11.

[396] Covered Tax Agreements are bilateral tax treaties that a jurisdiction chooses to be amended by the MLI.

[397] Cf. *Reimer*, IStR 2017, 1 (2 et seq.); OECD, Frequently Asked Questions on the Multilateral Instrument (MLI), p. 4, question 11.

[398] Cf. *Benz/Römer*, ISR 2017, 27 (31); *Böhmer*, in: W/A/D (Eds.), Betriebsstätten-Handbuch, para. 14.135. For justification of treaty override cf. BVerfG, 15 Dec. 2015, 2 BvL 1/12, BVerfGE 141,1.

[399] Cf. BVerfG, 15 Dec. 2015, 2 BvL 1/12, BVerfGE 141,1; BFH, 25 May 2016, I R 64/13, BStBl. II 2017, 1185.

[400] Cf. *Bendlinger*, SWI 2017, 2 (2).

at the headquarters of the OECD in Paris, where the MLI was signed by 67 countries, covering 68 jurisdictions from all continents and all levels of development.[401] Meanwhile, more countries joined the MLI, bringing the total number of Signatories to 95.[402]

Upon signature of the MLI, each of the Signatories has to deposit a document with the OECD, which contains the so-called 'MLI Position'[403]. The MLI Position comprises several elements: First of all, an enumeration of the tax treaties to which the Convention shall apply (CTAs) and secondly, each jurisdiction reveals its preliminary positions and notifies whether or not reservations to the provisions of the MLI are made and if so, what kind of reservations with regard to each of the provisions of the MLI shall be considered.[404] Furthermore, since several provisions of the MLI contain different options or alternatives from which the jurisdictions can choose from, the Signatories have to inform the OECD of the options or alternatives selected.[405] To ensure transparency and clarity about the application of the MLI, it is also required that the jurisdictions notify the OECD about their existing provisions that shall be modified by the MLI provision.[406]

In the event of a notification conflict, i.e. a tax treaty has been listed by one jurisdiction but not by the other, the respective tax treaty remains unchanged.[407] Germany notified the OECD that it wants 35 DTAs to be amended by the MLI.[408]

---

[401] Cf. OECD, BEPS, Progress Report 2017, p. 11.

[402] Number of Signatories as of 18 Feb. 2021. A comprehensive and regularly updated list of signatories and parties to the MLI is available at: http://www.oecd.org/tax/treaties/beps-mli-signatories-and-parties.pdf.

[403] The MLI Positions of the respective jurisdictions are available at: http://www.oecd.org/tax/treaties/beps-mli-signatories-and-parties.pdf.

[404] Cf. *Böhmer*, in: W/A/D (Eds.), Betriebsstätten-Handbuch, para. 14.136; *Bendlinger*, SWI 2017, 2 (3).

[405] Cf. *Bendlinger*, SWI 2017, 2 (3).

[406] Cf. detailed OECD, Explanatory Statement to the Multilateral Convention, paras. 15 et seqq.

[407] Cf. also *Böhmer*, in: W/A/D (Eds.), Betriebsstätten-Handbuch, para. 14.136.

[408] The tax treaties with the following jurisdictions were notified: The Republic of Austria; the Republic of Bulgaria; the People's Republic of China; the Republic of Costa Rica; the Republic of Croatia; the Republic of Cyprus; the Czech Republic; the Kingdom of Denmark; the Republic of Estonia; the Republic of Finland; the French Republic; the Republic of Hungary; Ireland; the State of Israel; the Italian Republic; Japan; the Republic of Korea; the Republic of Latvia; the Principality of Liechtenstein; the Republic of Lithuania; the Grand Duchy of Luxembourg; Malta; the Republic of Mauritius; the United Mexican States; the Kingdom of the Netherlands; New Zealand; Romania; the Russian Federation; the Republic of Slovakia; the Republic of Slovenia; the Kingdom of Spain; the Republic of Turkey; the

A comparison of the notifications reveals that only three jurisdictions that were listed by Germany, namely the Republic of Estonia, the United Arab Emirates and the United States of America, do not want to amend their tax treaties with Germany by the MLI.[409]

In order to become effective, the MLI is subject to each Signatories treaty procedure for ratification, acceptance or approval.[410] The appropriate term depends on domestic legal requirements.[411] In Germany, the implementation of the MLI requires the transposition in form of a federal law according to Article 59(2) GBL.[412] The MLI was ratified after approval by the German legislative bodies through the MLI Implementation Act[413] in December 2020 and will enter into force in Germany on 1 April 2021. Compared to the 35 DTAs Germany notified to the OECD at the time of signature of the MLI the number of Covered Tax Agreements were reduced to 14 in the MLI Implementation Act. Only the DTAs between Germany and the Republic of Austria, the Republic of Croatia, the Czech Republic, the French Republic, the Hellenic Republic, the Republic of Hungary, the Italian Republic, Japan, the Grand Duchy of Luxembourg, Malta, Romania, the Republic of Slovakia, the Kingdom of Spain and the Republic of Turkey are enumerated in the MLI Implementation Act.[414] DTAs not covered by the Act shall be revised through a bilateral revision agreement or a protocol of amendment to the existing DTA.[415]

The MLI entered into force three months after the deposit of the fifth instrument of ratification, acceptance or approval with the OECD.[416] That fifth deposit took place on 22 March 2018 by Slovenia.[417] Consequently, the MLI entered

---

United Arab Emirates; the United Kingdom of Great Britain and Northern Ireland and the United States of America, cf. OECD, MLI Positions Germany, available at: http://www.oecd.org/tax/treaties/beps-mli-position-germany.pdf.

409 Cf. *Gradl/Kiesewetter*, IStR 2018, 1 (3); *Benz/Böhmer*, DB 2017, 2308 (2309 et seq.). For a regularly updated overview of the Signatories and Parties to the MLI cf. OECD, BEPS Signatories and Parties to the Multilateral Convention.

410 Cf. Art. 27 (2) MLI.

411 Cf. OECD, Explanatory Statement to the Multilateral Convention, para. 263.

412 Cf. *Fischer/Pitzer*, IStR 2017, 804 (805); *Benz/Böhmer*, ISR 2017, 27 (32); *Reimer*, IStR 2017, 1 (5); *Böhmer*, in: W/A/D (Eds.), Betriebsstätten-Handbuch, para. 14.137.

413 MLI Implementation Act, 22 Nov. 2020, BGBl. II 2020, 946.

414 Cf. MLI Implementation Act, 22 Nov. 2020, BGBl. II 2020, 1015 et seq.

415 Cf. BT-Drs. 19/20979, 3.

416 Cf. Art. 34 (1) MLI.

417 Cf. OECD, Milestone in BEPS implementation, Press Release of 22 Mar. 2018.

into force on 1 July 2018. Earlier, the Republic of Austria (22 September 2017), the Isle of Man (19 October 2017), Jersey (15 December 2017), and Poland (23 January 2018) deposited their instruments with the OECD. From then on, the MLI enters into force for a particular jurisdiction on the first day of the month following the expiration of a period of three calendar months after the date of the deposit of its instrument of ratification with the OECD.[418]

The MLI provisions generally enter into effect with respect to a specific CTA at different dates. With respect to taxes withheld at source, Article 35(1) lit. a) MLI specifies that the provisions enter into effect after the first day of the following calendar year that begins on or after the latest of the dates on which the MLI enters into force for each of the Signatories to the CTA. With respect to all other taxes levied by a contracting jurisdiction, Article 35(1) lit. b) MLI specifies that the provisions enter into effect six calendar months[419] from the latest of the dates on which the Convention entered into force for each of the Signatories to the CTA.

Based on the latest provisional positions taken so far by the Signatories, it is estimated that the recommendations of BEPS Action 7 will only be implemented in a rather limited number of bilateral tax agreements.[420] More precisely, it is estimated that the changes to Article 5(5) OECD MC (revised dependent agent definition) would apply to approximately 17% and the changes to Article 5(4) OECD MC (revised provision defining specific-activity exemption) would apply to approximately 22% of bilateral tax treaty agreements covered by the MLI.[421]

c. German MLI Position

With regard to the Articles that deal with the avoidance of the PE status (Article 12–15 MLI), Germany decided that only changes proposed in Article 13 (Artificial Avoidance of Permanent Establishment Status through the Specific Activity Exception) of the MLI shall be implemented in their tax treaties.[422] In this respect,

[418] Cf. Art. 34 (2) MLI.

[419] That period can also be shorter, if all contracting states notify the OECD that they intend to apply that shorter period, cf. Art. 35 (1) lit. b) MLI.

[420] Cf. OECD, BEPS Action 1: Interim Report 2018, para. 272.

[421] Cf. OECD, BEPS Action 1: Interim Report 2018, para. 272.

[422] Cf. OECD, MLI Positions Germany, pp. 24 et seqq.; MLI Implementation Act, 22 Nov. 2020, BGBl. II 2020, 1019.

the MLI proposes two options for modification.[423] Option A[424], which by Germany has chosen,[425] relativises the list of exceptions in the sense that all activities listed must explicitly be of a preparatory or auxiliary nature.[426] In other words, this option limits the availability of the specific activity exemption to cases where the activity is of a preparatory or auxiliary nature. Option B[427] clearly defines that the activities listed under Article 5(4) lit. a)-d) OECD MC are per se exceptions, regardless of whether the activities listed are of a preparatory or auxiliary nature.[428] Additionally, Article 13(4) MLI provides for the implementation of an anti-fragmentation provision that was not chosen by Germany.[429]

V. Interim Conclusion

The previous analysis outlined the main elements of the PE definition as set out in Section 12 GFC and Article 5 OECD MC and examined similarities and differences between the German and the OECD approach. Table 1 provides an overview of the two approaches and summarises the main findings.

---

423 See in more detail with regard to the options for modification *Grotherr*, Ubg 2017, 188 (189 et seq.).

424 Cf. Article 13(2) MLI.

425 Cf. OECD, MLI Positions Germany, p. 25; MLI Implementation Act, 22 Nov. 2020, BGBl. II 2020, 1019.

426 Cf. OECD, Explanatory Statement to the Multilateral Convention, paras. 170 et seq.

427 Cf. Article 13(3) MLI.

428 Cf. OECD, Explanatory Statement to the Multilateral Convention, para. 173.

429 Cf. OECD, MLI Positions Germany, p. 25; MLI Implementation Act, 22 Nov. 2020, BGBl. II 2020, 1019.

Table 1 Main Elements of the PE Definition

	German approach	OECD approach
Place of business	• fixed place of business or facility	• fixed place of business
Duration of business activity	• certain degree of permanency • point of reference: minimum period of 6 months • recurrent activities only lasting for a short time (less than six months) but are repeated periodically do not qualify	• certain degree of permanency • 6 months guidance that allows tolerance in both directions • recurrent activities that last only for a short period of time (less than six months) but are repeated periodically may qualify
Right of disposal	• required	• required
Characteristic of fixed place of business	• fixed place of business or facility must 'serve' the business of an enterprise • wider meaning	• fixed place of business 'through which' the business of an enterprise is wholly or partly carried on
Places of business that trigger a PE	• stand-alone list provided in Section 12 sentence 2 GFC that give rise to a PE a priori	• list provided in Article 5(2) OECD MC • no stand-alone list (i.e. places of business listed only give rise to a PE if the requirements laid down in Article 5(1) OECD MC are met)
Exemption of certain activities	• no specific exceptions as long as activities carried out serve the business of the enterprise	• exemption of activities that are of a preparatory or auxiliary character as listed in Article 5(4) OECD MC
Building sites or construction or installation projects	• part of positive list (Section 12 sentence 2 no. 8 GFC) • time threshold: 6 months	• implemented in Article 5(3) OECD MC • time threshold: 12 months

(continued)

The overview illustrates that the PE definition of Article 5 OECD MC and Section 12 GFC have many features in common. However, it has become evident that the PE threshold under Article 5 OECD MC remains rather narrow compared

Table 1 (continued)

	German approach	OECD approach
Agent-PE	• concept of Agent PE does not exist • permanent representative triggers non-resident tax liability in its own right according to Section 13 GFC in conjunction with Section 49(1) no. 2 lit. a ITA • Section 13 GFC has a broader scope than Agent-PE under Article 5(5) and Article 5(6) OECD MC	• dependent and independent agent may constitute a PE according to Article 5(5) and Article 5(6) OECD MC
Server PE	• recognised if general requirements for the existence of a PE are met	• recognised if general requirements for the existence of a PE are met • no Server PE if activities carried on are merely of a preparatory or auxiliary character
Service PE	• not recognised	• recognised • optional extension of the PE threshold provided by Article 5 para. 155 OECD MC Commentary

Source: Own illustration.

to the PE threshold under German domestic law if the permanent representative is included in the latter concept.[430] In this sense, Article 5 OECD MC may function as a safeguard that defends the country of residence against taxation in the country of source.

[430]Cf. *Wassermeyer/Kaeser*, in: W/K/S/D (Eds.), Doppelbesteuerung, Art. 5 MA, para. 9; *Kahle/Schulz*, DStZ 2008, 784 (788); *Kahle/Ziegler*, DStZ 2009, 834 (341); *Kruse*, StuW 2003, 344 (348); *Schnitger/Bildstein*, Ubg 2008, 444 (447); *Kahle/Baschnagel/Kindich*, FR 2016, 193 (195); *Heinsen*, in: Looks/Heinsen (Eds.), Betriebsstättenbesteuerung, para. 276.

Nevertheless, a tendency can be observed that the threshold for triggering a PE under Article 5 OECD MC was constantly reduced throughout the past decades.[431] This is reflected, e.g., by Article 5 para. 155 OECD MC Commentary that provides for an optional extension of the PE threshold for the so-called Service PE or Article 5 para. 17 OECD MC Commentary introducing the 'painter-example' whose interpretation is officially rejected by Germany. Also, the latest changes to Article 5(4), (5) and (6) OECD MC and the corresponding Commentary through BEPS Action 7 confirm and even enhance this trend.[432]

This trend of lowering the PE threshold leads to the existence of potentially many more PEs. However, while the recognition and administration of these additional PEs results in an increase of compliance obligations for taxpayers, the increase in the number of PEs may not necessarily result in an increase of taxable profits in the jurisdiction where the PE is established. The reason for this observation is rooted in the mechanism for profit attribution to a PE which will be analysed in detail in the following.

[431] Cf. *Wassermeyer/Kaeser*, in: W/K/S/D (Eds.), Doppelbesteuerung, Art. 5 MA, para. 1.

[432] Cf. also *Wassermeyer/Kaeser*, in: W/K/S/D (Eds.), Doppelbesteuerung, Art. 5 MA, para. 1.

D. The Attribution of Profits to Permanent Establishments

I. The Attribution of Profits to PEs under Tax Treaty Law

1. Specifics of Profit Attribution in the PE Context

While Article 5 OECD MC is crucial for determining whether business profits of an enterprise may be subject to taxation in the source state, it does not itself allocate taxing rights.[1] Consequently, when an enterprise carries out business activities in another country through a PE, it is substantial to determine what, if any, profits of the enterprise can be taxed in the country where the PE is established. The fundamental principle that deals with the attribution of business profits between the residence state and the source state can be found in Article 7 OECD MC. According to Article 7(1) OECD MC 'profits of an enterprise of a Contracting State shall be taxable only in that State unless the enterprise carries on business in the other Contracting State through a permanent establishment therein'. Thus, it is not the actual geographic location of the business activity generating the profit that matters for the proper allocation of taxing rights, but the fact that the profits generated through the business activity are attributable to a PE.[2] Accordingly, the source state is entitled to tax the profits that are attributable to the PE, while the residence state has to mitigate double taxation by eliminating or reducing its tax claims according to Article 23A OECD MC (exemption method) or Article 23B

[1] Cf. OECD MC Commentary 2017, Art. 7, para. 2.

[2] Cf. *Pěchota*, in: Brugger/Plansky (Eds.), Permanent Establishments in International and EU Tax Law, 171 (175); *Plansky*, Die Gewinnzurechnung zu Betriebsstätten im Recht der Doppelbesteuerungsabkommen, 89.

S. Hentschel, *The Taxation of Permanent Establishments*, Hallesche Schriften zur Betriebswirtschaft 37, https://doi.org/10.1007/978-3-658-34000-1_4

OECD MC (credit method), depending on the method implemented in the bilateral DTAs.[3] This fundamental rule for the allocation of business profits can be found in most modern bilateral DTAs.[4]

However, in contrast to a group's subsidiary, an enterprise and its PE belong to the same legal entity.[5] Consequently, a PE is a dependent part of the enterprise. Since an entity cannot contract with itself, contractual arrangements between the PE and the rest of the enterprise are not recognised from a legal perspective and qualify as so-called 'dealings'.[6] These legal circumstances have created substantial problems with regard to the attribution of profits to PEs.

2. Methods of Profit Attribution

a. Preliminary Remarks

The fundamental structure of the profit attribution rule under Article 7 OECD MC (pre-2010 version) followed two methods, namely the direct (transaction-based) and the indirect (profit-oriented) method.[7] While the legal basis for the direct method of profit attribution can be derived from Article 7(2) OECD MC and the corresponding domestic legislation, Article 7(4) OECD MC (pre-2010 version) provided for the application of the indirect method of profit attribution.[8] With the update of the OECD MC in 2010 the indirect method of profit attribution as implemented in Article 7(4) OECD MC (pre-2010 version) has been deleted as its application had become very exceptional and due to concerns expressed that

---

[3] Cf. OECD MC Commentary 2017, Art. 7, para. 18. Detailed for the exemption versus credit method and its consequences with regard to achieving capital import versus capital export neutrality see *Reimer*, in: Reimer/Schmid/Orell (Eds.), Permanent Establishments, Part 3 [C], paras. 217 et seqq.

[4] Cf. *Reimer*, in: Reimer/Schmid/Orell (Eds.), Permanent Establishments, Part 3 [C], para. 80.

[5] Cf. *Kaeser*, in: W/K/S/D (Eds.), Doppelbesteuerung, Art. 7 MA (2010), para. 371. See in more detail for the differences between a group's subsidiary and a PE *Huibregtse/Verdoner/Valutyte/Offermanns*, ET 2015, 363 (365).

[6] Cf. *Looks*, in: Looks/Heinsen (Eds.), Betriebsstättenbesteuerung, para. 726; *Huibregtse/Verdoner/Valutyte/Offermanns*, ET 2015, 363 (365).

[7] Cf. *Reimer*, in: Reimer/Schmid/Orell (Eds.), Permanent Establishments, Part 3 [C], para. 87. For an overview with regard to the subcategories of the direct and the indirect method cf. *Reimer*, in: Reimer/Schmid/Orell (Eds.), Permanent Establishments, Part 3 [C], para. 84; *Endres/Spengel*, International Company Taxation and Tax Planning, § 8.03[A], 316.

[8] Cf. *Melicher*, in: Brugger/Plansky (Eds.), Permanent Establishments in International and EU Tax Law, 219 (223).

it was very difficult to ensure that the results of its application are in accordance with the arm's length principle.[9]

Nevertheless, due to the fact that Article 7(4) OECD MC (pre-2010 version) is still used in older bilateral treaties, the fundamental idea of both methods shall be explained in more detail.

b. Direct Method

The direct method of profit attribution follows a bottom-up approach. This means that the attribution of profits to a PE follows from the calculation of the profits or losses from all its activities, which includes a) transactions with independent enterprises, b) transactions with associated enterprises, and c) dealings with other parts of the enterprise.[10]

Under this method, the PE must be treated as if it were a distinct and separated enterprise.[11] Consequently, dealings between the PE and other parts of the enterprise must be regarded as if the PE carried on such dealings with another third enterprise at prices and under conditions prevailing in the ordinary market.[12] Key feature of this method is that the valuation of all transactions and dealings must be at arm's length to come as close as possible to the right amount of profits attributable to the PE.[13]

Treating the PE as a separate and independent enterprise implies that the PE does not share the same economic success as the overall enterprise. Consequently, profits may be attributed to the PE even though the enterprise as a whole has not made any profits.[14] Conversely, the application of the direct method may result in no profits being attributed to the PE even though the enterprise as a whole has generated substantial amounts of profits. In principle, such an approach requires separate accounting by each part of the enterprise.[15] Even though the

---

[9]Cf. OECD MC Commentary 2017, Art. 7, para. 41.

[10]Cf. OECD MC Commentary 2017, Art. 7, para. 20.

[11]Cf. OECD MC Commentary 2017, Art. 7, para. 15.

[12]Cf. *Kahle/Mödinger*, DB 2011, 2338 (2339).

[13]Cf. *Melicher*, in: Brugger/Plansky (Eds.), Permanent Establishments in International and EU Tax Law, 219 (224).

[14]Cf. OECD MC Commentary 2017, Art. 7, para. 17.

[15]Cf. *Reimer*, in: Reimer/Schmid/Orell (Eds.), Permanent Establishments, Part 3 [C], para. 89; *Kahle/Kindich*, in: Lübbehüsen/Kahle (Eds.), Brennpunkte der Besteuerung von Betriebsstätten, para. 4.21.

direct method of profit attributión guarantees a higher degree of accuracy, it is more difficult to administer.[16]

c. Indirect Method

The indirect method of profit attribution follows a top-down approach. This means that this method takes the total profits of the enterprise as a starting point and then apportions these total profits of the enterprise to its various parts.[17] The attribution of profits is done on the basis of a certain formula which may employ criteria such as premiums, cash-flow, cost of sales, book value of assets, turnover, cost of capital, wages and material or a combination of criteria that are weighted accordingly.[18]

It follows that in contrast to the direct method the PE shares the same economic success as the overall enterprise under this approach.[19] In other words, in case the enterprise as a whole makes a profit, a profit can also be attributed to the PE proportionally. However, if the enterprise as a whole makes a loss, the PE shares a part of that loss. This ultimately leads to an intra-enterprise and cross-border compensation of the overall performance.[20]

Separate accounts for the head office and the PE are not needed under this method, which makes it easier to apply and to administer.[21] Furthermore, dealings between the head office and the PE do not influence the overall profits and therefore do not affect the tax base relevant for the application of the indirect method. Consequently, the question of whether dealings between the PE and the head office are in accordance with the arm's length principle is dispensable.[22]

However, the main issue with regard to this method is the determination of the appropriate apportionment formula. Since that formula determines the way how the overall profit of the enterprise is distributed among to the various parts of the enterprise, it is of high significance. While turnover is considered suitable

---

[16] Cf. *Pěchota*, in: Brugger/Plansky (Eds.), Permanent Establishments in International and EU Tax Law, 171 (176).DF

[17] Cf. OECD MC Commentary 2017, Art. 7, para. 41.

[18] Cf. *Baker/Collier*, Cahiers de droit fiscal international, General Report 2006, 21 (30); *Reimer*, in: Reimer/Schmid/Orell (Eds.), Permanent Establishments, Part 3 [C], para. 90.

[19] Cf. *Ritter*, JbFSt 1976/1977, 288 (294).

[20] Cf. *Kahle/Mödinger*, DB 2011, 2338 (2342).

[21] Cf. *Reimer*, in: Reimer/Schmid/Orell (Eds.), Permanent Establishments, Part 3 [C], para. 90; *Kahle/Kindich*, in: Lübbehüsen/Kahle (Eds.), Brennpunkte der Besteuerung von Betriebsstätten, para. 4.21.

[22] Cf. *Kahle/Kindich*, in: Lübbehüsen/Kahle (Eds.), Brennpunkte der Besteuerung von Betriebsstätten, para. 4.16.

for enterprises manufacturing goods with high profit margin or in the service industry, the derivation of the profit from the capital structure is more appropriate for enterprises operating in the banking and finance industry.[23] Nevertheless, all respective apportionment formulas have in common that it is very difficult to ensure that the result of the application of this method is in accordance with the arm's length principle.[24] Therefore, the indirect method was deleted with the update of the OECD MC in 2010.[25]

Even though Article 7(4) OECD MC, as the legal basis for the application of the indirect method of profit attribution will be abolished as more and more OECD states follow the 2010 version of Article 7 OECD MC, the European Union takes an opposite approach with the work on the introduction of a Common Consolidated Corporate Tax Base (CCCTB).[26] In short, the CCCTB is a single set of corporate tax rules that shall be applied throughout the EU member states, with profits being consolidated at the level of the group[27] first and then in a second step apportioned to the respective member states on the basis of a predetermined formula, before being taxed at domestic tax rates.[28] The CCCTB was scheduled to be implemented in a two-step approach with the introduction of the common corporate tax base (CCTB)[29] in a first step in 2019 and the introduction of the consolidation rules (CCCTB)[30] in a second step in 2021. However, this ambitious plan could not be achieved. Even though the European Commission presently

---

[23]Cf. *Melicher*, in: Brugger/Plansky (Eds.), Permanent Establishments in International and EU Tax Law, 219 (227 et seq.). The OECD MC 2008 differentiates three categories with regard to the most common criteria on which the allocation keys are based on, cf. OECD MC Commentary 2008, Art. 7, paras. 54 et seqq. See in more detail with regard to hybrid methods which are more feasible for practical reasons but less accurate such as the 'Peer Entrepreneur Approach' or the 'Residual Profit Split Method' *Melicher*, in: Brugger/Plansky (Eds.), Permanent Establishments in International and EU Tax Law, 219 (228 et seq.).

[24]Cf. OECD MC Commentary 2017, Art. 7, para. 41.

[25]Cf. OECD MC Commentary 2017, Art. 7, para. 41.

[26]Cf. *Schön*, in: Maisto (Ed.), International and EC Tax Aspects of Groups and Companies, 542 (543). For a detailed analysis of the CCCTB and its effects on the taxation of PEs cf. *Kraft/Hentschel/Apler*, RIW 2017, 473 (473 et seqq.).

[27]The scope of the group comprises all PEs located in the EU and tax resident companies within the EU. For comments on the scope of the CCTB and the CCCTB cf. *Gutmann/Raingeard de la Blétière*, EC Tax Review 2017, 233 (23 et seq.).

[28]Cf. *Bhogal/Swanson*, TNI 84 (2016), 1093 (1093).

[29]EC, 25 Oct. 2016, COM(2016) 685 final.

[30]EC, 25 Oct. 2016, COM(2016) 683 final.

solely focuses on the CCTB, it is questionable whether this project will ever be implemented.[31]

As further discussed in chapter F the current work of the OECD on Pillar One as the answer to the tax challenges arising from the digitalisation of the economy also proposes an indirect method of profit attribution.

3. Interpretation of Article 7 OECD MC (pre-2010 version)

a. Relationship between Article 7(2) and Article 7(3) OECD MC

Since the early days of treaty rules, the attribution of profits to PEs has been one of the most disputed issues in international and national tax law and has created substantial problems of double taxation as well as double non-taxation.[32] This is, especially, due to the 'old' wording of Article 7(2) OECD MC (pre-2010 version) and its relation to Article 7(1) and Article 7(3) OECD MC (pre-2010 version).[33] The relationship between the respective provisions has been interpreted differently by the various OECD member countries.[34] According to Article 7(2) OECD MC (pre-2010 version), profits which a PE 'might be expected to make if it were a distinct and separate enterprise engaged in the same or similar activities under the same or similar conditions and dealing wholly independently with the enterprise of which it is a permanent establishment' shall be attributed to the PE. This paragraph lays down a twofold fiction that sets the essential requirements for the application of the arm's length principle in the PE context.[35] For the purpose of profit attribution the PE shall be treated as a separate enterprise, despite the fact that the enterprise and its PE belong to the same legal entity. This fiction ultimately enables the existence of dealings between the enterprise and its PE.[36]

In this regard, it is particularly controversial how the reference in Article 7(2) OECD MC (pre-2010 version) to Article 7(3) OECD MC (pre-2010 version) ought to be interpreted. According to Article 7(3) OECD MC (pre-2010 version), 'expenses which are incurred for the purpose of the permanent establishment,

[31] Cf. for a recent analysis of the CCTB *Aumayr/Mayr*, ET 2019, 153 (153 et seqq.); *Mock*, ET 2019, 209 (209 et seqq.).

[32] Cf. OECD, PE Report 2008, Preface, para. 3.

[33] Cf. *Hentschel/Kraft/Moser*, ET 2018, 73 (73).

[34] Cf. *Kroppen*, in: Kessler/Förster/Watrin (Eds.), Unternehmensbesteuerung—Festschrift Herzig, 1071 (1071 et seqq.); *Hentschel/Kraft/Moser*, ET 2018, 73 (73).

[35] Cf. OECD MC Commentary 2017, Art. 7, para. 16.

[36] Cf. OECD MC Commentary 2017, Art. 7, para. 16.

including executive and general administrative expenses' shall be deductible when determining the profits of the PE. While the purpose of this paragraph seems to be in the allocation of expenses to the PE without considering any profit margin, it seems to be contrary to Article 7(2) OECD MC (pre-2010 version), which requires a pricing at arm's length which ultimately includes an appropriate profit margin.[37] As a result, there has been a continuous discussion especially among German scholars with regard to the extent of hypothetical independence of the PE. On the one side, it is argued that the hypothetical independence of the PE should be limited to transactions with other enterprises.[38] Consequently, dealings between the enterprise and its PE shall not be priced at arm's length, but only with the actual incurred costs.[39] On the other side, it is argued that the reference in Article 7(2) OECD MC (pre-2010 version) to Article 7(3) OECD MC (pre-2010 version) is merely declaratory and shall not affect the hypothetical independence of the PE with regard to dealings.[40] Consequently, also dealings between the enterprise and its PE have to be priced at arm's length.

---

[37] Cf. *Pěchota*, in: Brugger/Plansky (Eds.), Permanent Establishments in International and EU Tax Law, 171 (176).

[38] Advocates of the limited hypothetical independence of the PE include: *Debatin*, DB 1989, 1692 (1692); *Debatin*, DB 1989, 1739 (1739 et seqq.); *Kleineidam*, IStR 1993, 395 (395 et seqq.); *Kleineidam*, IStR 1993, 349 (349 et seqq.); *Bierlaagh*, Intertax 1992, 156 (156); *Brülisauer*, ST 2005, 720 (723); *Ritter*, JbFSt 1976/1977, 288 (300); *Roser*, DStR 2008, 2389 (2391); *Hemmelrath*, in: Vogel/Lehner (Eds.), DBA-Kommentar, Art. 7, paras. 77 et seqq.; *Wassermeyer*, IStR 2004, 733 (733 et seqq.); BFH, 17 July 2008, I R 77/06, BFH/NV 2008, 1941; BFH, 20 July 1988, I R 49/84, BStBl. II 1989, 140; BFH, 27 July 1965, I 110/63 S, BStBl. III 1966, 24; BMF, 24 Dec. 1999, IV B 4—S 1300—111/99, BStBl. I 1999, 1076.

[39] Cf. *Kußmaul/Ruiner/Delarber*, Ubg 2011, 837 (838).

[40] Advocates of the unlimited hypothetical independence of the PE include: *Bähr*, Gewinnermittlung ausländischer Zweigbetriebe, 84; *Baranowski*, Besteuerung von Auslandsbeziehungen, 112 et seq.; *Becker*, EuStZ 1971, 95 (100); *Beiser*, DB 2008, 2724 (2726 et seq.); *Ditz*, in: Schönfeld/Ditz (Eds.), DBA-Kommentar, Art 7 (2008), para. 112; *Ditz/Schneider*, DStR 2010, 81 (82 et seq.); *Fink*, RIW 1988, 43 (48 et seq.); *Kluge*, StuW 1975, 294 (304); *Kroppen*, in: Gosch/Kroppen/Grotherr/Kraft (Eds.), DBA-Kommentar, Art. 7, para. 119; *van Raad*, Intertax 2000, 162 (163 et seq.); BFH, 21 Jan. 1972, III R 57/71, BStBl. II 1972, 374; *Ditz*, Internationale Gewinnabgrenzung bei Betriebsstätten, 167 et seqq.; *Kroppen*, IStR 2005, 74 (74 et seq.); *Sieker*, DB 1996, 110 (112 et seqq.); *Becker*, DB 1990, 392 (392 et seq.); *Becker*, DB 1989, 10 (10 et seqq.); *Kramer*, StuW 1991, 151 (153); *Haiß*, Gewinnabgrenzung bei Betriebsstätten im Internationalen Steuerrecht, 363; *Institut der Wirtschaftsprüfer*, Intertax 1988, 427 (427); *Kroppen*, IWB 2005, 727 (732); *Kumpf*, in: Herzig/Curtius-Hartung/Niemann (Eds.), StbJb 1988/1989, 399 (417 et seqq.); *Plansky*, Die Gewinnzurechnung zu Betriebsstätten im Recht der Doppelbesteuerungsabkommen, 112 et seqq.; *Storck*, Ausländische Betriebsstätten im Ertrag- und Vermögensteuerrecht, 324 et seqq.

b. Interpretation of the Term 'Profits of an Enterprise'

(1) Preliminary Remarks

While German literature mainly focused on the extend of hypothetical independence of the PE and therefore on the interpretation of Article 7(2) OECD MC (pre-2010 version), the discussion at the level of the OECD mainly focused on the meaning of the term 'profits of an enterprise' in Article 7(1) OECD MC (pre-2010 version).[41] Beyond confirming that 'the right to tax does not extend to profits that the enterprise may derive from that State otherwise than through the permanent establishment'[42], the OECD acknowledged that the Commentary on Article 7 OECD MC (pre-2008 version) provides little guidance on how to interpret the term.[43] As a result, historical practice has developed a number of alternative approaches with regard to the attribution of profits to a PE which can generally be grouped into the 'Relevant Business Activity' approach and the 'Functionally Separate Entity' approach.[44] Besides these two broad interpretations, further variations exist that may have to be taken into account.[45] However, in the following, only the two broad interpretations will be discussed in more detail.

(2) Relevant Business Activity Approach

Under the 'Relevant Business Activity' approach the term 'profits of the enterprise' is defined as referring only to the profits of business activities in which the PE is participating in.[46] In this regard, Article 7(1) OECD MC (pre-2010 version) imposes a limit on the profits of the enterprise that may be attributed under Article 7(2) OECD MC (pre-2010 version). More specifically, under this approach, the attributed profits cannot exceed the overall profits of the enterprise earned from the relevant business activity.[47] Key feature of the approach is that profits of the enterprise are only those earned from transactions with associated enterprises as

---

[41] Cf. *Plansky*, Die Gewinnzurechnung zu Betriebsstätten im Recht der Doppelbesteuerungsabkommen, 105.

[42] OECD MC Commentary 2005, Art. 7, para. 5.

[43] Cf. OECD, PE Report 2008, Part I, para. 60.

[44] Cf. detailed for the two approaches OECD, PE Report 2008, Part I, paras. 61 et seqq.

[45] For an overview of the methods for the allocation of profits within the enterprise cf. *Reimer,* in: Reimer/Schmid/Orell (Eds.), Permanent Establishments, Part 3 [C], para. 84; also *Endres/Spengel*, International Company Taxation and Tax Planning, § 8.03[B], 316.

[46] Cf. OECD, PE Report 2008, Part I, para. 61. This method may also be referred to as the 'single enterprise' approach, cf. *Baker/Collier,* Cahiers de droit fiscal international, General Report 2006, 21 (30); *Kobetsky*, International Taxation of Permanent Establishments, 199.

[47] Cf. OECD, PE Report 2008, Part I, para. 62.

well as profits earned with third parties.[48] If transactions with associated enterprises do not reflect a price at arm's length, corresponding adjustments will need to be made.[49] No profits are earned from dealings between the PE and the enterprise of which the PE is a part of.[50] It follows that the hypothetical independence of the PE ends in situations where the enterprise and its PE cannot act like unrelated third parties.[51]

The term 'profits of the enterprise' comprises both, profits as well as losses that the overall enterprise derives from its business activities.[52] Profits of the enterprise attributable to the PE under Article 7(1) OECD MC (pre-2010 version) are those derived from the relevant business activity carried on by the PE.[53] In this context, all parts of the enterprise which engage in the respective business activity have an impact on the profits attributable to the PE.[54] Consequently, if other parts of the enterprise engage in a particular business activity and a loss is incurred on those activities, that loss suffered by the other parts of the enterprise effectively reduces the profit attributable to the PE because the loss reduces the overall profit of the enterprise derived from that business activity.[55]

(3) Functionally Separate Entity Approach

Under the 'Functionally Separate Entity' approach, profits which can be attributed to the PE are not limited to those profits earned by the enterprise as a whole or by particular business activities in which the PE has participated in.[56] Accordingly, Article 7(1) OECD MC (pre-2010 version) is interpreted in a way that it does not affect the amount of profits that are attributed to the PE. Rather, it merely provides specific confirmation that the host country's right to tax does not extend

---

[48] Cf. OECD, PE Report 2008, Part I, para. 62.

[49] Cf. OECD, PE Report 2008, Part I, para. 62.

[50] Cf. *Baker/Collier,* Cahiers de droit fiscal international, General Report 2006, 21 (30); *Bernales*, in: Gutiérrez/Perdelwitz (Eds.), Taxation of Business Profits in the 21st Century, 135 (142).

[51] Cf. *Hemmelrath*, in: Vogel/Lehner (Eds.), DBA-Kommentar, Art. 7, para. 79; *Pinkernell/Ditz*, FR 2001, 1271 (1271 et seqq.); *Kußmaul/Ruiner/Delarber*, Ubg 2011, 837 (838).

[52] Cf. OECD, PE Report 2008, Part I, para. 63.

[53] Cf. OECD, PE Report 2008, Part I, para. 63.

[54] Cf. *Kobetsky*, International Taxation of Permanent Establishments, 199.

[55] Cf. OECD, PE Report 2008, Part I, para. 63.

[56] Cf. OECD, PE Report 2008, Part I, para. 69. This method may also be referred to as the 'separate enterprise' approach, cf. *Baker/Collier,* Cahiers de droit fiscal international, General Report 2006, 21 (30).

to the profits that the enterprise may derive from the respective state otherwise than through the PE.[57]

Key feature of this 'Functionally Separate Entity' approach is that the profits to be attributed to the PE comprise all profits that the PE would have earned at arm's length, in particular also those profits that the PE derives in its dealings with other parts of the enterprise.[58] Therefore, profits may be attributed to the PE even though the enterprise as a whole has never made any profits.[59]

According to this approach, Article 7(3) OECD MC (pre-2010 version) is only intended to ensure that expenses are taken into account when attributing profits to the PE, wherever such an expense is incurred, or whether the expense is incurred exclusively for the PE.[60]

4. Implementation of the Authorised OECD Approach

a. Development of the Authorised OECD Approach

(1) PE Report 2008 and its Implications for Article 7 OECD MC

The lack of a common interpretation has led the Committee on Fiscal Affairs to develop a more consistent interpretation and application of the rules of Article 7 OECD MC.[61] This work resulted in the release of the OECD report entitled 'Attribution of Profits to Permanent Establishments' (hereinafter: PE Report 2008) on 17 July 2008.[62] As explicitly stated by the OECD, the approach developed was neither constrained by the original intent nor by the historical practice and interpretation of Article 7 OECD MC.[63]

Throughout the work on the PE Report 2008, a 'Working Hypothesis' was developed by Working Party No. 6 in order to examine the preferred approach for the attribution of profits to PEs under Article 7 OECD MC.[64] In this context,

[57] Cf. OECD, PE Report 2008, Part I, para. 69.

[58] Cf. OECD, PE Report 2008, Part I, para. 69.

[59] Cf. OECD, PE Report 2008, Part I, para. 69.

[60] Cf. *Baker/Collier,* Cahiers de droit fiscal international, General Report 2006, 21 (31).

[61] Cf. OECD, PE Report 2008, Part I, para. 3. For a chronology of the work of the OECD Working Parties with regard to Art. 7 OECD MC cf. *Bernales,* in: Gutiérrez/Perdelwitz (Eds.), Taxation of Business Profits in the 21st Century, 135 (144 et seqq.); *Kroppen,* in: Kessler/Förster/Watrin (Eds.), Unternehmensbesteuerung—Festschrift Herzig, 1071 (1071 et seq.); *Kobetsky,* International Taxation of Permanent Establishments, 351 et seqq.

[62] Cf. OECD, PE Report 2008.

[63] Cf. OECD, PE Report 2008, Part I, para. 4.

[64] Cf. OECD, PE Report 2008, Part I, para. 3.

specifically the two general interpretations with regard to the term 'profits of an enterprise' in Article 7(1) OECD MC (pre-2010 version) were analysed by the Committee on Fiscal Affairs, namely the 'Functionally Separate Entity' approach and the 'Relevant Business Entity' approach.[65] After a thorough analysis of the merits of both approaches, the 'Functionally Separate Entity' approach was adopted as the 'Authorised OECD Approach' (AOA) and therefore considered as the preferred interpretation of Article 7 OECD MC.[66] Accordingly, profits to be attributed to the PE are those which the PE would have earned if it were a legally separate and distinct enterprise performing the same or similar functions under the same or similar conditions, which can be determined by applying the arm's length principle under Article 7(2) OECD MC.[67] Consequently, the term 'profits of an enterprise' used in Article 7(1) OECD MC should not be interpreted in a way that it affects the determination of the amount of profits that are attributable to the PE.[68]

The Committee on Fiscal Affairs concluded that the best way in order to remove potential for different interpretations with regard to Article 7 OECD MC and to provide maximum certainty to taxpayers and tax administrations is to redraft Article 7 OECD MC together with its accompanying Commentary.[69] Even though most aspects of the AOA were seen as mere enhancements or refinements of the interpretation provided by the Commentary on Article 7 OECD MC (pre-2008 version), the Committee on Fiscal Affairs acknowledged that some aspects in the PE Report 2008, especially the conclusions drawn with regard to the degree of the recognition of dealings between the PE and other parts of the enterprise, were not in line with the Commentary on Article 7 OECD MC (pre-2008 version).[70] Therefore, the OECD decided to use a two-step procedure to implement the AOA.

In a first step, those aspects of the PE Report 2008 were implemented in a revised version of the Commentary on Article 7 OECD MC (2008 version) that did not conflict with the existing text of the Commentary on Article 7 OECD MC (pre-2008 version).[71] This sort of interim version of the Commentary

[65] Cf. OECD, PE Report 2008, Part I, para. 9. See in more detail for the two approaches chapter D.I.3.b.(2) and (3) of this thesis.

[66] Cf. OECD, PE Report 2008, Part I, para. 9.

[67] Cf. OECD, PE Report 2008, Part I, para. 10.

[68] Cf. OECD, PE Report 2008, Part I, para. 10.

[69] Cf. OECD, PE Report 2008, Preface, para. 8.

[70] Cf. OECD, PE Report 2008, Preface, para. 8.

[71] Cf. OECD, PE Report 2010, Part I, para. 4.

aimed to provide more certainty for the interpretation of treaties that had already been concluded on the basis of the wording of Article 7 OECD MC (pre-2010 version).[72]

In a second step, the AOA was fully implemented through a new version of Article 7 OECD MC (2010 version)[73], together with its accompanying Commentary (2010 version)[74] and a revised version of the PE Report (PE Report 2010)[75] which were approved for publication by the OECD Council on 22 July 2010.[76]

(2) Overview of the Modifications to Article 7 OECD MC

The wording of Article 7 OECD MC (pre-2010 version) and Article 7 OECD MC (2010 version) reads as follows:

Table 1 Article 7(1) OECD MC (pre-2010 version vs. 2010 version)

Article 7(1) OECD MC (pre-2010 version)	Article 7(1) OECD MC (2010 version)
The profits of an enterprise of a Contracting State shall be taxable only in that State unless the enterprise carries on business in the other Contracting State through a permanent establishment situated therein. If the enterprise carries on business as aforesaid, the profits of the enterprise may be taxed in the other State but only so much of them as is attributable to that permanent establishment	Profits of an enterprise of a Contracting State shall be taxable only in that State unless the enterprise carries on business in the other Contracting State through a permanent establishment situated therein. If the enterprise carries on business as aforesaid, the profits that are attributable to the permanent establishment in accordance with the provisions of paragraph 2 may be taxed in that other State.

Source: Own illustration.

Article 7(1) sentence 1 OECD MC (2010 version) was slightly rephrased. The term 'The profits of an enterprise' was replaced by the term 'Profits of an enterprise'. Furthermore, Article 7(1) sentence 2 OECD MC (2010 version) explicitly

---

[72]Cf. OECD MC Commentary 2017, Art. 7, para. 7. See in more detail for changes to Commentary on Article 7 OECD MC *Baker/Collier*, BIT 2009, 199 (199 et seqq.).

[73]OECD, Model Tax Convention on Income and on Capital 2010.

[74]OECD, Commentaries on the Articles of the Model Tax Convention 2010.

[75]OECD, PE Report 2010. The PE Report 2008 refers several times to the wording of Art. 7 OECD MC (2008 version). In order to facilitate a harmonious reading of the conclusions of the PE Report 2008, the revised version of the PE Report 2010 was prepared which includes the new wording and noting of Art. 7 OECD MC (2010 version).

[76]Cf. OECD, PE Report 2010, Part I, paras. 5 et seq.

refers to paragraph 2 of Article 7 OECD MC and the phrases 'profits of the enterprise' and 'only so much of them' in Article 7(1) sentence 2 OECD MC (pre-2010 version) were not adopted in Article 7 OECD MC (2010 version). These changes were made in order to emphasise that the provision of Article 7(1) OECD MC shall not impose a limit on the profits of the enterprise that may be attributable under Article 7(2) OECD MC.[77] In other words, the attributable profit to the PE can exceed the overall profits of the enterprise.

With regard to Article 7(2) OECD MC, the following modifications have been made:

Table 2 Article 7(2) OECD MC (pre-2010 version vs. 2010 version)

Article 7(2) OECD MC (pre-2010 version)	Article 7(2) OECD MC (2010 version)
Subject to the provisions of paragraph 3, where an enterprise of a Contracting State carries on business in the other Contracting State through a permanent establishment situated therein, there shall in each Contracting State be attributed to that permanent establishment the profits which it might be expected to make if it were a distinct and separate enterprise engaged in the same or similar activities under the same or similar conditions and dealing wholly independently with the enterprise of which it is a permanent establishment.	For the purposes of this Article and Article [23A] [23B], the profits that are attributable in each Contracting State to the permanent establishment referred to in paragraph 1 are the profits it might be expected to make, in particular in its dealings with other parts of the enterprise, if it were a separate and independent enterprise engaged in the same or similar activities under the same or similar conditions, taking into account the functions performed, assets used and risks assumed by the enterprise through the permanent establishment and through the other parts of the enterprise.

Source: Own illustration.

Besides a modified introductory remark, Article 7(2) OECD MC (2010 version) provides that the PE shall be treated as a completely hypothetical 'separate and independent enterprise' for the purpose of profit attribution, both in its transactions with other enterprises and 'in particular in its dealings with other parts of the enterprise'. The chosen phrases and the reference to the 'functions performed, assets used, and risks assumed' in the last half sentence of Article 7(2) OECD

[77]Cf. also *Mödinger*, Internationale Erfolgs- und Vermögensabgrenzung zwischen Stammhaus und Betriebsstätte nach der Neufassung des Art. 7 OECD MC, 103; *Kahle/Kindich*, in: Lübbehüsen/Kahle (Eds.), Brennpunkte der Besteuerung von Betriebsstätten, para. 4.43; *Plansky*, Die Gewinnzurechnung zu Betriebsstätten im Recht der Doppelbesteuerungsabkommen, 253; *Bennett/Russo*, ITPJ 2009, 73 (75).

MC (2010 version) can be regarded as a clear commitment of the OECD to the 'Functionally Separate Entity' approach as the preferred interpretation of Article 7 OECD MC.

Article 7(3) OECD MC (pre-2010 version), which has led to controversial discussions among scholars,[78] in particular on the question of the extent of hypothetical independence of the PE, was completely deleted in the 2010 version of Article 7 OECD MC and was replaced with a new paragraph dealing with the relief from double taxation.[79]

Article 7(4) OECD MC (pre-2010 version) as the legal basis for the application of the indirect method of profit attribution to the PE on the basis of a certain formula has been deleted in the 2010 version of Article 7(4) OECD MC. Therefore, the application of the indirect method will no longer be applicable for tax treaties that are based on the wording of Article 7 OECD MC (2010 version).

b. The 2-Step Approach of the AOA

(1) Conceptual Approach

The attribution of profits to a PE under Article 7(2) OECD MC (2010 version) is based on the determination of the profits that a PE derives from all its activities.[80] As it follows from the fundamental concept of the AOA, such activities not only include transactions with independent and associated enterprises, but also dealings between the PE and other parts of the enterprise.[81] Since the head office and the PE belong to the same legal entity, the profit attribution to the different parts of the enterprise requires a two-step process in order to make sure that the principles for associated enterprises of Article 9 OECD MC can be applied in the PE context by analogy.[82]

Under the first step of the AOA, the PE is hypothesised as a separate and independent enterprise. As required by Article 7(2) OECD MC (2010 version), the 'functions performed, assets used, and risks assumed by the enterprise through the permanent establishment and through the other parts of the enterprise' shall be taken into account when attributing profits to the PE. In order to do so, a functional and factual analysis must be carried out in accordance with the TP Guidelines

---

[78]See in more detail in this regard chapter D.I.3.a of this thesis.

[79]See in more detail with regard to Art. 7(3) OECD MC (2010 version) *Kobetsky*, International Taxation of Permanent Establishments, 375 et seqq.

[80]Cf. OECD, PE Report 2010, Part I, para. 10.

[81]Cf. OECD, PE Report 2010, Part I, para. 10.

[82]Cf. OECD, PE Report 2010, Part I, para. 10.

that serve to identify the economically significant activities and responsibilities undertaken by the PE.[83]

The approach taken in the TP Guidelines in linking earnings of profits of the enterprise to the performance of functions is able to be applied in the PE context as well by equating functions to activities.[84] Nevertheless, in order to carry out functions it is required that assets ('assets follow functions') and risks ('risks follow functions') are attributed to the different parts of the enterprise. Since the PE is only a dependent part of the enterprise it cannot obtain legal ownership of assets or assume risks.[85] Therefore, the OECD supplements the functional analysis used in the context of Article 9 OECD MC for associated enterprises by the concept of the 'significant people function'. Accordingly, in the PE context, the attribution of risks is contingent upon the identification of significant people functions relevant for the assumption of risks and the attribution of ownership of assets is contingent upon the identification of significant people functions relevant for the economic ownership of assets.[86] Since the PE shall have sufficient capital in order to support the functions it performs, the risks it assumes and the assets it economically owns, also 'free capital' shall be attributed to it.[87] Additionally, it is necessary to recognise and determine the dealings between the PE and the rest of the enterprise under the first step.[88]

In the second step, the recognised dealings between the PE and other parts of the enterprise are priced on an arm's length basis by applying the full transfer pricing toolset used in the context of Article 9 OECD MC for associated enterprises by analogy.[89] This process requires a) the determination of comparability

[83]Cf. OECD, PE Report 2010, Part I, para. 10. For differences with regard to the application of the TP Guidelines in the PE context see *Mödinger,* Internationale Erfolgs- und Vermögensabgrenzung zwischen Stammhaus und Betriebsstätte nach der Neufassung des Art. 7 OECD-MA, 107 et seq.; *Margerie*, Gewinnermittlung und Gewinnabgrenzung bei Betriebsstätten, 106 et seq. As a matter of fact it must be noted that the functional and factual analysis in the context of Article 7 OECD MC is different from the functional analysis in the context of Article 9 OECD MC. As the title suggests the functional and factual analysis is broader than the factual analysis since the factual analysis also takes account of the hypothetical independence of the PE, cf. OECD, PE Report 2010, Part I, para. 15. See in more detail *van Wanrooij*, Intertax 2009, 298 (303); *Margerie*, Gewinnermittlung und Gewinnabgrenzung bei Betriebsstätten, 106.

[84]Cf. OECD, PE Report 2010, Part I, para. 57.

[85]Cf. *Wassermeyer/Kaeser*, in: W/K/S/D (Eds.), Doppelbesteuerung, Art. 5 MA, para. 371.

[86]Cf. OECD, PE Report 2010, Part I, para. 59.

[87]Cf. OECD, PE Report 2010, Part I, paras. 15, 28.

[88]Cf. OECD, PE Report 2010, Part I, para. 33.

[89]Cf. OECD, PE Report 2010, Part I, para. 10.

between dealings and uncontrolled transactions based on the functional and factual analysis, and b) the selection and application of the most appropriate transfer pricing method for the respective dealings between the PE and other parts of the enterprise.[90]

Figure 1 summarises the 2-step approach of the AOA and illustrates the interrelations within and between the respective steps of the approach.

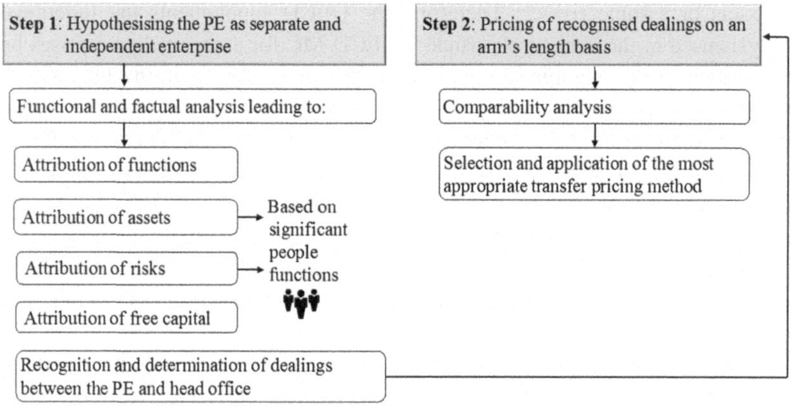

Figure 1 2-Step Approach of the AOA (Source: Own illustration)

(2) Step 1: Hypothesising the PE as a Separate and Independent Enterprise

(a) Functional and Factual Analysis

i. Fundamentals

Due to the absence of legally binding contracts or other ascertainable legal arrangements in the PE context, there is no single part of the enterprise which legally assumes the risk, owns the assets or possesses the capital.[91] Neither is there a single part of the enterprise which concludes contracts with other enterprises.[92]

[90] Cf. OECD, PE Report 2010, Part I, para. 44.

[91] Cf. OECD, PE Report 2010, Part I, para. 14.

[92] Cf. OECD, PE Report 2010, Part I, para. 14.

Rather, from a legal perspective, risks, assets, capital and the rights and obligations which arise out of transactions with other separate enterprises belong to the enterprise as a whole and not to any one part of the enterprise.[93]

Consequently, the use of a legal analysis to determine the profits to the respective parts of the enterprise is of no help. Instead, the OECD decided to adopt the concept of the functional and factual analysis, since there is already considerable guidance available in the TP Guidelines on how this analysis must be conducted under Article 9 OECD MC.[94] It follows that the guidance on the functional and factual analysis provided by the TP Guidelines can be applied 'fairly directly'[95] in the PE context.[96] However, in order to take the specifics of a PE into account, it proves necessary to supplement the functional analysis under Article 9 OECD MC.[97] Accordingly, it shall be identified what kind of economically significant activities and responsibilities the PE undertakes in the context of the entire enterprise.[98] In this regard, it is also necessary to attribute those rights and obligations to the PE which derive from transactions of the enterprise with other separated enterprises.[99] The objective is to identify those transactions of the enterprise with associated enterprises which would have been attributed to the PE if it were a separate and independent enterprise.[100] Additionally, the exact nature of the functions being performed and in what capacity these functions are performed shall be identified.[101] In this respect, it is conceivable that the PE carries out functions relatively autonomous and independent from the head office or mainly acts as a service provider for other parts of the enterprise.[102]

The determination of the specific activities and responsibilities that are associated with the PE is contingent upon the form of the PE within the meaning of Article 5(1) OECD MC. In cases where the PE is constituted through a fixed place of business according to Article 5(1) OECD MC, the determination of the

---

[93] Cf. OECD, PE Report 2010, Part I, para. 15.

[94] Cf. OECD, PE Report 2010, Part I, para. 15.

[95] OECD, PE Report 2010, Part I, para. 61.

[96] Cf. OECD, PE Report 2010, Part I, para. 60 with reference to para 1.42 of the TP Guidelines 2010. With the update of the TP Guidelines in 2017 the details on how to carry out a functional analysis can now be found in paras. 1.51 et seqq. of the TP Guidelines 2017.

[97] Cf. OECD, PE Report 2010, Part I, para. 15.

[98] Cf. OECD, TP Guidelines 2017, para 1.51; OECD, PE Report 2010, Part I, para. 10.

[99] Cf. OECD, PE Report 2010, Part I, para. 98.

[100] Cf. OECD, PE Report 2010, Part I, para. 98.

[101] Cf. OECD, PE Report 2010, Part I, para. 67.

[102] Cf. *Ditz*, in: Schönfeld/Ditz (Eds.), DBA-Kommentar, Art. 7 (2017), para 23; *Kroppen*, in: Kessler/Förster/Watrin (Eds.), Unternehmensbesteuerung—Festschrift Herzig, 1071 (1076).

specific activities and responsibilities should be based on an analysis of the fixed place of business that constitutes the PE and the functions that are performed at that fixed place.[103] In cases of a PE that is constituted by a dependent agent within the meaning of Article 5(5) OECD MC, the functions undertaken by the dependent agent on behalf of the enterprise have to be taken into account by the functional analysis.[104]

ii. Identification and Attribution of People Functions

In order to identify the economically significant activities and responsibilities the PE undertakes, the PE Report 2010 refers to the functions carried out by the personnel of the enterprise in the PE ('people functions').[105] A precise definition of the term 'people function' or 'function' is not provided by the OECD.[106] However, for the purpose of the functional analysis between associated enterprises the OECD enumerates a few examples of what functions may be in the TP Guidelines.[107] Accordingly, 'design, manufacturing, assembling, research and development, servicing, purchasing, distribution, marketing, advertising, transportation, financing and management'[108] are examples that may constitute a function. Due to the fact that the functional and factual analysis shall be carried out in accordance with the TP Guidelines,[109] the examples provided by the OECD may also constitute functions carried out by the personnel for the purpose of the functional and factual analysis in the PE context under Article 7 OECD MC.

It needs to be assessed what significance (if any) such people functions have for the purpose of generating profits for the business.[110] The OECD distinguishes

---

[103] Cf. OECD, PE Report 2010, Part I, para. 60.

[104] Cf. OECD, PE Report 2010, Part I, para. 60.

[105] Cf. OECD, PE Report 2010, Part I, para. 62.

[106] Cf. in more detail for the term function in the context of business restructurings *Hentschel*, Deutsche Regelungen zur internationalen Funktionsverlagerung, 31 et seqq.

[107] Cf. OECD, TP Guidelines 2010, para. 1.42. The updated TP Guidelines 2017 do not list these examples anymore. However, some of these examples can be found throughout the explanations within chapter D.1.2 of the TP Guidelines 2017 which deals with the functional analysis, cf. OECD, TP Guidelines 2017, paras. 1.51 et seqq.

[108] OECD, TP Guidelines 2010, para. 1.43. The updated TP Guidelines 2017 do not contain such an enumeration of examples that may constitute a function. The new TP Guidelines rather provide additional guidance on how to identify such a function, cf. OECD, TP Guidelines 2017, paras. 1.51 et seqq.

[109] Cf. OECD, PE Report 2010, Part I, paras. 10, 13.

[110] Cf. OECD, PE Report 2010, Part I, para. 62.

between 'ancillary or support functions' and 'significant people functions'.[111] In this context, it shall be examined which persons within the enterprise carry out what kind of activities and take on what kind of responsibilities in which parts of the enterprise.[112] Ultimately, this examination determines what kind of assets and risks shall be attributed to the PE. In that sense, it is of particular importance to identify the significant people functions since the OECD determines that the attribution of economic ownership of assets and the attribution of risks to the PE shall be based on the significant people functions.[113] As explicitly emphasised in the PE Report 2010, the significant people function relevant to the economic ownership of assets and the significant people function relevant to the assumption of risk may differ and will vary dependent upon the respective business sector and from enterprise to enterprise even within the same business sector.[114] By linking the significant people function to the generation of profit, the OECD ultimately considers the significant people function as operational functions which significantly contribute to the value creation of the enterprise and entail risks and responsibilities for asset creation and utilisation of the enterprise.[115] Consequently, if such functions are carried out by the PE a corresponding attribution of a fraction of the profits may be justified.

Furthermore, a function carried out by the personnel of the enterprise in the PE can only be considered a significant people function, if the personnel at the PE's location have a) actual capabilities (e.g. knowledge or skills) to carry out that function, b) the competence to assume responsibility, and c) the control to manage the underlying risks of the function.[116]

The attribution of the respective functions either to the PE or to other parts of the enterprise depends on where within the enterprise the significant people functions are carried out by the personnel. Consequently, the key question in determining economic ownership of assets and the assumption of risks is where

---

[111] Cf. OECD, PE Report 2010, Part I, para. 62.

[112] Cf. *Kroppen*, in: Kessler/Förster/Watrin (Eds.), Unternehmensbesteuerung—Festschrift Herzig, 1071 (1076); *Delarber*, Steuerliche Einflüsse auf die grenzüberschreitende Betriebsstättenbesteuerung, 194.

[113] Cf. OECD, PE Report 2010, Part I, paras. 15 et seq.

[114] Cf. OECD, PE Report 2010, Part I, para. 16. Cf. in more detail with regard to financial enterprises cf. OECD, PE Report 2010, Part I, para. 16 with reference to Part II, II and IV of the PE Report 2010.

[115] Cf. *Fris/Llinares/Gonnet*, TPTP 2008, 1 (2); *Margerie*, Gewinnermittlung und Gewinnabgrenzung bei Betriebsstätten, 112.

[116] Cf. *Kamphuis*, TMTPR 2008, 300 (301); *Margerie*, Gewinnermittlung und Gewinnabgrenzung bei Betriebsstätten, 111.

within the enterprise the significant people function is carried out.[117] It follows that in the event the significant people function is carried out by the personnel of the PE at the PE's location, the significant people function and based on that the attribution of economic ownership of assets and the attribution of risks shall be attributed to the PE.[118] This approach is very intuitive and straightforward in its application. Nevertheless, no clarifications on specific challenges, such as the attribution of overlapping people functions, e.g. monitoring or management activities, are addressed in the PE Report 2010, leaving a lot of flexibility for the taxpayer.[119] In practice, the preparation of an organisation chart may be of help for determining where within the enterprise the significant people functions are carried out.[120]

In this context, it is important to stress the fact that there is no presumption that functions that do not constitute significant people functions are automatically of low value.[121] This finding ultimately leads to the conclusion that profits may also be attributed to a PE in cases where only ancillary or support functions and consequently no significant people functions are carried out by the personnel at the PE's location.[122]

iii. Absence of Personnel

As pointed out earlier also, server, pipelines or fully automated facilities where manpower is substituted by autonomous operating systems may constitute a PE.[123] All these PEs have in common that they usually operate without the presence of personnel. In that regard, it is of particular interest how the functional and factual analysis might be conducted since the attribution of economic ownership

---

[117] Cf. OECD, PE Report 2010, Part I, para. 94.

[118] Cf. OECD, PE Report 2010, Part I, para. 68.

[119] Cf. *Ditz*, ISR 2012, 48 (53); *Looks,* in: Looks/Heinsen (Eds.), Betriebsstättenbesteuerung, para. 759.

[120] Cf. *Kraft/Dombrowski*, FR 2014, 1105 (1108).

[121] Cf. *Bernales*, in: Gutiérrez/Perdelwitz (Eds.), Taxation of Business Profits in the 21st Century, 135 (160 et seq.).

[122] Cf. *Andresen*, in: W/A/D (Eds.), Betriebsstätten-Handbuch, para. 5.18; *Bernales*, in: Gutiérrez/Perdelwitz (Eds.), Taxation of Business Profits in the 21st Century, 135 (161, note 105).

[123] Advocates of the conclusion that a PE can be triggered without the presence of personnel: cf. *Bernütz,* IStR 1997, 353 (356); *Hutter/Schmidt*, IStR 2000, 650 (653); *Arndt/Fetzer*, BB 2001, 1175 (1176). Critical *Portner*, IStR 1998, 553 (554); *Portner*, IStR 1999, 641 (643); *Hidien/Rodenhäuser*, DStZ 2007, 689 (693). See in more detail in this context chapter C.IV.3.c.(2) of this thesis.

of assets and the attribution of risks to the PE shall be based on the significant people functions. However, due to the absence of personnel working at the PEs location, no significant people functions can be identified.[124]

In the PE Report 2010 the case of PEs that operate without personnel is discussed with regard to Server PEs.[125] For such cases, the OECD emphasises that the same principles developed under the AOA shall apply.[126] However, due to the absence of personnel working at the PEs location and consequently the lack of significant people functions, the functional and factual analysis shall determine which so-called 'automated functions' are performed by the PE.[127] The automated nature of these functions carried out by a Server PE results in the circumstance that only assets and risks which are directly associated with the server hardware can be attributed to a Server PE.[128] In the case of a Server PE it may therefore be appropriate to attribute the server hardware itself to the PE.[129] Nevertheless, since no significant people functions are carried out in the Server PE, only little or no profit can be attributed to such a PE.[130]

In this context, the analysis of the economically relevant characteristics important to the performance of the automated functions as part of the functional and factual analysis under the first step is of high importance.[131] This analysis aims to identify all economically relevant parameters of the PE in order to accurately undertake the comparability analysis under the second step of the AOA and ultimately determine prices of the dealings between the PE and the rest of the enterprise and transactions between independent enterprises which are at arm's

[124]Cf. *Kaeser*, in: W/K/S/D (Eds.), Doppelbesteuerung, Art. 7 MA (2010), para. 450.; *Delarber*, Steuerliche Einflüsse auf die grenzüberschreitende Betriebsstättenbesteuerung, 195.

[125]Cf. OECD, PE Report 2010, Part I, para. 66.

[126]Cf. OECD, PE Report 2010, Part I, para. 66.

[127]Cf. OECD, PE Report 2010, Part I, para. 66.

[128]Cf. OECD, PE Report 2010, Part I, para. 66.

[129]Cf. *Kaeser*, in: W/K/S/D (Eds.), Doppelbesteuerung, Art. 7 MA (2010), para. 450; *Ditz/Tcherveniachki*, ISR 2020, 145 (150). Also para. 75 of the PE Report 2010 supports the conclusion that the server hardware itself shall be attributed to the place where it is used, cf. OECD, PE Report 2010, Part I, para. 75.

[130]Cf. OECD, PE Report 2010, Part I, para. 66; same conclusion *Greinert/Metzner*, Ubg 2014, 307 (309); *Kaeser*, in: W/K/S/D (Eds.), Doppelbesteuerung, Art. 7 MA (2010), para. 450; *Andresen*, in: W/A/D (Eds.), Betriebsstätten-Handbuch, para. 5.19. Critical with regard to PEs in e-commerce *Mödinger*, Internationale Erfolgs- und Vermögensabgrenzung zwischen Stammhaus und Betriebsstätte nach der Neufassung des Art. 7 OECD-MA, 214 et seqq.

[131]Cf. *Kaeser*, in: W/K/S/D (Eds.), Doppelbesteuerung, Art. 7 MA (2010), para. 450.

length.[132] In order to illustrate the significance of the analysis of the economically relevant characteristics for profit attribution, the sample case of the Server PE shall be stressed one more time. Insofar as the server is left for the use by another third party, a relevant share of the profit can be attributed to the PE since such an activity is of economical relevance.[133] However, in cases where the server is only used for internal purposes, such as internal distribution purposes, it is of less economical relevance.[134] Consequently, only a small portion of the profit can be attributed to the Server PE.[135]

(b) Attribution of Assets

i. Fundamentals

From a legal perspective, assets belong to the enterprise as a whole of which the PE is a part. Consequently, no one part of an enterprise factually 'owns' assets.[136] However, in applying the first step of the AOA a mechanism had to be found in order to attribute assets to the PE.[137] Due to the fact that legal contracts cannot be used as a criterion for the attribution of assets, the OECD introduced the concept of 'economic ownership'.[138] For the purpose of defining the term 'economic ownership' the OECD refers to the equivalent of ownership for income tax purposes by a separate enterprise.[139] Hereby, the economic owner on the one side enjoys all the benefits, but on the other side also bears the burdens related to the assets. In this regard, the OECD enumerates the following examples: the right to the income which is attributable to the ownership of the asset, e.g. royalties, the potential exposure to gains or losses from the appreciation or depreciation of the asset and the right to depreciate a depreciable asset.[140] The underlying idea of this concept is to attribute income generated from the assets to those parts of

---

[132] Cf. OECD, PE Report 2010, Part I, para. 64.

[133] Cf. *Kaeser*, in: W/K/S/D (Eds.), Doppelbesteuerung, Art. 7 MA (2010), para. 450.

[134] Cf. *Kaeser*, in: W/K/S/D (Eds.), Doppelbesteuerung, Art. 7 MA (2010), para. 450.

[135] Cf. *Kaeser*, in: W/K/S/D (Eds.), Doppelbesteuerung, Art. 7 MA (2010), para. 450; also *Delarber*, Steuerliche Einflüsse auf die grenzüberschreitende Betriebsstättenbesteuerung, 196.

[136] Cf. OECD, PE Report 2010, Part I, paras. 18, 72.

[137] Cf. OECD, PE Report 2010, Part I, para. 72.

[138] Cf. OECD, PE Report 2010, Part I, para. 18.

[139] Cf. OECD, PE Report 2010, Part I, para. 14, note 4.

[140] Cf. OECD, PE Report 2010, Part I, para. 14, note 4.

the enterprise that bear the risks of and the profits from the upside potential of the respective income-generating asset.[141]

In order to attribute economic ownership, the OECD distinguishes between tangible assets and intangibles.[142]

ii. Attribution of Tangible Assets

The OECD notes that the member countries expressed different views with regard to the attribution of tangible assets to the PE. On the one side, an attribution based on the significant people function relevant for the economic ownership of the tangible assets by means of a functional and factual analysis was found to be the most appropriate approach.[143] On the other side, the view was expressed that an attribution of tangible assets to the 'place of use' should be the sole attribution criterion.[144]

As a pragmatic solution the OECD prefers the second concept, an attribution of the tangible assets to the part of the enterprise where the tangible asset is used unless the specific circumstances of the case warrant a different view.[145] Such specific circumstances would result in an attribution of the tangible asset to the part of the enterprise where the significant people function relevant to the economic ownership of the tangible asset is carried on.[146]

Circumstances which could make an attribution of the tangible asset based on the significant people function appropriate might exist in the event of lease, rental or license agreements.[147] In such cases, the place of use of the tangible asset may not be identified clearly or might change frequently.[148] By way of example, the use of machines at a building or construction site for a rather short period

---

[141] Cf. *Kahle/Mödinger*, IStR 2010, 757 (760); *Ditz*, in: Schönfeld/Ditz (Eds.), DBA-Kommentar, Art. 7 (2017), para 25; *Kosch*, IStR 2010, 42 (43); *Ziehr*, Einkünftezurechnung im internationalen Einheitsunternehmen, 172; *Jeitler*, in: Brugger/Plansky (Eds.), Permanent Establishments in International and EU Tax Law, 185 (193).

[142] Cf. OECD, PE Report 2010, Part I, paras. 72 et seqq.

[143] Cf. OECD, PE Report 2010, Part I, para. 75.

[144] Cf. OECD, PE Report 2010, Part I, para. 75.

[145] Cf. OECD, PE Report 2010, Part I, para. 75. See for discussion of the two concepts *Ditz/Tcherveniachki*, ISR 2020, 145 (150).

[146] Cf. OECD, PE Report 2010, Part I, para. 75; also *Margerie*, Gewinnermittlung und Gewinnabgrenzung bei Betriebsstätten, 121.

[147] Cf. *Kosch*, IStR 2010, 42 (43); *Margerie*, Gewinnermittlung und Gewinnabgrenzung bei Betriebsstätten, 122.

[148] Cf. *Kosch*, IStR 2010, 42 (43); *Margerie*, Gewinnermittlung und Gewinnabgrenzung bei Betriebsstätten, 122.

of time could justify the assumption of a lease and should not lead to a notional transfer of the economic ownership of the machines to the place of use, i.e. the building or construction site, which would ultimately lead to a disclosure of the hidden reserves at the time of the transfer.[149] In such cases a comparable lease and consequently a dealing between the PE and the other part of the enterprise could be assumed.[150]

The OECD emphasises that both approaches should arrive at the same result or at least at a result which is not significantly different.[151] On the one side, the PE is treated as the economic owner of the asset and is therefore generally entitled to deductions for depreciations and/or interest expenses in case the asset is partly or wholly debt-financed.[152] On the other side, the PE is treated as the lessee of the respective tangible asset and is therefore generally entitled to deduct the rent for the used asset.[153] While both approaches may result in different profit allocations in the short term, the two cases may not differ significantly over the overall lifetime of the tangible asset.[154]

In cases where the tangible asset cannot be attributed clearly, the OECD also allows for a pro rata attribution to the parts of the enterprise in which the significant people functions are performed.[155] Especially, situations where a tangible asset was developed by different parts of the enterprise under a cost contribution arrangement splitting the costs for the development between the different parts of

[149] Cf. *Kaeser*, in: W/K/S/D (Eds.), Doppelbesteuerung, Art. 7 MA (2010), para. 475; *Bendlinger*, Die Betriebsstätte in der Praxis des internationalen Steuerrechts, 327; *Margerie*, Gewinnermittlung und Gewinnabgrenzung bei Betriebsstätten, 121; *Jeitler*, in: Brugger/Plansky (Eds.), Permanent Establishments in International and EU Tax Law, 185 (193).

[150] Cf. *Jeitler*, in: Brugger/Plansky (Eds.), Permanent Establishments in International and EU Tax Law, 185 (193).

[151] Cf. OECD, PE Report 2010, Part I, para. 75. Critical *Bernales* who argues that the attribution of the tangible assets to the part of the enterprise where the assets is used leads to the situation that the PE state keeps more taxing rights, cf. *Bernales*, in: Gutiérrez/Perdelwitz (Eds.), Taxation of Business Profits in the 21st Century, 135 (162); also *Margerie*, Gewinnermittlung und Gewinnabgrenzung bei Betriebsstätten, 122.

[152] Cf. OECD, PE Report 2010, Part I, para. 75.

[153] Cf. OECD, PE Report 2010, Part I, para. 75.

[154] Cf. OECD, PE Report 2010, Part I, para. 75.

[155] Cf. *Ditz*, in: Schönfeld/Ditz (Eds.), DBA-Kommentar, Art. 7 (2017), para. 26; *Looks*, in: Looks/Heinsen (Eds.), Betriebsstättenbesteuerung, para. 775; *Kraft*, in: Kraft (Ed.), AStG—Kommentar, § 1 AStG, para. 672.

the enterprise in a manner consistent with the contemplated use of the tangible asset could justify a pro rata attribution to different parts of the enterprise.[156]

iii. Attribution of Intangibles

With regard to the attribution of intangibles to the different parts of the enterprise, the PE Report 2010 distinguishes between trade intangibles[157] and marketing intangibles[158].[159] In case of trade intangibles another distinction is made between internally developed trade intangibles[160] and acquired trade intangibles[161]. A definition of the different types of intangibles is not provided by the PE Report 2010.[162] However, while the Report enumerates that in particular the logo and the name of the company or the brand can be regarded as examples that constitute marketing intangibles, the category of trade intangibles can be regarded as a so-called residuary clause which shall cover all other intangibles.[163] Nevertheless, since the criteria for the attribution of economic ownership do not differ with

---

[156]Cf. OECD, PE Report 2010, Part I, para. 197; also *Looks*, in: Looks/Heinsen (Eds.), Betriebsstättenbesteuerung, para. 775; *Ditz*, ISR 2012, 48 (50); *Kraft*, in: Kraft (Ed.), AStG—Kommentar, § 1 AStG, para. 672.

[157]Cf. OECD, PE Report 2010, Part I, paras. 83 et seqq.

[158]Cf. OECD, PE Report 2010, Part I, paras. 96 et seqq.

[159]In this context, the PE Report 2010 refers to chapter VI of the TP Guidelines and emphasises that the Guidelines distinguish between marketing intangibles and commercial intangibles, which are referred to as trade intangibles. According to the OECD this concept can be applied by analogy in the PE context. Cf. OECD, PE Report 2010, Part I, para. 79; OECD, TP Guidelines 2017, paras. 6.1 et seqq.

[160]Cf. OECD, PE Report 2010, Part I, paras. 83 et seqq.

[161]Cf. OECD, PE Report 2010, Part I, paras. 92 et seqq.

[162]A definition of the term intangible can be found in the OECD TP Guidelines 2017. Accordingly, an intangible 'is intended to address something which is not a physical asset or a financial asset, […] which is capable of being owned or controlled for use in commercial activities, and whose use or transfer would be compensated had it occurred in a transaction between independent parties in comparable circumstances. Rather than focusing on accounting and legal definitions, the thrust of a transfer pricing analysis in a case involving intangibles should be the determination of the conditions that would be agreed upon between independent parties for a comparable transaction', OECD, TP Guidelines 2017, para. 6.6. See in more detail for the changes to chapter VI of the TP Guidelines 2017 through BEPS Actions 8–10 chapter D.I.4.b.(2)(h)iii of this thesis.

[163]Cf. *Andresen*, in: W/A/D (Eds.), Betriebsstätten-Handbuch, para. 5.26.

regard to the different types of intangibles, a precise differentiation is not required at this point.[164]

Due to the fact that it is quite common for intangibles to be used simultaneously by various parts of the enterprise,[165] the place of use does not constitute a practicable criterion for the attribution of economic ownership to the different parts of the enterprise.[166] Therefore, the OECD determined that, in contrast to tangible assets, it is not the place of use which is decisive for the attribution of economic ownership of intangibles but rather the significant people functions which requires active decision-making with respect to the taking on and the corresponding management of risks that are associated with the intangible.[167]

More precisely, with regard to internally developed trade intangibles (e.g. specialised software), the significant people functions decisive for the attribution of economic ownership shall be those which require active decision-making regarding the taking on and corresponding management of risks associated with the development of the internally developed intangibles.[168] However, this does not necessarily mean that the active decision-making takes place at the strategic level of senior management and is therefore simply a matter of saying 'yes' or 'no' to an investment proposal.[169] Rather, the economic ownership shall be determined by the people functions which are responsible to actively manage the development programme of the intangible and which actively manage the risks associated with the respective development programme.[170] Even though the OECD emphasises that the identification of the significant people function may vary depending on the facts and circumstances of the case and shall therefore be determined on a case-by-case basis, the following people functions are enumerated in the PE Report 2010 which may be relevant in this regard:

---

[164] For a discussion on the different types of intangibles see *Nientimp/Stein/Schwarz/Holinski*, BB 2017, 407 (408); *Collier/Andrus*, Transfer Pricing and the Arm's Length Principle after BEPS, paras. 6.53 et seqq.; *Schmidtke*, IStR 2015, 120 (122).

[165] Cf. OECD, PE Report 2010, Part I, para. 77.

[166] Cf. *Jeitler*, in: Brugger/Plansky (Eds.), Permanent Establishments in International and EU Tax Law, 185 (194).

[167] Cf. OECD, PE Report 2010, Part I, paras. 85, 94, 97.

[168] Cf. OECD, PE Report 2010, Part I, para. 85. For a detailed analysis with regard to the attribution of internally developed trade intangibles see *Looks,* in: Looks/Heinsen (Eds.), Betriebsstättenbesteuerung, paras. 780 et seqq.

[169] Cf. OECD, PE Report 2010, Part I, para. 87; cf. also in this regard *Looks,* in: Looks/Heinsen (Eds.), Betriebsstättenbesteuerung, para. 781.

[170] Cf. OECD, PE Report 2010, Part I, para. 87.

- design of test specifications and development processes;
- review and evaluation of data produced by the tests;
- setting the stage posts at which the decisions are taken; and
- taking the decision on whether further resources shall be committed to the project or abandon it.[171]

For acquired intangibles, the significant people functions related to active decision-making with respect to the taking on of risk and the corresponding management of such risk might comprise:

- the evaluation of the acquired intangibles;
- the management of and evaluation of such risks which is associated with deploying the acquired intangible; and
- the performance of various follow-on development activities.[172]

Just as with trade intangibles, the key question in determining economic ownership of marketing intangibles is where within the enterprise the significant people function is carried out. Such people functions are those that are related to the initial assumption and subsequent management that are associated with marketing intangibles, such as:

- creation of and control over the branding strategies;
- maintenance of established marketing intangibles, and trade name; and
- trademark protection.[173]

If economic ownership of an intangible can be explicitly attributed to one part of the enterprise and that asset is used by another part of the enterprise, compensation at arm's length is to be paid to the part of the enterprise which owns the asset economically.[174] However, since the complexity of intangibles creates difficulties with respect to the question of where the decision-making and management process of risks lies within the enterprise, the attribution of economic ownership of

[171] Cf. OECD, PE Report 2010, Part I, para. 88.

[172] Cf. OECD, PE Report 2010, Part I, para. 94. For a detailed analysis with regard to the attribution of acquired trade intangibles see *Looks,* in: Looks/Heinsen (Eds.), Betriebsstättenbesteuerung, paras. 793 et seqq.

[173] Cf. OECD, PE Report 2010, Part I, para. 97. For a detailed analysis with regard to the attribution of marketing intangibles see *Looks,* in: Looks/Heinsen (Eds.), Betriebsstättenbesteuerung, paras. 809 et seqq.

[174] Cf. OECD, PE Report 2010, Part I, paras. 200 et seqq.

an intangible to a specific part of the enterprise might not be accurate.[175] In this context, it is conceivable that different parts of the enterprise carry out the significant people function that is relevant for the attribution of economic ownership. Therefore, the OECD does not only provide for the possibility of attributing sole ownership but also joint ownership of an intangible to the different parts of the enterprise.[176] However, in case the taxpayer makes use of such a pro rata attribution of economic ownership of an intangible to different parts of the enterprise, problems of demarcation and documentation are expectable, which will ultimately lead to legal uncertainty for the taxpayer.[177]

(c) Attribution of Risks

In contrast to associated enterprises, contractual arrangements between the head office and the PE are not legally binding.[178] Consequently, it is the enterprise as a whole which bears the risks from a legal perspective.[179] However, by hypothesising the PE as a separate and independent enterprise under the AOA, it is possible, even in the absence of a legally binding contractual arrangement which allocates risk to a particular part of the enterprise, to treat the PE as assuming risk.[180] In this context, the PE shall assume any risk for which the significant people functions crucial to the assumption of such risk are performed by the relevant personnel of the PE at the PE's location.[181]

Significant people functions decisive for the assumption of risk are those which require active decision-making by the personnel regarding the acceptance and/or

[175] Cf. *Bernales*, in: Gutiérrez/Perdelwitz (Eds.), Taxation of Business Profits in the 21st Century, 135 (163).

[176] Cf. OECD, PE Report 2010, Part I, paras. 83 et seqq., 200; *Andresen*, in: W/A/D (Eds.), Betriebsstätten-Handbuch, para. 5.27; *Margerie*, Gewinnermittlung und Gewinnabgrenzung bei Betriebsstätten, 128.

[177] Cf. *Andresen*, in: W/A/D (Eds.), Betriebsstätten-Handbuch, para. 5.27.

[178] Cf. *Kroppen*, in: Kessler/Förster/Watrin (Eds.), Unternehmensbesteuerung—Festschrift Herzig, 1071 (1076); *Bendlinger*, Die Betriebsstätte in der Praxis des internationalen Steuerrechts, 326; *Ditz*, in: Schönfeld/Ditz (Eds.), DBA-Kommentar, Art. 7 (2017), para. 24.

[179] Cf. OECD, PE Report 2010, Part I, para. 68.

[180] Cf. OECD, PE Report 2010, Part I, para. 68.

[181] Cf. OECD, PE Report 2010, Part I, para. 68; detailed in this context see *Andresen*, in: W/A/D (Eds.), Betriebsstätten-Handbuch, para. 5.27; *Kahle/Kindich*, in: Lübbehüsen/Kahle (Eds.), Brennpunkte der Besteuerung von Betriebsstätten, para. 4.52; *Kroppen*, in: Kessler/Förster/Watrin (Eds.), Unternehmensbesteuerung—Festschrift Herzig, 1071 (1076); *Ditz*, in: Schönfeld/Ditz (Eds.), DBA-Kommentar, Art. 7 (2017), para. 24.

management of such risks.[182] In this context, the extent of the decision-making depends on the nature of the risk which is involved.[183] The logic behind this concept is to attribute the economic consequences of business decisions to the people who are responsible for the respective decisions.[184] It follows that in case the active decision-making by the personnel is performed at the PE, provisions booked in relation to such risks are also to be attributed to the PE.[185] Consequently, the PE also bears the fiscal consequences of adding back or deducting allowances to these provisions and the exposure to potential losses or gains from the realisation or the non-realisation of such risks.[186] Relevant risks may be credit risk, inventory risk, interest rate risk, currency risk, product liability and warrant risks, market risks and/or regulatory risk, to name just a few.[187]

By way of example, assume that products are manufactured at the head office and then delivered to the PE for sale to customers in the jurisdiction where the PE is located. Consequently, the PE acts as a distributor for the products of the head office. If, in the case at hand, the PE makes the active decisions related to the levels of inventory and is in charge for the decision to conclude a sale to a specific customer after a careful examination of the creditworthiness of that customer, the excess inventory risk and credit risk is to be attributed to the PE in such a case.[188]

(d) Attribution of Rights and Obligations

From a legal perspective, rights and obligations which arise out of transactions with other separate enterprises are contractually tied to the enterprise as a whole and not to one part of the enterprise.[189]Also, the profits or losses of a PE, which shall be treated as a separate and independent enterprise for tax purposes, are based on all activities performed by the PE. This includes not only dealings with other parts of the enterprise to which the PE belongs to but also transactions with related enterprises and transactions with other unrelated enterprises.[190] Therefore,

---

182Cf. OECD, PE Report 2010, Part I, para. 22.

183Cf. OECD, PE Report 2010, Part I, para. 22.

184Cf. *Schön*, TNI 46 (2007), 1059 (1067); *Schön*, in: Lüdicke (Ed.), Besteuerung von Unternehmen im Wandel, 71 (100); *Ditz*, Internationale Gewinnabgrenzung bei Betriebsstätten, 207 et seqq.; *Kosch*, IStR 2010, 42 (43); *Kahle/Mödinger*, IStR 2010, 757 (760); *Kahle/Kindich*, in: Lübbehüsen/Kahle (Eds.), Brennpunkte der Besteuerung von Betriebsstätten, para. 4.52.

185Cf. OECD, PE Report 2010, Part I, para. 70.

186Cf. OECD, PE Report 2010, Part I, para. 70.

187Cf. OECD, PE Report 2010, Part I, para. 68.

188Cf. OECD, PE Report 2010, Part I, para. 24.

189Cf. *Kaeser*, in: W/K/S/D (Eds.), Doppelbesteuerung, Art. 7 MA (2010), para. 487.

190Cf. OECD, PE Report 2010, Part I, para. 98.

it is necessary to attribute the corresponding rights and obligations to the PE which arise out of the transactions of the enterprise with separate enterprises and which are properly attributable to the PE.[191]

The PE Report 2010 dedicates only one paragraph to the clarification of the respective attribution approach. Accordingly, the enterprise's transactions which should be hypothesised to have been entered into by the PE shall be determined by analysing the PE's functions in light of its assets used and risk assumed.[192] A specific significant people function relevant for the attribution of rights and obligations to the PE is not mentioned by the PE Report 2010.[193] Rather, the overall circumstances (attributed assets, attributed risks, performed significant people functions) shall be considered when attributing rights and obligations to the respective PE.[194]

The profits or losses of the PE attributable to a particular participation in the transactions can be computed either directly if the transactions were entered into with unrelated enterprises or by applying the TP Guidelines 2017 under Article 9 OECD MC if the transaction was entered into with related enterprises.[195]

(e) Attribution of Free Capital

i. Fundamentals

After assets, risks, rights and obligations are attributed to the PE, the next essential step under the AOA is the attribution of a proper amount of 'free' capital to the PE. In this regard, the term free capital is defined by the OECD as 'funding that does not give rise to a tax-deductible return in the nature of interest'[196]. The underlying idea behind that approach is the consideration that a PE should have sufficient capital to support the functions performed, the risks assumed and the assets used and is seen as a cushion against crystallisation of risk in this context.[197] In other words, capital needed to support the risks assumed by the PE has to be attributed to the PE by reference to the risks that are attributed to it ('capital follows risk'[198]) and not the other way around.[199] Consequently, the

---

[191] Cf. OECD, PE Report 2010, Part I, para. 98.

[192] Cf. OECD, PE Report 2010, Part I, para. 98.

[193] Cf. OECD, PE Report 2010, Part I, para. 98.

[194] Cf. *Froitzheim*, Steuerliche Selbstständigkeitsfiktion der Betriebsstätte, 63 et seq.

[195] Cf. OECD, PE Report 2010, Part I, para. 98.

[196] OECD, PE Report 2010, Part I, para. 28.

[197] Cf. OECD, PE Report 2010, Part I, para. 28.

[198] OECD, PE Report 2010, Part I, para. 26.

[199] Cf. OECD, PE Report 2010, Part I, para. 29.

part of the enterprise that carries out the significant people functions relevant to the assumption of risks shall be attributed the capital necessary to support such risks.[200]

This process involves two steps. First, the risks and assets attributed to the PE must be measured respectively valued in order to determine the overall amount of funding necessary.[201] In order to value the assets, the OECD provides different valuation options, such as the use of market values, book values or the use of the original purchase price or cost of the asset.[202] The process of measuring risks is more difficult, which leads the OECD to conclude that even an enterprise's own risk management system may be used as a starting point in this regard.[203]

Second, the free capital needed to support the risks and assets attributed to the PE must be determined.[204] In order to do so, no single internationally accepted approach was developed in the consultation process due to a lack of consensus amongst governments and business.[205] Rather, several approaches are considered in the PE Report 2010 which can broadly be classified in methods which are based on the actual capital structure of the enterprise (the capital allocation approach and the economic capital allocation approach) and methods which are based on the capital structure of comparable enterprises (thin capitalisation approach and the safe harbour approach).[206] Other methods illustrated in the PE Report 2010 developed specifically for banks, enterprises carrying on global trading of financial instruments and insurance companies will not be considered here.[207]

---

[200] Cf. OECD, PE Report 2010, Part I, para. 26.

[201] See in more detail OECD, PE Report 2010, Part I, paras. 108–114. See in more detail regarding the 2-step approach *Kaeser*, in: W/K/S/D (Eds.), Doppelbesteuerung, Art. 7 MA (2010), paras. 499 et seqq.

[202] Cf. OECD, PE Report 2010, Part I, paras. 109 et seq.

[203] Cf. OECD, PE Report 2010, Part I, para. 113.

[204] Cf. OECD, PE Report 2010, Part I, para. 107.

[205] Cf. OECD, PE Report 2010, Part I, para. 147.

[206] Cf. *Hoogterp*, ITPJ 2009, 396 (398). For detailed discussion with regard to the four methods see OECD, PE Report 2010, Part I, paras. 121 et seqq.; *Ditz*, in: Schönfeld/Ditz (Eds.), DBA-Kommentar, Art. 7 (2017), para. 27; *Kahle/Kindich*, in: Lübbehüsen/Kahle (Eds.), Brennpunkte der Besteuerung von Betriebsstätten, paras. 4.56 et seqq.; *Nouel*, in: Gutiérrez/Perdelwitz (Eds.), Taxation of Business Profits in the 21st Century, 183 (200 et seqq.); *Truffer*, in: Brugger/Plansky (Eds.), Permanent Establishments in International and EU Tax Law, 203 (212 et seqq.); *Malherbe/Daenen*, BIT 2010, 359 (363 et seq.).

[207] See in more detail with regard to the capital attribution to banks OECD, PE Report 2010, Part II, paras. 84 et seqq. See in more detail with regard to capital attribution to enterprises carrying on global trading of financial instruments OECD, PE Report 2010, Part III, paras.

ii. Attribution Methods

01. The Capital Allocation Approach

According to the capital allocation approach, free capital is attributed to the PE in accordance with the attribution of risks assumed and assets economically owned.[208] More specifically, a proportion of the entity's equity corresponding to the proportion of risks assumed and assets owned is attributable to the PE.[209] By way of example, if 50% of the overall assets and/or risks of the enterprise are attributed to the PE, 50% of free capital will be attributed to the PE under this approach.[210]

However, the OECD acknowledges that difficulties may arise in applying this approach, especially in cases where the PE carries on a very different type of business compared to the enterprise as a whole or in situations when the market conditions in the PE's host country are substantially different from the conditions that apply to the other parts of the enterprise.[211] In such circumstances, the capital allocation approach might not arrive at a result which is in line with the arm's length principle. Appropriate adjustments to account for the aforesaid differences are possible.[212] Nevertheless, the applicability of the capital allocation approach has its limitations. Especially in situations where the enterprise itself is thinly capitalised or in the opposite case when the enterprise has a high amount of capital due to specific circumstances such as temporary cash surplus for a potential acquisition or from selling a business.[213]

02. Economic Capital Allocation Approach

The economic capital allocation approach seeks to determine the amount of free capital a PE needs to hold in order to cover potential negative cash flows at a certain risk tolerance level and thereby aims to limit the possibility of bankruptcy over a specific time horizon.[214] This approach is explicitly based on measuring

---

232 et seqq. See in more detail with regard to capital attribution to enterprises carrying on global trading of financial instruments OECD, PE Report 2010, Part IV, paras. 139 et seqq.

[208] Cf. OECD, PE Report 2010, Part I, para. 121.

[209] Cf. OECD, PE Report 2010, Part I, para. 121.

[210] Cf. OECD, PE Report 2010, Part I, para. 121.

[211] Cf. OECD, PE Report 2010, Part I, para. 124.

[212] Cf. OECD, PE Report 2010, Part I, para. 124; see also with examples for such adjustments *Looks,* in: Looks/Heinsen (Eds.), Betriebsstättenbesteuerung, para. 875.

[213] Cf. OECD, PE Report 2010, Part I, paras. 124 et seqq.

[214] Cf. *Nouel*, in: Gutiérrez/Perdelwitz (Eds.), Taxation of Business Profits in the 21st Century, 183 (204).

risk from an economic perspective and is derived from risk measurement systems established in the financial industry where risk measurement is part of the regulatory framework.[215]

However, the OECD authorises this approach also for application in the non-financial industry and puts forward by way of example that the economic capital allocation approach might be appropriate, especially in circumstances where substantial development risks exist, e.g. when patented technology is developed by a PE.[216] In this respect, economically validated risk measurement systems such as the Monte Carlo simulation might be appropriate for determining the appropriate amount of free capital that shall be attributed to a PE.[217] However, given the fact that such risk measurement systems are extremely contestable the economic capital allocation approach is of subordinate importance in practice.[218]

03. Thin Capitalisation Approach

The thin capitalisation approach fully departs from the actual amount of the enterprise's equity capital as a whole by trying to attribute an appropriate amount of free capital to the PE on an autonomous basis, which may even lead to the situation that the amount of free capital attributed to the PE exceeds the actual amount of the enterprise's equity capital.[219]

According to the thin capitalisation approach, in a first step, assets and risks to be attributed to the PE are identified and analysed in order to determine the amount of overall funding that is required by the PE in order to support its respective functions, assets and risks.[220] In a second step, the allocation of the overall funding into free capital and interest-bearing debt is determined by analysing the debt-to-equity ratio of comparable independent enterprises in the host country of

---

[215]Cf. OECD, PE Report 2010, Part I, para. 128.

[216]Cf. OECD, PE Report 2010, Part I, para. 128.

[217]Cf. *Looks,* in: Looks/Heinsen (Eds.), Betriebsstättenbesteuerung, para. 876; *Malherbe/Daenen*, BIT 2010, 359 (363).

[218]Cf. *Andresen*, in: W/A/D (Eds.), Betriebsstätten-Handbuch, para. 5.39.

[219]Cf. OECD, PE Report 2010, Part I, para 134; Since the thin capitalisation approach may arrive at the result that the capital attributed to the PE exceeds the capital of the enterprise of which the PE is a part, the maximum amount available always needs to be determined and considered when applying this approach, cf. *Delarber*, Steuerliche Einflüsse auf die grenzüberschreitende Betriebsstättenbesteuerung, 204. The German Federal Tax Court determined that the amount of free capital in the enterprise as a whole is the maximum amount that can be attributed to the different parts of the enterprise, cf. BFH, 23 Aug. 2000, I R 98/96, BStBl. II 2002, 207.

[220]Cf. OECD, PE Report 2010, Part I, para 129.

the PE.[221] In case appropriate comparables are available, the approach has the advantage that no further limitations[222] to the capital structure apply.[223] However, the wide range of debt-to-equity ratios observable at arm's length, especially due to the various external and internal factors by which the ratio is influenced, such as the market conditions, the nature and quality of the assets, the business sector itself and preferences of the shareholder, makes the comparability analysis more complicated and may lead to increased compliance costs and ultimately leads to legal uncertainty for the taxpayer.[224] Consequently, even though the thin capitalisation approach is an appropriate method to arrive at an amount of free capital of the PE that complies with the arm's length principle,[225] its limitations may make this method more suitable as an approach to validate the results of the other methods suggested by the OECD.[226]

04. Safe Harbour Approach: Quasi Thin Capitalisation Approach

The fourth approach discussed by the OECD which is also called the 'regulatory minimum capital approach' requires the PE to hold at least the same amount of free capital required for regulatory purposes as would an independent enterprise that operates in the host country.[227] Even though this approach provides remarkable administrative simplicity compared to the other approaches discussed, there are a couple of problems that result in the fact that the OECD concludes that the safe harbour approach is not an authorised OECD approach.[228] This is mainly due to the fact that the approach ignores certain conditions of the AOA such as the circumstance that the PE shares the same creditworthiness as the enterprise

---

[221] Cf. OECD, PE Report 2010, Part I, para 129.

[222] Since the thin capitalisation approach fully departs from the actual amount of free capital of the enterprise as a whole, no difficulties arise in situations where the enterprise as a whole is entirely debt-funded, cf. OECD, PE Report 2010, Part I, para 134.

[223] Cf. *Truffer*, in: Brugger/Plansky (Eds.), Permanent Establishments in International and EU Tax Law, 203 (215).

[224] Cf. OECD, PE Report 2010, Part I, paras. 132 et seq.

[225] For a numerical example with regard to the application of the thin capitalisation approach see *Delarber*, Steuerliche Einflüsse auf die grenzüberschreitende Betriebsstättenbesteuerung, 204 et seq.

[226] Cf. *Kaeser*, in: W/K/S/D (Eds.), Doppelbesteuerung, Art. 7 MA (2010), para. 514. Critical in this regard also *Looks* who emphasises that besides difficulties with regard to compliance issues, also the assumption of the AOA that the PE generally enjoys the same creditworthiness as the enterprise of which it is a part is not considered by the thin capitalisation approach, cf. *Looks*, in: Looks/Heinsen (Eds.), Betriebsstättenbesteuerung, para. 877.

[227] Cf. OECD, PE Report 2010, Part I, para. 135.

[228] Cf. OECD, PE Report 2010, Part I, para. 135.

as a whole.[229] Further difficulties arise since its application outside the regulated financial sector may be very limited.[230] This is mainly due to the fact that the approach relies on sector benchmarks which ultimately may not meet the comparability standards.[231] Consequently, the applicability of the safe harbour approach is mostly limited to financial and insurance sector.[232]

05. Special Case: Entire Enterprise is Thinly Capitalised

It is emphasised in the PE Report 2010 that circumstances are possible where the entire enterprise is thinly capitalised (e.g. enterprise is entirely debt financed), leaving the PE thinly capitalised even if the entire free capital of the enterprise would be attributed to the PE.[233] In that case, the OECD suggests two possible approaches for the attribution of free capital to the PE.

A first approach would be the thin capitalisation approach which looks at the capital structure of comparable independent enterprises in comparable circumstances and derived an appropriate amount of free capital for the PE.[234] A second approach would first adjust the free capital of the enterprise to an amount that is at arm's length and then allocate free capital to the PE through the capital allocation approach.[235]

(f) Attribution of Interest-Bearing Debt

It is acknowledged by the OECD that a PE requires a certain amount of funding, consisting of both free capital and interest-bearing debt.[236] Once the amount of free capital has been determined and attributed on the basis of the aforementioned attribution approaches, the amount of interest-bearing debt results as a

---

[229] Cf. OECD, PE Report 2010, Part I, para. 135.

[230] Cf. *Looks*, in: Looks/Heinsen (Eds.), Betriebsstättenbesteuerung, para. 878; OECD, PE Report 2010, Part I, para. 136; *Andresen*, in: W/A/D (Eds.), Betriebsstätten-Handbuch, para. 5.41.

[231] Cf. OECD, PE Report 2010, Part I, para. 137.

[232] Cf. *Looks*, in: Looks/Heinsen (Eds.), Betriebsstättenbesteuerung, para. 878; *Kaeser*, in: W/K/S/D (Eds.), Doppelbesteuerung, Art. 7 MA (2010), para. 515; *Andresen*, in: W/A/D (Eds.), Betriebsstätten-Handbuch, para. 5.41.

[233] Cf. OECD, PE Report 2010, Part I, para. 140.

[234] Cf. OECD, PE Report 2010, Part I, para. 141.

[235] Cf. OECD, PE Report 2010, Part I, para. 142. See in more detail *Looks*, in: Looks/Heinsen (Eds.), Betriebsstättenbesteuerung, para. 880; *Kaeser*, in: W/K/S/D (Eds.), Doppelbesteuerung, Art. 7 MA (2010), para. 516.

Cf. OECD, PE Report 2010, Part I, para. 155.

[236] Cf. OECD, PE Report 2010, Part I, para. 150.

residuum.[237] It follows that no specific attribution methods are provided by the OECD. Rather, the amount of interest-bearing debt can be calculated as follow:

Interest-bearing debt = overall amount of funding—free capital.

In this context, the question arises on how to attribute external interest expense of the enterprise to its PE. Just as there exists more than one approach authorised by the OECD for the attribution of free capital to a PE, there exists also more than one approach for the attribution of external interest expense of the enterprise to its PE. In this context, the OECD focuses on two approaches, namely the so-called 'tracing approach' and the 'fungibility approach'.[238] Under the tracing approach, any external debt attributed to the PE must be traced back to its original source.[239] The interest rate for the external debt attributed to the PE is determined to be exactly the same as the actual interest rate incurred by the enterprise to the third party provider of the funding.[240] In certain circumstances, the tracing approach is to be evidenced by internal interest dealings that allocate the incurred interest expense of the enterprise to the PE.[241] The application of the tracing approach seems appropriate if large amounts of debt were borrowed for the business operations of the PE.[242] However, if the external debt attributed to the PE cannot be traced back to its original source, the tracing method will fail in its application, suggesting another method: the fungibility approach.[243]

The second approach, the fungibility approach, is based on the idea that each PE is attributed a portion of the whole enterprise's interest expense that was actually paid to third parties on a pre-determined basis.[244] Thus, the approach is built on the notion that the PE generally enjoys the same creditworthiness and capital structure as the enterprise of which it is a part.[245] Since there is no need to trace the movements of funds within the enterprise, the recognition of internal interest dealings would be of no use under the fungibility approach.[246] As far as

[237]Cf. OECD, PE Report 2010, Part I, para. 150.

[238]Cf. OECD, PE Report 2010, Part I, para. 154.

[239]Cf. OECD, PE Report 2010, Part I, para. 154.

[240]Cf. OECD, PE Report 2010, Part I, para. 154.

[241]Cf. OECD, PE Report 2010, Part I, para. 154.

[242]Cf. *Kaeser*, in: W/K/S/D (Eds.), Doppelbesteuerung, Art. 7 MA (2010), para. 521.

[243]Cf. *Kaeser*, in: W/K/S/D (Eds.), Doppelbesteuerung, Art. 7 MA (2010), para. 521.

[244]Cf. OECD, PE Report 2010, Part I, para. 154.

[245]Cf. *Kaeser*, in: W/K/S/D (Eds.), Doppelbesteuerung, Art. 7 MA (2010), para. 521. For creditworthiness of the PE see OECD, PE Report 2010, Part I, paras. 99.

[246]Cf. OECD, PE Report 2010, Part I, para. 154.

the capital allocation approach was used in order to attribute capital to the PE, it appears appropriate that also financing expenses are attributed to the PE based on an allocation key and therefore to favour the fungibility approach over the tracing approach.[247]

However, both, the tracing approach and the fungibility approach face difficulties in their application,[248] causing the OECD to conclude that 'it does not seem possible to develop a single approach for determining the amount of attributable interest expense that could be applicable in all circumstances'[249]. Therefore, the OECD recognises not only the tracing approach and the fungibility approach as authorised approaches for the attribution of external interest expense to the PE, but also authorises other approaches as long as the amount of interest expenses attributed to the PE does not exceed an arm's length amount.[250]

(g) Recognition of Dealings

Key feature of the 'Functionally Separate Entity' approach is that the profits to be attributed to the PE comprise all profits that the PE would have earned at arm's length, in particular also those profits that the PE derives in its dealings with other parts of the enterprise.[251] However, since dealings between the PE and other parts of the enterprise have no legal consequences for the enterprise as a whole, a greater scrutiny of dealings and its documentation is necessary compared to transactions between associated enterprises.[252] In this context, the term scrutiny means that a certain threshold must be passed in order for dealings to be accepted as equivalent to transactions between associated enterprises.[253]

It is assumed by the OECD that dealings between the PE and other parts of the enterprise are more susceptible to being restructured or disregarded for tax purposes by the respective tax administrations than transactions that would have taken place between associated enterprises.[254] Due to the fact that a dealing can only be reflected in the attribution of profits under Article 7(2) OECD MC in case the aforementioned threshold is passed, the OECD outlines certain criteria that shall be considered by the taxpayer in this regard. In principle, to identify

---

[247] Cf. *Kaeser*, in: W/K/S/D (Eds.), Doppelbesteuerung, Art. 7 MA (2010), para. 520.

[248] Cf. OECD, PE Report 2010, Part I, para. 155.

[249] OECD, PE Report 2010, Part I, para. 156.

[250] Cf. OECD, PE Report 2010, Part I, para. 156.

[251] Cf. OECD, PE Report 2010, Part I, para. 8.

[252] Cf. OECD, PE Report 2010, Part I, para. 175.

[253] Cf. OECD, PE Report 2010, Part I, paras. 34, 176.

[254] Cf. OECD, PE Report 2010, Part I, para. 176.

whether a dealing is relevant for the attribution of profits under Article 7(2) OECD MC, it must be determined whether there has been any economically significant transfer of risk, benefits as well as responsibilities between the PE and other parts of the enterprise as a result of that dealing.[255] In this sense, the OECD suggests the use of internal documentation and accounting records of the PE that shows the purported existence of a dealing as a starting point.[256] Additionally, in order to be relevant for the purpose of profit attribution, the dealing as documented needs to be related to a real and identifiable event.[257] In other words, the dealing must actually have taken place between the PE and the other part of the enterprise.

It is the responsibility of the taxpayer to prove that a dealing has taken place. With regard to tangible assets, a cross-border transfer could for example be verified with the help of customs documents.[258] The verification of a cross-border performance of a service could be verified with the help of the travel documents of the person who performed the service.[259] In this context, the use of quasi-contracts for such dealings—notwithstanding its lack of legal effect—is not only recommended due to the fact that it encourages the taxpayer to prepare contemporaneous documentation of the respective dealings but it also reduces the potential for controversies regarding the application of the AOA.[260]

Tax administrations are encouraged to recognise the documentation prepared by the taxpayer, provided that:

- the documentation is consistent with the actual economic reality as revealed by the functional and factual analysis;
- the arrangements of the documented dealings do—in their entirety—not differ from arrangements which would have been agreed to by comparable independent enterprises, or if they do differ, the arrangements don't practically impede the respective tax administrations from determining a transfer price for such arrangements which is in line with the TP Guidelines;

---

[255] Cf. OECD, PE Report 2010, Part I, paras. 36, 178.

[256] Cf. OECD, PE Report 2010, Part I, para. 177.

[257] Cf. OECD, PE Report 2010, Part I, para. 177.

[258] Cf. *Andresen*, in: W/A/D (Eds.), Betriebsstätten-Handbuch, para. 5.51.

[259] Cf. *Andresen*, in: W/A/D (Eds.), Betriebsstätten-Handbuch, para. 5.51.

[260] Cf. OECD, PE Report 2010, Part I, para. 36; *Andresen*, in: W/A/D (Eds.), Betriebsstätten-Handbuch, para. 5.51; *Delarber*, Steuerliche Einflüsse auf die grenzüberschreitende Betriebsstättenbesteuerung, 210.

- the dealing documented does not violate the fundamental principles of the AOA as put forward in the PE Report 2010.[261]

The OECD also deals with the recognition of internal interest dealing, so-called 'treasury dealings'. While the movement of funds between the different parts of an enterprise is not necessarily recognised as a dealing, there may be circumstances where such movements give rise to treasury dealing.[262] In most cases, it is appropriate to reward a PE that provides the funds (so-called treasury PE) as a service provider and remunerate the routine service on a cost plus basis or with a reimbursement of any administration costs incurred.[263] Only if the treasury PE is doing more than merely acting as a conduit, i.e. the PE carries out the significant people function relevant for the determination of economic ownership of assets and must therefore be treated as the economic owner of the assets, the PE would be entitled to an associated return on the assets attributed.[264]

(h) Analysis of the Modifications to the TP Guidelines through BEPS Actions 8-10 Affecting Step 1 of the AOA

i. Overview

As previously discussed, the OECD/G20 initiative on BEPS resulted in far reaching changes effecting the taxation of PEs. Besides significant changes to the PE definition through BEPS Action 7 dealing with the prevention of the artificial avoidance of the PE status, also other BEPS Action points effect the taxation of PEs.[265] Especially, the outcome of BEPS Actions 8–10 led to an overhaul of the TP Guidelines.[266] Since parts of the guidance provided in the TP Guidelines are applicable either fairly directly in the PE context or may prove to provide valuable

---

[261] Cf. OECD, PE Report 2010, Part I, para. 36.

[262] Cf. OECD, PE Report 2010, Part I, para. 152.

[263] Cf. OECD, PE Report 2010, Part I, para. 159.

[264] Cf. OECD, PE Report 2010, Part I, paras. 159 et seq. Detailed for the pricing of the return for a fully-fledged treasury dealing see OECD, PE Report 2010, Part I, paras. 160, 165.

[265] For an overview of the BEPS Action points influencing the taxation of PEs see chapter E.II of this thesis, see also *Böhmer*, in: W/A/D (Eds.), Betriebsstätten-Handbuch, paras. 14.138 et seqq.

[266] The following chapters of the TP Guidelines 2017 were revised or supplemented as a result of BEPS Actions 8–10: chapter I.D., paras. 1.33–1.173; chapter II, paras. 2.18–2.22, 2.114–2.183 and annex II; chapter VI and annex; chapter VII; chapter VIII and annex. See in more detail with regard to the modifications through BEPS Actions 8–10 *Jerabek/Kofler/Kroppen/Rasch*, in: Kofler/Schnitger (Eds.), BEPS-Handbuch, chapter I, paras. 4 et seqq.

additional guidance in order to carry out the first step of the AOA, the following analysis illustrates the changes to the TP Guidelines 2017 through BEPS Actions 8–10. Thereby, the analysis focuses on these aspects of the changes to the TP Guidelines through BEPS Actions 8–10 which are of relevance for the first step of the AOA.[267]

ii. Modifications Affecting the Functional and Factual Analysis

As the title of BEPS Actions 8–10 suggests, the work under these action points aims to ensure that transfer pricing outcomes are in line with value creation.[268] For this purpose, the OECD amended, among others, the guidance for applying the arm's length principle illustrated in Section D of chapter I of the TP Guidelines[269], which, as noted earlier, also apply by analogy in the PE context.

Accordingly, it is stated in paragraph 1.36 of chapter I of the TP Guidelines 2017 that a functional analysis shall take into account how functions 'relate to the wider generation of value by the MNE group to which the parties belong, the circumstances surrounding the transaction, and industry practices'[270]. This guidance can be understood as a clear reference to a value chain analysis which might be a valuable tool to use in this process.[271] However, while the functional analysis is performed based on the separate entity approach, a value chain analysis rather focuses on the operations carried out by the whole enterprise.[272] It follows that the value chain analysis disregards jurisdictional barriers or any legal frame.[273] Despite the fact that a value chain analysis is not characterised through an exactly defined set of process and consequently can take various forms and can be carried out to a lesser or greater level of detail, its core purpose is the identification of

---

[267] Detailed regarding the significance of the changes to the TP Guidelines through BEPS Actions 8–10 for step 2 of the AOA see chapter D.I.4.b.(3)(d) of this thesis.

[268] Cf. OECD, BEPS Actions 8–10: Final Report 2015, p. 13.

[269] Cf. OECD, TP Guidelines 2017, paras. 1.51 et seqq.

[270] OECD, TP Guidelines 2017, para. 1.36.

[271] Cf. *Petruzzi/Buriak*, TNI 90 (2018), 91 (102).

[272] This finding can be concluded from the following statement by the OECD in para 1.35 of the TP Guidelines 2017: 'The process then narrows to identify how each MNE within that MNE group operates, and provides an analysis of what each MNE does (e.g. a production company, a sales company) and identifies its commercial or financial relations with associated enterprises as expressed in transactions between them.', cf. *Petruzzi/Buriak*, TNI 90 (2018), 91 (102).

[273] Cf. *Petruzzi/Buriak*, TNI 90 (2018), 91 (102).

key value drivers of the whole company and in this regard distinguishes between important functions, assets and risks from less important ones.[274]

In this context, it is legitimate to ask what purpose the value chain analysis has in the PE context and how it fits into the process of the functional and factual analysis. First and foremost it must be emphasised that the value chain analysis does not replace the functional analysis and is therefore certainly not a substitute.[275] Rather, it can be regarded as a useful tool which supplements the functional analysis.[276] To this end, the performance of the functional and factual analysis in the PE context and the identification of significant people functions can be based on a value chain analysis in order to define how the individual dealings contribute to the key value activities of the enterprise. It follows that the value chain analysis might improve the outcome of the functional and factual analysis as part of the first step of the AOA. Furthermore, the value chain analysis might also be of value for the comparability analysis and for the selection of the most appropriate transfer pricing method as part of the second step of the AOA.

iii. Modifications Affecting the Attribution of Intangibles

The treatment of intangibles for transfer pricing purposes has been a source of concern for many years.[277] At the time the project on BEPS commenced, the OECD's Working Party 6 was already working on a project aiming to rewrite chapter VI of the TP Guidelines dealing with intangibles.[278] This work was subsumed into the BEPS Action plan and incorporated in the final report on BEPS Actions 8–10. More precisely, the OECD dedicated the whole BEPS Action Point 8 "Guidance on Transfer Pricing Aspects of Intangibles" to deal with intangible-related topics aiming to develop guidance which seeks to address the prevention of base erosion and profit shifting by moving intangibles among members of an MNE group.[279] Considering the fact that according to a recent study conducted by the Ponemon Institute LLC states that intangibles accounted for 84% of the

---

[274] Cf. OECD, BEPS Action 7: Comments on Discussion Draft (Part II), p. 345; *Petruzzi/Buriak*, TNI 90 (2018), 91 (102).

[275] Cf. OECD, BEPS Action 7: Comments on Discussion Draft (Part II), p. 345; *Petruzzi/Buriak*, TNI 90 (2018), 91 (102, note 52).

[276] Cf. OECD, BEPS Action 7: Comments on Discussion Draft (Part II), p. 345.

[277] Cf. *Collier/Andrus*, Transfer Pricing and the Arm's Length Principle after BEPS, para. 6.53; *Schmidtke*, IStR 2015, 120 (120 et seq.); *Naumann/Groß*, IStR 2014, 906 (906 et seqq.).

[278] Cf. *Collier/Andrus*, Transfer Pricing and the Arm's Length Principle after BEPS, para. 6.53.

[279] OECD, BEPS Actions 8–10: Final Report 2015, p. 63.

value of the S&P 500 firms in 2018 (up from 17% in 1975),[280] it is of no surprise that the treatment of intangibles for transfer pricing purposes is of high relevance within the BEPS Project.

Among others, the guidance developed resulted in a revision of chapter VI of the TP Guidelines dealing with intangibles. Even though the TP Guidelines are specifically tailored for determining arm's length prices for transactions between associated enterprises, the newly incorporated chapter provides supplemental guidance for specific matters involving intangibles that can also prove useful in the PE context.[281]

In this regard, two aspects of the newly incorporated chapter VI of the TP Guidelines 2017 must be highlighted. First, the definition of the term 'intangible'[282] was clarified and put in more precise terms. Accordingly, an intangible shall be something which is neither a physical nor a financial asset that can be owned or controlled for use in commercial activities and whose transfer or use would be compensated if it were part of a transaction between independent parties in comparable circumstances.[283] In this regard, it is neither required that an intangible is recognised as an intangible for accounting purposes,[284] nor is it necessary that an intangible is characterised by a separate transferability.[285]

---

[280] Cf. Ponemon Institute LLC, 2019 Intangible Assets Financial Statement Impact Comparison Report, p. 1.

[281] Para. 79 of the PE Report 2010 states that chapter VI of the OECD TP Guidelines can be applied by analogy in the PE context, cf. OECD, PE Report 2010, Part I, para. 79. *Nientimp/Stein/Schwarz/Holinski* and *Böhmer* emphasise that the changes to chapter VI of the TP Guidelines can be taken into account in the PE context and provide further detail in this regard, cf. *Nientimp/Stein/Schwarz/Holinski*, BB 2017, 407 (408 et seq.); *Böhmer*, in: W/A/D (Eds.), Betriebsstätten-Handbuch, para. 14.143.

[282] The term 'intangible property' used in the TP Guidelines 2010 and adopted in the PE Report 2010 was dropped in the TP Guidelines 2017 and changed to the more inclusive term 'intangible', see in more detail *Collier/Andrus*, Transfer Pricing and the Arm's Length Principle after BEPS, para. 6.58.

[283] Cf. OECD, TP Guidelines 2017, para. 6.6. For a non-exhaustive list of items that may constitute an intangible see OECD, TP Guidelines 2017, paras. 6.19 et seqq. Accordingly, patents, know-how, trade secrets, trademarks, trade names, brands, rights under contracts and government licenses, licenses and similar limited rights in intangibles as well as goodwill and ongoing concern value. However, the TP Guidelines 2017 emphasise that these items shall not be used as a substitute for a detailed analysis, cf. OECD, TP Guidelines 2017, para. 6.18. Critical with regard to the circumstance that also goodwill and an ongoing concern shall constitute an intangible *Jerabek/Kofler/Kroppen/Rasch*, in: Kofler/Schnitger (Eds.), BEPS-Handbuch, chapter I, para. 80.

[284] Cf. OECD, TP Guidelines 2017, para. 6.7.

[285] Cf. OECD, TP Guidelines 2017, para. 6.8.

Furthermore, it is clarified that no attempt is made in the TP Guidelines 2017 to distinguish between different categories of intangibles.[286] However, such a distinction was made in the TP Guidelines 2010,[287] namely a distinction between marketing intangibles and commercial intangibles (also referred to as trade intangibles), which was adopted and referred to in the PE Report 2010.[288] Since the PE Report 2010 was not revised within the course of the BEPS project and, as a consequence, still distinguishes between marketing and trade intangibles, the guidance in para. 6.16 of the TP Guidelines 2017 is of importance in this context. Accordingly, generic reference to such categories does neither relieve the taxpayer nor the tax administration to identify intangibles with specificity nor shall the use of such categories lead to the conclusion that a different approach shall be applicable in the determination of arm's length conditions for transactions or dealings that involve either trade or marketing intangibles.[289] Nevertheless, since the criteria for the attribution of economic ownership to the PE do not differ with regard to the aforementioned categories of intangibles, the changed terminology introduced in the TP Guidelines 2017 does not result in modifications regarding the attribution of intangibles to the PE.

Another definitory issue dealt with in the TP Guidelines 2017 is the distinction between intangibles on the one side and items that shall rather be analysed as comparability factors. The TP Guidelines 2017 assert that market specific characteristics, including location cost savings and local market features such as the size of the market or the rate of development and MNE group synergies cannot be owned or controlled and are therefore not to be treated as intangibles.[290] However, since such features can affect prices for transactions in the market, they should be taken into account in the comparability analysis.[291] It follows that such features shall be considered as part of the second step of the AOA in the PE context.

---

[286]Cf. OECD, TP Guidelines 2017, para. 6.15.

[287]Cf. OECD, TP Guidelines 2010, paras. 6.1 et seqq.

[288]Cf. OECD, PE Report 2010, Part I, para. 79.

[289]Cf. OECD, TP Guidelines 2017, para. 6.16.

[290]Cf. OECD, TP Guidelines 2017, paras. 6.30 et seq. This finding is in contrast to the view of the UN Practical Manual on Transfer Pricing for Developing Countries elaborating that such features may be considered to constitute an intangible depending on the facts and circumstances of the case, cf. UN, Practical Manual on Transfer Pricing for Developing Countries 2017, para. B.1.6.11. Especially the tax administrations of China and India consider location specific advantages as intangibles, cf. *Jerabek/Kofler/Kroppen/Rasch*, in: Kofler/Schnitger (Eds.), BEPS-Handbuch, chapter I, para. 84.

[291]Cf. OECD, TP Guidelines 2017, paras. 1.139 et seqq.

The second aspect that must be highlighted is the new guidance dealing with the ownership and entitlement to profits derived from the use of intangibles. The TP Guidelines 2017 assert that the determination of ownership of intangibles based on legal rights and contractual arrangements forms the starting point in a transfer pricing analysis involving intangibles.[292] The legal owner will be considered to be the owner of the intangible for transfer pricing purposes and may initially accrue the return from the exploitation of the intangible.[293] However, legal ownership of intangibles is not regarded sufficient in order to retain the entire amount of the intangible-related return.[294] If other members of the MNE group performed functions, used assets and assumed risks with regard to the development, enhancement, maintenance, protection and exploitation (hereinafter: DEMPE) of the intangible, they must be compensated by the legal owner of the intangible.[295] Consequently, two trends can be identified in the post-BEPS era. On the one hand, the weight of contractual arrangements, mere funding provided by a member of the MNE group and ownership which formed the foundation for the application of the arm's length standard in the pre-BEPS era was reduced.[296] On the other hand, territorial presence of people, functions and activities performed by them can be identified as the new foundation which shall have a decisive impact on intangible-related returns aiming to ensure that transfer pricing outcome is in line with value creation and real economic activity.[297]

---

[292] Cf. OECD, TP Guidelines 2017, para. 6.35. The guidelines further assert that the terms of the transaction involving intangibles may be found in public records such as trademark or patent registrations, written contracts or correspondence among the parties, cf. OECD, TP Guidelines 2017, para. 6.35.

[293] Cf. OECD, TP Guidelines 2017, para. 6.42. In the event no legal ownership can be identified, the member of the MNE group that controls decisions with regard to the economic exploitation of the intangible and has the actual capacity to restrict others from the use of the intangible may be considered the legal owner of that intangible for the purpose of determining appropriate transfer prices, OECD, TP Guidelines 2017, para. 6.40. In German accounting and tax law, the described circumstance is usually defined as economic ownership, see in more detail *Wenzel*, in: Kroppen/Rasch (Eds.), Handbuch Internationale Verrechnungspreise, OECD-Kap VI, para. 271.

[294] Cf. OECD, TP Guidelines 2017, para. 6.42.

[295] Cf. OECD, TP Guidelines 2017, para. 6.32. Since difficulties may arise in finding comparable transactions for such functions, the compensation of MNE group members may take the form of a particular share of the profits which may require the use of the transactional profit split methods, ex ante valuations or other methods that take both sides of the transaction into account, cf. OECD, TP Guidelines 2017, paras. 6.57 et seq.; *Collier/Andrus*, Transfer Pricing and the Arm's Length Principle after BEPS, para. 6.64.

[296] Cf. *Schön*, BTR 2015, 417 (419).

[297] Cf. *Schön*, BTR 2015, 417 (419).

In this context, the OECD puts strong emphasis on the notion of control over the DEMPE functions and highlights that certain important functions entailed by the DEMPE concept have special significance and therefore deserve particularly sizable compensation if performed by other members of the MNE group.[298] Functions of special significance may include: control and management of budgets, strategic design and control of research and marketing programmes, strategic decisions regarding intangible development programmes, direction of and establishing priorities for creative undertakings including determining the course of 'blue-sky' research, decisions regarding defence and protection of intangibles as well as ongoing quality control over the functions performed by independent or associated enterprises that may have material effects on the value of intangibles.[299] Since the actual performance and control of DEMPE functions by the members of the MNE group determines the ultimate entitlement of intangible related return, in literature the term 'functional ownership' is used describing the actual conduct of functions with respect to DEMPE of intangibles.[300]

Even though chapter VI of the TP Guidelines 2017 does not mention the concept of economic ownership which, as examined earlier, is the decisive concept for the attribution of intangibles to a PE, similarities between the newly introduced DEMPE concept (or 'functional ownership') and the concept of economic ownership exist. While the PE Report 2010 puts strong emphasis on the active decision-making with respect to the taking on and the corresponding management of risks that are associated with the intangible in order to attribute intangibles to a PE, the newly developed chapter VI of the TP Guidelines 2017 emphasises that intangible-related return should be based on the performance or control of DEMPE functions related to intangibles. A comparison of the functions relevant for the attribution of economic ownership to a PE and the DEMPE functions relevant for the entitlement to return from the exploitation of the intangible reveals that a majority of the remunerated functions in the PE Report 2010[301] and the TP Guidelines 2017[302] overlap.

---

298 Cf. OECD, TP Guidelines 2017, paras. 6.50 et seqq. For variations of the DEMPE concept used, e.g., by the UN or China see in more detail *Dziwiński/Peng*, in: Lang/Storck/Petruzzi/Risse (Eds.), 3 (12 et seq.). Critical with regard to the DEMPE concept cf. *Kroppen/Eigelshoven*, TPI 2019, 2 (3); *Kroppen/Dawid/Keil*, TPI 2019, 98 (101 et seq.).

299 Cf. OECD, TP Guidelines 2017, para. 6.56.

300 Cf. *Dziwiński/Peng*, in: Lang/Storck/Petruzzi/Risse (Eds.), 3 (10 et seq.).

301 Cf. OECD, PE Report 2010, Part I, paras. 88 et seqq.

302 Cf. OECD, TP Guidelines 2017, paras. 6.50 et seqq.

Despite the fact that the concept of economic ownership in the PE context and the DEMPE concept are not aligned and serve a different purpose (economic ownership: attribution of intangibles in the PE context vs. DEMPE concept: determination of an arm's length return based on the performance and control of important functions by members of the MNE group), the new and detailed guidance in the TP Guidelines 2017 may provide valuable additional assistance in the PE context, both for the attribution of intangibles to the PE (first step of the AOA) and the determination of an arm's length compensation between the PE and the other parts of the enterprise (second step of the AOA).[303]

iv. Modifications Affecting the Attribution of Risks

As explicitly outlined in the final report, BEPS Actions 9 and 10 mandate the development of 'rules to prevent BEPS by transferring risks among, or allocating excessive capital to, group members. This will involve adopting transfer pricing rules or special measures to ensure that inappropriate returns will not accrue to an entity solely because it has contractually assumed risks or has provided capital.'[304]

In the pre-BEPS era, the contractual allocation of risk between associated enterprises was respected as the parties agreed to in the contract unless the economic substance of the respective transaction differed from the contractual agreement.[305] In that case, the allocation of risks was determined in line with the 'control over risk' approach,[306] which was regarded as an exception rather than a standard in the context of Article 9 OECD MC.[307] In this regard, the term 'control' is defined by the OECD TP Guidelines 2010 as 'the capacity to make decisions to take on the risk (decision to put the capital at risk) and decisions on whether and how to manage the risk, internally or using an external provider'[308].

In the post-BEPS era, contractual arrangements between associated enterprises still play a pivotal role, just as they do in the context of intangibles, since they are the starting point when it comes to the determination of how the respective parties to the transaction allocate risk.[309] However, in the post-BEPS era, the

[303] Cf. also *Nientimp/Stein/Schwarz/Holinski*, BB 2017, 407 (409); *Böhmer*, in: W/A/D (Eds.), Betriebsstätten-Handbuch, para. 14.143.

[304] OECD, BEPS Actions 8–10: Final Report 2015, p. 13.

[305] Cf. OECD, TP Guidelines 2010, para. 1.49.

[306] For an example see OECD, TP Guidelines 2010, para. 9.21.

[307] Cf. *Tracana*, Intertax 2017, 411 (414).

[308] OECD, TP Guidelines 2010, para. 9.23.

[309] Cf. OECD, TP Guidelines 2017, para. 1.42; *Tracana*, Intertax 2017, 411 (414).

question of whether the contractual allocation of risk is at arm's length is not only tested if a lack of economic substance can be identified, but rather in all situations.[310] Therefore, the TP Guidelines 2017 employ a reshaped 'control over risk' approach, which focuses on the identification of the actual performance of the 'decision-making function' and the financial capacity to assume the risk.[311] More precisely, the performance of the decision-making function requires people who are experienced and knowledgeable in the area of the particular risk and who possess an understanding of the impact their decision has on the business to actually perform such functions.[312]

Given the mandate of BEPS Actions 9 and 10 to prevent base erosion and profit shifting by transferring risks among group members, the approach of the OECD to base the question on whether an enterprise carries out the functions relevant to have the control over the risk on the performance of the actual decision-making function can be regarded as well-chosen since it cannot be manipulated easily.[313] It is fairly obvious that the developments in this regard are not novel, since this concept very closely employs the approach of the AOA, according to which a PE assumes any risk for which the significant people functions crucial to the assumption of such risk are performed by the relevant personnel of the PE.[314] Significant people functions decisive for the assumption of risk according to the AOA are those which require 'active decision-making' by the personnel regarding the acceptance and/or management of such risks.

Besides minor differences in the wording ('decision making' vs. 'active decision making')[315] and other deviations linked to the legal differences between

---

[310]Cf. *Tracana*, Intertax 2017, 411 (414). It is argued that the departure from contractual arrangements in favour of a more substance-based approach goes even beyond the arm's length principle and contains characteristics of the formulary apportionment approach, cf. *Schön*, BIT 2014, 280 (286).

[311]Cf. detailed on the reshaped 'control over risk' approach OECD, TP Guidelines 2017, paras. 1.61 et seqq.

[312]Cf. OECD, TP Guidelines 2017, para. 1.66.

[313]See also *Petruzzi/Peng*, TPI 2017, 110 (111); critical *Schön*, StuW 2015, 69 (82 et seqq.); critical also *Heggmair* who expressed the concern that 'local tax authorities will feel encouraged to reallocate risks—and, accordingly, ownership of intangible assets—to local entities more or less based simply on their subjective evaluation of local people's activities', *Heggmair*, ITPJ 2017, 263 (266).

[314]Cf. OECD, PE Report 2010, Part I, para. 68.

[315]The comments from PwC suggest that the difference in the wording, more precisely the additional word 'active', might also lead to differences with regard to the attributions of risks: 'In the case of the SPF concept, our interpretation is there seems to be a much greater focus on the decision-making being active if it is to count for SPF identification, including the

associated enterprises and a PE,[316] the developments through BEPS Actions 9 and 10 result in the situation that the approach to allocate risk under Article 9 OECD MC and Article 7 OECD MC can be described as rather similar.[317] Consequently, situations may occur where the risk control function under Article 9 OECD MC overlaps with the concept of the significant people function used to attribute risk to the PE under Article 7 OECD MC.[318] However, as explicitly emphasised by the OECD, the two concepts are not aligned and can therefore not be used interchangeably.[319] It is further elaborated that, in order to avoid double taxation, risk that has already been attributed under Article 9 OECD MC cannot be attributed again under Article 7 OECD MC.[320] Additional comments with regard to the similarities and distinctions between the two concepts are neither provided by the Final Report on BEPS Actions 8–10 nor by the additional guidance on BEPS Action 7 of the OECD, which leaves the question unanswered whether the guidance developed under BEPS Actions 9 and 10 may be applicable in the PE context, especially in the absence of more detailed guidance on the definition of the significant people function for the attribution of risks in certain cases. Even though it is argued in literature that the guidance developed under BEPS Actions 9 and 10 can be regarded applicable in the PE context to the extent that the

suggestion that economic ownership of assets and risks will often be determined by functions performed below the strategic level of senior management given that this is the level at which the active management occurs and where the ability to actively manage the risk lies.', OECD, BEPS Action 7: Comments on Discussion Draft (Part II), p. 311. Critical in this regard also *Gonnet*, in: Lang/Storck/Petruzzi (Eds.), Transfer Pricing in a Post-BEPS World, 33 (39).

316 As outlined above, in order for an enterprise to have the 'control over risk', it must also have the financial capacity to assume such risk. In contrast, under the AOA capital is attributed to the PE after assets and risks are attributed. In this context, the amount of capital attributable to the PE must be sufficient in order to support the functions performed, the risks assumed and the assets used and is seen as a cushion against crystallisation of risk. In other words, capital needed to support the risks assumed by the PE is to be attributed to the PE by reference to the risks which are attributed to it ('capital follows risk'). See in more detail in this regard *Tracana*, Intertax 2017, 411 (415).

317 Cf. *Petruzzi/Peng*, TPI 2017, 110 (112); *Tracana*, Intertax 2017, 411 (415); *Gonnet*, in: Lang/Storck/Petruzzi (Eds.), Transfer Pricing in a Post-BEPS World, 33 (39). In this context, see especially the comments from PwC where it is emphasised that for the purpose of practical application of Article 7 OECD MC and Article 9 OECD MC it could be argued that 'the risk control threshold required as part of the Article 9 analysis is equivalent to the SPF threshold required through the AOA', cf. OECD, BEPS Action 7: Comments on Discussion Draft (Part II), p. 311.

318 Cf. OECD, BEPS Action 7: Additional Guidance 2018, para. 41.

319 Cf. OECD, BEPS Action 7: Additional Guidance 2018, para. 40.

320 Cf. OECD, BEPS Action 7: Additional Guidance 2018, para. 41.

deviations rooted in the legal differences between associated enterprises and the PE are taken into account,[321] the new guidance issued by the OECD suggests a different view.[322]

v. Modifications Affecting the Capital Attribution

Despite the fact that the BEPS Action plan does not specifically deal with any of the four capital allocation approaches suggested by the OECD in the PE Report 2010, the work of the OECD on other aspects of the BEPS Action plan might also be of value for the attribution of capital in the PE context.

One of the basic principles for the attribution of capital to the PE is that 'capital follows risk'[323]. Put differently, the part of the enterprise that carries out the significant people functions relevant to the risk assumption shall be attributed the capital necessary to support such risks.[324] Consequently, the additional guidelines introduced by the OECD through BEPS Actions 8–10, which, among others, aim 'to prevent BEPS by transferring risks among, or allocating excessive capital to, group members'[325], might influence the amount of capital attributed to the PE. Especially, the new guidance on the allocation of risk, which, as outlined in the previous chapter, emphasises that risk that has already been attributed under Article 9 OECD MC cannot be attributed again under Article 7 OECD MC and the examples provided by the additional guidelines on BEPS Action 7 may also impact the amount of capital attributed to the PE.

Furthermore, the additional guidance for the application of the transactional profit split method (hereinafter: TPSM), which was developed as part of Action 10 of the BEPS Action plan, may also be of help in this regard.[326] As outlined by *Petruzzi/Peng*, 'one may borrow the profit splitting factors applied in the profit split method, which represent the relative value of the contributions made by the different parts of the enterprise in the notional dealing, in a contribution analysis for the use of attributing capital to the PE'[327]. However, while this approach may be of practical help, it is not considered one of the four authorised OECD

[321] Cf. *Tracana*, Intertax 2017, 411 (416).

[322] Cf. OECD, BEPS Action 7: Additional Guidance 2018, paras. 40 et seqq. Critical also *Gonnet*, in: Lang/Storck/Petruzzi (Eds.), Transfer Pricing in a Post-BEPS World, 33 (39).

[323] OECD, PE Report 2010, Part I, para. 26.

[324] Cf. OECD, PE Report 2010, Part I, para. 26.

[325] OECD, BEPS Actions 8–10: Final Report 2015, p. 13.

[326] Cf. OECD, BEPS Action 10: Revised Guidance on TPSM 2018. See in more detail with regard to the changes made to the TPSM through BEPS chapter D.I.4.b.(3)(d)iii of this thesis.

[327] *Petruzzi/Peng*, TPI 2017, 168 (169).

approaches for capital attribution to the PE.[328] Consequently, the taxpayer may face legal uncertainty when applying this method for capital attribution to the PE, especially if tax authorities of the jurisdictions where the enterprise operates share different views with regard to the applicability of the approach.

vi. Interim Conclusion

Overall, it has become evident that the guidance developed under BEPS Actions 8–10 and implemented in the TP Guidelines 2017 undoubtedly influences certain aspects of the first step of the AOA. This influence is due to the fact that the PE Report 2010 either directly refers to certain aspects of the TP Guidelines which can be applied fairly directly in the PE context (e.g. guidance regarding the functional and factual analysis)[329] or the limited guidance provided in the PE Report 2010 regarding certain aspects concerning the first step of the AOA makes the revised TP Guidelines 2017 a valuable additional source of guidance to the extent examined in the previous chapters (e.g. guidance regarding the definition of intangibles and its remuneration if used by another group member of the MNE as well as guidance regarding the allocation of risk and capital).

Against this background, two developments as a result of BEPS Actions 8–10 must be highlighted. First, the guidance developed in Section D of chapter I of the TP Guidelines 2017 refer to a value chain analysis which might be a valuable tool to use supplementing the functional and factual analysis in order to distinguish between important functions, assets and risks from less important ones.[330] Used in this context, it might improve the outcome of the functional and factual analysis as part of the first step of the AOA.

Second, a key takeaway from the BEPS project is the 'substance over form' approach adopted in the revised TP Guidelines. Accordingly, contractual arrangements between associated enterprises still play a pivotal role. However, as examined above, in the post-BEPS era a) the entitlement to intangible-related return should be based on the financial and functional (DEMPE) contributions to the value creation of intangibles (substance), and b) the allocation of risk should be determined on a reshaped 'control over risk' approach focusing on the identification of the actual performance of the 'decision-making function' performed by 'people' and the financial capacity to assume the risk (substance).

---

[328] See in more detail with regard to the four authorised OECD approaches for capital attribution to the PE chapter D.I.4.b.(2)(e)ii of this thesis.

[329] OECD, PE Report 2010, Part I, para. 61.

[330] Cf. OECD, BEPS Action 7: Comments on Discussion Draft (Part II), p. 345; *Petruzzi/Buriak*, TNI 90 (2018), 91 (102).

The developments under BEPS Actions 8–10 which were implemented in the TP Guidelines 2017 can be regarded as valuable and insightful. To the extent examined, the amended TP Guidelines should serve as additional guidance on certain aspects concerning the first step of the AOA. Overall, the developments bring the taxation of associated enterprises closer in line with the taxation of PE structures.

(3) Step 2: Pricing of Dealings

(a) Conceptual Approach

In the second step of the AOA, the recognised dealings between the PE and the other parts of the enterprise must be priced on an arm's length basis.[331] This approach requires a) the determination of comparability between dealings and uncontrolled transactions based on the functional and factual analysis, and b) the selection and application of the most appropriate transfer pricing method for the respective dealings between the PE and the other parts of the enterprise in order to arrive at an arm's length compensation for these dealings.[332]

While the PE Report 2010 provides detailed guidance with regard to the application of the second step of the AOA to commonly occurring dealings such as a change in the use of a tangible asset,[333] the use of intangibles,[334] cost contribution arrangements,[335] and internal services,[336] the general explanations with regard to the comparability analysis and the selection and application of the appropriate transfer pricing methods are rather short.[337] This is due to the fact that the PE Report 2010 refers with regard to the comparability analysis and the selection and

[331] Cf. OECD, PE Report 2010, Part I, para. 10. In this sense, also transactions between the PE and associated enterprises must be priced on an arm's length basis. However, the determination of comparability between such transactions and uncontrolled transactions and the selection and application of the most appropriate transfer pricing method to the circumstances of the case can be carried out by applying the TP Guidelines 2017, cf. OECD, PE Report 2010, Part I, para. 44. The following explanations focus on the pricing of the dealings between the PE and the rest of the enterprise.

[332] Cf. OECD, PE Report 2010, Part I, paras. 44, 67.

[333] Cf. OECD, PE Report 2010, Part I, paras. 194 et seqq.

[334] Cf. OECD, PE Report 2010, Part I, paras. 200 et seqq.

[335] Cf. OECD, PE Report 2010, Part I, paras. 211 et seqq.

[336] Cf. OECD, PE Report 2010, Part I, paras. 216 et seqq.

[337] For a detailed analysis of the four particular circumstances cf. *Delarber*, Steuerliche Einflüsse auf die grenzüberschreitende Betriebsstättenbesteuerung, 219 et seqq.; *Kaeser*, in: W/K/S/D (Eds.), Doppelbesteuerung, Art. 7 MA (2010), paras. 567 et seqq.; *Kroppen*, in: Kessler/Förster/Watrin (Eds.), Unternehmensbesteuerung—Festschrift Herzig, 1071 (1082 et seqq.); *Ditz*, in: Schönfeld/Ditz (Eds.), DBA-Kommentar, Art. 7 (2017), paras. 32 et seqq.;

application of the most appropriate transfer pricing method to the TP Guidelines which shall be applied by analogy.[338]

However, a direct application of the TP Guidelines with regard to the second step of the AOA is not possible since, as already indicated in the context of the first step of the AOA, the TP Guidelines are conceptualised for legally separated enterprises. Even though the PE is hypothesised as a separate and independent enterprise under the AOA, the fact remains that the head office and the PE belong to the same legal entity. Consequently, while e.g. the starting point for the comparability analysis between associated enterprises in the context of Article 9 OECD MC is usually the contractual terms the transacting parties agreed to, legally binding contractual agreements between the PE and another part of the enterprise do not exist. Instead, documental evidence such as internal documentation or accounting records plays a pivotal role.[339] It follows that in order to find comparable uncontrolled transactions in the PE context, a greater focus is necessary on activities performed by the PE's personnel in order to recognise a dealing properly and as a matter of fact to find out what the actual terms of a dealing are.[340] Despite such differences, the principles stated in the TP Guidelines can be applied for step 2 of the AOA to a great extent.[341]

(b) Comparability Analysis

The comparability analysis, which is 'at the heart of the application of the arm's length principle'[342], seeks to identify whether a dealing between the PE and the other parts of the enterprise can be compared to an uncontrolled transaction between independent enterprises.[343] In this context, the term comparability means that differences that may exist between the dealing and an uncontrolled transaction between independent enterprises do not affect the measure that is used to attribute profits to the PE materially, or in case the identified differences affect the attribution of profits to the PE materially, reasonable accurate adjustments (e.g.

Margerie, Gewinnermittlung und Gewinnabgrenzung bei Betriebsstätten, 169 et seqq.; *Looks*, in: Looks/Heinsen (Eds.), Betriebsstättenbesteuerung, paras. 913 et seqq.

[338] Cf. OECD, PE Report 2010, Part I, para. 183.

[339] Cf. OECD, PE Report 2010, Part I, para. 179.

[340] Cf. OECD, PE Report 2010, Part I, para. 190.

[341] Cf. *Tracana*, Intertax 2017, 411 (412 et seqq.).

[342] OECD, TP Guidelines 2017, para. 1.33.

[343] Cf. *Kaeser*, in: W/K/S/D (Eds.), Doppelbesteuerung, Art. 7 MA (2010), para. 562.

adjustments with regard to volume or the terms of transportation and insurance) can be made in order to eliminate such differences.[344]

Five factors are identified in the TP Guidelines which determine comparability between uncontrolled and controlled transactions: contractual terms,[345] functional analysis,[346] characteristics of property or services,[347] economic circumstances,[348] and business strategies[349]. With the exception of contractual terms which can only be observed between legally separate enterprises, the remaining four comparability factors can be applied directly in the PE context as they are essentially based on facts.[350] However, as explicitly mentioned in the TP Guidelines, '[t]he terms of a transaction may also be found in communications between the parties other than a written contract'[351]. Therefore, by analogy, in the PE context, the 'contractual terms' may be found in the accounting records or any contemporaneous internal documentation which refer to the transfer of risks, benefits and responsibilities from one part of the enterprise to another.[352]

With the 2010 update of the TP Guidelines, the OECD dedicated an entire new chapter to the topic of comparability and introduced, among other things, a well-developed nine-step approach that can be followed by the taxpayer when performing a comparability analysis. Accordingly, the following fundamental, non-linear steps which are rather considered as an accepted good practice, but not as a compulsory process, should be undertaken:[353]

- Step 1: Determine the years to be covered.
- Step 2: Carry out a broad-based analysis of the taxpayer's circumstances.[354]

[344]Cf. OECD, PE Report 2010, Part I, paras. 40, 183.

[345]Cf. OECD, TP Guidelines 2017, paras. 1.42 et seqq.

[346]Cf. OECD, TP Guidelines 2017, paras. 1.51 et seqq.

[347]Cf. OECD, TP Guidelines 2017, paras. 1.107 et seqq.

[348]Cf. OECD, TP Guidelines 2017, paras. 1.110 et seqq.

[349]Cf. OECD, TP Guidelines 2017, paras. 1.114 et seqq.

[350]Cf. PE Report 2010, Part I, para. 190.

[351]OECD, TP Guidelines 2017, para. 1.42.

[352]Cf. OECD, PE Report 2010, Part I, para. 179; also *Kaeser*, in: W/K/S/D (Eds.), Doppelbesteuerung, Art. 7 MA (2010), para. 549.

[353]Cf. OECD, TP Guidelines 2017, para. 3.4. Please note that the wording of the nine-step process was slightly adjusted in order to be directly applicable in the PE context.

[354]See in more detail OECD, TP Guidelines 2017, para. 3.7.

- Step 3: Understand the controlled transaction (dealing)[355] based on a functional analysis.[356]
- Step 4: Review the existing internal comparables (if any).[357]
- Step 5: Determine available sources of information on external comparables.[358]
- Step 6: Select the most appropriate transfer pricing method and determine the relevant financial indicators needed for the method chosen.[359]
- Step 7: Identify potential comparables.[360]
- Step 8: Determine and make comparability adjustments in cases where appropriate.[361]
- Step 9: Interpret and use the data collected and determine an arm's length remuneration.[362]

According to this process, the determination of the degree of comparability of the potential comparables identified as well as the performance of comparability adjustments shall be carried out after the most appropriate transfer pricing method has been selected and applied by the taxpayer. In the following, the main transfer pricing methods that are applicable in the PE context will be presented in more detail.

(c) Selection and Application of the Transfer Pricing Method

i. Fundamentals

In order to determine an appropriate compensation at arm's length for the dealings between the PE and the rest of the enterprise, the OECD refers to the application of the TP Guidelines that shall be applied in the PE context by analogy.[363] In principle, the TP Guidelines provide for the application of the traditional transfer pricing methods (comparable uncontrolled price method (hereinafter: CUP

---

[355] In the PE context, this step must be applied by analogy, meaning that not the controlled transaction(s) but the dealing(s) shall be understood based on the functional analysis.

[356] Detailed OECD, TP Guidelines 2017, paras. 3.8–3.23.

[357] Detailed OECD, TP Guidelines 2017, paras. 3.27–3.28.

[358] Detailed OECD, TP Guidelines 2017, paras. 3.29–3.39 et seqq.

[359] Detailed OECD, TP Guidelines 2017, paras. 2.1–2.155 et seqq.

[360] Detailed OECD, TP Guidelines 2017, paras. 3.40–3.46 et seqq.

[361] Detailed OECD, TP Guidelines 2017, paras. 3.47–3-54 et seqq.

[362] Detailed OECD, TP Guidelines 2017, paras. 3.55–3.66 et seqq.

[363] Cf. OECD, PE Report 2010, Part I, para. 39.

method)[364], resale price method[365], cost plus method[366]) and the transactional profit methods (transactional net margin method (hereinafter: TNMM)[367], TPSM[368]).

In the 1995-version of the OECD TP Guidelines it is pointed out that the transactional profit methods were considered as methods of last resort which can only be applied in exceptional circumstances.[369] Consequently, the TP Guidelines 1995 contained a clear preference of the traditional transfer pricing methods over the transactional profit methods.[370] With the update of the TP Guidelines on 22 July 2010, this hierarchy was eliminated and replaced by the concept of the 'most appropriate method for a particular case'[371].[372] In other words, the taxpayer can choose a transfer pricing method in order to arrive at an arm's length compensation for the dealings that suit the circumstances of the particular case best.[373]

As a consequence, cases are possible where the application of transactional profit methods are more appropriate than a traditional transfer pricing method, e.g. in situations where both parties of the transaction make valuable and unique contributions in relation to the controlled transaction.[374] Nevertheless, in situations in which a traditional transfer pricing method and a transactional profit method can be applied in an equally reliable manner, the OECD points out that the application of the traditional transfer pricing method is preferable.[375] Moreover, the

[364] Detailed OECD, TP Guidelines 2017, paras. 2.14 et seqq.

[365] Detailed OECD, TP Guidelines 2017, paras. 2.27 et seqq.

[366] Detailed OECD, TP Guidelines 2017, paras. 2.45 et seqq.

[367] Detailed OECD, TP Guidelines 2017, paras. 2.64 et seqq.

[368] Detailed OECD, TP Guidelines 2017, paras. 2.114 et seqq.

[369] Cf. OECD, TP Guidelines 1995, para. 3.50.

[370] Cf. OECD, TP Guidelines 1995, paras. 2.49, 3.49; for same conclusion cf. *Kofler,* in: Reimer/Rust (Eds.), Klaus Vogel on Double Taxation Conventions, Art. 9, para. 78. For an overview of the historical development and a detailed analysis of the hierarchy of the transfer pricing methods in the 1979-version and 1995-version of the TP Guidelines see *Ahmadov*, ITPJ 2011, 184 (184 et seqq.).

[371] Cf. OECD, TP Guidelines 2017, para. 2.2.

[372] Cf. in more detail for the revision of the TP Guidelines in 2010 *Förster*, IStR 2009, 720 (720 et seqq.); *Förster*, IStR 2011, 20 (20 et seqq.); *Rasch/Feistle*, IWB 2009, 982 (982 et seqq.); *Kurzewitz*, IWB 2010, 95 (95 et seqq.); *Luckhaupt*, Ubg 2010, 646 (646 et seqq.).

[373] Cf. OECD, TP Guidelines 2017, para. 2.2.

[374] Cf. OECD, TP Guidelines 2017, para. 2.4.

[375] Cf. OECD, TP Guidelines 2017, para. 2.3.

CUP method is preferred over all other methods if applicable in an equally reliable manner.[376]

There is no need to decide for one single method for the remuneration of the identified dealings between the PE and the other parts of the enterprise.[377] Rather, different methods can be applied to different dealings, depending on the individual circumstances of the dealing examined. When selecting the transfer pricing method for a particular dealing, several factors should be considered, such as the appropriateness of the method in view of the nature of the dealing, the availability of reliable data on uncontrolled transactions, the degree of comparability between the dealing and the uncontrolled transactions (taking into account comparability adjustments needed in order to eliminate material differences between the dealing and the uncontrolled transactions), as well as the particular strengths and weaknesses of the transfer pricing methods.[378]

In the following, the different methods shall be discussed briefly and put in more precise terms with regard to their applicability for dealings between the PE and other parts of the enterprise. In the following, a distinction is made between the traditional transfer pricing methods and the transactional profit methods.

ii. Traditional Transfer Pricing Methods

01 Comparable Uncontrolled Price Method

The CUP method derives the transfer price from prices charged for the same or a comparable property or services to third parties in comparable circumstances.[379] This price is then compared to the price charged for the dealing between the PE and the other part of the enterprise. Differences between the prices may indicate that the conditions of the financial and commercial relations are not at arm's length and that the price charged for the dealing may need to be substituted for tax purposes by the price charged to third parties.[380] Difficulties with regard to this method arise in circumstances where prices for the exact same property or services cannot be observed or reasonable reliable comparability adjustments cannot be made.[381] Such adjustments might be necessary in cases where, e.g., the

---

[376] Cf. OECD, TP Guidelines 2017, para. 2.3.

[377] Cf. *Kaeser*, in: W/K/S/D (Eds.), Doppelbesteuerung, Art. 7 MA (2010), para. 554.

[378] Cf. OECD, TP Guidelines 2017, para. 2.2.

[379] Cf. OECD, TP Guidelines 2017, para. 2.14.

[380] Cf. *Kofler*, in: Reimer/Rust (Eds.), Klaus Vogel on Double Taxation Conventions, Art. 9, para. 82.

[381] Cf. *Kaeser*, in: W/K/S/D (Eds.), Doppelbesteuerung, Art. 7 MA (2010), para. 555; *Kofler*, in: Reimer/Rust (Eds.), Klaus Vogel on Double Taxation Conventions, Art. 9, para. 82; OECD,

comparable third party operates in a different country, the quantity of the comparable property or service sold varies; specific supplementary service agreement or warranty extensions were agreed upon which might influence the price agreed upon.[382]

The OECD exemplifies the use of this method in the PE context by means of a PE that purchases products from its head office which were also manufactured by the head office and then sold to third parties.[383] In case these products are also sold to third party distributors operating in comparable circumstances to those of the PE, the price charged to these third party distributors might be used as the 'comparable uncontrolled price'.[384] The profit that can be attributed to the PE in that case is determined by deducting the price notionally charged by the head office for the products sold to the PE from the revenues attributed to the PE from third party customer sales.[385] In case the price notionally charged by the head office for the products sold to the PE is not at arm's length, adjustments are necessary.

02. Resale Price Method

The resale price method derives the arm's length price that shall be charged for a specific dealing between the PE and another part of the enterprise, for tax purposes, by looking at an independent third-party customer sales price for the product which is deemed purchased by the PE and then deducts an arm's length gross margin—the so-called 'resale price margin' from the market-based resale price of that product.[386] In this respect, the gross margin represents the amount out of which an independent third-party reseller operating in comparable circumstances would seek to cover the costs for the sale and all other operating expenses incurred and, in consideration of the functions performed, make an appropriate

---

TP Guidelines 2017, para. 2.17. For further difficulties that arise with regard to this method cf. *Wittendorff*, Transfer Pricing and the Arm's Length Principle in International Tax Law, 713 et seq.; *Baumhoff*, in: Wassermeyer/Baumhoff (Eds.), Verrechnungspreise international verbundener Unternehmen, paras. 5.13 et seq.

[382]Cf. *Kaeser*, in: W/K/S/D (Eds.), Doppelbesteuerung, Art. 7 MA (2010), para. 555. For further details on comparability adjustments cf. *Wittendorff*, Transfer Pricing and the Arm's Length Principle in International Tax Law, 715 et seq.; OECD, TP Guidelines 2017, paras. 3.47 et seqq.

[383]Cf. OECD, PE Report 2010, Part I, para. 185.

[384]Cf. OECD, PE Report 2010, Part I, para. 185.

[385]Cf. OECD, PE Report 2010, Part I, para. 185.

[386]Cf. OECD, TP Guidelines 2017, para. 2.27.

profit.[387] As outlined in the TP Guidelines, this method is most useful when it is applied to marketing operations,[388] and easiest applied in circumstances where the reseller of the product does not add significantly to the value of the respective product.[389]

With regard to the example illustrated above, in which the PE distributes products produced by the head office to independent third parties, the resale price method is easiest to apply if the PE does not carry out any significant people functions besides the distribution function, since gross margins for mere distribution activities are easy to obtain from databases.[390]

03. Cost Plus Method

The cost plus method starts with the costs incurred by the supplier of services or property in a controlled transaction/dealing for services provided or property transferred to an associated purchaser and then adds an appropriate cost plus mark-up to the incurred costs of the supplier.[391] The cost plus mark-up compensates the part of the enterprise which sells the services or property for the costs of services or property sold and leaves an appropriate profit reflecting the functions performed (taking into account the assets used and risks assumed) and the market conditions.[392] Ideally, the cost plus mark-up should be established by reference to internal comparables, while external comparables can serve as a guide.[393] After the cost plus mark-up is added to the costs incurred, the result can be regarded as an arm's length price of the original dealing.[394]

This method can also be applied with regard to the example illustrated above. However, an application is only appropriate if the PE does not only act as a mere distributor for the products manufactured and supplied by the head office.[395] More

---

[387] Cf. OECD, TP Guidelines 2017, para. 2.27.

[388] Cf. OECD, TP Guidelines 2017, para. 2.27.

[389] Cf. OECD, TP Guidelines 2017, para. 2.35.

[390] Cf. *Baumhoff*, in: Wassermeyer/Baumhoff (Eds.), Verrechnungspreise international verbundener Unternehmen, para. 5.31; *Cousins*, in: Heimert/Michaelson/Duff&Phelps (Eds.), Guide to International Transfer Pricing, § 2.01 [B], 77; *Kaeser*, in: W/K/S/D (Eds.), Doppelbesteuerung, Art. 7 MA (2010), para. 556.

[391] Cf. OECD, TP Guidelines 2017, para. 2.45.

[392] Cf. OECD, TP Guidelines 2017, para. 2.45, also *Wittendorff*, Transfer Pricing and the Arm's Length Principle in International Tax Law, 726.

[393] Cf. *Kofler*, in: Reimer/Rust (Eds.), Klaus Vogel on Double Taxation Conventions, Art. 9, para. 84; OECD, TP Guidelines 2017, para. 2.46.

[394] Cf. OECD, TP Guidelines 2017, para. 2.45.

[395] Cf. OECD, PE Report 2010, Part I, para. 186.

precisely, in circumstances in which the functional and factual analysis reveals that the PE performs significant people functions that add significant value to the product (e.g. in case a valuable marketing intangible associated with the product is attributed to the PE since the PE carries out significant people functions associated with the marketing intangibles) and as a consequence also assumes higher risks then the mere distribution risks, the application of the cost plus method might be appropriate to determine the notional price of the transfer of goods from the head office to the PE.[396]

In the PE context, the cost plus method is most useful where semi-finished goods are sold between the PE and another part of the enterprise, where the PE and another part of the enterprise have long term buy-and-supply arrangements or where services are provided between the PE and another part of the enterprise.[397]

iii. Transactional Profit Methods

01. Transactional Net Margin Method

The TNMM is closely related to the above explained resale price method and the cost plus method.[398] However, while these two transactional transfer pricing methods consider gross margins, the TNMM focuses on net profit indicators.[399] More specifically, in the PE context the TNMM derives the net margin for a specific dealing between the PE and another part of the enterprise from the net margin which the PE earns in comparable transactions with third parties (internal comparables) or if such data is not available, the net margin for a specific dealing can be derived from the net margin that would have been earned by third parties in a comparable transaction (external comparables).[400] The net margin usually relates to the ratio of a profit indicator, e.g. operating income or EBIT to a) sales (so-called sales margin), b) full or partial costs (so-called profit margin or

---

[396] Cf. OECD, PE Report 2010, Part I, para. 186.

[397] Cf. *Looks*, in: Looks/Heinsen (Eds.), Betriebsstättenbesteuerung, para. 908. With regard to the applicability of the cost plus method for associated enterprises see OECD, TP Guidelines 2017, para. 2.45; *Kofler*, in: Reimer/Rust (Eds.), Klaus Vogel on Double Taxation Conventions, Art. 9, para. 84; *Baumhoff*, in: Wassermeyer/Baumhoff (Eds.), Verrechnungspreise international verbundener Unternehmen, para. 5.40.

[398] Cf. OECD, TP Guidelines 2017, para. 2.64.

[399] Cf. *Luckhaupt/Overesch/Schreiber*, in: Schön/Konrad (Eds.), Fundamentals of International Transfer Pricing in Law and Economics, 91 (104).

[400] Cf. OECD, TP Guidelines 2017, para. 2.64.

'Berry ratio'[401]) or c) capital employed (so-called return on assets or return on net assets).[402]

Since the TNMM belongs to the one-sided methods, it may be applied in cases where only one party to the dealing makes all the valuable and unique contributions, while the other party to the dealing does not make such contributions, e.g. uses non-unique intangibles like non-unique market knowledge or non-unique business processes.[403] It follows that this method is usually not appropriate in cases where each party to a dealing makes valuable and unique contributions and in cases where both parties perform a multitude of functions.[404] For such highly integrated dealings the application of the TPSM will probably be most appropriate.[405]

02. Transactional Profit Split Method

Even though the TPSM belongs to one of the five authorised transfer pricing methods of the OECD, it is quite different from the other four methods illustrated before. First of all, the TPSM is—in contrast to the other four methods—a two-sided method.[406] This means that both sides of the dealing, the PE and the other part of the enterprise, are considered to access their relative contributions. Consequently, it boasts of being a more reliable proxy of business reality.[407] Secondly, the TPSM is a profit-based method which is regarded to be the least direct method among the authorised transfer pricing methods.[408]

---

[401] The Berry ratio is usually applied with regard to distribution enterprises and is defined as the ratio of gross profit to operating expenses. See in more detail OECD, TP Guidelines 2017, paras. 2.106 et seqq.; also *Oestreicher/Vormoor*, IStR 2004, 95 (103); *Jacobs*, Internationale Unternehmensbesteuerung, 579; *Wittendorff*, Transfer Pricing and the Arm's Length Principle in International Tax Law, 745 et seq.

[402] Cf. *Ditz*, in: W/A/D (Eds.), Betriebsstätten-Handbuch, para. 6.203.

[403] Cf. OECD, TP Guidelines 2017, paras. 2.65 et seq.

[404] Cf. OECD, TP Guidelines 2017, para. 2.65.

[405] Cf. OECD, TP Guidelines 2017, para. 2.65. For strengths and weaknesses of this method see OECD, TP Guidelines 2017, paras. 2.68 et seqq.

[406] Cf. OECD, TP Guidelines 2017, 2.119 et seqq. (as amended through BEPS Action 10 in 2018). Due to the fact that the functional and factual analysis, which must be conducted in accordance with the OECD TP Guidelines, is a two-sided approach anyhow, some practitioners argue that the threshold between one and two-sided methods is diminished, cf. *Petruzzi/Peng*, TPI 2017, 44 (44, note 2).

[407] Cf. *Petruzzi/Peng*, TPI 2017, 44 (44).

[408] Cf. *Petruzzi/Peng*, TPI 2017, 44 (44); *Petruzzi*, in: Lang/Storck/Petruzzi (Eds.), Transfer Pricing in a Post-BEPS World, 1 (25). For strengths and weaknesses of the TPSM see OECD, TP Guidelines 2017, 2.119 et seqq. (as amended through BEPS Action 10 in 2018).

The TPSM follows a two-step procedure. In a first step, the combined profit which results from the dealing between the PE and the other part of the enterprise is identified and then, in a second step, splits the combined profit between the parties involved in the dealing.[409] In this regard, the combined profit should be split in relation to the profits that unrelated third parties would expect in comparable transactions.[410]

The TPSM can normally be applied by means of two approaches, depending on the information available and the specific characteristics of the dealing.[411] Most commonly, the 'contribution analysis' and the 'residual analysis' are used in this context.[412] However, the economic rationale of both approaches is slightly different.[413] Under the contribution analysis, on the one side, the combined profits derived from a dealing are allocated between the PE and the other part of the enterprise in a single step, based upon the functions performed, assets attributed and risks assumed by the respective parts of the enterprise.[414] While there is a broad agreement that the actual profit split shall be based upon a functional analysis of the contributions by the parties, the approach by which the value of the parties' contributions is quantified is controversial.[415] In practice, possible

---

[409]Cf. OECD, TP Guidelines 2017, para. 2.114 (as amended through BEPS Action 10 in 2018). For a detailed discussion of how to determine the profits to be split cf. OECD, TP Guidelines 2017, paras. 2.154 et seqq. (as amended through BEPS Action 10 in 2018); also *Wittendorff*, Transfer Pricing and the Arm's Length Principle in International Tax Law, 756 et seqq.; *Dawid*, in: Kroppen/Rasch (Eds.), Handbuch Internationale Verrechnungspreise, OECD-Kap. II, para. 465.

[410]Cf. OECD, TP Guidelines 2017, para. 2.114 (as amended through BEPS Action 10 in 2018).

[411]Despite the fact that various approaches exist, the OECD only discusses the Contribution Analysis and the Residual Profit Split Method, cf. OECD, TP Guidelines 2017, paras. 2.149 et seqq. (as amended through BEPS Action 10 in 2018). Other possible approaches are, e.g., the Capital Employed Method or the Comparable Profit Split Method, see in more detail *Ditz*, in: W/A/D (Eds.), Betriebsstätten-Handbuch, para. 6.207.

[412]Cf. *Luckhaupt/Overesch/Schreiber*, in: Schön/Konrad (Eds.), Fundamentals of International Transfer Pricing in Law and Economics, 91 (105).

[413]Cf. *Petruzzi/Peng*, TPI 2017, 44 (44).

[414]Cf. *Wittendorff*, Transfer Pricing and the Arm's Length Principle in International Tax Law, 763.

[415]Cf. OECD, BEPS Actions 8–10: Final Report 2015, p. 59, para. 13. Detailed in this regard *Chand/Wagh*, ITPJ 2014, 402 (402). *Bilaney* suggests the use of economic theory, such as game theory as profit splitting factor, cf. *Bilaney*, BIT 2017, 239 (241 et seq.). For a discussion on adopting economic-based approaches cf. *Petruzzi/Peng*, TPI 2017, 44 (52 et seqq.).

mechanisms include functional contributions, costs, invested capital, weighting of factors and equalised expected rates of return.[416]

Under the residual analysis, on the other side, the combined profits are divided into two categories, which are attributed to the participants of the dealing. Profits attributable to contributions which can be benchmarked on a reliable basis, typically less complex contributions, are in the first category.[417] This initial remuneration can be determined by the application of the one-sided methods discussed above, such as the CUP method, the resale price method, the cost plus method or the TNMM.[418] The second category of contributions consists of valuable and unique contributions and/or is attributable to the shared assumption of economically significant risks or to a high level of integration.[419] Since the mechanism for the splitting of profits for the contributions of the second category is no different from the contribution analysis, the aforementioned difficulties also occur in this context.[420] The residual analysis may be preferred to the contribution analysis in circumstances where one party makes less complex contributions to the dealing, but which are capable of being benchmarked through a reference to uncontrolled transactions which are comparable.[421]

Compared to the other four authorised transfer pricing methods of the OECD, the application of the TPSM provides certain advantages. In essence, the TPSM offers flexibility by taking specific and unique facts and circumstances of the associated enterprises into account that may not be observed in independent enterprises.[422] A further strength is that the method does not generate any extreme and improbable profit splitting results, since both parties of the transaction are directly

---

416 Cf. OECD, BEPS Actions 8–10: Final Report 2015, p. 59, para. 13.

417 Cf. OECD, TP Guidelines 2017, para. 2.152 (as amended through BEPS Action 10 in 2018).

418 Cf. OECD, TP Guidelines 2017, para. 2.152 (as amended through BEPS Action 10 in 2018).

419 Cf. OECD, TP Guidelines 2017, para. 2.152 (as amended through BEPS Action 10 in 2018).

420 With regard to the mechanism of the residual analysis cf. *Petruzzi/Peng*, TPI 2017, 44 (44); *Higinbotham*, Tax Management Transfer Pricing Special Report 1996, 1 (4).

421 Cf. OECD, TP Guidelines 2017, para. 2.149 (as amended through BEPS Action 10 in 2018).

422 Cf. OECD, TP Guidelines 2017, para. 2.121 (as amended through BEPS Action 10 in 2018).

evaluated.[423] Therefore, tax authorities tend to favour the use of this method in order to settle tax disputes.[424]

(d) Analysis of the Modifications to the TP Guidelines through BEPS Actions 8-10 Affecting Step 2 of the AOA

i. Overview

Due to the fact that the TP Guidelines shall be applied in the PE context by analogy,[425] modifications to the TP Guidelines also effect the second step of the AOA. As illustrated before, the work of the OECD on BEPS Actions 8–10 focused on certain shortcomings of the existing TP Guidelines, especially with regard to the interpretation of the arm's length principle. The corresponding amendments to the TP Guidelines were approved by the OECD Council on 23 May 2016. The follow-up work set out in the report on BEPS Actions 8–10 for revised guidance on the application of the TPSM was published on 21 June 2018.[426] This guidance was incorporated into the TP Guidelines, replacing the previous Section C of Part III, chapter II on the TPSM.

The following explanations focus on the revisions made to the TP Guidelines, which have an impact on key areas of the second step of the AOA, namely the comparability analysis and the selection and application of the transfer pricing methods.

ii. Modifications Affecting the Comparability Analysis

Relevant changes to the TP Guidelines 2017 as a result of the work under BEPS Actions 8–10, which also affect the comparability analysis in the PE context, can be identified in several areas (comparability adjustments for location savings and local market features[427], assembled workforce[428], group synergies[429]). In this

---

[423] Cf. OECD, TP Guidelines 2017, para. 2.122 (as amended through BEPS Action 10 in 2018).

[424] Cf. *Peng*, ITPJ 2016, 378 (384); *Petruzzi/Peng*, TPI 2017, 44 (44).

[425] Cf. OECD, PE Report 2010, Part I, para. 10.

[426] Cf. OECD, BEPS Action 10: Revised Guidance on TPSM 2018.

[427] Cf. OECD, TP Guidelines 2017, paras. 1.139 et seqq.

[428] Cf. OECD, TP Guidelines 2017, paras. 1.152 et seqq.

[429] Cf. OECD, TP Guidelines 2017, paras. 1.157 et seqq.

context, the following explanations focus on a) the need of comparability adjustments for group synergies[430], location savings and other local market features within MNEs, and b) changes with regard to the reliance on the comparability analysis in general.

While the TP Guidelines 2010 already acknowledged that due to the narrow, transaction-based scope of the comparability analysis, the arm's length principle 'may not always account for the economies of scale and interrelation of diverse activities created by integrated businesses'[431], no guidance for the consideration of such synergies was provided in the TP Guidelines 2010.[432] This lack is explicitly addressed in the revised TP Guidelines 2017.[433] Therein, it is clarified that group synergies, e.g. implicit support that arises entirely from being part of an MNE, are usually incidental and, as a consequence, cannot be considered as intra-group services.[434] However, if synergies arise due to deliberate concerted group actions and constitute a clearly identifiable structural advantage or disadvantage over other market participants that are not part of the MNE, the benefits that arise out of such synergies should be shared by the members of the group in proportion to their respective contribution to the creation of the synergies.[435] As a starting point, the OECD suggests to seek for comparables from independent enterprises.[436] However, since it might be difficult to find comparables for such unique synergies, the TP Guidelines 2017 provide for a three-step approach in order to split the benefits or burdens that arise out of such synergies.[437] In a first step, the nature of the advantage or disadvantage must be identified; secondly the benefit

---

[430]In this regard, group synergies can take many different forms, e.g. integrated systems, streamlined management, purchasing or borrowing power, elimination of costly duplication of effort, etc., cf. OECD, TP Guidelines 2017, para. 6.30.

[431]OECD, TP Guidelines 2010, para. 1.10.

[432]Cf. *Tracana*, Intertax 2017, 411 (412); *Schoueri*, BIT 2015, 690 (698).

[433]A reference to MNE group synergies can be found in Section D of chapter I (The Arm's Length Principle), Section A of chapter VI (Specific Considerations for Intangibles) and Section B of chapter VII (Specific Considerations for Intra-Group Services) of the TP Guidelines 2017 which constitute the theoretical basis for the application of the transfer pricing methods illustrated in chapter II (Transfer Pricing Methods), cf. *Petruzzi/Peng*, TPI 2017, 110 (113).

[434]Cf. OECD, TP Guidelines 2017, para. 1.158.

[435]Cf. OECD, TP Guidelines 2017, paras. 1.159, 1.162.

[436]Cf. *Petruzzi/Peng*, TPI 2017, 110 (113).

[437]Cf. OECD, TP Guidelines 2017, para. 1.161.

or burden must be quantified, and thirdly it must be assessed how the benefit or burden should be divided among the members of the multinational enterprise.[438] To account for the identified group synergies, comparability adjustments may be required.[439]

Additionally, the TP Guidelines 2017 provide further guidance on the issue of location savings which were already included in the context of business restructurings (chapter IX) of the TP Guidelines 2010. The TP Guidelines 2017 clarify two main issues with regard to location savings. Firstly, it is pointed out that the principles described in chapter IX of the TP Guidelines 2017 shall not only be applicable in cases of business restructurings but in all situations where location savings exist.[440] Secondly, a four-step approach is introduced in Section D.6 of chapter I of the TP Guidelines 2017 which covers the topic of location savings and other local market features from a general tax perspective.[441] In order to share the benefits of location savings and other local market features between members of an MNE, the following steps shall be carried out:[442]

- Step 1: Identify whether or not location savings exist.
- Step 2: Quantify the additional profits that arise from location savings.
- Step 3: Determine whether location savings are passed on to independent suppliers or customers.
- Step 4: Allocate the location savings (if any) in an arm's length manner if they are not fully shifted.

With regard to the second issue, the reliance on the comparability analysis in general, it is worth highlighting that the additional guidance implemented in the TP Guidelines 2017 amended the reliance on the comparability analysis for the

---

[438]Cf. OECD, TP Guidelines 2017, para. 1.161. To allocate benefits that arise from group synergies all five transfer pricing methods might be appropriate and shall be considered equally and comprehensively. Instead of choosing the profit split method as a default method for the allocation of group synergies, the 'most appropriate method to the circumstances of the case' shall be selected, cf. *Petruzzi/Peng*, TPI 2017, 110 (113).

[439]Cf. OECD, TP Guidelines 2017, para. 1.163. For examples on how to adjust for group synergies cf. OECD, TP Guidelines 2017, paras. 1.164 et seqq.

[440]Cf. OECD, TP Guidelines 2017, para. 1.140.

[441]Cf. OECD, TP Guidelines 2017, paras. 1.139 et seqq.

[442]Cf. OECD, TP Guidelines 2017, para. 1.141. With regard to other local market features, a similar procedure is provided by the TP Guidelines 2017, cf. OECD, TP Guidelines 2017, para. 1.146.

application of transfer pricing methods that heavily rely on that analysis to a certain extent.[443] The additional guidance added to Section B.1 of Part II in chapter II,[444] which provides for the use of quoted prices[445] as a reference to determine the arm's length price for controlled commodity transactions, can be regarded as an example in this context. The reference to quoted prices for the use of the CUP method seems to put less emphasis on the comparability of the respective transaction by replacing the comparability analysis with a method which is based more on proxies for simplification purposes.[446] Another example is the work of the OECD on the application of the cost plus method for low value-adding services which provides an elective and simplified approach, which ultimately leads to a decreased reliance on the comparability analysis for such transactions.[447]

However, despite the additional guidance and simplifications provided by the OECD with regard to the application of the comparability analysis, this step of the OECD approach to transfer pricing can be regarded as its 'Achilles heel'.[448] As a matter of fact, in circumstances where comparables are hard to find and where the assessment of transfer prices becomes a matter of broad discretion, opportunities for profit shifting undoubtfully increase.[449] Therefore, the OECD

---

[443]Cf. *Petruzzi*, in: Lang/Storck/Petruzzi (Eds.), Transfer Pricing in a Post-BEPS World, 1 (25); *Petruzzi/Peng*, TPI 2017, 44 (45, note 16).

[444]The additional guidance on commodity transactions was implemented in paras. 2.18–2.22 of the TP Guidelines 2017.

[445]As explained by the OECD, the term 'quoted price' in this context 'refers to the price of the commodity in the relevant period obtained in an international or domestic commodity exchange market', OECD, TP Guidelines 2017, para. 2.18.

[446]Cf. *Petruzzi*, in: Lang/Storck/Petruzzi (Eds.), Transfer Pricing in a Post-BEPS World, 1 (25).

[447]The provisions of chapter VII (Low Value-Adding Intra-Group Services) of the TP Guidelines 2010 were replaced entirely as a result of BEPS Actions 8–10. Cf. in more detail for the simplified approach to determine the arm's length price of low value-adding intra group services OECD, TP Guidelines 2017, paras. 7.43–7.65. See for further remarks in this regard *Hüning/Hewera/Geyik*, IWB 2016, 298 (298 et seqq.); *Petruzzi*, in: Lang/Storck/Petruzzi (Eds.), Transfer Pricing in a Post-BEPS World, 1 (27); *Hüning/Hewera/Geyik*, IWB 2016, 298 (298 et seqq.); *Groß*, IStR 2016, 233 (238).

[448]Cf. *Luckhaupt/Overesch/Schreiber*, in: Schön/Konrad (Eds.), Fundamentals of International Transfer Pricing in Law and Economics, 91 (106).

[449]Cf. OECD, BEPS Actions 8–10: Final Report 2015, p. 9; also *Luckhaupt/Overesch/Schreiber*, in: Schön/Konrad (Eds.), Fundamentals of International Transfer Pricing in Law and Economics, 91 (106).

approached the issues that arise in the context of the comparability analysis with a twofold strategy. Besides reducing the dependency on the comparability analysis for methodologies which rely heavily on its application, the OECD also provided more significance to the applicability of methods which are less reliant on the comparability analysis, such as the TPSM and other methods[450] than the five authorised OECD methods.[451] The following chapter will shed light on some of the major enhancements to the TP Guidelines 2017 as revised through BEPS Actions 8–10.

iii. Modifications Affecting the Selection and Application of the Transfer Pricing Method

As highlighted earlier, one of the most prevalent issues in determining arm's length transfer prices is the identification of appropriate comparables. These challenges are exacerbated as business models gain complexity and intercompany transactions are embedded in highly integrated value chains.[452] If the use of one-sided transfer pricing methods proves difficult or less likely to determine reliable arm's length transfer prices to the case at hand, the application of the TPSM might constitute the most appropriate method.[453]

Throughout the BEPS project, several discussion drafts[454] on the matter of the TPSM were published which set notable progress on clarifying the application of the TPSM.[455] The findings and conclusions of the discussion drafts led to the publication of the 'Revised Guidance on the Application of the Transactional Profit Split Method' on 21 June 2018, developed as part of Action 10 of the BEPS Action Plan. The new guidance replaces Section C of Part III in chapter II of the

---

[450]The TP Guidelines 2017 emphasise that 'the use of other alternatives may also be appropriate', OECD, TP Guidelines 2017, para. 6.136. For details with regard to the valuation techniques cf. OECD, TP Guidelines 2017, paras. 6.153–6.178.

[451]Cf. *Petruzzi/Peng*, TPI 2017, 44 (45, note 16); *Petruzzi*, in: Lang/Storck/Petruzzi (Eds.), Transfer Pricing in a Post-BEPS World, 1 (26).

[452]Cf. *Treidler*, TNI 84 (2016), 277 (277).

[453]Detailed for the TPSM see chapter D.I.4.b.(3)(c)iii.02 of this thesis.

[454]For discussion draft no. 1 cf. OECD, BEPS Action 10: Discussion Draft on the Use of Profit Split in the Context of Global Value Chains 2014; for discussion draft no. 2 cf. OECD, BEPS Actions 8–10: Revised Guidance on Profit Splits 2016; for discussion draft no. 3 cf. OECD, BEPS Action 10: Revised Guidance on Profit Splits 2017.

[455]For a detailed analysis with regard to each of the discussion drafts see *Petruzzi/Peng*, TPI 2017, 44 (44 et seqq.).

TP Guidelines 2017 and retains the fundamental premise that the TPSM should be applied in situations where it is found to be the most appropriate method to the circumstances of the case.[456] Rather than purely prescriptive guidance, the OECD offers indicators for the use of the TPSM and explains each of the situations where it might be proper to apply thoroughly.[457] Additionally, Annex II to chapter II of the TP Guidelines includes sixteen examples in order to demonstrate how the TPSM is applied in practice which can be considered as valuable and insightful.

More precisely, the new guidance clarifies that the clearest indicator that the TPSM may be appropriate to apply is the existence of unique and valuable contributions by the parties involved in the controlled transaction/dealing.[458] Other indicators that the TPSM may be the most appropriate method to apply could include the shared assumption of economically significant risks by the parties involved and/or a high level of integration in the business operation to which the transactions/dealings relate.[459] This is in particular the case if the participating enterprises perform similar functions in highly integrated operations which would prevent the evaluation of the contributions of the parties in isolation.[460] However, the indicators may not be regarded as mutually exclusive and may rather often be found jointly in a single case.[461]

---

[456] Cf. OECD, TP Guidelines 2017, para. 2.116 (as amended through BEPS Action 10 in 2018).

[457] Cf. *Lewis/Athanasious*, TNI 86 (2017), 1175 (1176).

[458] Cf. OECD, TP Guidelines 2017, para. 2.116 (as amended through BEPS Action 10 in 2018).

[459] Cf. OECD, TP Guidelines 2017, para. 2.126 (as amended through BEPS Action 10 in 2018).

[460] Cf. OECD, TP Guidelines 2017, paras. 2.130 et seqq. (as amended through BEPS Action 10 in 2018). See in more detail in this regard *Stähli*, ITPJ 2018, 280 (280 et seqq.).

[461] Cf. OECD, TP Guidelines 2017, para. 2.126 (as amended through BEPS Action 10 in 2018).

Concerns raced in the December 2014 discussion draft emphasising that the TPSM might automatically be used in the absence of reliable comparables, without even considering whether the TPSM is appropriate for the case at hand was explicitly dealt with by BEPS Action 10.[462] Accordingly, a lack of comparables is, by itself, not sufficient to warrant the use of the TPSM.[463] Put differently, the TPSM is not a residual method which automatically applies when other methods are not applicable. In this context, it is also clarified that enterprises operating through global value chains can be regarded as a rather general feature of MNEs as well as the fact that group synergies normally exist in intra-group transactions or dealings and therefore do not automatically enable the application of the TPSM.[464]

Furthermore, additional guidance is provided on the determination of the profits to be split and profit-splitting factors. With regard to the question whether actual or anticipated profits shall be used in order to determine the profit to be split, the OECD distinguished between two scenarios. According to the TP Guidelines, the use of the profit split of actual profits may only be appropriate 'where the accurate delineation of the transaction shows that the parties either share the assumption of the same economically significant risks associated with the business opportunity or separately assume closely related, economically significant risks associated with the business opportunity and consequently share in the resulting profits or losses'[465]. Alternatively, a split of the anticipated profits may be more appropriate if one of the parties does not share in the assumption of the economically significant risks associated with the business opportunity which plays out after the transaction was entered.[466] In general, the use of anticipated profits goes hand in hand with the use of valuation techniques. However, irrespective whether actual or anticipated profits are split, the arm's length principle applies in both cases indiscriminately.[467]

In this regard, it is worth mentioning that the new guidance also makes sure that the TPSM does not contain any elements of formulary apportionment which

---

[462] Cf. OECD, BEPS Actions 8–10: Final Report 2015, p. 58, para. 7.

[463] Cf. OECD, TP Guidelines 2017, para. 2.143 (as amended through BEPS Action 10 in 2018).

[464] Cf. *Petruzzi/Peng*, TPI 2017, 44 (49 et seq.).

[465] OECD, TP Guidelines 2017, para. 2.159 (as amended through BEPS Action 10 in 2018).

[466] Cf. OECD, TP Guidelines 2017, para. 2.160 (as amended through BEPS Action 10 in 2018).

[467] Cf. *Petruzzi/Peng*, TPI 2017, 44 (50).

would divide the profits of a group by a pre-determined formula.[468] Rather, the TPSM determines the profits on a transaction-by-transaction basis. The new guidance emphasise that the profits should be split on an economically valid basis that reflects the relative contributions of the participating parties to the transaction/dealing. However, the criteria and profit splitting factors (e.g. profit split based on assets, capital or costs) to achieve a result that is at arm's length should not be prescriptive but rather be suitable to the circumstances of the case.[469] Furthermore, it is emphasised by the OECD that the splitting factors or criteria used to split the profits should be independent of any transfer pricing policy formulation, verifiable and supported by comparable data, internal data, or both.[470]

As examined earlier, the work on BEPS Actions 8–10 also resulted in a revision of chapter VI of the TP Guidelines 2017 dealing with intangibles. In this context, it is noted that intangibles raise unique issues. Especially, the search for comparables, the selection of an appropriate transfer pricing method and the determination of arm's length conditions for transactions involving intangibles may prove difficult to resolve.[471] Section D of the TP Guidelines 2017 provides supplemental guidance for determining arm's length conditions in cases relating to intangibles.[472] In principle, the guidance moves away from the use of one-sided analyses and demands a thorough examination of the contribution to value creation of the two sides of the transactions.[473] It thereby rejects the assumption that the entire residual profit of the enterprise should automatically go to the owner of the intangible after the provider of a routine function is provided with modest reward.[474] In circumstances where valuation of the intangible is highly uncertain

---

[468] Cf. *Petruzzi/Peng*, TPI 2017, 44 (51). Cf. in more detail for formula apportionment *Higinbotham*, Tax Management Transfer Pricing Special Report 1996, 1 (23); *McLure*, BIT 2002, 586 (586 et seqq.); *Altshuler/Grubert*, NTJ 2010, 1145 (1145 et seqq.); *Morse*, VTR 2010, 593 (594 et seqq.); *Sadiq*, BIT 2001, 275 (275 et seqq.); *Avi-Yonah*, WTJ 2010, 3 (3 et seqq.).

[469] Cf. OECD, TP Guidelines 2017, para. 2.166 (as amended through BEPS Action 10 in 2018) and cf. in more detail for the profit split factors Cf. OECD, TP Guidelines 2017, para. 2.171 (as amended through BEPS Action 10 in 2018).

[470] Cf. OECD, TP Guidelines 2017, para. 2.166 (as amended through BEPS Action 10 in 2018).

[471] Cf. OECD, TP Guidelines 2017, paras. 6.33, 6.108.

[472] Cf. OECD, TP Guidelines 2017, paras. 6.107 et seqq.

[473] Cf. *Collier/Andrus*, Transfer Pricing and the Arm's Length Principle after BEPS, para. 6.66.

[474] Cf. OECD, TP Guidelines 2017, para. 6.133.

at the time of the transaction and where reliable comparable uncontrolled transactions for a transfer of intangibles cannot be identified, valuation techniques (such as cash flows derived from the exploitation of intangibles being valued or the calculation of the discounted value expected from projected future income streams) may be appropriate to use.[475] According to the OECD, such valuation techniques may be used by taxpayers as well as tax administrations either as part of one of the five transfer pricing methods authorised by the OECD (CUP method, resale price method, cost plus method, TNMM, TPSM) or as a tool that may support the identification of an appropriate transfer price.[476]

Even though the additional flexibility introduced with such valuation techniques can also be applied for dealings between the PE and other parts of the enterprise and is generally to be welcomed, it is correctly pointed out in literature that the new tool box introduced in the TP Guidelines 2017 opens up for a whole set of new challenges, e.g. necessary assumptions with regard to the discount rates, growth rates and tax rates and accuracy issues regarding financial projections that might lead to additional uncertainty for the taxpayer with regard to the application of such techniques.[477]

iv. Interim Conclusion

The analysis undertaken reveals that the work of the OECD on BEPS undoubtedly influences and enlightens the way in which the second step of the AOA is carried out. The contributions made can be regarded as valuable and insightful.

Two developments can be identified in this regard. On the one hand, the OECD placed more emphasis and provides enhanced guidance on the performance of the comparability analysis, e.g. detailed guidance for comparability adjustments for group synergies, location savings and other local market features within MNEs.[478] The additional guidance is to be welcomed and tackles some of the flaws and shortcomings of the TP Guidelines 2010. On the other side, more relevance is put to the use of methodologies which are less reliant on the comparability analysis such as the newly proposed approach to use the CUP method and the cost plus method for certain circumstances or the enhanced guidance to the use of the

[475] Cf. OECD, TP Guidelines 2017, para. 6.153. See for discussion *Baumhoff/Liebchen*, in: Wassermeyer/Baumhoff (Eds.), Verrechnungspreise international verbundener Unternehmen, para. 5.148.

[476] Cf. OECD, TP Guidelines 2017, para. 6.153.

[477] Cf. *Petruzzi*, in: Lang/Storck/Petruzzi (Eds.), Transfer Pricing in a Post-BEPS World, 1 (27); *Collier/Andrus*, Transfer Pricing and the Arm's Length Principle after BEPS, para. 6.67.

[478] Cf. *Petruzzi*, in: Lang/Storck/Petruzzi (Eds.), Transfer Pricing in a Post-BEPS World, 1 (27).

TPSM. Especially, the more pragmatic and reliable guidance provides a straightforward and well-defined scope for the application of the TPSM, which can be regarded as neither too broad nor too narrow. Together with the examples included in the revised guidance, it will allow taxpayers to take advantage of the flexibility provided by the method.[479] Especially in situations where both parties make unique and valuable contributions to the dealing (e.g. when significant people functions attributed to the PE are linked to value creation and intangibles)[480], where economically significant risks are shared and/or where business operations are highly integrated such that the contributions of the parties cannot be reliable evaluated, the new guidance will be helpful for its application. With business operations becoming more and more integrated and the digitalisation of the economy on its rise, the use of the TPSM will gain in importance.[481]

The developments outlined ultimately reveal that the arm's length principle has become an economic principle which is increasingly influenced by market principles and business rationales.[482] In this context, thorough documentation proving the arm's length nature of the profit determination has become increasingly important. The following chapter provides a detailed overview of the documentation requirements that are of importance in the PE context.

---

[479]Cf. *Petruzzi/Peng*, TPI 2017, 110 (119); *Treidler*, TNI 84 (2016), 277 (277).

[480]Cf. *Bernales*, in: Gutiérrez/Perdelwitz (Eds.), Taxation of Business Profits in the 21st Century, 135 (171).

[481]Cf. also *Kadet*, TNI 77 (2015), 1183 (1184 et seq.). The revised TP Guidelines 2017 also contain an indirect statement to a broader application of the TPSM, cf. *Greil*, Intertax 2017, 624 (627).

[482]Cf. *Petruzzi*, in: Lang/Storck/Petruzzi (Eds.), Transfer Pricing in a Post-BEPS World, 1 (28).

5. Documentation Requirements

a. Preliminary Remarks

For quite some time, the work on transfer pricing documentation requirements and its harmonisation has been given increased importance.[483] This work culminated in the publication of the final report on BEPS Action 13: 'Transfer Pricing Documentation and Country-by-Country Reporting' on 5 October 2015. BEPS Action 13 aims to re-examine rules for transfer pricing documentation to enhance transparency for tax administrations, taking into account compliance costs for businesses.[484] The final report on BEPS Action 13 resulted in a complete rewrite of chapter V of the TP Guidelines 2017.

Due to the fact that the PE Report 2010 refers to the guidance on the documentation set out in chapter V of the TP Guidelines which shall be applied by analogy, the changes through BEPS Action 13 are highly relevant in the PE context.[485] In general, the OECD states that 'the same standards would apply to the documentation of the arm's length nature of the profit determination relating to dealings as currently apply to the documentation of transactions'[486]. The new chapter V of the TP Guidelines 2017 provides for a three-tiered standardised approach for transfer pricing documentation. In this context, a PE may not only be obliged to prepare transfer pricing documentation in the country where it is situated but may also constitute a reporting entity for transfer pricing documentation purposes itself.

---

[483] Transfer pricing documentation requirements were first introduced by the United States in 1994, see Sec. 482 of the US Internal Revenue Code, 1994 Final Transfer Pricing Regulation of the United States. Since then the number of countries requiring transfer pricing documentation increased year by year. The first transfer pricing documentation guidelines on the level of the OECD were introduced on 27 June 1995 in chapter V of the TP Guidelines 1995. However, at that time chapter V of the TP Guidelines 1995 neither provided for a list of transfer pricing documents that shall be included in a documentation package nor did it provide for clear guidance with regard to the link between the documentation process for transfer pricing, the burden of proof and the administration of penalty. Cf. OECD, White Paper on Transfer Pricing Documentation, 30 July 2013, p. 4; OECD, BEPS Actions 13: Final Report 2015, p. 11, para. 2. For an overview of the development of the transfer pricing documentation requirements see *Kaeser/Bremer*, in: Lang/Storck/Petruzzi (Eds.), Transfer Pricing in a Post-BEPS World, 187 (190 et seqq.).

[484] Cf. OECD, BEPS Actions 13: Final Report 2015, p. 9.

[485] Cf. OECD, PE Report 2010, Part I, paras. 224 et seqq.

[486] OECD, PE Report 2010, Part I, para. 224.

In general, the OECD elaborates that the three-tiered approach to transfer pricing documentation shall consist of:[487]

- a master file which is supposed to provide high-level information regarding an MNE's transfer pricing policies and global business operations;
- a local file containing more detailed information of each country referring specifically to material transactions by the local taxpayer and the amounts involved in such transactions; and
- a Country-by-Country (hereinafter: CbC) Report which contains an overview of where employees, sales, assets and profits are located and where taxes are accrued and payed.

Figure 2 provides an overview of the three-tiered standardised approach to transfer pricing documentation and CbC Reporting.

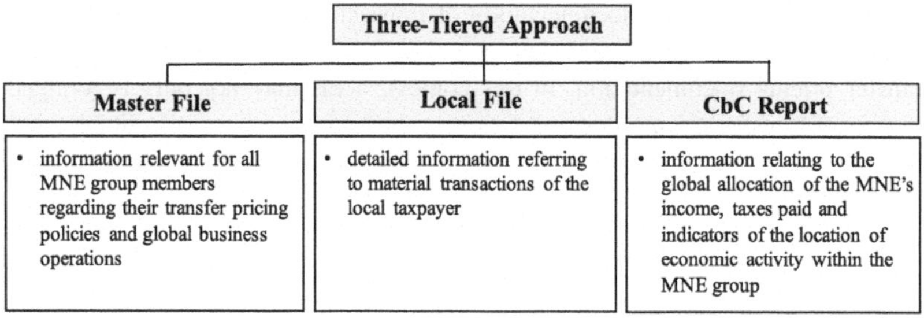

Figure 2 Three-Tiered Approach to Transfer Pricing Documentation (Source: Own illustration)

While the master file and the local file were already known, but not obligatory through the code of conduct on transfer pricing documentation for associated

[487] Cf. OECD, TP Guidelines 2017, para. 5.16.

enterprises in the European Union (EU TPD),[488] the CbC Reporting can be regarded as a new tool that has not been in use internationally.[489] The three-tiered standardised approach will be described in more detail in the following.

b. Three-Tiered Approach to Transfer Pricing Documentation

(1) Master File

The master file aims at providing a high-level overview of the MNE's group business as a whole.[490] Rather than requiring exhaustive listings of minutiae, taxpayers may limit the data provided to the important and general relevant information for the whole MNE group, such as the overall transfer pricing policies, the nature of its global business operations and its global allocation of economic activities and income.[491] In determining the appropriate level of detail provided in the master file, taxpayers should use prudent business judgement, keeping in mind the overall purpose of the master file in providing a high-level overview.[492] The information required can be found in Annex I to chapter V of the TP Guidelines 2017 and can be grouped into the following categories: a) the group's organisational structure, b) a description of the business and a brief functional analysis, c) the group's intangibles, d) the group's intercompany financial activities, and e) the group's financial and tax position.[493]

The master file shall be submitted by the taxpayer along with the tax return of the Ultimate Parent Entity of the MNE group and shall be made accessible

---

[488] EU, Code of Conduct for Transfer Pricing Documentation, 2006/C 176/01, 28 July 2006, 1. For further details with regard to the approaches see *Rasch/Mank/Tomson*, IStR 2015, 424 (424 et seqq.); *Kroppen/Rasch*, ISR 2014, 358 (364); *Kaeser/Bremer*, in: Lang/Storck/Petruzzi (Eds.), Transfer Pricing in a Post-BEPS World, 187 (195).

[489] So far, a CbC Report was only obligatory for commodity companies and banks, cf. *Böhmer*, in: W/A/D (Eds.), Betriebsstätten-Handbuch, para. 14.121. See in more detail in this regard *Tomson*, in: Kroppen/Rasch (Eds.), Handbuch Internationale Verrechnungspreise, OECD-Kap. V, para. 57 et seqq. Critical with regard to CbC Reporting *Böhmer*, in: W/A/D (Eds.), Betriebsstätten-Handbuch, para. 14.121; *Pinkernell*, FR 2014, 964 (971); *Ditz/Quilitzsch*, DStR 2014, 127 (127 et seqq.); *Rasch/Mank/Tomson*, IStR 2015, 424 (428 et seq.); *Kroppen/Rasch*, ISR 2014, 358 (363).

[490] Cf. OECD, TP Guidelines 2017, paras. 5.18, 5.20.

[491] Cf. OECD, TP Guidelines 2017, para. 5.18; *Kaeser/Bremer*, in: Lang/Storck/Petruzzi (Eds.), Transfer Pricing in a Post-BEPS World, 187 (195).

[492] Cf. OECD, TP Guidelines 2017, para. 5.18.

[493] Cf. OECD, TP Guidelines 2017, para. 5.19 in conjunction with Annex I to chapter V of the TP Guidelines 2017, pp. 501 et seqq. For an overview of the information that shall be included in the master file see table 1 in the Annex of this thesis.

to each jurisdiction in which the MNE operates.[494] In this sense, the master file shall be reviewed and, in case changes are necessary, updated by the due date of the tax return for the Ultimate Parent Entity of the MNE group.[495]

(2) Local File

Compared to the master file, the local file aims to provide more detailed information which relates to specific intercompany transactions and the amounts involved in such transactions.[496] Consequently, the information provided in the local file supplements the master file and helps to prove whether the taxpayer complies with the arm's length principle with respect to its material transfer pricing positions which affect a particular jurisdiction.[497]

More specifically, the content of the local file shall, i.a., consist of relevant financial information with regard to transactions taking place between the local country affiliate and associated enterprises in the various countries, a comparability analysis and reasoning with regard to the selection and application of the most appropriate transfer pricing method.[498] Detailed information with respect to the items that shall be included in the local file can be found in Annex II to chapter V of the TP Guidelines 2017.[499] In general, the scope of information to be included in the local file does, in many cases, not exceed the level of information which was required in many local country regulations before the OECD/G20 BEPS Project.[500] However, it needs to be considered that countries can require further information to be included in the local file, since the recommendations of the OECD only set a minimum standard.[501]

The local file shall be submitted to the responsible tax authority by each local taxpayer no later than the due date for filing the tax return for the respective fiscal year.[502]

---

[494] Cf. *Böhmer*, in: W/A/D (Eds.), Betriebsstätten-Handbuch, para. 14.122.

[495] Cf. OECD, TP Guidelines 2017, para. 5.30.

[496] Cf. OECD, TP Guidelines 2017, para. 5.22.

[497] Cf. OECD, TP Guidelines 2017, para. 5.22.

[498] Cf. OECD, TP Guidelines 2017, para. 5.22.

[499] Cf. Annex II to chapter V of the TP Guidelines 2017, pp. 505 et seqq. For an overview of the information that shall be included in the local file see table 2 in the Annex of this thesis.

[500] Cf. *Wehnert*, in: Lang/Storck/Petruzzi (Eds.), Transfer Pricing Developments Around the World 2018, 141 (145).

[501] Cf. *Wehnert*, in: Lang/Storck/Petruzzi (Eds.), Transfer Pricing Developments Around the World 2018, 141 (145).

[502] Cf. OECD, TP Guidelines 2017, para. 5.30.

(3) Country-by-Country Reporting

(a) Preliminary Remarks

While the first two pillars of the documentation requirements implemented through BEPS Action 13, namely the local and the master file, can be regarded as a useful tool to understand the transfer pricing policy of MNEs, the main purpose of the third pillar, the CbC Report, is to serve as a tool for risk assessment.[503] More precisely, the CbC Report, which belongs to one of the four BEPS minimum standards,[504] shall enable tax authorities to effective high-level risk assessment by providing them with aggregated information which relate to the global allocation of income, the corresponding taxes paid and specific indicators of the location of economic activity in each of the jurisdictions where the MNE group operates.[505] Accordingly, Annex III, A to chapter V of the TP Guidelines 2017 provides a model template (table one) that enables the taxpayer to record such information in a comprehensive manner.[506] In addition, two more tables are provided in Annex III, A to chapter V of the TP Guidelines 2017. Table two requires the taxpayer to identify each entity within the MNE group doing business in a particular jurisdiction and provides an indication of the main business activities the individual MNE group entities are engages in.[507] The last table enables the taxpayer to provide additional information, e.g. information that would facilitate the understanding of the compulsory information provided in the CbC Report.[508]

While the information required by the taxpayer for the purpose of the CbC Report seems quite straightforward, practice has shown that the interpretation

---

[503] Cf. *Petruzzi*, in: Lang/Storck/Petruzzi (Eds.), Transfer Pricing Developments Around the World 2017, 1 (8).

[504] See for an overview of the minimum standards of the BEPS project OECD, BEPS Project—Explanatory Statement, para. 11. See for an overview of the implementation process OECD, BEPS Progress Report 2020.

[505] Cf. OECD, TP Guidelines 2017, para. 5.59.

[506] Besides the amount of revenue and profits before income tax and income tax paid and accrued also the number of employees, stated capital, retained earnings and tangible assets shall be reported in the template. See in more detail, OECD, TP Guidelines 2017, Annex III, A to chapter V, Table 1(in Chapter C), p. 510. For an illustration of table one of the Model template for the CbC Report see also table 3 in the Annex of this thesis.

[507] Cf. OECD, TP Guidelines 2017, Annex III, A to chapter V, Table 1, p. 511; OECD, BEPS Action 13: CbC Reporting—Compilation of Peer Review Reports (Phase 1), p. 11, para. 1. For an own illustration of table two of the Model template for the CbC Report see also table 4 in the Annex of this thesis.

[508] Cf. OECD, TP Guidelines 2017, Annex III, A to chapter V, Table 2, p. 511. For an own illustration of table three of the Model template for the CbC Report see also table 5 in the Annex of this thesis.

of some of the individual figures remain unclear.[509] Therefore, the OECD regularly updates its guidance on CbC Reporting. In this regard, two publications can be highlighted. First, the 'Guidance on the Implementation of the Country-by-Country Reporting'[510] updated by the OECD on a regular basis which addresses certain key issues of interpretation in the interest of certainty and consistent implementation of the CbC Reporting for both the taxpayer and the tax administrations. Second, the 'Guidance on the appropriate use of information contained in CbC Reports'[511] of 9 September 2017 dealing with the meaning of the phrase 'appropriate use', consequences in case of non-compliance with the appropriate use condition and approaches that may be used by tax authorities in order to ensure the appropriate use of the information provided in the CbC Report.

Much of the information available in the CbC Report does not allow for any conclusions on the actual transfer pricing system in place by an MNE group.[512] Nevertheless, much ink has been spilled on the question whether the information provided by the CbC Report could potentially lead to the creation of taxable bases by means of some kind of formulary apportionment.[513] The OECD explicitly addressed this issue and emphasised that the CbC Report 'should not be used by tax administrations to propose transfer pricing adjustments based on a global formulary apportionment of income'[514]. Neither shall the information provided by the CbC Report be used as a substitute for a thorough transfer pricing analysis of the individual transactions and prices based on a complete functional and comparability analysis.[515]

[509] Cf. *Rasch*, in: Kroppen/Rasch (Eds.), Handbuch Internationale Verrechnungspreise, GAufzV, para. 24; see in more detail *Rasch/Mank/Tomson*, IStR 2013, 424 (424 et seqq.); *Mank/Salihu*, IWB 2017, 902 (902 et seqq.); *Mank/Totzek*, IWB 2017, 922 (922 et seqq.).

[510] OECD, BEPS Action 13: Guidance on the Implementation of CbC Reporting.

[511] OECD, BEPS Actions 13: Guidance on the appropriate use of information contained in Country-by-Country Reports 2017.

[512] Cf. *Petruzzi*, in: Lang/Storck/Petruzzi (Eds.), Transfer Pricing Developments Around the World 2017, 1 (8).

[513] Cf. *Petruzzi*, in: Lang/Storck/Petruzzi (Eds.), Transfer Pricing Developments Around the World 2017, 1 (8). Critical in this regard *Böhmer*, in: W/A/D (Eds.), Betriebsstätten-Handbuch, para. 14.124; *Kaeser/Bremer*, in: Lang/Storck/Petruzzi (Eds.), Transfer Pricing in a Post-BEPS World, 187 (201 et seqq.).

[514] OECD, TP Guidelines 2017, para. 5.25.

[515] Cf. OECD, TP Guidelines 2017, para. 5.25.

(b) Treatment of PEs in the CbC Report

For the purpose of the CbC Report, a PE may be regarded as a Constituent Entity of the MNE group if a) the PE is part of a separate business unit of the MNE group that is either included in the consolidated financial statements of the MNE group or excluded from that consolidated financial statements solely on size or materiality grounds, and b) a separate financial statement for regulatory, tax reporting, internal management control or financial reporting purposes is prepared for the PE.[516]

In this context, data for a PE should not be reported by reference to the tax jurisdiction of residence of the head office, but instead must be reported by reference to the tax jurisdiction in which the PE is situated.[517] This approach is in line with the AOA.[518] Consequently, financial data related to the PE should be excluded by the residence tax jurisdiction of the head office. However, pursuant to the TP Guidelines 2017, this general reporting requirement shall not apply for data to be provided in the eighth and ninth column of table 1(in Chapter C) of the CbC Report: the stated capital and the accumulated earnings.[519] Such data shall be reported by reference to the tax jurisdiction of the head office.[520] An exception applies to the stated capital if there is a defined capital requirement in the tax jurisdiction of the PE for regulatory purposes such as in the banking or insurance industry. In that case the minimum capital as required for regulatory purposes shall be reported by reference to the tax jurisdiction in which the PE is situated.[521]

The approach to report the stated capital by reference to the tax jurisdiction of the head office is not in line with the fundamental principles of the AOA.[522] Even though this approach might be favourable for the taxpayer since most accounting systems of MNEs might not provide the stated capital for the PE explicitly,[523] the approach taken might lead to data misinterpretation.

---

[516]Cf. OECD, TP Guidelines 2017, Annex III, B to chapter V, p. 512.

[517]Cf. OECD, TP Guidelines 2017, Annex III, B to chapter V, p. 512.

[518]Cf. also *Grotherr*, IStR 2016, 991 (995); *Busch*, in: W/A/D (Eds.), Betriebsstätten-Handbuch, para. 13.181.

[519]Cf. OECD, TP Guidelines 2017, Annex III, B to chapter V, p. 515.

[520]Cf. OECD, TP Guidelines 2017, Annex III, B to chapter V, p. 515.

[521]Cf. OECD, TP Guidelines 2017, Annex III, B to chapter V, p. 515.

[522]Cf. *Busch*, in: W/A/D (Eds.), Betriebsstätten-Handbuch, para. 13.181. Critical in this regard also *Grotherr* who argues that it makes no sense to report the stated capital by reference to the tax jurisdiction of the head office, cf. *Grotherr*, IStR 2016, 991 (1001).

[523]Cf. *Busch*, in: W/A/D (Eds.), Betriebsstätten-Handbuch, para. 13.181.

(c) Submission Requirements

The CbC Report shall be submitted by the Ultimate Parent Entity of the MNE group to the tax administration in its jurisdiction of tax residence.[524] Upon receipt of the CbC Report, the responsible tax administration shall automatically exchange the report with all tax administrations in the jurisdictions in which the MNE group has a Constituent Entity resident for tax purposes as indicated in the CbC Report.[525] This process shall be carried out under an international agreement[526] which permits automatic exchange of information.[527] In case the jurisdiction of tax residence of the Ultimate Parent Entity of the MNE group fails to provide information to another jurisdiction in which the MNE group has a Constituent Entity resident for tax purposes because a) the Ultimate Parent Entity of the MNE group is not obligated to file a CbC Report in its jurisdiction of tax residence, b) no competent authority agreement between the respective jurisdictions is in place for the exchange of the CbC Report, or c) the responsible jurisdiction fails in its obligation to automatically exchange the report with other jurisdictions even though it has agreed to do so, a secondary mechanism through local filing or through filing of the CbC Report by a designated member of the MNE group which acts in place of the Ultimate Parent Entity of the MNE group is accepted as appropriate.[528]

An exemption from the general filing requirement is provided for MNE groups with annual consolidated group revenue in the immediately preceding fiscal year of less than EUR 750 million or an equivalent amount in the respective domestic

---

[524]Cf. OECD, BEPS Action 13: CbC Reporting—Compilation of Peer Review Reports (Phase 1), p. 11, para. 2.

[525]Cf. OECD, BEPS Action 13: CbC Reporting—Compilation of Peer Review Reports (Phase 1), p. 11, para. 2.

[526]In this context, an international agreement could be an agreement such as a) a Double Tax Convention, b) a Tax Information Exchange Agreement or c) the Multilateral Convention on Mutual Administrative Assistance in Tax Matters cf. OECD/Council of Europe, The Multilateral Convention on Mutual Administrative Assistance in Tax Matters; OECD, BEPS Action 13: CbC Reporting—Compilation of Peer Review Reports (Phase 1), p. 11, para. 2. Within the European Union, an exchange of information is also possible on the basis of the EU Mutual Assistance Directive, cf. European Council, 15 Feb. 2011, Directive 2011/16/EU. This Directive was amended by the EU Council Directive of 25 May 2016 as regards mandatory automatic exchange of information in the field of taxation, cf. European Council, 25 May 2016, Directive 2016/881.

[527]Cf. OECD, BEPS Action 13: CbC Reporting—Compilation of Peer Review Reports (Phase 1), p. 11, para. 2.

[528]Cf. OECD, TP Guidelines 2017, para. 5.60. See in this regard also *Lappé/Schmidtke*, IStR 2015, 693 (694).

currency.[529] It is believed by the OECD that this exemption will exclude between 85% and 90% of MNE groups from the obligation to file a CbC Report.[530] Nevertheless, at the same time it is believed that the report will be filed by MNE groups controlling around 90% of corporate revenue.[531]

(d) Modalities of Global Implementation

It is recommended by the OECD that the first CbC Reports shall be filed for fiscal years beginning on or after 1 January 2016.[532] Considering that MNE groups shall be allowed one year to file the actual CbC Report, starting from the close of the fiscal year to which the CbC Report relates to, this means that the first CbC Report and with it the automatic exchange of information among the tax administrations of the respective jurisdictions starts by 31 December 2017.[533] However, it is acknowledged by the OECD that some jurisdictions may need more time in order to follow their specific domestic legislation process to make the necessary adjustments to national law.[534] In order to ensure accurate and timely implementation and thus safeguard the implementation on equal footing, the CbC Reporting requirements are subject to a peer review process which focuses on a) the domestic administrative and legal framework, b) the exchange of information framework, and c) the appropriate use and the confidentiality of the CbC Report.[535] While the first annual peer review[536] and second annual peer review[537] were already

---

[529] Cf. OECD, TP Guidelines 2017, para. 5.52.

[530] Cf. OECD, TP Guidelines 2017, para. 5.53.

[531] Cf. OECD, TP Guidelines 2017, para. 5.53.

[532] Cf. OECD, TP Guidelines 2017, para. 5.50.

[533] Cf. OECD, TP Guidelines 2017, para. 5.50; also *Böhmer*, in: W/A/D (Eds.), Betriebsstätten-Handbuch, para. 14.128.

[534] Cf. OECD, BEPS Action 13: CbC Reporting—Compilation of Peer Review Reports (Phase 1), p. 16, para. 8.

[535] For the findings of the peer review process see OECD, BEPS Action 13: CbC Reporting—Compilation of Peer Review Reports, p. 11.

[536] Cf. OECD, BEPS Action 13: CbC Reporting—Compilation of Peer Review Reports (Phase 1).

[537] Cf. OECD, BEPS Action 13: CbC Reporting—Compilation of Peer Review Reports (Phase 2).

released in May 2018 and September 2019 respectively, the last and final annual peer review[538] was published in October 2020.[539]

The final report on BEPS Action 13 also contains suggestions on how to facilitate a swift and consistent implementation of the CbC Report.[540] These suggestions became part of the CbC 'Reporting Implementation Package' of the TP Guidelines 2017.[541] This Reporting Implementation Package contains, among others, a model legislation which can be used by the countries participating in the BEPS project.[542] Jurisdictions are able to adapt this model legislation and if required by national legislation, make changes to the model legislation.[543] Additionally, the OECD releases the periodically updated 'Guidance on the implementation of Country-by-Country Reporting'[544]. This guidance aims to address certain key issues of interpretation in order to provide the framework for a consistent implementation of the CbC Reporting.

c. Evaluation of the Documentation Requirements

The implementation of the three-tiered standardised approach to transfer pricing documentation recommended by the OECD enables tax authorities to gain access to an unprecedented amount and detail of information which undoubtfully increases their ability to carry out an effective tax risk assessment.[545] However, at the same time it is apparent that the new three-tiered documentation approach creates several challenges, especially for large MNE groups.

While the requirements imposed through the local file are mostly consistent with the documentation requirements most transfer pricing legislations have already had in place for quite some time, most of the high level information requested for the master file and the CbC Report were not contemplated in most of

---

[538] Cf. OECD, BEPS Action 13: CbC Reporting—Compilation of Peer Review Reports (Phase 3).

[539] For the respective findings of the annual peer reviews with regard to the implementation of the CbC Report in Germany see chapter D.II.5.d.(5) of this thesis.

[540] Cf. OECD, BEPS Actions 13: Final Report 2015, p. 20, paras. 48 et seqq.

[541] See in more detail with regard to the CbC Reporting Implementation Package OECD, TP Guidelines 2017, Annex IV to chapter V, pp. 512 et seqq.

[542] Cf. OECD, TP Guidelines 2017, Annex IV to chapter V, pp. 512 et seqq.

[543] Cf. OECD, TP Guidelines 2017, Annex IV to chapter V, p. 512.

[544] OECD, BEPS Action 13: Guidance on the Implementation of CbC Reporting.

[545] Cf. *Silberztein/Le Naourès*, ITPJ 2018, 3 (3).

the previous transfer pricing legislations and consequently impose major challenges for most MNEs.[546] In this sense, it can be expected that the tax authorities in the different jurisdictions will have different perceptions on the level of information discloure. With regard to the master file, e.g. the OECD states that 'taxpayers should use prudent business judgment in determining the appropriate level of detail for the information supplied'[547]. However, no clear guidance is provided by the OECD on how to determine which factors shall be considered to be material, leading to increased uncertainty for the taxpayer and the potential for penalties imposed in certain jurisdictions.[548]

Additionally, two observations can be highlighted regarding the implementation of the local and the master file. While many countries adhered to the recommendations set out in chapter V of the TP Guidelines 2017, it can be noted that especially countries that had already transfer pricing documentation regulation in place before the BEPS project complemented the recommendations set out by the OECD with additional documentation requirements, which typically relate to the local file.[549] However, such deviations may result in a lack of consistency on a worldwide scale which undoubtedly undermines the goal of the OECD. Fortunately, the worldwide implementation of the recommendations with regard to the master file seems pretty consistent with the approach of the OECD.[550]

However, concerning the three-tiered approach to transfer pricing documentation, the implementation of the new transparency requirements introduced through the CbC Report can be regarded as the biggest challenge for both tax authorities and taxpayer.[551] As already elaborated in the previous chapter, the CbC Report requires MNE groups to generate a global footprint which reveals jurisdiction specific data on, e.g., taxable income, taxes paid, number of employees and the

---

[546] Cf. *Kaeser/Bremer*, in: Lang/Storck/Petruzzi (Eds.), Transfer Pricing in a Post-BEPS World, 187 (197, 200).

[547] Cf. OECD, TP Guidelines 2017, para. 5.18.

[548] Cf. *Kaeser/Bremer*, in: Lang/Storck/Petruzzi (Eds.), Transfer Pricing in a Post-BEPS World, 187 (198).

[549] Cf. *Wehnert*, in: Lang/Storck/Petruzzi (Eds.), Transfer Pricing Developments Around the World 2018, 141 (147).

[550] Cf. *Wehnert*, in: Lang/Storck/Petruzzi (Eds.), Transfer Pricing Developments Around the World 2018, 141 (147).

[551] Cf. *Willmanns*, in: Oestreicher (Ed.), BEPS konkret und weitere Entwicklungen im deutschen Steuerrecht, 7 (15); *Wehnert*, in: Lang/Storck/Petruzzi (Eds.), Transfer Pricing Developments Around the World 2018, 141 (147).

main business activities such as R&D activities. Two main concerns must be highlighted in this context: a) the risk of data misinterpretation, and b) the dilution of the arm's length principle.

The first concern, the risk of data misinterpretation, is caused by the fact that the informative value of the data provided by the CbC Report is questionable.[552] Especially, conclusions on whether the amount of country-specific taxes payed is compatible with the annual result in a specific fiscal year cannot be drawn.[553] Also, the individual reporting requirements asked for in the CbC Report are not fully in line with international accounting standards, which may result in different interpretations of the various positions, not only by the taxpayer but also by the tax administrations of the different jurisdictions.[554] This bears a considerable risk of double taxation. It would have been preferable if the OECD could have followed established international accounting standards.[555] Further risk of data misinterpretation can be identified in the PE context. While data of the PE shall be reported by reference to the tax jurisdiction in which the PE is situated, which is in line with the AOA, an exception from that principle applies for the stated capital and the accumulated earnings which shall be reported in the jurisdiction where the head office is located.

The second concern, which is linked to the first issue, relates to the fact that a number of emerging countries demand information to be included in the CbC Report that exceed the information recommended to be included by the OECD.[556]

---

[552] Cf. *Rasch/Mank/Tomson*, IStR 2015, 424 (428). Also, *Ditz/Bärsch/Engelen* critisise that the qualitative approach of the arm's length principle and the quantitative approach of the CbC Report are not compatible resulting in a limited degree to identify inappropriate transfer prices, cf. *Ditz/Bärsch/Engelen*, IStR 2016, 840 (859). For further risks of data misinterpretation see *Grotherr*, RIW 2017, 1 (15 et seq.).

[553] As argued by *Kaeser/Bremer*, this is due to the fact that 'income taxes affecting payments encompass tax prepayments for the current year (versus 'Income Tax Accrued' to the fiscal year only) and also tax prepayments for subsequent years, closing payments for prior periods, and supplementary payments or refunds due to tax audits or legal proceedings', *Kaeser/Bremer*, in: Lang/Storck/Petruzzi (Eds.), Transfer Pricing in a Post-BEPS World, 187 (201). See also in this regard *Rasch/Mank/Tomson*, IStR 2015, 424 (428); *Hanlon*, BIT 2018, 209 (214).

[554] Cf. *Willmanns*, in: Oestreicher (Ed.), BEPS konkret und weitere Entwicklungen im deutschen Steuerrecht, 7 (15); *Rasch/Mank/Tomson*, IStR 2015, 424 (428); *Kaeser/Bremer*, in: Lang/Storck/Petruzzi (Eds.), Transfer Pricing in a Post-BEPS World, 187 (201); *Hanlon*, BIT 2018, 209 (214 et seq.).

[555] Cf. *Rasch/Mank/Tomson*, IStR 2015, 424 (428); *Wehnert*, in: Lang/Storck/Petruzzi (Eds.), Transfer Pricing Developments Around the World 2018, 141 (148).

[556] Cf. *Kaeser/Bremer*, in: Lang/Storck/Petruzzi (Eds.), Transfer Pricing in a Post-BEPS World, 187 (202).

Especially in circumstances where a mismatch between profitability and the number of employees can be observed, e.g. in the case of automated PEs in which autonomous systems replace people, there is concern that such additional information might prelude to formulary apportionment and as a consequence will erode the arm's length principle.[557] This, again, bears a considerable risk of double taxation.

Moreover, confidentiality concerns were raised in literature.[558] Despite the fact that the OECD emphasised that tax administrations should take all reasonable steps to ensure that commercially sensitive data contained in the three-tiered approach to transfer pricing documentation are not disclosed publicly, considerable differences in the context of tax secrecy exist in the various jurisdictions.[559] Consequently, there is a fear that competitors might gain access to the data disclosed, particularly access to R&D results, trade secrets or confidential financial data.[560] Therefore, tax administrations are advised to follow the OECD Guide 'Keeping It Safe'[561] on how such information can be kept safe. Confidentiality concerns can also be identified in cases where disclosure is required in judicial decisions or public court proceedings. Even though the OECD emphasises that information shall only be disclosed to the extent needed,[562] sensitive data that is published during such judicial decisions or public court proceedings, can no longer be regarded confidential.[563]

---

557 Cf. *Kraft/Hentschel/Apler*, RIW 2017, 473 (479); *Grotherr*, RIW 2017, 1 (15); *Petruzzi*, in: Lang/Storck/Petruzzi (Eds.), Transfer Pricing Developments Around the World 2017, 1 (8 et seq.); *Kaeser/Bremer*, in: Lang/Storck/Petruzzi (Eds.), Transfer Pricing in a Post-BEPS World, 187 (206); *Hanlon*, BIT 2018, 209 (215 et seq.).

558 Cf. *Pinkernell*, FR 2014, 964 (969 et seq.); *Rasch/Mank/Tomson*, IStR 2015, 424 (428); *Hunt/Educate/Wentland*, TNI 85 (2017), 835 (835 et seqq.); *Petruzzi*, in: Lang/Storck/Petruzzi (Eds.), Transfer Pricing Developments Around the World 2017, 1 (8 et seq.); *Kaeser/Bremer*, in: Lang/Storck/Petruzzi (Eds.), Transfer Pricing in a Post-BEPS World, 187 (197); *Böhmer*, in: W/A/D (Eds.), Betriebsstätten-Handbuch, paras. 14.124 et seqq.

559 Cf. OECD, TP Guidelines 2017, para. 5.44.

560 This fear was also expressed several times in the comments to the discussion draft on BEPS Action 13. A list of the comments received on the discussion draft on transfer pricing documentation and CbC Reporting OECD is available at: http://www.oecd.org/tax/transfer-pricing/comments-discussion-draft-transfer-pricing-documentation.htm. See in this regard also *Rasch/Mank/Tomson*, IStR 2015, 424 (428); *Kaeser/Bremer*, in: Lang/Storck/Petruzzi (Eds.), Transfer Pricing in a Post-BEPS World, 187 (197).

561 OECD, Keeping It Safe—The OECD Guide on the Protection of Confidentiality of Information Exchanged for Tax Purposes.

562 Cf. OECD, TP Guidelines 2017, para. 5.44.

563 Cf. *Rasch/Mank/Tomson*, IStR 2015, 424 (428).

Only time can tell whether the new documentation requirements and especially the CbC Report will be a useful tool to standardise transfer pricing documentation requirements on an international level. As of now, the additional compliance costs for the taxpayer and the risk for misuse of the CbC Report by tax administrations outpace the ability of the documents to create a more transparent environment.

II. The Attribution of Profits to PEs under National Tax Law

1. Need for National Implementation of the AOA Approach

As elaborated in chapter C.IV.1.a, DTAs establish an independent mechanism aiming to avoid double taxation by restricting tax claims where overlapping claims by the respective treaty states are expected and therefore draw 'boundaries' on domestic taxation.[564] The extent to which a treaty state levies taxes—within the boundaries established by the DTA—is exclusively determined by its own domestic law.[565] It follows that the AOA as implemented in Article 7 OECD MC is not 'self-executing', but rather sets a limit on the amount of attributable profits that the host country of the PE may tax.[566] For the AOA to be fully applicable, it is necessary to implement national provisions into the tax laws of the respective jurisdictions.[567] In Germany, the AOA was implemented into national tax law through the Mutual Assistance Directive Implementation Act,[568] which resulted in Section 1 ETRA being amended.[569] According to Section 21(20) sentence 3 ETRA, the new provision is applicable for fiscal years starting after 31 December 2012.

The corresponding Ordinance on the application of the arm's length principle to PEs under Section 1(5) ETRA, the so-called 'Ordinance on the Allocation of

---

[564] Cf. *Kraft*, in: Kraft (Ed.), AStG—Kommentar, § 1 AStG, para. 610.

[565] Cf. *Vogel/Rust*, in: Reimer/Rust (Eds.), Klaus Vogel on Double Taxation Conventions, Introduction, paras. 52 et seqq.

[566] Cf. *Kraft*, in: Kraft (Ed.), AStG—Kommentar, § 1 AStG, para. 610.

[567] Cf. *Hentschel/Kraft/Moser*, ET 2018, 73 (74).

[568] Mutual Assistance Directive Implementation Act, 26 June 2013, BGBl. I 2013, 1809.

[569] Cf. *Hentschel/Kraft/Moser*, ET 2018, 73 (74). Critical with regard to the implementation of the AOA in Section 1 ETRA cf. *Kraft*, in: Kraft (Ed.), AStG—Kommentar, § 1 AStG, para. 621; *Wassermeyer*, IStR 2012, 277 (277 et seq.); *Gosch*, IWB 2012, 779 (785); *Schnitger*, IStR 2012, 633 (633); *Baldamus*, IStR 2012, 317 (318); *Ditz*, ISR 2013, 261 (262); *Schaumburg*, ISR 2013, 197 (198 et seq.); *Kußmaul/Ruiner*, BB 2012, 2029 (2029).

Profits of Permanent Establishments'[570] and the 'Administrative Principles on the Allocation of Profits of Permanent Establishments'[571] (hereinafter: VWG BsGa), were issued by the Federal Ministry of Finance on 17 October 2014 and 22 December 2016, respectively. Pursuant to Section 40 BsGaV, the new Ordinance is applicable for fiscal years starting after 31 December 2014.

2. Implementation of the AOA Approach in Section 1 ETRA

a. Conceptual Approach

In order to extent the scope of application of the arm's length principle to dealings between an enterprise and its PE, several amendments were made to Section 1 ETRA. First, the term 'business relations' as one of the requirements for the applicability of Section 1 ETRA was extended, resulting in the fact that also dealings between the PE and the rest of the enterprise are regarded as business transactions according to Section 1(4) sentence 1 no. 2 ETRA. Second, the two-step approach of the AOA hypothesising the PE as a separate and independent enterprise for the application of the arm's length principle was implemented in Section 1(5) ETRA.

Additionally, Section 1 ETRA was extended by paragraph six, authorising the Federal Ministry of Finance to issue a regulation in order to stipulate more detailed provisions on the arm's length principle as described in Section 1(1), (3) and (5) ETRA, as well as principles for determining the free capital as described in Section 1(5) sentence 3 no. 4 ETRA.

The above illustrated modifications to Section 1 ETRA will be described in more detail in the following.

b. Extension of the Scope of Application of Section 1 ETRA to PEs

Since a PE is a dependent part of the enterprise, *in personam* agreements between a PE and the rest of the enterprise are not possible.[572] Nevertheless, in order to extent the scope of application of the arm's length principle to business transactions between a PE and the rest of the enterprise, the German legislator introduced so-called 'notional *in personam* agreements' or so-called 'dealings'

[570] BsGaV, 13 Oct. 2014, BGBl. I 2014, 1603.

[571] BMF, 22 Dec. 2016, IV B 5—S 1341/12/10001–03, BStBl. I 2017, 182.

[572] Cf. BMF, 22 Dec. 2016, IV B 5—S 1341/12/10001–03, BStBl. I 2017, 182, para. 164; *Wassermeyer/Leonhardt*, in: F/W/B/S (Eds.), Außensteuerrecht—Kommentar, § 1 AStG, para. 2749.

in Section 1(4) sentence 1 no. 2 ETRA. Hence, not only individual or multiple connected economic transactions between the taxpayer and a related party to the taxpayer (Section 1(4) sentence 1 no. 1 ETRA) but also business transactions (dealings) between the head office and its PE (Section 1(4) sentence 1 no. 2 ETRA) are regarded as business transactions for the purpose of the application of the arm's length principle within the meaning of Section 1 ETRA.

In this context, Section 1(5) sentence 1 ETRA determines that Section 1(1), (3) and (4) ETRA are only applicable if the transfer prices for such dealings are not consistent with the arm's length principle and result in either a reduction of the domestic income of a taxpayer with limited tax liability in Germany or an increase of the foreign income of a taxpayer with unlimited tax liability in Germany.[573] Both scenarios would negatively impact the amount of taxable income in Germany and shall therefore be covered by the respective provision.[574] In other words, an adjustment of income in the PE context is only possible if the transfer prices for the dealings between the head office and the PE negatively impact the amount of taxable income in Germany. This asymmetry results in a lack of recognition of business expenses for notional service charges (such as charges for licence, rental or other services) for PEs that are subject to limited tax liability in Germany.[575] Thus, the implementation of the AOA in Section 1 ETRA, as a provision dealing with the adjustment of income, is rightly criticised in literature.[576] To achieve the concept of the AOA as a provision for the determination and allocation of income between the PE and the rest of the enterprise, an implementation of the concept in the German ITA would have been more suitable.[577]

The reference in Section 1(5) sentence 1 ETRA to Section 1(1), (3) and (4) ETRA leads to the fact that the principles set out in these paragraphs not only apply to individual or multiple connected economic transactions between the taxpayer and a related party to the taxpayer, but also to dealings between the PE and

---

[573]Cf. Section 1(5) sentence 1 ETRA.

[574]Cf. *Kaeser*, in: W/K/S/D (Eds.), Doppelbesteuerung, Art. 7 (2010), para. 707; *Kraft*, in: Kraft (Ed.), AStG—Kommentar, § 1 AStG, para. 637.

[575]Cf. *Kraft*, in: Kraft (Ed.), AStG—Kommentar, § 1 AStG, para. 621.

[576]Critical regarding the implementation of the AOA in Section 1 ETRA see *Wassermeyer*, IStR 2012, 277 (277 et seq.); *Gosch*, IWB 2012, 779 (785); *Schnitger*, IStR 2012, 633 (633); *Baldamus*, IStR 2012, 317 (318); *Ditz*, ISR 2013, 261 (262 et seq.); *Schaumburg*, ISR 2013, 197 (198 et seq.); *Kußmaul/Delarber/Müller*, IStR 2014, 466 (473); *Kußmaul/Ruiner*, BB 2012, 2025 (2029).

[577]Cf. *Wassermeyer*, IStR 2012, 277 (277 et seq.); *Kußmaul/Ruiner*, BB 2012, 2027 (2029); *Ditz*, ISR 2013, 261 (262).

other parts of the enterprise. Especially, the principles set out in Section 1(3) sentence 1–8 ETRA, dealing with the determination of appropriate transfer prices, are also applicable for dealings between the PE and other parts of the enterprise. Also, the provisions of Section 1(3) sentence 9–12 ETRA dealing with the relocation of functions are applicable in the PE context.[578]

c. Hypothesising the PE as a Separate and Independent Enterprise

When applying the arm's length principle, a PE must be treated as a separate and independent enterprise, unless the PE's relationship to the enterprise requires a different treatment.[579] Consequently, despite the fact that a PE is a legally dependent part of the enterprise, it shall be treated otherwise for tax purposes.

According to the governments reasoning and the VWG BsGa the fact that the PE is a dependent part of the enterprise from a legal perspective leads to the assumption that the PE shares the same creditworthiness as the enterprise as a whole and is insofar not to be treated as a separate and independent enterprise.[580] Furthermore, the VWG BsGa outlines some of the provisions implemented in the BsGaV which are necessary in order to account for the differences between a PE and a separate and independent enterprise.[581] On 17 December 2019 the Federal Ministry of Finance supplemented the VWG BsGa by a new paragraph 6a outlining that the PE's relationship to the enterprise may also require a different treatment in cases where no significant people functions are carried out in the PE (e.g. wind and solar power plants).[582]

---

[578]Cf. *Kraft*, in: Kraft (Ed.), AStG—Kommentar, § 1 AStG, para. 645; *Schnitger*, IStR 2012, 633 (638); *Richter/Heyd*, Ubg 2013, 418 (420). See in more detail with regard to the issue of the reallocation of functions *Hentschel*, Deutsche Regelungen zur internationalen Funktionsverlagerung.

[579]Cf. Section 1(5) sentence 2 ETRA. Detailed for circumstances which justify a different treatment of the PE to the enterprise of which it is a part *Melhem/Dombrowski*, IStR 2015, 912 (912 et seqq.).

[580]Cf. BT-Drs. 17/10000, 64; BMF, 22 Dec. 2016, IV B 5—S 1341/12/10001–03, BStBl. I 2017, 182, para. 7. Insofar the German legislator follows the OECD approach, cf. OECD, PE Report 2010, Part I, paras. 99 et seq.

[581]See in more detail BMF, 22 Dec. 2016, IV B 5—S 1341/12/10001–03, BStBl. I 2017, 182, para. 6.

[582]Cf. BMF, 17 Dec. 2019, IV B 5—S 1341/19/10010:003 03, BStBl. I 2020, 84. Detailed for consequences of this additional paragraph see chapter D.II.3.b.(1)(c).

3. The 2-Step Approach According to Section 1(5) Sentence 3 and 4 ETRA in conjunction with the Provisions of the BsGaV

a. Preliminary Remarks

From a systematic perspective, the approach taken by the German legislator for the attribution of income for tax purposes to the PE generally follows the 2-step approach of the AOA as developed by the OECD. In a first step, the PE must be treated as a separate and independent enterprise.[583] In order to do so, a function and risk analysis of the business activities of the PE as part of the business activities of the enterprise's business activities must be performed.[584] On the basis of this analysis, the people functions that are either attributed to the PE or the rest of the enterprise must be determined, especially, the significant people functions.[585] Due to the fact that assets as well as opportunities and risks cannot be attributed based on legal contracts, Section 1(2) no. 1 BsGaV determines that the attribution of assets as well as opportunities and risks shall be based on the identified significant people functions.[586] Furthermore, free capital and liability items as well as business transactions of the enterprise with independent third parties and related parties must be attributed to the PE.[587] Also, dealings within the meaning of Section 1(4) sentence 1 no. 2 ETRA must be determined.[588]

In the second step, a comparability analysis based on the function and risk analysis must be performed in order to determine transfer prices for the business relations as defined in Section 1(4) ETRA that are in line with the arm's length principle.[589]

---

[583] Cf. Section 1(5) sentence 3 ETRA.

[584] Cf. Section 1(1) sentence 1 BsGaV. Details on how to carry out the function and risk analysis are neither provided in the BsGaV nor in the VWG BsGa. However, the cross-reference in para. 26 of the VWG BsGa to the OECD PE Report 2010 which itself refers to the TP Guidelines indicates that the explanations provided by the PE Report 2010 and the TP Guidelines—despite the fact that they only constitute 'soft-law' and, thus, are not legally binding—can also be used as guidance in order to carry out the function and risk analysis for the purpose of Section 1(5) sentence 3 ETRA. Detailed for the function and risk analysis see *Puls*, in: Wassermeyer/Baumhoff (Eds.), Verrechnungspreise international verbundener Unternehmen, 279 et seqq.

[585] Cf. Section 1(5) sentence 3 no. 1 ETRA in conjunction with Section 1(2) no. 1 BsGaV.

[586] Cf. Section 1(5) sentence 3 no. 2–3 ETRA in conjunction with Section 1(2) no. 2 BsGaV.

[587] Cf. Section 1(2) nos. 3–5 BsGaV.

[588] Cf. Section 1(2) no. 6 BsGaV.

[589] Cf. Section 1(5) sentence 4 ETRA in conjunction with Section 1(1) sentence 2 BsGaV.

In the following the 2-step approach as implemented in Section 1(5) sentence 3 and 4 ETRA in conjunction with the provisions of the BsGaV will be elaborated in further detail. Each of the stages within the 2-step approach will be discussed and compared to the OECD approach.

b. Step 1: Hypothesising the PE as a Separate and Independent Enterprise

(1) Attribution of People Functions

(a) The Terms 'People Function' and 'Own Personnel'

On the basis of the function and risk analysis of the PEs business activities people functions must be determined and attributed to the PE and the rest of the enterprise, particularly the significant people functions.[590] A clarification of the term 'people function' is provided in Section 2(3) sentence 1 BsGaV. Accordingly, a people function is a business activity which is performed for the enterprise by the enterprise's own personnel. Section 2(3) sentence 2 BsGaV provides a list of the following nine activities which are deemed to constitute a people function: use, acquisition, production, management, sale, development, protection, risk management and the decision to undertake changes regarding opportunities and risks. The activities provided are only of an exemplary nature and cannot be regarded as exhaustive.[591]

In this context, the enterprise's own personnel shall include any individual who performs activities for the enterprise based upon an employment agreement or a partnership with the enterprise.[592] Also individuals who are hired out from another enterprise based upon an employment contract which is restricted to such hiring shall be part of the enterprise's own personnel.[593] The VWG BsGa further clarifies that individuals from another enterprise working for the enterprise on the legal basis of a service agreement shall not be part of the enterprise's own personnel.[594] This approach was criticised in literature as being outdated and not in line with Section 1(5) sentence 3 half-sentence 1 ETRA, since the non-recognition of

---

[590]Cf. Section 1(2) BsGaV.

[591]Cf. *Kraft*, in: Kraft (Ed.), AStG—Kommentar, § 1 AStG, para. 655; *Andresen*, in: W/A/D (Eds.), Betriebsstätten-Handbuch, para. 4.65.

[592]Cf. Section 2(4) sentence 1 BsGaV.

[593]Cf. Section 2(4) sentence 2 BsGaV; BMF, 22 Dec. 2016, IV B 5—S 1341/12/10001–03, BStBl. I 2017, 182, para. 37.

[594]Cf. BMF, 22 Dec. 2016, IV B 5—S 1341/12/10001–03, BStBl. I 2017, 182, para. 38. The differentiation between the posting of workers and services is in line with the administrative principles dealing with the posting of workers, cf. BMF, 9 Nov. 2001, IV B 4—S 1341—20/01, BStBl. I 2011, 796, para. 2.1.

such service agreements for the determination of people functions does not reflect the approach to treat the PE as a separate and independent enterprise.[595] Furthermore, individuals who perform activities for the enterprise without contractual agreements are part of the enterprise's own personnel if they are an entrepreneur, partner or shareholder of the enterprise or are related to the enterprise of the partners or shareholders of the enterprise as described in Section 1(2) ETRA.[596]

After the identification of the people functions, it needs to be assessed what significance such people functions have for the purpose of generating profits for the enterprise. The Ordinance distinguishes between significant and non-significant functions.[597] Since the attribution of assets, opportunities and risks and of business transactions to the PE shall be based on the significant people functions,[598] it is of particular importance to identify these functions. According to Section 2(5) sentence 1 BsGaV, a people function is deemed to be significant for the attribution of assets, opportunities and risks and business transactions to the PE if the performance of the people function in the regular course of the business is most important for the aforementioned items, in relation to the people functions which are performed in other PEs of the enterprise.[599] Whether a people function performed in the PE can be regarded as significant is contingent upon the specific relationship of the people function with regard to the item that shall be attributed and must be decided on a case-by-case basis.[600] In this respect, it is not decisive where within the enterprise hierarchy the decision is taken formally. People functions that are merely supportive in nature (e.g. administrative activities such as legal and tax consultancy, accounting or internal audit)[601] or relate solely to the enterprise's general business policy (e.g. strategy functions)[602] are not deemed to be significant.[603]

Despite the fact that non-significant people functions are irrelevant for the attribution of assets, they must still be attributed to the relevant part of the enterprise, since such functions might be subject of a dealing within the meaning

---

[595] Cf. *Andresen*, in: W/A/D (Eds.), Betriebsstätten-Handbuch, para. 4.70.

[596] Cf. Section 2(4) sentence 3 BsGaV.

[597] Cf. Section 2(5) BsGaV.

[598] Cf. Section 1(2) BsGaV.

[599] Cf. Section 2(5) sentence 1 BsGaV.

[600] Cf. BMF, 22 Dec. 2016, IV B 5—S 1341/12/10001–03, BStBl. I 2017, 182, para. 40.

[601] Cf. *Haverkamp,* in: Mössner et al. (Eds.), Steuerrecht international tätiger Unternehmen, para. 5.175.

[602] Cf. BMF, 22 Dec. 2016, IV B 5—S 1341/12/10001–03, BStBl. I 2017, 182, para. 40.

[603] Cf. Section 2(5) sentence 2 BsGaV.

of Section 16(1) no. 2 lit. a BsGaV (e.g. notional surrender of use or notional services) and as a consequence influence the profit attribution of the PE.[604] This finding ultimately leads to the conclusion that profits may also be attributed to the PE in cases where only non-significant functions are carried out by the personnel at the PE's location.

(b) Fundamental Attribution Approach

With regard to the attribution of people functions it is determined by Section 4(1) sentence 1 BsGaV that a people function shall be attributed to the PE in which it is performed (presumption rule). In other words, the attribution of the people functions to either the PE or another part of the enterprise is contingent upon where within the enterprise the significant people functions are carried out by the personnel. In this context, it should be stressed that it is the people function that is to be attributed to the PE and not the personnel working for the PE itself.[605] Moreover, while the personnel of the enterprise might perform various people functions successively that may be attributed to different PEs, the people function itself can only be attributed to one PE.[606]

While employment contracts shall usually provide the necessary information where within the enterprise the personnel actually carries out work, situations may arise where the personnel carries out work in various PEs of the enterprise making a clear attribution challenging.[607] In such circumstances, Section 4(1) sentence 2 BsGaV determines that a people function is not to be attributed to a PE if it has no material connection with the business activities of the PE and is performed in the PE for less than 30 days within a fiscal year. Conversely, a people function carried out in a PE shall be attributed to that PE if it has material connection with the business activities of the PE or is carried out in the PE for more than 30 days. A pragmatic solution that may be of help for the identification of the place where the personnel of the enterprise carry out work is the preparation of an organisation chart.[608]

However, difficulties may still arise in situations where people functions cannot be attributed to specific locations, e.g. in cases of sales representatives or when

[604] Cf. BMF, 22 Dec. 2016, IV B 5—S 1341/12/10001–03, BStBl. I 2017, 182, para. 48.

[605] Cf. *Kraft*, in: Kraft (Ed.), AStG—Kommentar, § 1 AStG, para. 657.

[606] Cf. BMF, 22 Dec. 2016, IV B 5—S 1341/12/10001–03, BStBl. I 2017, 182, para. 36.

[607] Cf. *Haverkamp,* in: Mössner et al. (Eds.), Steuerrecht international tätiger Unternehmen, para. 5.178.

[608] Cf. *Kraft/Dombrowski*, FR 2014, 1105 (1108).

posting workers. Also, the board of directors or similar decision-making committees may consist of members who reside in different countries making decisions via video conferencing or other means of communication.[609] In such cases where the people function is performed neither in the PE nor in the rest of the enterprise or in cases where the people function has no material connection with the business activities of the PE and is performed in the PE for less than 30 days within a fiscal year (cases of Section 4(1) sentence 2 BsGaV), the people function must be attributed to the PE to which it has the closest material connection.[610] Neither the BsGaV nor the VWG BsGa provides for a definition of the term 'material connection'. However, the scope of evaluation permitted by the BsGaV shall be justified by objective criteria and evidence on a case-by-case basis.[611]

If a people function cannot be attributed clearly on the basis of these attribution rules, it must be attributed in a manner which does not conflict with Section 4(1) and (2) BsGaV.[612] This provision can be regarded as a residuary clause which provides a high level of leeway for the taxpayer.[613] Consequently, an adequate and thorough documentation which also includes the reasons for the attribution decision is recommended in order to reduce possible discussions with the tax administration.[614] Otherwise, an estimate according to Section 162(3) GFC is to be feared.[615] As explicitly emphasised in the VWG BsGa, a pro rata attribution of a people function to different PEs is not accepted.[616]

---

[609] Cf. *Kraft*, in: Kraft (Ed.), AStG—Kommentar, § 1 AStG, para. 658. See in more detail in this regard *Leonhardt/Tcherveniachki*, in: F/W/B/S (Eds.), Außensteuerrecht—Kommentar, § 1 AStG, para. 3013; *Kroppen*, DB 2014, 2134 (2134); *Roeder/Friedrich*, BB 2015, 1053 (1055).

[610] Cf. Section 4(2) BsGaV.

[611] Cf. *Haverkamp*, in: Mössner et al. (Eds.), Steuerrecht international tätiger Unternehmen, para. 5.179.

[612] Cf. Section 4(3) BsGaV. Cf. in more detail for the issue of split functions and rivalry of functions BMF, 22 Dec. 2016, IV B 5—S 1341/12/10001–03, BStBl. I 2017, 182, paras. 42 et seq.

[613] Cf. *Kraft*, in: Kraft (Ed.), AStG—Kommentar, § 1 AStG, para. 659.

[614] Cf. *Haverkamp*, in: Mössner et al. (Eds.), Steuerrecht international tätiger Unternehmen, para. 5.179. See in this regard also BMF, 22 Dec. 2016, IV B 5—S 1341/12/10001–03, BStBl. I 2017, 182, para. 75.

[615] Cf. BMF, 22 Dec. 2016, IV B 5—S 1341/12/10001–03, BStBl. I 2017, 182, para. 75.

[616] Cf. BMF, 22 Dec. 2016, IV B 5—S 1341/12/10001–03, BStBl. I 2017, 182, para. 75.

(c) PEs without Personnel

In this context, an issue of high relevance is the question of how to treat PEs which operate without personnel. Such PEs are of no rare occurrence nowadays. Examples of such PEs are servers, pipelines or fully automated facilities where manpower is substituted by autonomous operating systems, to name just a few. As already elaborated in chapter C.III.2.c.(2) the presence of personnel is in principle not required for a PE to exist as long as the activity carried on by the fully automated facility serves the business purpose.[617] However, given the attribution approach of Section 1 BsGaV in conjunction with Section 4 BsGaV, the absence of personnel does not allow for the attribution of 'people' functions to such PEs. As a consequence the attribution approach of the AOA results in the circumstance that no assets, opportunities and risks and therefore also no profits can be attributed to such PE's.[618]

Unfortunately, neither the legislator nor the BsGaV provide for any further clarification in this regard. The paragraph in the draft version of the VWG BsGa[619] stating that only little or no profit can be attributed to underground pipelines (pipeline PEs) did not make it into the final version of the VWG BsGa, leaving room for interpretation at the expense of legal certainty for the taxpayer.[620] Nevertheless, this result does not reflect the economic reality and illustrates a failure of the AOA since fully automated PEs without personnel might very well contribute to the value creation process and would therefore also justify the attribution of a certain amount of profit to such PEs.[621]

To circumvent this shortcoming of the AOA principles, it was discussed in literature whether the so-called 'escape-clause' pursuant to Section 1(5) sentence 2 half-sentence 2 ETRA, stating that a PE shall be treated as a separate and independent enterprise unless the PEs relationship to the enterprise requires a different

[617] Cf. BFH, 30 Oct. 1996, II R 12/92, BStBl. II 1997, 12.

[618] Cf. *Kraft/Hentschel/Apler*, Ubg 2017, 318 (325); *Kraft*, in: Kraft (Ed.), AStG—Kommentar, § 1 AStG, para. 663.

[619] Cf. BMF, 13 Mar. 2016, draft version, para. 49.

[620] Cf. *Kraft/Hentschel/Apler*, Ubg 2017, 318 (325); *Kraft*, in: Kraft (Ed.), AStG—Kommentar, § 1 AStG, para. 663. The reason for deleting the respective para. in the final version of the VWG BsGa was probably driven by politically considerations, especially against the background of Action Point 1 'Addressing the Tax Challenges of the Digital Economy', cf. *Haverkamp,* in: Mössner et al. (Eds.), Steuerrecht international tätiger Unternehmen, para. 5.179.

[621] Cf. *Kraft/Hentschel/Apler*, Ubg 2017, 318 (325); also *Kahle/Baschnagel/Kindich*, FR 2016, 193 (201); *Heggmair/Riedl/Wutschke*, IStR 2015, 92 (96).

treatment, can be applied for PEs which operate without personnel.[622] Put in different words, Section 1(5) sentence 2 half-sentence 2 ETRA allows for deviations from the AOA principles in certain cases. However, neither the legislator nor the BsGaV specifies the cases justifying the application of Section 1(5) sentence 2 half-sentence 2 ETRA. As argued by *Kraft/Hentschel/Apler*[623], a PE without personnel is indeed different and might justify a profit attribution which deviates from the AOA principles.[624] While *Kahle/Baschnagel/Kindich*[625] argue that the justification of the law[626] does not support such a view, *Melhem/Dombrowski*[627] argue that the aforementioned justification does not provide any additional insight supporting either way.[628]

Given the uncertainty that surrounds the applicability of Section 1(5) sentence 2 half-sentence 2 ETRA, the circular of the Federal Ministry of Finance from 17 December 2019 supplementing the VWG BsGa by a new paragraph 6a is to be welcomed.[629] Accordingly, in cases where no significant people functions are carried out by the PE the PE's relationship to the enterprise may require a different treatment (and therefore the applicability of the 'escape-clause' pursuant to Section 1(5) sentence 2 half-sentence 2 ETRA).[630] In this context, the circular refers to para. 66 of the PE-Report 2010. As outlined earlier,[631] para. 66 of the PE-Report 2010 states that in the case of a Server PE the functional and factual analysis shall determine which so-called 'automated functions' are performed by the PE.[632] The automated nature of these functions carried out by a Server PE

[622] Cf. *Kraft/Hentschel/Apler*, Ubg 2017, 318 (325 et seq.); *Melhem/Dombrowski*, IStR 2015, 912 (912 et seq.); *Kraft*, in: Kraft (Ed.), AStG—Kommentar, § 1 AStG, para. 664.

[623] *Kraft/Hentschel/Apler*, Ubg 2017, 318 (326).

[624] Also *Melhem/Dombrowski* argue for the applicability of the escape-clause for such PEs, cf. *Melhem/Dombrowski*, IStR 2015, 912 (912 et seq.).

[625] Cf. *Kahle/Baschnagel/Kindich*, FR 2016, 193 (201).

[626] Cf. BT-Drs. 17/10000, 64.

[627] Cf. *Melhem/Dombrowski* who argue that the examples provided by the justification of the law for the applicability of Section 1(5) sentence 2 half-sentence 2 ETRA are only exemplary and consequently non-exhaustive, cf. *Melhem/Dombrowski*, IStR 2015, 912 (912 et seq.).

[628] Cf. *Kraft/Hentschel/Apler*, Ubg 2017, 318 (326).

[629] Cf. for the circular BMF, 17 Dec. 2019, IV B 5—S 1341/19/10010:003 03, BStBl. I 2020, 84.

[630] Cf. BMF, 17 Dec. 2019, IV B 5—S 1341/19/10010:003 03, BStBl. I 2020, 84.

[631] See chapter D.I.4.b.(2)(a)iii of this thesis.

[632] Cf. OECD, PE Report 2010, Part I, para. 66.

results in the circumstance that only assets and risks which are directly associated with the server hardware can be attributed to a Server PE.[633]

Nevertheless, the OECD concludes that since no significant people functions are carried out in the Server PE, only little or no profit can be attributed to such a PE.[634] This result may not be satisfactory considering that also fully automated PEs which carry on business activities without personnel might very well contribute to the value creation process and would therefore also justify the attribution of a higher amount of profit to such PEs.[635] However, compared to the result without the

(d) Comparison to the OECD Approach

In general, both the OECD and the German legislator follow the same approach regarding the concept of people functions. However, the OECD approach can be regarded as rather broad and flexible compared to the German approach outlining very specific provisions.[636] Some of the major differences of the two concepts that may potentially lead to a different attribution of people functions to PEs shall be pointed out in the following.

While the term 'people function' is defined in Section 2(3) sentence 1 BsGaV as a business activity performed for the enterprise by the enterprise's own personnel, the PE Report 2010 does not explicitly provide a definition for the term. It is only determined that the functional and factual analysis shall take account of the functions 'performed by the personnel of the enterprise'[637]. Given the underlying economic approach of the PE Report 2010 and the fact that it is not explicitly emphasised by the OECD that 'own' personnel is required in this sense, it is argued in literature that individuals from another enterprise working for the enterprise on the legal basis of a service agreement shall also be part of the enterprise's personnel.[638] However, this approach is not in line with the principles outlined in the VWG BsGa explicitly emphasising that such personnel shall not be part

---

[633] Cf. OECD, PE Report 2010, Part I, para. 66.

[634] Cf. OECD, PE Report 2010, Part I, para. 66; same conclusion *Greinert/Metzner*, Ubg 2014, 307 (309); *Kaeser*, in: W/K/S/D (Eds.), Doppelbesteuerung, Art. 7 MA (2010), para. 450; *Andresen*, in: W/A/D (Eds.), Betriebsstätten-Handbuch, para. 5.19. Critical with regard to PEs in e-commerce *Mödinger*, Internationale Erfolgs- und Vermögensabgrenzung zwischen Stammhaus und Betriebsstätte nach der Neufassung des Art. 7 OECD-MA, 214 et seqq.

[635] See in more detail for discussion *Kraft/Hentschel/Apler*, Ubg 2017, 318 (325 et seq.).

[636] Cf. *Andresen*, ITPJ 2015, 77 (79).

[637] OECD, PE Report 2010, Part I, para. 62.

[638] Cf. *Andresen*, in: W/A/D (Eds.), Betriebsstätten-Handbuch, para. 5.19.

of the enterprise's own personnel.[639] It follows that the OECD approach can be regarded as broader and rather based on real economic activity than on legal circumstances.[640]

When it comes to the attribution of profits to the PE, both the OECD and the German legislator refer to the concept of the people functions.[641] While the PE Report 2010 distinguishes between significant people functions and support or ancillary people functions,[642] Section 2(5) BsGaV differentiates significant from non-significant people functions. Both the PE Report 2010 and the BsGaV emphasise that the attribution of assets, opportunities and risks and of business transactions to the PE shall be based on the significant people functions.[643] Since the German tax administration refers to the PE Report 2010 when determining whether or not a people function is deemed to be significant for the attribution of assets, opportunities and risks as well as business transactions to a PE, it can be assumed that the approaches are in line with each other.[644]

Another issue that must be stressed relates to the attribution of people functions to the PE. While both approaches follow the same fundamental concept, namely the attribution of the people function to the PE in which it is performed geographically, the devil is in the detail. On the one side, Section 4(1) sentence 2 BsGaV determines that the outlined fundamental approach is not acceptable if the people function has no material connection to the PE's business activities and is performed in the PE on less than 30 days within a fiscal year. Only then and in cases where the people function is neither performed in the PE nor in the rest of the enterprise, Section 4(2) BsGaV provides for an attribution of the people function to the PE to which it has the closest material connection. On the other side, the PE Report 2010 does not provide for an attribution of people functions other than to the PE in which they are performed geographically.[645] Consequently, the illustrated deviations from the fundamental concept implemented in Section 4 (1) sentence 2 and Section 4(2) and (3) BsGaV might lead to a different attribution

[639] Cf. BMF, 22 Dec. 2016, IV B 5—S 1341/12/10001–03, BStBl. I 2017, 182, para. 38.

[640] Cf. *Andresen*, in: W/A/D (Eds.), Betriebsstätten-Handbuch, para. 5.19.

[641] Cf. OECD, PE Report 2010, Part I, para. 62.

[642] Cf. OECD, PE Report 2010, Part I, para. 62.

[643] Cf. OECD, PE Report 2010, Part I, para. 59; Section 1(2) BsGaV.

[644] The German tax administration refers in para. 40 of the VWG BsGa to para. 16 of Part I of the PE Report 2010.

[645] Cf. *Ditz*, ISR 2012, 48 (53); *Looks*, in: Looks/Heinsen (Eds.), Betriebsstättenbesteuerung, para. 759.

of the people function, especially in circumstances illustrated in Section 4(1) sentence 2 BsGaV. Moreover, while the OECD does not provide any clarifications regarding overlapping people functions such as monitoring or management activities,[646] the BsGaV provides guidance for such issues implemented in Section 4(2) and Section 4(3) BsGaV. Guidance is also provided for the specific cases of split functions and rivalry of functions by the German tax administration.[647] Despite the fact that the German approach leaves certain leeway for interpretation as well (e.g. the term 'material connection' is neither specified by the BsGaV nor the VWG BsGa), it can be concluded that the BsGaV and the VWG BsGa provide more detailed guidance and, as a matter of fact, results in a more consistent application regarding the attribution of people functions to the PE than the guidance provided by the OECD.

An issue of growing importance is the question of how to treat PEs which operate without personnel. While there is consensus that the presence of personnel is in principle not required for a PE to exist,[648] it was questionable whether the escape clause implemented in Section 1(5) sentence 2 half-sentence 2 ETRA can be applied for such PEs. Against this background, the circular issued by the Federal Ministry of Finance on 17 December 2019 stating that the escape clause of Section 1(5) sentence 2 half-sentence 2 ETRA can be applied for PEs which operate without personnel is to be welcomed. The reference in the circular of the Federal Ministry of Finance to para. 66 of the PE-Report 2010 suggests that no differences to the OECD approach are intended.

Table 3 provides an overview of the OECD and the German approach with respect to the attribution of people functions.

(2) Attribution of Assets

(a) The Term 'Assets'

According to Section 1(5) sentence 3 no. 2 ETRA, assets needed to perform the designated business functions must be attributed to the PE. Before taking a closer look at the attribution rules for such assets, it shall be clarified what is actually meant by the term 'assets' in this context. This fundamental question is tackled in the BsGaV as well as in the VWG BsGa.

---

[646] Cf. *Ditz*, ISR 2012, 48 (53); *Looks*, in: Looks/Heinsen (Eds.), Betriebsstättenbesteuerung, para. 759.

[647] Cf. in more detail for the issue of split functions and rivalry of functions BMF, 22 Dec. 2016, IV B 5—S 1341/12/10001–03, BStBl. I 2017, 182, paras. 42 et seq.

[648] Cf. for OECD view OECD, PE Report 2010, Part I, para. 66. Cf. for view of the German Federal Tax Court BFH, 30 Oct. 1996, II R 12/92, BStBl. II 1997, 12.

Table 3 OECD vs. German Approach for Attribution of People Functions

<table>
<tr><th></th><th>OECD approach</th><th>German approach</th></tr>
<tr><td>Definition and scope of the term people function</td><td>• no definition provided
• paraphrased as a function performed by the personnel of the enterprise
• can range from support or ancillary people functions to significant people functions</td><td>• business activity performed for the enterprise by the enterprise's own personnel
• can range from significant to non-significant people functions</td></tr>
<tr><td>Personnel</td><td>• no definition provided
• broad understanding of the term which shall also include individuals from another enterprise working for the enterprise on the legal basis of a service agreement</td><td>• only own personnel which includes individuals who
– perform activities on the basis of an employment agreement
– are hired out from another enterprise
– are an entrepreneur or partner or shareholder of the enterprise are is related to that individual within the meaning of Section 1(2) ETRA
• explicitly excluded: individuals from another enterprise working for the enterprise on the legal basis of a service agreement</td></tr>
<tr><td rowspan="2">Attribution of people functions</td><td colspan="2">• significant people function as the relevant people function for attribution of assets, opportunities, risks and business transactions
• general rule: attribution of the people function to the PE where it is performed geographically</td></tr>
<tr><td>• no exceptions from the general rule
• rather broad and flexible compared to German approach</td><td>• exceptions from general rule apply according to Section 4(1) sentence 2 BsGaV and Section 4(2) and (3) BsGaV
• more detailed and consistent in its application than OECD pproach</td></tr>
</table>

(continued)

While Section 2(6) BsGaV points out that assets are economic goods and benefits which shall, in particular, include a) tangible assets, b) intangible values, including intangibles, c) stakes, and d) financial assets, the VWG BsGa sheds

Table 3 (continued)

	OECD approach	German approach
Treatment of PEs without personnel	• no significant people function can be attributed to such PEs	
	• for Server PEs: concept of automated functions → allow for the attribution of assets and risks which are directly associated with the server hardware • only little or no profit can be attributed	• Section 1(5) sentence 2 half sentence 2 ETRA applicable • reference to para. 66 of the PE Report 2010 through the circular of the Federal Ministry of Finance suggests that no difference to the OECD approach is intended • consequently, only little or no profit can be attributed to PEs without personnel

Source: Own illustration.

more light on the term. In principle, the scope of the term can be regarded as very broad. Definitions of the term assets provided by the national or international accounting standards shall not be decisive in this context.[649] Neither shall it be of significance whether the assets are included in the auxiliary and ancillary accounts of the PE.[650] In contrast to the term assets used for the purpose of tax and commercial accounting, also non-accounted assets (such as internally developed intangibles)[651] or assets that are not accountable[652] on the balance sheet (such as expenses for setting up a company or expenses for raising equity) shall be a relevant asset since they might be subject of a dealing within the meaning of Section 1(4) sentence 1 no. 2 ETRA and therefore of importance for the purpose of attributing profits to the PE.[653]

Benefits within the meaning of Section 2(6) sentence 1 BsGaV can only be subject of a dealing within the meaning of Section 1(4) sentence 1 no. 2 ETRA if they are suitable, i.e. they must have their 'own value'.[654] Examples of benefits are provided by the VWG BsGa.[655] Accordingly, e.g. financial instruments within the meaning of Section 254 German Commercial Code (hereinafter: GCC), which are

---

[649] Cf. BMF, 22 Dec. 2016, IV B 5—S 1341/12/10001–03, BStBl. I 2017, 182, para. 49.

[650] Cf. BMF, 22 Dec. 2016, IV B 5—S 1341/12/10001–03, BStBl. I 2017, 182, para. 49.

[651] For non-accounted assets on the balance sheet see Section 248(2) sentence 2 GCC.

[652] For assets not accountable on the balance sheet see Section 248(1) GCC.

[653] Cf. BMF, 22 Dec. 2016, IV B 5—S 1341/12/10001–03, BStBl. I 2017, 182, para. 49.

[654] Cf. *Rasch/Wenzel*, ISR 2015, 128 (129).

[655] Cf. BMF, 22 Dec. 2016, IV B 5—S 1341/12/10001–03, BStBl. I 2017, 182, para. 50.

no assets but are used for the hedging of assets within the meaning of Section 11 BsGaV, shall constitute a benefit in this respect.[656]

(b) Fundamental Attribution Approach

i. Overview

The rules for the attribution of assets to the PE are laid down in Sections 5–8 BsGaV. In this regard, the BsGaV distinguishes between the attribution of tangible assets (Section 5 BsGaV), intangibles (Section 6 BsGaV), stakes, financial assets and similar assets (Section 7 BsGaV) as well as other assets (Section 8 BsGaV). Even though the specific criteria for the attribution of the illustrated assets differ from asset to asset, especially with regard to the relevant significant people function, the underlying attribution approach is the same and shall be outlined in the following.

Subsection one of the specific Sections determines that the respective asset must be attributed to the PE where the significant people function is performed (Subsection 1: presumption rule). If another people function performed in another PE is clearly of 'greater importance' for the relevant asset, this asset shall be attributed to that other PE (Subsection 2: derogation rule). The third Subsection specifies Subsection 2 by stating that in cases where the people functions which are of greater importance are simultaneously performed in multiple PEs, the asset shall be attributed to the PE whose other people function is of the greatest importance for the relevant asset (Subsection 3: specification of derogation rule). If an asset cannot be attributed clearly, Subsection 4 of the relevant Section provides a margin of discretion for the taxpayer by determining that the respective asset can be attributed in a manner that does not conflict with Subsection 1–3 (Subsection 4: escape-clause). However, when applying the escape-clause, the burden of proof that an attribution according to Subsection 1–3 does not lead to unambiguous results lies with the taxpayer and must be documented properly.[657]

ii. Attribution of Tangible Assets

According to Section 5(1) BsGaV, the significant people function for the attribution of tangible assets to a PE shall be its use. If the tangible asset is later used in another PE on a long-term basis, it must be attributed to the other PE from that point in time onward.[658] This change of attribution must be regarded as a notional

---

[656] Cf. BMF, 22 Dec. 2016, IV B 5—S 1341/12/10001–03, BStBl. I 2017, 182, para. 50.

[657] Cf. *Haverkamp,* in: Mössner et al. (Eds.), Steuerrecht international tätiger Unternehmen, para. 5.171. For documentation requirements see in further detail chapter D.II.5 of this thesis.

[658] Cf. Section 5(1) sentence 2 BsGaV.

sale and insofar constitutes a dealing within the meaning of Section 16(1) no. 1 BsGaV.[659] Temporary changes of use to another PE shall not lead to a change in attribution. Rather the use of the relevant asset leads to a notional surrender of use and insofar also constitutes a dealing within the meaning of Section 16(1) no. 2 lit. a BsGaV. In cases of frequent changes of use, i.e. more than two times in a fiscal year, the tangible asset must be attributed to the PE for whose business activity the tangible asset is used predominantly.[660] This way, notional sales within the meaning of Section 16(1) no. 1 BsGaV which may lead to the taxation of hidden reserves can be avoided.[661]

Exceptions to the presumption rule of Section 5(1) BsGaV are illustrated in Section 5(2) BsGaV. Accordingly, a tangible asset must be attributed to the PE other than that in which it is used if the importance of another people function (e.g. acquisition, production, sale or management of the relevant tangible asset) performed in the other PE is of greater importance. A divergent attribution other than outlined in Section 5(1) BsGaV is only appropriate if such an attribution leads to a result that is rather in line with the arm's length principle in the specific circumstances of the case, both, from a business perspective as well as from the perspective of the other parts of the enterprise.[662]

When applying the derogation rule of Section 5(2) BsGaV, the taxpayer faces the challenge of how to determine whether another people function is of greater importance. Such decisions almost always contain subjective elements.[663] Therefore, it is of importance to assess the facts of the case thoroughly and decide on a case-by-case basis.[664] As emphasised by the Ordinance, qualitative aspects shall be decisive in this context.[665] In order to objectify the analysis, at least in some way, the use of a balance scorecard was suggested in literature which would enable the taxpayer to evaluate the importance of certain people functions

---

[659]Cf. BMF, 22 Dec. 2016, IV B 5—S 1341/12/10001–03, BStBl. I 2017, 182, para. 77.

[660]Cf. Section 5(1) sentence 3 BsGaV; BMF, 22 Dec. 2016, IV B 5—S 1341/12/10001–03, BStBl. I 2017, 182, para. 79.

[661]Cf. BMF, 22 Dec. 2016, IV B 5—S 1341/12/10001–03, BStBl. I 2017, 182, para. 79.

[662]Cf. BR-Drs. 401/14, 58.

[663]Cf. also *Kahle/Kindich*, in: Lübbehüsen/Kahle (Eds.), Brennpunkte der Besteuerung von Betriebsstätten, para. 4.239.

[664]Cf. BMF, 22 Dec. 2016, IV B 5—S 1341/12/10001–03, BStBl. I 2017, 182, para. 80.

[665]Cf. BMF, 22 Dec. 2016, IV B 5—S 1341/12/10001–03, BStBl. I 2017, 182, para. 80.

by putting a 'weight' on the respective people functions.[666] This way, the relative significance of each part of the enterprise for the tangible asset could be identified.

An exception applies for immovable property in which the business activities of the PE are performed. Such assets must always be attributed to the PE where the asset is located (situs-principle).[667]

If other people functions (except the use) within the meaning of Section 5(2) sentence 1 BsGaV are simultaneously performed in more than one PE, the tangible asset must be attributed to the PE whose other people function is of the greatest importance for the respective tangible asset.[668] Again, the use of a balance scorecard might be of help in order to identify a people function which is of greater importance.

Section 5(4) BsGaV provides for an 'escape' if the tangible asset cannot be attributed clearly. In that case, the attribution is of the discretion of the taxpayer as long as the attribution does not conflict with Section 5(1) to (3) BsGaV. The decision regarding an attribution pursuant to Section 5(4) BsGaV must be recorded by the time the auxiliary and ancillary account is prepared and the reasons for the respective attribution must be explained on the basis of the records to be prepared pursuant to Section 90(3) GFC.[669] Otherwise, an estimate according to Section 162(3) GFC is to be feared.[670]

In cases where no significant people function is carried out in the PE due to the absence of personnel, the outlined attribution approach of Section 5 BsGaV does not allow for the attribution of tangible assets (except immovable property)[671] to

---

[666] Cf. *Roeder/Friedrich*, BB 2015, 1053 (1056); *Kahle/Kindich*, in: Lübbehüsen/Kahle (Eds.), Brennpunkte der Besteuerung von Betriebsstätten, para. 4.239; *Kraft/Dombrowski*, FR 2014, 1105 (1108).

[667] Cf. Section 5(2) sentence 3 BsGaV. This approach is in line with international tax law for immovable property such as Article 6 OECD MC dealing with the taxation of immovable property. Accordingly, it is the state where the immovable property is situated that has the right of taxation. Also the German tax administration refers to Article 6 OECD MC in this regard, cf. BMF, 22 Dec. 2016, IV B 5—S 1341/12/10001–03, BStBl. I 2017, 182, para. 82.

[668] Cf. Section 5(3) BsGaV.

[669] Cf. BMF, 22 Dec. 2016, IV B 5—S 1341/12/10001–03, BStBl. I 2017, 182, para. 84. Detailed for the documentation requirements see chapter D.II.5 of this thesis.

[670] Cf. BMF, 22 Dec. 2016, IV B 5—S 1341/12/10001–03, BStBl. I 2017, 182, para. 84.

[671] Whether a server or wind and solar power plants can be regarded as immovable property which would allow for an attribution of such assets to the PE according to Section 5(2) is questionable, cf. *Ditz/Tcherveniachki*, ISR 2020, 145 (150); *Brüninghaus*, in: Vögele/Borstell/Engler (Eds.), Verrechnungspreise, para. K 121.

the PE.[672] Since this approach would result in the circumstance that not even tangible assets which are the actual reason for the existence of the PE (e.g. server, wind and solar power plants) can be attributed to the PE the Federal Ministry of Finance states in its circular from 17 December 2019 that the 'escape-clause' pursuant to Section 1(5) sentence 2 half-sentence 2 ETRA shall be applicable in such cases.[673] The reference in the circular to para. 75 of the PE-Report 2010 suggests that the Federal Ministry of Finance may consider it appropriate to attribute tangible assets (e.g. server, wind and solar power plant) to the place of use (i.e. the place where it is physically located) despite the lack of a significant people function carried out by the PE.[674] Insofar, also profits associated with the operation of the tangible assets could be attributed to such PEs. This approach is certainly a step in the right direction and allows to partially patch the design flaw of the German AOA implementation approach in general and Section 5 BsGaV in particular.[675]

As explicitly emphasised in the VWG BsGa, a pro rata attribution of tangible assets to the PEs is not accepted.[676] Such a pro rata attribution is only accepted for intangibles which shall be dealt with in the following.

iii. Attribution of Intangibles

Due to the fact that intangibles are commonly used by various parts of the enterprise simultaneously, the use as the significant people function does not constitute a practicable criterion for the attribution of intangibles.[677] Rather, an intangible (e.g. patent, brand, know-how or goodwill) must be attributed to a particular PE if the intangible was created (1. presumption rule) or acquired (2. presumption rule) by that PE.[678] Put differently, the significant people function decisive for

---

[672] Cf. also *Kraft/Hentschel/Apler*, Ubg 2017, 318 (325 et seq.); *Ditz/Tcherveniachki*, ISR 2020, 145 (150); *Brüninghaus*, in: Vögele/Borstell/Engler (Eds.), Verrechnungspreise, para. K 121. For a different view see *Van der Ham/Retzer* arguing that the German AOA principles allow for the attribution of tangible assets to the PE where no significant people functions are carried out as Section 1(5) sentence 3 ETRA does not make the attribution of assets contingent upon the attribution of people functions, cf. *Van der Ham/Retzer*, IWB 2020, 86 (89 et seqq.).

[673] Cf. BMF, 17 Dec. 2019, IV B 5—S 1341/19/10010:003 03, BStBl. I 2020, 84.

[674] See for the same conclusion *Ditz/Tcherveniachki*, ISR 2020, 145 (150).

[675] See in more detail for the flaws of the German AOA implementation approach in general and Section 5 BsGaV in particular *Kraft/Hentschel/Apler*, Ubg 2017, 318 (325 et seqq.).

[676] Cf. BMF, 22 Dec. 2016, IV B 5—S 1341/12/10001–03, BStBl. I 2017, 182, para. 84.

[677] Cf. *Kraft*, in: Kraft (Ed.), AStG—Kommentar, § 1 AStG, para. 673.

[678] Cf. Section 6(1) sentence 1 BsGaV; BMF, 22 Dec. 2016, IV B 5—S 1341/12/10001–03, BStBl. I 2017, 182, para. 85.

the attribution of the intangibles to the PE is either the creation or the acquisition. In this context, 'creation' of intangibles shall mean the performance of a people function which is decisive for the development of the intangible. This may not only encompass research and development activities, but also the design of test specifications and development processes; the review and evaluation of data produced by the tests; setting the stage posts of the projects and the decision to finance a specific research project.[679]

Correspondingly, 'acquisition' of an intangible shall mean the performance of a people function which is decisive for the acquisition of the intangible.[680] Besides the performance of the actual acquisition process, also the evaluation of the need for the intangible in question; the decision to acquire a specific intangible instead of creating it; the inspection of the intangible; the performance of various follow-on development activities and the decision on how to use the acquired intangible are activities of importance when acquiring an intangible.[681]

As outlined in the VWG BsGa, the significant people functions which require active decision-making regarding the taking on and corresponding management of risks associated with the development or the acquisition of the intangibles are of particular importance for the attribution of intangibles to the PE.[682] Especially, in cases where intangibles were developed 'in-house', the taking on and corresponding management of risks associated with the development of the intangible shall be of particular significance with regard to the attribution of such intangibles.[683] In this context, it shall be of no significance who actually takes the formal decisions, especially if the person who formally takes the decision does not possess the qualification to take a responsible decision.[684] If the relevant people function is performed in various PEs, the intangible must be attributed to the PE whose people function is of the greatest importance for the intangible.[685]

---

[679] Cf. BMF, 22 Dec. 2016, IV B 5—S 1341/12/10001–03, BStBl. I 2017, 182, para. 86. In practice the attribution of the intangible to another PE than the one where the research and development activities are carried out should be a rare occurrence, cf. *Kraft/Dombrowski*, FR 2014, 1105 (1110).

[680] Cf. BMF, 22 Dec. 2016, IV B 5—S 1341/12/10001–03, BStBl. I 2017, 182, para. 87.

[681] Cf. BMF, 22 Dec. 2016, IV B 5—S 1341/12/10001–03, BStBl. I 2017, 182, para. 87.

[682] Cf. BMF, 22 Dec. 2016, IV B 5—S 1341/12/10001–03, BStBl. I 2017, 182, para. 88 with cross-reference to OECD, PE Report 2010, Part I, paras. 84 et seqq.

[683] Cf. *Nientimp/Stein/Schwarz/Holinski*, BB 2017, 407 (409). Cf. in more detail for typical risks associated with research and development activities *Stein/Schwarz/Holinski*, DStR 2017, 118 (120 et seq.).

[684] Cf. BMF, 22 Dec. 2016, IV B 5—S 1341/12/10001–03, BStBl. I 2017, 182, paras. 40, 89.

[685] Cf. Section 6(1) sentence 2 BsGaV.

The operationalisation of these specifications in practice may create considerable challenges for the taxpayer since the above analysis is of high complexity, especially for research-intensive MNEs.[686] In this regard, further guidance can be obtained from the TP Guidelines 2017 revised through BEPS Actions 8–10. As illustrated earlier,[687] the new guidelines provide that members of an MNE group shall be compensated for their contributions to the value of the intangible under the arm's length principle. This shall be accomplished by compensating the MNE group members based on the functions performed, assets used and risks assumed in the development, enhancement, maintenance, protection and exploitation (so-called DEMPE-functions) of the intangibles.[688]

By way of derogation from the presumption rule of Section 6(1) BsGaV, an intangible must be attributed to another PE according to Section 6(2) BsGaV if another people function (e.g. the use, management, development, protection or sale)[689] performed in that other PE is clearly of greater importance than the creation or acquisition. A divergent attribution other than outlined in Section 6(1) BsGaV is only appropriate if such an attribution leads to a result that is better in line with the arm's length principle in the specific circumstances of the case, both, from a business perspective as well as from the perspective of the other parts of the enterprise.[690]

The approach for the attribution of other people functions within the meaning of Section 6(2) BsGaV when simultaneously performed in multiple PEs (Section 6(3) BsGaV) and the approach for the attribution of an intangible which cannot be attributed clearly (Section 6(4) BsGaV) follow the approaches of Section 5(3) and (4) BsGaV with regard to tangible assets except of one significant exception implemented in Section 6(4) sentence 2 BsGaV. According to this exception, a pro rata attribution of an intangible to the PE in which the most important people functions are performed on a long-term basis is possible in cases where such assets cannot be attributed clearly to one PE. Especially in cases where the intangible was developed in more than one part of the enterprise, e.g. under a pool agreement, the possibility to attribute intangibles to different parts of the enterprise is generally to be welcomed.[691]

---

686 Cf. Nientimp/Stein/Schwarz/Holinski, BB 2017, 407 (409).

687 See chapter D.I.4.b.(2)(h)iii of this thesis.

688 Cf. OECD, TP Guidelines 2017, para. 6.32.

689 Cf. Section 6(2) sentence 2 BsGaV.

690 Cf. BR-Drs. 401/14, 61.

691 Cf. *Kraft*, in: Kraft (Ed.), AStG—Kommentar, § 1 AStG, para. 677.

However, Section 6(4) sentence 2 BsGaV does not provide any 'scale' on how to attribute intangibles on a pro rata basis to the different parts of the enterprise. Fundamentally, an intangible which was developed by multiple PEs could, for example, be attributed to the respective PEs based upon the contribution of the respective PEs to the added value with regard to the intangible by using a value chain analysis or on basis of the costs incurred for the development of the intangible.[692] Nevertheless, another criterion, which is more suitable in consideration of the legal consequences of a pro rata attribution, is the attribution based upon the 'use' of the intangible.[693] As pointed out in the VWG BsGa, notional royalties may be avoided completely if the pro rata attribution of the intangible to the PEs corresponds to the relative use of the intangible by the different PEs.[694] Also, the Ordinance's explanatory statement elaborates that a pro rata attribution may be appropriate if dealings between the different parts of the enterprise can be avoided on a long-term basis.[695] Consequently, if the taxpayer decides to attribute an intangible on a pro rata basis to different parts of the enterprise, an attribution based on the relative use of the intangible by the respective parts of the enterprise is recommended.[696]

Another interesting issue arising in this context is the question of how the royalties would then be attributed to the different PEs if the intangible is licenced to third parties. The answer is straightforward: The respective royalties must be attributed in proportion to the pro rata attribution of the intangible to the different PEs.[697]

---

[692] Cf. *Leonhardt/Tcherveniachki*, in: F/W/B/S (Eds.), Außensteuerrecht—Kommentar, § 1 AStG, para. 3061.

[693] Cf. *Leonhardt/Tcherveniachki*, in: F/W/B/S (Eds.), Außensteuerrecht—Kommentar, § 1 AStG, para. 3061.

[694] Cf. BMF, 22 Dec. 2016, IV B 5—S 1341/12/10001–03, BStBl. I 2017, 182, para. 101.

[695] Cf. BR-Drs. 401/14, 63.

[696] Cf. *Leonhardt/Tcherveniachki*, in: F/W/B/S (Eds.), Außensteuerrecht—Kommentar, § 1 AStG, para. 3061.

[697] Cf. *Ditz/Luckhaupt*, ISR 2015, 1 (6).

iv. Attribution of Stakes, Financial Assets and Similar Assets

The significant people function for the attribution of stakes,[698] financial assets[699] or similar assets[700] to a PE is the use.[701] Consequently, a stake, financial asset or similar asset must be attributed to a particular PE if the respective stake, financial asset or similar asset is used in that PE. In this context, the term 'use' requires a functional connection with the business activity of the PE.[702]

The chosen attribution approach can only surprise since it could be expected that the attribution would follow the attribution approach chosen for intangibles.[703] Both, intangibles as well as stakes, financial assets or similar assets are characterised by their lack of tangibility. Consequently, an attribution based on the active decision-making with respect to the taking on and the corresponding management of risks that are associated with the stakes, financial assets or similar assets would be more consistent.[704] However, such an attribution approach is only provided by the derogation rule in Section 7(2) BsGaV and applicable if the importance of another people function is greater than the use. According to Section 7(2) sentence 2 BsGaV, such people functions that may be of greater importance are, in particular, those related to the acquisition, risk management or sale of a stake, financial asset or a similar asset.

---

[698] With regard to the term 'stake' within the meaning of Section 2(6) sentence 2 no. 3 BsGaV, it must be referred to Section 271(1) sentence 1 GCC defining a stake as a share held in other enterprises which are intended to serve the enterprise's own business purpose by creating a permanent affiliation to such other enterprises intended. Cf. detailed in this regard *Leonhardt/Tcherveniachki*, in: F/W/B/S (Eds.), Außensteuerrecht—Kommentar, § 1 AStG, para. 2958.

[699] With regard to the term 'financial asset' within the meaning of Section 2(6) sentence 2 no. 4 BsGaV, it must be referred to Section 266(2) A.III no. 2, 4 and 6 GCC. Accordingly, the term shall cover loans to affiliated companies (Section 266(2) A.III no. 2 GCC); loans to companies linked by virtue of a participating interest (Section 266(2) A.III no. 4 GCC) and other loans (Section 266(2) A.III no. 6 GCC), cf. *Leonhardt/Tcherveniachki*, in: F/W/B/S (Eds.), Außensteuerrecht—Kommentar, § 1 AStG, para. 2959.

[700] A definition of the term 'similar assets' can neither be found in the GCC, the BsGaV nor in the VWG BsGa. Therefore, the term can only be determined by interpretation and shall encompass financial assets held as long-term investment, cf. *Leonhardt/Tcherveniachki*, in: F/W/B/S (Eds.), Außensteuerrecht—Kommentar, § 1 AStG, para. 3071.

[701] Cf. Section 7(1) sentence 1 BsGaV.

[702] Cf. Section 7(1) sentence 2 BsGaV.

[703] Cf. *Kraft*, in: Kraft (Ed.), AStG—Kommentar, § 1 AStG, para. 681; *Kraft/Dombrowski*, FR 2014, 1105 (1110).

[704] Cf. *Kraft*, in: Kraft (Ed.), AStG—Kommentar, § 1 AStG, para. 681.

The attribution rules for other assets determined in Section 7(3) and 7(4) BsGaV follow the fundamental attribution approach outlined above. Accordingly, if other people functions within the meaning of Section 7(2) sentence 1 BsGaV are performed in multiple PEs, stakes, financial assets or similar assets must be attributed to the PE whose other staff function is most important.[705] If the aforementioned asset cannot be attributed clearly or if the predominant functional connection changes frequently, the asset must be attributed in a manner that does not violate the attribution principles outlined in Section 7(1) to (3) BsGaV. A pro rata attribution of stakes, financial assets or similar assets to different parts of the enterprise is not possible.[706]

v. Attribution of Other Assets

Section 8 BsGaV, dealing with the attribution of 'other assets', can be regarded as a residuary clause which shall encompass all assets that are not covered by Section 5 to 7 BsGaV.[707] As pointed out in the Ordinance's explanatory statement, a residuary clause is necessary since the provisions of Section 5–7 BsGaV deal with the attribution of very specifically defined assets.[708] However, also other assets not covered by Sections 5–7 BsGaV are of significance for the determination of accurate transfer prices between the different parts of the enterprise.[709] A definition of the term 'other assets' can neither be found in the BsGaV nor in the VWG BsGa. The VWG BsGa does not even provide examples for assets which can be regarded as other assets. The examples included in the draft version of the BsGaV, namely receivables and goodwill, were not adopted in the final version.[710] Nevertheless, other assets within the meaning of Section 8 BsGaV shall mostly include assets that belong to the current assets of the enterprise including stakes and financial assets not covered by Section 7 BsGaV.[711]

---

705 Cf. Section 7(3) BsGaV.

706 Cf. BMF, 22 Dec. 2016, IV B 5—S 1341/12/10001–03, BStBl. I 2017, 182, para. 107.

707 Cf. *Kraft*, in: Kraft (Ed.), AStG—Kommentar, § 1 AStG, para. 683.

708 Cf. BR-Drs. 401/14, 63.

709 Cf. BR-Drs. 401/14, 63; *Kraft*, in: Kraft (Ed.), AStG—Kommentar, § 1 AStG, para. 683.

710 Cf. BMF, 5 Aug. 2013, BsGaV-Draft, p. 45. For possible reasons why the examples were not included in the final version of the BsGaV see *Kraft*, in: Kraft (Ed.), AStG—Kommentar, § 1 AStG, para. 684.

711 Cf. *Haverkamp,* in: Mössner et al. (Eds.), Steuerrecht international tätiger Unternehmen, para. 5.208. For further examples of assets which may belong to the category of 'other assets' cf. *Andresen*, in: W/A/D (Eds.), Betriebsstätten-Handbuch, para. 4.113.

In principle, the attribution approach outlines in Section 8 BsGaV follows the attribution approach for intangibles illustrated in Section 6 BsGaV.[712] The only difference can be identified when it comes to the possibility of a pro rata attribution. In contrast to Section 6(4) BsGaV, the possibility for such an attribution is not provided by Section 8(4) BsGaV and shall not be possible as outlined in the VWG BsGa.[713]

(c) Comparison to the OECD Approach

i. Fundamentals

Even though the provisions of the BsGaV dealing with the attribution of assets (Sections 5–8 BsGaV) do not explicitly mention the concept of 'economic ownership' as the guiding concept for the attribution of assets to the PE—as set out in the PE Report 2010[714]—the fundamental attribution approaches for assets to the PE are mostly in line with the OECD approach.[715] However, differences exist, especially with respect to the possibility of a pro rata attribution of assets to the PE. The most significant differences which may create problems of double taxation are discussed in more detail in the following.

ii. Attribution of Tangible Assets

While the presumption rule set out in Section 5(1) BsGaV provides for the attribution of tangible assets to the part of the enterprise where the significant people function of use is carried out, the OECD approach departs from the fundamental approach of allocating assets to the part of the enterprise where the significant people function is carried out.[716] Rather, the tangible asset shall be attributed to the part of the enterprise where it is used irrespective of the existence of people operating in the PE where the tangible asset is attributed to.[717] In most cases the place of use and the part of the enterprise where the significant people function of use is carried out should be the same. However, in cases where no significant people function is carried out by the PE due to the absence of personnel differences between the German and the OECD approach could occur. Nevertheless,

---

[712] A precise definition of the term 'other asset' is neither provided by the BsGaV nor by the VWG BsGa.

[713] Cf. BMF, 22 Dec. 2016, IV B 5—S 1341/12/10001–03, BStBl. I 2017, 182, para. 111.

[714] Cf. OECD, PE Report 2010, Part I, para. 18.

[715] Cf. *Andresen*, in: W/A/D (Eds.), Betriebsstätten-Handbuch, para. 5.20.

[716] See in more detail for the OECD approach chapter D.I.4.b.(2)(b)ii of this thesis.

[717] For the OECD approach cf. OECD, PE Report 2010, Part I, para. 75.

as stated by the Federal Ministry of Finance, such cases may allow for the application of the 'escape-clause' pursuant to Section 1(5) sentence 2 half-sentence 2 ETRA.[718] The application of the escape clause would enable the taxpayer for the attribution of tangible assets (e.g. server, wind and solar power plants) to the PE, especially if such assets are the actual reason for the existence of the PE.[719] Insofar, also profits associated with the operation of the tangible assets could be attributed to such PEs. This approach is to be welcomed as it a) better reflects economic reality and b) aligns the German AOA principles with the principles set out in the PE-Report 2010.

However, difficulties may arise with regard to the exceptions to the presumption rule which are implemented in Section 5(2) sentence 1 and 2 BsGaV. As outlined above, this so-called derogation rule sets out four examples for alternative criteria for the attribution of the tangible asset, namely, acquisition, production, sale and management, if such people functions are of greater importance for the tangible asset.[720] Even though also the PE Report 2010 provides for the possibility to attribute tangible assets to another PE than to the PE where the asset is used if the 'circumstances in a particular case'[721] justify such a different attribution, it is questionable whether the other treaty state provides for the same alternative criteria for the attribution of tangible assets. In order to reduce the potential for double taxation, it is recommended to depart from the criteria of use only in situations where the circumstances of the case clearly justify another attribution.[722]

Furthermore, a significant deviation of the two approaches can be identified when it comes to the possibility of a pro rata attribution of tangible assets. While the German tax administration emphasises that such a pro rata attribution of tangible assets is not accepted,[723] the PE Report 2010 provides for such an attribution.[724] Especially, situations where a tangible asset was developed by different parts of the enterprise under a cost contribution arrangement, splitting the costs for the development between the different parts of the enterprise in a manner

---

[718] Cf. BMF, 17 Dec. 2019, IV B 5—S 1341/19/10010:003 03, BStBl. I 2020, 84.

[719] Cf. reference in the circular of the Federal Ministry of Finance to para. 75 of the PE-Report 2010. Para. 75 of the PE-Report 2010 outlines that an attribution of tangible assets to the place of use is in particular for cases 'where a fixed place of business PE [...] existed precisely due to the presence in the host country of those tangible assets.', OECD, PE Report 2010, Part I, para. 75. See in more detail chapter D.I.4.b.(2)(b)ii of this thesis.

[720] Cf. *Andresen*, in: W/A/D (Eds.), Betriebsstätten-Handbuch, para. 5.22.

[721] OECD, PE Report 2010, Part I, para. 75.

[722] Cf. *Andresen*, in: W/A/D (Eds.), Betriebsstätten-Handbuch, para. 5.24.

[723] Cf. BMF, 22 Dec. 2016, IV B 5—S 1341/12/10001–03, BStBl. I 2017, 182, para. 84.

[724] Cf. OECD, PE Report 2010, Part I, paras. 197 et seq.

consistent with the contemplated use of the tangible asset, could justify a pro rata attribution to different parts of the enterprise.[725]

iii. Attribution of Intangibles

For the attribution of intangibles, the PE Report 2010—in contrast to the BsGaV—distinguishes between trade intangibles[726] and marketing intangibles[727] without consequences resulting from this distinction for the attribution approach.[728] With regard to the attribution of intangibles, it is determined by the OECD that the significant people functions that are decisive for the attribution of economic ownership shall be those which require active decision-making with respect to the taking on and the corresponding management of risks that are associated with the creation or the acquisition of the intangible.[729] Even though the presumption rule of Section 6(1) BsGaV only refers to the creation or acquisition to constitute the significant people function and does not require the active decision-making with respect to the taking on and the corresponding management of risks that are associated with the creation and the development of the intangible, paragraph 88 of the VWG BsGa emphasises that the decision-making with respect to the taking on and the corresponding management of risks that are associated with the creation and the acquisition of the intangible shall be of particular significance.[730] Consequently, no deviation from the fundamental attribution approach of the OECD is intended.[731] However, differences regarding

[725]Cf. OECD, PE Report 2010, Part I, para. 197; see also *Looks,* in: Looks/Heinsen (Eds.), Betriebsstättenbesteuerung, para. 775; *Ditz,* ISR 2012, 48 (50); *Kraft,* in: Kraft (Ed.), AStG—Kommentar, § 1 AStG, para. 672.

[726]Cf. OECD, PE Report 2010, Part I, paras. 83 et seqq.

[727]Cf. OECD, PE Report 2010, Part I, paras. 96 et seqq.

[728]With the revision of the TP Guidelines through BEPS-Actions 8–10, the categorisation of intangibles was dropped in the TP Guidelines 2017. Due to the fact that the PE Report 2010 refers to the TP Guidelines in para. 79 and adopted the categorisation of the TP Guidelines 2010, the drop of the categorisation in favour of the general term 'intangibles' in the TP Guidelines 2017 is in line with the approach of the BsGaV and the VWG BsGa.

[729]Cf. OECD, PE Report 2010, Part I, paras. 85, 97.

[730]Cf. BMF, 22 Dec. 2016, IV B 5—S 1341/12/10001–03, BStBl. I 2017, 182, para. 88. The stronger focus on the taking on and the corresponding management of risks is also in line with the recent developments in the TP Guidelines 2017 as an outcome of BEPS Actions 8–10 putting more emphasis on the control over risk and the financial capacity to assume the risk, cf. OECD, TP Guidelines 2017, paras. 1.98 et seq.

[731]For further references of the VWG BsGa to the PE Report 2010 illustrating the similarities of the two approaches see BMF, 22 Dec. 2016, IV B 5—S 1341/12/10001–03, BStBl. I 2017, 182, paras. 86, 87, 89, 90. However, *Andresen* argues that differences regarding the

the attribution of intangibles may occur if the taxpayer chooses to attribute the intangibles according to one of the alternative attribution approaches provided by Section 6(2)–(4) BsGaV. Such a different attribution may lead to double taxation.

Both approaches provide for the possibility to attribute intangibles on a pro rata basis to different parts of the enterprise. However, the taxpayer must bear in mind that a pro rata attribution must be documented thoroughly. As outlined in the previous chapter, an attribution based on the relative use of the intangible by the respective parts of the enterprise is recommended if a pro rata attribution is considered to be appropriate for the specific circumstances of the case. Even though it cannot be guaranteed that the tax administrations in the different jurisdictions agree with the chosen pro rata attribution, the risk of double taxation is still lower compared to the scenario that such a possibility of a pro rata attribution does not exist.[732]

iv. Attribution of Stakes, Financial Assets and Similar Assets

As outlined above, the OECD does not differentiate between the attribution of intangibles and the attribution of stakes, financial assets or similar assets.[733] Rather, the attribution approach for stakes, financial assets or similar assets follows the attribution approach for intangibles.[734] Accordingly, the significant people functions decisive for the attribution shall be those which require active decision-making regarding the taking on and corresponding management of risks associated with the stakes, financial assets or similar assets. However, this understanding is not in line with the presumption rule of Section 7(1) BsGaV, determining that the use shall be the significant people function for the attribution of stakes, financial assets or similar assets to a PE. An attribution which would be in line with the OECD approach is only provided by the derogation rule of Section 7(2) BsGaV. Nevertheless, the derogation rule, as its name suggests, can

---

application of the fundamental attribution approach might occur in practice, cf. *Andresen*, in: W/A/D (Eds.), Betriebsstätten-Handbuch, para. 5.28.

[732] Cf. *Kraft*, in: Kraft (Ed.), AStG—Kommentar, § 1 AStG, para. 679.

[733] Cf. *Kraft*, in: Kraft (Ed.), AStG—Kommentar, § 1 AStG, para. 681; *Kraft/Dombrowski*, FR 2014, 1105 (1110); *Kußmaul/Delarber/Müller*, IStR 2014, 466 (471).

[734] As correctly argued by *Häck*, stakes are, by nature, intangibles and therefore the attribution approach for intangibles of the OECD is to be followed, cf. *Häck*, ISR 2015, 113 (116). In this context, also financial or similar assets can be regarded as intangibles resulting in the respective application of the attribution rules for intangibles. See in this regard also *Leonhardt/Tcherveniachki*, in: F/W/B/S (Eds.), Außensteuerrecht—Kommentar, § 1 AStG, para. 3072; *Kraft*, in: Kraft (Ed.), AStG—Kommentar, § 1 AStG, para. 681; *Kraft/Dombrowski*, FR 2014, 1105 (1110); *Kußmaul/Delarber/Müller*, IStR 2014, 466 (471).

only be applied subordinately if the importance of another people function is of greater importance than the use. In many cases, the application of the derogation rule will not be possible leaving the taxpayer with the potential risk of double taxation if the tax administration of another jurisdiction follows the OECD approach.[735]

v. Attribution of Other Assets

Given the above, the attribution approach for other assets within the meaning of Section 8 BsGaV follows the attribution approach for intangibles, except of the fact that the possibility for a pro rata attribution of other assets is not provided by Section 8 BsGaV. In contrast, the OECD does not provide for any specific attribution rules for this category of assets. Rather, they are covered by the attribution approach for intangibles as outlined in the PE Report 2010.[736] As a consequence, the same deviations that were already identified in the context of intangibles can be also be outlined in this context.[737] The only, yet important, difference is that the PE Report 2010 does provide for the possibility of a pro rata attribution for intangibles,[738] while such an attribution approach—as emphasised above—is not provided by Section 8 BsGaV.

vi. Interim Conclusion

Table 4 provides an overview of the OECD and the German approach with respect to the attribution of assets to a PE and can be regarded as a summary of the above analysis.

(3) Attribution of an Enterprise's Business Transactions

(a) Fundamental Attribution Approach

In order to determine the profits for the hypothesised separate and independent PE, not only people functions and assets must be attributed to the PE but also business transactions (including the related business income and business expenses) within the meaning of Section 1(4) sentence 1 no. 1 ETRA. In this context, not only purchase or sales contracts but also lease and rental agreements shall

[735]Cf. *Kraft/Dombrowski*, IWB 2015, 87 (90); *Leonhardt/Tcherveniachki*, in: F/W/B/S (Eds.), Außensteuerrecht—Kommentar, § 1 AStG, para. 3061.

[736]Cf. OECD, PE Report 2010, Part I, paras. 76 et seqq.

[737]See in more detail for the deviations with regard to intangibles chapter D.II.3.b.(2)(b)iii of this thesis.

[738]Cf. OECD, PE Report 2010, Part I, para. 72.

be recognised.[739] The mechanism for the attribution is determined by Section 9 BsGaV.

According to Section 9(1) BsGaV, business transactions that the enterprise has concluded with either an independent third party or with a related party must be attributed to a particular PE if the people function that gives rise to the business

Table 4 OECD vs. German Approach for Attribution of Assets

	OECD approach	**German approach**
Attribution of tangible assets	• fundamental attribution of the tangible asset to the place of use	• fundamental attribution of the tangible asset to the part of the enterprise where significant people function (use of tangible asset) is carried on
	• exceptions if circumstances in a particular case justify a different attribution → then attribution according to significant people function	• exceptions if importance of another people function is clearly greater than the use (e.g. acquisition, production, management or sale) • exception if no significant people function is carried on in PE (due to the absence of personnel) → then place of use possible
	• pro rata attribution possible	• pro rata attribution not possible
Attribution of intangibles	• significant people function: active decision-making with respect to taking on and management of risk associated with creation or acquisition	• significant people function: creation or acquisition • exceptions if importance of another people function is clearly greater (e.g. use, management, development, protection or sale)
	• pro rata attribution possible	
Attribution of stakes, financial assets or similar assets	• no separate attribution approach → attribution approach for intangibles applicable • significant people function: active decision-making with respect to taking on and management of risk associated with creation or acquisition	• significant people function: use (functional connection) • exceptions if importance of another people function is clearly greater (e.g. acquisition, management, risk management or sale)

(continued)

[739]Cf. *Frotscher*, Internationales Steuerrecht, para. 447.

Table 4 (continued)

	OECD approach	German approach
	• pro rata attribution possible	• pro rata attribution not possible
Attribution of other assets	• no separate attribution approach → attribution approach for intangibles applicable • significant people function: active decision-making with respect to taking on and management of risk associated with creation or acquisition	• significant people function: creation or acquisition • exceptions if importance of another people function is clearly greater (e.g. use, management, risk management or sale)
	• pro rata attribution possible	• pro rata attribution not possible

Source: Own illustration.

transaction is performed in that PE. Thus, the activity that gives rise to the business transaction is regarded as the significant people function.[740] The invoicing or the name of the contracting partners can only be regarded as an indication.[741] Rather, it is crucial where within the enterprise the people function is performed that is decisive and therefore significant for concluding the relevant business transaction and for the taking on of the risks related thereto.[742] If multiple PEs simultaneously perform such a people function, the business transaction must be attributed to the PE whose people function is of the greatest importance for this transaction.[743] As elaborated earlier, decisive for the determination of the greatest significance are qualitative aspects. An attribution based on quantitative aspects such as the costs are only appropriate if an attribution based on qualitative aspects is not possible.[744]

If the importance of another people function is clearly greater than the people function that gives rise to the business transaction, Section 9(2) BsGaV determines that the business transaction is to be attributed to the PE where the people function of greater importance is performed. Such people functions are, in particular, those related to the fulfilment of obligations arising from the business

[740] For difficulties related to the fundamental attribution approach cf. *Looks*, in: Looks/Heinsen (Eds.), Betriebsstättenbesteuerung, para. 846.

[741] Cf. BMF, 22 Dec. 2016, IV B 5—S 1341/12/10001–03, BStBl. I 2017, 182, para. 112.

[742] Cf. BMF, 22 Dec. 2016, IV B 5—S 1341/12/10001–03, BStBl. I 2017, 182, para. 112.

[743] Cf. Section 9(1) sentence 2 BsGaV.

[744] Cf. BMF, 22 Dec. 2016, IV B 5—S 1341/12/10001–03, BStBl. I 2017, 182, paras. 42, 113.

transactions or to its management or risk management.[745] If such people functions are simultaneously performed in multiple PEs of the enterprise, the business transaction are to be attributed to the PE whose other people function can be regarded of the greatest importance for the business transaction.[746] A divergent attribution other than outlined in Section 9(1) BsGaV is only appropriate if such an attribution leads to a result that is rather in line with the arm's length principle in the specific circumstances of the case, both from a business perspective as well as from the perspective of the other parts of the enterprise.[747]

If a business transaction cannot be attributed clearly, Section 9(4) BsGaV provides a margin of discretion for the taxpayer by determining that the respective business transaction can be attributed in a manner that does not conflict with Section 9(1)-(3) BsGaV. A pro rata attribution to different parts of the enterprise is not possible.[748]

(b) Comparison to the OECD Approach

Compared to the OECD approach, dedicating only one paragraph to the attribution of rights and obligations, the German approach outlined in Section 9 BsGaV and clarified by paragraph 112–116 VWG BsGa can be regarded as a lot more detailed that provides for various possibilities regarding the attribution of business transactions to the PE contingent upon the circumstances of the case. However, it is recognised by both the PE Report 2010 as well as by the BsGaV that from a legal perspective, rights and obligations which arise out of business transactions with other independent third parties and with related parties are contractually tied to the enterprise as a whole and not to any one part of the enterprise and must therefore be attributed to the PE for the purpose of treating the PE as a separate and independent enterprise.[749]

Despite the fact that the OECD concludes that the overall circumstances (attributed assets, attributed risks, performed significant people functions) shall be decisive when attributing rights and obligations to the respective PE, instead of determining any specific significant people function, the fundamental attribution

---

[745] Cf. Section 9(2) sentence 2 BsGaV.

[746] Cf. Section 9(3) BsGaV.

[747] Cf. BR-Drs. 401/14, 72.

[748] Cf. BMF, 22 Dec. 2016, IV B 5—S 1341/12/10001–03, BStBl. I 2017, 182, para. 116.

[749] Cf. OECD, PE Report 2010, Part I, para. 98; BMF, 22 Dec. 2016, IV B 5—S 1341/12/10001–03, BStBl. I 2017, 112 et seqq.

approach of Section 9(1) BsGaV and the OECD is in line with each other.[750] As elaborated earlier, it is also crucial for the fundamental attribution approach of Section 9(1) BsGaV to identify where within the enterprise the people function is performed that is decisive and therefore significant for concluding the relevant business transaction and for the taking on of the risks related thereto.[751]

However, differences may arise if the circumstances of the case justify an attribution according to Section 9(2)–(4) BsGaV. Since the PE Report 2010 does not provide for such deviating attribution approaches, the risk of double taxation exists.[752]

Table 5 summarises the main similarities and differences of the attribution approaches.

Table 5 OECD vs. German Approach for Attribution of Business Transactions

	OECD approach	German approach
Attribution approach	• attribution contingent upon the overall circumstances (attributed assets, attributed risks, performed significant people functions)	• significant people function: people function which gives rise to the business transaction • exceptions if importance of another people function is clearly greater than the one which gives rise to the transaction (e.g. fulfilment of obligations arising from the transaction or to its management or risk management)

Source: Own illustration.

(4) Attribution of Opportunities and Risks

(a) Fundamental Attribution Approach

As determined by Section 1(5) sentence 3 no. 3 ETRA, the enterprise's opportunities and risks that are assumed on the basis of the business functions performed

750 Cf. *Andresen*, in: W/A/D (Eds.), Betriebsstätten-Handbuch, para. 5.31. Critical *Froitzheim*, Steuerliche Selbstständigkeitsfiktion der Betriebsstätte, 63 et seq.

751 Cf. BMF, 22 Dec. 2016, IV B 5—S 1341/12/10001–03, BStBl. I 2017, 182, para. 112.

752 Similar *Andresen*, in: W/A/D (Eds.), Betriebsstätten-Handbuch, para. 5.31.

and assets assigned to it must also be attributed to the PE. In this context, the Ordinance's explanatory statement points out that chances and risks are a direct result of entrepreneurial activities and are therefore directly or indirectly linked to the assets and business relations (e.g. currency fluctuations, commodity prices, market developments).[753] Against this backdrop, the attribution approach implemented in Section 10 BsGaV shall be understood.

Fundamentally, the attribution of opportunities and risks to a PE depends on its relation to an asset (within the meaning of Sections 5–8 BsGaV) or a business transaction (within the meaning of Section 9 BsGaV). If opportunities and risks are directly related to an asset or business transaction, Section 10(1) BsGaV determines that these opportunities and risks must be attributed to the PE to which the relevant asset or transaction is attributed. It follows that opportunities and risks share the same fate than the assets to which they are directly linked to.[754]

In contrast, other opportunities and risks that are not directly related to an asset or business transaction (e.g. general market risks) but are based on a PE's people function, this people function shall be the significant and therefore the relevant people function for attributing opportunities and risks to a PE.[755] If, for instance, the use of a tangible asset by a PE does not result in a corresponding change of attribution of the asset to that PE, risks that are related to the use of the tangible asset (e.g. improper operation by personnel of the PE) must be attributed to that PE, irrespective of the fact that the asset itself is attributed to another part of the enterprise.[756] In case people functions are simultaneously performed in multiple PEs, the opportunities and risks shall be attributed to the PE whose people function is regarded to be of the greatest importance for such opportunities and risks.[757]

Only if the importance of another people function performed in another PE is of greater importance than the people function referred to in Section 10(2) BsGaV, the derogation rule of Section 10(3) BsGaV emphasises that opportunities and risks must then be attributed to a PE other than that whose people

[753] Cf. BR-Drs. 401/14, 50.

[754] Cf. *Kraft*, in: Kraft (Ed.), AStG—Kommentar, § 1 AStG, para. 688.

[755] Cf. Section 10(2) sentence 1 BsGaV.

[756] For an example dealing with this issue see BMF, 22 Dec. 2016, IV B 5—S 1341/12/10001–03, BStBl. I 2017, 182, para. 118. In this context, also *Haverkamp*, in: Mössner et al. (Eds.), Steuerrecht international tätiger Unternehmen, para. 5.212.

[757] Cf. Section 10(2) sentence 2 BsGaV.

function gave rise to these opportunities and risks.[758] Such other people functions could for example include those related to the management, risk management or the realisation of opportunities and risks or decisions to undertake changes related to opportunities and risks. In case such other people functions are simultaneously performed in multiple PEs, opportunities and risks must be attributed to the PE whose people function is of greater importance for such opportunities and risks.[759]

If the circumstances of the case do not provide for a clear attribution of opportunities and risks, Section 10(5) BsGaV provides a margin of discretion for the taxpayer by determining that the relevant opportunities and risks can be attributed in a manner that does not conflict with Section 10(1)-(4) BsGaV.

(b) Comparison to the OECD Approach

In contrast to Section 1(5) sentence 3 no. 3 ETRA and Section 1(2) no. 2 BsGaV in conjunction with Section 10 BsGaV, the OECD does not explicitly refer to the attribution of opportunities and risks in the PE Report 2010, but instead only emphasises the risks that must be attributed to the PE. However, a closer look into the PE Report 2010 confirms that also 'the attendant benefits and burdens, in particular the potential exposure to gains or losses from the realisation or non-realisation of said risks'[760] shall be considered. It followed that no differences can be identified in this regard.

In principle, the OECD and the German approach for the attribution of risks (and opportunities) to a PE are in line with each other.[761] Even though the OECD does not differentiate whether the risks (and opportunities) are directly or indirectly related to an asset or a business transaction, the resulting attribution should, in most cases, not deviate. While the attribution approach of the OECD, determining that the PE shall assume any risk for which the significant people functions crucial to the assumption of such risks are performed by the relevant personnel of the PE at the PE's location,[762] is reflected by Section 10(2) BsGaV, the attribution approach implemented in Section 10(1) BsGaV emphasises that opportunities and

[758] Cf. Section 10(3) BsGaV.

[759] Cf. Section 10(4) BsGaV.

[760] Cf. OECD, PE Report 2010, Part I, para. 21.

[761] Cf. also *Andresen*, in: W/A/D (Eds.), Betriebsstätten-Handbuch, para. 5.31; *Froitzheim*, Steuerliche Selbstständigkeitsfiktion der Betriebsstätte, 223 et seqq.; *Margerie*, Gewinnermittlung und Gewinnabgrenzung bei Betriebsstätten, 245 et seq.

[762] Cf. OECD, PE Report 2010, Part I, para. 68.

risks that are directly related to an asset or business transaction must also be attributed to the PE to which the relevant asset or transaction is attributed. However, the attribution approach set out in Section 10(1) BsGaV emphasising that opportunities and risks share the same fate than the assets to which they are directly linked to can rather be regarded as a clarification which does not conflict with the OECD approach.[763]

Differences may arise if the circumstances of the case justify an attribution according to Section 10(3)-(5) BsGaV.[764] Table 6 summarises the main similarities and differences of the attribution approaches.

Table 6 OECD vs. German Approach for Attribution of Opportunities and Risks

	OECD approach	**German approach**
Attribution approach	• attribution to PE which performs the significant people functions crucial to the assumption of risk	• risks directly related to asset/ transaction: – PE to which the relevant asset or transaction is attributed • risks not directly related to asset/ transaction: – PE which performs the significant people functions crucial to the assumption of risks • exceptions if importance of another people function is clearly greater than that which gives rise to the transaction (e.g. management, risk management or realisation of opportunities and risks or decision to undertake changes)

Source: Own illustration.

[763] Cf. also *Andresen*, in: W/A/D (Eds.), Betriebsstätten-Handbuch, para. 5.31; *Margerie*, Gewinnermittlung und Gewinnabgrenzung bei Betriebsstätten, 245 et seq.

[764] Similar *Andresen*, in: W/A/D (Eds.), Betriebsstätten-Handbuch, para. 5.31.

(5) Attribution of Free Capital

(a) Preliminary Remarks

In the next step, the PE should be attributed an adequate amount of the enterprise's equity in order to support the functions performed, the assets used as well as the opportunities and risks assumed.[765] Since the amount of attributed capital ultimately influences the capital structure of the PE and therefore the deductibility of interest expense, its attribution plays an essential part in determining the profits of the PE. In this context, the BsGaV distinguishes between domestic PEs of foreign enterprises (Section 12 BsGaV) and foreign PEs of domestic enterprises (Section 13 BsGaV). Remarkably, both approaches differ with regard to the attribution methods and are contingent upon the fact whether the PE is located in Germany or abroad.

In general, the attribution rules are only applicable to PEs of enterprises that are required to keep accounts either under foreign law (foreign enterprise) or domestic law (domestic enterprise).[766] Regardless of the PE's location, the amount of free capital must be attributed to the PE on a yearly basis, always at the beginning of each fiscal year.[767] It follows that the principle of 'balance sheet continuity' within the meaning of Section 252 (1) no. 1 GCC does not hold for the auxiliary and ancillary accounts that must be prepared for a PE pursuant to Section 3 BsGaV.[768]

In the following, the different attribution approaches implemented in Section 12 BsGaV and Section 13 BsGaV shall be examined in more detail.

(b) Free Capital of Domestic PE of Foreign Enterprise

i. Fundamental Attribution Approach

In general, free capital of a domestic PE of a foreign enterprise shall be attributed in accordance with the capital allocation method.[769] Accordingly, the domestic PE

---

[765] Cf. Section 1(2) no. 3 BsGaV; BR-Drs. 401/14, 75.

[766] Cf. BR-Drs. 401/14, 76. Provisions dealing with the attribution of financing expenses of enterprises that are not required to keep accounts are implemented in Section 15(4) and (5) BsGaV.

[767] Cf. Section 12(1) and 13(1) BsGaV.

[768] Cf. *Busch*, DB 2014, 2490 (2496); *Kahle/Kindich*, in: Lübbehüsen/Kahle (Eds.), Brennpunkte der Besteuerung von Betriebsstätten, para. 4.309. See in more detail for auxiliary and ancillary accounts chapter D.II.5.b of this thesis.

[769] Cf. Section 12(1) BsGaV. Prior to the capital allocation method, the German tax authority suggested the use of the 'Kapitalspiegelmethode', cf. BMF, 24 Dec. 1999, IV B 4—S 1300—111/99, BStBl. I 1999, 1076, para. 1.1.1.1 and para. 2.5.1. This approach was rejected by the German Federal Tax Court several times, cf. BFH, 27 July 1965, I 110/63 S, BStBl.

must be attributed a proportion of the enterprise's equity capital which equates to the proportion of assets owned and opportunities and risks assumed by the domestic PE at the beginning of each fiscal year.

Although the amount of the foreign enterprise's equity capital must be determined in accordance with German tax law,[770] Section 12(2) sentence 2 BsGaV provides for an exception for simplification purposes. Accordingly, contributed capital plus reserves and profit carried forward and less loss carried forward as it is shown in the enterprise's foreign balance sheet may be used as the general basis for allocation purposes.[771] However, this simplified approach is only permitted if evidence is provided that a) the amount of equity capital determined from the enterprise's foreign balance sheet does not substantially differ from the amount of equity capital to be applied under German tax law, or b) appropriate adjustments can be made for deviations, leading to a result that does not substantially differ (less than 10%)[772] from the amount of the foreign enterprise's equity capital determined pursuant to German tax law.[773] Nevertheless, also this simplified approach requires the taxpayer to adjust the respective figures of the foreign balance sheet in accordance with German tax law.[774]

For the application of the capital allocation method, it is necessary to determine the capital ratio of the domestic PE. In order to do so, the assets of the domestic PE and the rest of the enterprise must be measured at values that comply with the arm's length principle and adequately take account of opportunities and risks.[775] For reasons of simplification, it is conceded to use book or similar values from the enterprise's records if evidence is provided by the enterprise that such a valuation results in a capital ratio that does not substantially differ from the capital ratio that would otherwise result from using values that comply with the arm's length

III 1966, 24; BFH, 25 June 1986, II R 213/83, BStBl. II 1986, 785; BFH, 1 Apr. 1987, II R 186/80, BStBl. II 1987, 550. Critical with regard to the 'Kapitalspiegelmethode' also *Looks*, in: Looks/Heinsen (Eds.), Betriebsstättenbesteuerung, para. 875; *Nouel*, in: Gutiérrez/Perdelwitz (Eds.), Taxation of Business Profits in the 21st Century, 183 (201).

770Cf. Section 12(2) sentence 1 BsGaV; BMF, 22 Dec. 2016, IV B 5—S 1341/12/10001–03, BStBl. I 2017, 182, para. 133.

771Cf. Section 12(2) sentence 2 BsGaV.

772Cf. BMF, 22 Dec. 2016, IV B 5—S 1341/12/10001–03, BStBl. I 2017, 182, para. 134.

773Cf. Section 12(2) sentence 2 BsGaV; BMF, 22 Dec. 2016, IV B 5—S 1341/12/10001–03, BStBl. I 2017, 182, para. 134.

774Cf. BMF, 22 Dec. 2016, IV B 5—S 1341/12/10001–03, BStBl. I 2017, 182, para. 134; critical with regard to this approach *Kraft*, in: Kraft (Ed.), AStG—Kommentar, § 1 AStG, para. 695.

775Cf. Section 12(3) sentence 1 BsGaV.

principle, or existing differences can be balanced through adjustments so that the result does not substantially differ (less than 10%)[776] from the result obtained by using values that comply with the arm's length principle and adequately take account of opportunities and risks.[777]

The capital allocation method shall not be applied if the foreign enterprise to which the PE belongs is part of a group of enterprises within the meaning of Section 18 of the Stock Corporation Act (hereinafter: SCA) and the application of the capital allocation method leads to an amount of free capital for the PE that would not be accepted by a prudent and conscientious manager.[778] This may be the case when the foreign enterprise in thinly capitalised and the amount of loans attributed to the PE and the corresponding interest expenses result in a scenario that would plunge the PE into a permanent loss-making situation.[779] In that case, a portion of the group's consolidated equity capital (determined in accordance with Section 12(2) BsGaV) is to be attributed to the PE as free capital on a consolidated basis.[780]

The minimum level of free capital that must be attributed to a domestic PE is determined by Section 12(5) BsGaV. Accordingly, the capital actually shown in domestic commercial accounts of the domestic PE can be regarded as the lower boundary and must therefore be attributed to the PE. In other words, the capital actually shown in domestic commercial accounts must always be attributed to the PE if it is higher than the free capital that results from the application of the capital allocation method under Section 12(1) to (3) BsGaV or the alternative approach of Section 12(4) BsGaV.[781]

As determined by Section 12(1) BsGaV, the amount of free capital attributable to the PE must be determined at the beginning of each fiscal year. However, if the attributed people functions, assets or opportunities and risks to the domestic PE change over the course of a fiscal year and would result in a significant change in the amount of free capital attributable to the domestic PE, the amount of free capital must be adjusted accordingly within the fiscal year.[782] In the tax authority's

---

[776] Cf. BMF, 22 Dec. 2016, IV B 5—S 1341/12/10001–03, BStBl. I 2017, 182, para. 139.

[777] Cf. Section 12(3) sentence 2 BsGaV; BMF, 22 Dec. 2016, IV B 5—S 1341/12/10001–03, BStBl. I 2017, 182, para. 138.

[778] Cf. Section 12(3) sentence 1 BsGaV.

[779] Cf. *Kraft*, in: Kraft (Ed.), AStG—Kommentar, § 1 AStG, para. 697; *Andresen*, in: W/A/D (Eds.), Betriebsstätten-Handbuch, para. 4.149.

[780] Cf. Section 12(4) BsGaV.

[781] Cf. *Leonhardt/Tcherveniachki*, in: F/W/B/S (Eds.), Außensteuerrecht—Kommentar, § 1 AStG, para. 3218.

[782] Cf. Section 12(6) BsGaV.

view, a change in the amount of free capital must be regarded as 'significant' if the amount of free capital to be attributed to the domestic PE at the beginning of the following fiscal year, resulting from the change of the attributed people functions, assets or opportunities and risks, is more than 30% compared to the amount of free capital attributed to the domestic PE at the beginning of the fiscal year.[783] However, this shall only be of relevance if the absolute deviation amounts to at least EUR 2 million.[784] As explicitly emphasised by the tax authority, a decrease of free capital attributed to the PE shall be accepted only insofar as it is proven that the foreign enterprise has drawn the necessary tax consequences abroad respectively.[785] The purpose of this approach is to ensure that, in particular, interest expenses are not deducted twice.[786]

ii. Comparison to the OECD Approach

Both the OECD and the German tax authority agree upon the fact that a PE should be attributed sufficient capital to support the functions performed, the assets used and the opportunities and risks assumed.[787] However, the approach on how to attribute free capital to the PE differs in certain aspects. While the OECD acknowledges that different capital structures may be in accordance with the arm's length principle and illustrates various methods (e.g. capital allocation approach, the economic capital allocation approach and the thin capitalisation approach) that may be appropriate for the attribution of capital to a PE,[788] the German tax authority puts forward very 'prescriptive' provisions on how free capital must be attributed to a PE. In this regard, a distinction is made between the attribution of free capital to a domestic PE of a foreign enterprise (Section 12 BsGaV) and the attribution of free capital of a foreign PE of a domestic enterprise (Section 13 BsGaV).

As outlined above, the fundamental method that must be applied for the attribution of free capital to a PE located in Germany is the capital allocation approach.

---

[783] Cf. BMF, 22 Dec. 2016, IV B 5—S 1341/12/10001–03, BStBl. I 2017, 182, para. 139.

[784] Cf. BMF, 22 Dec. 2016, IV B 5—S 1341/12/10001–03, BStBl. I 2017, 182, para. 139.

[785] Cf. BMF, 22 Dec. 2016, IV B 5—S 1341/12/10001–03, BStBl. I 2017, 182, para. 143.

[786] Cf. *Leonhardt/Tcherveniachki*, in: F/W/B/S (Eds.), Außensteuerrecht—Kommentar, § 1 AStG, para. 3219.

[787] Cf. OECD, PE Report 2010, Part I, para. 28; BMF, 22 Dec. 2016, IV B 5—S 1341/12/10001–03, BStBl. I 2017, 182, para. 139.

[788] Cf. OECD, PE Report 2010, Part I, paras. 121 et seqq. Even though the OECD also illustrates the safe harbour approach, it is concluded by the OECD that this method is not an authorised OECD approach, cf. OECD, PE Report 2010, Part I, para. 135.

This method is also covered by the PE Report 2010.[789] Nevertheless, even if the jurisdiction where the foreign enterprise is located provides for the application of the capital allocation approach, deviations resulting from differences in its application by the jurisdiction where the foreign head office is located may occur. In this context, a possible deviation may arise due to differences in the determination of the foreign enterprise's equity capital. While the PE Report 2010 does not provide any guidance in this regard, Section 12(2) sentence 1 BsGaV determines that the amount of the foreign enterprise's equity capital must be determined in accordance with German tax law. A 'simplified' approach based on the enterprise's foreign balance sheet is provided by Section 12(2) sentence 2 BsGaV. However, since the requirements for the application of this simplified approach are firstly quite difficult to prove[790] and secondly very strict,[791] its scope should prove very limited.[792]

In order to determine the capital ratio needed for the application of the capital allocation approach, the German tax authority emphasises that assets of the PE and the rest of the enterprise must be measured at values that comply with the arm's length principle and take account of opportunities and risks.[793] This approach is covered by the PE Report 2010, outlining a variety of possible approaches.[794] Despite the fact that also the use of book values, acknowledged by the German tax authority as a simplified approach in order to measure the value of assets, is covered by the OECD approach, the actual use of this alternative approach is very difficult in its application and loses any meaning, especially in cases where the domestic PE uses non-accounted assets such as internally developed intangibles.[795]

[789] Similar *Andresen*, in: W/A/D (Eds.), Betriebsstätten-Handbuch, para. 5.42.

[790] Cf. *Kraft*, in: Kraft (Ed.), AStG—Kommentar, § 1 AStG, para. 697; *Kraft/Dombrowski*, FR 2014, 1105 (1111); *Kraft/Dombrowski*, Ubg 2015, 143 (148); *Leonhardt/Tcherveniachki*, in: F/W/B/S (Eds.), Außensteuerrecht—Kommentar, § 1 AStG, para. 3210.

[791] Cf. *Leonhardt/Tcherveniachki*, in: F/W/B/S (Eds.), Außensteuerrecht—Kommentar, § 1 AStG, para. 3210.

[792] For the requirements see BMF, 22 Dec. 2016, IV B 5—S 1341/12/10001-03, BStBl. I 2017, 182, para. 134.

[793] Cf. Section 12(3) sentence 1 BsGaV.

[794] Cf. OECD, PE Report 2010, Part I, paras. 109 et seq. Also *Margerie* sees the German approach in line with the OECD approach, cf. *Margerie*, Gewinnermittlung und Gewinnabgrenzung bei Betriebsstätten, 247.

[795] Cf. *Oestreicher/van der Ham/Andresen*, insert to issue 4 IStR 2014, 1 (17); *Kraft*, in: Kraft (Ed.), AStG—Kommentar, § 1 AStG, para. 696; *Leonhardt/Tcherveniachki*, in: F/W/B/S (Eds.), Außensteuerrecht—Kommentar, § 1 AStG, para. 3215.

Circumstances where the application of the capital allocation approach is not appropriate are outlined in Section 12(4) and 12(5) BsGaV. Both approaches are not covered by the PE Report 2010 and therefore bear the risk for double taxation if applied by the taxpayer or the tax authorities.[796]

Clarifications with regard to the question whether the amount of free capital must be adjusted within the fiscal year if the attributed people functions, assets, opportunities and risks to the domestic PE change over the course of the fiscal year, resulting in a significant change in the amount of free capital as determined by Section 12(6) BsGaV, are not provided in the PE Report 2010.

Table 7 summarises the OECD and the German approach with regard to the attribution of free capital to a domestic PE of a foreign enterprise.

(c) Free Capital of Foreign PE of Domestic Enterprise

i. Fundamental Attribution Approach

Free capital of a foreign PE of a domestic enterprise must be determined in accordance with the minimum capital approach, i.e. free capital shall only be attributed to a foreign PE if evidence is provided that such an attribution is required for commercial reasons.[797] Commercial reasons in this sense are, e.g., a negative payment balance either occurred in the past or expected for future business activities, a replacement of a loan or expiring supplier loans.[798] Thus, in order to attribute free capital to a foreign PE, the taxpayer is explicitly required to provide proof; otherwise no free capital can be attributed.

According to Section 12(2) BsGaV, the foreign PE may also be attributed a higher amount of free capital if this higher amount is more in line with the arm's length principle. Nevertheless, if the taxpayer is able to prove that such a higher amount of free capital is more suitable for the specific circumstances of the case, Section 13(2) sentence 2 BsGaV specifies a limit of attributable free capital. More precisely, the free capital attributed to the foreign PE must not exceed the amount that would result from the application of the capital allocation approach in accordance with Section 12(1)–(3) BsGaV.[799] An even higher amount of free capital is only permitted if non-tax provisions (e.g. minimum capital requirements

---

[796] Cf. *Kraft*, in: Kraft (Ed.), AStG—Kommentar, § 1 AStG, para. 698; *Andresen*, in: W/A/D (Eds.), Betriebsstätten-Handbuch, para. 5.42.

[797] Cf. Section 13(1) BsGaV.

[798] Cf. *Andresen*, in: W/A/D (Eds.), Betriebsstätten-Handbuch, para. 4.156; *Leonhardt/Tcherveniachki*, in: F/W/B/S (Eds.), Außensteuerrecht—Kommentar, § 1 AStG, para. 3231.

[799] Cf. Section 13(2) sentence 2 BsGaV. As explicitly emphasised in the Ordinance, the calculation of this maximum amount must be based on the book values relevant for taxation.

Table 7 OECD vs. German Approach for Attribution of Free Capital to Domestic PE of Foreign Enterprise

	OECD approach	German approach
Attribution method	• different methods outlined: – capital allocation approach – economic capital allocation approach – thin capitalisation approach – quasi thin capitalisation approach (only acceptable as a safe harbour under certain conditions)	• in general: capital allocation approach • exceptions apply mostly in cases of thin capitalisation (Section 12(4) and (5) BsGaV)
Minimum amount of free capital	• no specified minimum amount provided by PE Report 2010	• capital actually shown in domestic commercial accounts of the domestic PE (Section 12 (5) BsGaV)
Adjustments within the fiscal year	• not addressed in the PE Report 2010	• adjustments necessary if attributed people functions, assets, opportunities and risks changes over the course of the fiscal year resulting in a significant change of free capital to the PE • meaning of significant change: – 30% compared to amount of free capital at the beginning of the fiscal year – absolute deviation at least EUR 2 million

Source: Own illustration.

in banking and insurance) of the state in which the PE is located require such an amount.[800]

Other amounts are only permitted if it would lead to a result that better complied with the arm's length principle, cf. Section 13(2) sentence 3 BsGaV.

[800]Cf. Section 13(3) BsGaV.

In contrast to Section 12(5) BsGaV, determining that the capital actually shown in domestic commercial accounts shall constitute the minimum amount of free capital that must be attributed to a domestic PE, Section 13(4) BsGaV determines that the capital actually shown in foreign commercial accounts shall constitute the maximum amount of free capital that must be attributed to a foreign PE. This is intended to prevent that free capital attributed to the foreign PE is increased subsequently and arbitrary.[801]

In analogy to Section 12(6) BsGaV, Section 13(5) BsGaV deals with the adjustment of free capital within the fiscal year. Accordingly, if the attributed people functions, assets or opportunities and risks to the foreign PE change over the course of a fiscal year and would result in a significant change in the amount of free capital attributable to the foreign PE, the amount of free capital must be adjusted accordingly within the fiscal year.[802] As already elaborated in the context of domestic PEs, in the German tax authority's view, a change in the amount of free capital must be regarded as 'significant' if the amount of free capital to be attributed to the foreign PE at the beginning of the following fiscal year, resulting from the change of the attributed people functions, assets or opportunities and risks, is more than 30% compared to the amount of free capital attributed to the foreign PE at the beginning of the fiscal year.[803] This shall only be of relevance if the absolute deviation amounts to at least EUR 2 million.[804] An increase of free capital attributed to the foreign PE shall be accepted only insofar as it is proven that the domestic enterprise has drawn the necessary tax consequences abroad respectively.[805] This shall ensure that interest expenses are not deducted twice.[806]

ii. Comparison to the OECD Approach

In contrast to the OECD, emphasising that '[a]ll business activity involves some kind of risk'[807] and therefore requires a certain amount of free capital that should be attributed to a PE as a 'cushion against the crystallisation of risks into actual losses'[808], the German tax authority determines the minimum capital approach

---

801 Cf. BR-Drs. 401/14, 82.

802 Cf. Section 13(5) BsGaV.

803 Cf. BMF, 22 Dec. 2016, IV B 5—S 1341/12/10001–03, BStBl. I 2017, 182, para. 151.

804 Cf. BMF, 22 Dec. 2016, IV B 5—S 1341/12/10001–03, BStBl. I 2017, 182, para. 151.

805 Cf. BMF, 22 Dec. 2016, IV B 5—S 1341/12/10001–03, BStBl. I 2017, 182, para. 151.

806 Cf. *Leonhardt/Tcherveniachki*, in: F/W/B/S (Eds.), Außensteuerrecht—Kommentar, § 1 AStG, para. 3239.

807 OECD, PE Report 2010, Part I, para. 71.

808 OECD, PE Report 2010, Part I, para. 71.

as the general approach for the attribution of free capital to a foreign PE of a domestic enterprise. It follows that no free capital can be attributed to a foreign PE at all if the taxpayer is unable to provide proof that free capital is required. The minimum capital approach is not one of the authorised OECD approaches outlined in the PE Report 2010 and, when applied, leads to a situation that an excessive amount of financing expenses is attributed to a foreign PE of a domestic enterprise.[809] A higher amount of free capital can only be attributed to a foreign PE if proof is provided by the taxpayer.[810] However, even then the free capital attributed to the foreign PE shall not exceed the amount that results from the application of the capital allocation approach.[811]

Compared to the inbound scenario, where the capital allocation approach constitutes the fundamental approach for the attribution of free capital, it is quite obvious that the German tax authority disproportionately treats outbound and inbound scenarios. This asymmetric treatment of domestic and foreign PEs shall ensure that the profit of the part of the enterprise located in Germany is as high as possible, resulting in a higher tax payment. By way of example, as higher the amount of free capital attributed to a foreign PE as lower the attributable liabilities to this PE, resulting in a lower amount of financing expenses attributable to the foreign PE.[812] This, however, could ultimately lead to the situation that the financing expenses are deducted at the level of the domestic enterprise and decrease the amount of profits in Germany, resulting in a lower tax payment in Germany. Since the minimum capital approach ensures that the foreign PE can only be attributed a minimum amount of free capital and therefore a higher amount of financing expenses, the German approach must be regarded as fiscally motivated and puts PEs located abroad in disadvantage compared to PEs located in Germany.[813] This unequal treatment of outbound and inbound investments causes considerable legal uncertainty and may lead to double taxation if the foreign jurisdiction follows another approach for the attribution of free capital.[814]

---

809 Cf. *Kraft*, in: Kraft (Ed.), AStG—Kommentar, § 1 AStG, para. 703.

810 Cf. BMF, 22 Dec. 2016, IV B 5—S 1341/12/10001-03, BStBl. I 2017, 182, para. 146.

811 Cf. Section 13(2) BsGaV.

812 Cf. BR-Drs. 401/14, 80.

813 Critical also *Busch*, DB 2014, 2490 (2493); *Kraft*, in: Kraft (Ed.), AStG—Kommentar, § 1 AStG, para. 703; *Kraft/Dombrowski*, FR 2014, 1105 (1112); *Nientimp/Ludwig/Stein*, IWB 2014, 815 (823 et seq.); *Oestreicher/van der Ham/Andresen*, insert to issue 4 IStR 2014, 1 (18 et seq.); *Kußmaul/Delarber/Müller*, IStR 2014, 466 (473); *Strothenke/Holtrichter*, IWB 2013, 730 (734); *Kahle/Kindich*, in: Lübbehüsen/Kahle (Eds.), Brennpunkte der Besteuerung von Betriebsstätten, para. 4.347.

814 Cf. *Hentschel/Kraft/Moser*, ET 2018, 73 (78).

As elaborated above, the German approach provides for three upper limits for the attribution of free capital to a foreign PE. Firstly, the amount that results from the application of the capital allocation approach,[815] secondly the amount as required under non-tax provisions,[816] and thirdly the amount of capital actually shown in the foreign commercial account of the foreign PE.[817] The OECD does not provide for any specified maximum amount of free capital attributable to a foreign PE in the PE Report 2010. While the first upper limit—if exhausted by the taxpayer—may lead to a result that turns out to be in line with the OECD approach, since the capital allocation approach is one of the methods illustrated in the PE Report 2010,[818] the other two limits are not mentioned in the PE Report 2010. Especially, the third limit, the capital actually shown in the foreign commercial account of the foreign PE, bears the potential for double taxation if the German tax authority insists to apply this limit in the course of a tax audit.[819]

As outlined in the previous chapter, clarifications whether the amount of free capital must be adjusted within the fiscal year if the attributed people functions, assets, opportunities and risks to the domestic PE change over the course of the fiscal year, resulting in a significant change in the amount of free capital as determined by Section 13(5) BsGaV, are not provided in the PE Report 2010.

Table 8 summarises the OECD and the German approach with regard to the attribution of free capital to a foreign PE of a domestic enterprise.

(6) Attribution of Remaining Liability Items and Financing Expenses

(a) Attribution of Remaining Liability Items

i. The Term 'Remaining Liability Items'

A definition of the term 'remaining liability items' is neither provided by the BsGaV nor by the VWG BsGa. Given the intention that the interplay between the outlined attribution methods shall result in a notional tax balance sheet for the PE for profit determination purposes, the remaining liability items should encompass all liability items that do not constitute equity within the meaning

---

[815] Cf. Section 13(2) sentence 2 BsGaV.

[816] Cf. Section 13(3) BsGaV.

[817] Cf. Section 13(4) BsGaV.

[818] See in more detail for the capital allocation approach OECD, PE Report 2010, Part I, paras. 121 et seqq. and chapter D.I.4.b.(2)(e)ii.01 of this thesis.

[819] Cf. *Andresen*, in: W/A/D (Eds.), Betriebsstätten-Handbuch, para. 5.42.

Table 8 OECD vs. German Approach for Attribution of Free Capital to Foreign PE of Domestic Enterprise

	OECD approach	German approach
Attribution method	• different methods outlined: – capital allocation approach – economic capital allocation approach – thin capitalisation approach – quasi thin capitalisation approach (only acceptable as a safe harbour under certain conditions)	• in general: minimum capital approach • exceptions apply (Section 13(2) to 13(4) BsGaV)
Maximum amount of free capital	• no specified maximum amount provided by PE Report 2010	• <u>first upper limit:</u> – amount that results from the application of the capital allocation method • <u>second upper limit:</u> – amount as required under non-tax provisions • <u>third upper limit:</u> – capital actually shown in foreign commercial accounts of the PE
Adjustments within the fiscal year	• not addressed in the PE Report 2010	• adjustments necessary if attributed people functions, assets, opportunities and risks changes over the course of the fiscal year resulting in a significant change of free capital to the PE • meaning of significant change: – 30% compared to amount of free capital at the beginning of the fiscal year – absolute deviation at least EUR 2 million

Source: Own illustration.

of Section 266(3) lit. A GCC.[820] Accordingly, remaining liability items for the purpose of Section 14 BsGaV that must be attributed to the PE are provisions within the meaning of Section 266(3) lit. B.1. to B.3. GCC, liabilities within the meaning of Section 266(3) lit. C.1. to C.8. GCC and deferrals within the meaning of Section 266(3) lit. D GCC.[821] Provisions for risks within the meaning of Section 10 BsGaV, such as warranty provisions that must be shown in the auxiliary and ancillary accounts,[822] do not belong to the remaining liability items within the meaning of Section 14 BsGaV.

ii. Fundamental Attribution Approach

In general, remaining liability items can only be attributed to the PE if there is a shortfall on the liability side of the auxiliary and ancillary account of the PE, after risks that must be shown in this account and free capital was attributed to the PE.[823] In other words, if the amount of risks as shown in the auxiliary and ancillary accounts and free capital equals the amount of assets, no remaining liability items can be attributed to the PE. Table 9 provides an example for an auxiliary and ancillary account that must be prepared for a PE according to Section 3 BsGaV. After assets, free capital and risks were attributed to the PE, the amount of remaining liability items attributable to the PE must be determined.

Table 9 Example for Auxiliary and Ancillary Account

Auxiliary and ancillary account (within the meaning of Section 3 BsGaV)			
Assets	100 EUR	Free Capital	60 EUR
		Warranty Provisions (Risks)	10 EUR
		Remaining Liability Items	?
Sum	100 EUR	Sum	100 EUR

Source: Own illustration.

[820] Cf. *Andresen*, in: W/A/D (Eds.), Betriebsstätten-Handbuch, para. 4.167; *Leonhardt/Tcherveniachki*, in: F/W/B/S (Eds.), Außensteuerrecht—Kommentar, § 1 AStG, para. 3261.

[821] Cf. *Andresen*, in: W/A/D (Eds.), Betriebsstätten-Handbuch, para. 4.167.

[822] For an example see BMF, 22 Dec. 2016, IV B 5—S 1341/12/10001–03, BStBl. I 2017, 182, para. 153.

[823] Cf. *Kraft*, in: Kraft (Ed.), AStG—Kommentar, § 1 AStG, para. 704. Critical *Kraft/Dombrowski*, FR 2014, 1105 (1112).

The attribution must be determined based on Section 14 BsGaV. In this sense, a two-step approach must be followed. In a first step, the remaining liability items that are directly related to the attributed assets as well as the opportunities and risks must be attributed to the PE (direct attribution).[824] Such liabilities shall include, e.g., loan liabilities taken for assets that are attributed to the PE.[825] This approach shall ensure that assets and its source of financing are not separated from each other.[826]

Even though the auxiliary and ancillary account cannot be regarded as an actual tax balance sheet, the sum of its assets and the sum of its free capital, risks and remaining liability items must still correspond according to amount.[827] Against this background, Section 14(2) BsGaV determines that remaining liability items must be reduced on a pro rata basis if the sum of the remaining liability items that can be attributed to the PE directly exceeds the remaining amount after risks and free capital were attributed to the PE. The remaining liability items that had to be reduced on a pro rata basis must be attributed to the other parts of the enterprise.[828]

In case there is a shortfall of liability items in the auxiliary and ancillary account after the directly attributable liability items were attributed to the PE, this shortfall must be made up in a second step with remaining liability items of the enterprise according to Section 14(3) BsGaV (indirect attribution).

iii. Comparison to the OECD Approach

As examined earlier, it is acknowledged by the OECD that a PE requires a certain amount of funding which is made up of free capital and interest-bearing debt.[829] A mechanism on how to attribute interest-bearing debt to a PE is not provided by the OECD.[830] Rather, the amount of interest-bearing debt results as a residuum

---

[824] Cf. Section 14(1) BsGaV.

[825] Cf. BR-Drs. 401/14, 83.

[826] Cf. BR-Drs. 401/14, 83.

[827] Cf. *Kahle/Kindich*, in: Lübbehüsen/Kahle (Eds.), Brennpunkte der Besteuerung von Betriebsstätten, para. 4.352.

[828] Cf. BR-Drs. 401/14, 83. Critical *Kraft/Dombrowski*, FR 2014, 1105 (1112); *Kraft*, in: Kraft (Ed.), AStG—Kommentar, § 1 AStG, para. 704.

[829] Cf. OECD, PE Report 2010, Part I, para. 150.

[830] Cf. *Kaeser*, in: W/K/S/D (Eds.), Doppelbesteuerung, Art. 7 MA (2010), para. 499. The OECD only elaborates that 'there is more than one authorised approach to attributing interest-bearing debt and to determine the rate of interest to be applied to that debt', cf. OECD, PE Report 2010, Part I, para. 151.

after free capital has been attributed to a PE.[831] Other liability items such as provisions or deferrals are not mentioned in this context.[832] However, also the OECD acknowledges that provisions booked in relation to risks (such as warranty provisions) must be attributed to a PE if the significant people function relevant for the assumption of that risk is performed by this PE.[833]

In contrast to the OECD approach, Section 14 BsGaV does not only deal with the attribution of interest-bearing debt, but also the attribution of provisions (other than those related to risk that must be shown in the auxiliary and ancillary account) and deferrals. As illustrated in table 9, the amount of remaining liability items also results as a residuum after free capital and risks were attributed to the PE. However, Section 14 BsGaV provides a more detailed attribution approach than the OECD which allows for two assessments.

First, Section 14(1) BsGaV determines that remaining liability items that are directly related to the assets as well as the opportunities and risks must be attributed to the PE. In case the sum of the attributable free capital, the risks and the directly attributable liability items exceed the amount of assets attributed to the PE, the amount of the directly attributable remaining liability items must be reduced on a pro rata basis.[834] Further explanations on how such a reduction on a pro rata basis shall be carried out can neither be found in the BsGaV nor in the VWG BsGa. Only an example used in the VWG BsGa in order to illustrate the mechanism of a pro rata reduction of directly attributable remaining liability suggests that a pro rata reduction shall be carried out on a linear basis.[835] Such a linear reduction should indeed provide the least amount of leeway and should therefore reduce the probability of disputes with the tax authority and is recommended in this context.[836]

Secondly, even though a reduction of directly attributable liability items is not in line with the idea to treat a PE as a separate and independent enterprise, this

---

[831]Cf. *Kaeser*, in: W/K/S/D (Eds.), Doppelbesteuerung, Art. 7 MA (2010), para. 499.

[832]Cf. *Andresen*, in: W/A/D (Eds.), Betriebsstätten-Handbuch, para. 5.44.

[833]Cf. OECD, PE Report 2010, Part I, para. 70; *Looks*, in: Looks/Heinsen (Eds.), Betriebsstättenbesteuerung, para. 850; *Kaeser*, in: W/K/S/D (Eds.), Doppelbesteuerung, Art. 7 MA (2010), para. 456; *Margerie*, Gewinnermittlung und Gewinnabgrenzung bei Betriebsstätten, 129.

[834]Cf. Section 14(2) BsGaV.

[835]Cf. BMF, 22 Dec. 2016, IV B 5—S 1341/12/10001–03, BStBl. I 2017, 182, para. 153.

[836]Another suggestion by *Looks* is that the pro rata reduction could be based upon the maturity of the liabilities, cf. *Looks*, in: Looks/Heinsen (Eds.), Betriebsstättenbesteuerung, para. 895. However, such a reduction would imply new difficulties and thus cannot be recommended.

mechanism is a direct result of the attribution approach determining to attribute free capital and risks first and then the remaining liability items in a second step. However, *Andresen* and *Leonhardt/Tcherveniachki* must be followed who emphasise that a pro rata reduction is only appropriate for liability items within the meaning of Section 266(3) lit. C.1. to C.7. GCC.[837] A reduction of provisions within the meaning of Section 266(3) lit. B.1. to B.3. GCC, liability items within the meaning of Section 266(3) lit. C.8. GCC and deferrals within the meaning of Section 266(3) lit. D GCC would not be appropriate since such items directly relate to the business situation of the PE.[838] The example used in the VWG BsGa clarifies that provisions for risks within the meaning of Section 11 BsGaV, such as warranty provisions that must be shown in the auxiliary and ancillary accounts, must be attributed to the PE before remaining liability items within the meaning of Section 14 BsGaV are attributed to the PE and must therefore not be reduced on a pro rata basis.[839]

Table 10 provides an overview of the German and the OECD approach with regard to the attribution of interest bearing debt/remaining liability items to a PE and can be regarded as a summary of the above analysis.

(b) Attribution of Financing Expenses

i. The Term 'Financing Expenses'

A definition of the term 'financing expenses' is neither provided by the BsGaV nor by the VWG BsGa. However, given the overall intention of the AOA, financing expenses within the meaning of Section 16 BsGaV shall encompass those items that constitute interests and other expenses within the meaning of Section 275(2) no. 13 GCC or Section 275(3) no. 12 GCC.[840]

[837] Cf. *Andresen*, in: W/A/D (Eds.), Betriebsstätten-Handbuch, para. 4.170; *Leonhardt/Tcherveniachki*, in: F/W/B/S (Eds.), Außensteuerrecht—Kommentar, § 1 AStG, para. 3264.

[838] Cf. *Leonhardt/Tcherveniachki*, in: F/W/B/S (Eds.), Außensteuerrecht—Kommentar, § 1 AStG, para. 3264.

[839] Cf. BMF, 22 Dec. 2016, IV B 5—S 1341/12/10001-03, BStBl. I 2017, 182, para. 153. According to Section 14(1) BsGaV, 'risks that must be shown in the auxiliary and ancillary accounts' must be attributed to the PE before remaining liability items.

[840] Cf. *Andresen*, in: W/A/D (Eds.), Betriebsstätten-Handbuch, para. 4.174; *Leonhardt/Tcherveniachki*, in: F/W/B/S (Eds.), Außensteuerrecht—Kommentar, § 1 AStG, para. 3291.

Table 10 OECD vs. German Approach for Attribution of Interest-Bearing Debt

	OECD approach	German approach
Attribution approach	• no specific attribution approach provided • interest-bearing debt results as a residuum → interest-bearing debt = overall amount of financing–free capital	• 2-step approach for attribution: – 1-step: direct attribution → attribution of remaining liability items that are directly related to the assets and to the opportunities and risks of the PE → reduction on a pro rata basis if amount of directly attributable liability items exceeds attributable amount – 2-step: indirect attribution → attribution of remaining liability items of the enterprise → only if there is a shortfall of liability items for the PE

Source: Own illustration.

ii. Fundamental Attribution Approach

The approach for the attribution of financing expenses follows the approach used for remaining liability items. Consequently, financing expenses that are related to liability items that must directly be attributed to a PE according to Section 14(1) BsGaV must be attributed to this PE as well.[841] Also, as far as directly attributable liability items must be reduced on a pro rata basis pursuant to Section 14(2) BsGaV, financing expenses directly related to such liability items must be reduced accordingly.[842] However, a pro rata reduction of financing expenses that are related to items covered by Section 266(3) lit. B. and C.8. GCC, e.g. interests within the meaning of Sections 233 et seqq. GFC, would not be appropriate since such items directly relate to the business situation of the PE.[843]

[841]Cf. Section 15(1) BsGaV.

[842]Cf. Section 15(2) BsGaV.

[843]Cf. *Andresen*, in: W/A/D (Eds.), Betriebsstätten-Handbuch, para. 4.175; *Leonhardt/Tcherveniachki*, in: F/W/B/S (Eds.), Außensteuerrecht—Kommentar, § 1 AStG, para. 3292.

If a direct attribution of financing expenses to the PE is not possible or would cause disproportionate efforts, Section 15(3) sentence 1 BsGaV determines that the attribution of financing expenses to the PE shall be carried out on a pro rata basis in accordance with the indirect attribution of the liability items. For reasons of simplicity, the PE's portion of the financing expenses shall be determined on the basis of the ratio resulting at the beginning of the relevant fiscal year.[844] The advantage of referring to the beginning of the relevant fiscal year is that the ratio is not influenced by ongoing business transactions or dealings as long as no significant changes pursuant to Section 12(6) BsGaV or Section 13(5) BsGaV occur within the fiscal year.[845] By way of derogation from Section 15(3) sentence 1 and 2 BsGaV, the PE's portion of financing expenses can be determined differently if this leads to a result for the PE that better complies with the arm's length principle.[846] Such a different determination according to Section 15(3) sentence 3 BsGaV is appropriate e.g. in case an adjustment of free capital attributed to the PE is necessary according to Section 12(6) BsGaV or Section 13(5) BsGaV.[847]

Section 15(4) BsGaV and Section 15(5) BsGaV contain a particular approach for the attribution of financing expenses applicable if the enterprise is not required to keep accounts and does not, in fact, keep accounts. In that case, a domestic PE of a foreign enterprise (Section 15(4) BsGaV), respectively a foreign PE of a domestic enterprise (Section 15(5) BsGaV), can only be attributed financing expenses that are directly related to the PE's business activities.[848] In contrast to domestic PEs, foreign PEs must be attributed a minimum portion of financing expenses that equates to its portion of the domestic enterprise's external sales.[849] A different attribution is only possible if a result is produced for the PE that is more in line with the arm's length principle.[850]

---

[844]Cf. Section 15(3) sentence 2 BsGaV.

[845]Cf. *Looks,* in: Looks/Heinsen (Eds.), Betriebsstättenbesteuerung, para. 896.

[846]Cf. Section 15(3) sentence 3 BsGaV. In this regard, *Kraft/Dombrowski* appropriately criticise that such an attribution by derogation from Section 15(3) sentence 1 and 2 BsGaV is only possible for financing expenses that are related to liability items that were indirectly attributed to the PE within the meaning of Section 14(3) BsGaV and not for financing expenses of liability items that were directly attributed to the PE, ultimately putting PEs that have a transparent financing structure at a disadvantage, cf. *Kraft/Dombrowski*, FR 2014, 1105 (1112).

[847]Cf. BMF, 22 Dec. 2016, IV B 5—S 1341/12/10001-03, BStBl. I 2017, 182, para. 160.

[848]Cf. *Kahle/Kindich*, in: Lübbehüsen/Kahle (Eds.), Brennpunkte der Besteuerung von Betriebsstätten, para. 4.365.

[849]Cf. Section 15(5) sentence 2 BsGaV.

[850]Cf. Section 15(5) sentence 3 BsGaV.

iii. Comparison to the OECD Approach

For the attribution of financing expenses, the OECD primarily discusses two approaches that may be appropriate contingent upon the specific circumstances of the case: the tracing approach and the fungibility approach.[851] Elements of both approaches are included in Section 15 BsGaV.[852] While the attribution approach implemented in Section 15(1) BsGaV follows the tracing approach, the attribution approach implemented in Section 15(3) BsGaV follows the fungibility approach.[853] Insofar, no inherent risk of double taxation can be identified.

However, the approach for the attribution of financing expenses implemented in Section 15(4) BsGaV and Section 15(5) BsGaV, applicable if the enterprise is not required to keep accounts and does not, in fact, keep accounts, reveals that the German tax authority treats inbound and outbound PEs disproportionately. While the approach implemented in Section 15(4) BsGaV limits the deductibility of interest expenses for inbound PEs by determining that the PE's remaining result from its business activities (after the deduction of interest expenses) must comply with the arm's length principle, Section 15(5) BsGaV determines that a foreign PE must be attributed a minimum portion of financing expenses that equates to its portion of the domestic enterprise's external sales.[854] In other words, the approach chosen intends to safeguard the German tax base by a) setting a limit for the amount of attributable interest expenses to PEs located in Germany and at the same time, b) determining a minimum portion of attributable financing expenses to PEs located abroad which ultimately ensures that this amount does not reduce the German tax base of the domestic enterprise.[855] The 'escape-clause' implemented in Section 15(5) sentence 3 BsGaV determining that a different attribution of financing expenses to foreign PEs is only possible if such a different attribution produces a result that is more in line with the arm's length principle, imposes an additional administrative burden for the taxpayer and should prove to be difficult

---

[851] See in more detail chapter D.I.4.b.(2)(f) of this thesis.

[852] Cf. *Andresen*, in: W/A/D (Eds.), Betriebsstätten-Handbuch, para. 5.44; *Froitzheim*, Steuerliche Selbstständigkeitsfiktion der Betriebsstätte, 239.

[853] Cf. *Margerie*, Gewinnermittlung und Gewinnabgrenzung bei Betriebsstätten, 251.

[854] Cf. *Kahle/Kindich*, in: Lübbehüsen/Kahle (Eds.), Brennpunkte der Besteuerung von Betriebsstätten, para. 4.368; *Kraft*, in: Kraft (Ed.), AStG—Kommentar, § 1 AStG, para. 708.

[855] Cf. *Kahle/Kindich*, in: Lübbehüsen/Kahle (Eds.), Brennpunkte der Besteuerung von Betriebsstätten, para. 4.368: *Looks*, in: Looks/Heinsen (Eds.), Betriebsstättenbesteuerung, para. 897. Also critical regarding the approach chosen by the German tax authority *Haverkamp*, in: Mössner et al. (Eds.), Steuerrecht international tätiger Unternehmen, para. 5.242; *Andresen*, in: W/A/D (Eds.), Betriebsstätten-Handbuch, paras. 4.179 et seqq.; *Kraft*, in: Kraft (Ed.), AStG—Kommentar, § 1 AStG, para. 708.

to benefit from in practice.[856] If the taxpayer is unable to provide proof and is therefore unable to attribute an amount of financing expenses to a foreign PE that is more in line with the arm's length principle, an inherent risk of double taxation exists. This is due to the fact that it cannot be expected that the other jurisdiction where the foreign PE is located follows such an approach.

Even though the OECD concludes that 'it does not seem possible to develop a single approach for determining the amount of attributable interest expense that could be applicable in all circumstances'[857], it is also explicitly emphasised by the OECD that regardless of the approach chosen, the amount of interest expenses attributed to the PE shall not exceed an arm's length amount.[858] However, if the attribution of a minimum portion of financing expenses to a foreign PE that equates to its portion of the domestic enterprise's external sales as determined by Section 15(5) sentence 2 BsGaV is too high and the taxpayer fails to prove that this amount exceeds an arm's length amount simply due to bureaucratic hurdles, this result would not be in line with the OECD approach and may lead to double taxation.[859]

Table 11 provides an overview of the German and the OECD approach with regard to the attribution of financing expenses to a PE and can be regarded as a summary of the above analysis.

c. Step 2: Recognition and Pricing of Dealings

(1) Recognition of Dealings

(a) Conceptual Approach

On the basis of the attributions carried out under Section 1(5) sentence 3 ETRA in conjunction with Sections 5–15 BsGaV, the type of business relations between the enterprise and its PE must be determined.[860] As elaborated earlier, business transactions between the enterprise and its PE are regarded as notional *in personam* agreements or so-called 'dealings' pursuant to Section 1(4) sentence 1 no. 2 ETRA.

According to Section 16(1) BsGaV, a dealing within the meaning of Section 1(4) sentence 1 no. 2 ETRA shall exist if economic transactions between

---

[856] Cf. *Haverkamp,* in: Mössner et al. (Eds.), Steuerrecht international tätiger Unternehmen, para. 5.242.

[857] OECD, PE Report 2010, Part I, para. 156.

[858] Cf. OECD, PE Report 2010, Part I, para. 156.

[859] Critical also *Haverkamp,* in: Mössner et al. (Eds.), Steuerrecht international tätiger Unternehmen, para. 5.242.

[860] Cf. Section 1(5) sentence 4 ETRA.

Table 11 OECD vs. German Approach for Attribution of Financing Expenses

	OECD approach	German approach
Attribution approach	• tracing and fungibility approach discussed as possible approaches for the attribution of financing expenses • other approaches applicable as long as the amount of financing expenses attributed to the PE does not exceeds an arm's length amount	• 2-step approach for attribution: – 1-step: direct attribution → direct attribution to PE where directly attributable liability items were attributed → reduction on a pro rata basis if directly attributable liability items must be reduced on a pro rata basis – 2-step: indirect attribution → only if direct attribution is not possible or would involve disproportionate effort • specific provisions for enterprises that are not required to keep accounts (Section 15(4) and (5) BsGaV

Source: Own illustration.

a PE and the rest of the enterprise can be identified that would either require a change to the attribution pursuant to Sections 5–11 BsGaV, or—if the PE and the rest of the enterprise were independent enterprises—would be regulated by *in personam* agreements or result in an assertion of legal positions.[861] Thus, for a dealing to exist, a real and identifiable event is required.[862] Such an event usually refers to the people functions carried out.[863] In this context, a threshold needs to be passed before a dealing between a PE and the rest of the enterprise is accepted as equivalent to a transaction between independent enterprises.[864] A non-exclusive list of general economic transactions between the PE and the rest of the enterprise that may constitute a dealing within the meaning of Section 1(4) sentence 1 no. 2

[861] Cf. Section 16(1) no. 1 and 2 BsGaV.

[862] Cf. BMF, 22 Dec. 2016, IV B 5—S 1341/12/10001–03, BStBl. I 2017, 182, para. 165; see also *Haverkamp,* in: Mössner et al. (Eds.), Steuerrecht international tätiger Unternehmen, para. 5.244.

[863] Cf. BMF, 22 Dec. 2016, IV B 5—S 1341/12/10001–03, BStBl. I 2017, 182, para. 165.

[864] Cf. BMF, 22 Dec. 2016, IV B 5—S 1341/12/10001–03, BStBl. I 2017, 182, para. 165.

ETRA is provided in the VWG BsGa. Accordingly, dealings shall, in particular, exist:[865]

- If the people function with regard to an asset changes (e.g. an asset that is attributed to a PE is used by another PE [notional surrender of use], or an asset that is attributed to a PE is to be attributed to another PE due to a change of the people function [notional sale]);
- if a supportive people function is carried out for another PE of the enterprise (e.g. a people function concerning risk, such as the supervision or management of risk, is carried out by a PE which is not the significant people function decisive for the attribution of the respective assets [notional service]), and
- if the economic activities between the PE and another part of the enterprise would result in an assertion of legal positions by independent third parties.

The reasons for the existence of dealings and the kind of the dealing (e.g. notional surrender of use, notional sale, notional service) must be recorded and is part of the documentation that must be prepared according to Section 90(3) GFC.[866]

By contrast, the use of financial resources of the rest of the enterprise by the PE (notional loan) does, in general, not qualify as a dealing within the meaning of Section 1(4) sentence 1 no. 2 ETRA.[867] According to the governments reasoning, this approach is mainly justified by two reasons. First, it is argued that the use of financial resources of the enterprise by the PE results in assets that are to be attributed to the PE in accordance with Sections 5–8 BsGaV and with it the corresponding free capital and the remaining liability items pursuant to Sections 12–15 BsGaV. The recognition of a dealing between the PE and the other parts of the enterprise for the use of financial resources would result in the situation that the attributed free capital and the remaining liability items would need to be reviewed

---

[865] Cf. BMF, 22 Dec. 2016, IV B 5—S 1341/12/10001–03, BStBl. I 2017, 182, para. 166; BR-Drs. 401/14, 89. For a list of economic transactions that are of significance with regard to the identification of dealings see BMF, 22 Dec. 2016, IV B 5—S 1341/12/10001–03, BStBl. I 2017, 182, para. 168. See in more detail in this regard also *Haverkamp,* in: Mössner et al. (Eds.), Steuerrecht international tätiger Unternehmen, paras. 5.247 et seqq.; *Andresen,* in: W/A/D (Eds.), Betriebsstätten-Handbuch, paras. 4.192 et seqq.; *Kahle/Kindich,* in: Lübbehüsen/Kahle (Eds.), Brennpunkte der Besteuerung von Betriebsstätten, paras. 4.375 et seqq.; *Leonhardt/Tcherveniachki,* in: F/W/B/S (Eds.), Außensteuerrecht—Kommentar, § 1 AStG, paras. 3322 et seqq.

[866] Cf. Section 3 (3) no. 1 BsGaV; BMF, 22 Dec. 2016, IV B 5—S 1341/12/10001–03, BStBl. I 2017, 182, para. 166. See in more detail for the documentation requirements in accordance with Section 90(3) GFC chapter D.II.5.c of this thesis.

[867] Cf. Section 16(3) BsGaV.

and, if necessary, adjusted which would significantly increase the complexity of taxation.[868] Second, since a PE enjoys the same creditworthiness as the enterprise of which it is a part, the impact of such dealings for profit determination purposes would be very limited anyway.[869]

By way of derogation from Section 16(3) sentence 1 BsGaV, a dealing between the PE and the rest of the enterprise must be considered if the PE either hosts a financing function within an enterprise[870] or generates financial resources as a result of a PE's business activities that are made available to the entire enterprise of which the PE is a part (notional short term loan).[871] Nevertheless, a notional short term loan can be accepted as a dealing only for a period that does not exceed one year and therefore ends, at the latest, at the end of the current fiscal year or upon adjustment of the free capital pursuant to Section 12(6) BsGaV or Section 13(5) BsGaV.[872]

If the PE hosts a financing function within an enterprise, i.e. the PE performs liquidity management for one or several other PEs of the same enterprise, assets and liability items related to the financial resources shall generally not be attributed to the PE.[873] Rather, the performance of that function within the enterprise shall be considered a service that must be remunerated on a cost-based transfer pricing method, i.e. cost plus method or transactional net margin method.[874] However, in specific cases it is also possible to attribute assets and liability items to the PE that performs the financing function; but only in cases where the people functions in respect of assets, liability items created and opportunities and risks are performed in the financing PE.[875]

---

[868] Cf. BR-Drs. 401/14, 89.

[869] Cf. BR-Drs. 401/14, 89.

[870] Cf. Section 16(3) sentence 2 no. 1 BsGaV.

[871] Cf. Section 16(3) sentence 2 no. 2 BsGaV.

[872] Cf. Section 16(3) sentence 3 BsGaV.

[873] Cf. Section 17(2) sentence 1 BsGaV.

[874] Cf. Section 17(2) sentence 2 BsGaV; BMF, 22 Dec. 2016, IV B 5—S 1341/12/10001–03, BStBl. I 2017, 182, para. 182 with reference to paras. 2.39 et seqq. and paras. 2.92 et seqq. of the TP Guidelines 2017. If the costs incurred cannot be linked to a specific other PE that is using the funds or this would involve disproportioned effort, Section 17(3) BsGaV allows for an indirect allocation of the costs according to the 'costs-by-cause' principle.

[875] Cf. Section 17(7) no. 1 BsGaV. For examples see BMF, 22 Dec. 2016, IV B 5—S 1341/12/10001–03, BStBl. I 2017, 182, para. 191.

(b) Comparison to the OECD Approach

At first glance, the requirements for the existence of a dealing under German national law seem quite 'soft' and less strict than the OECD requirements.[876] This is mainly due to the fact that the German tax administration emphasises that all different kinds of dealings are possible and provides a list of 25 circumstances where a dealing between the PE and the rest of the enterprise must be assumed.[877] However, both the OECD and the German approach recognise that a certain threshold must be passed before a dealing between a PE and the rest of the enterprise is accepted as equivalent to a transaction that would have occurred between independent enterprises.[878] In this regard, the VWG BsGa explicitly refers to the respective paragraphs in the PE Report 2010 which emphasises that the German tax administration does not intend to deviate from the OECD approach. It is also emphasised by both the PE Report 2010 and the VWG BsGa that a real and identifiable event that has occurred between the PE and another part of the enterprise is a requirement for a dealing to exist.[879] Insofar no significant differences to the OECD approach can be identified.

With respect to the use of financial resources, the OECD and the German approach are very similar.[880] However, deviations and therefore the risk of double taxation can be identified if the provisions that allow for a different treatment regarding the use of financial resources implemented in Section 16(3) sentence 2 no. 2 BsGaV (i.e. the PE generates funds as a result of its business activities which are made available for the enterprise as a whole) are applied by either the taxpayer or the tax authority.

Table 12 provides an overview of the German and the OECD approach with regard to the recognition of dealings and can be regarded as a summary of the above analysis.

---

[876] *Andresen* and *Margerie* argue that the requirements for the dealing to exist between the PE and another part of the enterprise are formulated very soft (*Andresen*) and open (*Margerie*) which could ultimately result in the fact that more dealings are deemed to exist under German national law, cf. *Andresen*, in: W/A/D (Eds.), Betriebsstätten-Handbuch, para. 5.53; *Margerie*, Gewinnermittlung und Gewinnabgrenzung bei Betriebsstätten, 254.

[877] Cf. BMF, 22 Dec. 2016, IV B 5—S 1341/12/10001-03, BStBl. I 2017, 182, para. 164. For a list of economic transactions that are of significance with regard to the identification of

Table 12 OECD vs. German Approach for Recognition of Dealings

<table>
<tr><th></th><th>OECD approach</th><th>German approach</th></tr>
<tr><td>Requirements</td><td colspan="2">• existence of a dealing requires:
– a certain threshold that must be passed
– a real and identifiable event
• events that may trigger a dealing: notional surrender of use, notional sale, notional service between PE and the rest of the enterprise</td></tr>
<tr><td rowspan="2">Treatment of internal interest dealings</td><td colspan="2">• no dealing exists if PE uses financial resources of the enterprise
• if PE performs financing function, the assets and liability items shall generally not be attributed to PE → financing function shall be considered a notional service and remunerated on a cost-based transfer pricing method</td></tr>
<tr><td>• <u>exception:</u>
– fully fledged treasury function where PE performs significant people function relevant for the determination of economic ownership of assets PE → is economic owner of assets and entitled to an associated return</td><td>• <u>exceptions:</u>
– Section 17(7) no. 1 BsGaV: PE performs significant people function relevant for the attribution of assets and liability items → assets and liability items shall be attributed to PE
→ PE is entitled to an associated return on assets
– Section 16(3) sentence 2 no. 2 BsGaV: PE generates funds as a result of its business activities which are made available for the enterprise as a whole → short term dealing</td></tr>
</table>

Source: Own illustration.

dealings see BMF, 22 Dec. 2016, IV B 5—S 1341/12/10001–03, BStBl. I 2017, 182, para. 168.

[878]Cf. BMF, 22 Dec. 2016, IV B 5—S 1341/12/10001–03, BStBl. I 2017, 182, para. 165 with reference to OECD, PE Report 2010, Part I, paras. 35, 176.

[879]Cf. BMF, 22 Dec. 2016, IV B 5—S 1341/12/10001–03, BStBl. I 2017, 182, para. 165 with reference to OECD, PE Report 2010, Part I, paras. 35, 176.

[880]Cf. *Andresen*, in: W/A/D (Eds.), Betriebsstätten-Handbuch, para. 5.46.

(2) Determination of Transfer Prices for PE's Business Relations

(a) Comparability Analysis[881]

For the recognised dealings between the PE and the rest of the enterprise as well as for other business transactions between the PE and related parties, transfer prices must be determined that comply with the arm's length principle.[882] In order to do so, a comparability analysis of the PE's business activities must be carried out according to Section 1(1) sentence 2 BsGaV.

The comparability analysis seeks to identify whether a dealing between the PE and the other parts of the enterprise or a business transaction between the PE and related parties can be compared to an uncontrolled transaction between independent enterprises.[883] Explanations on how to carry out a comparability analysis can neither be found in the BsGaV nor in the VWG BsGa. Nevertheless, criteria that must be considered when determining comparability between a controlled and an uncontrolled business transaction can be derived from jurisprudence[884], promulgations issued by the German tax authority[885] as well as from the TP Guidelines[886]. Accordingly, comparability exists if the comparative facts correspond in their nature, characteristics, scale and with regard to the particular circumstances of the relevant markets.[887]

---

[881] The Draft Legislation on the Withholding Tax Relief Modernisation Act as of 22 Jan. 2021 provides for amendments influencing the comparability analysis. Besides the implementation of a definition of the term 'comparability analysis' that shall be implemented in Section 1(3) sentence 3 ETRA (cf. BR-Drs. 50/21, 15), the governments reasoning refers to the use of the comparability factors as outlined in the TP Guidelines (cf. OECD, TP Guidelines 2017, paras. 1.36 et seqq.) to determine the 'actual circumstances' underlying the respective business transaction and the performance of the comparability analysis in line with the guidance provided in the TP Guidelines (cf. OECD, TP Guidelines 2017, paras. 3.1 et seqq.), cf. BR-Drs. 50/21, 76 et seqq.

[882] Cf. Section 1(1) sentence 2 BsGaV.

[883] Cf. *Kaeser*, in: W/K/S/D (Eds.), Doppelbesteuerung, Art. 7 MA (2010), para. 562.

[884] Cf. BFH, 1 Feb. 1967, I 220/64, BStBl. III 1967, 497; BFH, 17 Oct. 2001, I R 103/00, BStBl. II 2004, 171.

[885] Cf. BMF, 23 Feb. 1983, IV C 5—S 1341—4/83, BStBl. I 1983, 218, para. 3.1.2; BMF, 12 Apr. 2005, IV B 4—S 1341—1/05, BStBl. I 2005, 570, para. 3.4.12.7.

[886] Cf. OECD, TP Guidelines 2017, paras. 1.36 et seqq.

[887] Cf. *Baumhoff/Liebchen,* in: Mössner et al. (Eds.), Steuerrecht international tätiger Unternehmen, para. 4.119. For the use of databases when assessing comparability see *Baumhoff/Liebchen,* in: Mössner et al. (Eds.), Steuerrecht international tätiger Unternehmen, para. 4.108; *Baumhoff*, IStR 2003, 1 (3 et seqq.); *Oestreicher/Duensing*, IStR 2005, 134 (134 et seqq.); *Rehkugler/Vögele*, BB 2002, 1937 (1937 et seqq.); *Kopecek/Zehetner*, TPI 2017, 252 (252 et seqq.).

More detailed, when assessing comparability, the German tax authority specifies five factors that are important to consider:[888]

- characteristics of goods (quality, physical features, kind of intangibles, availability, reliability, quantity delivered) and services;
- functions performed, risks assumed, and assets used;
- contractual terms (contract period, terms of payment);
- economic circumstances in the relevant markets;
- business strategies.

The TP Guidelines 2017 contain similar comparability factors (contractual terms,[889] functional analysis,[890] characteristics of property or services,[891] economic circumstances,[892] and business strategies[893]) that shall determine comparability between uncontrolled and controlled transactions. The fact that the German tax authority cross-refers to the TP Guidelines with regard to each of the listed comparability factors underlines that the TP Guidelines—despite the fact that they only constitute 'soft-law' and are thus not legally binding—provide an additional valuable source of guidance that can be used for interpretation purposes.[894] Also, the VWG BsGa and the government's reasoning to Section 1(1) sentence 2 BsGaV cross-refer to the PE Report 2010, which again cross-refers to the comparability analysis described in the TP Guidelines that shall be applied, by analogy, in the PE context.[895] Accordingly, also the changes to the TP Guidelines 2017, emphasising that the following three additional criteria:

---

[888]Cf. BMF, 12 Apr. 2005, IV B 4—S 1341—1/05, BStBl. I 2005, 570, para. 3.4.12.7.

[889]Cf. OECD, TP Guidelines 2017, paras. 1.36. See in more detail 1.42 et seqq.

[890]Cf. OECD, TP Guidelines 2017, paras. 1.36. See in more detail 1.51 et seqq.

[891]Cf. OECD, TP Guidelines 2017, paras. 1.36. See in more detail 1.107 et seqq.

[892]Cf. OECD, TP Guidelines 2017, paras. 1.36. See in more detail 1.110 et seqq.

[893]Cf. OECD, TP Guidelines 2017, paras. 1.36. See in more detail 1.114 et seqq.

[894]Cf. BMF, 12 Apr. 2005, IV B 4—S 1341—1/05, BStBl. I 2005, 570, para. 3.4.12.7. The reference of the tax authority to the TP Guidelines 1995 is due to the date of publication. Nevertheless, the updated TP Guidelines 2017 contain the five factors which determine comparability between uncontrolled and controlled transactions as well and shall be used for interpretation purposes.

[895]Cf. BR-Drs. 401/14, 44 and BMF, 22 Dec. 2016, IV B 5—S 1341/12/10001-03, BStBl. I 2017, 182, para. 27 with reference to paras. 39–43 of the PE Report 2010.

- location savings and local market features;[896]
- assembled workforce;[897]
- group synergies[898]

may affect comparability and shall therefore be considered.[899]

Since the selection and application of the relevant transfer pricing method is contingent upon the availability of comparables, a thorough comparability analysis is of great importance and underlines the fact that the concept of comparability is the 'heart and soul'[900] when it comes to the determination of transfer prices.

(b) Determination of Transfer Prices[901]

The reference in Section 1(5) sentence 1 ETRA to Section 1(1), (3) and (4) ETRA implies that the principles set out in these paragraphs do not only apply to business transactions between a taxpayer and a related party to the taxpayer but also to dealings between a taxpayer's enterprise and its PE. Especially, the principles set out in Section 1(3) sentence 1–8 ETRA, dealing with the approach on how to determine appropriate transfer prices, are also applicable to dealings between a taxpayer's enterprise and its PE.[902] When applying the arm's length principle, it shall firstly be assumed that unrelated third parties have knowledge of all

---

[896] Cf. OECD, TP Guidelines 2017, paras. 1.139 et seqq.

[897] Cf. OECD, TP Guidelines 2017, paras. 1.152 et seqq.

[898] Cf. OECD, TP Guidelines 2017, paras. 1.157 et seqq.

[899] See in more detail *Baumhoff/Liebchen*, in: F/W/B/S (Eds.), Außensteuerrecht—Kommentar, § 1 AStG, paras. 245 et seqq.

[900] *Treidler/Grothe/Paprotny*, TNI 85 (2017), 921 (921).

[901] The Draft Legislation on the Withholding Tax Relief Modernisation Act as of 22 Jan. 2021 provides changes to the determination of transfer prices, see in more detail for the proposed changes BR-Drs. 50/21, 15 et seqq. According to the governments reasoning the changes shall ensure that the internationally recognized procedure for determining and examining arm's length prices are implemented in a declaratory, concretising and comprehensible manner. This shall ensure that the international understanding of the application of the arm's length principle is disclosed in order to contribute to legal certainly, cf. BR-Drs. 50/21, 76. Most prominently, the draft provides for the elimination of the hierarchy among the transfer pricing methods. This hierarchy shall be replaced with the concept of the 'most appropriate transfer pricing method' for the particular case as used in the TP Guidelines, cf. BR-Drs. 50/21, 15.

[902] In this context, it shall also be mentioned that the provisions of Section 1(3) sentence 9–12 ETRA, dealing with the relocation of functions, are applicable in the PE context. See in more detail for the provisions of Section 1(3) sentence 9–12 ETRA, dealing with the reallocation of functions *Hentschel*, Deutsche Regelungen zur internationalen Funktionsverlagerung, 29 et seqq.

the significant circumstances of the business relations and secondly that these unrelated third parties act in accordance to the principles applied by prudent and conscientious business managers.[903]

The selection and application of the transfer pricing method for a particular business transaction depends on the availability of comparables. In this context, Section 1(3) sentence 1–8 ETRA sets out a three-level approach.[904] The first level requires that fully comparable arm's length prices can be determined, following appropriate adjustments with regard to the business functions performed, the assets used and the risks and opportunities assumed.[905] In that case, the transfer price must be determined by applying primarily one of the traditional transfer pricing methods, namely the CUP method, the resale price method or the cost plus method.[906] The selection of the appropriate method shall depend on the specific circumstances and may vary from case to case.[907] The wording of the legislator, determining that the traditional transfer pricing methods shall be applied 'primarily', indicates that also transactional profit methods may be applicable.

However, in practice it is rarely possible to identify such fully comparable arm's length prices, even after appropriate adjustments were performed.[908] Therefore, Section 1(3) sentence 2 ETRA determines that in case such fully comparable arm's length prices cannot be determined, the taxpayer must use partly comparable prices, following appropriate adjustments, as a basis for selecting a transfer

---

[903] Cf. Section 1(1) sentence 3 ETRA.

[904] See in more detail *Hentschel*, Deutsche Regelungen zur internationalen Funktionsverlagerung, 18 et seqq.; *Baumhoff/Liebchen*, in: Wassermeyer/Baumhoff (Eds.), Verrechnungspreise international verbundener Unternehmen, paras. 5.149 et seqq. See critical with regard to the three-level approach *Kahle/Schulz*, in: Haun/Kahle/Goebel/Reiser (Eds.), Außensteuerrecht, § 1 Abs. 3 AStG, paras. 14 et seqq.

[905] In this context, full comparability must exist after the arm's length prices were adjusted appropriately in respect of the business functions performed as well as the assets used and the opportunities and risks assumed, cf. Section 1(3) sentence 1 ETRA.

[906] Cf. Section 1(3) sentence 1 ETRA; BMF, 12 Apr. 2005, IV B 4—S 1341—1/05, BStBl. I 2005, 570, para. 3.4.10.3.a). See in more detail for requirements of full comparability as considered by the German tax authority BMF, 12 Apr. 2005, IV B 4—S 1341—1/05, BStBl. I 2005, 570, para. 3.4.12.7.a).

[907] Cf. BFH, 17 Oct. 2001, I R 103/00, BStBl II 2004, 171 (174 f.); *Kraft*, in: Kraft (Ed.), AStG Kommentar, § 1 AStG, para. 202; *Hentschel*, Deutsche Regelungen zur internationalen Funktionsverlagerung, 20.

[908] Cf. *Baumhoff/Liebchen*, in: Wassermeyer/Baumhoff (Eds.), Verrechnungspreise international verbundener Unternehmen, paras. 5.153, 5.161; *Hentschel*, Deutsche Regelungen zur internationalen Funktionsverlagerung, 20; *Förster*, IStR 2011, 20 (22).

pricing method (second level).[909] If multiple partly comparable arm's length prices can be determined, the range that results must be narrowed.[910] A concrete transfer pricing method that must be used by the taxpayer is not mentioned by the legislator. Rather, the wording 'suitable transfer pricing method'[911] used in Section 1 (3) sentence 2 ETRA indicates that all appropriate transfer pricing methods can be applied.[912] It follows that not only the traditional transfer pricing methods but also the transactional profit methods such as the TNMM and the TPSM can be applied on an equal footing.[913] Nevertheless, according to the German tax authority, the traditional transfer pricing methods take precedence over the TNMM and the TPSM.[914] While the application of the TNMM is only conceded by the German tax administration if the traditional transfer pricing methods cannot be applied due to a lack of comparable data and can only be used for enterprises performing routine functions, the TPSM is regarded as a method of last resort that can only be applied if the traditional transfer pricing methods cannot or cannot reliably be applied.[915] The use of the comparable profit method is not recognised by the German tax authority since this method does not follow a transactional based approach and does not lead to arm's length results.[916]

Provided that no partly comparable arm's length prices can be identified by the taxpayer, Section 1(3) sentence 5 ETRA determines that the hypothetical arm's

---

[909]Cf. Section 1(3) sentence 2 ETRA. See in more detail for requirements of partly comparability as considered by the German tax authority BMF, 12 Apr. 2005, IV B 4—S 1341—1/05, BStBl. I 2005, 570, para. 3.4.12.7.c).

[910]Cf. Section 1(3) sentence 3 ETRA. See in more detail on how to narrow the resulting range BMF, 12 Apr. 2005, IV B 4—S 1341—1/05, BStBl. I 2005, 570, para. 3.4.12.5; also *Kraft,* in: Kraft (Ed.), AStG Kommentar, § 1 AStG, paras. 270 et seqq.

[911]Section 1(3) sentence 2 ETRA.

[912]Cf. *Förster*, IStR 2011, 20 (22); also BMF, 12 Apr. 2005, IV B 4—S 1341—1/05, BStBl. I 2005, 570, para. 3.4.12.7.

[913]Cf. *Kußmaul/Müller*, StB 2013, 187 (191); *Hentschel*, Deutsche Regelungen zur internationalen Funktionsverlagerung, 24; *Baumhoff/Liebchen,* in: Wassermeyer/Baumhoff (Eds.), Verrechnungspreise international verbundener Unternehmen, para. 5.151.

[914]Cf. BMF, 12 Apr. 2005, IV B 4—S 1341—1/05, BStBl. I 2005, 570, para. 3.4.10.3.b) and c); *Baumhoff/Liebchen,* in: Mössner et al. (Eds.), Steuerrecht international tätiger Unternehmen, para. 4.289; *Baumhoff/Liebchen,* in: Wassermeyer/Baumhoff (Eds.), Verrechnungspreise international verbundener Unternehmen, paras. 5.159 et seqq.

[915]Cf. BMF, 12 Apr. 2005, IV B 4—S 1341—1/05, BStBl. I 2005, 570, para. 3.4.10.3.b) and c).

[916]Cf. BMF, 12 Apr. 2005, IV B 4—S 1341—1/05, BStBl. I 2005, 570, para. 3.4.10.3.d). See in more detail for this method *Baumhoff/Liebchen,* in: Mössner et al. (Eds.), Steuerrecht international tätiger Unternehmen, para. 4.212.

length method must be used (third level).[917] Accordingly, the taxpayer is obliged to carry out a functional analysis as well as internal planning calculations in order to determine the recipient's maximum price and the supplier's minimum price which shall constitute the arm's length range.[918] This approach requires taking adequate capitalisation interest rates for the functions performed and risks assumed into account. Pursuant to Section 1 (3) sentence 6 half-sentence 2 ETRA, the arm's length range is based on the recipient's and supplier's profit expectations (profit potential). In other words, a notional pricing process between two prudent and conscientious business managers must be simulated where the price within the arm's length range that is most likely to correspond to the arm's length principle must be chosen by the taxpayer.[919] In case no value within the arm's length range can be plausibly demonstrated, the taxpayer must choose the mean of the range.[920]

The application of the hypothetical arm's length method is not based on any of the transfer pricing methods presented.[921] It follows that the traditional transfer pricing methods (CUP method, resale price method, cost plus method) and the transactional profit methods (TNMM and TPSM) can only be applied if fully comparable or partly comparable arm's length prices can be determined.

(c) Comparison to OECD Approach

In order to determine transfer prices for dealings between a taxpayer's enterprise and its PE that are at arm's length, both the OECD and the German legislator allow for the application of the same principles, by analogy, as applied for business transactions between a taxpayer and a related party to the taxpayer. However, some differences between the OECD and the German approach exist which shall be outlined and discussed in the following.

Firstly, the German legislator assumes that in applying the arm's length principle unrelated third parties to the business transaction have knowledge of all

---

[917]See in more detail for requirements of incomparability BMF, 12 Apr. 2005, IV B 4—S 1341—1/05, BStBl. I 2005, 570, para. 3.4.12.7.b).

[918]Cf. Section 1 (3) sentence 6 ETRA.

[919]Cf. Section 1 (3) sentence 1 half-sentence 1 ETRA; *Baumhoff/Liebchen*, in: Wassermeyer/Baumhoff (Eds.), Verrechnungspreise international verbundener Unternehmen, para. 5.152.

[920]Section 1 (3) sentence 1 half-sentence 2 ETRA. Critical *Hentschel*, Deutsche Regelungen zur internationalen Funktionsverlagerung, 27.

[921]Cf. *Baumhoff/Liebchen*, in: Wassermeyer/Baumhoff (Eds.), Verrechnungspreise international verbundener Unternehmen, para. 5.152; *Baumhoff/Liebchen*, in: Mössner et al. (Eds.), Steuerrecht international tätiger Unternehmen, para. 4.316.

circumstances that are significant for the business relations and that they act according to the principles applied by prudent and conscientious business managers.[922] While the legal figure of the prudent and conscientious business managers is in line with the settled case-law of the German Federal Tax Court[923] and is merely a fiction in order to apply the arm's length principle, the assumption of the German legislator that unrelated third parties have knowledge of all significant circumstances of the business relations is undoubtedly a novelty in national and international tax law and not in line with the arm's length principle as interpreted by the OECD.[924] Rather, the OECD emphasises that both taxpayers and tax administrations 'often have difficulty in obtaining adequate information to apply the arm's length principle'[925] since information that is accessible may be incomplete or confidentiality concerns may make it impossible to access information from independent enterprises at all.[926] It follows that, in contrast to the German approach, only the accessible information can be used when applying the arm's length principle according to the OECD.[927]

Secondly, the comparability analysis can be regarded as the cornerstone for the application of the arm's length principle. Since the German tax administration cross-refers to the TP Guidelines with regard to each of the listed comparability factors, no differences between the two approaches can be identified insofar. Rather, the TP Guidelines can be seen as an additional valuable source of guidance in this regard. However, according to the OECD, the determination of the

[922]Cf. Section 1 sentence 3 ETRA.

[923]Cf. BFH, 17 May 1995, I R 147/93, BStBl. II 1996, 204; BFH, 6 Dec. 1995, I R 88/94, BStBl. II 1996, 383; BFH, 19 May 1998, I R 36/97, BStBl. II 1998, 689; BFH, 27 Mar. 2001, I R 27/99, BStBl. II 2002, 111; BFH, 17 Oct. 2001, I R 103/00, BStBl. II 2004, 171; BFH, 24 Apr. 2002, I R 18/01, BStBl. II 2002, 670; BFH, 28 Jan. 2004, I R 87/02, BFH/NV 2004, 736; BFH, 6 Apr. 2005, I R 15/04, BStBl. II 2006, 196; BFH, 6 Apr. 2005, I R 22/04, BStBl. II 2007, 658; BFH, 21 Aug. 2007, I R 27/07, HFR 2008, 367; BFH, 22 Aug. 2007, I R 32/06, BStBl. II 2007, 961; BFH, 5 Mar. 2008, I R 45/07, BFH, 17 Feb. 2010, I R 97/08, BFH/NV 2010, 1307.

[924]Cf. *Hentschel*, Deutsche Regelungen zur internationalen Funktionsverlagerung, 15; Critical also *Kraft*, in: Kraft (Ed.), AStG—Kommentar, § 1 AStG, para. 125; *Baumhoff*, in: Wassermeyer (Ed.), Doppelbesteuerung, 251 (254); *Frischmuth*, IStR 2007, 485 (486); *Wulf*, DB 2007, 2280 (2281); *Wassermeyer*, DB 2007, 535 (536).

[925]OECD, TP Guidelines 2017, para. 1.13.

[926]Cf. OECD, TP Guidelines 2017, para. 1.13.

[927]Cf. *Wassermeyer*, DB 2007, 535 (536); *Kraft*, in: Kraft (Ed.), AStG—Kommentar, § 1 AStG, para. 125; *Hentschel*, Deutsche Regelungen zur internationalen Funktionsverlagerung, 15; *Baumhoff/Liebchen*, in: F/W/B/S (Eds.), Außensteuerrecht—Kommentar, § 1 AStG, paras. 349 et seq.

degree of comparability of the potential comparables identified shall be carried out after the most appropriate transfer pricing method was chosen by the taxpayer.[928] Consequently, the determination of comparability refers to the specific transfer pricing method.[929] By contrast, according to German national law, the availability of comparables determines the transfer pricing method that can be applied by the taxpayer. Consequently, the determination of the degree of comparability must be identified first since the selection and application of the transfer pricing method for a particular business transaction depends on the availability of comparables.[930]

Thirdly, while the hierarchy among the transfer pricing methods was eliminated with the update of the TP Guidelines 2010 and replaced by the concept of the 'most appropriate method for a particular case'[931], the German legislator provides for a three-level approach in Section 1(3) sentence 1–8 ETRA, making the selection and application of the transfer pricing method contingent upon the availability of comparables. As examined above, in case fully comparable arm's length prices are available, the transfer price must be determined by applying primarily one of the traditional transfer pricing methods. Despite the fact that also the OECD is of the opinion that in situations in which a traditional transfer pricing method and a transactional profit method can be applied in an equally reliable manner, the application of one of the traditional transfer pricing methods is preferable, the German approach can be regarded as narrower. Nevertheless, fully comparable arm's length prices may only be identified if actual market prices or reliable internal comparables exist.[932] In such cases, however, also the OECD would prefer the application of the traditional transfer pricing methods over the transactional profit method. Consequently, the differences should only be of theoretical nature.[933] Besides, *Baumhoff/Liebchen* argue that the requirement of full

[928] Cf. OECD, TP Guidelines 2017, paras. 1.33, 3.4; *Baumhoff/Liebchen*, in: Wassermeyer/Baumhoff (Eds.), Verrechnungspreise international verbundener Unternehmen, para. 5.153.

[929] Cf. *Baumhoff/Liebchen*, in: Wassermeyer/Baumhoff (Eds.), Verrechnungspreise international verbundener Unternehmen, para. 5.153.

[930] See in more detail for the differences of the OECD and the German approach *Baumhoff/Liebchen*, in: Wassermeyer/Baumhoff (Eds.), Verrechnungspreise international verbundener Unternehmen, para. 5.153.

[931] Cf. OECD, TP Guidelines 2017, para. 2.2.

[932] Cf. *Förster*, IStR 2011, 20 (22).

[933] Cf. *Förster*, IStR 2011, 20 (22); *Baumhoff/Liebchen*, in: Wassermeyer/Baumhoff (Eds.), Verrechnungspreise international verbundener Unternehmen, para. 5.153.

comparability for applying transactional profit methods cannot be met in practice anyway.[934]

If only partly comparable arm's length prices can be identified, the taxpayer must use a 'suitable transfer pricing method' according to Section 1(3) sentence 3 ETRA. While this approach can be regarded as broader than the 'most appropriate method for a particular case' -approach of the OECD since only 'a' suitable and not 'the' most appropriate method must be used, the differences between the two approaches should be of no relevance in practice.[935] However, difficulties may occur, and therefore the risk of double taxation, due to the restrictive view of the German tax administration with regard to the applicability of the TNMM and the TPSM.[936] Such restrictions are not only inconsistent to Section 1(3) sentence 3 ETRA that allows for the use of all suitable transfer pricing methods on an equal footing but also seem 'outdated' considering the recently published enhanced OECD guidance for the use of the TPSM which contains an indirect statement to a broader application of this method.[937] As elaborated earlier, the application of the TPSM may be suitable in circumstances where both parties make unique and valuable contributions to the transaction, where economically significant risks are shared and where business operations are highly integrated such that the contributions of the parties cannot be reliable evaluated.[938] Given that business transactions become more and more integrated and the digitalisation of the economy is on the rise, the use of the TPSM will gain importance internationally.[939] Therefore, the German tax administration is advised to review its administrative principles, which were already published before the introduction of the three-level approach was implemented in German national law, and revise these principles so that they do not only comply with the legislative approach set out in Section 1(3)

---

[934] Cf. *Baumhoff/Liebchen*, in: Wassermeyer/Baumhoff (Eds.), Verrechnungspreise international verbundener Unternehmen, para. 5.153.

[935] This is mainly due to the fact that it is emphasised by the OECD in para. 2.8 of the TP Guidelines 2017 that selecting the most appropriate method for a particular case 'does not mean that all transfer pricing methods should be analysed in depth or tested in each case in arriving at the selection of the most appropriate method'. See in this context also *Baumhoff/Liebchen*, in: Wassermeyer/Baumhoff (Eds.), Verrechnungspreise international verbundener Unternehmen, para. 5.153.

[936] For the position of the German tax administration see BMF, 12 Apr. 2005, IV B 4—S 1341—1/05, BStBl. I 2005, 570, para. 3.4.10.3.b) and c).

[937] For the applicability of the TPSM cf. *Greil*, Intertax 2017, 624 (627).

[938] Cf. OECD, BEPS Action 10: Revised Guidance on TPSM 2018, 2.116 et seqq. See in more detail chapter D.I.4.b.(3)(d)iii of this thesis.

[939] Cf. *Kadet*, TNI 77 (2015), 1183 (1184 et seq.).

sentence 3 ETRA but are also aligned with the view of the OECD. This would a) provide more flexibility for the taxpayer in finding a 'suitable transfer pricing method', and b) decrease the risk of double taxation since the chance that other jurisdictions follow the OECD approach rather than the outdated approach of the German tax administration is certainly higher.

If no partly comparable arm's length prices can be identified by the taxpayer, Section 1(3) sentence 5 ETRA determines that the hypothetical arm's length method must be applied. Despite the fact that this approach is also based on the fiction of the prudent and conscientious business managers who have knowledge of all significant circumstances of the business transaction, which is not in line with the OECD approach as discussed earlier, the underlying idea to use valuation techniques in situations where reliable comparable uncontrolled transactions cannot be identified is not unknown internationally. In fact, chapter VI of the TP Guidelines 2017 which was amended as a result of the work on BEPS Action 8 provides for the use of such valuation techniques in order to determine transfer prices for transactions involving intangibles for which valuation is highly uncertain at the time of the transaction. However, as already pointed out earlier, the use of valuation techniques also raises challenges such as the need for assumptions with regard to the discount rates, growth rates and tax rates and accuracy issues regarding financial projections that might lead to additional uncertainty for the taxpayer when it comes to the application of such techniques.[940]

Table 13 provides an overview of the main differences and similarities of the German and the OECD approach concerning the determination of transfer prices in the PE context that can be regarded as a summary of the above analysis.

d. Interim Conclusion

As mentioned above, the AOA, as implemented in Article 7 OECD MC, is not self-executing but, when implemented in the respective tax treaty, sets a limit on the amount of attributable profit that the host country in which the PE is located may tax. To be able to exploit the taxing rights allocated by the respective tax treaty, it is necessary that jurisdictions implement national legislation.[941] In Germany, the concept of the AOA was implemented in Section 1(5) ETRA and the BsGaV.

Overall, it has become evident that the approach taken by the German legislator in Section 1(5) ETRA follows the two-step approach of the AOA as developed

[940] Cf. *Petruzzi*, in: Lang/Storck/Petruzzi (Eds.), Transfer Pricing in a Post-BEPS World, 1 (27).

[941] Cf. *Kraft*, in: Kraft (Ed.), AStG—Kommentar, § 1 AStG, para. 610.

Table 13 OECD vs. German Approach for Determination of Transfer Prices

	OECD approach	**German approach**
Comparability analysis	• comparability factors: – contractual terms – functional analysis – characteristics of property or services – economic circumstances – business strategies – location savings and local market features – assembled workforce – group synergies • determination of the degree of comparability of the potential comparables identified shall be carried out after the most appropriate transfer pricing method was chosen	• cross-reference of the German tax administration to the TP Guidelines suggests that comparability factors shall not differ from OECD approach • determination of the degree of comparability must be carried out first before the respective transfer pricing method can be applied
Applicable transfer pricing methods	• fundamental concept: 'most appropriate method for a particular case' -approach • traditional transfer pricing methods: – CUP method – resale price method – cost plus method • transactional profit methods: – TNMM – TPSM • other valuation techniques (only for intangibles under certain conditions) • if traditional transfer pricing methods and transactional profit methods can be applied in an equally reliable manner the application of traditional transfer pricing method is preferable	• three-level approach contingent upon availability of comparables • first level: – fully comparable arm's length prices → preferred application of traditional transfer pricing methods • second level: – only partly comparable arm's length prices → 'suitable transfer pricing method' -approach – allows for the use of the traditional transfer pricing methods and the transactional profit methods • third level: – no partly comparable arm's length prices → hypothetical arm's length method

Source: Own illustration.

by the OECD. Despite this general uniform framework, certain areas have been identified throughout the analysis where deviations exist. These deviations are caused by the situation that the German tax administration provides for provisions in the BsGaV that are not in line with the principles set out in the PE Report 2010.

Most of the deviations identified result from an unequal treatment of inbound and outbound PEs. It has been shown that such deviations are fiscally motivated and intend to safeguard the German tax base. The following examples can be outlined in this regard:

- The approach for the attribution of free capital to inbound and outbound PEs. While the BsGaV determines the minimum capital approach (Section 13(1) BsGaV)—which is not an authorised OECD approach—as the general approach for the attribution of free capital to a foreign PE of a domestic enterprise, the capital allocation approach (Section 12(1) BsGaV) shall be the guiding principle for domestic PEs of foreign enterprises.
- The approach for the attribution of financing expenses for enterprises that are not required to keep accounts implemented in Section 15(4) BsGaV and Section 15(5) BsGaV, setting a limit for the amount of attributable interest expenses to PEs located in Germany and at the same time determining a minimum portion of attributable financing expenses to PEs located abroad which ultimately ensures that this amount does not reduce the German tax base of the domestic enterprise.

Other deviations are caused by the fact that certain provisions in the BsGaV put forward attribution rules that can be regarded as very prescriptive compared to the rather broad and flexible approach outlined by the OECD. Examples of such provisions are the following:

- While the PE Report 2010 determines that people functions shall be attributed to the PE in which they are performed geographically, Section 4(1) sentence 2 BsGaV provides for a different attribution if the people function has no material connection to the PE's business activities and is performed in the PE for less than 30 days.
- In contrast to the OECD approach, the German approach does not allow for a pro rata attribution of tangible assets (Section 5 BsGaV), stakes, financial assets, similar assets (Section 7 BsGaV) and other assets (Section 8 BsGaV).

Regardless of the kind of deviation, the hereby caused fundamental lack of consistency to the OECD approach may lead to double taxation if the foreign jurisdiction follows the concept of the AOA as outlined in the PE Report 2010.

Throughout the analysis it has been assumed that the foreign jurisdiction where the enterprise carries out business activities through a PE follows the AOA as implemented in the PE Report 2010. However, three observations must be outlined in this regard. First, even though the German tax authority generally assumes that other OECD member countries follow the AOA principles as implemented in Section 1(5) sentences 1–7 ETRA and the BsGaV,[942] ten OECD member countries have entered reservations on the 2010 version of Article 7 OECD reserving the right to use Article 7 OECD MC (pre-2010 version).[943] Outside the OECD, the adoption rate of the AOA is even lower.[944] Even before the final version of Article 7 OECD MC 2010 and the PE Report 2010 were released, the UN Committee of Experts rejected the AOA approach since the principles were considered to be in direct conflict with Article 7(3) UN Model.[945]

Second, the vast majority of the German DTAs are not yet based on the wording as implemented in the version of Article 7 OECD MC 2010. This is mainly due to the lengthy process of adoption. The MLI as an outcome of the OECD BEPS project was not available (and neither is the Article 7 OECD MC 2010 option included in the MLI) in order to adopt the AOA into the bilateral treaty network.[946] Rather, in order to adopt the AOA in full a renegotiation on a treaty-by-treaty basis would be necessary by the DTA states which turns the implementation process into a very lengthy and time consuming process that slows down the adoption rate even for those OECD member countries that are willing to take up the principles of the AOA.[947]

Third, even if the latest version of Article 7 OECD MC is implemented in the DTA between Germany and another state, tax disputes may still arise since it cannot be expected that the other state has an approach implemented in domestic law that provides for provisions which are consistent to the German approach as

---

[942] Cf. BMF, 22 Dec. 2016, IV B 5—S 1341/12/10001–03, BStBl. I 2017, 182, para. 427.

[943] Cf. OECD MC Commentary 2017, Art. 7, paras. 96–97 and paras. 99–100.

[944] Cf. *Collier/Vella*, WTJ 2019, 159 (167).

[945] Cf. UN, Model Double Taxation Convention 2011, Article 7 Commentary, para. 1. Article 7(3) UN Model disallows deductions other than reimbursements of actual expenses paid by a PE to the head office of the enterprise (e.g. royalties, fees or similar payments in return for the use of patents or other rights), cf. UN, Model Double Taxation Convention 2017, Article 7(3).

[946] Cf. *Collier/Vella*, WTJ 2019, 159 (166).

[947] Cf. *Collier/Vella*, WTJ 2019, 159 (166).

implemented in Section 1(5) sentences 1–7 ETRA and the BsGaV. As discussed above, certain provisions implemented in German national tax law (e.g. the approach for the attribution of free capital) are fiscally motivated and intend to safeguard the German national tax base. Consequently, even if the other state has exactly the same provisions implemented an inherent risk for double taxation still exists due to the unequal treatment of inbound and outbound investments.

Nevertheless, the German legislator was aware of the outlined difficulties and implemented an escape clause in Section 1(5) sentence 8 ETRA which mitigates the risk of double taxation in certain circumstances. The following chapter will analyse the escape clause in more detail.

4. Restricted Applicability of the German AOA Principles[948]

a. Issues Arising from Divergent German Tax Treaty Network

As mentioned above, the concept of the AOA was implemented in German national tax law as early as 2013. Nevertheless, most German tax treaties currently in force are not yet based on Article 7 OECD MC 2010. Thus, the concept of the AOA is not necessarily the governing principle for profit attribution to a PE in these treaties. This situation often results in a different treatment of PE issues from a German national tax law perspective in comparison to the treaty perspective. As a consequence, double taxation or double non-taxation issues may arise. In order to mitigate such a mismatch, Germany has enacted an 'escape clause' in Section 1(5) sentence 8 ETRA.

However, before taking a closer look at the escape-clause and the requirements for its application, the following analysis first examines the current German tax treaty network and develops a taxonomy of treaties that proves necessary in order to examine whether the escape clause of Section 1(5) sentence 8 ETRA can be applied with regard to each of the categories identified.

b. Classification of the German Tax Treaty Network

(1) Tax Treaties Following the Wording of Article 7 OECD MC 2010

Although Article 7 of the German 'Basis for Agreements for the Avoidance of Double Taxation and the Prevention of Fiscal Evasion with Respect to Taxes on

[948]The following chapter was already published in a slightly modified version and was incorporated into this thesis with the consent of the co-authors (© 2018 IBFD. Originally published as S. Hentschel, G. Kraft & T. Moser, Permanent-Establishment Taxation in Germany in the Post-AOA-Implementation Era: A Primer on Exceptions and Problem Areas in 58 Eur. Taxn. 2/3, Journals IBFD, 73 (76 et seqq.). Reproduced with permission.).

Income and on Capital'[949] is based on the idea that a PE shall be fully treated as a hypothetical separate and independent enterprise for the purpose of profit attribution and, therefore, explicitly contains the idea of the AOA, the vast majority of current German tax treaties are not yet based on the wording implemented in the version of Article 7 OECD MC 2010[950]. In fact, only five out of the 96 tax treaties currently concluded and ratified—namely the Income and Capital Tax Treaties with Armenia[951], Liechtenstein,[952] Luxembourg[953], Netherlands[954], and the Income Tax Treaty with Japan[955]—are based on the wording of Article 7 OECD MC 2010.[956] In addition, the AOA has been incorporated into the protocols to the Germany-Norway Income Tax Treaty,[957] the Germany-Cyprus,[958] the Germany-United Kingdom,[959] and the Germany-Ireland Income and Capital Tax Treaties[960]. Through an additional protocol of amendment of 1 June 2006, the unlimited hypothetical independence of the PE and, thus, the basic idea of

[949]Cf. BMF, 22 Aug. 2013, IV B 2—S 1301/13/10009.

[950]The wording of Art. 7 OECD MC 2010 and the latest version of the Art. 7 (i.e. Art. 7 OECD MC 2017) did not change. In order to allow for a clear delimitation of the changes resulting from the implementation of the AOA the following analysis refers to the Art. 7 OECD MC 2010 as the AOA version of the Art.

[951]DTA Federal Republic of Germany- Republic of Armenia, 29 June 2016, BGBl. II 2017, 1077.

[952]DTA Federal Republic of Germany- Principality of Liechtenstein, 17 Nov. 2011, BGBl. II 2012, 1462.

[953]DTA Federal Republic of Germany-Grandy Duchy of Luxembourg, 23 Apr. 2012, BGBl. II 2012, 1403.

[954]DTA Federal Republic of Germany-Kingdom of the Netherlands, 12 Apr. 2012, BGBl. II 2012, 1414.

[955]DTA Federal Republic of Germany-Japan, 18 July 2016, BGBl. II 2016, 1230.

[956]For an overview of the tax treaties concluded by Germany as of 1 Jan. 2021 see BMF, 18 Feb. 2021, IV B 2—S 1301/07/10017-12, BStBl. I 2021, 265.

[957]DTA Federal Republic of Germany-Kingdom of Norway, amended by protocol of 24 June 2013, BGBl. II 2014, 906.

[958]DTA Federal Republic of Germany-Cyprus, amended by protocol of 19 Feb. 2021, has not yet entered into force.

[959]DTA Federal Republic of Germany-United Kingdom of Great Britain and Northern Ireland, amended by protocol of 17 Mar. 2014, BGBl. II 2015, 1297.

[960]DTA Federal Republic of Germany-Ireland, amended by protocol of 3 Dec. 2014, BGBl. II 2015, 1322.

the AOA was also declared applicable with regard to the Germany-United States Income and Capital Tax Treaty.[961]

(2) Interpretation of the Different Tax Treaties

As previously illustrated, the OECD Commentary on the OECD MC, even though not legally binding, serves as a valuable assistance for the interpretation of the OECD MC.[962] Since the AOA was implemented in a two-step procedure, the question of whether a change in the Commentary may affect the interpretation of a tax treaty that was concluded before the Commentary was published (static versus dynamic approach)[963] is of particular importance when it comes to the interpretation of the provision that deals with the attribution of profits to a PE in the various tax treaties.

In general, tax treaties that contain the wording of Article 7 OECD MC 2010 and that were ratified after 22 July 2010 (i.e. tax treaties with unlimited hypothetical independence of the PE) are interpreted according to the Commentary on the OECD MC 2010 and the PE Report 2010.[964] Consequently, the AOA and its implications with regard to the attribution of profits to a PE are fully applicable in these instances. Yet, the interpretation of tax treaties that contain the wording of Article 7 OECD MC (pre-2010 version) and that were ratified before the incorporation of the AOA into the OECD MC (i.e. before 22 July 2010) is far more problematic. In this regard, a further distinction needs to be made between tax treaties that were ratified before 17 July 2008 and those ratified between 17 July 2008 and 22 July 2010.

While the Committee of Fiscal Affairs takes the view that tax treaties shall be interpreted dynamically in light of the latest Commentary, the German Federal Tax Court does not share this view and follows a static approach, i.e. the interpretation of a tax treaty can only be based on the Commentary as it was phrased at

---

[961] DTA Federal Republic of Germany-United States of America, amended by protocol of 1 June 2006, BGBl. II 2006, 1184; detailed cf. *Wolff*, in: W/K/S/D (Eds.), Doppelbesteuerung, Art. 7 USA, paras. 186 et seq.

[962] Cf. OECD MC Commentary 2017, Introduction, para. 15; *Vogel/Rust*, in: Reimer/Rust (Eds.), Klaus Vogel on Double Taxation Conventions, Introduction, paras. 29.1 et seqq.

[963] See for discussion *Gosch*, IStR 2015, 709 (709 et seq.); *Hemmelrath/Keppler*, IStR 2013, 37 (39 et seq.); *Kraft/Dombrowski*, IWB 2015, 87 (88 et seq.); *Kahle/Kindich*, in: Lübbehüsen/Kahle (Eds.), Brennpunkte der Besteuerung von Betriebsstätten, paras. 4.97 et seq.; *Lang/Brugger*, ATF 2008, 95 (98 et seq.). See also chapter C.IV.1.c.(2) of this thesis.

[964] Cf. *Hentschel/Kraft/Moser*, Ubg 2016, 144 (145); *Andresen*, ISR 2013, 320 (326). For legal considerations cf. *Ditz*, in: Schönfeld/Ditz (Eds.), DBA-Kommentar, Art. 7 (2017), paras. 6 et seq.

the time the tax treaty was negotiated.[965] Therefore, the concept of the AOA cannot apply to tax treaties that were concluded before 17 July 2008 and that follow the wording of Article 7 OECD MC (pre-2010 version; i.e. tax treaties with limited hypothetical independence of the PE). For tax treaties concluded between 17 July 2008 and 22 July 2010, however, containing the wording of Article 7 OECD MC (pre-2010 version; i.e. tax treaties with extended hypothetical independence of the PE), it can be argued that the contracting states were positively aware of the changes that were made to the Commentary on Article 7 OECD MC and thus based their treaty negotiations on these changes.[966]

Since there may be several years between the date of signature of a tax treaty and its effective ratification by the legislator, a clear time-based delimitation is important when deciding which version of the Commentary on the OECD MC can be used for the purpose of interpretation of the tax treaty. The German Federal Tax Court[967] rightly refers to the will of the contracting parties to determine which version of the Commentary on the OECD MC can be used for the interpretation of the respective tax treaties. Consequently, irrespective of the time of ratification or the time when the tax treaty entered into force, it is the time of the conclusion of the tax treaty that is relevant in this regard.[968] Therefore, it cannot be presumed that the contracting parties have the will to apply the Commentary on the OECD MC 2010 to tax treaties ratified between 17 July 2008 and 22 July 2010 but signed and therefore concluded before 17 July 2008. In these instances, new negotiations between Germany and the respective contracting state need to take place in order to adapt to the new will of the respective contracting states. Tax treaties with extended hypothetical independence of the PE are in place between Germany and

[965] Cf. BFH, 25 May 2011, I R 95/10, BFHE 234, 63; BFH, 9 Feb. 2011, I R 54/10, BStBl. II 2012, 106.

[966] Cf. *Hemmelrath/Keppler*, IStR 2013, 37 (40). See for the changes to the OECD MC Commentary chapter D.I.4.a.(1) of this thesis.

[967] Cf. BFH, 25 May 2011, I R 95/10, BFHE 234, 63; BFH, 9 Feb. 2011, I R 54/10, BStBl. II 2012, 106.

[968] Cf. *Hentschel/Kraft/Moser*, Ubg 2016, 144 (144 et seq.).

the following states: Albania[969], Australia[970], Bulgaria[971], Hungary[972], Malaysia[973], Syria[974] and the United Arab Emirates[975]. Also, the Income and Capital Tax Treaties with China[976], Costa Rica[977], Finland[978], Israel[979], Philippines[980], Tunisia[981] and the Income Tax Treaty with Mauritius[982], concluded after 22 July 2010, contain the wording of Article 7 OECD MC (pre-2010 version) and must, accordingly, be classified as tax treaties with extended hypothetical independence of the PE.

Table 14 provides an overview of the classification of the different German tax treaty network.

c. The Escape Clause

(1) Background

The German legislator did not distinguish between the different types of tax treaties when implementing the AOA into German tax law. Therefore, the provisions of Section 1(5) sentences 1–7 ETRA are applicable regardless of whether or not the AOA has been implemented in the respective tax treaties. Even if no tax treaty

---

[969] DTA Federal Republic of Germany-Republic of Albania, 6 Apr. 2010, BGBl. II 2011, 1186.

[970] DTA Federal Republic of Germany-Commonwealth of Australia, 12 Nov. 2015, BGBl. II 2016, 1114.

[971] DTA Federal Republic of Germany-Republic of Bulgaria, 25 Jan. 2010, BGBl. II 2010, 1286.

[972] DTA Federal Republic of Germany-Hungary, 28 Feb. 2011, BGBl. II 2011, 919.

[973] DTA Federal Republic of Germany-Malaysia, 23 Feb. 2010, BGBl. II 2010, 1310.

[974] DTA Federal Republic of Germany-Syrian Arab Republic, 17 Feb. 2010, BGBl. II 2010, 1359.

[975] DTA Federal Republic of Germany-United Arab Emirates, 1 July 2010, BGBl. II 2011, 538.

[976] DTA Federal Republic of Germany-People's Republic of China, 28 Mar. 2014, BGBl. II 2015, 1647.

[977] DTA Federal Republic of Germany-Republic of Costa Rica, 13 Feb. 2014, BGBl. II 2014, 917.

[978] DTA Federal Republic of Germany-Republic of Finland, 19 Feb. 2016, BGBl. II 2017, 466.

[979] DTA Federal Republic of Germany-State of Israel, 21 Aug. 2014, BGBl. II 2015, 1301.

[980] DTA Federal Republic of Germany-Republic of Philippines, 9 Sept. 2013, BGBl. II 2014, 822.

[981] DTA Federal Republic of Germany-Republic of Tunisia, 8 Feb. 2018, BGBl. II 2020, 154.

[982] DTA Federal Republic of Germany-Republic of Mauritius, 7 Oct. 2011, BGBl. II 2012, 1050.

Table 14 Classification of Different Tax Treaties from a German Tax Perspective

Tax treaty	Interpretation
• treaties with limited hypothetical independence of PE – wording of Article 7 OECD MC (pre-2010) – concluded before 17 July 2008	• commentary on OECD MC 2008 not applicable • interpretation can only be based on the commentary as it was phrased at the time the treaty was negotiated
• treaties with extended hypothetical independence of PE – wording of Article 7 OECD MC (pre-2010) – concluded after 17 July 2008	• commentary on OECD MC 2008 applicable • commentary on OECD MC 2010 not applicable
• treaties with unlimited hypothetical independence of PE – wording of Article 7 OECD MC 2010 – concluded after 22 July 2010	• commentary on OECD MC 2010 applicable

Source: Own illustration based on *Hentschel/Kraft/Moser*, Ubg 2016, 144 (146).

exists between Germany and the other state, the principles set out in Section 1(5) sentences 1–7 ETRA must be applied.

In this context, it is worth noting that the interest in implementing the AOA in future tax treaties[983] appears to be limited, especially for developing countries, as they potentially fear that their taxing rights may be infringed in implementing the AOA. This tendency does not promote a consistent application of the attribution of profits to PEs by the respective jurisdictions. The following example illustrates the potential risks of double taxation that may arise due to a divergent application of the AOA by different countries.

Example:[984]
S-GmbH, a corporation established under German law with its registered office and place of business management in Hamburg, produces semi-conductors for smartphones. In order to respond quickly and flexibly to customer requirements, S-GmbH decides to carry out the production and distribution for the foreign market through different PEs in China, India,

[983]Cf. *Bayer*, SWI 2011, 539 (542); *Valta*, ISR 2013, 186 (188); *Froitzheim*, Ubg 2015, 354 (357).

Liechtenstein and Spain. S-GmbH provides considerable support infrastructure such as IT, R&D as well as accounting functions for the PE's located abroad. The following figure illustrates the case (Figure 3).

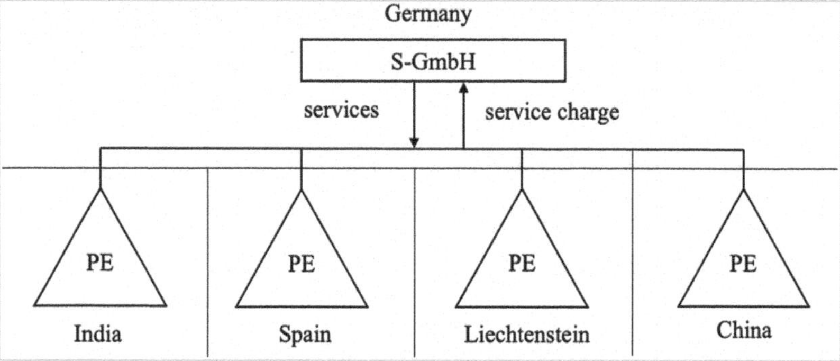

Figure 3 Example Illustrating the Necessity of the Escape Clause (Source: Own illustration based on *Hentschel/Kraft/Moser*, Ubg 2016, 144 (147))

984 Cf. *Hentschel/Kraft/Moser*, Ubg 2016, 144 (147).

Solution:
According to Section 1(4) sentence 1 no. 2 ETRA in conjunction with Section 16 BsGaV, the illustrated support functions carried out by the S-GmbH are regarded as dealings between the S-GmbH and the PEs located abroad. When attributing profit to the various parts of the enterprise, the respective dealings need to be considered. More precisely, according to Section 1(5) sentence 4 ETRA, the respective dealings have to be priced at arm's length. This legal consequence applies regardless of whether or not the concept of the AOA is actually implemented in the respective tax treaties between Germany and the other states where the PEs are located. It applies even if no tax treaty exists between Germany and the respective PE state.

To avoid double taxation, the corresponding service charges for the support functions need to be deductible at the level of the PE in the foreign state. However, it is highly questionable whether the notional service charges will be recognised as a business expense by the respective foreign tax authorities. In the case at hand, only the Germany-Luxembourg[985] Income and Capital Tax Treaty contains the wording of Article 7 OECD MC 2010 and can be regarded as a tax treaty with unlimited hypothetical independence of the PE. The Income and Capital Tax Treaties with India[986], Spain[987] and China[988] do not follow the wording of Article 7 OECD MC 2010 and, therefore, the risk exists that the service charges will be taxed at the level of S-GmbH but cannot be deducted as business expenses in the respective states where the other PEs are located.

The example reveals that in many instances double taxation may result from the unconditional application of the AOA provisions by Germany. Considering this finding, the following analysis examines cases in which the 'escape clause' of Section 1(5) sentence 8 ETRA can help to mitigate this risk of double taxation.

---

[985] DTA Federal Republic of Germany-Grandy Duchy of Luxembourg, 23 Apr. 2012, BGBl. II 2012, 1403.

[986] DTA Federal Republic of Germany-Republic of India, 19 June 1995, BGBl. II 1996, 706.

[987] DTA Federal Republic of Germany-Kingdom of Spain, 3 Feb. 2011, BGBl. II 2012, 18.

[988] DTA Federal Republic of Germany-People's Republic of China, 28 Mar. 2014, BGBl. II 2015, 1647.

(2) Requirements for the Application of the Escape Clause

(a) General Overview

The German legislator's idea is to address problems stemming from a divergent application of Article 7 OECD MC by the respective states through the application of the escape clause of Section 1(5) sentence 8 ETRA. Pursuant to this provision, the regulations of the tax treaty take precedence over Section 1(5) sentences 1–7 ETRA if:

a) the taxpayer claims that the provisions of the applicable tax treaty are contradictory to the legal provisions of Section 1(5) sentences 1–7 ETRA (burden of proof rule 1);
b) the taxpayer proves that the other state exercises its taxing right according to the regulations of the respective tax treaty (burden of proof rule 2); and
c) double taxation arises due to the application of the legal provisions of Section 1(5) sentences 1–7 ETRA (burden of proof rule 3).

Thus, the taxpayer is obliged to meet a threefold set of burden of proof rules. In this context, it is surprising that the obligation to assert and prove certain circumstances lies with the taxpayer. According to Section 88 GFC, it is generally the obligation of the tax authorities to regard the regulations of the tax treaties as directly applicable norms.[989] However, the fact that the respective regulations are only to be considered if the taxpayer completes the 'assignments' provided by Section 1(5) sentence 8 ETRA leads to the conclusion that the escape clause is a special form of 'treaty override'.[990] More specifically, in this context, the expression 'reverse treaty override'[991] has emerged. This expression refers to the fact that, in contrast to a typical derogation from tax treaties through domestic tax law, Section 1(5) sentence 8 ETRA explicitly requires proof that the other state is exercising its taxation rights according to the regulations of the respective tax treaty.[992]

---

989 Cf. *Schnitger*, IStR 2012, 633 (641).

990 For further information with regard to the term ‚treaty override' cf. *Hemmelrath/Keppler*, IStR 2013, 37 (41); *Brunsbach/Endres/Lüdicke/Schnitger*, Deutsche Abkommenspolitik, 64; *Gebhardt,* BB 2012, 2353 (2353 et seq.). The concerns of the German Federal Tax Court regarding the constitutional legitimacy of a treaty override (BFH, 10 Jan. 2012, I R 66/09, BFHE 236, 304) were not shared by the Federal Constitutional Court, cf. BVerfG, 15 Dec. 2015, 2 BvL 1/12, BVerfGE 141, 1.

991 *Andresen*, DB 2012, 879 (884).

992 Cf. *Kraft/Dombrowski*, IWB 2015, 87 (91 et seq.).

(b) Burden of Proof Rule 1

When a taxpayer endeavours to claim the application of the escape clause, the first challenge is to determine the circumstances in which the provisions of the applicable tax treaty are contradictory to Section 1(5) sentence 1–7 ETRA and how such a contradiction should be formally substantiated.

An answer to this can neither be found in the ETRA nor in BsGaV. In an attempt to clarify such ambiguities, the German tax authorities tried to provide examples of how the escape clause of Section 1(5) sentence 8 ETRA may be used to avoid international tax conflicts. The following three scenarios were identified:[993]

- **Scenario 1:** tax treaties containing a provision corresponding to Article 7 OECD MC 2010;
- **Scenario 2:** tax treaties with OECD member countries containing a provision corresponding to Article 7 OECD MC (pre-2010 version); and
- **Scenario 3:** tax treaties with non-OECD member countries containing a provision corresponding to Article 7 OECD MC (pre-2010 version) or Article 7 UN MC[994].

According to the German tax authority, tax treaties containing a provision that corresponds to Article 7 OECD MC 2010 and tax treaties in which the other contracting state declares that the principles of the AOA are applicable under the respective tax treaty (e.g. the United States), in general do not contradict the legal provisions of Section 1(5) sentences 1–7 ETRA.[995] However, tax disputes might arise in such scenarios due to divergent interpretations of the respective treaty provisions by the states.[996] As the following example illustrates, divergent interpretations of tax treaties arise, in particular, in situations in which the national legislator implements the provisions of the AOA into domestic law in a way that is favourable to national tax revenue.

---

[993] Cf. BMF, 22 Dec. 2016, IV B 5—S 1341/12/10001–03, BStBl. I 2017, 182, paras 424 et seq.

[994] Cf. UN, Model Double Taxation Convention, 2017.

[995] Cf. BMF, 22 Dec. 2016, IV B 5—S 1341/12/10001–03, BStBl. I 2017, 182, para. 425.

[996] Cf. *Hentschel/Kraft/Moser*, Ubg 2016, 144 (148).

Example continued:[997]
Referring to the example discussed above, S-GmbH now carries out a functional and factual analysis to attribute functions, assets and risks—as required by Section 1(5) sentence 3 ETRA in conjunction with Sections 4–11 BsGaV—to its PE in Liechtenstein. In the next step, free capital has to be attributed to the PE.

Solution:

According to Section 1(5) sentence 3 no. 4 ETRA in conjunction with Section 13(1) BsGaV, free capital can only be attributed to the PE in Liechtenstein if S-GmbH proves that such capital is necessary (minimum capital method). Otherwise, no capital at all can be attributed to the PE. As this approach is not consistent with the methods provided in the OECD's PE Report 2010,[998] it would not come as a surprise if the tax authority in Liechtenstein were to decide not to follow the German approach and instead attribute a higher amount of free capital to the PE by using a method that is in line with the PE Report 2010, for example, the capital allocation approach. Paradoxically, if the PE were to be located in Germany and the other part of the enterprise that provides the service in Liechtenstein, Section 12 BsGaV would require that the capital allocation approach be used to attribute free capital to the PE. This unequal treatment of inbound and outbound investments causes considerable legal uncertainty and can ultimately lead to double taxation, since the attribution of free capital also influences the deductibility of interest expenses.

One might think that the escape clause in Section 1(5) sentence 8 ETRA is a suitable instrument to avoid double taxation in the case at hand. However, as the reason for the tax conflict between Germany and Liechtenstein is not found in the legal conflict between the applicable tax treaty (tax treaty with unlimited hypothetical independence of the PE) and Section 1(5) sentences 1–7 ETRA, the escape clause cannot be applied in the case under consideration.[999] The German tax authority suggests that, in such scenarios, only the costly way of a mutual agreement procedure can help mitigate the effects of double taxation.[1000]

[997] Cf. *Hentschel/Kraft/Moser*, Ubg 2016, 144 (148).

[998] For an overview of the methods provided by the OECD cf. PE Report 2010, Part I, paras. 121 et seq. and chapter D.I.4.b.(2)(e) of this thesis.

[999] Cf. BMF, 22 Dec. 2016, IV B 5—S 1341/12/10001–03, BStBl. I 2017, 182, para. 425.

[1000] Cf. BMF, 22 Dec. 2016, IV B 5—S 1341/12/10001–03, BStBl. I 2017, 182, para. 426.

The second constellation addressed by the German tax authority covers tax treaties with OECD member countries that contain a provision that corresponds to Article 7 OECD MC (pre-2010 version). With regard to such constellations, the German tax authority generally assumes that the other OECD member countries follow the German approach as implemented in Section 1(5) sentences 1–7 ETRA and the BsGaV.[1001] Consequently, in general, no conflicts with the respective tax treaty should arise in view of the German tax authority.[1002] If, however, disagreements between the tax authorities occur, the German tax authority turns to mutual agreement procedures[1003] and, by doing so, ultimately accepts the risk of double taxation in such instances.[1004] Only in the event of a notional surrender of use will the German tax authority[1005] recognise a contradiction.[1006] However, this view is surprising since a conflict between a tax treaty that was concluded before 17 July 2008 containing the wording of Article 7 OECD MC (pre 2010 version, i.e. a tax treaty that provides for limited hypothetical independence of the PE) and Section 1(5) sentences 1–7 ETRA already exists—irrespective of whether the tax treaty was concluded with OECD member countries or non-OECD countries—due to the fact that the Commentary on the OECD MC 2008 and, thus, the basic concept of the AOA cannot be relied on in interpreting the tax treaty.[1007]

The issue of whether or not a conflict between the tax treaty and Section 1(5) sentences 1–7 ETRA exists is more complex for tax treaties that were concluded after 17 July 2008 and contain the wording of Article 7 OECD MC (pre-2010 version, i.e. tax treaties with extended hypothetical independence of the PE). With regard to such tax treaties, the Commentary on Article 7 OECD MC 2008 and, therefore, central elements of the AOA, such as the two-step approach to profit attribution and the recognition of dealings between the PE and another part of the enterprise, are available in interpreting the respective tax treaties. In this respect,

---

[1001] Cf. BMF, 22 Dec. 2016, IV B 5—S 1341/12/10001–03, BStBl. I 2017, 182, para. 427.

[1002] Cf. BMF, 22 Dec. 2016, IV B 5—S 1341/12/10001–03, BStBl. I 2017, 182, para. 427.

[1003] Cf. BMF, 22 Dec. 2016, IV B 5—S 1341/12/10001–03, BStBl. I 2017, 182, para. 428.

[1004] Cf. *Sennewald/Geberth*, DB 2017, 31 (33).

[1005] Cf. BMF, 22 Dec. 2016, IV B 5—S 1341/12/10001–03, BStBl. I 2017, 182, para. 428.

[1006] This is due to the fact that the OECD does not allow for a notional payment of royalties: '[i]n the case of intangible rights, the rules concerning the relations between enterprises of the same group (e.g. payment of royalties or cost sharing arrangements) cannot be applied in respect of the relations between parts of the same enterprise', OECD MC Commentary 2008, Art. 7, para. 34.

[1007] Cf. BFH, 25 May 2011, I R 95/10, BFHE 234, 63; BFH, 9 Feb. 2011, I R 54/10, BStBl. II 2012, 106.

no direct conflict with Section 1(5), sentences 1–7 ETRA can be identified. However, for tax treaties that were concluded between 17 July 2008 and 22 July 2010 and those that were concluded after 22 July 2010 but refer to the Commentary on the OECD MC 2008 with regard to the interpretation of the respective Article that deals with the attribution of profits to a PE, a conflict to Section 1(5), sentences 1–7 ETRA arises, since such tax treaties are in general to be interpreted according to the Commentary on the OECD MC 2008. The Commentary on the OECD MC 2008 does,e.g., not allow for deductions for internal debts and receivables.[1008] However, according to Section 16(3) sentence 1 BsGaV in conjunction with Section 17 BsGaV, the performance of a financing function within an enterprise is generally possible if certain conditions apply and must be remunerated at arm's length.[1009] This circumstance illustrates that also tax treaties concluded after 17 July 2008 and that contain the wording of Article 7 OECD MC (pre-2010 version) may conflict with Section 1(5), sentences 1–7 ETRA. Accordingly, the application of the escape-clause should be possible in such circumstances.

Further, the government's reasoning in respect of Section 1(5) sentence 8 ETRA supports this finding.[1010] Accordingly, the escape clause shall also be applicable in situations where the treaty contains the wording of Article 7 OECD MC (pre-2010 version) and the contracting state interprets the respective provision according to the Commentary on Article 7 OECD MC 2008.[1011] In this context, the fact that the German tax authority does not allow for the application of the escape clause in such instances and, instead, suggests the use of time-consuming mutual agreement procedures, has to be criticised.

A third and last constellation explicitly addressed by the German tax authority deals with tax treaties that are concluded with non-OECD member countries that contain a provision corresponding to Article 7 OECD MC (pre-2010 version) or Article 7 UN Model.[1012] For these tax treaties, the German tax authority recognises a conflict with Section 1(5) sentences 1–7 ETRA and therefore accepts the application of the escape clause.[1013] In these instances, the tax assessment is

---

[1008] Cf. OECD MC Commentary 2008, Art. 7, paras. 41 et seq.; detailed also *Buchner*, IStR 2013, 228 (228 et seqq.).

[1009] Cf. *Hentschel/Kraft/Moser*, Ubg 2016, 144 (148). See in more detail chapter D.II.3.c.(1)(a) of this thesis.

[1010] Cf. BT-Drs. 17/10000, 65.

[1011] Cf. BT-Drs. 17/10000, 65.

[1012] Cf. BMF, 22 Dec. 2016, IV B 5—S 1341/12/10001–03, BStBl. I 2017, 182, paras. 430 et seqq.

[1013] Cf. BMF, 22 Dec. 2016, IV B 5—S 1341/12/10001–03, BStBl. I 2017, 182, paras. 430, 432.

carried out in line with the common understanding of the tax treaty at the time of its conclusion, making a mutual agreement procedure unnecessary.[1014]

(c) Burden of Proof Rule 2

If a conflict between the applicable tax treaty and Section 1(5) sentences 1–7 ETRA becomes apparent, in a second step, the taxpayer has to prove that the other state is exercising its taxing right according to the provisions of the respective tax treaty. According to the government's reasoning, such proof can, in general, be provided by submitting the respective foreign tax declaration and additional documents.[1015] The types of additional documents that are required are not mentioned by the legislator. The German tax authority has clarified, however, that in addition to the national and foreign tax declaration, the respective tax assessment of the foreign state must also be submitted.[1016] If such information is not available at the time of submission, it is to be sent without undue delay.[1017]

In this respect, the taxpayer faces two challenges. First, it is questionable whether or not the German tax authority will accept a tax assessment that is in another language than German. It is possible that the tax authorities will refer to Section 87(1) and 87(2) GFC and ask the taxpayer for a translation of the tax assessment into the German language.[1018] Second, several years might pass between the submission of the tax declaration in the respective treaty state and the receipt of the tax assessment.

Moreover, a foreign tax audit—which sometimes takes place several years after the tax assessment was issued—might assess the facts of the case differently and revise the tax assessment. Thus, the question that arises is when the respective taxing right is considered to have been exercised. This shall be deemed to have occurred if it is foreseeable—for example through tax assessments issued in former years—that the foreign state will claim its corresponding taxing right.[1019] The position of the German tax authority is favourable to the taxpayer in this regard. The administrative principles state that the German tax authority is to examine whether the other state exercises its taxing right in line with the PE Report 2010.

[1014] Cf. BMF, 22 Dec. 2016, IV B 5—S 1341/12/10001–03, BStBl. I 2017, 182, para. 430.

[1015] Cf. BT-Drs. 17/10000, 65.

[1016] Cf. BMF, 22 Dec. 2016, IV B 5—S 1341/12/10001–03, BStBl. I 2017, 182, para. 430.

[1017] Cf. BMF, 22 Dec. 2016, IV B 5—S 1341/12/10001–03, BStBl. I 2017, 182, para. 430.

[1018] Cf. *Kahle/Kindich*, in: Lübbehüsen/Kahle (Eds.), Brennpunkte der Besteuerung von Betriebsstätten, para. 4.454; *Hentschel/Kraft/Moser*, Ubg 2016, 144 (149).

[1019] Cf. *Hentschel/Kraft/Moser*, Ubg 2016, 144 (149).

If no official public statement exists, the respective tax authority might request information from the Federal Central Tax Office in Germany.[1020]

In this context, it should be mentioned that a special treatment for 'old' tax treaties (tax treaties with limited or extended hypothetical independence of the PE), in respect of which the other state already makes the profit attribution according to the AOA, is necessary. Since most[1021] OECD member countries have agreed to the PE Report 2010 and, therefore, have accepted the basic principles of the AOA as the accurate interpretation of Article 7 OECD MC, this constellation is of particular importance. In these instances, the actual interpretation of the tax treaty differs from the initial interpretation at the time of the treaty's conclusion.

This point is illustrated by the Austria-Germany Income and Capital Tax Treaty.[1022] This tax treaty can be classified as a tax treaty that provides for limited hypothetical independence of the PE. Consequently, the Commentary on the OECD MC 2008 and the PE Report 2008 are not accessible in interpreting such tax treaties since they did not exist at the time of the conclusion of this treaty. The principles of the AOA are, however, to be applied according to the Austrian TP Guidelines—but only to the extent that there is no conflict with the OECD MC 2008. Given a narrow interpretation of the wording of Section 1(5) sentence 8 ETRA, proof that the contracting state exercises its taxing right in accordance with the regulations of the respective tax treaty would not be possible, despite the existing contradictions between the OECD MC 2008 and OECD MC 2010. Consequently, the escape clause cannot be used.

Considering the government's reasoning, however, it is clear that such a narrow interpretation is not appropriate. As pointed out herein, according to the government's reasoning, Section 1(5) sentence 8 ETRA shall also be applied in situations in which the contracting state interprets the respective provision according to Article 7 OECD MC 2008.[1023] Thus, conflicts that arise between the Commentary on Article 7 OECD MC 2008 and the Commentary on Article 7 OECD MC 2010

[1020] Cf. BMF, 22 Dec. 2016, IV B 5—S 1341/12/10001–03, BStBl. I 2017, 182, para. 431.

[1021] The following exceptions apply: New Zealand does not agree with the approach reflected in Part I of the PE Report 2010 and, therefore, reserves the right to use the pre-2010 version of Art. 7 OECD MC, cf. OECD MC Commentary 2017, Art. 7, para. 95. Also, Austria, Chile, Greece, Mexico, the Slovak Republic, Turkey, Portugal, Australia and Latvia reserve the right to use the pre-2010 version of Art. 7 OECD MC, cf. OECD MC Commentary 2017, Art. 7, paras. 96–97 and paras. 99–100.

[1022] Cf. DTA Federal Republic of Germany-Republic of Austria, 26 Mar. 2002, BGBl. II 2002, 734.

[1023] Cf. BT-Drs. 17/10000, 65.

fall within the scope of the escape clause implemented in Section 1(5) sentence 8 ETRA.

(d) Burden of Proof Rule 3

To prove the fact that double taxation would arise if the other state exercises its taxing rights according to the tax treaty, it is not entirely clear what kind of documents are necessary to prove such double taxation.[1024] In accordance with the principle of proportionality, the requirements for proof of double taxation should not be excessive. Otherwise, administrative obstacles could potentially exclude certain taxpayers from the use of the escape clause.[1025]

In practice, it may be helpful to carry out the following steps in order to prove double taxation to the German tax authorities. If the contracting state does not follow the AOA, it seems advisable for the taxpayer to initially declare the income in the foreign state according to the understanding of the tax treaty at the time of its conclusion.[1026] Upon request, the taxpayer needs to clarify the underlying principles according to which the income is taxed abroad.[1027] In this regard, the auxiliary and ancillary account, to be drawn up pursuant to Section 3 BsGaV, as well as the transfer pricing documentation required under Section 90(3) GFC, is of particular importance.

Furthermore, the tax declaration in Germany must be filed—with reference to the fact that the AOA cannot be applied in the respective case—according to the former understanding of the tax treaty.[1028] In addition, the German tax authority will likely expect a comparability calculation from the taxpayer that illustrates how the individual dealings between the PE and the other parts of the enterprise

[1024] See also *Brüninghaus*, in: Vögele/Borstell/Engler (Eds.), Verrechnungspreise, para. K 109.

[1025] Cf. *Hentschel/Kraft/Moser*, Ubg 2016, 144 (150 et seq.); *Kahle/Kindich*, in: Lübbehüsen/Kahle (Eds.), Brennpunkte der Besteuerung von Betriebsstätten, para. 4.455.

[1026] Cf. BMF, 22 Dec. 2016, IV B 5—S 1341/12/10001–03, BStBl. I 2017, 182, paras. 429 et seq.

[1027] Cf. BMF, 22 Dec. 2016, IV B 5—S 1341/12/10001–03, BStBl. I 2017, 182, para. 433.

[1028] For the former understanding of the German tax authorities the BMF, 22 Dec. 2016, IV B 5—S 1341/12/10001–03, BStBl. I 2017, 182 refers to BMF, 24 Dec. 1999, IV B 4—S 1300–111/99, BStBl. I 1999, 1076.

would have been recorded according to the AOA.[1029] The deviations need to be quantified[1030] and submitted to the respective tax authorities.[1031]

If it later turns out that the foreign tax assessment deviates from the foreign tax declaration, e.g. due to a different assessment of the case as a result of a foreign tax audit, it should be determined whether or not an amendment to the tax declaration is appropriate, e.g. through the use of Section 175 GFC.

(3) Application with Respect to Non-Tax Treaty States

The escape clause of Section 1(5) sentence 8 ETRA cannot be applied if no tax treaty has been concluded between Germany and the respective state wherein the PE is located. However, since the provision of Section 1(5) sentences 1–7 ETRA is applicable regardless of whether or not a tax treaty has been concluded between the respective states, the legal consequences directly affect the taxpayer.[1032] In such instances, the potential risk of double taxation can only be mitigated through the application of the unilateral imputation or deduction method. For outbound PEs, the possibility for a tax credit and tax deduction is implemented in Section 26 CITA in conjunction with Section 34c (1)-(3) in conjunction with Section 34d ITA.[1033]

d. Interim Conclusion

The analysis undertaken allows for multiple assessments regarding the relationship between the implementation of the AOA into German domestic tax law and the provisions of current German tax treaties. First, despite the problems outlined herein, the rapid implementation of the AOA into German domestic law is generally to be welcomed, as, in the long run, swift implementation will promote the earliest possible consistent application of AOA principles. However, since most German tax treaties are still based on the 'old' wording of Article 7 OECD MC (pre-2010 version), the mismatch between German domestic law and the respective tax treaties currently leads to significant legal uncertainty regarding the attribution of profits to PEs. In this context, the German legislator's attempt to

[1029] Cf. *Hentschel/Kraft/Moser*, Ubg 2016, 144 (151).

[1030] Deviations that emerge from different treatments of the national law of the other contracting state are not to be regarded in making the respective quantification, cf. *Kaeser*, in: W/K/S/D (Eds.), Doppelbesteuerung, Art. 7 MA (2010), para. 711.

[1031] Cf. BMF, 22 Dec. 2016, IV B 5—S 1341/12/10001–03, BStBl. I 2017, 182, paras. 429 et seq.

[1032] Cf. *Kraft/Dombrowski*, IWB 2015, 87 (93).

[1033] Cf. in more detail *Kraft/Dombrowski*, IWB 2015, 87 (93 et seq.).

implement an escape clause into domestic law to address these problems deserves—in principle—positive reception. The fact that the escape clause can only be applied if the taxpayer succeeds in proving specific circumstances of the case must, however, be viewed critically and shows that the escape clause can—at best—mitigate the problems outlined therein but does not solve them.

Additionally, due to the static approach taken by the German Federal Tax Court in terms of tax treaty interpretation, it is necessary to classify existing German tax treaties for the purposes of applying the escape clause. This especially holds true considering that the German tax authority follows a dynamic approach and set its own guidelines and tax treaty typology for the application of treaties.

As outlined previously, the approach taken by the German tax authorities will ultimately lead to two effects: first, the taxpayer will face legal uncertainty with regard to the applicability of the escape clause in Section 1(5) sentence 8 ETRA, as the German tax authority, in a somewhat debatable manner, limits its scope of application to specific cases. Second, the number of time-consuming and costly mutual agreement procedures will increase. Given this background, the mismatch between the AOA provisions implemented under German domestic law and the wording of existing tax treaties will remain a problem for cross-border PE taxation in the near future. Current developments in this regard should, accordingly, be closely monitored by tax practitioners dealing with cross-border transactions with Germany.

In any case, an adequate and thorough documentation of the individual circumstances relevant for the particular business transactions by the taxpayer—not only in order to meet the threefold set of burden of proof rules set out in Section 1(5) sentence 8 ETRA but also in order to comply with the documentation and reporting requirements under German national tax law—is mandatory. The following chapter attempts to provide an overview of the documentation and reporting requirements the taxpayer must comply with in the PE context. Throughout the analysis, specific focus is given to the changes to the national documentation and reporting requirements as a result of BEPS Action 13. In this regard, also the question whether the overhauled national documentation and reporting requirements can be regarded as a useful tool to standardise transfer pricing documentation requirements on an international level is to be examined.

5. Documentation Requirements under German National Law

a. Evolution of Documentation Requirements in Germany

(1) Landmark Decision of the German Federal Tax Court

The introduction of documentation and reporting requirements in the transfer pricing context can be traced back to a landmark decision of the German Federal Tax Court on 17 October 2001.[1034] In this judgement, the German Federal Tax Court specifically ruled that no legal documentation requirements were in place under the existing tax law at that time which obliged the taxpayer to prepare documents proving the appropriateness of the determined transfer prices.[1035] As a consequence, the German Federal Tax Court put the burden of proof for the failure of the taxpayer to adhere to the arm's length principle on the tax authority.[1036]

Against this background, Section 90(3) GFC was introduced through the 'Act on the Reduction of Tax Benefits and Exceptions'[1037] dealing with the obligation of the taxpayer to prepare and, upon request, to provide the required documentation illustrating the nature and the content of business transactions with a foreign nexus.[1038] The corresponding Ordinance substantiating the provision, the 'Ordinance on the Type, Content and Scope of Records as Referred to in Section 90 Subsection (3) of the Fiscal Code' (hereinafter: GAufzV)[1039], was introduced in

[1034] BFH, 17 Oct. 2001, I R 103/00, BStBl II 2004, 171. In this case, the German Federal Tax Court had to decide on a case which was subject to a tax audit covering the years 1985 to 1990.

[1035] Cf. BFH, 17 Oct. 2001, I R 103/00, BStBl II 2004, 171. See in this context also *Thies* in: Heimert/Michaelson/Duff&Phelps (Eds.), Guide to International Transfer Pricing, § 10.07 [B], 546; *Kroppen/Rasch*, IWB 2013, 830 (830 et seqq.).

[1036] Cf. *Wassermeyer*, DB 2003, 1535 (1535); *Busch*, in: W/A/D (Eds.), Betriebsstätten-Handbuch, para. 13.92; *Thies* in: Heimert/Michaelson/Duff&Phelps (Eds.), Guide to International Transfer Pricing, § 10.07 [B], 546.

[1037] Act on the Reduction of Tax Benefits and Exceptions, 20 May 2003, BGBl. I 2003, 660.

[1038] For an overview of the provision see *Kroppen/Rasch*, IWB 2013, 830 (830 et seq.); *Schnorenberger*, DB 2003, 1241 (1241 et seqq.); *Seer*, IWB 2012, 350. According to Article 97 Section 22(1) sentence 1 EGAO, the documentation and reporting requirements according to Section 90(3) GFC shall be provided by the taxpayer for fiscal years starting after 31 Dec. 2002. The additional documentation requirements introduced through the 'Act Implementing the Amendments of the Mutual Administrative Cooperation Directive and of Further Measures Against Base Erosion and Profit Shifting' are applicable for fiscal years starting after 31 Dec. 2016 according to Article 97 Section 22(1) sentence 4 EGAO.

[1039] GAufzV, 13 Nov. 2003, BGBl. I 2003, 2296, last amended through Article 7 of the Mutual Assistance Directive Implementation Act, 26 June 2013, BGBl. I 2013, 1809. This Ordinance expired and was replaced by the GAufzV, 12 July 2017, BGBl. I 2017, 2367. According to

2004 and the respective administrative principles, the 'Principles for the Examination of Income Allocation between Related Parties with Cross-Border Business Relationships as regards Duties of Investigation and Coordination, Adjustments as well as Mutual Agreement Procedures and EU Arbitration Procedures'[1040] were issued by the Federal Ministry of Finance on 12 April 2005.

(2) Additional Documentation Requirements for Dealings

However, limitations with regard to the documentation requirements in the PE context were determined in Section 7 sentence 1 GAufzV in the version as of 13 November 2003. Accordingly, the documentation requirements of Section 1–6 GAufzV shall only apply for profit allocation purposes between the enterprise and its PE 'to the extent a profit must be reported for tax purposes by reason of assets transferred or services performed or to the extent expenditures must be apportioned with tax effect'[1041].

With the implementation of the AOA through the Mutual Assistance Directive Implementation Act in Section 1(4) and (5) ETRA in 2013 and the corresponding amendments to Section 7 GAufzV in the version as of 30 June 2013, the outlined limitations with regard to the documentation requirements in the PE context were abolished leading to the fact that the documentation requirements of Section 1–6 GAufzV fully apply to business transactions (dealings) between a taxpayer's enterprise and its PE.[1042]

Additionally, Section 3 BsGaV determines that the taxpayer has to prepare auxiliary and ancillary accounts which must include all relevant aspects that are necessary in order to determine the profit of the PE.[1043]

(3) Modifications through BEPS Action 13

Further changes with regard to the documentation and reporting requirements in the transfer pricing context were implemented as a result of the OECD/G20 BEPS Project. Specifically, the recommendations of BEPS Action 13 concerning the three-tiered approach to transfer pricing documentation have been taken up by

---

Section 7 GAufzV, the new Ordinance is applicable for fiscal years starting after 31 Dec. 2016.

[1040] BMF, 12 Apr. 2005, IV B 4—S 1341–1/05, BStBl. I 2005, 570.

[1041] Translation provided by KPMG (Ed.), German International Taxation, p. 215.

[1042] Cf. *Richter/Heyd*, Ubg 2013, 418 (422). See in more detail also *Busch*, in: W/A/D (Eds.), Betriebsstätten-Handbuch, para. 13.112.

[1043] Cf. Section 3(1) sentence 2 BsGaV. The BsGaV applies to fiscal years starting after 31 Dec. 2014, cf. Section 40 BsGaV.

the EU Commission in the EU Directive 2016/881 of 25 May 2016. Since an EU Directive is a legislative act that sets out a goal that all EU member states must achieve, it is necessary that an EU Directive is implemented into the national law of the respective member states by the national legislator. As explicitly stated in the Directive, member states should use the Final Report on BEPS Action 13 as a source of illustration or interpretation in order to ensure consistency of application across member states.[1044]

In Germany, the provisions of the EU Directive were incorporated by the German legislator through the 'Act Implementing the Amendments of the Mutual Administrative Cooperation Directive and of Further Measures against Base Erosion and Profit Shifting'[1045] promulgated on 23 December 2016.[1046] In this context, two major changes to the already existing documentation requirements to transfer pricing were implemented in the GFC. First, Section 90(3) GFC, dealing with the obligation of participants to cooperate, was extended. Besides a country-specific and company-specific documentation (local file) that is to be prepared by the taxpayer for all business relations as defined in Section 1(4) ETRA,[1047] also the master file concept was implemented in the respective section. As a result of the changes to Section 90(3) GFC, the GAufzV as of 13 November 2003 was replaced by a new GAufzV[1048] on 12 July 2017.[1049] Second, Section 138a GFC implementing the obligation to file a CbC Report was introduced.

[1044]Cf. European Council, 25 May 2016, Directive 2016/881, para. 17.

[1045]Mutual Administrative Cooperation Directive Implementation Act, 20 Dec. 2016, BGBl. I 2016, 3000.

[1046]For a general overview of the legal bases for information exchange in the area of taxation in Germany, cf. *Kraft/Ditz/Heider*, DB 2017, 2243 (2244).

[1047]The amended Section 90(3) GFC directly refers to business relations as defined in Section 1(4) ETRA which also includes business transactions (dealings) between a taxpayer's enterprise and its PE (Section 1(4) sentence 1 no. 2 ETRA).

[1048]GAufzV, 12 July 2017, BGBl. I 2017, 2367. For authorisation of the new Ordinance see Section 90(3) sentence 11 GFC.

[1049]Among other changes, the amended Section 1 GAufzV directly refers to business relations as defined in Section 1(4) ETRA which also includes business transactions (dealings) between the PE and the rest of the enterprise, cf. Section 1(4) sentence 1 no. 2 ETRA. See in more detail for changes between the GAufzV as of 13 Nov. 2003 and 12 July 2017 *Rasch*, in: Kroppen/Rasch (Eds.), Handbuch Internationale Verrechnungspreise, GAufzV, para. 23; *Hüning/Hennemann-Raschke/Kampes*, IWB 2017, 779 (779 et seqq.).

b. The Obligation to Prepare Auxiliary and Ancillary Accounts

For the purpose of treating the PE as a separate and independent enterprise, the documentation and reporting requirements are of particular importance. Key element in this context is the obligation to prepare auxiliary and ancillary accounts for the PE according to Section 3 BsGaV for fiscal years starting after 31 December 2014. Such accounts must be prepared at the beginning of each fiscal year, updated during the fiscal year, and closed at the end of the fiscal year.[1050] According to Section 3(1) sentence 2 BsGaV, the auxiliary and ancillary accounts shall include the result of the PE, meaning the income attributable to the PE under either Section 49(1) no. 2 lit. a ITA in case of a domestic PE or under Section 34d no. 2 lit. a ITA in case of a foreign PE.[1051] In other words, the taxpayer is obliged to prepare a notional tax balance sheet as well as a notional profit and loss account for the PE.[1052] The auxiliary and ancillary accounts must have been prepared by the date of filing the tax return of the enterprise or the domestic PE.[1053]

Furthermore, Section 3(2) BsGaV specifies that the auxiliary and ancillary accounts must include all components that are to be attributed to the PE based on its people functions, namely assets (Sections 5–8 BsGaV), free capital (Sections 12–13 BsGaV), remaining liability items (Section 14 BsGaV), business income and business expenses as well as notional business income and notional business expenses (Sections 16–17 BsGaV).[1054]

The records containing the reasons for the attribution of the components to the PE and the existence of dealings are not part of the obligation to prepare auxiliary and ancillary accounts and must therefore not be prepared by the date of filling the tax return. Rather, according to Section 3(3) BsGaV, such documentation requirements are part of the documentation to be prepared and submitted upon request under Section 90(3) GFC which will be explained in further detail in the following.[1055]

[1050] Cf. Section 3(1) sentence 1 BsGaV.

[1051] Cf. Section 3(1) sentence 2 BsGaV; see also *Andresen*, ITPJ 2015, 77 (79).

[1052] Cf. *Kraft*, in: Kraft (Ed.), AStG—Kommentar, § 1 AStG, para. 728; *Leonhardt/Tcherveniachki*, in: F/W/B/S (Eds.), Außensteuerrecht—Kommentar, § 1 AStG, para. 2989.

[1053] Cf. Section 3(1) sentence 2 et seq. BsGaV.

[1054] Cf. Section 3(3) no. 1 and 2 BsGaV.

[1055] Section 3(3) BsGaV is applicable for the first time to fiscal years starting after 31 Dec. 2016, cf. Section 40 sentence 2 BsGaV.

c. Documentation Requirements in Accordance with Section 90(3) GFC

(1) Local File

(a) Obligation to Submit a Local File

Section 90(3) sentence 1 GFC requires the taxpayer to keep records of the nature and content of their business relations that fall under the definition provided in Section 1(4) ETRA. As outlined above, by referring to Section 1(4) ETRA, the legislator ensures that the documentation requirements do not only apply for transactions between the taxpayer and a related party within the meaning of Section 1(2) ETRA but also for dealings between the enterprise and its PE.[1056]

The corresponding Ordinance substantiating the provision contains a catalogue of country-specific and company-related documentation requirements in Section 4 GAufzV that should be prepared by the taxpayer to the extent it is material to the examination of business relationships within the meaning of Section 90(3) sentence 1–2 GFC.[1057] According to Section 90(3) sentence 2 GFC, the local file shall encompass a) the documentation of facts, and b) the documentation of commensurateness.

Exceptions apply for smaller enterprises and taxpayers which generate other income than income from a surplus income type from its transactions with related parties.[1058] In that case, the parties concerned do not need to provide a local file as long as the already exciting documentation meets the requirements of Section 2(1) GAufzV.[1059] In this regard, Section 6(2) GAufzV determines that an enterprise is considered small if, for the current fiscal year, a) the total remuneration for the delivery of goods and merchandise with related parties does not exceed EUR 6 million,[1060] and b) the total remuneration for business operations other than the delivery of goods and merchandise with related parties does not exceed EUR 600.000.[1061]

(b) Documentation of Facts

With regard to the first obligation, the documentation of facts, Section 1(2) GAufzV clarifies that it is necessary to prepare documentation on the nature,

---

[1056]Cf. *Busch*, in: W/A/D (Eds.), Betriebsstätten-Handbuch, para. 13.112.

[1057]For an overview of the information that shall be included in the local file see table 6 and table 7 in the Annex of this thesis.

[1058]Cf. Section 6(1) GAufzV.

[1059]Cf. Section 6(1) GAufzV.

[1060]Cf. Section 6(2) no. 1 GAufzV.

[1061]Cf. Section 6(2) no. 2 GAufzV.

scope and execution of the transactions as well as on their economic and legal framework. More specifically, the country-specific and company-related documentation of facts shall encompass general information on ownership relationships between the taxpayer and related parties within the meaning of Section 1(2) no. 1 and 2 ETRA and general information on the business and the organisational structure.[1062] Additionally, the documentation shall include a description of the business relationships with related parties, an overview of the nature and scope of these business relationships and an overview of the contracts underlying these business relationships as well as a compilation of the material intangibles that are owned or used by the taxpayer or made available for use by others in the context of its business relationships with related parties.[1063]

Special consideration within the documentation process is given to the functional and risk analysis. Besides information on the functions performed and risks assumed, including any changes therein, information on business strategies adapted, material assets used, contractually agreed terms and conditions and material aspects of the competitive and market situation shall be documented.[1064] Furthermore, a description of the value chain and delineation of the taxpayer's contribution to the value added relative to the value added of the related parties with which business relationships exist shall be included.[1065]

(c) Documentation of Commensurateness

Regarding the second obligation, the documentation of commensurateness, Section 90(3) sentence 2 GFC determines that the taxpayer is obliged to keep records of legal and economic aspects of any arm's length agreement on terms of business, especially transfer prices. It is further determined that additional information on when the transfer prices were set, which transfer pricing method was used and details on which comparability data were used shall be documented by the taxpayer.[1066] Even though the German tax administration prefers to determine transfer prices for business transactions prior to the time when the transaction is carried on (*ex ante* approach), it is at the discretion of the taxpayer to choose

---

[1062] Cf. Section 4(1) no. 1 GAufzV.

[1063] Cf. Section 4(1) no. 2 GAufzV.

[1064] Cf. Section 4(1) no. 3 lit. a GAufzV.

[1065] Cf. Section 4(1) no. 3 lit. b GAufzV.

[1066] Cf. Section 90(3) sentence 2 GFC. See in more detail with regard to the transfer pricing analysis in this regard Section 4(1) no. 4 GAufzV.

when to determine the respective transfer prices.[1067] In this regard, the principle of proportionality applies meaning that it is sufficient if the taxpayer shows the sincere effort to comply with the arm's length principle.[1068] This ultimately implies that an appropriate cost-benefit ratio should be maintained keeping the compliance costs for the taxpayer at a reasonable level.[1069]

(d) Specific Requirements for PEs

Section 3(3) BsGaV, dealing with auxiliary and ancillary accounts for PEs, explicitly determines that the records to be prepared under Section 90(3) GFC must set out the reasons why the components were attributed to the PE. In this context, the term 'components' probably refers to the components of the auxiliary and ancillary accounts within the meaning of Section 3(2) BsGaV, i.e. especially assets, free capital, remaining liability items, business income and business expenses as well as notional business income and business expenses.[1070] Moreover, the reasons for the attribution of the enterprise's business transactions (Section 9 BsGaV), opportunities and risks (Section 10 BsGaV) as well as hedging transactions (Section 11 BsGaV) must be documented.[1071] The documentation must also contain the reasons for the existence of the dealings between the taxpayer's enterprise and its PE.[1072]

Despite the fact that the people function itself is not part of the auxiliary and ancillary accounts, the reasons for the attribution of the respective functions must be documented for the purpose of the documentation requirements under Section 90(3) GFC.[1073]

The required documentation to be prepared by the taxpayer in the PE context for the purpose of the local file complies with the recommendations of the OECD in the PE Report 2010, stating that tax administrations shall 'encourage documentation efforts by taxpayers [...] so as to ensure that dealings are in fact

---

1067 Cf. *Kraft*, in: Kraft (Ed.), AStG—Kommentar, § 1 AStG, para. 817; *Ditz/Bärsch/Engelen*, IStR 2016, 789 (792).

1068 Cf. *Kraft*, in: Kraft (Ed.), AStG—Kommentar, § 1 AStG, para. 818.

1069 Cf. *Kraft*, in: Kraft (Ed.), AStG—Kommentar, § 1 AStG, para. 818; *Eigelshoven/Kratzer*, IStR 2004, 30 (32).

1070 Cf. *Kraft*, in: Kraft (Ed.), AStG—Kommentar, § 1 AStG, para. 728; *Leonhardt/Tcherveniachki*, in: F/W/B/S (Eds.), Außensteuerrecht—Kommentar, § 1 AStG, para. 2991.

1071 Cf. Section 3(3) no. 1 BsGaV.

1072 Cf. Section 3(3) no. 2 BsGaV.

1073 Cf. *Leonhardt/Tcherveniachki*, in: F/W/B/S (Eds.), Außensteuerrecht—Kommentar, § 1 AStG, para. 2991.

adequately documented for purposes of their recognition, and also that the arm's length nature of the profit determinations relating to those dealings is adequately documented'[1074]. The required documentation is also in line with the recommendations of the OECD with regard to the information to be included in the local file.

(2) Master File

(a) Obligation to Submit a Master File

The modified Section 90(3) GFC introduces the obligation for the taxpayer to prepare a so-called 'Stammdokumentation', which is equivalent to the master file concept established by the OECD. More specifically, Section 90(3) sentence 3 GFC determines that enterprises which form part of an MNE group are subject to the submission of an overview of the type of business activities conducted and the transfer pricing methods used by the group. An exemption only applies for enterprises with revenue in the previous year which totalled less than EUR 100 million.[1075] In this regard, an MNE group is any group comprised of two or more enterprises that are related within the meaning of Section 1(2) ETRA and that are resident in different countries, or any group comprised of two or more enterprises with at least one PE in another country.[1076] By linking the obligation to submit a master file to the revenue of the previous year, the legislator provides certainty for the taxpayer with regard to the question of whether or not a master file must be prepared.

(b) Required Information

The master file aims at providing a high-level overview of an MNE group business as a whole. Consequently, the information prepared by the taxpayer shall provide a blueprint of the entire MNE group. In this regard, Section 5 GAufzV and the corresponding Annex to Section 5 GAufzV substantiate the taxpayer's obligation under Section 90(3) sentence 3 and 4 GFC. More specifically, the Annex to Section 5 GAufzV provides for the scope of the master file by enumerating 18 elements that shall be contained in the master file.[1077] In this regard, the information required is in line with the recommendations of BEPS Action 13 as implemented

---

[1074] OECD, PE Report 2010, Part I, para 226.

[1075] Cf. Section 90(3) sentence 3 GFC.

[1076] Cf. Section 90(3) sentence 4 GFC.

[1077] For an overview of the information that shall be included in the master file see table 8 and table 9 in the Annex of this thesis.

in the TP Guidelines 2017.[1078] Besides information on the group's organisational structure,[1079] a description of the business and a brief functional analysis,[1080] the group's intangibles,[1081] and the group's intercompany financial activities[1082], the German tax administration also requires information on the group's financial and tax position.[1083] Especially, information on the group's organisational structure and its main business activities as well as information on the group's transfer pricing policy related to intangibles and intra-group financial transactions are of increased importance and a key focus in tax audits.[1084] According to Section 5(2) GAufzV, the taxpayer should use prudent business judgement for the preparation of the master file, keeping in mind to achieve the purpose of the master file with proportionate effort. Consequently, the level of detail of the information provided in the master file shall not be too high. Otherwise it would run counter to the objective of providing a high-level overview of the MNE group's business as a whole.

(3) Submission Requirements and Penalties

In contrast to the recommendations of the OECD proposing to finalise the local file by the time the tax return is filed for the fiscal year in question and to review the master file and, if necessary, to update the documentation no later than the tax return due date for the Ultimate Parent Entity of the MNE group,[1085] the German legislator follows a different approach. Accordingly, German tax authorities should require the submission of documents only for the purpose of conducting an external audit.[1086] In this regard, the request of the tax authorities shall specify the business segments and business relationships that form the intended subject of the tax audit.[1087]

[1078] See in more detail for the required information for the master file OECD, TP Guidelines 2017, paras. 5.18 et seqq. in conjunction with Annex I to chapter V of the TP Guidelines 2017. See in more detail chapter D.I.5.b.(1) of this thesis.

[1079] Cf. Annex to Section 5 GAufzV, no. 1.

[1080] Cf. Annex to Section 5 GAufzV, nos. 2–7.

[1081] Cf. Annex to Section 5 GAufzV, nos. 8–13.

[1082] Cf. Annex to Section 5 GAufzV, nos. 14–16.

[1083] Cf. Annex to Section 5 GAufzV, nos. 17–18.

[1084] Cf. *Busch*, in: W/A/D (Eds.), Betriebsstätten-Handbuch, para. 13.155.

[1085] Cf. OECD, TP Guidelines 2017, para. 5.30.

[1086] Cf. Section 90(3) sentence 5 GFC.

[1087] Cf. Section 2(6) GAufzV.

While the submission of the documentation shall be made upon request within a period of 60 days,[1088] records of exceptional business transactions within the meaning of Section 3(2) GAufzV shall be compiled as soon as possible and submitted within a period of 30 days upon request.[1089] Considering the recommendations of the OECD and the fact that many countries require documentation to be finalised by the time the tax return is filed,[1090] the submission requirements in German national law can be regarded as quite moderate.[1091] The documentation shall generally be prepared in German language.[1092] At the taxpayers' request, the tax authorities may permit exceptions.[1093]

The documentation and reporting requirements set out in Section 90(3) GFC as amended by the Mutual Administrative Cooperation Directive Implementation Act[1094] as well as the new GAufzV as of 12 July 2017 are applicable for fiscal years starting after 31 December 2016.[1095]

If the taxpayer breaches his obligations to cooperate under Section 90(3) GFC, Section 162 GFC provides for corresponding penalties. In cases where the taxpayer fails to submit records of a business transaction, the submitted information are essentially of no use, or the documentation of an exceptional business transaction were not compiled in a timely manner, it is rebuttably presumed that the taxable income of the taxpayer is higher than the income declared.[1096] In such cases the tax authorities can conduct an estimate.[1097] By doing so, tax authorities may unfavourably limit the range, e.g. on the basis of a price band, to the detriment of the taxpayer.[1098]

1088 Cf. Section 90(3) sentence 7 GFC.

1089 Cf. Section 90(3) sentence 8 GFC. In this regard, records are still regarded as promptly prepared if they are prepared within a period of six months following the end of the fiscal year in which the transaction has occurred, cf. Section 3(1) sentence 2 GAufzV.

1090 Cf. OECD, TP Guidelines 2017, para. 5.29.

1091 Cf. also *Wilmanns*, in: Oestreicher (Ed.), BEPS konkret und weitere Entwicklungen im deutschen Steuerrecht, 7 (13).

1092 Cf. Section 2(5) sentence 1 GAufzV.

1093 Cf. Section 2(5) sentence 2 GAufzV.

1094 Mutual Administrative Cooperation Directive Implementation Act, 20 Dec. 2016, BGBl. I 2016, 3000.

1095 With regard to the applicability of Section 90(3) GFC see Article 97 Section 22(1) sentence 4 EGAO. With regard to the applicability of the provisions of the GAufzV see Section 7 GAufzV.

1096 Cf. Section 162(3) sentence 1 GFC.

1097 Cf. Section 162(3) sentence 2 GFC.

1098 Cf. Section 162(3) sentence 2 GFC.

Additionally, Section 162(4) GFC determines that tax authorities shall impose a penalty if the taxpayer does not comply with the documentation requirements under Section 90(3) GFC. In cases where the taxpayer fails to submit records for a business transaction or the submitted records for the business transaction are essentially of no use, a penalty of 5–10% shall be imposed, but at least EUR 5.000, of the additional income that results from the correction under Section 162(3) GFC.[1099] In cases where unusable records are submitted late, the penalty shall be at least EUR 100 for each full day following the expiration of the deadline and shall total up to EUR 1 million.[1100]

As illustrated, the approach taken by Section 162(3) and (4) GFC is based on the documentation of business transactions. It follows that these provisions on penalties can in principle not be used in order to sanction non-compliance with the documentation requirements of the master ˆfile.[1101] This is due to the fact that the master file aims at providing a high-level overview of the MNE group's business as a whole such as the overall transfer pricing policies, the nature of its global business operations and its global allocation of economic activities and income rather than requiring exhaustive listings of individual business transactions.[1102]

d. CbC Reporting

(1) Obligation to Submit a CbC Report

In contrast to the obligation to submit a local and a master file according to Section 90(3) GFC, the third pillar of the three-tiered standardised approach to transfer pricing documentation—the obligation to submit a CbC Report—was not implemented in Section 90(3) GFC. Rather, the German legislator introduced the obligation to file a CbC Report by MNEs in Section 138a GFC. The implementation of the CbC Report under the subchapter dealing with the duties of disclosure appears appropriate since an adjustment of income based purely on the data available in the CbC Report is not possible.[1103] As examined earlier, the CbC Report can rather be regarded as a tool that shall enable tax authorities to effective high-level risk assessment by providing them with aggregated information which relate to the global allocation of income, the corresponding taxes paid

[1099] Cf. Section 162(4) sentence 1 GFC.

[1100] Cf. Section 162(4) sentence 2 GFC.

[1101] Cf. *Kraft*, in: Kraft (Ed.), AStG—Kommentar, § 1 AStG, para. 850.

[1102] Cf. OECD, TP Guidelines 2017, paras. 5.18, 5.20.

[1103] Cf. *Schreiber/Greil*, DB 2017, 10 (13); *Kraft*, in: Kraft (Ed.), AStG—Kommentar, § 1 AStG, para. 870.

and specific indicators of the location of economic activity in each of the jurisdictions where the MNE group operates.[1104] Consequently, the information provided in the CbC Report is not appropriate to propose transfer pricing adjustments.[1105] It is also explicitly emphasised by the OECD and the German legislator that the information provided in the CbC Report shall, in particular, not be used by tax administrations for a global formulary apportionment of income.[1106]

According to Section 138a(1) GFC a domestic enterprise[1107] that prepares or must prepare consolidated financial statements is obliged to submit a CbC Report to the Federal Central Tax Office (hereinafter: FCTO) if

- the consolidated financial statements cover at least one enterprise with effective place of management or registered office in another country or at least one foreign PE; and
- the previous fiscal year's consolidated revenue, as reported in the consolidated financial statements, totals to at least EUR 750 million.

The determined threshold for the consolidated revenue of EUR 750 million aims at capturing only large MNE groups to file a CbC Report and follows the recommendations of the OECD (soft law)[1108] and the requirements of the EU (hard law)[1109].[1110]

The obligation to submit a CbC Report shall not apply if the domestic enterprise is included in the consolidated financial statement of another enterprise,[1111] unless the domestic group company has been obliged by the foreign group parent to submit the CbC Report for the group (so-called surrogate parent entity)[1112] or if the domestic group company is subject to specific cooperation obligations (so-called secondary mechanism).[1113]

[1104] See in more detail for the purpose of the CbC Report chapter D.I.5.b.(3)(a) of this thesis.

[1105] Cf. OECD, TP Guidelines 2017, para. 5.25.

[1106] Cf. OECD, TP Guidelines 2017, para. 5.25; BT-Drs. 18/9536, 37.

[1107] A domestic enterprise is defined as an enterprise with registered office (within the meaning of Section 11 GFC) or effective place of management (within the meaning of Section 10 GFC) in Germany, cf. Section 138a(1) GFC.

[1108] Cf. OECD, TP Guidelines 2017, para. 5.52.

[1109] Cf. European Council, 25 May 2016, Directive 2016/881, Annex III, Section 1 no. 4.

[1110] Cf. *Kraft*, in: Kraft (Ed.), AStG—Kommentar, § 1 AStG, para. 872.

[1111] Cf. Section 138a(1) sentence 2 GFC.

[1112] Cf. Section 138a(3) GFC.

[1113] See in more detail for the specific cooperation obligations Section 138a(4) GFC.

(2) Required Information

According to Section 138a(2) GFC, the CbC Report shall consist of three parts which are further clarified by the Federal Ministry of Finance.[1114] Among others, the administrative principles published on 11 July 2017 contain three tables that are mostly in line with the model templates suggested by the OECD.[1115]

The first part shall contain an overview, broken down by tax jurisdictions, revealing how the business activities of the MNE group are distributed throughout the tax jurisdictions where the enterprises or PEs are engaged.[1116] Based on the consolidated financial statement, the overview shall contain the following information per tax jurisdiction:

a) revenue and other income from business transactions with related parties;
b) revenue and other income from business transactions with unrelated parties;
c) total revenue and other income pursuant to letters a) and b) above;
d) income taxes paid during the financial year;
e) income taxes paid and accrued during the financial year for that financial year;
f) profit (loss) before income taxes;
g) stated capital;[1117]
h) accumulated earnings;
i) number of employees; and
j) tangible assets.[1118]

Part two of the CbC Report shall contain a list of all enterprises and PEs of the MNE group, broken down by tax jurisdictions which are covered by the information reported under part one and the most important business activity(ies) they are engaged in.[1119] In this regard, the administrative principles further clarify that the nature of the business activity(ies) shall be determined. In order to do so, a list of the following potential business activit(ies) is provided:[1120]

[1114] Cf. BMF, 11 July 2017, IV B 5—S 1300/16/10010:002, BStBl. I 2017, 974.

[1115] See for details on the deviations from the OECD approach chapter D.II.5.d.(5) of this thesis. For the three tables published in the German Federal Tax Gazette and their English translation see tables 35–40 in the Annex of this thesis.

[1116] Cf. Section 138a(2) no. 1 GFC.

[1117] See for a critical analysis of the term and possible deviations to the OECD approach chapter D.II.5.d.(5) of this thesis.

[1118] Cf. Section 138a(2) no. 1 lit. a-j GFC.

[1119] Cf. Section 138a(2) no. 2 GFC.

[1120] Cf. BMF, 11 July 2017, IV B 5—S 1300/16/10010:002, BStBl. I 2017, 974, Annex, table 1.

research and development; holding or managing intellectual property; purchasing or procurement; manufacturing or production; sales, marketing or distribution; administrative, management or support services; provision of services to unrelated parties; internal group finance; regulated financial services; insurance; holding shares or Securities of a Participating nature; dormant activities, and other[1121].[1122] To reduce the chance of misinterpretation, the data shall be consistent with the data in the local and master file.[1123]

Pursuant to Section 138a(2) no. 3 GFC, the third part of the CbC Report shall contain any additional information that are considered necessary or that facilitate the understanding of the compulsory information provided in part one and two of the CbC Report. Among others, the additional information may include a short description of the data source used with regard to the stated information, a description of 'other' business activities insofar as such activities are stated in part two of the report, information with regard to the enterprises and PEs covered in the report, explanations on extreme values, e.g. losses that might lead to lower tax payments in the following years as well as explanations on the number of employees or the treatment of partnerships.[1124] In general, it is recommended that all data provided in part one and two that may lead to misinterpretation shall be explained in this part of the CbC Report.

(3) Treatments of PEs in the CbC Report

Pursuant to Section 138a(4) sentence 5 GFC, a domestic PE may also be a Constituent Entity and therefore be obliged to submit a CbC Report to the FCTO under the secondary filing mechanism if the FCTO has not received a CbC Report from the foreign group parent.[1125]

However, it remains unclear whether the data of the PE shall be reported by reference to the tax jurisdiction in which the PE is situated or by reference to the tax jurisdiction of residence. Neither the German legislator nor the German tax administration deal with this issue. Nevertheless, considering that it is not only emphasised in the administrative principles issued by the Federal Ministry of

---

[1121] The nature of 'other' business activities shall be specified in part three where additional information can be provided.

[1122] Cf. BMF, 11 July 2017, IV B 5—S 1300/16/10010:002, BStBl. I 2017, 974, Annex, table 1.

[1123] Cf. *Kraft*, in: Kraft (Ed.), AStG—Kommentar, § 1 AStG, para. 886; *Ditz/Bärsch/Engelen*, IStR 2016, 840 (846); *Busch*, in: W/A/D (Eds.), Betriebsstätten-Handbuch, para. 13.185.

[1124] Cf. *Busch*, in: W/A/D (Eds.), Betriebsstätten-Handbuch, para. 13.186.

[1125] With regard to the legal preconditions for filling obligations of the domestic PE see Section 138a(4) GFC.

Finance[1126] but also in the EU Directive that member states should use the Final Report on BEPS Action 13 as a source of illustration or interpretation in order to ensure consistency of application across member states, the only approach which results in a consistent application is the obligation to report the data for the PE by reference to the tax jurisdiction in which it is situated.[1127] Also the general instructions for filing in the CbC Report of the EU Directive follow the wording of the OECD and emphasises that PE data shall be reported by reference to the tax jurisdiction in which it is situated.[1128] However, both the OECD and the EU Directive clarify that this general reporting requirement shall not apply for data to be provided in the eighth and ninth column of table 1(in Chapter C) of the CbC Report: the stated capital and the accumulated earnings.[1129] Such data shall be reported by the legal entity of which it is a PE.[1130] An exception applies to the stated capital if there is a defined capital requirement in the tax jurisdiction of the PE for regulatory purposes such as in the banking or insurance industry. In that case, the minimum capital as required for regulatory purposes shall be reported by reference to the tax jurisdiction in which the PE is situated.[1131] With regard to the aim to ensure a consistent application of the CbC Report among countries, the taxpayer is advised to follow the approach of the OECD and the EU Directive.[1132]

[1126]The administrative principles contain a link to the website relating to CbC Reporting: http://www.bzst.de/DE/Steuern_International/CbCR/cbcr_node.html.

[1127]Cf. European Council, 25 May 2016, Directive 2016/881, para. 17.

[1128]Cf. European Council, 25 May 2016, Directive 2016/881, Annex III, Section III, chapter B, no. 2.

[1129]Cf. OECD, TP Guidelines 2017, Annex III, B to chapter V, p. 515; European Council, 25 May 2016, Directive 2016/881, Annex III, Section III, chapter C, nos. 1.6 and 1.7.

[1130]Cf. OECD, TP Guidelines 2017, Annex III, B to chapter V, p. 515; European Council, 25 May 2016, Directive 2016/881, Annex III, Section III, chapter C, nos. 1.6 and 1.7.

[1131]Cf. OECD, TP Guidelines 2017, Annex III, B to chapter V, p. 515; European Council, 25 May 2016, Directive 2016/881, Annex III, Section III, chapter C, no. 1.6.

[1132]Also *Busch* and *Grotherr* argue in their explanations that the OECD approach is to be followed, cf. *Busch*, in: W/A/D (Eds.), Betriebsstätten-Handbuch, para. 13.181; *Grotherr*, IStR 2016, 991 (995 et seq.). However, with regard to the stated capital *Grotherr* and *Kraft/Heider* are at the opinion that the stated capital for the PE shall be reported by reference to the tax jurisdiction where the PE is situated, cf. *Grotherr*, IStR 2016, 991 (996); *Kraft/Heider*, DStR 2017, 1353 (1358).

(4) Submission Requirements and Penalties

The filling obligation for the CbC Report applies for fiscal years beginning on or after 1 January 2016, which is in line with the recommendations of the OECD.[1133] Generally, the CbC Report shall be submitted to the FCTO no later than one year after the end of the fiscal year for which the CbC Report is to be produced.[1134] According to Section 138a(6) sentence 3 GFC, the submission shall be made by using 'an officially prescribed data set via remote data transmission'. In this regard, the CbC Report shall be submitted to the FCTO in the XML schema[1135] through the mass data interface (ELMA).[1136]

The received CbC Reports shall then be forwarded by the FCTO to the respective tax authorities.[1137] If the CbC Report contains data of foreign enterprises or PEs, the FCTO shall forward the submitted CbC Reports to the competent authority of the respective contracting state.[1138] The exchange of information is done on the basis of a bilateral or multilateral international agreement. In this context, the legal instrument that covers most of the countries is the 'Multilateral Competent Authority Agreement on the Exchange of Country-by-Country Reports' (hereinafter: CbC MCAA), signed by the FCTO on 27 January 2016. The agreement has already been signed by 89 countries.[1139] Among member states of the EU, the exchange is primarily done on the basis of Article 8aa of the EU Council Directive of 25 May 2016.[1140] Other countries, such as the United States of America prefer bilateral competent authority agreements for the exchange of CbC

1133 Cf. Art. 97 Section 31 sentence 1 EGAO. For the recommendation of the OECD cf. OECD, TP Guidelines 2017, para. 5.50. An exception applies for enterprises that are obliged for secondary filing. In that case, the filling obligation to submit the CbC Report applies for fiscal years commencing on or after 1 Jan. 2017, cf. Art. 97 Section 31 sentence 2 EGAO.

1134 Cf. Section 138a(6) sentence 1 GFC.

1135 For details on the XML schema see OECD, Country-by-Country Reporting XML Schema: User Guide for Tax Administrations.

1136 Cf. BMF, 11 July 2017, IV B 5—S 1300/16/10010:002, BStBl. I 2017, 974, p. 1.

1137 Cf. Section 138a(7) sentence 1 GFC

1138 Cf. Section 138a(7) sentence 2 GFC.

1139 Number of Signatories as of 13 Jan. 2021. For a comprehensive and regularly updated list of the signatories of the Multilateral Competent Authority Agreement on the exchange of CbC Reports (CbC MCAA) and signing dates see: http://www.oecd.org/tax/treaties/beps-mli-signatories-and-parties.pdf.

1140 Cf. European Council, 25 May 2016, Directive 2016/881, para. 17.

Reports.[1141] Furthermore, the exchange can be based on a DTA or a Tax Information Exchange Agreement if the respective agreement contains a legal basis for the exchange of the CbC Report.[1142]

Violations against the reporting requirements of Section 138a GFC are dealt with under the chapter on administrative fines in the GFC. According to Section 379(2) no. 1c GFC, a reporting entity commits an administrative crime if it fails to submit a CbC Report fully or on time in violation of Section 138a(1), (3) or (4) GFC or fails to provide notification fully or on time in violation of Section 138a(4) sentence 3 GFC. Violations may be punished with an administrative fine of up to EUR 10.000.[1143] In the case the violation is considered as a reckless understatement of tax according to Section 378 GFC, the administrative offence may be punished with a monetary fine of up to EUR 50.000. However, considering that the CbC Report is merely a tool that shall enable tax authorities to effective high-level risk assessment, the application of Section 378 GFC is not appropriate for violations against the reporting requirements of Section 138a GFC.[1144]

(5) Comparison to the OECD Approach

While the requirements with regard to the information to be provided for the local and the master file according to Section 90(3) GFC in conjunction with Article 4 and 5 GAufzV are mostly[1145] in line with the recommendations of the OECD outlined in the TP Guidelines,[1146] several deviations can be identified with regard to the requirement on the CbC Report.

[1141] For an overview of the CbC Reporting status of the United States of America see https://www.irs.gov/businesses/country-by-country-reporting-jurisdiction-status-table. See detailed for the exchange of CbC Reports between Germany and the United States of America *Ditz/Heider*, ISR 2018, 399 (399 et seqq.).

[1142] Cf. *Busch*, in: W/A/D (Eds.), Betriebsstätten-Handbuch, para. 13.173.

[1143] Cf. Section 379(4) GFC. In cases of negligence the administrative fine may be up to EUR 5.000 according to Section 377(2) GFC in conjunction with Section 17(2) of the Act on Regulatory Offences.

[1144] Cf. *Kraft*, in: Kraft (Ed.), AStG—Kommentar, § 1 AStG, para. 890.

[1145] For existing deviations see *Mank/Totzek*, IWB 2017, 922 (923 et seq.).

[1146] For the recommendations of the OECD with regard to the master file see OECD, TP Guidelines 2017, chapter V, paras. 5.18 et seqq. in conjunction with Annex I to chapter V, pp. 501 et seqq. For the recommendations of the OECD with regard to the local file see OECD, TP Guidelines 2017, chapter V, paras. 5.22 et seq. in conjunction with Annex II to chapter V, pp. 505 et seqq.

First, Section 138a(2) no. 1 GFC determines that the data provided for the purpose of part 1 of the CbC Report shall be based on the consolidated financial statement of the group. Additionally, it is elaborated in the government's reasoning that aggregated data for all enterprises and PEs which are part of the consolidated financial statement shall be considered for the purpose of the CbC Report.[1147] This wording can be interpreted as meaning that data for business entities which are excluded from the consolidated financial statement of the group solely on size or materiality grounds shall not be separately disclosed in the CbC Report.[1148] However, it is explicitly determined by the OECD that also business units 'excluded from the MNE group's consolidated financial statement solely on size or materiality grounds' shall be considered a Constituent Entity and therefore be separately disclosed for the purpose of completing the CbC Report.[1149]

Even though the simplified approach of the German legislator is in general to be welcomed since the additional knowledge gained from the inclusion of business entities which are excluded from the consolidated financial statement of the MNE group on size or materiality grounds would in most cases not be worth the additional effort of gathering the data, the approach is not in line with the recommendations of the OECD.[1150] Consequently, the requirement of the German legislator seems to be a relief only at first glance since other tax administrations might require information on the excluded business entities subsequently.[1151]

This issue is also outlines in the peer review report of the OECD.[1152] However, in the report it is reasoned that, despite the fact that the reporting requirements at issue do not appear in Section 138a GFC, the German tax administration refers to the definitions contained in the CbC Report.[1153] Consequently, also business units which are excluded from the MNE group's consolidated financial statement solely on size or materiality grounds shall be regarded as a Constituent Entity for

1147 Cf. BT-Drs. 18/9536, 38.

1148 Cf. *Rasch*, in: Kroppen/Rasch (Eds.), Handbuch Internationale Verrechnungspreise, GAufzV, para. 26; *Kraft*, in: Kraft (Ed.), AStG—Kommentar, § 1 AStG, para. 879; *Busch*, in: W/A/D (Eds.), Betriebsstätten-Handbuch, para. 13.170.

1149 Cf. OECD, TP Guidelines 2017, Annex III to chapter V, p. 512.

1150 Cf. *Busch*, in: W/A/D (Eds.), Betriebsstätten-Handbuch, para. 13.180.

1151 Cf. *Busch*, in: W/A/D (Eds.), Betriebsstätten-Handbuch, para. 13.170.

1152 Cf. OECD, BEPS Action 13: CbC Reporting—Compilation of Peer Review Reports (Phase 1), p. 269, paras. 7 et seqq.

1153 Cf. OECD, BEPS Action 13: CbC Reporting—Compilation of Peer Review Reports (Phase 1), p. 269, para. 8; BMF, 11 July 2017, IV B 5—S 1300/16/10010:002, BStBl. I 2017, 974.

the purpose of the CbC Report.[1154] Against this background, it is recommended to follow the approach of the OECD and consider the data of such business units when preparing a CbC Report in Germany.

Another deviation which is connected to the first one refers to the question under what circumstances a PE shall be regarded a Constituent Entity and should therefore be considered in the CbC Report. According to the OECD, a PE should only be disclosed separately in the CbC Report if a separate financial statement for the PE is prepared for either regulatory, tax reporting, financial reporting or internal management control purposes.[1155] Nevertheless, Section 138a(2) no. 2 GFC requires all PEs to be disclosed separately as Constituent Entities as far as data of the PE is considered in table one of the CbC Report. However, in Germany a PE is generally not required to prepare a separate financial statement for the purpose of financial reporting under the accounting standards applicable.[1156] A PE is only treated as a Constituent Entity and should therefore be disclosed separately in the CbC Report if it exceptionally appears for internal management control purposes or for tax reporting as a distinct legal entity.[1157]

A third deviation can be identified with regard to the 'Stated Capital' as required by table one of the model template for the CbC Report of the OECD.[1158] The German version of the TP Guidelines 2017 translates the term with 'ausgewiesenem Kapital'.[1159] Instead of using this translation the German legislator decided to choose the term 'Eigenkapital' in Section 138a(2) lit. g GFC. However, the term 'Eigenkapital' has a broader notion and comprises not only the 'Stated Capital' but also the capital reserves. Since the capital reserves are part of the accumulated earnings which must be stated separately according to Section 138a(2) lit. h GFC, the German approach may lead to misinterpretations.[1160] Such misinterpretations might occur if the CbC Report is submitted to the FCTO in German language and then translated into English for the purpose of the automatic exchange of

[1154] Cf. OECD, BEPS Action 13: CbC Reporting—Compilation of Peer Review Reports (Phase 1), p. 269, para. 8.

[1155] Cf. BEPS Action 13: Country-by-Country Reporting, Annex I to chapter V, p. 31.

[1156] Cf. OECD, BEPS Action 13: CbC Reporting—Compilation of Peer Review Reports (Phase 1), p. 274, note 9.

[1157] Cf. OECD, BEPS Action 13: CbC Reporting—Compilation of Peer Review Reports (Phase 1), p. 274, note 9.

[1158] Cf. OECD, TP Guidelines 2017, chapter V, para. 5.26 in conjunction with Annex III to chapter V, p. 510.

[1159] Cf. OECD, TP Guidelines 2017, chapter V, para. 5.26 in conjunction with Annex III to chapter V (German Version), p. 546.

[1160] Detailed in this regard, *Grotherr*, IStR 2016, 991 (1001).

information. Since the language service of the Federal Ministry of Finance translates the term 'Eigenkapital' with the term 'Stated Capital'[1161] for the translation of the German Tax Code it is likely that the competent authority of the country receiving the CbC Report may not be aware of the broader meaning of the German term 'Eigenkapital'.[1162] In order to reduce the risk of misinterpretation, it is recommended to explain the interpretation of the term 'Eigenkapital' in table three of the CbC Report.

A fourth deviation can be outlined with regard to table two of the CbC Report. In contrast to the OECD approach, the template[1163] issued by the Federal Ministry of Finance does not contain the column asking for the 'Tax Jurisdiction of Organisation or Incorporation if Different from Tax Jurisdictions of Residence'[1164] which might indicate cases of dual residency for tax planning purposes.[1165]

Another difference existed with regard to the local filing obligation implemented in Section 138a(4) GFC which was different from the circumstances contemplated under paragraph 8 (c) iv. of the terms of reference of the OECD.[1166] This deviation was also pointed out in the peer review report of the OECD published on 23 May 2018, recommending that Germany shall 'assess its local filing requirements and its impact in practice, and ensure that they would apply in scenarios that should not differ from paragraph 8 (c) iv. of the terms of reference'[1167]. In this regard, the OECD lists the following examples where the German requirements differ from the terms of reference of the OECD:

[1161] Translation available at: https://www.gesetze-im-internet.de/englisch_ao/englisch_ao.html#p2500.

[1162] *Grotherr* argues that the competent authority of the respective contracting state receiving the CbC Report may add the 'accumulated earnings' and the 'stated capital' in order to receive the sum of the equity (Eigenkapital) of the Constituent Entity which would result in a higher amount for the equity, cf. *Grotherr*, IStR 2016, 991 (1001).

[1163] BMF, 11 July 2017, IV B 5—S 1300/16/10010:002, BStBl. I 2017, 974, Annex, table 1.

[1164] OECD, TP Guidelines 2017, Annex III, A to chapter V, Table 1, p. 511; also table 4 in the Annex of this thesis.

[1165] Cf. *Grotherr*, IStR 2016, 991 (1008).

[1166] For the terms of reference see OECD, BEPS Action 13: CbC Reporting—Compilation of Peer Review Reports (Phase 1), p. 270, para. 13.

[1167] OECD, BEPS Action 13: CbC Reporting—Compilation of Peer Review Reports (Phase 1), pp. 270 et seq., para. 14.

a) 'where the Ultimate Parent Entity of an MNE Group is required to file a CbC Report with the tax authority in its residence jurisdiction, but there is no international agreement between Germany and this jurisdiction'[1168];
b) 'where the Ultimate Parent Entity of an MNE Group is required to file a CbC Report with the tax authority in its residence jurisdiction, but has not complied with this obligation'[1169];
c) 'where the tax authority in the residence jurisdiction of the Ultimate Parent Entity of an MNE Group has failed to exchange the group's CbC Report with Germany, but this falls short of systematic failure.'[1170]

As pointed out in the second Peer Review Report 'Germany has issued internal guidance on this issue and will publish guidance and amend legislation in due course.[1171] This amended legislation was introduced through the 'Act on Further Tax Incentives for Electromobility and on the Amendment of other Tax Provisions' of 12. December 2019 amending, among others, Section 138a(4) GTC.[1172] The minor change[1173] in Section 138a(4) sentence 1 GTC shall be regarded sufficient in order to address the issues pointed out by the OECD. Also, the OECD removed its recommendations on this issue in the second Peer Review Report.[1174]

Besides the outlined deviations, the German implementation of the BEPS Action 13 in German national law follows the recommendations of the OECD and meets all applicable term of reference.[1175]

Table 15 provides an overview of the German and the OECD approach with regard to the documentation requirements.

[1168] OECD, BEPS Action 13: CbC Reporting—Compilation of Peer Review Reports (Phase 1), p. 270, para. 13, example 1.

[1169] OECD, BEPS Action 13: CbC Reporting—Compilation of Peer Review Reports (Phase 1), p. 270, para. 13, example 2.

[1170] OECD, BEPS Action 13: CbC Reporting—Compilation of Peer Review Reports (Phase 1), p. 270, para. 13, example 3.

[1171] OECD, BEPS Action 13: CbC Reporting—Compilation of Peer Review Reports (Phase 2), p. 215, para. 3.

[1172] Act on the Amendment of Tax Provisions, 12 Dec. 2019, BGBl. I 2019, 1451.

[1173] For the change to Section 138a(4) GTC see: https://www.buzer.de/gesetz/1966/al81223-0.htm.

[1174] Cf. OECD, BEPS Action 13: CbC Reporting—Compilation of Peer Review Reports (Phase 2), p. 215, para. 3.

[1175] See also OECD, BEPS Action 13: CbC Reporting—Compilation of Peer Review Reports (Phase 3), p. 173, para. 3

Table 15 Overview of the Documentation Requirements in the PE Context

	OECD	German domestic law
Language	• master and local file: – commonly used languages • CbC Report: – commonly used languages	• auxiliary and ancillary accounts: – German • master and local file: – German; English only upon request • CbC Report: – table I and II: German or English – table III: only English
Submission deadline	• master and local file: – no later than the due date for the filing of the tax return for the fiscal year • CbC Report: – one year after the last day of the reporting fiscal year	• auxiliary and ancillary accounts: – must be prepared by the date of filling the tax return • master and local file: – within 60 days (30 days for extraordinary transactions) upon request of a tax audit • CbC Report: – one year after the last day of the reporting fiscal year
Thresholds	• master and local file: – no specifications • CbC Report: – previous fiscal year's consolidated revenue ≥ EUR 750 million	• auxiliary and ancillary accounts: – no threshold • local file: – remuneration for goods and merchandise ≤ EUR 6 million – other business operations ≤ EUR 600.000 • master file: – previous fiscal year's revenue ≥ EUR 100 million • CbC Report: – previous fiscal year's consolidated revenue ≥ EUR 750 million

(continued)

Table 15 (continued)

	OECD	German domestic law
Treatment of PEs	• master and local file: – dealings between the enterprise and its PE shall be documented • CbC Report: – PE may be regarded as a Constituent Entity – in general, data for the PE shall be reported by reference to the tax jurisdiction in which it is situated – exception: stated capital and accumulated earnings shall be reported by reference to the tax jurisdiction of the head office (counter-exception for stated capital if required for regulatory purposes)	• auxiliary and ancillary accounts: – must comprise all components to be attributed to the PE as well as the result of the PE • master and local file: – documentation requirements apply for PEs subject to limited tax liability in Germany – dealings within the meaning of Section 1(4) sentence 1 no. 2 ETRA between the enterprise and its PE must be documented and the reasons for the attribution of the components to the PE • CbC Report: – PE may be regarded as a Constituent Entity – no further specifications by German legislator and German tax administration

Source: Own illustration.

e. Evaluation of the Documentation Requirements

The analysis of the German documentation and reporting requirements in the transfer pricing context allows for multiple assessments. Firstly, the obligation to prepare auxiliary and ancillary accounts, which must include the result of the PE as required by Section 3 BsGaV, obliges the taxpayer to prepare a notional tax balance sheet as well as a notional profit and loss account for the PE.[1176] However, it is questionable whether a legal basis exists for such an additional obligation in the PE context. Section 1(6) ETRA authorises the Federal Ministry of Finance only to issue an Ordinance in order to stipulate more detailed provisions on the

[1176]Cf. *Kraft*, in: Kraft (Ed.), AStG—Kommentar, § 1 AStG, para. 728; *Leonhardt/Tcherveniachki*, in: F/W/B/S (Eds.), Außensteuerrecht—Kommentar, § 1 AStG, para. 2989.

arm's length principle as described in Section 1(1), (3) and (5) ETRA as well as principles for determining the free capital as described in Section 1(5) sentence 3 no. 4 ETRA. Consequently, the Federal Ministry of Finance is not authorised to oblige the taxpayer to prepare a notional tax balance sheet as well as a notional profit and loss account for the PE.[1177]

Secondly, in order to implement the concept of the local and master file, Section 90(3) GFC, dealing with the obligations of participants to cooperate, was extended along with the replacement of the GAufzV. While most of the requirements with regard to the local file were already incorporated in German national law before the outlined changes to Section 90(3) GFC and the GAufzV were made, the obligation to submit a master file is entirely new.[1178] As outlined in the previous chapter, the new requirements with regard to the local and master file are mostly in line with the recommendations of the OECD outlined in the TP Guidelines 2017.

Thirdly, Section 138a GFC was introduced in German national law implementing the obligation to file a CbC Report.[1179] Besides the outlined deviations from the OECD approach, the German legislation meets all applicable terms of reference as explicitly stated in the Peer Review Reports of the OECD.[1180] However, despite the fact that the German tax authority became an unprecedented amount and detail of information which increases their ability for an effective tax risk assessment, the new requirements impose major compliance costs for most enterprises. The assumption of the German legislator estimating the average compliance costs for the preparation of the CbC Report to EUR 53,60 were already criticised in literature as a loss of reality.[1181]

[1177]Cf. *Kraft*, in: Kraft (Ed.), AStG—Kommentar, § 1 AStG, para. 728.

[1178]For an overview of the changes see e.g., *Rasch*, in: Kroppen/Rasch (Eds.), Handbuch Internationale Verrechnungspreise, GAufzV, paras. 17 et seq.; *Ditz/Bärsch/Engelen*, IStR 2016, 789 (789 et seqq.).

[1179]For an overview of the documentation and reporting requirements in the transfer pricing context in German national law see *Rasch*, in: Kroppen/Rasch (Eds.), Handbuch Internationale Verrechnungspreise, GAufzV, para. 18.

[1180]Cf. OECD, BEPS Action 13: CbC Reporting—Compilation of Peer Review Reports (Phase 1), p. 270, para. 13; also OECD, BEPS Action 13: CbC Reporting—Compilation of Peer Review Reports (Phase 2), p. 215, para. 2; OECD, BEPS Action 13: CbC Reporting—Compilation of Peer Review Reports (Phase 3), p. 173, para. 3.

[1181]Cf. *Grotherr*, IStR 2016, 991 (1008).

Fourthly, the fact that it is emphasised by both the administrative principles of the Federal Ministry of Finance[1182] and the EU Directive[1183] that the Final Report on BEPS Action 13 shall be used as a source of interpretation in order to ensure a consistent understanding with respect to the terms and requirements of the CbC Report is to be welcomed. Especially for issues where the German legislation lacks specific requirements, e.g. the treatment of PEs in the CbC Report, this approach is helpful. Consequently, it was reasoned that data for the PE shall be reported by reference to the tax jurisdiction in which it is situated. An exception applies for the data of the stated capital and the accumulated earnings, which shall be reported by reference to the tax jurisdiction of the head office.

Whether the new three-tiered standardised approach for transfer pricing documentation implemented in German national law will prove to be a useful tool to standardise transfer pricing documentation requirements on an international level is yet to be seen. In the short term, the new requirements impose challenges and create uncertainty for the taxpayer.

The information that must be prepared by the taxpayer in order to comply with the documentation requirements under national tax law, especially the information that must be prepared for the CbC Report may also prove useful in order to comply with the currently discussed approach on how to address the tax challenges arising from the digitalisation of the economy by Inclusive Framework under Pillar One. In this context, the CbC Report may not only provide a possible infrastructure for filing and exchange of information, but the gross revenue threshold of EUR 750 million could also be used as a threshold in order to determine whether a business is within the scope of the new approach discussed under Pillar One.[1184] Nevertheless, before elaborating this approach in further detail in chapter F and discussing the possible role of the CbC Report in this context the following chapter E will first set the stage for this discussion by providing an overview of the digitalisation of the economy and its implications for the PE concept.

1182 The administrative principles contain a link to the website relating to CbC Reporting: http://www.bzst.de/DE/Steuern_International/CbCR/cbcr_node.html.

1183 Cf. European Council, 25 May 2016, Directive 2016/881, para. 17.

1184 However, as explicitly pointed out by the OECD, the CbC Report shall not be used by tax administrations to propose transfer pricing adjustments based on global formulary apportionment, cf. OECD, TP Guidelines 2017, para. 5.25. Therefore, any approach put forward by the OECD using information provided by the CbC Report in order to derive or determine profits taxable via a formulaic approach would be problematic, see in more detail chapter D.I.5.c of this thesis.

E. Digitalisation of the Economy and Its Implications for the PE Concept

I. Tax Challenges Arising from the Digitalisation of the Economy

1. Preliminary Remarks

The PE threshold, as implemented in both treaty law and German domestic tax law, requires a certain level of physical presence in the source jurisdiction. Therefore, despite the fact that some changes have been made to the PE concept over time in order to address certain changes in business conditions,[1] the fundamental concept is still build on the notion of a 'brick and mortar' economy.[2] As a consequence, a growing stock of literature argues that the current tax rules no longer meet the requirements of today's digitalised world,[3] 'where businesses rely

[1] See for the historical development of the PE concept chapter C.I of this thesis.

[2] Cf. EC, 21 Sep. 2017, COM(2017) 547 final, pp. 2, 6; OECD, BEPS Action 1: Final Report 2015, para. 36.

[3] See most recently, e.g., *Brauner* arguing that '[t]he international tax regime has [...] struggled to adopt to this transformation of the global economy, mainly because it had been designed for a long gone, pure bricks-and-mortar economy, one that has begun to change almost from the very beginning of the regime itself.', *Brauner*, Intertax 2018, 462 (462); *Petruzzi/Buriak*, arguing that '[u]nder the current rules, tax authorities do not appear to have sufficient mechanisms by which to tax the business profits of companies that are derived from the value generated by the digitalization of the economy', *Petruzzi/Buriak*, TNI 90 (2018), 91 (92); *Kemmeren*, arguing that 'the current term permanent establishment is out of date', *Kemmeren*, EC Tax Review 2018, 72 (73); *Kofler/Mayr/Schlager* arguing that '[i]n particular in times of intensifying international tax competition, [...] new business models reveal possible weaknesses in the current international direct tax framework, which was originally designed for "brick and mortar" business', *Kofler/Mayr/Schlager*, ET 2017, 523 (526); *de Wilde*, arguing that '[...]

S. Hentschel, *The Taxation of Permanent Establishments*, Hallesche Schriften zur Betriebswirtschaft 37, https://doi.org/10.1007/978-3-658-34000-1_5

heavily on hard-to-value intangibles, data and automation, which facilitate online trading across borders with no physical presence'[4].

Indeed, digitalisation has induced a structural transformation of the economy, which is having a widespread impact,[5] not only for businesses but also for tax policy makers who need to respond to the changing environment. Several—very different—proposals on how the current international tax law and its underlying principles may be adjusted or reformed in order to adopt to the challenges imposed by the digital economy have been presented by academic scholars[6] and

today's international corporate tax system have long become outdated, and updates to the international tax framework in its current form have not kept pace with the evolution of present-day business models and practices', de *Wilde*, Intertax 2018, 466 (466). Critical in this regard *Schön* who argues that '[t]ax law, like any area of the law, is meant to express long-term value judgements and political agreements that have been transformed into legislative language. These norms show a general character and can be applied to new facts irrespective of changes in the real world, whether these are changes in technology or changes in the way business is done.', *Schön*, BIT 2018, 278 (278).

[4]EC, 21 Sep. 2017, COM(2017) 547 final, p. 2.

[5]Cf. OECD, BEPS Action 1: Interim Report 2018, para. 375.

[6]E.g. suggestions on amending the PE threshold: *Collin/Colin* arguing that the collection of data via regular and systematic monitoring of users in a country should in itself create a taxable presence in that country, cf. *Collin/Colin*, Task Force on Taxation of the Digital Economy, pp. 114 et seqq.; *Hongler/Pistone* suggesting a new PE nexus based on physical presence that consists of four main requirements or elements: (1) digital services, (2) user threshold, (3) a certain time threshold and (4) a *de minimis* revenue threshold, cf. *Hongler/Pistone*, Blueprints for a New PE Nexus, IBFD Working Paper 2015, pp. 22 et seqq. Moreover, suggestions for the development of specific transfer pricing guidelines for the digital economy were made, cf. i.a. *Olbert/Spengel*, WTJ 2017, 3 (33 et seqq.). Also, suggestions for the introduction of a withholding tax for digital transactions were presented, i.a. *Brauner/Báez*, Withholding Taxes in the Service of BEPS Action 1, IBFD Working Paper 2015, pp. 4 et seqq.; *Báez/Brauner*, Taxing the Digital Economy Post BEPS ... Seriously, University of Florida Levin College of Law Research Paper No. 19-16, pp. 7 et seqq. For an overview and evaluation of the different proposal cf. *Pfister*, Die Besteuerung der digitalen Wirtschaft, 178 et seqq. Furthermore, *Förster/Greil/Hilse* propose a 'kind of amount A system' in which consolidated profits are considered as the result of value-creating elements, which are then allocated to the different countries in proportion to their respective contributions to value creation as well as modifications to Amount B and C, see in more detail for the concept *Förster/Greil/Hils,* ITPJ 2020, 3 (12 et seqq.). *Schön* proposes a concept of 'digital investment' that would allow market jurisdictions to claim a larger share of the overall tax revenue. Under this concept, taxing rights are not allocated based on sales, but rather on the invested capital in a particular market for the purpose of accessing a specific

supranational institutions[7]. Nevertheless, there is a general consensus among academic scholars[8] and supranational institutions[9] that the attempt to ring-fence the digital economy from the rest of the economy for tax purposes would not be feasible because of the increasingly pervasive nature of digitalisation. The Final Report on BEPS Action 1 identified a number of emerging technologies, such as the Internet of Things, the sharing economy, digital (crypto-)currencies, 3-D printing, advanced robotics as well as open government data, which are combining in innovative ways, emphasising the increasingly central role of digital technologies.[10]

In order to better grasp the tax challenges raised by the digitalisation of the economy and its implications for the PE concept, this chapter proceeds as follows. First, commonly observed key characteristics of digitalised businesses and its implications for the current PE concept are discussed. Second, common business models deployed by enterprises operating in the digitalised economy are

customer base, see in more detail for the concept *Schön*, BIT 2018, 278 (288 et seqq.). Another approach presented by *Devereux/Auerbach/Keen/Oosterhuis/Schön/Vella* is the 'residual profit allocation by income' approach, in which the right to tax routine profits is allocated to the country where functions and activities take place and the right to tax residual profits to the market country where sales are made to third parties, see in more detail for the concept *Devereux/Auerbach/Keen/Oosterhuis/Schön/Vella*, Residual profit allocation by income, Working Paper 2019.

[7]E.g. the European Union proposed the introduction of a Digital Service Tax at EU level at a rate of 3% on gross revenue from digital services as an interim measure and a long-term approach for taxing revenues derived from a significant digital presence. For the Significant Digital Presence proposal cf. EC, 21 Mar. 2018, COM(2018) 147 final. For the Digital Service Tax proposal see EC, 21 Mar. 2018, COM(2018) 148 final.

[8]Cf. *Olbert/Spengel*, WTJ 2017, 4 (5); *Blum*, BIT 2015, 314 (314); *Spinosa/Chand*, Intertax 2018, 476 (476). Critical *Schön* who argues that the 'plea against "ring-fencing" [of] the digital economy is correct in general terms, one should not overlook that one sometimes has to break down general principles of tax law for specific cases in order to get useful practical outcomes.' Therefore, so *Schön*, 'it can make sense to develop specific rules for the digitalized economy.' Nevertheless, such 'rules should be in line with general assumptions about the scope and structure of the international tax regime and the allocation of taxing rights between countries.', *Schön*, BIT 2018, 278 (281).

[9]Cf. OECD, BEPS Action 1: Final Report 2015, para. 115; OECD, BEPS Action 1: Interim Report 2018, para. 375; OECD, BEPS Action 1 – Public Consultation Document 2019, para. 1; EC, 28 May 2014, Commission Expert Group on Taxation of the Digital Economy – Report, p. 11.

[10]Cf. OECD, BEPS Action 1: Interim Report 2018, para. 9.

classified according to the concept put forward by *Hagiu/Wright*[11]. Third, different concepts of value creation are outlined and specified with regard to its suitability for the identified business models.

2. Common Characteristics of Digitalised Business Models and their Tax Implications

Although the term 'digital economy' has been in use for quite some time, neither the OECD nor the European Commission provide for a definition of the term. A report of the European Commission Expert Group on Taxation of the Digital Economy rather notes that '[d]efining what constitutes the digital economy has proven problematic, because of the ever-changing technologies of the ICT sector and the widespread diffusion of the digital economy within the whole economy'[12]. Nevertheless, key characteristics frequently observed in digitalised business models were identified in the OECD Interim Report on the tax challenges arising from digitalisation (hereinafter: OECD Interim Report 2018)[13]. Accordingly, the following three key characteristics prevalent in digitalised business models, which will be of increasingly significance of an even larger number of businesses as the trend of digitalisation continues, were identified by the OECD: Cross-jurisdictional scale without mass; heavy reliance on intangibles (especially IP); as well as the importance of data, user participation and their synergies with IP.[14]

Since an understanding of these characteristics is important for understanding the challenges imposed by digitalised businesses to the PE concept, the following explanations examine the aforementioned key characteristics and its implications for the existing tax framework in more detail:

- <u>Cross-jurisdictional scale without mass</u>: Digitalisation has created a highly connected and integrated world where businesses can locate different stages of their production process across various jurisdictions and at the same time reach customers around the globe without being physically present in the respective

[11] *Hagiu/Wright*, Management Science 2015, 184 (184 et seqq.); *Hagiu/Wright*, International Journal of Industrial Organization 2015, 162 (162 et seqq.).

[12] EC, 28 May 2014, Commission Expert Group on Taxation of the Digital Economy – Report, p. 11.

[13] Cf. OECD, BEPS Action 1: Interim Report 2018.

[14] Cf. OECD, BEPS Action 1: Interim Report 2018, paras. 33 et seqq., 130 et seqq.

jurisdictions where they carry on business activities.[15] The phenomenon of economic presence without physical presence is not only limited to large enterprises and is not unique to digitalised businesses.[16] Small and medium-sized enterprises operating in more traditional businesses can reach global markets and generate profits in the various countries without any physical presence as well.[17] In other words, digitalisation has increased the pace at which globalisation is possible and allows businesses to achieve local scale without local mass.[18] Since the PE concept is predominantly rooted in physical presence requirements, the phenomenon of cross-jurisdictional scale without mass challenges the ability of the market jurisdiction to tax the corresponding profits that are generated within its borders.[19]

- Heavy reliance on intangibles: Most business models of enterprises operating in the digital economy are characterised by a growing importance and, at the same time, dependence on investments in intangibles (software, algorithms, patents etc.).[20] Such intangibles are key for their business models since they support platforms, websites and many other business functions of the enterprise.[21] Given the fact that certain functions, including decision making capabilities, previously performed by local personnel is now performed cross-border by sophisticated algorithms and software programmes,[22] the market jurisdiction's capability to tax profits derived from the performance of such intangibles is challenged. Even if a nexus is established in the market jurisdiction through a PE (e.g. local warehouse or server performing automated functions), the current mechanism of the AOA results in the situation that the profits derived from the performance of the intangibles are attributed to the jurisdiction where the significant people function relevant for the creation or acquisition of such assets are performed.[23] Since such functions are mainly performed by the head office of the enterprise, an attribution of a substantial

[15] Cf. OECD, BEPS Action 1: Interim Report 2018, paras. 33, 131.

[16] Cf. OECD, BEPS Action 1: Interim Report 2018, para. 134.

[17] Cf. OECD, BEPS Action 1: Interim Report 2018, para. 133.

[18] Cf. OECD, BEPS Action 1: Interim Report 2018, paras. 33, 134.

[19] Cf. *Spinosa/Chand*, Intertax 2018, 476 (479); *Hadzhieva*, Impact of Digitalisation on International Tax Matters, p. 10; OECD, BEPS Action 1: Interim Report 2018, para. 379.

[20] Cf. OECD, BEPS Action 1: Interim Report 2018, paras. 33, 135; *Schön*, BIT 2018, 278 (278).

[21] Cf. OECD, BEPS Action 1: Interim Report 2018, para. 33.

[22] Cf. OECD, BEPS Action 1: Final Report 2015, paras. 253 et seq.

[23] See in more detail chapter D.I.4.b.(2)(b)iii of this thesis.

amount of the profits derived from the performance of the intangibles to jurisdictions other than the one where the head office is located is not possible under the current mechanism of the AOA.

- Data, user participation and their synergies with IP: Typically, the significance of data, user participation, network effects as well as the provision of user-generated content are common characteristics of business models of rather highly digitalised businesses.[24] While data generated from users is valuable for any business, the benefits from data analysis are of particular significance for most highly digitalised enterprises. However, the degree of user participation depends on the core business model of the enterprise and does not necessarily correlate with the degree of digitalisation.[25] While user participation plays a crucial role for certain business models and actually enables businesses to create user generated content and network effects (e.g. social networks) in the first place, other business models such as cloud computing involve only limited user participation.[26] In this regard, the question arises on how jurisdictions may tax value that results from such data, user participation as well as network effects. The existing international tax framework does neither take such factors into account when allocating taxing rights over enterprises' profit nor captures a concept of value creation.[27] Although the dependence on data and user participation varies contingent upon the business model employed by the enterprise, as illustrated in the next chapter, the range of businesses significantly benefiting from data and user participation tends to increase as the digitalisation of the economy intensifies.[28] This circumstance also poses challenges to the existing nexus rules if the enterprise does not have a physical PE or a subsidiary established in the market jurisdiction where the ultimate customer, from whom the enterprise exploits user-generated content and data, resides.[29]

Despite the fact that the members of the Inclusive Framework generally acknowledge the existence of all of the above examined characteristics of digitalised business models, no consensus on their relevance and importance to the identity of the value creator and the location of value creation exists among members.[30]

---

[24] Cf. OECD, BEPS Action 1: Interim Report 2018, paras. 35, 139.

[25] Cf. OECD, BEPS Action 1: Interim Report 2018, para. 35.

[26] Cf. OECD, BEPS Action 1: Interim Report 2018, para. 35.

[27] Cf. *Devereux/Vella*, BTR 2018, 387 (391).

[28] Cf. OECD, BEPS Action 1: Interim Report 2018, para. 386.

[29] Cf. *Schön*, BIT 2018, 278 (278).

[30] Cf. OECD, BEPS Action 1: Interim Report 2018, para. 36.

General agreement exists that even though the increased reliance on intangibles and cross-jurisdictional scale without mass are not unique or exclusive to digitalised businesses, they can be highly relevant for value creation.[31] However, views differ regarding the question of whether and to what extent data and user participation contribute to value creation by the enterprises.[32]

Before investigating the process of value creation in the digital economy in more detail, the following chapter classifies and discusses existing digitalised business models.

3. Classification of Digitalised Business Models

The scale and pace of digitalisation has led to an economic environment where existing business models are rapidly evolving and new and innovative business models are emerging.[33] This situation makes it challenging to classify digitalised business models. Academic scholars[34] and supranational institutions[35] have put forward various approaches on how to classify digitalised business models. However, since the author believes that any solution developed in order to address the tax challenges arising from the digitalisation of the economy can only be resolved at the level of the OECD, the following explanations are based on the classification set out in the OECD Interim Report 2018.

---

[31] Cf. OECD, BEPS Action 1: Interim Report 2018, para. 36.

[32] Cf. OECD, BEPS Action 1: Interim Report 2018, para. 37.

[33] Cf. *Hadzhieva*, Impact of Digitalisation on International Tax Matters, p. 10. For an overview of new business models see OECD, BEPS Action 1: Final Report 2015, paras. 116 et seqq.

[34] See for example *Spinosa/Chand* who identify five broad categories of businesses operating in the digital sphere: a) businesses selling physical products through an online platform, b) businesses selling digitalised products and content through an online platform, c) businesses providing an online marketplace for the sale of goods and services, d) businesses providing online services, and e) businesses providing online solutions, cf. *Spinosa/Chand*, Intertax 2018, 476 (477). Another approach is taken by *Schön* who singled out those companies that have formed an alliance and submitted comments to the OECD's consultation under the name of the 'Digital Economy Group' which comprises ten of the post innovative and powerful Europe-based and US-based internet firms, see for the classification *Schön*, BIT 2018, 278 (281 et seq.).

[35] For the classification approach put forward by the OECD see OECD, BEPS Action 1: Interim Report 2018, para. 58. The EU-Commission put forward a non-exhaustive list in order to highlight new ways of doing business in the digital economy and distinguish between a) the online retailer model, b) the social media model, c) the subscription model, and d) the collaborative platform model, cf. EC, 21 Sep. 2017, COM(2017) 547 final, p. 5.

Based on the work of *Hagiu/Wright*[36], the OECD Interim Report 2018 categorises business models or, differently said, business lines, identified in digital markets.[37] In this context, not entire enterprises are categorised but rather business models (business lines), resulting in the situation that enterprises could be engaged in more than one business model.[38] The following four business models are distinguished by the OECD:

- Multi-sided platforms: Multi-sided platforms essentially provide intermediation services to different groups of end users and therefore play an essential role in bringing together the two sides of the market (e.g. hosts and guests [hotels.com, bookings.com, Airbnb]; drivers and passengers [BlaBlaCar, Uber, Didi Chuxing]; sellers and buyers [Amazon Marketplace, eBay, AliExpress]) and in facilitating exchange.[39] The economic success of such platforms depends on reaching a high number of end-users on either side of the market.[40] It follows that multi-sided platforms are characterised by the presence of indirect network effects, i.e. an increase in end-users on the one side of the market (e.g. hosts, drivers, sellers) increases the utility of end-users on the other side of the market (e.g. guests, passengers, buyers) and vice versa.[41] In this regard, control rights[42] and liabilities[43] towards the customer are left with

[36] *Hagiu/Wright*, Management Science 2015, 184 (184 et seqq.); *Hagiu/Wright*, International Journal of Industrial Organization 2015, 162 (162 et seqq.).

[37] Cf. OECD, BEPS Action 1: Interim Report 2018, para. 58.

[38] Cf. OECD, BEPS Action 1: Interim Report 2018, para. 58.

[39] Cf. *Caillaud/Jullien*, The RAND Journal of Economics 2003, 309 (309 et seq.); *Rosenblat/Stark*, International Journal of Communication 2016, 3758 (3758 et seqq.); OECD, BEPS Action 1: Interim Report 2018, paras. 52, 58.

[40] Cf. OECD, BEPS Action 1: Interim Report 2018, para. 52.

[41] Cf. *Hagiu/Wright*, International Journal of Industrial Organization 2015, 162 (163); OECD, BEPS Action 1: Interim Report 2018, para. 58.

[42] This means that the supplier (business customer) retains control of the input necessary to provide the service, e.g. if an owner of an apartment rents out that apartment through a multi-sided platform to a guest, the owner of that apartment will retain control and ownership of the apartment, cf. OECD, BEPS Action 1: Interim Report 2018, p. 30, note 6.

[43] This means that the supplier (business customer) is responsible for potential damage inflicted to the customers, e.g. the apartment owner is responsible that the apartment remains in habitable condition, cf. OECD, BEPS Action 1: Interim Report 2018, p. 30, note 7.

the supplier in most cases.[44] The OECD distinguishes between e-commerce intermediaries[45] and service intermediaries[46].

- Reseller: The business model of resellers is constructed in a way that they acquire products, including exploitation and commercialisation rights, from certain suppliers and then resell these products to buyers.[47] It follows that resellers only act as intermediaries and do not produce the final good sold.[48] Thereby, resellers not only have the ability to control prices for the products provided but also assume liability towards customers. Businesses acting as a reseller are characterised by three main features: they do not allow end-users to interact on the platform with each other, they do not necessarily require their customer to affiliate to the respective online platform, and they benefit from indirect network effects.[49] The OECD distinguishes between resellers of tangible goods[50] and resellers of intangible goods & digital content[51].

---

[44] Cf. OECD, BEPS Action 1: Interim Report 2018, para. 58.

[45] With regard to e-commerce intermediaries, another distinction is made by the OECD between e-commerce intermediaries for tangible goods (e.g. AliExpress, eBay, Amazon Marketplace and Etsy) and e-commerce intermediaries for intangible goods (e.g. Trivago, Hotels.com, Bookings.com, Kayak, Apple iTunes store and Google Play), cf. OECD, BEPS Action 1: Interim Report 2018, p. 43, figure 2.5.

[46] With regard to service intermediaries another distinction is made by the OECD between service intermediaries for collaborative consumption/sharing economy (e.g. BlaBlaCar, AirBnB, Drivy, Uber, Turo, Didi Chuxing, Ola, Foodora, Deliveroo, Upwork and TaskRabbit), service intermediaries for social networks (e.g. Linkedin, Facebook, Sina Weibo, Twitter, Tencent Weibo, Nice, Kuaishou and Qzone), service intermediaries for online gaming and gambling, service intermediaries for search engines (e.g. Google, Yahoo, Bing, Baidu, NetEase), service intermediaries for Email (e.g. Gmail, Hotmail, Yahoo, NetEase), service intermediaries for online content (e.g. YouTube, SoundCloud, Dailymotion, TripAdvisor reviews and Vimeo) and service intermediaries for e-payments (e.g. PayPal, Alipay, TransferWise and Worldpay), cf. OECD, BEPS Action 1: Interim Report 2018, p. 43, figure 2.5.

[47] Cf. OECD, BEPS Action 1: Interim Report 2018, para. 58.

[48] Cf. *Hagiu/Wright*, International Journal of Industrial Organization 2015, 162 (170); OECD, BEPS Action 1: Interim Report 2018, para. 58, figure 2.1.

[49] Cf. OECD, BEPS Action 1: Interim Report 2018, para. 58; *Hagiu/Wright*, Management Science 2015, 184 (184 et seqq.).

[50] The following enterprises can be regarded as examples for resellers of intangible goods: Amazon retail, Alibaba, Tencent, Walmart, JD.com, cf. OECD, BEPS Action 1: Interim Report 2018, p. 43, figure 2.5.

[51] With regard to resellers of tangible goods and digital content another distinction can be made between resellers of creative content (e.g. Spotify, Netflix, Tencent's music distribution business line, Amazon Audible, Deezer and Sony (films/music)), and resellers of software (e.g. Best-Buy, Amazon), cf. OECD, BEPS Action 1: Interim Report 2018, p. 43, figure 2.5.

- Vertically integrated firms: As the name suggests, vertically integrated firms are characterised by the fact that they acquired certain suppliers and integrate these suppliers within their business.[52] Such businesses do not act as intermediary but rather produce the final product and sell that product directly to the customers.[53] In this regard, price control rights and liabilities towards the customers are left to the vertically integrated firm. While the user affiliation can be regarded as low, vertically integrated firms benefit from indirect network effects.[54] Vertically integrated firms may not only sell manufactured goods such as tangible/intangible goods and digital content but also professional services.[55]
- Input supplier: Input suppliers can be defined as businesses that supply intermediary inputs that are required for the production process of goods or services of another business.[56] In contrast to resellers and multi-sided platforms, input suppliers are not intermediaries and therefore do not interact with the final customer.[57] Rather, they carry on business with other firms which produce the final good.[58] It follows that users are not affiliated with the input supplier and indirect network effects do not exist.[59]

---

[52] Cf. OECD, BEPS Action 1: Interim Report 2018, para. 58.

[53] Cf. *Hagiu/Wright*, International Journal of Industrial Organization 2015, 162 (164); OECD, BEPS Action 1: Interim Report 2018, para. 58.

[54] Cf. *Hagiu/Wright*, International Journal of Industrial Organization 2015, 162 (164, 170); OECD, BEPS Action 1: Interim Report 2018, para. 58.

[55] Examples for vertically integrated firms selling tangible goods are the following: Coca Cola, Unilever, Siemens, GE, BMW, Ikea as well as the hardware business of Apple, Microsoft, Huawei, Sony, Intel, Cisco, IBM, Tsinghua Unigroup and Xiomi. With regard to manufacturers of intangible goods and digital content another distinction can be made between enterprises creating content such as Disney, Sony and Netflix and enterprises selling standard software packages such as Adobe, SAP, Dropbox, Google Drive, Weiyun or Microsoft. Vertically integrated firms selling professional services can be distinguished into firms involved in Internet of Things (IoT) consulting (such as GE and Siemens) and firms involved in data analysis, cf. OECD, BEPS Action 1: Interim Report 2018, p. 43, figure 2.5.

[56] Cf. OECD, BEPS Action 1: Interim Report 2018, para. 58. Companies that create goods for sale to resellers are, e.g., Intel or Tsinghua Unigroup. However, also computing power may be supplied to other businesses such as Infrastructure as a service (e.g. Alibaba, Microsoft, AWS, Huawei, Intel or Cisco) and product as a service (e.g. Alibaba, AWS, IBM, Microsoft or SAP), cf. OECD, BEPS Action 1: Interim Report 2018, p. 43, figure 2.5.

[57] Cf. OECD, BEPS Action 1: Interim Report 2018, para. 58.

[58] Cf. OECD, BEPS Action 1: Interim Report 2018, para. 58.

[59] Cf. OECD, BEPS Action 1: Interim Report 2018, para. 58, figure 2.1.

While vertically-integrated firms and resellers have already been employed as typical organisational structures far before the digitalisation of the economy started, the emergence of multi-sided platforms and input suppliers can be regarded as business models that are essentially based on digitalisation.[60] Figure 1 provides an overview of the four broad business models which can currently be identified in digital markets. Nevertheless, while this classification captures the current business models deployed by enterprises operating in the digital economy, new technologies are likely to encourage the emergence of new and even more innovative business models which may currently not even be foreseeable.

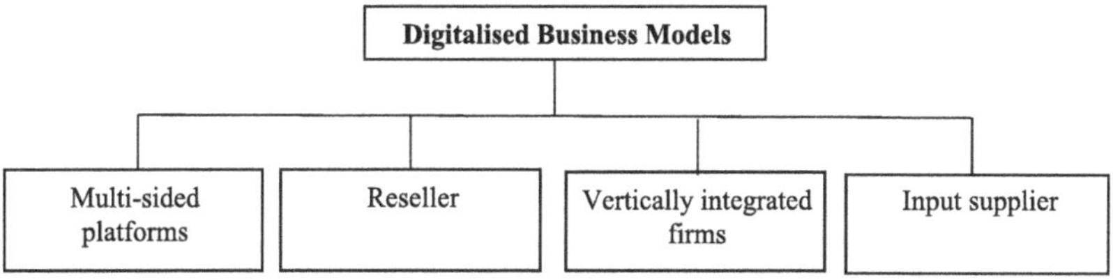

Figure 1 Classification of Digitalised Business Models (Source: Own illustration)

4. Value Creation in the Digital Economy

Since the inception of the BEPS project, the concept of value creation has emerged as a politically significant benchmark.[61] The core of all of the OECD's anti-BEPS Action points rally around the intention to 'ensure that profits are taxed where economic activities take place and value is created'[62]. Screening the scholarly publications on this issue, it was rightly pointed out that, despite the fact that the OECD introduced the concept of value creation as the central point of

[60] Cf. OECD, BEPS Action 1: Interim Report 2018, para. 60.

[61] Cf. *Schön*, BIT 2018, 278 (280). Cf. also *Hey*, arguing that the concept of value creation has emerged as a political idea, *Hey*, BIT 2018, 203 (205). Moreover, the European Commission claims that 'the international tax framework needs to be reformed so that it effectively captures the value created from new business models', EC, 21 Sep. 2017, COM(2017) 547 final, p. 3.

[62] Cf. OECD, BEPS Project – Explanatory Statement, para. 1.

reference to justify the allocation of taxing rights, the concept has not been clarified within the course of the OECD/G20 BEPS initiative.[63] This shortcoming was tackled in the OECD Interim Report 2018. The explanations provided can be regarded as useful in order to analyse the different business models and their source of value creation.[64]

In general, the OECD discusses three concepts or tools that can be used to understand and analyse the process of value creation relevant in the context of digitalisation: the value chain, the value network and the value shop.[65] The first concept, developed by *Michael Porter*[66], aims at understanding how superior value is created for a firm by dividing an enterprise into discrete business activities.[67] This concept can be regarded as suitable for the identification of value creation, where such value is generated by an enterprise through converting particular input factors into specific outputs by performing discrete and related sequential activities.[68] With reference to the business models outlined above, the value chain may prove suitable for the following business models:[69]

- Vertically-integrated manufacturing firms operating linear production processes which produce either tangible goods (e.g. Siemens, BMW, Coca Cola), or intangible goods and services such as software, movies or games (e.g. Microsoft, Disney, Sony);

---

[63]Cf. *Hey*, BIT 2018, 203 (203). See also *Olbert/Spengel* who criticise that the OECD Report on BEPS Action 1 'does not give any definition or interpretation of value creation', *Olbert/Spengel*, WTJ 2017, 3 (9); similar *Schön*, BIT 2018, 278 (280).

[64]For the analysis of the OECD on the three concepts of value creation see OECD, BEPS Action 1: Interim Report 2018, paras. 66 et seqq. While the benchmark of value creation seemed to be the central benchmark for all of the BEPS Action points, the current work under Pillar One aiming to address the tax challenges arising from the digitalisation of the economy does not put much emphasis on the concept of value creation anymore, cf. for a detailed analysis in this context *Hentschel/Hörnicke/Kraft*, Ubg 2019, 673 (673 et seqq.).

[65]Cf. OECD, BEPS Action 1: Interim Report 2018, paras. 66 et seqq.

[66]Cf. *Porter*, Competitive Advantage: Creating and Sustaining Superior Performance.

[67]In this regard, two categories of activities are distinguished: Primary activities (inbound logistics, operations, outbound logistics, marketing & sales and service) and support activities (infrastructure, human resource management, technology development and procurement), cf. *Porter*, Competitive Advantage: Creating and Sustaining Superior Performance, 36 et seqq.

[68]Cf. OECD, BEPS Action 1: Interim Report 2018, para. 74.

[69]Cf. OECD, BEPS Action 1: Interim Report 2018, para. 79. With regard to the limited applicability to services see in more detail *Stabell/Fjeldstad,* SMJ 1998, 413 (413 et seqq.). With regard to the limited ability to value created from information flows see *Rayport/Sviokla*, HBR 1995, 75 (75 et seqq.).

- Resellers operating websites for the sale of either tangible goods (e.g. Alibaba, Walmart, Amazon retail) or intangible goods & digital content (e.g. Netflix [purchased content], Spotify);
- Input suppliers (e.g. Intel) or companies that have developed apps for the sale through app stores.

Even though the concept has been broadly used, not only by academia but also by real-life business, Porter's value chain has been criticised due to its limited applicability to services, to firms that operate on a global basis and its limited ability to integrate value that is created from information flows.[70] Since all of these criticised elements are highly relevant in the context of digitalisation, the application of the value chain as a one-size-fits-all approach for the examination of value creation is not suitable.[71] Therefore, the OECD discusses two alternative tools to broaden the concept of value creation: the value network and the value shop, first introduced by *Stabell/Fjeldstad*.[72]

In a value network, value is created through direct linking (e.g. where users are brought together through a social network) or indirect linking (e.g. in a common pool of funds where customers are not linked directly to each other, but a group of customers is linked).[73] Put differently, in a value network, value is created through the facilitation and organisation of exchange between users.[74] Primary activities that comprise a value network are network promotion and contract management, service provisioning and network infrastructure operations.[75] Revenue may be generated through pay-as-you-go fees (e.g. BlaBla car, Airbnb), subscription fees (e.g. LinkedIn Premium) or targeted advertising (e.g. Facebook, Instagram, Google, Twitter).[76] The aforementioned examples already indicate that with reference to the business models outlined above, the value network approach may prove suitable for the determination of value creation for multi-sided platforms, such as social networks (e.g. Facebook, Twitter), collaborative consumption forms (e.g.

[70] Cf. OECD, BEPS Action 1: Interim Report 2018, para. 67; *Spinosa/Chand*, Intertax 2018, 476 (478, note 23); *Stabell/Fjeldstad,* SMJ 1998, 413 (413 et seqq.); *Rayport/Sviokla*, HBR 1995, 75 (75 et seqq.).

[71] Cf. OECD, BEPS Action 1: Interim Report 2018, para. 80.

[72] Cf. *Stabell/Fjeldstad,* SMJ 1998, 413 (413 et seqq.).

[73] Cf. *Stabell/Fjeldstad,* SMJ 1998, 413 (427).

[74] Cf. OECD, BEPS Action 1: Interim Report 2018, para. 83.

[75] Cf. *Stabell/Fjeldstad,* SMJ 1998, 413 (429).

[76] Cf. OECD, BEPS Action 1: Interim Report 2018, para. 87.

BlaBla cars, AirBnB) and e-commerce intermediaries (e.g. Amazon Marketplace, Apple's App Store).[77]

The third concept, the value shop, may prove suitable for service business models that operate in single-sided markets where business activities are performed with one specific type of customer (user) and do not depend upon a network relationship.[78] A value shop's objective is to solve a specific customer demand or problem.[79] The process of value creation is characterised by the use of intensive technologies in order to solve unique customer demands with either standardised or highly customised solutions, contingent upon the specific customer demand or problem.[80] The value shop is a cyclical value system with the following primary activities: problem finding and acquisition, problem-solving, choice, execution, and control and evaluation.[81] In this sense, the last step of evaluation can become the problem-finding activity and may trigger a new problem-solving cycle.[82] With reference to the business models outlined above, the value shop may prove suitable for vertically-integrated professional service firms or input suppliers of computing power to other businesses such as cloud computing businesses (e.g. AWS, Alibaba, IBM).[83]

II. BEPS Action Points Affecting Taxation of PE's

1. Preliminary Remarks

The previous chapter illustrated that the way how enterprises carry out business and the process of value creation have fundamentally evolved over time. These changes have put pressure on the PE concept, which was developed almost a century ago, at a time when the factors that contribute to value creation were relatively immobile and dependent upon the intensive use of tangible assets and labour.[84]

---

[77] Cf. OECD, BEPS Action 1: Interim Report 2018, para. 87.

[78] Cf. OECD, BEPS Action 1: Interim Report 2018, para. 89.

[79] Cf. *Stabell/Fjeldstad,* SMJ 1998, 413 (420).

[80] Cf. OECD, BEPS Action 1: Interim Report 2018, para. 92.

[81] Cf. *Stabell/Fjeldstad,* SMJ 1998, 413 (423 et seq.).

[82] Cf. *Stabell/Fjeldstad,* SMJ 1998, 413 (423 et seq.).

[83] Cf. OECD, BEPS Action 1: Interim Report 2018, para. 97.

[84] Cf. OECD, BEPS Action 1: Interim Report 2018, paras. 375, 378.

The primary focus of the existing international tax framework has been to align the allocation of taxing rights with the place where economic activities take place, which includes the property and the people that are employed in that activity.[85] The OECD Interim Report 2018 outlines the significance of both principles: a) the PE threshold as the nexus determining the circumstances in which a non-residence enterprise is considered to carry on the necessary level of economic activity in a jurisdiction to justify taxation in that jurisdiction, and b) the arm's length principle as the internationally accepted principle underlying profit allocation.[86] In this regard, physical presence is a central element of both principles.[87]

Throughout the BEPS Project, both principles were strengthened aiming to realign the location where profits of an enterprise are taxed with the location where real economic activities take place and where value is created.[88] Especially, BEPS Action 7 focusing on the prevention of the artificial avoidance of the PE status and BEPS Actions 8–10 focusing on the alignment of transfer pricing outcomes with value creation, can be regarded as substantial milestones in this context.[89] Nevertheless, as value creation becomes less dependent on actual physical presence of property and people, the effectiveness of the reinforced principles and even the whole conceptual approach is challenged by the digitalisation of the economy.[90] Other BEPS measures that are of importance to capture the challenges imposed by digitalisation include BEPS Action 3[91] on CFC rules, BEPS Action 5[92] on harmful tax practices, and BEPS Action 6[93] on treaty abuse.

Also, new guidelines and implementation mechanisms for the VAT treatment of B2C supplies of various services and intangibles by foreign suppliers operating in e-commerce were agreed under BEPS Action 1 to level the playing field between foreign and domestic suppliers.[94] As noted in the OECDs Progress Report,

[85] Cf. OECD, BEPS Action 1: Interim Report 2018, para. 379.

[86] Cf. OECD, BEPS Action 1: Interim Report 2018, para. 378.

[87] While the PE threshold requires either a 'fixed place of business' or a dependent agent physically present in the source country, the arm's length principle essentially focuses on the functions performed by the people (personnel) and the assets used, cf. OECD, BEPS Action 1: Interim Report 2018, para. 378.

[88] Cf. OECD, BEPS Action 1: Interim Report 2018, para. 379.

[89] Cf. OECD, BEPS Action 1: Interim Report 2018, para. 258.

[90] Cf. also OECD, BEPS Action 1: Interim Report 2018, para. 379.

[91] See in more detail for the measure BEPS Action 3: Final Report 2015.

[92] See in more detail for the measure BEPS Action 5: Final Report 2015.

[93] See in more detail for the measure BEPS Action 6: Final Report 2015.

[94] Cf. OECD, BEPS Action 1: Interim Report 2018, paras. 252, 256. As described in the Interim Report 2018, a majority of G20 and OECD countries have adopted rules for the VAT treatment

over 50 jurisdictions have already adopted rules with regard to the application of VAT to B2C intangibles and services from online sales by foreign vendors.[95] For all participating countries, the revenue raised by the implementation of these measures alone amounts to EUR 10.2 billion.[96]

Furthermore, several new policy alternatives to address broader direct tax challenges raised by the digitalisation of the economy, which depart from the existing international tax framework, were analysed by the Task Force on the Digital Economy (hereinafter: TFDE) in the Final Report on BEPS Action 1, namely a withholding tax on certain types of digital transactions, an equalisation levy, and a new nexus in the form of a significant economic presence.[97] However, none of these three options were recommended as internationally agreed standards for implementation in the domestic laws of the various countries by the OECD in the Final Report on BEPS Action 1.[98] Rather, it is expected by the OECD that certain aspects of the broader direct tax challenges that are raised by the digitalisation of the economy will be mitigated once the other BEPS measures are implemented. Nevertheless, as the fear exists that countries might introduce their own unilateral measures out of disappointment over the lack of an agreed standard for implementation in the domestic laws in order to overcome the challenges raised by the digitalisation of the economy, the OECD concludes that countries may introduce any of the three suggested options as additional safeguards against BEPS, provided that the implemented measures respect existing tax treaty obligations.[99]

---

of B2C suppliers of services and intangibles by foreign suppliers and the corresponding duties of compliance recommended in the Final Report on BEPS Action 1, cf. OECD, BEPS Action 1: Interim Report 2018, para. 256. In Germany, the recommendations were implemented in Section 3a(5) sentence 2 no. 3 of the Value Added Tax Act (hereinafter: VAT Act) and the provision concerning the Mini-One-Stop-Shop was implemented in Section 18(4c), (4d), (4e) and Section 18h of the VAT Act, cf. *Benz/Böhmer*, DB 2018, 1233 (1234). For further clarifications on the modifications of the VAT Guidelines see *Erdbrügger*, DStR 2018, 593 (593 et seqq.).

[95]Cf. OECD, BEPS Progress Report 2019, p. 6.

[96]Cf. OECD, BEPS Progress Report 2019, p. 6.

[97]See in more detail OECD, BEPS Action 1: Final Report 2015, paras. 273 et seqq. Critical *Moreno*, Intertax 2018, 560 (561).

[98]Cf. detailed for the options developed in order to address the broader direct tax challenges of the digital economy OECD, BEPS Action 1: Final Report 2015, paras. 273 et seqq. Cf. detailed for an evaluation of the options developed in order to address the broader direct and indirect tax challenges raised by the digital economy OECD, BEPS Action 1: Final Report 2015, paras. 340 et seqq.

[99]Cf. OECD, BEPS Action 1: Final Report 2015, para. 357. However, it is emphasised by the OECD that adoption of any of the three measures in domestic law requires further calibration

Given the above, this chapter will proceed as follows. In order to evaluate the effectiveness of the BEPS measures in addressing the challenges imposed by digitalisation of the economy, first a brief overview of the different measures is provided. Thereby, the discussion is restricted to the outcomes of BEPS Action 7, BEPS Actions 8–10 and BEPS Action 3 due to its significance for the digital sector.[100] Secondly, based on these findings, the appropriateness of the presented measures on meeting the tax challenges raised by the digital economy is critically evaluated.

2. BEPS Action 7: Prevention of the Avoidance of the PE Status

As outlined in the final report on BEPS Action 1, the TFDE considers the work done with respect to BEPS Action 7 a crucial area of focus for addressing BEPS risks in the digital economy.[101] BEPS Action 7 identified the PE threshold as in need of updating and recommended changes to the definition of the PE implemented in Article 5 OECD MC as to prevent its avoidance through artificial arrangements. More precisely, two crucial areas were cited in the report that are of particular importance in the digital economy, namely the artificial avoidance of the PE status through a) commissionaire arrangements and similar strategies, and b) specific activity exceptions implemented in Article 5(4) OECD MC.[102] As a result of BEPS Action 7, both areas were tackled by the OECD through the amendment of key provisions of Article 5 OECD MC and its corresponding Commentary.

With regard to the first issue, the artificial avoidance of the PE status through commissionaire arrangements and similar strategies, the report on BEPS Action 7 resulted in the change of Article 5(5) OECD MC and Article 5(6) OECD MC

of the different options in order to provide further clarity on the details and some adaptation in order to ensure consistency with already existing international legal commitments, cf. OECD, BEPS Action 1: Final Report 2015, para. 357.

[100]See in more detail for a description of the progress of implementation of the other BEPS Actions not described in this thesis, namely BEPS Action 3, BEPS Action 5 and BEPS Action 6 cf. OECD, BEPS Action 1: Interim Report 2018, paras. 252 et seqq.

[101]Cf. OECD, BEPS Action 1: Final Report 2015, para. 215.

[102]Cf. OECD, BEPS Action 1: Final Report 2015, paras. 216 et seqq. The third amendment suggested by the OECD in the final report on BEPS Action 7 deals with the artificial avoidance of the PE status through the practice of splitting up contracts between closely related enterprises in order to take advantage of the 12-month threshold provided by Article 5(3) OECD MC. However, this strategy applies to construction sites and is therefore not further examined in this context. See in more detail in this regard chapter C.IV.6.a.(2) of this thesis.

and thereby tightened the requirements of the Agent PE.[103] The new approach considers it sufficient that a person acting in a contracting state on behalf of the enterprise plays the principal role leading to the conclusion of contracts which are afterwards routinely concluded without material modifications by the enterprise.[104] With regard to Article 5(6) OECD MC, the modifications result in the situation that the measures of proof for an independent agent were increased substantially.

Where the recommendations of Action 7 are implemented arrangements specifically used by highly digitalised businesses, e.g. the online provision of advertising services where contracts are substantially negotiated in a market jurisdiction through a local subsidiary but then finalised by an automated system managed overseas by the parent company, can no longer be used in order to avoid a dependent Agent PE if the local workforce plays the principal role for the conclusion of these contracts which are then routinely concluded by the parent company without any material modifications.[105]

The second issue, the avoidance of the PE status through the reliance on specific activity exceptions in Article 5(4) OECD MC, was tackled by the OECD through the modification of Article 5(4) OECD MC. Accordingly, the exceptions listed in subparagraphs a) to d) of Article 5(4) OECD MC are only excluded from the PE exemption if they are of a preparatory or auxiliary character. Furthermore, an anti-fragmentation rule was introduced in order to ensure that it will no longer be possible to benefit from the exceptions listed in subparagraphs a) to d) of Article 5(4) OECD MC through the fragmentation of business activities among enterprises that are closely related.[106]

With regard to digitalised business models, the changes result in the situation that activities which have become increasingly significant for companies operating in the digital economy and which are therefore not of a merely preparatory and auxiliary character for these companies can no longer benefit from the exceptions listed in subparagraphs a) to d) of Article 5(4) OECD MC. By way of example, the maintenance of a large and complex warehouse (e.g. used by multi-sided platforms such as Amazon Marketplace or resellers such as Amazon retail) for the delivery of goods to customers purchased on a company's online website can no

---

[103] See in more detail chapter C.IV.6.c.(2) of this thesis.

[104] Cf. Art. 5(5) OECD MC.

[105] Cf. OECD, BEPS Action 1: Final Report 2015, para. 216. See also the 'Additional Guidance on the Attribution of Profits to a Permanent Establishment under BEPS Action 7' published on 22 Mar. 2018, which contains further examples on a commissionaire structure for an online advertising sales structure, the sale of goods and a procurement structure.

[106] Cf. OECD, BEPS Action 1: Final Report 2015, para. 217.

longer be regarded as an activity of merely preparatory and auxiliary character.[107] Rather, such business activities must be regarded as core activities of the aforementioned business models, since they heavily rely on the need for fast delivery and the proximity to customers. It follows that the changes to the PE definition in Article 5(4) OECD MC led to the situation that such warehouses constitute a PE for the online seller.[108] Further guidance with regard to the changes to Article 5(4) OECD MC and its implications for the attribution of profits to these PEs is provided by the report 'Additional Guidance on the Attribution of Profits to a Permanent Establishment under BEPS Action 7' published on 22 March 2018 by the OECD.[109]

As elaborated earlier, the outcomes of BEPS Action 7 are currently being implemented through the MLI and bilateral tax treaty negotiations.[110] While OECD projections indicate a relatively low adoption rate of the changes recommended under BEPS Action 7 through the MLI,[111] these projections do not necessarily reflect the full impact of the outcome of BEPS Action 7. As pointed out by the OECD, this is mainly due to the fact that several digitalised MNEs have started to restructure their international trade structures, e.g. by changing from a remote sales business structure to a commercial sales business structure where the online sales of the MNE with 'in-country' customers are recognised

---

[107] Cf. OECD, BEPS Action 1: Final Report 2015, para. 217.

[108] Cf. OECD, BEPS Action 1: Final Report 2015, para. 217. Germany decided that the changes to the PE definition shall be implemented in their DTAs through the MLI (Article 13: Artificial Avoidance of Permanent Establishment Status through the Specific Activity Exception). In this regard, Article 13 provided for two options of implementation. Since Germany decided to choose Option A, which relativises the list of exceptions in the sense that all activities listed must explicitly be of a preparatory or auxiliary nature, only 15 bilateral tax treaties could be amended by the MLI, cf. OECD, MLI Positions Germany, p. 25. The additional option to implement an anti-fragmentation provision according to Article 13(4) MLI was not chosen by Germany, cf. OECD, MLI Positions Germany, p. 25. See in more detail in this regard chapter C.IV.5.b of this thesis.

[109] Cf. OECD, BEPS Action 7: Additional Guidance 2018.

[110] The relevant Article dealing with the artificial avoidance of the PE status through commissionaire arrangements and similar strategies is Article 12 MLI. Germany decided that only the changes proposed in Article 13 of the MLI dealing with the artificial avoidance of PE status through specific activity exception shall be implemented in their tax treaties. See in more detail for German MLI position chapter C.IV.7.c of this thesis.

[111] As indicated by the OECD, only around 22% of the 1246 bilateral tax agreements covered by the MLI are effected by the revised provision of Article 5(4) OECD MC dealing with specific-activity exemptions and even less (only around 17%) are effected by the revised dependent Agent-PE definition in Article 5(5) OECD MC, cf. OECD, BEPS Action 7: Additional Guidance 2018, para. 272.

within a local entity (i.e. PE or subsidiary).[112] As a result, the local taxpayer of the respective MNE group is no longer characterised as a provider of routine services usually remunerated on a cost plus basis, but instead the income generated from the sales with the 'in-country' customers is recognised at the level of the local PE or subsidiary of the MNE. In most cases, these changes should result in the attribution of a higher share of the MNEs group's income to the market country where the actual customers are located.[113]

3. BEPS Actions 8–10: Aligning Transfer Pricing Outcomes with Value Creation

BEPS Actions 8–10 are expected to tackle BEPS behaviour exacerbated by digitalisation and broader tax challenges of the digitalisation by ensuring that profit allocation is in line with value creation and real economic activity.[114] More specifically, in view of the OECD, the guidance developed is expected to address tax-driven transfer pricing strategies that are of specific relevance for highly digitalised MNEs.[115] Particularly, strategies involving intangibles or their associated rights that were typically transferred to low-tax jurisdictions that may have lacked the people functions to control such intangibles and the associated risk shall be tackled by BEPS Actions 8–10.[116]

The guidance provided by the OECD aims to ensure that legal ownership of intangibles, financing provided and the contractual allocation of risk shall not automatically lead to the entitlement to large parts of the return from the exploitation of intangibles.[117] Rather, the OECD puts more emphasis on territorial presence of people and activities or functions performed by them. Stated differently, if members of an MNE group perform functions, use assets and assume risks with regard to the development, enhancement, maintenance, protection and exploitation (DEMPE functions) of intangibles they must be compensated appropriately by the legal owner of the intangible.[118] Furthermore, contractual allocation of risk shall be determined on a reshaped 'control over risk' approach,

[112]Cf. OECD, BEPS Action 1: Interim Report 2018, para. 309.
[113]Cf. OECD, BEPS Action 1: Interim Report 2018, para. 309.
[114]Cf. OECD, BEPS Action 1: Interim Report 2018, para. 264.
[115]Cf. OECD, BEPS Action 1: Interim Report 2018, para. 277.
[116]Cf. OECD, BEPS Action 1: Interim Report 2018, para. 275.
[117]Cf. BEPS Actions 8–10: Final Report 2015, p. 13
[118]Cf. OECD, TP Guidelines 2017, para. 6.32.

where the contractual allocation of risk is only respected if supported by actual decision-making by people.[119]

Furthermore, BEPS Actions 8–10 led to the implementation of a clear but rather broad definition of the term 'intangibles' in the TP Guidelines aiming to ensure that certain items do not fall outside the scope of the definition and can, as a consequence, not be transferred to other tax jurisdictions without appropriate compensation.[120] Even though no specific elaboration on the definition and detection of intangibles within digital business models is provided, it is clarified that group synergies and market specific characteristics which are of particular relevance for certain digital business models shall not be treated as intangibles and should rather be taken into account within the comparability analysis.[121]

The OECD also acknowledges that MNEs operating in the digital economy tend to employ highly integrated value chains on a global basis making the enforcement of the arm's length principle increasingly difficult.[122] Therefore, enhanced guidance on the application of the TPSM was developed by the OECD which may prove to be of particular relevance if unique intangibles are used in digital business models in the context of global value chains.[123]

As pointed out in the Interim Report 2018, the measures introduced led MNEs to take steps to align their corporate structure with real economic activity, through, e.g., business restructurings or changes to their transfer pricing positions such as the re-evaluation of the location of people functions, risk management and risk assumption.[124] Furthermore, an 'on-shoring' of assets can be observed, i.e. a reallocation of intangibles and risks from low-tax jurisdictions to jurisdictions where real economic activities take place.[125]

---

[119] Cf. OECD, TP Guidelines 2017, para. 1.65.

[120] Cf. OECD, TP Guidelines 2017, para. 6.6. Critical with respect to the width of the definition of the term intangible cf. *Ditz/Pinkernell/Quilitzsch*, IStR 2014, 45 (49); *Olbert/Spengel*, WTJ 2017, 4 (14); *Hey*, BIT 2018, 203 (206). See in more detail for the term intangible chapter D.I.4.b.(2)(b)iii.

[121] Cf. OECD, TP Guidelines 2017, paras. 6.30 et seq., 1.139 et seqq.; *Olbert/Spengel*, WTJ 2017, 4 (14).

[122] Cf. OECD, BEPS Actions 8–10: Final Report 2015, p. 55, also OECD, BEPS Action 1: Final Report 2015, paras. 231 et seq.; *Olbert/Spengel*, WTJ 2017, 4 (14).

[123] Cf. *Olbert/Spengel*, WTJ 2017, 4 (14). For guidance developed with respect to the TPSM cf. OECD, BEPS Action 10: Revised Guidance on TPSM 2018.

[124] Cf. OECD, BEPS Action 1: Interim Report 2018, para. 308.

[125] Cf. OECD, BEPS Action 1: Interim Report 2018, para. 308.

4. BEPS Action 3: Designing Effective CFC Rules

Another OECD Action Point that is of relevance for the taxation of highly digitalised business models is BEPS Action 3. The final report on BEPS Action 3 sets out six building blocks for the design of effective CFC rules.[126] The measures recommended shall prevent MNEs from allocating an extensive amount of income to group members of an MNE (usually characterised by limited personnel and the performance of little business functions) located in low-tax jurisdictions through the allocation of key intangibles which are then used in order to remotely sell digital goods and services by these group members of an MNE via the internet to third-party customers located in other jurisdictions.[127]

Such a structure results in the situation that the income which arises from the remote sale will only be subject to a minimal or no taxation in the low tax jurisdiction in many cases while no tax liability arises in the jurisdiction where the actual customers are located.[128] Furthermore, the payments by the customers are generally not subject to domestic taxation in the ultimate residence country at the level of the ultimate shareholder (so-called parent company) since many jurisdictions do not have a CFC regime at all, or if they have such a regime, it either poorly covers particular categories of passive or highly mobile income (e.g. income generated from third-party customers or from online sales), or can be avoided easily by using hybrid mismatch arrangements.[129]

The recommendations set out in the final report on BEPS Action 3 aim to ensure that income typically earned by many highly digitalised MNEs (e.g. income earned from the remote sale of digital goods and services or income from intangible property) to which only little or no value was added by the CFC, would be subject to tax in the jurisdiction where the ultimate parent entity (hereinafter: UPE) is located.[130] In this respect, BEPS Action 3 recommends that CFC rules should also apply to PEs if their income earned raises BEPS concerns which are not addressed through other measures.[131] More precisely, two recommendations are set out in the final report on BEPS Action 3 tackling the importance of CFC

[126]The following building blocks are set out in the final report on BEPS Action 3: Definition of a CFC, CFC exemptions and threshold requirements, definition of income, computation of income, attribution of income, prevention and elimination of double taxation. See in more detail OECD, BEPS Actions 3: Final Report 2015, pp. 8 et seq.

[127]Cf. OECD, BEPS Action 1: Interim Report 2018, para. 281.

[128]Cf. OECD, BEPS Action 1: Interim Report 2018, para. 282.

[129]Cf. OECD, BEPS Action 1: Interim Report 2018, para. 282.

[130]Cf. OECD, BEPS Action 1: Interim Report 2018, para. 282.

[131]Cf. OECD, BEPS Action 3: Final Report 2015, para. 24.

rules for PEs. First of all, CFC rules should be designed in a way that they are broad enough to potentially be applicable in circumstances where a foreign entity has a PE in another country.[132] Secondly, in situations where income of a PE is exempt in the parent jurisdiction but this income raises the same concerns as income arising in a foreign subsidiary, the parent jurisdiction could address these concerns by applying CFC rules to the PE.[133]

Since the final report on BEPS Action 3 has been published, many countries have already implemented or amended their CFC rules. For example, under the EU Council's Anti-Tax Avoidance Directive (ATAD)[134] the EU member states are required to introduce CFC rules that tackle income earned from a CFC.[135] Similar, the United States have implemented a tax on global intangible low-taxed income (so-called 'GILTI') which is a new feature in its CFC regime ensuring a certain minimum effective corporate tax rate (combined US and foreign). Also, countries like Japan, Columbia or Chile have adopted certain aspects of the recommendations set out in BEPS Action 3.[136]

5. Evaluation of the Effectiveness of the BEPS Actions

Overall, it has become evident that the measures developed by the OECD throughout the course of the BEPS project help to tackle specific BEPS behaviour exacerbated by the digitalisation of the economy and by doing so help to realign profit allocation with real economic activity and value creation. However, none of the aforementioned BEPS measures that are of specific significance in the PE context became minimum standards.[137] Considering the non-binding nature of the OECD recommendations, the implementation process may become like 'cherry picking', where countries implement the measures that work in favour for them

[132] Cf. OECD, BEPS Action 3: Final Report 2015, para. 28.

[133] Cf. OECD, BEPS Action 3: Final Report 2015, para. 28.

[134] European Council, 12 July 2016, Directive 2016/1164.

[135] For a critical review of the provisions of the EU Anti-Tax Avoidance Directive regarding CFC rules cf. *Moser/Hentschel*, Intertax 2017, 606 (623).

[136] While the measures introduced by Japan take the specific recommendations regarding intangible property and income earned from online services and sales into account, the measure introduced by Columbia and Chile were not specifically designed to tackle BEPS risks raised by online sales and services as well as intangibles property, cf. OECD, BEPS Action 1: Interim Report 2018, para. 286.

[137] For an overview of the minimum standards of the BEPS project see OECD, BEPS Project – Explanatory Statement, para. 11.

and disregard the ones that would result in a reduction of the overall tax revenue. While it will certainly take time to evaluate the overall success of the BEPS project, three main observations with respect to its effectiveness in tackling the challenges imposed by the digitalisation of the economy and its implications for the PE concept can already be outlined.

Firstly, as pointed out in the OECD Interim Report 2018, the outcome of the BEPS Actions has led several heavily digitalised MNEs—more or less voluntarily—to restructure their international trade structures so that online sales of MNEs with 'in-country' customers are recognised within a local entity (i.e. PE or subsidiary).[138] This should result in the attribution of a higher share of the MNE group's income to the market jurisdiction where the actual customers are located.[139] However, besides such restructurings—provoked also through public pressure exercised by media and the fear of a poor corporate image related to the use of tax avoidance strategies—the illustrated BEPS Actions do not provide an answer to the question of how to address tax challenges that arise from rather highly digitalised business models, e.g. multi-sided platforms such as service intermediaries like Google or Facebook. These business models significantly benefit from data obtained from its users that reside in various jurisdictions. Nevertheless, in many cases no physical PE or subsidiary is established in the market jurisdiction where the ultimate customer, from whom the enterprise exploits user-generated content and data, resides.[140] Despite the fact that users and data generated from them in the market jurisdictions play an important role for three of the four identified business models, namely multi-sided platforms, resellers and vertically integrated firms, the new concepts introduced through BEPS still solely rely on supply-side factors (i.e. production factors, such as labour, risk and capital) while the role of the market side in destination countries, where such factors are not needed in order to establish a demand side, remains insignificant.[141]

Secondly, while the title of BEPS Action 7 'Preventing the Artificial Avoidance of the Permanent Establishment Status' suggests that only aggressive tax planning strategies shall be tackled, it was illustrated that the scope of BEPS Action 7 actually goes beyond aggressive tax planning strategies mainly carried out by heavily digitalised MNEs.[142] Rather, the measures introduced extend the

---

[138] Cf. OECD, BEPS Action 1: Interim Report 2018, para. 309.

[139] Cf. OECD, BEPS Action 1: Interim Report 2018, para. 309.

[140] Cf. *Schön*, BIT 2018, 278 (278).

[141] Cf. *Dourado*, Intertax 2018, 565 (567); *Hadzhieva*, Impact of Digitalisation on International Tax Matters, p. 32; *Schön*, BIT 2014, 280 (290).

[142] Cf. *Schön*, BIT 2014, 280 (292).

reach of the PE concept in favour of market countries regardless of whether the structure established seeks for any tax abuse.[143] Nevertheless, despite the existence of these 'new' PEs, not much profit can be attributed to these PEs under the current profit attribution rules of the AOA.[144] This finding as well as the fact that the introduction of the new PE rules under BEPS Action 7 will result in an increase of rather smaller PEs ultimately leading to higher compliance costs and an increased possibility for double taxation may be the reason why the OECD projections indicate a relatively low adoption rate of the changes recommended under BEPS Action 7 through the MLI.[145]

Thirdly, the work on BEPS Actions 8–10 resulted in the amendment of the TP Guidelines, which equipped tax administrations with instruments in order to tackle BEPS more effectively. In the PE context, the revised and enhanced guidance developed may prove to be valuable for the identification of intangibles, the attribution of intangibles, risk and capital to the PE and the application of the TPSM that may prove to be of particular relevance in cases where unique intangibles are used in digital business models in the context of global value chains.[146] The new concept which puts more emphasis on the control over risk and the performance of DEMPE functions certainly helps to tackle some aggressive tax planning strategies such as cash boxes mostly used by highly digitalised MNEs. However, the new approach has been criticised in literature, in particular for its unclear and imprecise meaning of the concepts of 'value creation' and 'real economic activity' and its lack of consistency with respect to the traditional application of the arm's length principle.[147] As the new approach puts less emphasis on legal contracts, higher compliance costs and a higher risk of tax disputes are very likely calling for effective dispute resolution mechanisms. Furthermore, it is broad forward that the potential for tax planning is not diminished since one

143 Cf. *Schön*, BIT 2014, 280 (294); similar *Brauner*, WTJ 2014, 10 (28). For an analysis of the changes through BEPS Action 7 to Article 5(4) OECD MC and an evaluation of the modifications with respect to the tax principles of neutrality, efficiency, certainty and simplicity, effectiveness and fairness, flexibility and equity cf. *Pinto*, CTJ 2017, 291 (307 et seq.).

144 Cf. *Benz/Böhmer*, DB 2018, 1233 (1234). See in this context also the case studies in the following Section.

145 Critical with regard to the outcome of Action 7 cf. *Kroppen/Dawid/Keil*, TPI 2019, 98 (100); *Gerlach/Hagemann*, FR 2017, 1035 (1037).

146 Cf. *Olbert/Spengel*, WTJ 2017, 4 (14). For guidance developed with respect to the TPSM cf. OECD, BEPS Action 10: Revised Guidance on TPSM 2018.

147 Cf. *Schön*, BTR 2015, 417 (420); *Schön*, BIT 2014, 280 (288); *Devereux/Vella*, Fiscal Studies 2014, 449 (464); *Olbert/Spengel*, WTJ 2017, 4 (13); *Hey*, BIT 2018, 203 (203).

allocation criterion (contractual allocation of risk) has been replaced by another (performance of people functions), which may also be subject to manipulation, e.g. via reallocation of senior employees.[148]

Summarising, the work carried out by the OECD within the course of the BEPS project helps to tackle specific BEPS behaviour exacerbated by the digitalisation of the economy. However, most of the key challenges posed by highly digitalised companies remain largely unaddressed by the BEPS measures. As value creation becomes less dependent on actual physical presence of property and people, the effectiveness of the reinforced principles and even the whole conceptual approach is challenged by the digitalisation of the economy.[149]

The following case studies illustrate the effectiveness of the discussed BEPS Action points and identify the main challenges for the international tax system.

III. Case Studies Illustrating the Challenges Arising from the Digitalisation of the Economy for the PE Concept

1. Case Study 1: Online Retailer[150]

a. Facts of the Case

AmazCo, a corporation resident in Country X, sells various kinds of physical goods through an online platform in different markets including Germany. In order to respond quickly and flexible to customer requirements, AmazCo decides to carry out the distribution for the European market through very large warehouses that are located in different EU member states. Incoming sales orders from customers that log on to the website of AmazCo are automatically accepted and processed through a server. That server is owned and operated by AmazCo and located within the premises of the head office in Country X. Furthermore, the

[148]Cf. *Majdowski/Bronzewska*, Intertax 2018, 210 (223); *Wittendorff*, TNI 81 (2016), 331 (332); *Hadzhieva*, Impact of Digitalisation on International Tax Matters, p. 31. Critical with respect to the allocation criterion of people function cf. *Jerabek/Kofler/Kroppen/Rasch*, in: Kofler/Schnitger (Eds.), BEPS-Handbuch, Section I, paras. 38 et seqq; *Kroppen*, in: Lüdicke/Schnitger/Spengel (Eds.), Besteuerung Internationaler Unternehmen: Festschrift Endres, 199 (202).

[149]Cf. OECD, BEPS Action 1: Interim Report 2018, para. 379; see also *Fehling/Valta*, in: Kofler/Schnitger (Eds.), BEPS-Handbuch, Section B, para. 49.

[150]The following case study is based on *Kraft/Hentschel/Apler* and was modified for the purpose of this thesis, cf. *Kraft/Hentschel/Apler*, Ubg 2017, 318 (319 et seqq.).

processing of payments and the selection of the appropriate warehouse that ensures delivery of the goods in a timely and reliable manner to the customers are performed automatically through the server.

One of these warehouses operated by AmazCo is located in Germany. This warehouse is staffed with a significant number of employees that handle the receipt of shipment from various suppliers, the stocking of the received goods as well as the execution of deliveries to customers that is carried out by using independent service providers. All other significant business functions, such as the purchasing of goods from unrelated third parties for resale, the performance of the marketing and sales concept for the EU market as well as the performance of key decisions and the management of associated risks with regard to the development and enhancement of the intellectual property, especially the logistic concept used by the warehouses, is carried out by AmazCo.

Figure 2 illustrates the case:

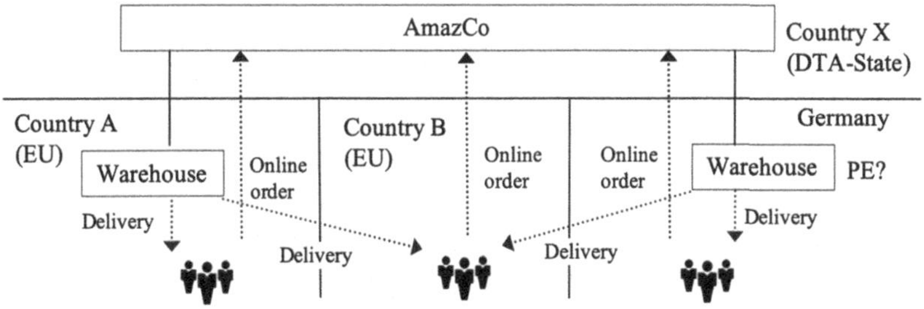

Figure 2 Business Structure of AmazCo (Source: Own illustration)

Assume that in the case under consideration a DTA between Country X and Germany is in place that contains the latest changes to the OECD MC through the BEPS Action points (i.e. DTA based on the OECD MC 2017, hereinafter: DTA Germany-Country X). In this context, the question arises whether the warehouse operated in Germany constitutes a PE for AmazCo in Germany and if so what amount of the profits derived by the online retailer can be taxed in Germany.

b. Nexus in Market Jurisdiction

For the determination of whether Germany may tax a certain amount of the profits derived by the online retailer, a two-step approach must be followed. First, it is to be determined whether AmazCo is liable to taxation in Germany. If that is the case, in a second step, it must be analysed whether the DTA between Germany and Country X allows Germany to tax a certain amount of the profits derived by the online retailer.

Since AmazCo has neither its registered office nor its effective place of management in Germany, AmazCo is not subject to unlimited German corporate tax liability pursuant to Section 1(1) no. 1 CITA. However, according to Section 2 no. 1 CITA, Section 8(1) sentence 1 CITA, Section 49(1) no 2 lit. a ITA in conjunction with Section 12 and 13 GFC, AmazCo is subject to limited German corporate tax liability if AmazCo generates domestic-source income through the operation of a PE or a permanent representative. In the case at hand, the physical goods sold through the online platform of AmazCo to German or other customers in the EU are stored in the warehouse located in Germany until they are delivered to the customers who ordered the product online. According to Section 12 sentence 2 no. 5 GFC, such a warehouse constitutes a PE for AmazCo in Germany. Therefore, as a result of the first step, it can be concluded that AmazCo is subject to limited German tax liability with its income generated through the operation of the warehouse PE in Germany.[151]

However, due to the fact that DTAs establish an independent mechanism aiming to avoid double taxation by restricting tax claims where overlapping claims by the respective treaty states are expected and therefore draw 'boundaries' on domestic taxation,[152] in a second step, it must be determined whether the DTA between Germany and Country X allows Germany to tax a certain amount of the profits of AmazCo through the operation of the warehouse PE in Germany. Since the DTA between Germany and Country X follows the wording of the latest version of the OECD MC, Article 7(1) of the DTA Germany-Country X determines that profits attributable to the warehouse shall be taxable in Germany if AmazCo carries on business in Germany through a PE in Germany. In order to determine whether the warehouse constitutes a PE for AmazCo in Germany, it is not the PE definition according to Section 12 GFC that is decisive but the PE definition pursuant to Article 5 DTA Germany-Country X.

While the warehouse in the case at issue can be regarded as a fixed place of business through which the business of AmazCo is wholly or partly carried on as required by Article 5(1) DTA Germany-Country X,[153] Article 5(4) DTA

[151] Cf. *Kraft/Hentschel/Apler*, Ubg 2017, 318 (320).

[152] Cf. *Kraft*, in: Kraft (Ed.), AstG – Kommentar, § 1 AStG, para. 610.

[153] See in more detail for explanations of the essential characteristics of the PE definition of Article 5(1) OECD MC chapter C.IV.3 of this thesis.

Germany-Country X lists a number of business activities that are treated as exceptions to Article 5(1) DTA Germany-Country X. Among others, Article 5(4) lit. a DTA Germany-Country X determines that the term PE shall be deemed not to include 'the use of facilities solely for the purpose of storage, display or delivery of goods or merchandise belonging to the enterprise'. This provision by itself (as used before the update of the OECD MC 2017) would lead to the result that the described warehouse activities carried on by AmazCo in Germany would not constitute a PE for AmazCo. However, with the update of the OECD MC 2017 the exceptions listed by Article 5(4) lit. a DTA Germany-Country X must explicitly be of a preparatory or auxiliary nature in order to avoid triggering a PE.[154] Nevertheless, the described activities carried out in the warehouse in Germany cannot be regarded as merely preparatory or auxiliary activities. This is mainly due to the fact that storage and delivery activities that are performed through that warehouse constitute an essential part of the business model of AmazCo.[155] Especially, the execution of deliveries to customers in a timely and reliable manner is a core aspect of the business model and can therefore not be regarded as a merely preparatory or auxiliary activity.[156]

It follows that the warehouse operated by AmazCo in Germany constitutes a PE according to Article 5 DTA Germany-Country X. Therefore, the DTA allocates the right to tax the profits derived from the operation of the PE in Germany. This situation raises another question: How to determine the profit, if any, generated by the operation of the PE that are subject to taxation in Germany? This question is discussed in the next chapter.

---

[154] As discussed earlier, none of the DTA concluded between Germany and other States are yet based on the latest version of the OECD MC 2017 as assumed in this case study. However, the MLI aims to streamline the implementation of treaty related BEPS measures by allowing countries to quickly amend their bilateral tax treaty network without the need to implement the respective changes on a treaty-by-treaty basis. Germany decided that only changes proposed in Article 13 (Artificial Avoidance of Permanent Establishment Status through the Specific Activity Exception) of the MLI shall be implemented in their tax treaties. In this context, Germany decided to implement Option A that relativises the list of exceptions in the sense that all activities listed must explicitly be of a preparatory or auxiliary nature. As a consequence, 15 German bilateral tax treaties could be amended by the MLI. For a list of countries see chapter C.IV.7.c of this thesis.

[155] This reasoning is in line with the OECD MC Commentary 2017, cf. OECD MC Commentary 2017, Art. 5, para. 62. See also OECD, BEPS Action 1: Interim Report 2018, para. 271.

[156] For a detailed discussion see *Kraft/Hentschel/Apler*, Ubg 2017, 318 (321 et seq.).

c. Profit Attribution to Market Jurisdiction

In order to determine the profits attributable to the PE of AmazCo in Germany, the two-step approach of the AOA as implemented in Section 1(5) sentence 3 and 4 ETRA in conjunction with the provisions of the BsGaV must be applied.[157] Accordingly, the profits attributable to the warehouse PE of AmazCo are those that the warehouse PE would have derived if it were a separate and independent enterprise that performs the same storage and delivery activities.[158]

Under step one, the function and risk analysis reveals that the warehouse in Germany is in charge of the following functions:

- receipt of shipments from various suppliers,
- stocking of the received goods, and
- execution of deliveries to customers using independent service providers.

According to the facts of the case all other functions, especially the performance of key decisions and the management of associated risks with regard to the:

- processing of payments and country specific customer data analysis,
- development and enhancement of the intellectual property for the logistic concept used by the warehouses (e.g. server software),
- set up of new warehouses and the performance of the marketing and sales concept for the EU market, as well as the
- analysis of specific customer data

are performed by AmazCo in Country X.

It follows that besides certain tangible assets (e.g. the warehouse facility and the machines and instruments inside the warehouse) that are to be attributed to the PE,[159] most of the other assets, especially the intangibles that contribute significantly to the value creation of the enterprise (e.g. the logistic concept that is a major part of the business model), are to be attributed to the head office in Country X since the significant people functions relevant for the development

---

[157] See in more detail for the two-step approach chapter D.I.4.b of this thesis.

[158] A similar case from a treaty perspective is discussed by the OECD in the additional guidance on the attribution of profits to PEs, cf. OECD, BEPS Action 7: Additional Guidance 2018, paras. 11 et seqq.

[159] Cf. Section 5(1) sentence 1 BsGaV in conjunction with Section 5(2) sentence 3 BsGaV.

and enhancement of the intangibles used by the warehouse are performed by the head office.[160]

On the basis of the attributions carried out under Section 1(5) sentence 3 ETRA in conjunction with Section 5–15 BsGaV, the type of business relations between AmazCo and the warehouse PE in Germany must be determined.[161] In the case at hand the dealing that is to be hypothesised between AmazCo and the warehouse PE is the provision of storage and delivery services by the warehouse in Germany to the head office in County X that must be compensated at arm's length in the second step according to Section 1(5) sentence 4 ETRA.

In order to price the storage and delivery services at arm's length a comparability analysis must be carried out aiming to determine the amount that AmazCo would have had to pay to an independent enterprise for the provision of such storage and delivery services.[162] Taking into consideration that, among others, the key decisions and the management of the associated risks with regard to the development and enhancement of the intellectual property for the logistic concept used by the warehouses are carried out by the head office in Country X, the remaining functions carried out by the warehouse in Germany (i.e. receipt of shipments, stocking of received goods, execution of deliveries) can be considered to be routine in nature that only justifies a compensation on a cost-based method such as the cost plus method or the TNMM with costs as profit level indicator.[163]

[160] According to Section 6(1) sentence 1 BsGaV, an intangible (e.g. patent, brand, know-how or goodwill) must be attributed to a particular PE if the intangible was created (1. presumption rule) or acquired (2. presumption rule) by that PE. By way of derogation from the presumption rule of Section 6(1) BsGaV an intangible must be attributed to another part of the enterprise according to Section 6(2) BsGaV if another people function (e.g. the use) performed in that other part of the enterprise is clearly of greater importance than the creation or acquisition. In the case under consideration, another attribution according to Section 6(2) BsGaV does not seem appropriate since the use in the PE in Germany does not have a greater importance than the actual creation of the intangible in the head office in Country X.

[161] Cf. Section 1(5) sentence 4 ETRA.

[162] Cf. also OECD, BEPS Action 7: Additional Guidance 2018, para. 20.

[163] The application of the cost plus method or the TNMM is regarded appropriate for the provision of routine services, cf. OECD, TP Guidelines 2017, para. 2.45 (for cost plus method), para. 2.93 (for TNMM). The application of another transfer pricing method (e.g. the TPSM) that may attribute a higher profit to the market jurisdiction cannot be regarded appropriate for the case at hand. As emphasised in the amended TP Guidelines 2017, the clearest indicator that the TPSM may be appropriate to apply is the existence of unique and valuable contributions by the parties involved in the controlled transaction or in the case at issue, the dealing between the head office and the warehouse, cf. OECD, TP Guidelines 2017, para. 2.116 (as amended through BEPS Action 10 in 2018). Also, other indicators mentioned by the OECD such as the shared assumption of economically significant risks by the parties involved and/or a high level

Consequently, the profits earned by the warehouse PE operated in Germany can be regarded as a compensation for the routine functions carried out and any other costs that incur for running the warehouse.[164]

d. Evaluation

The case study illustrates that even though the revisions to Article 5 OECD MC and its corresponding Commentary through BEPS Action 7 led to a situation in which the warehouse operated by AmazCo in Germany can be regarded as a PE from a treaty perspective, no significant profits can be attributed to this PE. Irrespective of the fact that the warehouse operated by AmazCo is a key element for the overall success of the enterprise and constitutes an important part in the value chain, the mechanism of the AOA results in the situation that Germany as the market jurisdiction may only tax a small portion of the overall profits generated by AmazCo.[165] Also, the changes through BEPS Actions 8–10 to the OECD TP Guidelines that can be applied to a certain extend by analogy in the PE context (e.g. amended guidance regarding intangibles (DEMPE concept) or the application of the profit split method) do not result in a higher amount of profits attributable to the warehouse operated in Germany. While this situation may not be satisfactory for the German market jurisdiction from a tax perspective, other market jurisdictions where no warehouses are established and whose customers are delivered through warehouses established in other jurisdictions (e.g. from the German warehouse) are not even able to tax any of the retailer's profits.

This situation shows that the current international tax rules may lead to unsatisfactory results in the market jurisdictions where the customers reside. Considering the fact that the examined business model of a classical reseller is not a new business model that emerged in the context of digitalisation but is rather a refined form of the traditional mail order with regard to the way how goods are presented, contracts are concluded and payments are made via the use of the internet, it may come as a surprise to see the challenges imposed to the international

---

of integration in the business operation to which the transactions relate are not existent in the case at issue, cf. OECD, TP Guidelines 2017, para. 2.126 (as amended through BEPS Action 10 in 2018). For a case study that would justify the application of the TPSM for warehouse activities (warehouse carries out more significant people functions) cf. *Dutriez*, ITPJ 2018, 185 (194 et seqq.).

[164]Costs that could incur for the warehouse in the case under consideration are, e.g., salaries paid to the employees of the warehouse, expenses for leasing the warehouse to an independent third party, delivery service expenses or costs for the usage of the software.

[165]For a detailed discussion on the profit attribution to a warehouse see *Kraft/Hentschel/Apler*, Ubg 2017, 318 (323 et seq.).

tax system by it.[166] However, while in the case at issue the market jurisdiction (i.e. Germany) may at least tax a certain amount of the profits generated by AmazCo through the PE that is operated in Germany, the following case study illustrates that new business models such as multisided platforms, that emerged through technological development, may obtain substantial value from user data and generate profits with these data without even establishing a taxable nexus in the market/user jurisdiction.

2. Case Study 2: Online Advertiser[167]

a. Facts of the Case

GoogCo, a corporation resident in Country X operates an online search engine and has a global market share of nearly 90% in that business. The search engine that is accessible to users through a website is available in different markets, including Germany. The business model of GoogCo can be clearly identified as a multi-sided platform that provides intermediary services to users of the search engine who obtain 'free' search services on the one side and advertisers who pay a service fee in order for their adds that are linked to particular content to appear among the Internet search results on the other side. To make it more likely that a user finds the website of GoogCo, the enterprise operates in Germany via a local domain name.

In order to provide targeted advertising services, GoogCo developed sophisticated software that allows GoogCo to track and trace users' online activities in order to segment users and ensure that only those advertisements are displayed that fit the specific user's needs. The entire infrastructure (e.g. server hardware, R&D facilities) needed to carry out the service offered by GoogCo as well as the entire R&D activities for the continuous development and enhancement of the software is carried out by GoogCo in Country X.

Besides the actual users of the search service and the advertisers that use the advertising service one more player is involved in the German structure, namely SupportGmbH. SupportGmbH is a local corporation that is 100% owned by GoogCo and established under the legal form of a GmbH. This GmbH has its registered office in Germany, operates independently and merely serves GoogCo to provide support services for the local market. These services are limited

166Cf. *Kofler/Mayr/Schlager*, ET 2017, 523 (526).

167The following case study is based on *Hentschel/Hörnicke/Kraft* and was modified for the purpose of this thesis, cf. *Hentschel/Hörnicke/Kraft*, Ubg 2019, 673 (675 et seqq.).

to marketing and promotion activities. The compensation received by GoogCo for the services provided is fixed and not contingent upon the overall amount of service fees received by the advertisers in Germany. Contracts with the advertisers located in Germany are directly concluded online with GoogCo without any intermediation service provided by SupportGmbH.

Figure 3 illustrates the case:

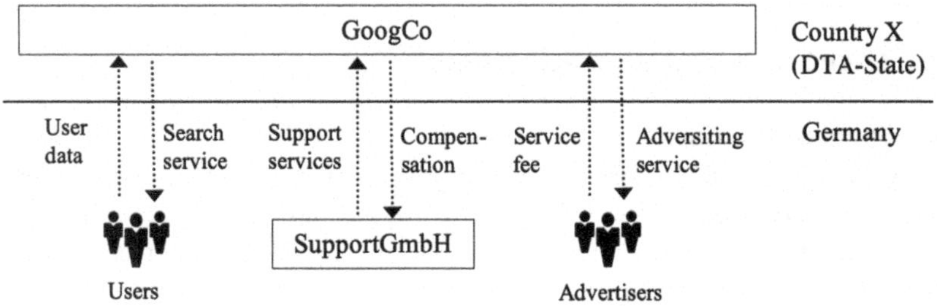

Figure 3 Business Structure of GoogCo (Source: Own illustration)

As in the previous case study, it shall be assumed that a DTA between Country X and Germany is in place that contains the latest changes to the OECD MC through the BEPS Action points (i.e. DTA based on the OECD MC 2017). The following analysis will focus on the question as to whether the activities (i.e. the operation of a multi-sided platform) carried out by GoogCo in Germany constitute a taxable nexus in Germany that would enable Germany to levy taxes on the profits generated from the advertisement activities.

b. Nexus in Market Jurisdiction

In order to determine whether the profits generated by GoogCo through the business activities carried out are subject to taxation in Germany, it must be determined whether GoogCo is liable to German taxation. According to the facts of the case, GoogCo has neither its registered office nor its effective place of management in Germany. Consequently, the corporation is not subject to unlimited German corporate tax liability pursuant to Section 1(1) no. 1 CITA. However, GoogCo as a non-resident corporation may be subject to limited German corporate tax liability pursuant to Section 2 no. 1 CITA, provided that domestic income according to Section 49(1) ITA is earned by GoogCo.

The catalogue of Section 49(1) ITA provides for the following types of domestic income that may be of relevance in the case under consideration:

- income from trade or business for which a domestic PE is maintained or a domestic permanent representative is appointed (Section 49(1) no. 2 lit. a) ITA),
- income from trade or business derived from the rental, lease or sale of interrelated objects[168] or rights that have a domestic nexus (Section 49(1) no. 2 lit. f) sentence 1 ITA), or
- other income derived from the use of tangible movable property in Germany or from the right to use know-how[169] in Germany (Section 49(1) no. 9 ITA).

The first type of domestic income, that is income derived through the operation of a PE within the meaning of Section 12 GFC or a permanent representative within the meaning of Section 13 GFC, was already elaborated in more detail for the purpose of case study 1. In the case at hand, the business model of GoogCo is organised in a way that a PE or a permanent representative is neither required nor actually employed in Germany. Rather, contracts with the advertisers located in Germany are directly concluded online with GoogCo. While the website of GoogCo operated under a local domain does not qualify as a fixed place of business and can therefore not be considered to establish a PE for GoogCo in Germany, the actual server hardware of GoogCo is located in Country X. Consequently, no PE is established for GoogCo in Germany through the operation of the website and the server hardware. Also, the mere existence of a market with users on the one side and advertisers on the other side does not lead to the existence of a PE or a permanent representative in Germany.

Furthermore, the activities carried on by the personnel of SupportGmbH are limited to mere support services such as marketing and promotion activities. The personnel employed by SupportGmbH is neither subject to substantive instructions from GoogCo nor are they involved in the conclusion or the procurement of contracts between GoogCo and the advertisers as required for the existence of a permanent representative within the meaning of Section 13 GFC. Rather, GoogCo's market share of 90% suggests that such intermediary services are not required for the business model established. It follows that GoogCo does not derive any income pursuant to Section 49(1) no. 2 lit. a ITA in Germany.

---

[168] DE: Sachinbegriffe.

[169] In this context, the term 'know-how' shall comprise commercial, technical, scientific, and similar experience, knowledge, and skills, such as plans, models, and processes, cf. Section 49(1) no. 9 ITA. Fundamental with regard to the term 'know-how' see BFH, 16 Dec. 1970, I R 44/67, BStBl. II, 1971, 235. Subsequent rulings provided further guidance on the term, see BFH, 13 Nov. 2002, I R 90/01, BStBl. II, 2003, 249; BFH, 23 Nov. 1988, II R 209/82, BStBl. II, 1989, 82.

Nevertheless, as outlined above, domestic income within the meaning of Section 49(1) ITA may be derived even without the presence of a PE or a permanent representative in Germany. According to Section 49(1) no. 2 lit. f) sentence 1 ITA, income derived from the rental, lease or sale of domestic immovable property, groups of interrelated objects or rights that are situated in the domestic territory or recorded in a domestic public book or register or that are exploited in a domestic PE or another facility constitutes domestic source income for purposes of non-resident income tax liability.[170] However, the rights in the search engine of GoogCo are neither situated in Germany nor recorded in a domestic public book or register[171]. It follows that the income earned by GoogCo in Germany is not covered by Section 49(1) no. 2 lit. f) sentence 1 ITA.[172]

Since the income derived by GoogCo is neither taxable under Section 49(1) no. 2 lit. a) ITA nor under Section 49(1) no. 2 lit. f) sentence 1 ITA, the provision of Section 49(1) no. 9 ITA may be of relevance. This is the case, in particular, if income is derived a) from the use of tangible movable property in Germany, or b) from the right to use know-how in Germany. While income derived from option a) would require the provision of advertising services to qualify as tangible movable property within the meaning of Section 90 of the German Civil Code that is clearly not the case,[173] only option b) deserves a closer look.

According to *Hruschka,* head of the Bavarian tax audit department, advertising revenue derived from a foreign search engine operator must be regarded as a compensation for the provision of the use of processes (algorithms) to the domestic advertiser and therefore constitutes income within the meaning of Section 49(1) no. 9 ITA for the foreign search engine operator.[174] As a consequence, so

---

[170] See in more detail for the requirements of the applicability of Section 49(1) no. 2 lit. f) sentence 1 ITA BMF, 27 Oct. 2017, IV C 5 – S 2300/12/10003:004, BStBl. I 2017, 1448; also *Kraft*, NWB 2018, 868 (870). With specific reference to the surrender of use of software cf. *Kraft*, NWB 2018, 937 (937 et seqq.).

[171] A register in this context could be the patent register, cf. *Kraft*, NWB 2018, 868 (870).

[172] Cf. *Kraft*, NWB 2018, 868 (870 et seq.); *Hruschka*, DStR 2019, 88 (89); *Heil/Pupeter*, BB 2019, 604 (606 et seqq.); *Nürnberg*, Ubg 2019, 219 (220). This conclusion was also confirmed by the German Federal Ministry of Finance, cf. BMF, 3 Apr. 2019, IV C 5 – S 2411/11/10002, BStBl. I 2019, 256. As a consequence, the principles of the German Federal Ministry of Finance cannot be applied in this context, cf. *Hruschka*, DStR 2019, 88 (89).

[173] For detailed reasoning with regard to the non-qualification of databanks and software as tangible movable property see *Kraft*, NWB 2018, 868 (872).

[174] Cf. *Hruschka*, DStR 2019, 88 (89 et seqq.). Even though it is emphasised in the Article that it only reflects the personal opinion of *Hruschka* and was not written in his professional role as head of the Bavarian tax audit department, his view represented the view taken by the Bavarian tax audit department at the time, cf. *Heil/Pupeter*, BB 2019, 604 (604).

Hruschka, the payment debtors (i.e. the advertiser in Germany) are obliged to withhold a tax of 15% plus solidarity surcharge pursuant to Section 50a(1) no. 3 ITA in conjunction with Section 50a(2) ITA at source.[175] While such a procedure would directly affect the earnings and the liquidity of the domestic advertiser,[176] the foreign search engine operator can (if a DTA exists between the two countries that contains an Article consistent to Article 12 OECD MC as it does in the case between Country X and Germany)[177] request a refund of the taxes payed (Section 50d(1) ITA) or an exemption of future tax payments (Section 50d(2) ITA) at the Federal Central Tax Office.[178] Nevertheless, as pointed out by *Hildebrandt*, the foreign platform operators would in many cases not even have an interest in requesting such an exemption certificate since the general business terms and conditions of most advertising contracts usually provide for a compensation based on a net payment ultimately leading to the situation that the domestic advertiser would bear the tax burden.[179]

The position expressed by *Hruschka* and practised by the Bavarian tax audit department was rightly criticised by the prevailing view in literature.[180] However, a circular issued by the Federal Ministry of Finance clarifies that compensations received by foreign platform operators and internet service providers for the placement or intermediation of online advertisement on websites are not subject to

---

[175]Cf. *Hruschka*, DStR 2019, 88 (89 et seqq.).

[176]The tax to be withhold at source constitutes marketing expenses for the domestic advertiser using the services of the foreign search engine operator. As such they decrease the EBITDA of the domestic advertiser that directly affect its distribution capability and its business valuation, cf. *Hildebrandt*, NWB 2019, 625 (625).

[177]Pursuant to Article 12(1) OECD MC, 'Royalties arising in a Contracting State and beneficially owned by a resident of the other Contracting State shall be taxable only in that other State'. However, according to Section 50d(1) ITA, the restriction of the German right to tax at source according to Article 12(1) OECD MC does not apply directly but is contingent upon the verification (prior to the payment) that the taxpayer subject to limited tax liability is entitled to the benefits granted by the DTA. The eligibility must be verified at the Federal Central Tax Office. See in more detail *Kraft*, NWB 2018, 868 (873). In the non-DTA case, no refund of the taxes payed or exemptions for future tax payments is possible, cf. *Kraft*, NWB 2018, 868 (873).

[178]Nevertheless, this would only be the case if the requirements of Section 50d(3) ITA are met. For an analysis of Section 50d(3) ITA and its compatibility with European Union law cf. *Kraft*, NWB 2018, 868 (874); also *Haase*, DStR 2019, 761 (765 et seq.).

[179]Cf. *Hildebrandt*, NWB 2019, 625 (625).

[180]Cf. *Heil/Pupeter*, BB 2019, 604 (605 et seqq.); *Reichl/Wiedmann*, FR 2019, 201 (204 et seqq.); *Haase*, DStR 2019, 761 (761 et seqq.); *Hildebrandt*, NWB 2019, 625 (625); *Diffring/Saft*, DB 2019, 387 (387 et seqq.); *Nürnberg*, Ubg 2019, 219 (219 et seqq.); *Linn*, DStR 2019, 418 (418 et seqq.).

withholding tax pursuant to Section 50a(1) no. 3 ITA.[181] Such compensation is neither paid for a temporary transfer of the rights of use pursuant to Section 49(1) no. 2 lit. f ITA nor for the use of commercial, technical, scientific or similar experience, knowledge and skills pursuant to Section 49(1) no. 9 ITA.[182] The view expressed by the Federal Ministry of Finance is to be welcomed since the foreign platform operators (or in the case at hand: GoogCo) do not surrender the algorithms to the domestic advertisers. Rather, GoogCo uses the algorithms itself in order to place advertisement of the German advertisers effectively.[183] It follows that GoogCo does not surrender an algorithm but rather provides a service to the domestic advertiser and can therefore not derive income pursuant to Section 49(1) no. 9 ITA.

The above analysis illustrates that GoogCo is (under the current German tax rules) neither subject to unlimited nor limited corporate tax liability in Germany. Whether or not the DTA between Germany and Country X provides for the existence of a PE or a permanent representative in Germany does not change this finding since a DTA can only allocate taxing rights and limit the rights of source countries to tax income that may be taxed in the source country.[184] The extent to which a treaty state levies taxes—within the boundaries established by the DTA—is exclusively determined by its own domestic law.[185] Nevertheless, the structure employed by GoogCo in Germany would neither constitute a PE nor an Agent-PE under the pre- or post-BEPS framework. While the website of GoogCo operated under a local domain does not qualify as a fixed place of business and can therefore not be considered to constitute a PE for GoogCo in Germany (which is consistent to the approach taken within the meaning of Section 12 GFC), it may be argued that SupportGmbH constitutes an Agent PE for GoogCo in Germany. For the purpose of this case study it shall be assumed that the DTA between Germany and Country X is based on the latest changes to the OECD MC.[186] However, even after the changes to Article 5(5) and 5(6) OECD MC as a result

[181] Cf. BMF, 3 Apr. 2019, IV C 5 – S 2411/11/10002, BStBl. I 2019, 256.

[182] Cf. BMF, 3 Apr. 2019, IV C 5 – S 2411/11/10002, BStBl. I 2019, 256.

[183] See in more detail *Heil/Pupeter*, BB 2019, 604 (609); *Reichl/Wiedmann*, FR 2019, 201 (204 et seqq.).

[184] Cf. *Kraft*, in: Kraft (Ed.), AstG – Kommentar, § 1 AStG, para. 610.

[185] Cf. *Vogel/Rust*, in: Reimer/Rust (Eds.), Klaus Vogel on Double Taxation Conventions, Introduction, paras. 52 et seqq.

[186] In this context, it shall be emphasised that Germany decided that only the changes proposed in Article 13 (Artificial Avoidance of Permanent Establishment Status through the Specific Activity Exception) of the MLI shall be implemented in their tax treaty network. The changes to the Agent PE through Article 12 MLI (Artificial Avoidance of Permanent Establishment

of BEPS Action 7, SupportGmbH does not constitute an Agent PE for GoogCo in Germany since the activities carried out by SupportGmbH are merely limited to support services. Therefore, SupportGmbH cannot be seen as an entity that plays the principal role leading to the conclusion of contracts which are afterwards routinely concluded without material modifications by GoogCo as required by Article 5(5) OECD MC. Nevertheless, SupportGmbH has its registered office in Germany and is subject to unlimited German corporate tax liability pursuant to Section 1(1) no. 1 CITA.

These findings lead to the next question: Can Germany, as the market jurisdiction where the users (i.e. the targets of the advertisers) and the advertisers reside, tax any profits earned by GoogCo or SupportGmbH? This question will be discussed in the following.

c. Profit Attribution to Market Jurisdiction

With regard to GoogCo, the question of whether Germany may tax any of the profits derived from that business can be answered straightforward. Since GoogCo is neither subject to unlimited nor to limited German tax liability, the profits generated by GoogCo for the advertising services provided cannot be taxed in Germany.

The situation is different for SupportGmbH. This corporation, that is 100% owned by GoogCo, has its registered office in Germany and is therefore subject to unlimited German corporate taxation with its worldwide income pursuant to Section 1(1) no. 1 CITA in conjunction with Section 1(2) CITA. Yet, SupportGmbH only carries out support activities such as marketing and promotion activities for GoogCo. Such activities are routine in nature and are usually remunerated using a cost-based transfer pricing method such as the cost plus method or the TNMM with costs as profit level indicator that only leads to little tax revenue for Germany.[187]

d. Evaluation

As it has been pointed out above, GoogCo operates a business model that can be classified as a multisided platform characterised by the presence of indirect

---

Status through Commissionaire Arrangements and Similar Strategies) were not chosen by Germany, cf. OECD, MLI Positions Germany, p. 24.

[187] Cf. OECD, TP Guidelines 2017, para. 2.45 (for cost plus method), para. 2.93 (for TNMM). The application of the TPSM that may attribute a higher profit to SupportGmbH cannot be regarded appropriate for the case at hand since the activities performed by SupportGmbH do not justify its applicability. For activities that justify the application of the TPSM cf. OECD, TP Guidelines 2017, paras. 2.116 et seqq. (as amended through BEPS Action 10 in 2018).

network effects, i.e. a high number of users using the 'free' search service results in the availability of more data for GoogCo that can be utilised by the software employed in order to provide more targeted advertisement. Furthermore, the more users actively use the search service of GoogCo, the more ads can be displayed to the users leading to higher ad revenue and ultimately higher profits for GoogCo.

Though, the above analysis illustrated that, despite GoogCo's economic presence in Germany, the profits generated from the advertisement services provided are not liable to German corporate income taxation as GoogCo neither has its registered office or its effective place of management in Germany nor does the corporation derive any domestic income pursuant to Section 49(1) ITA with its business activities carried out in Germany. Also, from a treaty perspective, the structure employed by GoogCo does neither constitutes a PE nor an Agent PE under the pre- and post-BEPS framework and does therefore not lead to a taxable nexus in the market jurisdiction. The only profits that are taxable in Germany are the profits derived by SupportGmbH. However, since SupportGmbH merely performs support services for the business activities of GoogCo, remuneration for these support services on a cost-based transfer pricing method seems appropriate. While such remuneration only leads to little profits that are taxable in Germany, the actual profits generated from the advertising services can only be taxed in Country X.

Notwithstanding the above, users who access the search service in Germany certainly add value to the business model employed by GoogCo. Therefore, it can be argued that the current tax rules are not appropriate for coping with the tax challenges arising from the digitalisation of the economy and may lead to a misalignment between the location where value is added/created and the location where profits are taxed.[188]

IV. Taxing the Digitalised Economy

1. The Underlying Problem

The above case studies illustrate that physical presence of a corporation is not necessary in order to carry out business in a jurisdiction other than the jurisdiction of residence (cross-jurisdictional scale without mass). This situation presents a challenge for the international tax system which is based on physical presence as

188 Cf. also OECD, BEPS Action 1: Interim Report 2018, para. 387.

the nexus to assert a jurisdiction in order to tax the profits companies derive from operations in the market jurisdiction.

Another issue that was pointed out in the second case study is the fact that data and user participation play a crucial role in many business models, especially in highly digitalised business models such as multi-sided platforms. However, the existing tax framework does not capture the value that is derived from data and user participation. This circumstance poses challenges to the existing nexus rules, especially if the enterprise does not have a physical PE or a subsidiary established in the market jurisdiction where the ultimate customer, from whom the enterprise exploits user-generated content and data, resides. Although the dependence on data and user participation varies contingent upon the business model,[189] the range of businesses considerably benefiting from data and user participation tends to increase as the digitalisation of the economy intensifies.[190]

However, the ongoing digitalisation of the economy does not only challenge the effectiveness of the existing nexus rules but also the effectiveness of the existing profit allocation rules.[191] As pointed out in case study one, even though the outcome of BEPS Action 7 led to the existence of more PEs in the jurisdiction where cross-border business activities of corporations are carried out, this does not necessarily imply that a high amount of profits can be attributed to the market jurisdictions. In many cases, the activities carried out by these 'new' PEs are mostly limited to service activities that are usually compensated on a cost-based method such as the cost plus method or the TNMM with costs as profit level indicator.[192] Yet, the actual success of most highly digitalised business models is built on intangibles such as patents and algorithms.[193] Nevertheless, the approach taken by the AOA leads to the situation that intangibles and the profits derived from the performance of such intangibles must be attributed to the jurisdiction where the significant people functions relevant for the creation or acquisition of such assets are performed.[194] Since such functions are in many cases performed in the country of residence by the head office, an attribution of a substantial amount of profits derived from the performance of these intangibles to a jurisdiction other

---

[189] See in more detail chapter E.I.3 of this thesis.

[190] Cf. OECD, BEPS Action 1: Interim Report 2018, para. 386.

[191] Cf. OECD, BEPS Action 1: Interim Report 2018, para. 380.

[192] Cf. OECD, TP Guidelines 2017, para. 2.45 (for cost plus method), para. 2.93 (for TNMM).

[193] Cf. OECD, BEPS Action 1: Interim Report 2018, para. 34; EC, 21 Sep. 2017, COM(2017) 547 final, p. 2.

[194] See in more detail for the attribution of intangibles chapter D.I.4.b.(2)(b)iii of this thesis.

than the one where the head office is located is not possible under the current mechanism of the AOA.

Despite having only recently undergone 'the most significant re-write of the international tax rules in a century'[195] within the course of the BEPS project the outlined weaknesses illustrate that the effectiveness of the reinforced principles are challenged and do not appear sufficient in order to cope with the tax challenges that arise from the unique features observed in highly digitalised business models. Given the importance of this matter and the fact that finding a solution in order to cope with these challenges is 'possibly the biggest future challenge in the tax area'[196], it is not surprising that the viewpoints on how to overcome these challenges among the members of the Inclusive Framework fall across a broad spectrum.

2. Different Views by the Members of the Inclusive Framework

Although the views of the members of the OECD's Inclusive Framework on this issue are quite different, they can be divided into three groups.[197] The first group, which includes the EU, takes the view that the reliance on data and user participation challenges the existing nexus and profit allocation rules and may lead to a misalignment between the location where value is created and the location where profits are taxed.[198] Nevertheless, these countries are of support of the fundamental principles of the existing international tax framework and opt for targeted measures instead of a wide-ranging change.[199] Most of the countries in this group reject the idea that the mere provision of a market where a foreign enterprise may sell its goods and services should be regarded as a sufficient link to create a nexus in that country for tax purposes.[200]

---

[195] *Devereux/Vella*, BTR 2018, 387 (387).

[196] *Kofler/Mayr/Schlager*, ET 2017, 523 (524).

[197] Cf. OECD, BEPS Action 1: Interim Report 2018, para. 388.

[198] Cf. OECD, BEPS Action 1: Interim Report 2018, para. 387; *Hadzhieva*, Impact of Digitalisation on International Tax Matters, p. 74.

[199] Cf. OECD, BEPS Action 1: Interim Report 2018, para. 390; *Hadzhieva*, Impact of Digitalisation on International Tax Matters, p. 74.

[200] Cf. OECD, BEPS Action 1: Interim Report 2018, para. 390.

The second group of countries, which includes the US, recognises that the ongoing digital transformation of the economy poses challenges to the effectiveness of the current international tax framework for business profits in general.[201] However, in view of these countries, the challenges are not exclusive to highly digitalised business models. Rather, the changing global economy poses general challenges to the nexus issue (i.e. limited need for physical presence in the market jurisdiction for economic presence) and the profit allocation issue (i.e. an increasing amount of profits is dependent on mobile and non-physical value drivers).[202] Most of the countries in this group think that user data and user participation shall be treated not different than other business inputs sourced from independent third parties in its business' supply chain.[203] It follows that this group of countries holds the view that reform should extend to the whole system and should not only be limited to specific highly digitalised business models.[204] As put forward by *Devereux/Vella*, the difference between the first and the second group can be partly captured by identifying the actual source of the challenges which is the 'digital economy' for the first group and the 'digitalisation of the economy' for the second group.[205]

Members of the third group share the view that the BEPS measures generally addressed most of the concern related to double non-taxation and see no further need for a significant reform of the current international tax rules.[206]

The lack of consensus among the members of the Inclusive Framework on how to overcome the broader direct tax challenges raised by the digitalisation of the economy have led many countries to develop and implement unilateral measures in order to address concerns about the inadequacy of the current international corporate tax rules.[207]

3. Unilateral Actions Introduced by Countries

Even though the OECD provides for the implementation of any of the three suggested options, namely a withholding tax on certain types of digital transactions,

[201] Cf. OECD, BEPS Action 1: Interim Report 2018, para. 391.

[202] Cf. OECD, BEPS Action 1: Interim Report 2018, para. 392.

[203] Cf. OECD, BEPS Action 1: Interim Report 2018, para. 393.

[204] Cf. *Devereux/Vella*, BTR 2018, 387 (387 et seq.).

[205] Cf. *Devereux/Vella*, BTR 2018, 387 (388).

[206] Cf. OECD, BEPS Action 1: Interim Report 2018, para. 394.

[207] Cf. OECD, BEPS Action 1: Interim Report 2018, paras. 346, 376.

an equalisation levy, and a new nexus in the form of a significant economic presence in the Final Report on BEPS Action 1[208] as additional safeguards against BEPS, it demands consistency with existing tax treaty obligations.[209] While only some of the introduced unilateral measures are based upon elements of the three suggested options, they all respond to the desire to secure an appropriate tax base with regard to business activities that are performed in the market jurisdiction where the goods and services are supplied.[210] Given the wide range of measures, the OECD grouped the unilateral measures that are implemented in various jurisdictions into four categories as illustrated in Table 1.

The PE threshold as implemented in Article 5 OECD MC and in most national tax laws requires a certain level of physical presence in the source jurisdiction. Since digitalisation has enabled businesses to reach customers around the globe without being physically present in the respective jurisdictions where they carry on business activities, some countries that belong to the first category have amended the PE threshold aiming to dilute the PE requirement of being physical present in the source jurisdiction.[211] Relevant developments in this context include measures that draw upon some non-physical factors of 'digital presence' intending to evidence a sustained and purposeful interaction with the economy of a country through digital means.[212] By way of example, Israel[213] introduced a 'significant economic presence' test which is broadly defined by reference of factors[214] of digital presence, India[215] introduced a similar concept establishing a new nexus based on a revenue-linked as well as user-linked threshold that is based on the concept of significant economic presence and the Slovak Republic[216] expanded

[208] Cf. OECD, BEPS Action 1: Final Report 2015, para. 357.

[209] Cf. OECD, BEPS Action 1: Final Report 2015, para. 357.

[210] Cf. OECD, BEPS Action 1: Interim Report 2018, para. 346.

[211] Cf. OECD, BEPS Action 1: Interim Report 2018, para. 349.

[212] Cf. OECD, BEPS Action 1: Interim Report 2018, paras. 349 et seq.

[213] For a detailed overview of the interpretation of the domestic nexus rule for corporate income tax purposes as published in the Administrative Circular No. 04/2016 of 11 Apr. 2016 see PwC, Israeli Tax Authority releases first guidance related to e-commerce; see also *Turina*, Intertax 2018, 495 (505 et seq.).

[214] Such factors may capture, e.g., online contract conclusion, the use of digital products and services, multi-sided business models as well as localised websites, cf. OECD, BEPS Action 1: Interim Report 2018, p. 137, box 4.1.

[215] The new nexus rules became effective from 1 Apr. 2019 and were introduced through the amendment of Section 9(1) of the Indian Income Tax Act. See in more detail OECD, BEPS Action 1: Interim Report 2018, p. 138, box 4.2.

[216] According to Section 16(2) of the Slovakian Income Tax Law, intermediation services of a non-resident enterprise that facilitate the conclusion of contracts through an online platform

Table 1 Overview of Selected Unilateral Measures Introduced Globally

Alternative Application of the PE Threshold	Withholding Taxes	Turnover Taxes	Specific Regimes to Deal with Large MNEs
• measures incorporating digital presence factors: – Israel's significant economic presence test – India's new nexus based on significant economic presence – Slovakia's intermediation tax • extension of the service PE concept as implemented in Article 5(3) b UN MTC: – Saudi Arabia's and Kuwait's virtual service PE	• broadening of withholding tax for royalties: – Greece's and Philippine's withholding tax for payments for the use or the right to use software – Malaysia's withholding tax for payments for visual images of sounds transmitted through ICT • adoption of withholding tax on fees for technical services: – Brazilian's withholding tax on SaaS • introduction of new withholding taxes on income from online advertising: – Thailand's e-commerce withholding tax	• introduction of sectorial turnover taxes targeted at revenue from online advertising services: – Hungary's advertisement tax – India's equalisation levy – France's tax on physical and online distribution of audio-visual content – Italy's levy on digital transactions	• anti-abuse rules to address excessive use of base eroding payments: – United Kingdom's and Australia's Diverted Profit Tax – United States' BEAT

Source: Own illustration.

the definition of the term 'fixed place of business' for specific digital platforms in 2017.[217] All these measures have in common that they extend the PE threshold and allow for net-basis taxation without any physical presence of the non-resident enterprise in the source country.[218]

A further development that also aims for the extension of the PE threshold relates to the interpretation of the 'service PE' as implemented in Article 5(3) lit (b) of the UN MC.[219] While the prevailing interpretation goes in the direction that physical presence by a non-resident enterprise in the source country is required either through personnel or employees in order to establish a service PE in the source country, a minority view expressed by countries like Saudi Arabia[220] and Kuwait[221] goes in the direction that physical presence through personnel or employees shall no longer constitute a relevant requirement for the application of a service PE, in this case also referred to as a 'virtual' service PE.[222] However, as emphasised by the OECD, such measures could potentially reach far beyond online activities, and comprise any remote services that are supplied to a market.[223]

Other countries make use of withholding taxes (second category) for specific types of digital products and services in order to enforce taxing rights in the source country even in the absence of a physical presence through a PE of the non-resident enterprise that carries on business activities in the source jurisdiction.[224] Such measures include a) the broadening of the domestic definition for royalties subject to withholding taxes,[225] b) the adoption of the withholding tax on fees for

with respect to the provision of services of accommodation and transportation are deemed to constitute an activity carried out through a fixed place cf. OECD, BEPS Action 1: Interim Report 2018, p. 160, note 6.

[217]Cf. OECD, BEPS Action 1: Interim Report 2018, para. 351.

[218]Cf. OECD, BEPS Action 1: Interim Report 2018, para. 351.

[219]The OECD MC itself does not provide for a similar provision. Nevertheless, the update of the OECD MC 2008 brought about a substantial broadening of the PE notion and offers an optional extension of the PE threshold in Article 5 para. 155 of the OECD MC Commentary which is also referred to as the service PE, see in more detail chapter C.IV.6.d of this thesis.

[220]The view of Saudi Arabia on the interpretation of the service PE was expressed in an official letter of the Saudi Arabia Government (No 01/08/1436) published on 10 Feb. 2016.

[221]For an overview of Kuwait's virtual service PE concept see EY, Tax Insights, October 2015, p. 46.

[222]Cf. OECD, BEPS Action 1: Interim Report 2018, para. 354.

[223]Cf. OECD, BEPS Action 1: Interim Report 2018, para. 354.

[224]Cf. OECD, BEPS Action 1: Interim Report 2018, para. 356.

[225]Cf. OECD, BEPS Action 1: Interim Report 2018, para. 357. Such a broadening of the definition for royalties that brings certain transactions within the scope of withholding taxes

technical services such as cloud computing services,[226] and c) the introduction of withholding taxes on other categories of income,[227] e.g. income from online advertisement.[228]

The third category of relevant measures observed across the globe includes measures that have been taken outside the framework of corporate income taxes. These measures typically involve specific turnover taxes targeted at revenue generated from online advertising services provided by foreign-based suppliers of these services.[229] Such measures were introduced in various countries and include, i.a., Hungary's advertisement tax,[230] India's Equalisation Levy,[231] France's tax on physical and online distribution of audio-visual content[232] as well as Italy's levy on digital transactions.[233] In many cases, these measures apply not only to resident but also to non-resident enterprises and are commonly combined with broad nexus rules focussing on the respective destination of the supplies.[234]

---

can be found in the tax code of countries like the Philippines and Greece (payments for the use or right to use software) as well as Malysia (payments for visual images or sounds transmitted through ICT), cf. OECD, BEPS Action 1: Interim Report 2018, p. 161, notes 17 and 18.

[226] Cf. OECD, BEPS Action 1: Interim Report 2018, para. 357. Such a withholding tax on fees for technical services was added to Article 12 A(3) of the UN MC. Also, the Brazilian Federal Revenue Service has expressed through an answer to the Formal Consultation Request No. 191/2017 that cross-border payments for SaaS are subject to withholding tax, cf. Brazilian Federal Revenue Service, Advance Tax Ruling request No. 191/2017.

[227] E.g. payments to a provider of advertising services provided through the internet, or payments provided to those who act as an intermediary for an provider of such a service are subject to withholding tax in Thailand, cf. Presidential Decree No. 476, Official Gazette of 19 Dec. 2018 with further clarification by the Ministry of Treasury and Finance in the Communiqué No. 17 Amending the General Corporate Income Tax Communiqué No. 1 of 15 Feb. 2019.

[228] Cf. OECD, BEPS Action 1: Interim Report 2018, para. 357.

[229] Cf. OECD, BEPS Action 1: Interim Report 2018, para. 359.

[230] For an overview of Hungary's advertisement tax see PwC, Hungary: Corporate – Taxes on corporate income; see also OECD, BEPS Action 1: Interim Report 2018, p. 145, box 4.5.

[231] For an overview of India's Equalisation levy see *Wagh*, BIT 2016, 538 (538 et seqq.); *Hadzhieva*, Impact of Digitalisation on International Tax Matters, p. 44; *Jain*, in: Kerschner/Somare (Eds.), Taxation in a Global Digital Economy, 161 (180 et seq.). OECD, BEPS Action 1: Interim Report 2018, p. 142, box 4.3.

[232] For an overview of France's tax on physical and online distribution of audio-visual content see *Hadzhieva*, Impact of Digitalisation on International Tax Matters, p. 40; OECD, BEPS Action 1: Interim Report 2018, pp. 146 et seq., box 4.6.

[233] For an overview of Italy's levy on digital transactions see *Hadzhieva*, Impact of Digitalisation on International Tax Matters, p. 39; OECD, BEPS Action 1: Interim Report 2018, pp. 143 et seq., box 4.4.

[234] Cf. OECD, BEPS Action 1: Interim Report 2018, para. 360.

The last category comprises measures that are not targeted specifically towards highly digitalised business models but rather apply more generally to large MNEs.[235] A prominent measure in this regard is the Diverted Profit Tax (hereinafter: DPT) as implemented by the United Kingdom[236] and Australia[237] that both work as an anti-abuse rule for income tax purposes.[238] Rather than expanding the coverage of the income tax base, the DPT is usually tied to the already existing international standards on nexus (e.g. dependent agent PE) and profit attribution (e.g. transfer pricing rules and arm's length principle).[239] In principle, these measures target corporate structures that are established in order to avoid the recognition of a PE (mostly a dependent agent PE), or certain intra-group payments made in order to erode the tax base.[240] Another measure that falls into this category is the Base Erosion and Anti-Abuse Tax also referred to as BEAT adopted in the United States in 2017. This measure is not confined to structures used by highly digitalised business models but rather works as a minimum corporate income tax that disallows the deduction of certain outbound payments such as royalties, interests as well as specific services.[241]

[235] Cf. OECD, BEPS Action 1: Interim Report 2018, para. 363.

[236] For an overview of the DPT as introduced in the United Kingdom see HM Revenue & Customs, Diverted Profits Tax: Guidance; *Oppel*, IStR 2015, 333 (333 et seqq.); *Kofler/Mayr/Schlager*, BB 2017, 1751 (1753); *Jain*, in: Kerschner/Somare (Eds.), Taxation in a Global Digital Economy, 161 (179 et seq.); OECD, BEPS Action 1: Interim Report 2018, pp. 149 et seqq., box 4.7.

[237] The Australian DPT was implemented in two successive steps with the Multinational Anti-Avoidance Law in Dec. 2015 (Section 177 DA of the Income Tax Assessment Act[1936]) introducing a PE anti-avoidance rule and the DPT adopted in Apr. 2017 (Expansion of Part IV A of the Income Tax Assessment Act [1936] laid down in Section 177H to 177R) introducing an anti-abuse rule for transfer pricing purposes, cf. OECD, BEPS Action 1: Interim Report 2018, p. 162, note 32. For an overview of the Australian DPT see *Jain*, in: Kerschner/Somare (Eds.), Taxation in a Global Digital Economy, 161 (177 et seqq.); OECD, BEPS Action 1: Interim Report 2018, pp. 153 et seqq., boxes 4.8 and 4.9.

[238] Cf. OECD, BEPS Action 1: Interim Report 2018, para. 363.

[239] Cf. OECD, BEPS Action 1: Interim Report 2018, para. 364.

[240] Cf. OECD, BEPS Action 1: Interim Report 2018, para. 364.

[241] Cf. OECD, BEPS Action 1: Interim Report 2018, para. 366. BEAT was introduced in Section 59A of the Internal Revenue Code. For an overview and the effects of BEAT see *Linn*, DStR 2018, 321 (324 et seq.); *Schönfeld/Zinowsky/Rieck*, IStR 2018, 127 (132 et seqq.); OECD, BEPS Action 1: Interim Report 2018, p. 158, box 4.10.

4. The Need for a Common Approach

The previous chapter illustrated that quite a large number of jurisdictions are not satisfied with the outcomes produced by the current international tax rules and implemented their own unilateral measures due to the absence of any internationally agreed approach. However, unilateral measures come at the expense of internationally operating businesses that are, as described by *Kroppen/Dawid/Keil*, currently subject of an 'allocation battle' of national tax administrations aiming to receive a large portion of the taxable income of globally operating companies.[242] Yet, such measures not only induce uncertainty for taxpayers but also significantly increase compliance burdens as well as the risk of double taxation.

The pace at which unilateral measures have been introduced by various jurisdictions emphasises that the tax challenges that arise from the digitalisation of the economy have brought the international tax debate to a critical point. At this stage, it is not a question anymore whether the current international tax rules for corporate taxation need to be adapted. Rather, the spotlight is on the question how to adapt the current international tax rules for corporate taxation in order to deal with the challenges raised by the digitalisation of the economy. The political pressure to reach a consensus-based solution is high. If no consensus-based solution is reached, there is no doubt that more and more countries will proceed with the implementation of uncoordinated unilateral measures which will lead to an even more complex, fractured and distorted international tax system ultimately leading to an adverse impact on global investment and growth.[243]

Throughout the past years, academic scholars and political institutions have proposed various approaches on how to reshape the current international tax rules in order to cope with the tax challenges that arise from the digitalisation of the economy. Among others, approaches on an amendment of the PE threshold,[244] the development of specific transfer pricing guidelines for the digital economy[245]

---

[242] Cf. *Kroppen/Dawid/Keil*, TPI 2019, 98 (98).

[243] Cf. OECD, BEPS Action 1: Programme of Work 2019, para. 11.

[244] Cf. i.a. *Collin/Colin* arguing that the collection of data via regular and systematic monitoring of users in a country should in itself create a taxable presence in that country, cf. *Collin/Colin*, Task Force on Taxation of the Digital Economy, pp. 114 et seqq.; *Hongler/Pistone* suggesting a new PE nexus based on physical presence that consists of four main requirements or elements: (1) digital services, (2) user threshold, (3) a certain time threshold and (4) a *de minimis* revenue threshold, cf. *Hongler/Pistone*, Blueprints for a New PE Nexus, IBFD Working Paper 2015, pp. 22 et seqq.

[245] Cf. i.a. *Olbert/Spengel*, WTJ 2017, 3 (33 et seqq.).

and the introduction of a withholding tax for digital transactions[246] have been proposed and analysed in various academic papers.[247] Also, the European Union proposed the introduction of a Digital Service Tax at EU level at a rate of 3% on gross revenue from digital services as an interim measure and a long-term approach for taxing revenues derived from a Significant Digital Presence.[248]

One striking feature of these approaches is that they are all in favour of international tax reform in light of the digitalisation of the economy. However, it seems obvious that the introduction of more and more unilateral measures are obstructive in finding mutual solutions in order to cope with the tax challenges raised by the digitalisation of the economy. Therefore, it is to be welcomed that the Council of the European Union abandoned the proposal of introducing a Digital Service Tax as a short-term measure and emphasised that it would rather focus on the broader international tax discussion that is under way at the level of the OECD.[249]

Indeed, the Inclusive Framework, the key forum of the OECD dealing with BEPS Action 1 with a global membership of currently 139[250] countries and jurisdictions, seems to be the right forum in order to bring an international tax reform that addresses the tax challenges raised by the digitalisation of the economy on its way. In contrast to previous major tax projects that were mostly developed at the level of the G20 and the member states of the OECD consisting of mainly industrialised countries and only some emerging countries, the Inclusive Framework

[246] Cf. i.a. *Brauner/Báez*, Withholding Taxes in the Service of BEPS Action 1, IBFD Working Paper 2015, pp. 4 et seqq.; *Báez/Brauner*, Taxing the Digital Economy Post BEPS ... Seriously, University of Florida Levin College of Law Research Paper No. 19-16, pp. 7 et seqq.

[247] For an overview and evaluation of the different concepts see *Pfister*, Die Besteuerung der digitalen Wirtschaft, 178 et seqq.; *Kofler/Mayr/Schlager*, BB 2017, 1751 (1751 et seqq.); *Kofler/Mayr/Schlager*, BB 2017 1815 (1815 et seqq.).

[248] For the Significant Digital Presence proposal cf. EC, 21 Mar. 2018, COM(2018) 147 final. For the Digital Service Tax proposal see EC, 21 Mar. 2018, COM(2018) 148 final. After the EU's finance ministers failed to agree on the proposals due to opposition from countries like Denmark, Finland, Ireland and Sweden on 12 Mar. 2019 the EU abandoned the proposal of the Digital Service Tax and emphasised that it would rather focus on the broader international tax discussions that are underway at the level of the OECD. Only if progress was not made in the course of 2020 by the OECD the EU would then revisit the issue, cf. Council of the European Union, 12 Mar. 2019, Outcome of the Council Meeting, p. 6. The latest developments at the level of the OECD led the EU to postpone the timeframe for a possible unilateral EU response to mid-2021, cf. *Karaboytcheva*, Taxation of the digital economy: Latest developments, Dec. 2020, p. 1.

[249] Cf. Council of the European Union, 12 Mar. 2019, Outcome of the Council Meeting, p. 6.

[250] Number of members of the Inclusive Framework as of Feb. 2021. Cf. for a regularly updated overview of the members of the Inclusive Framework: https://www.oecd.org/tax/beps/inclusive-framework-on-beps-composition.pdf.

includes about 70% of non-OECD and non-G20 counties.[251] The fact that decisions at the level of the Inclusive Framework are made unanimously ensures that the proposals being made to the international tax rules will not only be influenced by the interests of export-oriented industrialised countries but also from the inputs and perspectives of developing countries.[252] While such a mechanism makes the process of finding a consensus solution on how to address the tax challenges arising from the digitalisation of the economy a challenging task, it is to be hoped that one's such a consensus solution is found by the members of the Inclusive Framework individual country efforts on implementing unilateral measures will be abandoned.

In the following chapter, the focus is shifted from the discussion of the tax challenges arising from the digitalisation of the economy and its implications for the PE concept to the analysis of the currently discussed approach on how to adopt the international tax system to the digitalisation of the economy under Pillar One. In order to do so, the next chapter provides, in a first step, a short overview of the most recent developments at the level of the OECD in this context. In a second step, the fundamental concept of the reform proposal under Pillar One is described in further detail and then, in a third step, evaluated with respect to the overarching principles of tax policy as presented in chapter B of this thesis.

[251] Cf. OECD, BEPS Progress Report 2019, p. 2.

[252] Cf. *Fehling*, IStR 2019, 656 (657).

F. Adapting the International Corporate Tax System to the Digitalisation of the Economy

I. Where Do We Stand in the Ongoing Debate

The work on developing a long-term solution to the broader tax challenges arising from the digitalisation of the economy has significantly picked up speed throughout the past years. While the Final Report on BEPS Action 1, published in 2015, and the Interim Report on the tax challenges arising from digitalisation, published in 2018, merely analysed potential tax policy alternatives in order to address broader direct tax challenges raised by the digitalisation of the economy but did not present any concrete solutions, in 2019 the Inclusive Framework pathed the road for the development of a potential consensus-based long-term solution in order to address the tax challenges raised by the digitalisation of the economy.[1]

In a Policy Note,[2] approved on 23 January 2019, the Inclusive Framework illustrates concrete proposals framed within two complementary pillars which could 'form the basis for consensus'[3]. Under the first pillar, new rules on the allocation of taxing rights (nexus) and on profit allocation are developed.[4] Under the second pillar, referred to as the GloBE proposal, remaining BEPS issues are focused on.[5] The Inclusive Framework decided to explore these proposals on a 'without prejudice'[6] basis, i.e. none of the members of the Inclusive Framework is committed to any of the proposals presented.

[1]Cf. *Schön*, IStR 2019, 647 (647); *Hentschel/Hörnicke/Kraft*, Ubg 2019, 673 (673).

[2]OECD, BEPS Action 1: Policy Note 2019.

[3]OECD, BEPS Action 1: Policy Note 2019, p. 1.

[4]Cf. OECD, BEPS Action 1: Policy Note 2019, p. 1

[5]Cf. OECD, BEPS Action 1: Policy Note 2019, p. 2.

[6]Cf. OECD, BEPS Action 1: Policy Note 2019, p. 2.

S. Hentschel, *The Taxation of Permanent Establishments*, Hallesche Schriften zur Betriebswirtschaft 37, https://doi.org/10.1007/978-3-658-34000-1_6

Since the release of the Policy Note, both pillars were further examined and put in more precise terms. As part of this examination, a public consultation document[7] was released on 13 February 2019 that drew response from over 200 stakeholders submitting over 2,000 pages of written comments.[8] The proposals, outlined in the public consultation document, can be traced back to different political forces.[9] With regard to Pillar One, three proposals are outlined in the public consultation document that would all require changes to the existing nexus as well as profit allocation rules.[10]

The first proposal, the 'user participation'[11] proposal suggested by the United Kingdom, focuses on certain highly digitalised businesses (i.e. social media platforms, search engines and online marketplaces)[12] and seeks to attribute parts of the profits derived from such businesses to jurisdictions where an 'active and engaged user base'[13] is located, irrespective of whether these businesses have a local physical presence in that jurisdiction.[14] The second proposal, the 'marketing intangibles'[15] proposal suggested by the United States, is broader in scope than the user participation proposal and requires that the residual or the non-routine income of an MNE group that can be attributed to marketing intangibles and their corresponding risks shall be allocated to the market jurisdiction.[16] The third proposal, the 'significant economic presence'[17] proposal suggested by the

[7]OECD, BEPS Action 1: Public Consultation Document 2019.

[8]Cf. OECD, BEPS Action 1: Programme of Work 2019, para. 9. The written submissions made to the Public Consultation Document are available at: https://www.oecd.org/tax/beps/public-comments-received-on-the-possible-solutions-to-the-tax-challenges-of-digitalisation.htm.

[9]Cf. *Schön*, IStR 2019, 647 (647).

[10]Cf. OECD, BEPS Action 1: Public Consultation Document 2019, para. 56. For an evaluation of the proposals see i.a. *Becker/van der Ham*, DB 2019, 502 (509).

[11]Cf. for the proposal OECD, BEPS Action 1: Public Consultation Document 2019, paras. 17–28.

[12]Cf. OECD, BEPS Action 1: Public Consultation Document 2019, para. 19.

[13]OECD, BEPS Action 1: Public Consultation Document 2019, para. 17.

[14]Cf. OECD, BEPS Action 1: Public Consultation Document 2019, paras. 21 et seq.

[15]For the proposal cf. OECD, BEPS Action 1: Public Consultation Document 2019, paras. 29–49. According to the OECD TP Guidelines 2017, marketing intangibles are intangibles that relate to marketing activities, aids in the commercial exploitation of a service or product and/or has an important promotional value for the service or product concerned. Marketing intangibles may include trade names, trademarks, customer relationships, customer lists and customer data, cf. OECD, TP Guidelines 2017, p. 27.

[16]Cf. OECD, BEPS Action 1: Public Consultation Document 2019, para. 43.

[17]Cf. for the proposal OECD, BEPS Action 1: Public Consultation Document 2019, paras. 50–55.

G-24 group of developing and emerging economies, seeks to establish a taxable presence in a jurisdiction when a non-resident enterprise has a purposeful and sustained interaction in this jurisdiction via digital technology and other automated means and suggests the use of the fractional apportionment method in order to allocate profits to such a significant economic presence.[18]

The second pillar, proposed by Germany and France, aims to develop taxing rights that strengthen the ability of jurisdictions to tax profits that have not been taxed in other jurisdictions because these jurisdictions have not exercised their primary rights or where the payment is otherwise only subject to no or only a low level of effective taxation.[19]

Given the different proposals and the various comments of the stakeholders, the Inclusive Framework further examined both pillars. The results of that examination are reflected in the 'Programme of Work to Develop a Consensus Solution to the Tax Challenges Arising from the Digitalisation of the Economy'[20], adopted in May 2019. On the basis of the published documents, the Inclusive Framework has continued work on a long-term solution that was scheduled to be delivered by the end of 2020.[21] As pointed out in the programme of work, the interaction between both pillars as well as a reduction of the number of options to be pursued under Pillar One shall be worked out.[22]

On 9 October 2019, the OECD Secretariat published a public consultation document proposing a 'Unified Approach' under Pillar One in order to advance international negotiations.[23] It becomes evident that no single proposal set out under Pillar One has reached consensus in isolation. Therefore, the Unified Approach does not focus on one single approach, but rather aims to combine the significant commonalities of the three proposals. The document identifies four commonalities. More precisely, it is examined that all proposals:

- aim to reallocate taxing rights in favour of the market jurisdiction, which is for some business models the jurisdiction where the users are located,
- envisage a new nexus rule that does not depend on physical presence in the market jurisdiction,

[18] Cf. G-24 Working Group, Proposal for Addressing Tax Challenges, 17 Jan. 2019, pp. 3 et seqq.; OECD, BEPS Action 1: Public Consultation Document 2019, para. 51.

[19] Cf. OECD, BEPS Action 1: Policy Note 2019, p. 2.

[20] OECD, BEPS Action 1: Programme of Work 2019.

[21] Cf. OECD, BEPS Action 1: Programme of Work 2019, para. 13.

[22] Cf. OECD, BEPS Action 1: Programme of Work 2019, para. 13.

[23] Cf. OECD, BEPS Action 1: Secretariat Proposal for a "Unified Approach" 2019.

- depart from the separate entity principle and go beyond the arm's length principle, and
- search for stability of the tax system, simplicity and increased tax certainty in implementation.[24]

While much work will still be needed in order to deliver a consensus based long-term solution, two main observations can already be made. First, the former discussion on the appropriate taxation of the digitalised economy has gone over to a discussion on the appropriate taxation of cross-border business activities in general.[25] In this context, all approaches illustrated under Pillar One have in common that they represent a shift from levying taxes by reference to the country of residence towards the market country in its roles as a destination country, i.e. the country of the consumer location or the relevant market.[26] Second, the discussion on finding solutions to address the tax challenges arising from the digitalisation of the economy is accompanied by the search for new sources of tax revenue that may arise from the digitalisation of the economy.[27] In this context, the danger arises that the discussion on finding a consensus solution which 'will have an impact on revenue and the overall balance of taxing rights'[28] is rather led by the interests of the individual members of the Inclusive Framework on receiving a higher share of the overall tax revenue than on sound economic principles.[29]

While discussions at the level of the Inclusive Framework continued on the elements outlined in the Secretariat Proposal in order to achieve the goal to reach an agreement of the architecture of the Unified Approach at the level of the Inclusive Framework by January 2020,[30] a letter[31] from the former US Treasury Secretary Steven Mnuchin, suggesting to make Pillar One a 'safe harbour' regime (i.e. MNE groups may elect to opt-out of any agreed solution), stalled negotiations and let

[24] Cf. OECD, BEPS Action 1: Secretariat Proposal for a "Unified Approach" 2019, para. 10.

[25] Cf. *Schön*, IStR 2019, 647 (648).

[26] See in this context *Collier/Vella*, WTJ 2019, 159 (182). See in more detail for the benefits of moving towards a tax system that rest upon the destination principle *Devereux/Vella*, in: Gupta/Keen/Shad/Verdier (Eds.), Digital Revolutions in Public Finance, 91 (103 et seqq.).

[27] Cf. *Kroppen/Dawid/Keil*, TPI 2019, 98 (105).

[28] OECD, BEPS Action 1: Programme of Work 2019, para. 13.

[29] *Kroppen/Dawid/Keil* argue that the principle of economic efficiency is of subordinate significance in the current international tax debate on finding a solution to the tax challenges arising from the digitalisation of the economy, cf. *Kroppen/Dawid/Keil*, TPI 2019, 98 (105).

[30] Cf. OECD, BEPS Action 1: Programme of Work 2019, para. 13.

[31] The letter can be accessed online under: https://www.orbitax.com/news/archive.php/U.S.-Treasury-Secretary-Sends--40283.

other members of the Inclusive Framework to voice concern on the approach suggested by the former US Treasury Secretary.[32] Nevertheless, a statement by the Inclusive Framework published on 31 January 2020 affirmed the commitment of the members of the Inclusive Framework to continue the work under both pillars.[33] Furthermore, the Inclusive Framework officially endorsed the Unified Approach as developed by the OECD Secretariat as the basis for further negotiations and emphasised its commitment to reach an agreement on a consensus-based solution by the end of 2020. Moreover, it is emphasised that the final decision on whether Pillar One may be implemented on a safe harbour basis, as suggested by the former US Treasury Secretary Steven Mnuchin, shall not be decided before the other elements of the consensus-based solution have been agreed upon.[34]

The outbreak of the COVID-19 pandemic in 2020 and political disagreement among the members of the Inclusive Framework slowed down the work on both pillars. Therefore, the initial intention to reach an agreement on the key policy features of a consensus-based solution to the Pillar One issues by July 2020 and to produce a final report by the end of 2020 could not be met.[35] Rather, in July 2020 the G20 mandated the Inclusive Framework to produce reports on the Blueprints of Pillar One and Pillar Two by the G20 Finance Ministers meeting in October 2020.[36] These reports together with the Cover Statement were published on 12 October 2020.[37] As emphasised in the Cover Statement, the Inclusive Framework aims at bringing the work on both Pillars to a successful conclusion by mid-2021.[38] While work on both Pillars continues, US Treasury Secretary Janet Yellen informed her counterparts at the virtual meeting of the G20 finance ministers on 26 February 2021 that the United States is no longer advocating a 'safe harbour'

---

[32]Cf. OECD, BEPS Action 1: Statement on the Two-Pillar Approach 2020, para. 3. The official letter of the OECD to the former US Treasury Secretary Steven Mnuchin can be accessed online under: http://www.oecd.org/tax/Letter-from-OECD-Secretary-General-Angel-Gurria-for-the-attention-of-The-Honorable-Steven-T-Mnuchin-Secretary-of-the-Treasury-United-States.pdf.

[33]Cf. OECD, BEPS Action 1: Statement on the Two-Pillar Approach 2020, para. 1.

[34]Cf. OECD, BEPS Action 1: Statement on the Two-Pillar Approach 2020, para. 3.

[35]For the timeline cf. OECD, BEPS Action 1: Statement on the Two-Pillar Approach 2020, Annex 1, para. 4.

[36]Cf. OECD, BEPS Action 1: Report on Pillar One Blueprint 2020, p. 4.

[37]For the Report on Pillar One Blueprint cf. OECD, BEPS Action 1: Report on Pillar One Blueprint 2020. For the Report on Pillar Two Blueprint cf. OECD, BEPS Action 1: Report on Pillar Two Blueprint 2020. For the Cover Statement by the Inclusive Framework on the Reports on the Blueprints of Pillar One and Pillar Two cf. OECD, BEPS Action 1: Cover Statement on the Blueprints 2020.

[38]Cf. OECD, BEPS Action 1: Cover Statement on the Blueprints 2020, para. 9.

implementation of Pillar One.[39] As this issue has been one of the main stumbling blocks to a mutual agreement among the members of the Inclusive Framework on Pillar One, the announcement of the US Treasury Secretary Janet Yellen certainly increases the changes to reach a mutual agreement on Pillar One by mid-2021.

In the following, the analysis focuses on Pillar One as outlined in the 'Report on Pillar One Blueprint' and approved by the Inclusive Framework on 8–9 October 2020. In a first step, the central elements of Pillar One are elaborated in further detail and then, in a second step, evaluated with respect to the overarching principles of tax policy.

II. Overview of Pillar One Blueprint

1. Conceptual Foundation

The fundamental architecture of Pillar One as outlined in the Pillar One Blueprint consists of three main elements: A new taxing right which is not dependent on actual physical presence of an enterprise in the market jurisdiction (Amount A), a new profit allocation mechanism (Amount A and Amount B) as well as improved tax certainty processes through the introduction of dispute prevention and dispute resolution mechanisms. While both types of taxable profits described by Amount A and Amount B encompass new and revised profit allocation rules, only Amount A aspires to introduce a new taxing right. More specifically, as proposed in the Pillar One Blueprint, Amount A shall reflect profits associated with the active and sustained engagement of qualified businesses in the market jurisdiction.[40] In order to meet this objective, a share of the residual profit shall be attributed to the market jurisdiction by means of a formulaic approach.[41] In this sense, Amount A constitutes the main response of Pillar One to the tax challenges arising from the digitalisation of the economy.[42]

Amount B provides for a fixed return for baseline marketing and distribution functions that are carried out in the market jurisdiction.[43] This fixed return shall be based on the arm's length principle and seeks to a) simplify the remuneration for such baseline activities, and b) reduce uncertainty and disputes regarding the

[39] Cf. *Johnson*, TNTF 2021, 39-7.

[40] Cf. OECD, BEPS Action 1: Report on Pillar One Blueprint 2020, para. 6.

[41] Cf. OECD, BEPS Action 1: Report on Pillar One Blueprint 2020, para. 7.

[42] Cf. OECD, BEPS Action 1: Statement on the Two-Pillar Approach 2020, Annex 1, para. 10.

[43] Cf. OECD, BEPS Action 1: Report on Pillar One Blueprint 2020, para. 7.

pricing for baseline marketing and distribution activities and thereby enhance tax certainty.[44]

The third key component of the Pillar One Blueprint aims for improved tax certainty processes through the introduction of dispute prevention and dispute resolution mechanisms.[45]

Figure 1 provides an overview of the main elements of Pillar One as part of the Two-Pillar Approach currently discussed under BEPS Action 1.

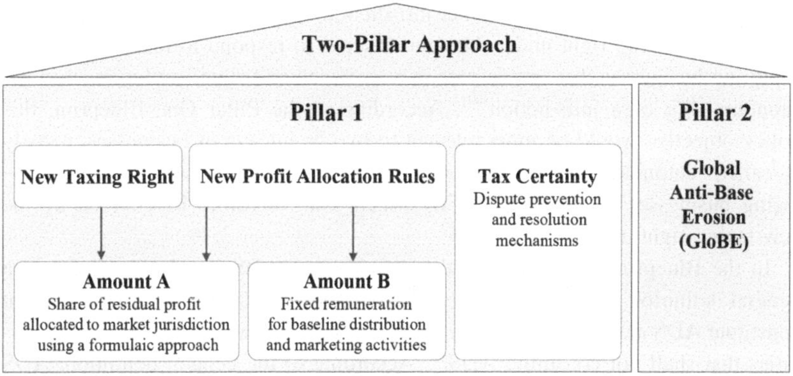

Figure 1 Main Elements of Pillar One as part of the Two-Pillar Approach (Source: Own Illustration)

[44] Cf. OECD, BEPS Action 1: Report on Pillar One Blueprint 2020, para. 11.

[45] Prior to the Pillar One Blueprint (i.e. in the Statement on the Two-Pillar Approach 2020) tax certainty processes through the introduction of dispute prevention and dispute resolution mechanisms were only a part of the so-called 'Amount C'. This Amount C also comprised any additional profit where in-country functions exceeded baseline activities compensated under Amount B, cf. OECD, BEPS Action 1: Statement on the Two-Pillar Approach 2020, Annex 1, para. 10. However, in the Pillar One Blueprint the term 'Amount C' was dropped since the Pillar One Blueprint does not provide for any additional profit where in-country functions exceeded baseline activities compensated under Amount B.

2. New Taxing Right (Amount A)

a. Scope

As has been shown in chapter E, physical presence of an enterprise in the jurisdiction where business activities are carried out is not necessary anymore in order to develop an active and sustained engagement in the market jurisdiction and thereby generate a substantial amount of profits in this jurisdiction. This situation presents a challenge for the international tax system which is based on physical presence as the nexus to assert a jurisdiction in order to tax the profits companies derive from operations in the market jurisdiction.

The new taxing right under Amount A seeks to respond to this challenge by capturing businesses that 'participate in a sustained and significant manner in the economic life of a jurisdiction'[46]. According to the Pillar One Blueprint, this policy objective would be most relevant to two broad sets of businesses, namely so-called 'automated digital services' (hereinafter: ADS) as well as 'consumer-facing businesses' (hereinafter: CFB) which shall therefore be covered by the new taxing right under Amount A.[47]

In the Blueprint on Pillar One the definition of ADS is structured around a general definition, supported by a positive list of services that shall in any event constitute ADS and therefore within scope of Amount A and a negative list of activities that shall not constitute ADS.[48] According to the general definition, ADS are a) digital, i.e. they are provided over the Internet or an electronic network; and b) automated, i.e. once the service is set up minimal human intervention on the part of the service provider is required to provide the service to a particular user.[49] The following non-exhaustive positive list of business activities shall be within the scope of ADS: online advertising services; sale or other alienation of user data; online search engines; social media platforms; online intermediation platforms; digital content services; online gaming; standardised online teaching services and cloud computing services.[50] Not included within the scope of the new taxing right under Amount A, and therefore part of the negative list, shall be the following business activities: customised professional services; customised online teaching services; online sale of goods and services other than ADS;

[46] OECD, BEPS Action 1: Report on Pillar One Blueprint 2020, para. 38.

[47] Cf. OECD, BEPS Action 1: Report on Pillar One Blueprint 2020, paras. 38 et seqq.

[48] Cf. OECD, BEPS Action 1: Report on Pillar One Blueprint 2020, paras. 39 et seqq.

[49] Cf. OECD, BEPS Action 1: Report on Pillar One Blueprint 2020, paras. 26, 43.

[50] Cf. OECD, BEPS Action 1: Report on Pillar One Blueprint 2020, para. 44; for detailed explanations see OECD, BEPS Action 1: Report on Pillar One Blueprint 2020, para. 45.

revenue from the sale of a physical good, irrespective of network connectivity as well as services providing access to the Internet or another electronic network.[51] Only in the event an activity is neither on the positive nor on the negative list it is necessary to consider whether it meets the conditions in the general definition.[52]

The second set of businesses that the Pillar One Blueprint intents to bring within the scope of Amount A are CFB that shall cover businesses that generate revenues from selling goods or services either directly or indirectly (e.g. through a broker, agent, intermediary or representative) to customers.[53] Also, businesses that generate revenue through licensing a consumer brand and commercial know-how as well as businesses that generate revenue from licensing rights over trademarked consumer products shall be regarded as consumer facing and shall therefore be covered by Amount A.[54]

Specific consideration is given to certain sectors which shall not be in scope of Amount A. These sectors include natural resources; financial services; construction, sale and leasing of residential property as well as international air and shipping business.[55] According to the Pillar One Blueprint, these scope exclusions should apply on a segment basis, meaning that for an MNE group operating multiple business lines, only those business lines that are explicitly listed shall be excluded from the scope of Amount A.[56]

Furthermore, two thresholds are considered to be applied to ensure that administrative and compliance costs are in proportion to the intended benefits of the new nexus rule. Against this backdrop, the new nexus rule shall only be applied to MNE groups that meet a certain global revenue threshold. The discussion currently revolves around the appropriateness of the EUR 750 million global gross revenue threshold as already used for the purpose of CbC Reporting.[57] Nevertheless, as explicitly emphasised in the Pillar One Blueprint, no decision has yet been taken by the Inclusive Framework on the precise amount or the design of the threshold.[58] The estimated number of MNE groups with a primary activity in ADS or CFB sectors that would fall in scope of Amount A after applying the

[51]Cf. OECD, BEPS Action 1: Report on Pillar One Blueprint 2020, para. 46; for detailed explanations see OECD, BEPS Action 1: Report on Pillar One Blueprint 2020, para. 47.

[52]Cf. OECD, BEPS Action 1: Report on Pillar One Blueprint 2020, para. 42.

[53]Cf. OECD, BEPS Action 1: Report on Pillar One Blueprint 2020, para. 39.

[54]Cf. OECD, BEPS Action 1: Report on Pillar One Blueprint 2020, paras. 33, 53.

[55]Cf. OECD, BEPS Action 1: Report on Pillar One Blueprint 2020, paras. 35, 105 et seqq.

[56]Cf. OECD, BEPS Action 1: Report on Pillar One Blueprint 2020, para. 108.

[57]Cf. OECD, BEPS Action 1: Report on Pillar One Blueprint 2020, para. 198.

[58]Cf. OECD, BEPS Action 1: Report on Pillar One Blueprint 2020, para. 175; note 36.

EUR 750 million threshold sums up to 2,300.[59] To avoid tax administrations being overwhelmed with the administration of the new taxing right, it is currently discussed to implement the global revenue threshold on a phased approach starting with a higher threshold in the beginning that could then i) gradually be reduced over a certain number of years; or ii) applied for a longer period and then be reduced after a post-implementation review has been undertaken.[60]

The second threshold outlined in the Pillar One Blueprint relates to the amount of foreign source in-scope revenue. This so-called 'de minimis foreign in-scope revenue test' shall ensure that the revenue from ADS and CFD earned outside the domestic market of the MNE group is above a certain threshold.[61] Discussions among the members of the Inclusive Framework revolved around a threshold of EUR 250 million.[62] However, the Pillar One Blueprint does not provide any concrete number with regard to the amount of this threshold.

b. Nexus

The Pillar One Blueprint suggests the introduction of a new nexus rule which does not depend on physical presence of an enterprise in the market jurisdiction. Rather, a new nexus shall be created based on indicators that evidence a significant and sustained engagement with the market jurisdiction, largely expressed through sales.[63] It is suggested to introduce this new nexus rule in a standalone provision to limit spill-over effects on other existing tax or non-tax rules.[64]

Primary evidence of a significant and sustained engagement with a market jurisdiction shall be the generation of in-scope revenue in a market jurisdiction.[65] However, while a certain market revenue threshold could be the only test required to create nexus for ADS in scope, the Pillar One Blueprint emphasises that mere sales into a market jurisdiction above a certain threshold may not suffice to create a new nexus for CFB.[66] Rather, additional factors or so-called 'plus' factors (e.g. existence of a subsidiary or a PE of the enterprise in the market jurisdiction or sales above an even higher threshold) are currently discussed in order to evidence

---

[59] Cf. OECD, BEPS Action 1: Report on Pillar One Blueprint 2020, para. 181.

[60] Cf. OECD, BEPS Action 1: Report on Pillar One Blueprint 2020, paras. 179 et seq.

[61] Cf. OECD, BEPS Action 1: Report on Pillar One Blueprint 2020, paras. 36, 182 et seqq.

[62] Cf. *Ditz/Pinkernell*, ISR 2020, 417 (419).

[63] Cf. OECD, BEPS Action 1: Report on Pillar One Blueprint 2020, paras. 186 et seqq.

[64] Cf. OECD, BEPS Action 1: Report on Pillar One Blueprint 2020, para. 189.

[65] Cf. OECD, BEPS Action 1: Report on Pillar One Blueprint 2020, para. 190.

[66] Cf. OECD, BEPS Action 1: Report on Pillar One Blueprint 2020, paras. 190 et seqq.

a significant and sustained engagement with the market jurisdiction.[67] Nevertheless, whether or not such 'plus' factors shall be part of the nexus requirement for CFB is still unclear and subject to discussion among the members of the Inclusive Framework.[68] The initial suggestion to set the market revenue threshold for ADS at EUR 1 million and for CFB at EUR 3 million does not appear in the Pillar One Blueprint.[69]

c. Revenue Sourcing Rules

To determine the revenue derived from a particular market jurisdiction the Pillar One Blueprint provides for different revenue sourcing rules.[70] In this context, sourcing principles are identified for each type of in-scope revenue which are accompanied by a list of specific indicators an MNE shall use to apply the sourcing principles.[71] These indicators are organised in a hierarchy, with the indicator that appears first in the hierarchy shall also be applied first by the MNE to identify the source jurisdiction unless this information is unreliable or unavailable.[72] By way of example, for online advertising services, the principle shall be to source the revenue based on the jurisdiction of the real-time location of the viewer of the advertisement, and the acceptable indicator would be (i) the jurisdiction of the geolocation of the device of the viewer at the time of display; or if unreliable or unavailable ii) the jurisdiction of the IP address of the device of the viewer at the time of display; or if unreliable or unavailable iii) other available information to determine the real-time location of the viewer.[73]

The revenue sourcing rules are not only important for applying the scope and nexus rules, but also for the application of the new profit allocation rules, which are further elaborated in the next chapter.

---

[67] Cf. OECD, BEPS Action 1: Report on Pillar One Blueprint 2020, para. 192.

[68] Cf. OECD, BEPS Action 1: Report on Pillar One Blueprint 2020, para. 191.

[69] The expression 'EUR X million' used in the Pillar One Blueprint indicates that no final decision on the market revenue threshold for ADS and CFB has been reached yet, cf. OECD, BEPS Action 1: Report on Pillar One Blueprint 2020, para. 192.

[70] See in more detail OECD, BEPS Action 1: Report on Pillar One Blueprint 2020, paras. 218 et seqq.

[71] Cf. OECD, BEPS Action 1: Report on Pillar One Blueprint 2020, para. 219.

[72] Cf. OECD, BEPS Action 1: Report on Pillar One Blueprint 2020, para. 220.

[73] Cf. OECD, BEPS Action 1: Report on Pillar One Blueprint 2020, paras. 238 et seq.

3. New Profit Allocation Rules (Amount A and B)

a. Amount A

(1) Overview

As pointed out above, Amount A is important on two counts: it aims at establishing a new taxing right and it shall be decisive for profit attribution to market jurisdictions. More precisely, Amount A shall represent a share of the residual profit of an MNE (either on a group or a segment basis) that shall be allocated to market jurisdictions based on a globally agreed formula.[74] It follows that the calculation of Amount A totally departs from the arm's length principle.

(2) Tax Base Determination

The calculation of Amount A shall be based on an adjusted profit before tax (hereinafter: PBT) measure derived from consolidated financial accounts prepared under IFRS (hereinafter: International Financial Reporting Standards) or other eligible[75] national Generally Accepted Accounting Principles (hereinafter: GAAP).[76] Book-to-book harmonisation adjustments to account for the variances between different GAAPs are considered not necessary.[77] Also, book-to-tax adjustments to align the tax base for Amount A with the corporate tax base of the Inclusive Framework members shall be limited to a minimum.[78]

Since the new taxing right under Amount A is to apply only to profits attributable to ADS and CFB, the need arises to segment the tax base. Nevertheless, in many cases such segmentation of the net profits attributable to ADS and CFB may not be possible.[79] Therefore, the Pillar One Blueprint provides for the use of the consolidated profit margin of the MNE group as a proxy for the in-scope profit

[74]Cf. OECD, BEPS Action 1: Report on Pillar One Blueprint 2020, paras. 10, 496.

[75]According to the Pillar One Blueprint an initial assessment has shown that the following GAAP shall be considered eligible for the Amount A calculation: GAAP of Australia, Canada, Hong Kong (China), Japan, New Zealand, the People's Republic of China, the Republic of India, the Republic of Korea, Singapore and the United States, cf. OECD, BEPS Action 1: Report on Pillar One Blueprint 2020, para. 420.

[76]Cf. OECD, BEPS Action 1: Report on Pillar One Blueprint 2020, para. 407.

[77]Cf. OECD, BEPS Action 1: Report on Pillar One Blueprint 2020, para. 408.

[78]According to the Pillar One Blueprint these book-to-tax adjustments shall include: exclusion of income tax expenses; exclusion of dividend income and gains or losses arising in connection with shares, exclusion of profits or losses derived from using the equity method of accounting and exclusion of expenses that are typically non-deductible or limited for public policy reasons, cf. OECD, BEPS Action 1: Report on Pillar One Blueprint 2020, paras. 409, 430 et seqq.

[79]Cf. OECD, BEPS Action 1: Report on Pillar One Blueprint 2020, para. 412.

margin.[80] This in-scope profit margin shall then be applied to in-scope revenues to produce a proxy for in-scope profits.[81] Moreover, to limit the number of MNE groups required to segment their Amount A tax base, the Pillar One Blueprint provides for a segmentation exemption for MNE groups that have a global revenue below a certain threshold.[82] The exact global revenue threshold below which the segmentation exemption shall apply has yet to be determined. Additionally, it is proposed that MNE groups may not be required to compute the Amount A tax base on a segmented basis if the disclosed segments have similar profit margins.[83]

As explicitly emphasised, Amount A is intended to apply not only to profits, but also to losses, in order to ensure that losses are brought into consideration. In this regard, loss-carry forward rules are suggested which shall apply through a so-called earn-out mechanism.[84]

(3) The Formula to Determine the Quantum of Amount A

The underlying idea of the Pillar One Blueprint is that Amount A shall apply only to a certain portion of the profits that exceed a particular level of profitability. Consequently, the calculation of Amount A must be based on a formula. However, the members of the Inclusive Framework did not yet agree on the precise parameters of such a formula. Rather, the Pillar One Blueprint sets out three steps that shall form the basic to determine the Amount A quantum. The following steps are outlined:[85]

- Step 1 (profitability threshold): To isolate the residual profits of a business potentially subject to reallocation, the Amount A formula shall include a profitability threshold based on a fixed percentage (PBT to revenue ration).
- Step 2 (reallocation percentage): To ensure that other factors such as trade intangibles, risk and capital continue to be remunerated and allocated residual profits, only a share of the residual profits shall be allocated to market jurisdictions. This allocation percentage shall be a fixed percentage of the residual profits.

[80] Cf. OECD, BEPS Action 1: Report on Pillar One Blueprint 2020, para. 412.
[81] Cf. OECD, BEPS Action 1: Report on Pillar One Blueprint 2020, para. 412.
[82] Cf. OECD, BEPS Action 1: Report on Pillar One Blueprint 2020, para. 412.
[83] Cf. OECD, BEPS Action 1: Report on Pillar One Blueprint 2020, para. 447.
[84] Cf. OECD, BEPS Action 1: Report on Pillar One Blueprint 2020, paras. 415 et seq.
[85] Cf. OECD, BEPS Action 1: Report on Pillar One Blueprint 2020, paras. 496 et seqq.

- Step 3 (allocation key): To distribute the allocable tax base among the eligible market jurisdictions an allocation key must be implemented which shall be based on locally sourced in-scope revenue.

However, the level of profitability above which Amount A shall apply, the portion of the residual profit that shall be allocated to the market jurisdictions and whether different percentages shall apply for different business activities are not yet decided and present only some of the issues that must still be addressed in further negotiations among the members of the Inclusive Framework.[86] Also, whether the formula to determine the quantum of Amount A shall be delivered through a profit-based (i.e. calculation would start with the Amount A tax base determined as a profit amount) or a profit margin-based approach (i.e. calculation would start with the Amount A tax base determined as a profit margin) is still unclear at this stage of the work of the Inclusive Framework.[87]

(4) Elimination of Double Taxation

As Amount A is an overlay to the arm's length based profit allocation rules, it is necessary that the profits allocated to the market countries under Amount A are deductible from the taxable profits in other countries. Otherwise double taxation would appear to be the ultimate result of such an overlay. In order to reconcile the two profit allocation systems, it is necessary to identify which entity/entities within the MNE group should bear the Amount A tax liability, which in turn determines which jurisdiction/jurisdictions must relieve the double taxation arising from Amount A.[88]

In this context, the Pillar One Blueprint suggests the use of a four-step approach to identify the paying entity/entities.[89] In a first step, entities within the MNE group performing activities that make a material and sustained contribution to the MNE group's ability to generate residual profits shall be identified.[90] To ensure that the entities identified in the first step actually have the capability to bear the Amount A tax liability, a profitability test shall be applied in a second

[86] Detailed for issues that must still be addressed in further negotiations among the members of the Inclusive Framework see OECD, BEPS Action 1: Report on Pillar One Blueprint 2020, paras. 554 et seqq.

[87] Cf. OECD, BEPS Action 1: Report on Pillar One Blueprint 2020, para. 497 and Annex B.

[88] Cf. OECD, BEPS Action 1: Report on Pillar One Blueprint 2020, para. 557.

[89] Cf. OECD, BEPS Action 1: Report on Pillar One Blueprint 2020, para. 560.

[90] See in more detail OECD, BEPS Action 1: Report on Pillar One Blueprint 2020, paras. 579 et seqq.

step.[91] Subsequently, in a third step, the Amount A tax liability is to be allocated to the entities that have a connection with the markets where Amount A is allocated.[92] If a sufficiently strong connection is not found, or where the entities with a market connection lack the required profit, the remaining tax liability is to be allocated to the remaining entities on a pro-rata basis.[93]

The Pillar One Blueprint contemplates that tax on Amount A could be relieved by paying entities using either the credit method or the exemption method.[94]

b. Amount B

Amount B aims to establish a standardised remuneration for so-called 'baseline marketing and distribution activities' carried on in the market jurisdiction by distributors either through a subsidiary or a PE.[95] As already pointed out above, Amount B does not establish any new taxing right but rather seeks to simplify the application of existing transfer pricing rules based on the arm's length principle for specific transactions.[96] Furthermore, it is emphasised in the Pillar One Blueprint that the introduction of Amount B also intends to reduce controversy between tax administrations and taxpayers and enhance tax certainty.[97]

The scope of Amount B shall not be subject to the scope limitations of Amount A.[98] In-scope 'baseline marketing and distribution activities' shall be defined by reference to a positive list of functions performed, assets owned and risks assumed at arm's length by routine distributors.[99] This positive list shall be supplemented by a negative list of activities that should not be performed by distributors to be considered in scope of Amount B.[100] Furthermore, certain

---

[91] See in more detail OECD, BEPS Action 1: Report on Pillar One Blueprint 2020, paras. 592 et seqq.

[92] See in more detail OECD, BEPS Action 1: Report on Pillar One Blueprint 2020, paras. 599 et seqq.

[93] See in more detail OECD, BEPS Action 1: Report on Pillar One Blueprint 2020, paras. 608 et seqq.

[94] Cf. OECD, BEPS Action 1: Report on Pillar One Blueprint 2020, para. 571.

[95] Cf. OECD, BEPS Action 1: Report on Pillar One Blueprint 2020, para. 650.

[96] Cf. OECD, BEPS Action 1: Report on Pillar One Blueprint 2020, para. 651.

[97] Cf. OECD, BEPS Action 1: Report on Pillar One Blueprint 2020, para. 651.

[98] Cf. OECD, BEPS Action 1: Report on Pillar One Blueprint 2020, para. 659.

[99] Cf. OECD, BEPS Action 1: Report on Pillar One Blueprint 2020, para. 664.

[100] Cf. OECD, BEPS Action 1: Report on Pillar One Blueprint 2020, paras. 664, 669.

quantitative indicators shall be used to support the identification of in-scope activities.[101] The 'next steps' enumerated in the Pillar One Blueprint indicate that various technical issues, including the identification of which baseline marketing and distribution activities shall be on the positive list as well as which activities, functions, and risks shall be on the negative list, remains to be addressed.[102]

Another issue that remains to be clarified is the quantum of the fixed return to remunerate baseline marketing and distribution activities under Amount B. As emphasised in the Pillar One Blueprint, the TNMM appears to be the most appropriate transfer pricing method for the remuneration of these baseline activities.[103] However, it shall be possible to rebut the application of Amount B by demonstrating that another method would be the most appropriate under the arm's length principle (escape-clause).[104] Also, the need for differentiated returns by regions, industries and functional intensity is currently explored.[105]

4. Tax Certainty

The Pillar One Blueprint dedicates an entire chapter to the issue of tax certainty and emphasises that tax certainty 'is a key component of Pillar One'[106]. The tax certainty dimension is broken down into two segments: i) dispute prevention and resolution for Amount A and ii) dispute prevention and resolution beyond Amount A.[107]

With respect to the first dimension, the Pillar One Blueprint provides a draft outline for a framework for a binding dispute avoidance and prevention mechanism to ensure that the application of all aspects of Amount A to a particular MNE group is agreed among all participating jurisdictions.[108] This mechanisms

---

[101] See in more detail OECD, BEPS Action 1: Report on Pillar One Blueprint 2020, para. 667 et seqq.

[102] For the next steps see OECD, BEPS Action 1: Report on Pillar One Blueprint 2020, para. 703.

[103] Cf. OECD, BEPS Action 1: Report on Pillar One Blueprint 2020, para. 686.

[104] Cf. OECD, BEPS Action 1: Report on Pillar One Blueprint 2020, para. 688.

[105] Cf. OECD, BEPS Action 1: Report on Pillar One Blueprint 2020, paras. 689 et seqq.

[106] Cf. OECD, BEPS Action 1: Report on Pillar One Blueprint 2020, para. 16.

[107] See in more detail for dispute prevention and resolution for Amount A OECD, BEPS Action 1: Report on Pillar One Blueprint 2020, paras. 713 et seqq. and for dispute prevention and resolution beyond Amount A OECD, BEPS Action 1: Report on Pillar One Blueprint 2020, paras. 792 et seqq.

[108] Cf. OECD, BEPS Action 1: Report on Pillar One Blueprint 2020, paras. 17, 706.

shall be based on a representative panel process that shall perform a review function and involve a review panel and, if necessary, a determination panel to ensure early tax certainty.[109] In cases where the MNE group does not opt for the early tax certainty process, the Pillar One Blueprint also provides enhanced dispute resolution features when disputes arise with respect to Amount A.[110]

With respect to the second dimension, the Pillar One Blueprint outlines three main steps to provide tax certainty beyond Amount A:[111]

- Step 1: Improvements to dispute prevention processes;
- Step 2: Improvements to the Mutual Agreement Procedures, and
- Step 3: A binding dispute resolution mechanism beyond Amount A.

III. Assessment of Pillar One Blueprint in Light of the Overarching Principles of Tax Policy

1. Preliminary Remarks

As emphasised earlier, the key elements of Pillar One are outlined in the Pillar One Blueprint, which was approved by the Inclusive Framework on 8–9 October 2020. Nevertheless, at its current stage the Pillar One Blueprint is not yet a fully developed approach that is ready for implementation in tax treaty law and national tax law. Rather, several technical, administrative, and key policy issues of the new approach on which there are differences of opinion among members of the Inclusive Framework still need to be bridged to reach a consensus-based solution by mid-2021.[112]

Nevertheless, the path the Inclusive Framework envisages to proceed with Pillar One seems quite clear and already allows for an assessment against the overarching principles of tax policy as elaborated in chapter B. In this context, the assessment not only identifies benefits and shortcomings of the basic architecture of the Pillar One Blueprint, but also develops recommendations on how certain aspects of the approach can be improved to be more compatible with the overarching principles of tax policy.

[109] Cf. OECD, BEPS Action 1: Report on Pillar One Blueprint 2020, para. 174.

[110] Cf. OECD, BEPS Action 1: Report on Pillar One Blueprint 2020, paras. 707, 786.

[111] Cf. OECD, BEPS Action 1: Report on Pillar One Blueprint 2020, paras. 794 et seqq.

[112] For an overview of the technical, administrative and key policy issues of the new approach see OECD, BEPS Action 1: Public Consultation Document 2020, pp. 3 et seqq.

2. Equity

a. Inter-Nation Equity

(1) Scope and Nexus

As elaborated in chapter B, the principle of inter-nation equity seeks an equitable allocation of taxing rights among countries to ensure that each country receives a fair share of tax revenue from cross-border transactions. While under current international tax law, business profits derived by an enterprise are solely taxable in the country of residence unless such profits are derived in another state through a PE situated therein, the new taxing right under Amount A envisages to expand the taxing rights of market jurisdictions. More precisely, the new taxing right shall not depend on actual physical presence of an enterprise but rather on an active and sustained engagement of an MNE group in market jurisdictions largely expressed through sales generated in these jurisdictions.[113]

A basic requirement of any new taxing right intended to enhance inter-nations equity is that it is based on a solid legitimation. Such a legitimation can be derived from the principle of economic allegiance, which is also used in order to justify PE taxation.[114] It can certainly be argued that also non-resident enterprises that do not maintain an actual physical presence in the market jurisdiction still benefit from the market jurisdiction's legal system, as businesses rely upon it to uphold intellectual property rights, enforce legal contracts as well as payments for transactions.[115] Also, the provision of a proper technical infrastructure from motorways to data highways could justify market-based taxation.[116] However, as argued earlier, while the principle of economic allegiance may be utilised to justify the existence of a 'genuine link' to the market jurisdiction in general and insofar does in principle allow taxation by the market jurisdiction, it is unable to provide clear guidance with regard to the sharing of taxing rights between jurisdictions.[117]

---

[113]Cf. OECD, BEPS Action 1: Report on Pillar One Blueprint 2020, paras. 6, 22.

[114]See for the use of that principle in order to justify PE taxation by the source jurisdiction i.a. *Schaumburg*, Internationales Steuerrecht, para. 18.215; *Ditz*, Internationale Gewinnabgrenzung bei Betriebsstätten, 100 et seqq.

[115]Cf. *Pinto*, E-Commerce and Source-Based Income Taxation, 22.

[116]Cf. *Schön*, BIT 2018, 278 (285).

[117]Cf. *Schön*, BIT 2018, 278 (287); *Hey*, IWB 2004, 2003 (2007 et seqq.); *Richman*, Taxation of Foreign Investment Income, 16; *Schön*, WTJ 2009, 67 (75 et seq.); *Schön*, Intertax 2019, 1003 (1008 et seqq.); *Schäfer*, International Company Taxation in the Era of Information and Communication Technologies, 80.

An entitlement to tax corporate profits in the demand jurisdiction can also be derived from the supply-demand approach, used in order to identify the profit's source.[118] Also, *Vogel* recognises the entitlement to tax corporate profits in the market jurisdiction and emphasises that '[t]here is no valid objection [...] against a claim of the sales state to tax part of the sales income.'[119] Nevertheless, as argued earlier, also the supply-demand approach lacks a workable benchmark for the allocation of taxing rights among countries.[120]

Even though, no commonly accepted benchmark for the allocation of taxing rights has evolved throughout taxation history,[121] all of the OECD's BEPS Action points rally around the notion to ensure that profits are taxed where value is created.[122] If the concept of value creation is used as the benchmark against which to evaluate whether the new taxing right under Amount A results in a more equitable allocation of taxing rights among countries, the result would not be satisfactory. As appropriately argued by *Petruzzi/Holzinger/Screpante/Buriak/Capristano Cardoso*, a new taxing right based on sales does not appear to be directly linked to value creation, since sales in the market jurisdiction generally do not create value.[123] *Förster/Greil/Hilse* also argue that even though 'the impact and value creation by digitalisation is *crystallized* at the point in time when revenue is generated, the value creation may have taken place outside the jurisdiction where sales are taking place'[124]. This may be the case, according to *Förster/Greil/Hilse*, if customer or user data obtained in a specific jurisdiction may also result in revenue generation outside the jurisdiction where sales are taking place.[125] It is therefore rightly argued that measuring the impact of digitalisation merely with a factor of sales does not seem to bring nexus and taxation rights in line with value creation.[126]

---

[118] See in more detail chapter B.II.2.a of this thesis.

[119] Cf. *Vogel*, Intertax 1988, 393 (401).

[120] Cf. *Ditz/Pinkernell*, ISR 2019, 377 (382). Also, *Vogel* argues that 'how much is contributed to the income by providing a market cannot be measured exactly', *Vogel*, Intertax 1988, 393 (401). See in more detail also chapter B.II.2 of this thesis.

[121] Cf. *Fuest*, ifo Schnelldienst 3/2020, 6 (9).

[122] See i.a. OECD, BEPS Project – Explanatory Statement, para. 1.

[123] Cf. *Petruzzi/Holzinger/Screpante/Buriak/Capristano Cardoso*, TPI 2019, 312 (314 et seq.).

[124] *Förster/Greil/Hilse*, ITPJ 2020, 3 (7).

[125] Cf. *Förster/Greil/Hilse*, ITPJ 2020, 3 (7).

[126] Cf. Dispute prevention, ITPJ 2020, 3 (7); similar *Petruzzi/Holzinger/Screpante/Buriak/Capristano Cardoso*, TPI 2019, 312 (315).

However, while the concept of value creation functioned quite effective throughout the BEPS project in order to fix existing shortcomings of the tax system and thereby addressing BEPS issues, especially by denying taxing rights to tax havens arguing that no value is created in such jurisdictions,[127] *Devereux/Vella* rightly point out that the concept of value creation can or should not be used 'as a guide for allocating taxing rights among countries'[128]. Given the diverse views of the members of the Inclusive Framework with regard to the question of whether active user participation creates value for the enterprise which should be covered by an additional taxing right, no consensus solution among the members of the Inclusive Framework seems possible on the grounds of the concept of value creation.[129] Besides, even though the OECD dedicated an entire chapter to the concept of value creation,[130] *Devereux/Vella* correctly argue that it seems impossible to know how much value users create.[131] Therefore, rather than trying to align taxation rights with the vague concept of value creation, the OECD's initiative for a reform of corporate taxation rules should ultimately aim to resolve existing conflicts and return to a tax framework that is not characterised by permanent double taxation caused through unilateral tax measures.[132]

Against this background, the fundamental approach of Pillar One, which moves away from the concept of value creation and rather focuses to justify the new taxing right with an active and sustained engagement of an enterprise in a market jurisdiction expressed through specific in-scope sales generated in this jurisdiction, seems to be a viable approach that could facilitate political compromise.[133] This approach acknowledges that customer/user interaction and engagement, may it be through the benefits received from powerful customer or user network effects or through the collection and exploitation of individual customer data, can substantially increase the sales of enterprises and could therefore

---

[127] Cf. *Das*, BIT 2020, 134 (142).

[128] Cf. *Devereux/Vella*, BTR 2018, 387 (405); similar *Das*, BIT 2020, 134 (142); *Fuest*, ifo Schnelldienst 3/2020, 6 (9).

[129] For the diverse views of the members of the Inclusive Framework cf. OECD, BEPS Action 1: Interim Report 2018, paras. 387 et seqq. and chapter E.IV.2 of this thesis. Critical regarding the use of the concept of value creation for establishing new taxing rights see also *Bräutigam/Kellermann/Spengel*, IStR 2020, 281 (283).

[130] See in more detail OECD, BEPS Action 1: Interim Report 2018, paras. 66 et seqq. and chapter E.I.4 of this thesis.

[131] Cf. *Devereux/Vella*, BTR 2018, 387 (399).

[132] Similar *Fuest*, ifo Schnelldienst 3/2020, 6 (10).

[133] The use of sales as a new nexus was already proposed by various scholars, see i.a. *Schreiber*, BIT 2018, 259 (259 et seqq.); *Schreiber/Fell*, WTJ 2017, 99 (99 et seqq.).

justify a new taxing right for market countries.[134] Insofar, the approach envisages to bring the new taxing right in line with the level of engagement in the market jurisdiction that cannot be captured by the current PE rules.

It can certainly be argued that using sales as a proxy for the level of engagement in the market jurisdiction may be arbitrary. However, a new taxing right based on sales also offers many advantages. Such a new taxing right would not only be difficult to circumvent due to the immobility of consumers/users,[135] but it would also provide a stable basis to which profit allocation rules can be linked. If combined with the commitment of the members of the Inclusive Framework to withdraw unilateral measures introduced as a response to the tax challenges arising from the digitalisation of the economy,[136] the fundamental idea of the new taxing right under Amount A could be a pragmatic basis to overcome existing shortcomings of the current PE rules resulting from the digitalisation of the economy which could enhance inter-nation equity.

(2) Profit Allocation Rules

Even though, many parameters of the new profit allocation mechanism under Amount A are still unclear at this point of time, the quantum of Amount A shall represent a share of the residual profit that is to be allocated to market jurisdictions in proportion to in-scope sales in the various market countries using a formulaic approach. As Amount A is an overlay to the arm's length based profit allocation rules, it is necessary that profits allocated to market countries are deductible from the taxable profits in other countries. Otherwise double taxation would appear to be the ultimate result of such an overlay.

As stated above, the Pillar One Blueprint provides for a mechanism to reconcile the new and the existing profit allocation rules to prevent double taxation.[137] This mechanism mainly results in the effect that residual profits allocated to the market countries shall be deducted from countries where the residual profits are currently allocated. While such an approach would be difficult to sell to countries which would lose out,[138] the OECD's economic impact assessment, published on 12 October 2020, reveals that it is expected that on average all income groups,

[134] Cf. OECD, BEPS Action 1: Report on Pillar One Blueprint 2020, para. 24.

[135] Cf. *Devereux/Vella*, BTR 2018, 387 (404).

[136] For an overview of unilateral measures introduced see chapter E.IV.3 of this thesis.

[137] See in more detail OECD, BEPS Action 1: Report on Pillar One Blueprint 2020, paras. 556 et seqq. and chapter F.II.3.a.(4) of this thesis.

[138] Cf. *Devereux*, The OECD Pillar One Proposal, University of Oxford Saïd Business School Blog.

ranging from low to high income countries, would experience an increase in corporate tax revenue.[139] Only investment hubs[140] would be expected to experience some loss in tax revenue.[141] Even though, it was rightly pointed out by *Vogel* that it is difficult to prove that something is equitable in the same way as this can be done with regard to empirical facts,[142] an approach which takes away ultimately taxable profits from investment hubs in favour of countries where businesses develop an 'active and sustained engagement' would probably be perceived as an approach which could enhance inter-nation equity by most countries.[143] Also, the estimate that the effect from the implementation of Amount A would result in a global revenue increase in a range of 0,2–0,5% seems to be an encouraging basis for reaching an agreement among the members of the Inclusive Framework.[144]

In the discussion of inter-nation equity, an issue of importance is also the treatment of losses in the context of Amount A. An asymmetrical system that only allocates residual profits to market jurisdictions seems unbalanced and not in line with the principle of inter-nation equity. However, as outlined above, the Pillar One Blueprint provides for a loss carry-forward regime to ensure that no Amount A shall be allocated to market jurisdictions if the relevant MNE group is not profitable over time. In this regard, the regime shall rely on an earn-out mechanism that allows past losses to be offset against future profits.[145]

While the quantum of Amount A departs from the arm's length principle, Amount B reflects efforts to improve the practical application of the arm's length principle by proposing a standardised remuneration of baseline marketing and

---

[139]Cf. OECD, BEPS Action 1: Economic Impact Assessment 2020, paras. 22, 102. The estimates are based on the assumption that Pillar One focuses on ADS and CFB with a global revenue threshold of EUR 750 million, a profitability threshold percentage of 10% (based on PBT/turnover), a reallocation percentage of 20% and a nexus revenue threshold of EUR 1 million for ADS and EUR 3 million for CFB, cf. OECD, BEPS Action 1: Economic Impact Assessment 2020, paras. 23, 102.

[140]Investment hubs are defined as jurisdictions with a total inward foreign direct investment above 150% of gross domestic product, cf. OECD, BEPS Action 1: Economic Impact Assessment 2020, para. 102.

[141]Cf. OECD, Update on Economic Analysis and Impact Assessment, slide 12.

[142]Cf. *Vogel*, Intertax 1988, 393 (393).

[143]Similar *Devereux* who argues that taking away taxable profits 'from jurisdictions with low tax rates (and high residual profit) [...] may be perfectly acceptable to most OECD members', *Devereux*, The OECD Pillar One Proposal, University of Oxford Saïd Business School Blog.

[144]Cf. OECD, Update on Economic Analysis and Impact Assessment, slide 12.

[145]Cf. for the estimates OECD, BEPS Action 1: Report on Pillar One Blueprint 2020, para. 10.

distribution activities based on the arm's length principle. If properly developed, Amount B could achieve a more equitable allocation of taxable profits among countries. This is mainly due to the fact that Amount B seeks to simplify the computation of the return for activities in scope, and in this respect may reduce disputes and uncertainties surrounding the computation of arm's length prices. Especially, countries whose tax administrations do not have the technological and administrative means to defend their tax base may benefit from such simplified rules.

Nevertheless, the success of the new profit allocation rules, and insofar also the evaluation of whether inter-nation equity can be improved through the new approach, depends largely on the ability of the Inclusive Framework to develop dispute prevention and dispute resolution mechanisms with regard to Amount A and beyond. The current outline of a new framework for dispute prevention and resolution for Amount A and beyond, as proposed in the Pillar One Blueprint, appears to be an encouraging foundation and can be seen as a step in the right direction.

(3) Interim Conclusion

Based on the above assessment, Table 1 evaluates the extent to which the basic architecture of the Pillar One Blueprint, differentiated by scope and nexus as well as profit attribution rules, complies with the tax policy principle of inter-nation equity and summarises the main reasons for this evaluation.

Table 1 Compatibility of Pillar One Blueprint with Inter-Nations Equity

	Scope and Nexus	**Profit Allocation Rules**
Evaluation	***	***
Reasoning	• new taxing right does not depend on physical presence of an enterprise in the market jurisdiction and insofar aims to overcome the shortcomings of the PE concept • approach acknowledges that customer/user interaction and engagement can substantially increase the sales of enterprises and could therefore justify a new taxing right for market countries • chosen point of reference for new taxing right (in-scope sales) could provide a stable basis to which profit allocation rules can be linked	• formulaic approach of Amount A seems a pragmatic approach to compensate market countries for active and sustained engagement of an MNE in the market jurisdiction • OECD's preliminary impact assessment suggests that all income groups except of investment hubs would experience an increase in corporate tax revenue, which could be considered to enhance inter-nations equity • Amount B seeks to simplify the computation of the return for activities in scope and makes it easier for countries to claim their share of tax revenue • success of new profit allocation rules largely depends on the ability of the Inclusive Framework to develop improved dispute prevention and resolution mechanisms

Scale:[146]
*Approach could adversely impact the overarching tax policy principle
**Approach could partially challenge the overarching tax policy principle
***Approach could be compatible with the overarching tax policy principle

Source: Own illustration.

[146]The scale used for the evaluation of the Pillar One Blueprint is based on the scale used by *Pistone/Nogueira/Andrade* for the evaluation of previous OECD proposals: the 'user participation' proposal, the 'marketing intangibles' proposal and the 'significant economic presence' proposal, see *Pistone/Nogueira/Andrade*, ITAXS 2019, Issue 2, 1 (40 et seq.).

b. Inter-Taxpayer Equity

(1) Scope and Nexus

While the principle of inter-nation equity seeks an equitable allocation of taxing rights among countries, the principle of inter-taxpayer equity seeks an equitable treatment of taxpayers, requiring that cross-border income of taxpayers is neither overtaxed nor undertaxed.

On the one side, overtaxation may occur from an uncertain and inconsistent application of taxation rules.[147] As the new taxing right under Amount A shall be implemented as an additional layer on top of the already existing taxation rules, uncertainties and inconsistencies related to the existing nexus rules would not be abandoned. Rather, the new taxing right would add an additional layer of complexity which could lead to additional uncertainties and inconsistencies.[148] On the other side, it is envisaged to tie any consensus-based agreement to the commitment of the members of the Inclusive Framework to withdraw unilateral measures introduced as a response to the tax challenges arising from the digitalisation of the economy.[149] Since unilateral measures flout tax treaty obligations and ultimately result in double taxation,[150] the approach could also provide a chance to reduce instances of overtaxation and insofar enhance inter-taxpayer equity.

Undertaxation in an international context occurs where income generated by an enterprise is not taxed anywhere or not fully taxed.[151] As outlined earlier, the new taxing right under Amount A envisages to link the taxation right to sales generated from transactions between the MNE and the consumer/user. Since consumers/users are relatively immobile and do not have an incentive to move to a low tax jurisdiction just for the sake of reducing the tax burden of the MNE from which they purchase products or use services, the new taxing right under Amount A could reduce leeway for tax planning and insofar may also reduce possibilities for undertaxation of income generated by taxpayers.[152]

---

[147]Cf. *Li*, CTJ 2002, 823 (840).

[148]See in more detail for uncertainties surrounding the new taxing right under Amount A chapter F.III.5 of this thesis.

[149]Cf. OECD, BEPS Action 1: Report on Pillar One Blueprint 2020, para. 848.

[150]Cf. *Parada*, TNI 96 (2019), 983 (989).

[151]Cf. *Li*, CTJ 2002, 823 (840).

[152]Even though leeway for tax planning appears limited opportunities exists, see in more detail chapter F.III.6.a of this thesis.

However, the principle of inter-taxpayer equity does not only demand to avoid overtaxation or undertaxation of income but also that taxpayers in similar circumstances should bear a similar tax burden.[153] In this regard, it is worth emphasising that the new taxation right under Amount A envisages to bring only specific businesses within the scope of the new taxing right, namely ADS and CFB which exceed certain revenue thresholds. This distinction between different business models not only leads to increased compliance costs for MNEs in scope, but very likely also to different tax payments for businesses in scope depending on the tax rate abroad. Likewise, the implementation of revenue thresholds could also lead to an unwanted discrimination of smaller MNEs, e.g. in the case the market jurisdiction provides for a lower tax rate than the residence jurisdiction.[154] In order to improve compatibility with the principle of inter-taxpayer equity, the possibility of an optional election to be taxed under the Amount A regime could be considered.[155] This would not only mitigate the effects of any arbitrary cut-off thresholds, but would also put smaller enterprises on equal footing to their larger competitors. To avoid 'cherry picking', this optional election could be bound to a certain period of time.[156]

(2) Profit Allocation Rules

As mentioned above, where profits are allocated on the basis of the arm's length principle, Amount A is an overlay to the current system as the arm's length principle already allocates the full MNE group profit to the respective parts of the enterprise.[157] Insofar, additionally to the already existing possibilities of overtaxation through unilateral transfer pricing increases in one tax jurisdiction without corresponding downward adjustments in another tax jurisdiction, Amount A adds further possibilities of overtaxation of the taxpayer.[158]

It is recognised that tax disputes over Amount A will likely affect taxation of Amount A in multiple jurisdictions.[159] Therefore, a mechanism that protects the taxpayer from unilateral increases of the portion of residual profits attributed to the market countries is necessary. Such a mechanism is outlined in the Pillar One

---

[153] Cf. OECD, BEPS Action 1: Final Report 2015, para. 11.

[154] Cf. *Förster/Greil/Hilse*, ITPJ 2020, 8.

[155] See also Bundessteuerberaterkammer, Comments on Secretariat Proposal, 4

[156] See also Bundessteuerberaterkammer arguing for a time period of three to five years, cf. Bundessteuerberaterkammer, Comments on Secretariat Proposal, 4.

[157] Cf. OECD, BEPS Action 1: Report on Pillar One Blueprint 2020, para. 556.

[158] See in more detail for potential sources of overtaxation chapter F.III.6.b of this thesis.

[159] Cf. OECD, BEPS Action 1: Statement on the Two-Pillar Approach 2020, Annex 1, para. 68.

Blueprint.[160] However, the different technical features of the tax certainty process for Amount A, including how to implement a binding outcome in jurisdictions, is still on the agenda of the Inclusive Framework.[161] Considering that the calculation of Amount A would apply to the profits of an MNE group as a whole (top-down approach) and not merely on an individual country and individual entity basis, such mechanisms seem essential to avoid overtaxation of the taxpayer.

At the same time, Amount A could partially reduce instances of undertaxation, as it could mitigate shortcomings of the arm's length principle which, even after the BEPS project, provides leeway to shift income to low-tax jurisdictions and reveals further weaknesses when applied to highly digitalised business transactions.[162] Insofar, the formulaic approach of Amount A could help to mitigate some of the shortcomings of the existing arm's length principle. Nevertheless, as pointed out in the TP Guidelines, a profit allocation mechanism based on a predetermined formula disregards the particular circumstances of an individual enterprise,[163] and insofar challenges the principle of inter-taxpayer equity.

Amount B may potentially reduce the risk of overtaxation of the taxpayer, as it envisages to reduce disputes and uncertainties with regard to the remuneration of baseline marketing and distribution activities by proposing a fixed return for the remuneration of these activities. Such a fixed return, if implemented by a significant number of jurisdictions, may decrease the risk of unilateral transfer pricing increases without corresponding downward adjustments and may insofar reduce the risk of overtaxation of such transactions, which in turn would promote inter-taxpayer equity. Against this background, the implementation of binding dispute prevention and resolution mechanisms, as envisaged by the Inclusive Framework, will form an essential part to comply with the principle of inter-taxpayer equity.

[160] Cf. OECD, BEPS Action 1: Report on Pillar One Blueprint 2020, paras. 704 et seqq.

[161] Cf. OECD, BEPS Action 1: Report on Pillar One Blueprint 2020, para. 804.

[162] See in more detail for the effectiveness of the BEPS measures chapter E.II of this thesis.

[163] Cf. OECD, TP Guidelines 2017, para. 1.25.

(3) Interim Conclusion

Based on the above assessment, Table 2 evaluates the extent to which the basic architecture of the Pillar One Blueprint, differentiated by scope and nexus as well as profit attribution rules, complies with the tax policy principle of inter-taxpayer equity and summarises the main reasons for this evaluation.

Table 2 Compatibility of Pillar One Blueprint with Inter-Taxpayer Equity

	Scope and Nexus	**Profit Allocation Rules**
Evaluation	**	**
Reasoning	• on the one side, new taxing right adds an additional layer of complexity which also introduces additional uncertainties and inconsistencies and may result in overtaxation of the taxpayer • on the other side, envisaged withdrawal of unilateral measures as part of a consensus-based solution could reduce instances of overtaxation • given the immobility of consumers/users, the new taxing right could reduce leeway for tax planning and insofar undertaxation of income • scope limitations challenge the principle of horizontal equity	• Amount A adds further possibilities of overtaxation of the taxpayer but could also mitigate instances of undertaxation • formulaic approach disregards the particular circumstances of an individual enterprise • Amount B could reduce the risk of overtaxation • overall evaluation of the approach depends on the ability of the Inclusive Framework to develop mandatory and binding dispute prevention and resolution mechanisms

Scale:
*Approach could adversely impact the overarching tax policy principle
**Approach could partially challenge the overarching tax policy principle
***Approach could be compatible with the overarching tax policy principle

Source: Own illustration.

3. Neutrality

a. Scope and Nexus

The OECD has repeatedly pointed out that 'it would be difficult, if not impossible, to ring-fence the digital economy from the rest of the economy'[164], as the digital economy is increasingly becoming the economy itself. In particular, the characteristics frequently observed in digitalised business models that pose a challenge to the international tax rules, i.e. cross-jurisdictional scale without mass, heavy reliance on intangibles and the importance of data, user participation and their synergies with IP,[165] can also be found in more traditional business models.[166] Against this background, the fundamental approach of the new taxing right under Amount A proposing to cover a wide range of businesses, namely CFB as well as ADS, which would not only bring highly digitalised businesses within the scope of the new taxing right but also more traditional business models is, in principle, positive from a neutrality perspective. However, it remains unclear why non-CFB as well as non-ADS shall not be covered by the new taxing right, considering that 'it would be difficult, if not impossible, to ring-fence the digital economy from the rest of the economy'[167].

Despite the fact that the notion of CFB as well as ADS appears quite broad at first glance, it provides for various limitations that are not conducive to neutrality. One of these limitations is that the notion of 'consumer-facing' may leave several B2B transactions out of scope.[168] As elaborated earlier, especially input suppliers are characterised by the fact that they do not interact with the final customer.[169] Consequently, in many cases they may not be captured by the term CFB. Even though some of these cases may be captured by the notion of ADS, the negative list of ADS outlined in the Pillar One Blueprint demonstrates that certain B2B transactions (e.g. B2B transactions that generate revenue from the sale of physical goods) are neither covered by the term CFB nor by ADS. Yet, from a neutrality perspective, also B2B transactions should be covered by the new taxing right.

---

[164] I.a. OECD, BEPS Action 1: Final Report 2015, paras. 115, 364; OECD, BEPS Action 1: Interim Report 2018, para. 375.

[165] See in more detail for the frequently observed characteristics of highly digitalised business models chapter E.I.2 of this thesis.

[166] Cf. OECD, BEPS Action 1: Interim Report 2018, para. 383.

[167] I.a. OECD, BEPS Action 1: Final Report 2015, paras. 115, 364; OECD, BEPS Action 1: Interim Report 2018, para. 375.

[168] See for B2B transactions which shall be covered by the notion of consumer-facing OECD, BEPS Action 1: Report on Pillar One Blueprint 2020, para. 53.

[169] See chapter E.I.3 of this thesis.

Otherwise, some highly profitable business lines of MNEs may potentially not be covered by the new taxing right under Amount A.

Another aspect that is of significance for the assessment of neutrality is the implementation of several thresholds as proposed in the Pillar One Blueprint.[170] While the use of such thresholds intents to limit the new taxing right to mostly very large businesses and insofar aims to reduce compliance as well as administrative burdens for the taxpayers and the tax authorities, any kind of size limitation could lead to an unwanted discrimination of enterprises below these thresholds.[171] A disadvantage for enterprises below the threshold could, e.g., result if the tax rate in the market jurisdiction is lower than in the country of residence. As estimated in the TP Guidelines 2017 within the context of the CbC Report, only a possible implementation of a gross revenue threshold of EUR 750 million by itself (applied on an MNE group basis) would effectively exclude 85–90% of MNE groups operating worldwide from the scope of the new taxing right.[172] Despite the fact that any kind of fixed quantitative threshold would be arbitrary, it may also prevent enterprises to grow beyond a certain size and insofar may potentially distort business decisions of enterprises.[173]

Furthermore, as outlined above, the Pillar One Blueprint proposes carve-outs for the following sectors: i) natural resources; ii) financial services; iii) construction, sale and leasing of residential property; and iv) international airline and shipping businesses.[174] These carve-outs are a form of ring-fencing and must be seen critical under the principle of neutrality.[175] Even though well-reasoned,[176] other business models such as the telecommunication and real estate industry could also bring forward sound arguments why their business models should be out of scope of the new taxing right.[177] However, in order to achieve neutrality,

[170]Cf. in more detail for the proposed threshold tests OECD, BEPS Action 1: Report on Pillar One Blueprint 2020, paras. 171 et seqq.

[171]Cf. also *Förster/Greil/Hilse*, ITPJ 2020, 3 (8).

[172]Cf. OECD, TP Guidelines 2017, para. 5.53.

[173]Cf. *Spengel/Fischer/Ludwig/Müller*, Comments on Secretariat Proposal, 2.

[174]Cf. OECD, BEPS Action 1: Report on Pillar One Blueprint 2020, para. 105.

[175]See also *Petruzzi/Holzinger/Screpante/Buriak/Capristano Cardoso*, TPI 2019, 312 (315); *Pistone/Nogueira/Andrade/Turina*, BIT 2020, 14 (15).

[176]Cf. in more detail for the reasoning for carve-outs OECD, BEPS Action 1: Report on Pillar One Blueprint 2020, paras. 106 et seqq.

[177]See i.a. Dorenkamp, who proposes carve-outs for the telecommunication and real estate industry, cf. *Dorenkamp*, FR 2020, 114 (116).

Amount A should apply broadly rather than merely zoning a part of the digital economy, which would be done through the implementation of the envisaged thresholds and carve-outs.[178]

b. Profit Allocation Rules

Even businesses falling within the scope of the new taxing right are not necessarily considered for Amount A liability, as Amount A shall only apply to the portion of profit exceeding a certain level of profitability.[179] Insofar, the scope of businesses is narrowed even further. Such an approach which excludes businesses not exceeding a certain level of profitability from the reallocation of residual profits to the market jurisdiction, does not appear to be neutral, as it treats enterprises differently depending on their level of profitability.

Furthermore, the approach raises the question of how to deal with MNE groups that carry out various CFB as well as ADS activities with some business lines with a high profit margin and some with a low profit margin. As appropriately pointed out by *Fügemann/Naess-Schmidt* from Copenhagen Economics, the 'use of industry/business line as tax unit would in principle be the most neutral with respect to firm's choice of business models and the sharing of profits between countries'[180]. Even though not clear at this stage, the Pillar One Blueprint seems to tend to the use of segmentation in specific cases[181] which would be positive from a neutrality point of view.

As illustrated earlier, Amount B proposes a fixed return for baseline marketing and distribution activities. Besides the lack of clarification on the quantum of the fixed return to remunerate such activities, it has not yet been decided whether a differentiation of the fixed remuneration should be made contingent on industries, regions and functional intensity.[182] Nevertheless, from a neutrality perspective

[178]Cf. *Harpaz*, TNI 96 (2019), 909 (909).

[179]Detailed for the profitability threshold cf. OECD, BEPS Action 1: Report on Pillar One Blueprint 2020, paras. 507 et seqq.

[180]Business at OECD, Comments on Secretariat Proposal, 3.

[181]The Pillar One Blueprint points out the case where a large MNE operates two substantially independent businesses with different profit margins. In such a case, it is suggested to compute the Amount A tax base on a segmented basis, see in more detail for the segmentation framework OECD, BEPS Action 1: Report on Pillar One Blueprint 2020, paras. 442 et seqq. Also, Annex A of the Pillar One Blueprint contains a detailed process map of Amount A, which includes the segmentation process under Step 4, cf. OECD, BEPS Action 1: Report on Pillar One Blueprint 2020, Annex A, p. 214.

[182]Cf. OECD, BEPS Action 1: Report on Pillar One Blueprint 2020, para. 703.

such a differentiation mechanism seems critical. In particular, regional differentiation appears critical in this respect, as such differentiation could distort MNE groups' business decisions on where to invest in distribution and marketing activities.[183] Differentiation by region could also encourage MNE groups to restructure certain business activities in order to minimise their overall tax payment.

c. Interim Conclusion

Based on the above assessment, Table 3 evaluates the extent to which the basic architecture of the Pillar One Blueprint, differentiated by scope and nexus as well as profit attribution rules, complies with the tax policy principle of neutrality and summarises the main reasons for this evaluation.

Table 3 Compatibility of Pillar One Blueprint with Neutrality

	Scope and Nexus	Profit Allocation Rules
Evaluation	**	**
Reasoning	• fundamental approach shall apply to a wide number of enterprises (CFB and ADS) • traditional business models are put on equal footing with enterprises operating highly digitalised business models • several B2B transactions may be out of scope • proposed thresholds and carve-outs lead to another kind of ring fencing that does not promote neutrality	• formulaic approach limits the liability to Amount A to MNE groups (or segments) with a high level of profitability • applicability of Amount A on segmented basis would be more neutral than MNE group approach • fixed return of Amount B could distort business decisions if differentiations contingent upon, e.g., regions are made

Scale:
*Approach could adversely impact the overarching tax policy principle
**Approach could partially challenge the overarching tax policy principle
***Approach could be compatible with the overarching tax policy principle

Source: Own illustration.

[183] Cf. Tax Foundation, Comments on Secretariat Proposal, 4.

4. Efficiency

a. Scope and Nexus

As outlined earlier, efficient tax rules are those which minimise both compliance costs for taxpayers and administration costs for the relevant tax authorities.[184] Under this premises, the new taxing right under Amount A must prove to be administrable for tax authorities and feasible under reasonable efforts for taxpayers. However, as illustrated in the following, doubts must be expressed whether the new taxing right under Amount A is compatible with these requirements.

On the one side, the envisaged introduction of several thresholds to limit the scope of the new taxing right is certainly to be welcomed from an efficiency point of view, as they would reduce associated administration and compliance costs and thus increase efficiency in the collection of taxes. Such thresholds, especially the discussed introduction of a gross revenue threshold of EUR 750 million,[185] would exclude certain businesses from the new taxing right, particularly small and medium sized businesses. Also, the envisaged carve-outs for certain sectors, such as natural resources; financial services; construction, sale and leasing of residential property as well as international airline and shipping businesses would reduce the number of businesses that may be confronted with the new taxing right, promoting efficiency.

On the other side, any new international taxation right introduced in addition to already existing taxation rights adds complexity for both taxpayers and tax authorities and, to that extent, increases compliance and administration costs.[186] In particular, the sales-based design of Amount A requires a system to locate sales and identify where the product or service is consumed/used.[187] As pointed out by Accountancy Europe, it 'is not always easy, or even possible, to trace the identity of the final consumer'[188]. The revenue sourcing rules provided for the different CFB and ADS outlined in the Pillar One Blueprint already indicate that the administration of the new taxing right will be highly complicated and

---

[184] Cf. OECD, Electronic Commerce: Taxation Framework Conditions 1998, para. 9; *Graetz*, TLR 2001, 261 (310).

[185] Cf. OECD, BEPS Action 1: Report on Pillar One Blueprint 2020, paras. 175 et seqq.

[186] Cf. also *Englisch*, Comments on Secretariat Proposal, 2, 4; *Förster/Greil/Hilse*, ITPJ 2020, 3 (9).

[187] Cf. *Förster/Greil/Hilse*, ITPJ 2020, 3 (10).

[188] Cf. Accountancy Europe, Comments on Secretariat Proposal, para. 14.

will demand detailed documentation to evidence the application of the chosen indicators for revenue sourcing.[189]

b. Profit Allocation Rules

It appears evident that determining the quantum of Amount A and allocating it to the different market jurisdictions in addition to the existing profit allocation mechanism based on the arm's length principle would increase compliance costs for taxpayers covered by the new profit allocation rules and administration costs for the relevant tax authorities. However, the proposal to base the calculation of Amount A on an adjusted PBT measure derived from consolidated group financial accounts[190] appears to be a pragmatic solution that seems to be administrable for the taxpayer under reasonable efforts.[191] Book-to-book harmonisation adjustments to account for variances between different GAAPs are not considered necessary according to the Pillar One Blueprint, which is to be welcomed from an efficiency point of view. Also, the development of simplified administrative processes, such as simplified reporting and registration-based mechanisms (e.g. a 'one stop shop' and exclusive filing in the ultimate parent jurisdiction), as envisaged, would be crucial to reduce administrative complexity resulting from the implementation of the new profit allocation rule under Amount A.[192]

Another issue relates to the need to compute the Amount A tax base on a segmented basis. Although the Pillar One Blueprint emphasises that segmentation may be required for some MNE's that generate global sales above a certain threshold, in many cases a simplified mechanism can be applied to ensure that additional compliance and administration costs are kept in proportion.[193] Considering the fact that segmentation for Amount A purposes may not necessarily be in line with segmentation for accounting purposes, the simplification mechanism is to be welcomed from an efficiency point of view.

Furthermore, approaches outlined in the Pillar One Blueprint to introduce digital as well as jurisdictional differentiation would increase both administrative and compliance costs and should therefore be viewed critically.[194]

---

[189] See in more detail regarding the required documentation in this context OECD, BEPS Action 1: Report on Pillar One Blueprint 2020, paras. 388 et seqq.

[190] Cf. OECD, BEPS Action 1: Report on Pillar One Blueprint 2020, para. 407.

[191] Cf. also *Englisch*, Comments on Secretariat Proposal, 3. For difficulties that arise from consolidated group financial accounts see chapter F.III.6.b of this thesis.

[192] See in more detail for thoughts on simplified administration processes OECD, BEPS Action 1: Report on Pillar One Blueprint 2020, paras. 816 et seq.

[193] Cf. OECD, BEPS Action 1: Report on Pillar One Blueprint 2020, para. 411.

[194] Cf. OECD, BEPS Action 1: Report on Pillar One Blueprint 2020, paras. 520 et seqq.

The proposed fixed return for baseline distribution and marketing activities under Amount B has the potential to reduce compliance costs for taxpayers and exonerate resources from tax administrations. Therefore, the fundamental idea of Amount B is to be welcomed from an efficiency point of view. However, the potential for reducing compliance and administrative costs is limited to distribution and marketing activities that fall within the scope of Amount B. Moreover, it appears that the increase of compliance and administrative costs introduced by Amount A cannot be offset by the simplification introduced by Amount B.[195]

The evaluation of the new profit allocation rules will also be influenced by the ability of the Inclusive Framework to develop binding dispute prevention and dispute resolution procedures. Without such procedures, any disputes between jurisdictions would need to be resolved on the basis of existing bilateral systems, such as mutual agreement procedures.[196] Since disputes between two jurisdictions over Amount A would likely also affect the taxation of Amount A in other jurisdictions,[197] such procedures seem essential to keep the additional compliance and administrative costs introduced by Pillar One proportionate.

c. Interim Conclusion

Based on the above assessment, Table 4 evaluates the extent to which the basic architecture of the Pillar One Blueprint, differentiated by scope and nexus as well as profit attribution rules, complies with the tax policy principle of efficiency and summarises the main reasons for this evaluation.

5. Certainty and Simplicity

a. Scope and Nexus

At its current stage, the new taxing right under Amount A does certainly not appear simple and is surrounded by several areas which cause uncertainty. Although this finding is also due to the fact that the approach developed under Pillar One is not yet fully developed and several political and technical issues are still being discussed, doubts must be expressed that an evaluation of the final version of Pillar One will deviate significantly from this assessment.

---

[195] Cf. also *Englisch*, ifo Schnelldienst 3/2020, 11 (12).

[196] Cf. OECD, BEPS Action 1: Statement on the Two-Pillar Approach 2020, Annex 1, para. 68.

[197] Cf. OECD, BEPS Action 1: Statement on the Two-Pillar Approach 2020, Annex 1, para. 68.

Table 4 Compatibility of Pillar One Blueprint with Efficiency

	Scope and Nexus	**Profit Allocation Rules**
Evaluation	**	**
Reasoning	• new taxation right adds an additional layer of complexity and increases compliance and administration costs • proposed thresholds and carve-outs exclude several businesses and are to be welcomed from an efficiency point of view • proposed revenue sourcing rules are very complicated and demand detailed documentation that will increase administration and compliance costs	• Amount A increases compliance costs for taxpayers and administration costs for tax authorities • proposed thresholds and exemptions lead to an increase in compliance costs only for certain MNE groups (depending on the specific design of the rules) • simplification measures for segmentation are to be welcomed • Amount B has the potential to lower compliance costs for taxpayers and exonerate resources from tax administrations • increase of compliance and administration costs by Amount A cannot be compensated by simplification measures that shall be introduced by Amount B • binding dispute prevention and resolution processes seem mandatory to keep additional compliance and administration costs introduced in proportion

Scale:
*Approach could adversely impact the overarching tax policy principle
**Approach could partially challenge the overarching tax policy principle
***Approach could be compatible with the overarching tax policy principle

Source: Own illustration.

One reason for this evaluation relates to the approach chosen to define in-scope activities for Amount A. The current definition of CFB in the Pillar One Blueprint is very broad and covers a wide variety of businesses. In practice, this approach raises various delineation issues and may often require a complex and costly segmentation of the existing business lines.[198] The approach for the definition of ADS, consisting of a positive list of ADS activities, a negative list of non-ADS

[198] Cf. *Englisch*, Comments on the Pillar One Blueprint, 2.

activities and a general definition, is in general to be welcomed. Especially, the positive and negative list provide some kind of certainty for MNEs whether or not they are covered by the new taxing right. However, in case a business is neither on the positive nor on the negative list, it needs to consider whether it meets the conditions of the general definition, which in turn may raise delineation issues. Against this background, the intention to cover all scope issues through an early tax certainty process is to be welcomed.[199]

Another issue relates to the revenue sourcing rules to determine the revenue that would be treated as derived from a particular market jurisdiction, which are outlined in the Pillar One Blueprint. These rules, which consist of a hierarchical list of acceptable indicators that an MNE group should use to determine the country of source for each type of activity, together with the documentation requirements provided, are very complex, prescriptive and difficult to implement.[200] Especially, the need to justify the use of another indicator that is further down the list and may be more appropriate to apply requires the MNE group to document that reasonable steps have been taken to obtain the information but have been unsuccessful (if the indicator is unavailable) or to prove that the indicator is unreliable (if the indicator is not a true representative of the principle in the source rule) can certainly not be regarded as simple.[201] Furthermore, the rules do not provide certainty for the MNE group, as it remains unclear whether a chosen indicator further down in the hierarchical list would be accepted by the tax administration.

Difficulties related to the revenue sourcing rules are particularly significant for MNE groups operating through independent distributors. As emphasised in the Pillar One Blueprint, enterprises selling consumer products indirectly through third party resellers shall be within the scope of the new taxing right.[202] Nevertheless, as argued earlier, such enterprises may not necessarily receive information on the location of the final consumer/user, which would be needed for the new taxing right under Amount A.[203] The Business at OECD Tax Committee rightly points out that '[a]ny look through provision that requires tracing direct sales to end users or consumers stands to introduce significant complexity for both taxpayers

[199] See in more detail OECD, BEPS Action 1: Report on Pillar One Blueprint 2020, paras. 25, 704 et seqq.

[200] Cf. similarly *Petruzzi/Buriak*, Comments on Pillar One Blueprint, 5.

[201] Cf. OECD, BEPS Action 1: Report on Pillar One Blueprint 2020, para. 222.

[202] Cf. OECD, BEPS Action 1: Report on Pillar One Blueprint 2020, para. 33.

[203] Cf. PwC, Comments on Secretariat Proposal, 6.

and tax authorities'[204]. Therefore, to increase tax certainty, appropriate methods for determining the location of the final customer with reasonable accuracy are needed. Unfortunately, such methods are not provided in the Pillar One Blueprint. Rather, in cases where the information is not reported by the independent distributor, the Pillar One Blueprint specifies that the MNE group must take reasonable steps to seek a change in the contractual arrangements with the distributor in order to obtain the information.[205] Only if the information is not available after reasonable steps have been taken by the MNE group it is conceded that other information already available, such as market research used for management reporting, may be used.[206] This approach can neither be referred to as simple nor can an MNE group be certain that the respective tax administration agrees with the assessment of the MNE group that reasonable steps have been taken to change the contract with the independent distributor, but has been unsuccessful in doing so.

Further uncertainties relate to the various thresholds and exemptions to be introduced through Pillar One. Since such thresholds and carve-outs would exclude several MNE groups from the scope of the new taxing right, it is crucial that these exceptions are clearly defined and applicable under reasonable efforts by the taxpayer. However, as outlined in the Pillar One Blueprint, no agreement has yet been reached on the amount/percentage of the proposed thresholds, including whether, e.g., a phased approach should be used for the global revenue test among the members of the Inclusive Framework.

Since the new taxing right under Amount A shall not replace, but rather complement the existing taxation rules, it can be concluded that the approach would add an additional layer of complexity which would certainly not simplify the international tax system.[207]

b. Profit Allocation Rules

Considering that Amount A could have a large impact on the portion of the residual profit to be allocated to the eligible market jurisdictions, it is key that all terms/concepts used to determine Amount A are absolutely precise and do not allow for any misinterpretation. However, the various open key features of the

---

[204]Cf. Business at OECD, Comments on Secretariat Proposal, para. 22.

[205]Cf. OECD, BEPS Action 1: Report on Pillar One Blueprint 2020, para. 378.

[206]Cf. OECD, BEPS Action 1: Report on Pillar One Blueprint 2020, para. 379.

[207]Cf. also *Schön*, ifo Schnelldienst 3/2020, 26 (28); *Englisch*, Comments on Secretariat Proposal, 12.

approach outlined in the Public Consultation Document illustrate that the new profit allocation rules under Amount A are surrounded by several unresolved issues.[208] The level of the appropriate profitability threshold and the reallocation percentage are just some of the issues on which agreement has not yet been reached. The large number of unresolved issues indicates that there is still much work ahead for the Inclusive Framework to present a final approach that secures tax certainty.

Furthermore, even though some elements of Amount A, such as the envisaged exploration of administrative simplification measures, are positive in principle, Amount A is an overlay to the current system based on the arm's length principle and, as such, does not seem to bring simplicity to the international tax system. Rather, the proposal would add another layer of uncertainty to the uncertainty that already exists with respect to the profit allocation rules based on the arm's length principle.[209] Considerations expressed in the Pillar One Blueprint on the potential implementation of digital as well as jurisdictional differentiation confirm the concern that the proposed profit allocation rules under Amount A would further increase the complexity of the new approach.[210] Similarly, the proposed segmentation framework, which requires the MNE group to compute the relevant measure of PBT by using segmented accounts in certain cases, will certainly increase the complexity of the approach.

Amount B follows a different rational and has the potential to simplify the application of existing transfer pricing rules for baseline marketing and distribution activities and, as a direct result, may increase tax certainty with regard to the pricing of such transactions. Particularly in light of the large number of tax disputes between taxpayers and tax administrations related to distribution functions, the basic idea of Amount B is a step in the right direction.[211] Moreover, the approach that the implementation of Amount B should be neither an elective nor a safe-harbour is important to achieve certainty and simplicity.[212] Otherwise, Amount B would provide more leeway with regard to the remuneration of such

[208] See in more detail OECD, BEPS Action 1: Public Consultation Document 2020, pp. 3 et seqq.

[209] Cf. also *Englisch*, Comments on Secretariat Proposal, 4.

[210] Cf. OECD, BEPS Action 1: Report on Pillar One Blueprint 2020, paras. 520 et seqq.

[211] Cf. *Ditz/Pinkernell*, ISR 2019, 377 (386).

[212] Cf. OECD, BEPS Action 1: Statement on the Two-Pillar Approach 2020, Annex 1, para. 58.

transaction and, to that extent, would fail in its objective of achieving a higher degree of tax certainty and simplification.[213]

Although not yet fully developed, the basic approach of having a positive list of baseline marketing and distribution activities that are intended to fall within the scope of Amount B and a negative list of activities, functions and risks that Amount B is not intended to cover is to be welcomed, as it increases certainty with regard to the applicability of Amount B. On the contrary, work that looks at differentiated returns by regions, industries and functional intensity would make the application of Amount B more complex.

Against this background, the planned introduction of dispute prevention and resolution mechanisms as part of Pillar One is an important step, as these mechanisms aim to increase tax certainty for tax administrations and taxpayers alike. Given that many tax treaties among the members of the Inclusive Framework (if such a treaty even exists) do not contain a mandatory arbitration clause,[214] the efforts of the Inclusive Framework are central to ensure tax certainty.

c. Interim Conclusion

Based on the above assessment, Table 5 evaluates the extent to which the basic architecture of the Pillar One Blueprint, differentiated by scope and nexus as well as profit attribution rules, complies with the tax policy principle of certainty and simplicity and summarises the main reasons for this evaluation.

[213]Oxfam also argues that 'Amount B should not operate as a safe harbour for taxpayers with an arm's length escape, otherwise it will fail to increase tax certainty or prevent disputes', Oxfam, Comments on Secretariat Proposal, 10.

[214]Cf. *Petruzzi/Holzinger/Screpante/Buriak/Capristano Cardoso*, TPI 2019, 312 (320).

Table 5 Compatibility of Pillar One Blueprint with Certainty and Simplicity

	Scope and Nexus	Profit Allocation Rules
Evaluation	*	*
Reasoning	• Amount A aims to introduce an additional nexus that complements the PE threshold and, as such, would certainly not simplify the international tax system • Pillar One Blueprint contains several unclear terms/concepts • revenue sourcing rules are very complex and do not provide certainty for the MNE groups, especially not for those operating through independent distributors • no decision yet on the proposed thresholds	• Amount A is an overlay to the current system based on the arm's length principle and, as such, does not seem to bring simplicity to the international tax system • multitude of unresolved issues demonstrates that the profit allocation rules under Amount A do not yet provide tax certainty for taxpayers • Amount B has the potential to simplify the application of transfer pricing rules and enhance tax certainty • binding dispute prevention and resolution mechanisms for Amount A and beyond is key to enhance tax certainty

Scale:
*Approach could adversely impact the overarching tax policy principle
**Approach could partially challenge the overarching tax policy principle
***Approach could be compatible with the overarching tax policy principle

Source: Own illustration.

6. Effectiveness and Fairness

a. Scope and Nexus

Whether a new taxing right largely based on sales would be able to produce the right amount of tax at the right time, as required by the principle of effectiveness and fairness,[215] depends on how someone looks at this requirement. As argued in the context of inter-nations equity, the result would not be satisfactory if measured against the benchmark of value creation, since sales do not appear to be directly linked to value creation.[216] However, rather than linking the new taxing right to

[215] See in more detail chapter B.VI of this thesis.

[216] Cf. *Petruzzi/Holzinger/Screpante/Buriak/Capristano Cardoso*, TPI 2019, 312 (314 et seq.).

value creation, the new taxing right is intended to reflect an MNEs active and sustained participation in the economy of a market jurisdiction, recognising that the allocation of taxing rights can no longer be merely circumscribed by reference to physical presence.[217]

Against this background, the approach to base the new taxing right on specific in-scope sales (as well as possible additional 'plus factors' for CFBs) seems to be a pragmatic approach to recognise that parts of the corporate profits also result from customer/user interaction and engagement in the market jurisdiction. Nevertheless, also small and medium sized businesses may be able to develop an active and sustained participation in the economy of a market jurisdiction that could justify such a taxing right. Against this background, the intention to limit the new taxing right to MNE groups that meet a certain gross revenue threshold leads to a trade-off between strict compliance with the underlying principle of the new taxing right and administrability of the approach. Despite this limitation, it appears too early to make a conclusive assessment of whether the new taxing right appears to produce the right amount of tax at the right time at this stage, as various details on scope and nexus are still subject to negotiation among the members of the Inclusive Framework.[218]

Another aspect of effectiveness and fairness relates to the requirement that taxation rules shall avoid double taxation as well as unintended double non-taxation,[219] which presupposes their implementation in tax treaties as well as domestic legislation. In this regard, not only robust mechanisms such as treaty changes or other instruments (e.g. a new multilateral convention)[220] are required, but also the simultaneous implementation of the new taxing right into domestic legislation of the participating countries.[221] Therefore, it is key that the new taxing right clearly defines all relevant terms under which taxable income arises in a certain country and, to that extent, provides as little leeway as possible for deviations in implementation. As shown in the previous chapter, the new taxing right does not meet this requirement at its current stage, as several uncertainties surround the new taxing right under Amount A.

---

[217]Cf. OECD, BEPS Action 1: Report on Pillar One Blueprint 2020, paras. 6, 22.

[218]See for the remaining work OECD, BEPS Action 1: Report on Pillar One Blueprint 2020, paras. 185, 216 et seq.

[219]Cf. OECD, BEPS Action 1: Final Report 2015, para. 10.

[220]Cf. OECD, BEPS Action 1: Report on Pillar One Blueprint 2020, para. 824. See in more detail for the necessity of a multilateral convention chapter F.IV.5 of this thesis.

[221]*Förster/Greil/Hilse* also emphasise the need that the simultaneous introduction of the new taxing right in a significant number of countries is necessary in order to allow the new system to work, cf. *Förster/Greil/Hilse*, ITPJ 2020, 3 (5).

In this context, it is also key that basic law requirements of the participating countries are met.[222] Within the EU, compliance with the fundamental freedoms and non-discrimination regulations is important.[223] Although it is still too early for a comprehensive analysis on these issues, doubts can already be expressed as to whether the envisaged thresholds and carve-outs for the new taxing rights would satisfy non-discrimination regulations.[224]

Furthermore, to prove effective and fair, it is required that taxation rules minimise the potential for tax evasion and tax avoidance.[225] Because Amount A is largely allocated upon sales in the market countries that are relatively immobile, as previously described, the proposal has the potential to reduce leeway for tax planning.[226] Also, the rather wide scope of the new taxing right seems to limit opportunities for tax evasion. Nevertheless, opportunities related to the global revenue and the de minimus foreign in-scope revenue threshold can still be identified. These opportunities may create new opportunities for tax planning and tax avoidance strategies and make the new taxing right more vulnerable to litigation.[227] In particular, MNE groups whose sales are slightly above a certain threshold and thus fall within the scope of the new taxing right may find it worthwhile to invest considerable effort to restructure certain business lines in order to remain below the threshold and thereby 'escape' the new taxing right under Amount A. In addition, the proposed carve-outs create opportunities for gaps and abusive practices that make the new taxing right less effective and fair.[228]

b. Profit Allocation Rules

The allocation mechanism under Amount A is designed in a way that it reallocates taxable profits already allocated based on the arm's length principle towards market countries. Insofar, the new profit allocation mechanism under Amount A ultimately reallocates a part of the taxable profits, which were allocated based on principles developed within the course of the BEPS project (i.a. newly developed

---

[222]Cf. *Förster/Greil/Hilse*, ITPJ 2020, 3 (5).

[223]Cf. *Förster/Greil/Hilse*, ITPJ 2020, 3 (5). See in more detail for the requirements with regard to EU law *Junkers*, IStR 2019, 850 (851). *Ditz/Pinkernell* outline several areas where potential problems of the Pillar One approach with EU law may arise, cf. *Ditz/Pinkernell*, ISR 2019, 377 (385 et seq.).

[224]See in more detail *Förster/Greil/Hilse*, ITPJ 2020, 3 (5).

[225]Cf. OECD, BEPS Action 1: Final Report 2015, para. 10.

[226]Cf. *Fuest*, ifo Schnelldienst 3/2020, 6 (9).

[227]Cf. also *Förster/Greil/Hilse*, ITPJ 2020, 3 (11).

[228]Cf. also *Parada*, TNI 96 (2019), 983 (985).

DEMPE concept) towards market countries.[229] Even though, a move away from the arm's length principle, one of the earliest international tax references,[230] in favour of a profit allocation mechanism based on a predetermined formula appears debatable,[231] as it disregards market conditions as well as the particular circumstances of the individual enterprises,[232] such an approach seems necessary given the objective of Amount A to allocate more taxing rights to the new nexus in the market countries. Also *Ditz/Pinkernell* argue that if the members of the Inclusive Framework accept a new taxing right that is intended to reflect the active and sustained participation of a business in the economy of a market jurisdiction based on sales, the use of a profit allocation mechanism allocating profits as a lump-sum appears necessary.[233]

Nevertheless, the final evaluation of whether the new profit allocation rule under Amount A may produce the right amount of tax at the right time largely depends on the final design of the formula and the mechanisms developed on how to avoid double taxation resulting from the circumstance that Amount A is an overlay to the arm's length-based profit allocation rules. Possible sources for double taxation may also result from:[234]

- the potential overlap of market jurisdictions taxing the same income;
- the potential overlap of residence jurisdictions taxing the same income allocated to market jurisdictions;
- the use of unclear terms;
- possibilities of different tax bases contingent upon how to calculate the quantum of Amount A; and
- a potential disconnect resulting from who is seen as the taxpayer for the purpose of the tax payment under Amount A and who is the taxpayer under domestic law.

---

[229] For a detailed analysis of the principles developed throughout the BEPS project see chapter D.I.4.b.(2)(h) of this thesis.

[230] Cf. *Graetz/Hear*, DLJ 1997, 1021 (1089).

[231] See critical with respect to a formulaic approach i.a. *Förster/Greil/Hilse*, ITPJ 2020, 3 (7); *Collier/Vella*, WTJ 2019, 159 (185).

[232] The TP Guidelines 2017 also state that 'predetermined formulae are arbitrary and disregard market conditions, the particular circumstances of the individual enterprise, and management's own allocation of resources, thus producing an allocation of profits that may bear no sound relationship to the specific facts surrounding the transaction.' OECD, TP Guidelines 2017, para 1.25.

[233] Cf. *Ditz/Pinkernell*, ISR 2019, 377 (387 et seq.).

[234] Cf. in more detail PwC, Comments on Secretariat Proposal, 20 et seq.

Against this background, the work carried out by the Inclusive Framework and the OECD Secretariat on a mechanism to reconcile the new taxing right and the existing profit allocation rules and the work on early dispute prevention and resolution processes indicates that the Inclusive Framework is aware of the outlined inherent risks of double taxation and envisages to solve them, which is certainly a step in the right direction.[235] Furthermore, the aim expressed in the Pillar One Blueprint that any consensus-based agreement must include the commitment of the members of the Inclusive Framework to withdraw unilateral actions implemented by the members seems absolutely necessary to reduce already existing instances of double taxation.[236]

Additional issues can arise from the determination of the tax base for Amount A, which shall be based on a PBT measure derived from consolidated financial accounts prepared under IFRS or other eligible national GAAPs.[237] Besides the lack of clear guidance on the consolidation scope,[238] the fact that book-to-book harmonisation adjustments are not considered necessary and book-to-tax adjustments shall be limited to a minimum could create opportunities for tax planning. Therefore, appropriate adjustments to harmonise the use of different financial accounting standards are necessary. Otherwise, as *Englisch* emphasises, this leeway might be the starting point for an 'international accounting competition' or an inversion to jurisdictions with accounting standards which would allow MNE groups to artificially reduce their consolidated group profit.[239] Further opportunities for tax planning could arise in cases where the Amount A tax base must be computed on a segmented basis as envisaged in specific cases.[240]

Moreover, while financial accounts mainly reflect the companies' ability to generate cash-flow and insofar allow investors to make forward-looking decisions, tax accounts are concerned with the respective profits and losses in a specific

[235] Similar *Ditz/Pinkernell*, ISR 2019, 377 (386).

[236] Cf. OECD, BEPS Action 1: Report on Pillar One Blueprint 2020, para. 808.

[237] Cf. OECD, BEPS Action 1: Report on Pillar One Blueprint 2020, para. 407.

[238] See in more detail on problems related to the consolidation scope *Petruzzi/Buriak*, Comments on Secretariat Proposal, 5.

[239] Cf. *Englisch*, Comments on Secretariat Proposal, 3; similar *Petruzzi/Holzinger/Screpante/Buriak/Capristano Cardoso*, TPI 2019, 312 (317).

[240] Cf. in more detail on the segmentation framework OECD, BEPS Action 1: Report on Pillar One Blueprint 2020, paras. 442 et seqq.

period and account for the taxpayer's ability to pay.[241] This divergence in objectives results in drawbacks when relying on accounting profits for tax purposes.[242] More precisely, the reliance on accounting profits for tax purposes may result in the inadequate effect that enterprises might have to pay taxes on profits not yet realised.[243] Furthermore, market jurisdictions might receive a taxing right for profits resulting from transactions solely taking place within a country, e.g. profits resulting from domestic restructuring processes.[244]

In contrast to Amount A, Amount B, if implemented consistently and multinational, could prove to be an effective way to compute the remuneration for baseline distribution and marketing activities, thereby reducing the potential for tax disputes.[245] Fears expressed by Oxfam[246] arguing that Amount B could facilitate tax avoidance through the allocation of excessively high profits to baseline distribution and marketing activities if implemented as an elective safe harbour are addressed, as Amount B shall neither be optional nor a safe-harbour.[247] Insofar, possibilities for tax planning resulting from Amount B appear rather limited.

While the approach for the remuneration of baseline distribution and marketing activities under Amount B is based on the arm's length principle and aims to make the computation of the return for activities in scope more simple and therefore also easier to enforce, the enforceability of Amount A largely depends on its final design and the tools provided. Even though it is still too early for a final evaluation, the work carried out by the Inclusive Framework and the OECD Secretariat and the willingness to actively engage external stakeholders, i.a. through public consultations, point in the right direction. Also, the intention to implement simplified administration processes (i.a. centralise the computation of Amount A and related compliance activities in a single entity, possibly the ultimate parent jurisdiction) and procedures for dispute prevention and resolution for Amount A and beyond in a multilateral convention are of importance with regard to the enforceability of the new nexus rules.[248]

---

[241] Cf. *Freedman,* in: Schön (Ed.), Tax and Corporate Governance, 75; PwC, Comments on Secretariat Proposal, 12.

[242] Cf. PwC, Comments on Secretariat Proposal, 12.

[243] Cf. *Blaufus/Jacobs*, Tax Related Implications of Fair Value Accounting, 254.

[244] Cf. *Förster/Greil/Hilse*, ITPJ 2020, 3 (11).

[245] Cf. *Petruzzi/Holzinger/Screpante/Buriak/Capristano Cardoso*, TPI 2019, 312 (319).

[246] Cf. Oxfam, Comments on Secretariat Proposal, 10.

[247] Cf. OECD, BEPS Action 1: Statement on the Two-Pillar Approach 2020, Annex 1, para. 58.

[248] See in more detail on implementation and administration OECD, BEPS Action 1: Report on Pillar One Blueprint 2020, paras. 806 et seqq.

c. Interim Conclusion

Based on the above assessment, Table 6 evaluates the extent to which the basic architecture of the Pillar One Blueprint, differentiated by scope and nexus as well as profit attribution rules, complies with the tax policy principle of effectiveness and fairness and summarises the main reasons for this evaluation.

Table 6 Compatibility of Pillar One Blueprint with Effectiveness and Fairness

	Scope and Nexus	**Profit Allocation Rules**
Evaluation	**	**
Reasoning	• approach to base the new taxing right largely on sales seems to be a pragmatic approach to reflect the active and sustained participation of a business in the economy of a market jurisdiction • envisaged gross revenue threshold leads to a trade-off between strict compliance with the underlying principle of the new taxing right and administrability of the approach • proposal provides little leeway for tax planning, but possibilities exist, especially with regard to the proposed global revenue and the de minimus foreign in-scope revenue threshold	• formulaic approach under Amount A appears necessary given the objective to allocate more profits to market jurisdictions • approach of Amount A provides for several possible sources of double taxation • use of consolidated financial statements introduces possibilities for tax planning • Amount B could prove to be an effective way to compute the remuneration of baseline activities in scope • possibilities for tax planning resulting from Amount B appear rather limited • development of early dispute prevention and resolution processes are mandatory to reduce inherent risks of double taxation

Scale:
*Approach could adversely impact the overarching tax policy principle
**Approach could partially challenge the overarching tax policy principle
***Approach could be compatible with the overarching tax policy principle

Source: Own illustration.

7. Flexibility

a. Scope and Nexus

The new taxing right does not only envisage to bring ADS but also CFB with a significant and sustained engagement in the market jurisdiction within the scope of Amount A. Even though no final definition of the terms CFB and ADS is yet provided, the scope of the new taxing right, as argued earlier, appears quite broad.[249] On the one side, this broad scope provides some flexibility to keep pace with new developments that can be captured through a measure of sales, whether through the emergence of new business models, changes in business practices or other changes induced by technological or commercial developments. On the other side, any kind of ring-fencing of specifically defined businesses does also come with the drawback that such definitions could become obsolete in the future.[250] Against this background, the approach for defining ADS in the Pillar One Blueprint, proposing an updatable positive list of ADS activities, an updatable negative list of non-ADS activities combined with a general definition could increase flexibility for future developments.

Furthermore, any kind of fixed monetary threshold reduces flexibility.[251] This is also the case for the proposed global revenue threshold as well as the de minimis foreign in-scope revenue test limiting the applicability of the new taxing right to MNE groups that exceed this threshold. The use of such thresholds does not provide flexibility to account for, e.g., inflation and may insofar lead to the erosion of the thresholds in 'real terms'.[252]

b. Profit Allocation Rules

The criticism expressed on the use of fixed monetary thresholds and its adverse impact on flexibility can be extended to the use of formulaic elements.[253] Although no final approach for the determination of the quantum of Amount A has

---

[249] See in more detail chapter F.III.3.a of this thesis.

[250] See also *Pistone/Nogueira/Andrade* with regard to the concept of the user participation proposal arguing that specific definitions of nexus rules 'could risk easily becoming obsolete, since there will always be new ways of conducting business remotely and benefiting from active user participation', *Pistone/Nogueira/Andrade,* ITAXS 2019, Issue 2, 1 (41).

[251] Cf. Business at OECD, Comments on Secretariat Proposal, para. 13.

[252] Cf. PwC, Comments on Secretariat Proposal, 7.

[253] Cf. Business at OECD, Comments on Secretariat Proposal, para. 13.

yet been presented, consensus exists that the approach shall be formula-based.[254] However, any kind of fixed formulaic elements make the new profit allocation rules under Amount A somehow static and unable to capture the dynamics of the digitalisation of the economy.[255] In particular, the fact that Amount A shall only apply to businesses within scope that exceed a certain level of profitability narrows the scope of Amount A to highly profitable businesses, which may not prove sufficient to address the challenges arising from the digitalisation of the economy. Nevertheless, technical work carried out on the implementation of a potential differentiation mechanism that includes both digital differentiation to account for different degrees of digitalisation and jurisdictional differentiation to account for substantial variations in profitability between market jurisdictions would increase the flexibility of the formulaic approach.

Amount B shall operate with a fixed return for baseline marketing and distribution activities based on the arm's length principle. While this approach, as emphasised earlier, would simplify the computation of the return for activities in scope,[256] it does not provide flexibility to take into account the individual circumstances and facts of the specific case (e.g. a distribution centre in China may be different from one in Germany causing different profitability margins). Against this background, the work carried out on differentiated returns by region and industry as well as functional intensity is to be welcomed from a flexibility point of view, as it would allow to adapt the fundamental approach followed by Amount B to be more in line with economic reality.

[254] Cf. OECD, BEPS Action 1: Report on Pillar One Blueprint 2020, para. 496.

[255] Cf. *Förster/Greil/Hilse*, ITPJ 2020, 3 (11).

[256] See in more detail chapter F.III.5.b of this thesis.

c. Interim Conclusion

Based on the above assessment, Table 7 evaluates the extent to which the basic architecture of the Pillar One Blueprint, differentiated by scope and nexus as well as profit attribution rules, complies with the tax policy principle of flexibility and summarises the main reasons for this evaluation.

Table 7 Compatibility of Pillar One Blueprint with Flexibility

	Scope and Nexus	**Profit Allocation Rules**
Evaluation	**	**
Reasoning	• broad scope of new taxing right and updatable positive list of ADS activities provides some flexibility to keep pace with new developments • use of fixed monetary thresholds (global revenue threshold, de minimis foreign in-scope revenue) reduces flexibility	• formulaic approach under Amount A makes approach static to capture the dynamics of the digitalisation of the economy • potential differentiation mechanism would increase flexibility of the formulaic approach • fixed return under Amount B does not provide flexibility to take into account the individual circumstances and facts of the case • differentiated returns by region, industry and functional intensity for Amount B would enhance flexibility

Scale:
*Approach could adversely impact the overarching tax policy principle
**Approach could partially challenge the overarching tax policy principle
***Approach could be compatible with the overarching tax policy principle

Source: Own illustration.

8. Overall Evaluation

Table 8 summarises the evaluation of the central elements of the Pillar One Blueprint, differentiated by scope and nexus as well as profit allocation rules, in light of the overarching tax policy principles that have formed the basis of the assessment (Table 8).

This assessment is based on the fundamental architecture of Pillar One as outlined in the Pillar One Blueprint, which was approved by the Inclusive Framework on 8–9 October 2020. However, as outlined in the Executive Summary

Table 8 Compatibility of Pillar One Blueprint with Overarching Tax Policy Principles

Tax Policy Principle	Scope and Nexus	Profit Allocation Rules
Inter-Nation Equity	***	***
Inter-Taxpayer Equity	**	**
Neutrality	**	**
Efficiency	**	**
Certainty and Simplicity	*	*
Effectiveness and Fairness	**	**
Flexibility	**	**

Scale:
*Approach could adversely impact the overarching tax policy principle
**Approach could partially challenge the overarching tax policy principle
***Approach could be compatible with the overarching tax policy principle

Source: Own illustration.

on the Pillar One Blueprint, there are still a number of open issues on some of the key features of the approach that are subject to further discussion among the members of the Inclusive Framework. Therefore, it would be premature to make a final judgement on Pillar One at this stage. Further work on the design of Pillar One will certainly have an impact on the evaluation. Nevertheless, the following conclusions can already be outlined:

The central element of Pillar One, Amount A, is an overlay to the current tax system based on the PE threshold and the arm's length principle. This ensures that the current corporate tax system, based on long-standing and sound principles, will not be abandoned. Rather, the approach proposes a partial reallocation of taxable profits towards market countries and, in this respect, attempts to provide a response to specific concerns arising from the digitalisation of the economy, where both the PE concept and the arm's length principle have proven insufficient and led to unsatisfactory results.[257] Using revenue as the predominant reference point for nexus and the allocation of a portion of the residual profits under Amount A to the various market jurisdictions appears a workable and pragmatic approach to facilitate political compromise. Moreover, the use of formulaic elements for the allocation of residual profits to market jurisdictions appears necessary in light of the objective of Amount A. In this respect, the basic idea of Amount A could lead to a more equitable allocation of taxation rights among jurisdictions.

[257] See in this context the case studies elaborated in chapter E.III of this thesis.

However, whether the benefits introduced through the new taxing right may outweigh the additional administrative and compliance costs introduced largely depends on the final design of the approach. While the use of carve-outs, high revenue thresholds and a high residual profit threshold may keep additional administrative and compliance costs in proportion, all these limitations do not only have a negative impact on the neutrality of the approach, which raises non-discrimination issues, but also weights on the effectiveness and fairness of the approach. As correctly pointed out by the OECD, 'it would be difficult, if not impossible, to ring-fence the digital economy from the rest of the economy'[258]. Therefore, any kind of scope-limitation comes at the expense of neutrality and the effectiveness and fairness of the approach, as not only large enterprises with high residual profits are able to develop an active and sustained engagement in the market jurisdictions. Moreover, as outlined above, any kind of monetary thresholds and formulaic elements also challenges the flexibility of the approach.

Furthermore, the analysis revealed that the Pillar One approach does not seem to bring simplicity to the international corporate tax system. In fact, the only simplification measure introduced through Pillar One would be the standardisation of the remuneration of routine distribution and marketing activities as part of Amount B.[259] Most of the other elements, especially the reallocation mechanism under Amount A, raise a multitude of procedural and technical issues.[260] Given the tight timeline and the multitude of other issues that need to be addressed, it seems very ambitious to resolve all of the remaining issues by mid-2021, as envisaged by the Inclusive Framework.

However, despite the criticism broad forward throughout the analysis, it seems worth to continue intensive work on Pillar One to reach a consensus-based solution among the members of the Inclusive Framework. Especially, when someone thinks of the alternatives to Pillar One. If the members of the Inclusive Framework cannot agree on a solution within the given framework of the Pillar One Blueprint, the alternative would be a state in which more and more countries continue to implement uncoordinated unilateral measures.[261] However, such measures would lead to an even more complex, fractured and distorted international tax system and ultimately increase the risk of double taxation.[262]

[258] I.a. OECD, BEPS Action 1: Final Report 2015, paras. 115, 364; OECD, BEPS Action 1: Interim Report 2018, para. 375.

[259] Cf. *Englisch*, Comments on Secretariat Proposal, 12.

[260] Cf. *Englisch*, Comments on Secretariat Proposal, 12.

[261] See similar *Schanz*, ifo Schnelldienst 3/2020, 14 (17).

[262] Cf. OECD, BEPS Action 1: Programme of Work 2019, para. 11.

Against this background, the following chapter does not discuss alternative solutions to the Pillar One approach that may potentially be more compatible with the overarching tax policy principles discussed. Several different alternative approaches were already presented in literature.[263] Nevertheless, as argued earlier, given the current stage of work of the Inclusive Framework, none of these alternatives seem to be a realistic option, as they depart from the fundamental architecture of Pillar One. Rather, the following chapter will provide recommendations on some of the remaining technical and policy issues that still need to be resolved under Pillar One. Since Amount A constitutes the primary response of Pillar One to the tax challenges arising from the digitalisation of the economy, the recommendations will focus on issues related to Amount A.

IV. Recommendations for Remaining Work

1. Scope of Amount A

As criticised in the previous chapters, the current definition of CFB in the Pillar One Blueprint is very broad and raises various delineation issues. Furthermore, the definition of ADS consisting of a positive list of ADS activities, a negative list of non-ADS activities and a general definition appears quite complicated and raises delineation issues, especially when a business is neither on the positive nor on the negative list. Against this background and the fact that the digital economy is increasingly becoming the economy itself, it seems advisable to include all

[263] For alternative approaches see i.a. *Förster/Greil/Hilse* proposing a 'kind of amount A system' where consolidated profits are considered as the result of value-creating elements which are then allocated to the different countries in proportion to their respective contributions to the value creation as well as modifications to Amount B, see in more detail for the concept *Förster/Greil/Hils*, ITPJ 2020, 3 (12 et seqq.). *Schön* proposes a concept of 'digital investment' which seems more in line with the existing tax framework and would still enable market jurisdictions to claim a larger part of the overall tax revenue. This concept does not allocate taxing rights based on sales but rather depends on the invested capital in a specific market for the purpose of accessing a specific customer base, see in more detail for the concept *Schön*, BIT 2018, 278 (288 et seqq.). Another approach presented by *Devereux/Auerbach/Keen/Oosterhuis/Schön/Vella* is the 'residual profit allocation by income' approach where the right to tax routine profit is allocated to the country where functions and activities take place and the right to tax residual profits to the market country where sales are made to third parties, see in more detail for the concept *Devereux/Auerbach/Keen/Oosterhuis/Schön/Vella*, Residual profit allocation by income, Working Paper 2019.

MNEs in-scope of Amount A as a starting point and then narrow this scope by the use of a) a passive catalogue, and b) revenue thresholds.

The passive catalogue could include certain businesses which shall explicitly be excluded from the scope of the new taxing right, e.g. businesses operating in sectors such as natural resources; financial services; construction, sale and leasing of residential property as well as international air and shipping business.[264] The use of a passive catalogue would not only provide more certainty for taxpayers and tax administrations alike, but would also provide less leeway for tax planning strategies. Furthermore, new and emerging business models (which may not fall within the definition of CFB and ADS) would automatically be captured by the new taxing right, unless explicitly excluded in the passive catalogue.

Despite the concerns expressed throughout the analysis on limiting the new taxing right to businesses that reach a certain revenue threshold,[265] the introduction of such a threshold seems necessary to keep the new taxing right administrable for both taxpayers and tax authorities. In the long run, the same revenue threshold should be used as for CbC-reporting, i.e. MNE groups with gross revenue exceeding EUR 750 million.[266] This threshold does not only allow to capture a very high percentage of the total profits of MNE groups,[267] but also allows to use the infrastructure for filing and exchange of information already established for CbC Reporting.[268] However, considering that under the EUR 750 million threshold an estimated number of 780 MNE groups[269] would be subject to Amount A taxation, which could all apply for the tax certainty procedure ultimately leading to an almost equal number of time consuming review

[264]For the proposed exclusions see OECD, BEPS Action 1: Report on Pillar One Blueprint 2020, paras. 105 et seqq.

[265]See in more detail chapter F.III.2.b(1), F.III.3.a., F.III.6.a., F.III.7.a of this thesis.

[266]This threshold is also considered in the proposal, cf. OECD, BEPS Action 1: Report on Pillar One Blueprint 2020, paras. 175 et seqq.

[267]An analysis of PwC indicates that the implementation of a EUR 750 million revenue threshold (and insofar the exclusion of all enterprises below this revenue threshold from Amount A) would still account for 93% of the total profits before tax from the sample of enterprises which was taken, see in more detail PwC, Comments on Secretariat Proposal, 7. Also, the economic impact assessment of the OECD shows that there is only a very little increase in the residual profits allocated to market jurisdictions from using a lower figure than EUR 750 million, OECD, BEPS Action 1: Economic Impact Assessment 2020, para. 24.

[268]Cf. OECD, BEPS Action 1: Statement on the Two-Pillar Approach 2020, Annex 1, para. 35. See in more detail for CbC Reporting chapter D.I.5 of this thesis.

[269]Under the premise of a profitability threshold of 10% and the scope and nexus limitations as set out in the Pillar One Blueprint, cf. OECD, BEPS Action 1: Report on Pillar One Blueprint 2020, para. 509.

panel procedures, it seems advisable to implement the global revenue threshold in a phased approach.[270] A higher initial global revenue threshold, such as EUR 3 billion would allow tax administrations to gain some experience with the new taxing right under Amount A and should therefore be considered in a starting phase.[271] This threshold could then be gradually reduced over a transition period of e.g. three or five years.

The second proposed threshold, the de minimis foreign in-scope revenue threshold, requires the MNE group to identify its domestic or home market. While the Pillar One Blueprint suggests to define the domestic or home market as the jurisdiction where the group is headquartered or where the UPE is tax resident, it seems more appropriate to determine the jurisdiction where the MNE group generated most in-scope revenue from as the 'domestic market'.[272] This approach could not only prevent manipulation, e.g. where the UPE may just operate as the group holding company without generating substantial revenue in this jurisdiction, but also makes this threshold more effective.

With regard to the level of the threshold, the Pillar One Blueprint proposes to set this threshold at an absolute number rather than a percentage in relation to the size of an MNEs domestic business.[273] Although the determination of the threshold seems to be largely a political issue and needs to be negotiated among the members of the Inclusive Framework, it seems appropriate to set this threshold at 1/3 of the respective global revenue threshold. It follows that the de minimis foreign in-scope revenue threshold could be set at EUR 1 billion in an initial starting phase and then be gradually reduced to EUR 250 million.

2. New Nexus Rule under Amount A

As emphasised in the Pillar One Blueprint, there is a need to define a new nexus rule which is based on indicators of 'significant and sustained engagement with market jurisdictions'[274]. In order to capture the 'significance' of the engagement with the market jurisdiction, it seems advisable to solely rely on market revenue

[270] Cf. also *Englisch*, Comments on Pillar One Blueprint, 2.

[271] As illustrated in the Economic Impact Assessment, the amount of global residual profit declines only relatively slowly when higher global revenue thresholds are considered, see in more detail OECD, BEPS Action 1: Economic Impact Assessment 2020, para. 24.

[272] Cf. *Englisch*, Comments on Pillar One Blueprint, 3. PwC also proposes this approach as one possible option, cf. PwC, Comments on Pillar One Blueprint, 9.

[273] Cf. OECD, BEPS Action 1: Report on Pillar One Blueprint 2020, para. 153.

[274] Cf. OECD, BEPS Action 1: Report on Pillar One Blueprint 2020, para. 194.

thresholds. Once an enterprise generates in-scope revenue above that threshold, it can be assumed that a significant engagement with the market jurisdiction exists. Such a market revenue threshold could prove effective in excluding from the new taxing right jurisdictions where MNE groups develop only a small or negligible engagement in the market jurisdiction. Although the Pillar One Blueprint does not provide any details with regard to the level of the market revenue threshold, it appears that not only different market revenue threshold are envisaged for ADS and CFB, but also the inclusion of additional 'plus-factors' for CFB. From a neutrality point of view, such a differentiation of ADS and CFB should be avoided. Moreover, PwC rightly points out that the use of plus factors for CFB would be 'inherently more complex and is likely to result also in further complexity so there may be concern that the burden on those with CFB could potentially outweigh the benefit'[275]. Furthermore, the proposed plus factors such as the existence of a subsidiary or a fixed place of business (e.g. a PE) seem to contradict the intention of the Inclusive Framework to establish a new taxing right that shall be unconstrained by physical presence.

For addressing the second part, the 'sustained' engagement of an MNE group in the market jurisdiction, i.e. an engagement of the MNE group maintained throughout an extended period of time, it could be considered that an MNE group only establishes a nexus in the market jurisdiction if the MNE group exceeds the revenue threshold in each of the past three years.[276] While this approach could avoid covering isolated or one-off transactions as well as mitigate the impact of cyclical changes and insofar avoid dipping into and rolling out of Amount A regularly,[277] other considerations, such as referring to the degree of permanence requirements found in the existing PE definition in the OECD MC[278], do not appear suitable.[279] As rightly pointed out by *Danon/Chand*, such an approach would depend on the circumstances and facts of each taxpayer and in this respect lead to uncertainties.[280]

---

[275] PwC, Comments on Pillar One Blueprint, 10.

[276] See also *Danon/Chand* who propose a time period of three to five years, cf. *Danon/*Chand, Comments on Secretariat Proposal, para. 33 and PwC proposing a threshold of three to five years, cf. PwC, Comments on Pillar One Blueprint, 10.

[277] Cf. PwC, Comments on Pillar One Blueprint, 10 et seq.

[278] Cf. OECD MC Commentary 2017, Art. 5, para. 28.

[279] See *Danon/Chand* who refer to this possibility as an option in order to address the temporal requirement of the nexus in the market jurisdiction, cf. *Danon/Chand*, Comments on Secretariat Proposal, para. 32.

[280] Cf. *Danon/Chand*, Comments on Secretariat Proposal, para. 32.

3. Tax Base Determination

The proposal outlined in the Pillar One Blueprint to base the calculation of Amount A on an adjusted PBT measure derived from consolidated financial statements appears appropriate, as such statements 'provide the most reliable source of financial information on a worldwide group'[281]. Nevertheless, MNE groups produce consolidated financial statements under different accounting standards.[282] Some of these accounting standards may however be inappropriate for determining taxable profits as they, e.g., provide leeway for individual accounting policies of businesses or are based on estimated values that have not yet been confirmed by actual market transactions.[283] Furthermore, as pointed out earlier, the reliance on accounting profits for tax purposes may result in inadequate effects, e.g. corporations might have to pay taxes on profits not yet realised[284] or market jurisdictions receive a taxing right for profits resulting from transactions solely taking place within a jurisdiction.[285]

Against this backdrop, it might come as a surprise that the Inclusive Framework does not provide for specific book-to-book harmonisation adjustments to account for variances between different accounting standards. Certainly, the significant additional compliance costs and complexity that excessive adjustments would introduce to the new taxing right and the burden they would impose on the ongoing negotiation process on Amount A justify that the Inclusive Framework does not envisages to introduce broad adjustments at this stage. Nevertheless, it seems advisable to develop reference tables that at least identify material differences between the accounting standards (e.g. reversal of impairments or financial asset classification)[286] that may produce materially inconsistent outcomes and may cause competitive distortions in the determination of the Amount A tax base among MNE groups and, as a consequence, require specific adjustments. The proposal discussed in the Pillar One Blueprint to implement an ongoing monitoring mechanism to identify material competitive distortions derived from existing or future differences across accounting standards that may require specific adjustments is certainly a step in the right direction and should be pursued.

---

[281] OECD, BEPS Action 4: Final Report 2015, para. 122.

[282] Cf. OECD, BEPS Action 1: Statement on the Two-Pillar Approach 2020, Annex 1, para. 43.

[283] Cf. *Englisch*, Comments on Secretariat Proposal, 3.

[284] Cf. *Blaufus/Jacobs*, Tax Related Implications of Fair Value Accounting, 254.

[285] Cf. *Förster/Greil/Hilse*, ITPJ 2020, 3 (11).

[286] See in more detail for the differences OECD, BEPS Action 1: Report on Pillar One Blueprint 2020, para. 424.

The proposed book-to-tax adjustments (exclusion of income tax expenses, exclusion of dividend income and gains or losses arising in connection with shares, exclusion of profits or losses derived from using the equity method of accounting and exclusion of expenses that are typically non-deductible or limited for public policy reasons)[287] are necessary given the different objectives of tax and accounting rules. Nevertheless, additional adjustments could be considered to prevent undesirable tax planning opportunities by MNE groups.

While several different profit level indicators were discussed for the calculation of Amount A (e.g. Profits Before Tax (PBT), Earnings Before Interest and Taxes (EBIT) and Earnings Before Interest, Taxes, Depreciation and Amortisation (EBITDA))[288], the use of PBT seems to be the most appropriate indicator to compute Amount A, as it is best suited to determine the true profitability of a business.[289] Against this background, it is to be welcomed that the Pillar One Blueprint refers to an adjusted PBT measure for the calculation of Amount A.

4. Revenue Sourcing Rules

As criticised above, the proposed revenue sourcing rules outlined in the Pillar One Blueprint are very complex, overly prescriptive and difficult to implement. Moreover, they do not provide certainty for MNE groups (especially not for those operating through independent distributors), as it remains unclear whether a selected indicator further down in the hierarchical list would be accepted by the tax administration.

Against this background, MNE groups should be given some more flexibility in the application of the indicators outlined in the list.[290] More specifically, it seems advisable to allow MNE groups to choose an appropriate indicator that best suits their available information, regardless of the hierarchical order set out in the proposal. Also, information already available to the MNE group for VAT

---

[287] Cf. OECD, BEPS Action 1: Report on Pillar One Blueprint 2020, paras. 409, 430 et seqq.

[288] See for the advantages and disadvantages of the different profit level indicators *Danon/Chand*, Comments on Secretariat Proposal, para. 44; PwC, Comments on Secretariat Proposal, 14 et seqq.; *Pistone/Nogueira/Andrade/Turina*, BIT 2020, 14 (19 et seq.).

[289] Cf. OECD, BEPS Action 1: Statement on the Two-Pillar Approach 2020, Annex 1, para. 44. For advantages of PBT see *Danon/Chand*, Comments on Secretariat Proposal, para. 44; *Chand*, Intertax 2019, 1023 (1037).

[290] Cf. also, i.a., PwC, Comments on Pillar One Blueprint, 11; *Keidanren*, Comments on Pillar One Blueprint, 5 et seqq.

purposes may be considered.[291] Such a 'practical best effort' approach could i) significantly reduce compliance costs for MNE groups and ii) reduce the complexity of the revenue sourcing rules. To ensure that tax administrations are able to understand the information provided, MNE groups may be required to document the adequacy of the information provided.

In addition, in cases where an MNE group sells products through independent distributors, it does not seem appropriate to require the MNE group to seek a change to the contractual arrangements with the independent distributor in order to comply with reporting requirements, as such a change may involve costs in form of a broader renegotiation of the contract.[292]

5. Segmentation Framework

Another issue that needs to be addressed relates to the question under what circumstances the Amount A tax base should be computed on a segmented basis. The analysis revealed that the need for segmentation may increase administration as well as compliance costs significantly. Nevertheless, segmentation appears necessary in certain cases to obtain accurate results. Otherwise, business lines generating high residual profits (e.g. Amazon's cloud computing AWS) may be blended by business lines with low or no residual profits (e.g. Amazon's retail business).[293] Also from a neutrality perspective, the computation of the Amount A tax base on a segmented basis appears to be the most neutral with respect to the firm's choice of the business model.[294]

Against this background, the proposal in the Pillar One Blueprint to compute the Amount A tax base on a segmented basis if the global revenue of the MNE group is above a certain revenue threshold and the segments do not generate similar profit margins seems appropriate. To provide a balance between additional complexity brought by the segmentation of the tax base and additional accuracy, the global revenue threshold for mandatory segmentation should be set well above the size threshold envisaged for defining in-scope MNE groups for Amount A purposes. Against this background, this threshold could initially be set at a higher

---

[291] Cf. also PwC, Comments on Pillar One Blueprint, 11.

[292] Cf. similar PwC, Comments on Pillar One Blueprint, 11.

[293] Cf. *Sullivan*, TNI 2020, 951 (951). See for calculations on the effects of calculating Amount A on a business line basis for Amazon, Alphabet, Netflix and Microsoft *Sullivan*, TNI 2020, 951 (951 et seqq.).

[294] Cf. similar Business at OECD, Comments on Secretariat Proposal, 3.

level, e.g. EUR 20 billion, and then lowered over a transition period of three or five years.[295]

In order to limit compliance and administration costs, disclosed segments as shown in the consolidated financial accounts should be used in the majority of cases as a basis for segmenting the Amount A tax base. Cases where the disclosed segments as shown in the consolidated financial accounts of the MNE groups may be rebutted by the tax administrations should be narrowly and precisely defined by guidelines.[296]

6. Implementation and Administration

With regard to the implementation of the new taxing right under Amount A, several options for implementation exist. One option would be to implement the new rules in a separate treaty article in order to limit spill-over effects on other existing tax treaty rules.[297] However, experiences with the implementation of the AOA revealed that amending a jurisdiction's bilateral tax treaty network may take very long, as changes on a treaty-by-treaty basis would be required. Furthermore, not even Germany has established bilateral tax treaties with all members of the Inclusive Framework.[298] Consequently, the introduction of the new taxing right solely through changes in tax treaties would not prove effective. Another option, the implementation of the new taxing right under Amount A through the MLI, as

[295]The Pillar One Blueprint provides for a similar approach, cf. OECD, BEPS Action 1: Report on Pillar One Blueprint 2020, para. 452.

[296]Cf. also *Keidanren*, Comments on Pillar One Blueprint, 9.

[297]Cf. also *Collier/Vella* and *Hentschel/Hörnicke/Kraft* emphasise that the implementation of rules dealing with any digital tax changes should not be implemented within the existing PE rules since the existence of a PE also needs to be taken into account for other Articles of the OECD MC such as Article 10 (Dividends), Article 11 (Interest), Article 12 (Royalties), Article 13 (Capital gains), Article 21 (Other income) and Article 22 (Capital), cf. *Collier/Vella*, WTJ 2019, 159 (184); *Hentschel/Hörnicke/Kraft*, Ubg 2019, 673 (680, note 108). See for detailed reasoning why the implementation of the new nexus rule would not be suitable in Article 5 OECD MC *Ditz/Pinkernell*, ISR 2019, 377 (383).

[298]See for an overview of the bilateral tax treaty network of Germany as of 1 Jan. 2021 BMF, 18 Feb. 2021, IV B 2 – S 1301/07/10017- 12, BStBl. I 2021, 265. See for a regularly updated list of the members of the Inclusive Framework https://www.oecd.org/tax/beps/inclusive-framework-on-beps-composition.pdf.

discussed in literature,[299] would face similar challenges, as the MLI is designed in a way that only existing tax treaties can be modified.[300]

Against this background, the implementation of the new taxing right under Amount A as well as the other elements of Pillar One through a new multilateral convention, as currently explored,[301] seems the only viable approach to allow all participating jurisdictions to implement the elements of Pillar One in a consistent and coherent manner and thereby close the gaps in treaty coverage.

The suggestion of the former US Treasury Secretary Steven Mnuchin to implement Pillar One as a 'safe harbour' regime should clearly be rejected as such an approach would not only fail to meet all of the OECD's policy objectives and insofar question the effectiveness of the entire project, but it can also not be expected that any kind of consensus agreement among the members of the Inclusive Framework seems possible on this basis.[302] Against this background, the latest developments at the virtual meeting of the G20 finance ministers on 26 February 2021, where US Treasury Secretary Janet Yellen informed her counterparts that the United States is no longer advocating a 'safe harbour' implementation of Pillar One,[303] seems very encouraging and is certainly a step in the right direction.

---

[299] Cf. i.a. *Danon/Chand*, Comments on Secretariat Proposal, para. 103.

[300] Cf. *Danon/Chand*, Comments on Secretariat Proposal, para. 103. Detailed for the MLI see BEPS Action 15: Final Report and chapter C.IV.7 of this thesis.

[301] Cf. OECD, BEPS Action 1: Report on Pillar One Blueprint 2020, paras. 837 et seqq.

[302] Cf. for concerns expressed OECD, BEPS Action 1: Statement on the Two-Pillar Approach 2020, para. 3.

[303] Cf. *Johnson*, TNTF 2021, 39-7.

G. Conclusion

The main objective of this thesis was to analyse the current rules governing the taxation of PEs and to evaluate whether these rules can be regarded appropriate to meet the challenges of the digitalisation of the economy. To do so, this thesis followed a two-step approach. In the first step, the PE threshold as well as the rules governing the attribution of profits to the PE as implemented in the OECD MC and German domestic law were analysed and deviations between the two approaches were identified. In this context, changes influencing the PE threshold as well as the profit attribution rules as a result of the BEPS Actions were analysed and critically evaluated. In the second step, the focus was shifted to the digitalisation of the economy and the challenges that arise from this ongoing development to the PE rules. The analysis undertaken allows for multiple assessments.

With regard to the PE threshold, it has become evident that the PE definition implemented in Article 5 OECD MC remains rather narrow compared to the PE definition under German domestic law if the permanent representative is included in the latter concept. In this sense, Article 5 OECD MC may function as a safeguard that defends the country of residence against taxation in the country of source. Nevertheless, the analysis showed that a strong trend can be observed for the PE threshold triggering a PE under Article 5 OECD MC to be constantly reduced over time. Especially, the latest changes to Article 5(4), (5) and (6) OECD MC and the corresponding Commentary through BEPS Action 7 confirm and even enhance this trend. However, even though this development may increase the number of existing PEs, ultimately leading to higher compliance costs for the taxpayer, it became evident that this development also introduces a number of operational difficulties and does not necessarily result in an increase of taxable profits in the jurisdiction where the PE is located.

S. Hentschel, *The Taxation of Permanent Establishments*, Hallesche Schriften zur Betriebswirtschaft 37, https://doi.org/10.1007/978-3-658-34000-1_7

The reason for this conclusion can be found in the mechanism that governs the attribution of profits to PEs: the AOA as implemented in Article 7(2) OECD MC. As outlined, the AOA is the result of a lengthy project of the OECD to address decades of uncertainty that resulted from different interpretations of Article 7 OECD MC. Nevertheless, the assessment whether the result of this project has been successful in its goal to bring about the intended uniformity for the attribution of profits to PEs is twofold.

On the one side, the AOA has brought certainty with regard to the explicit adoption of the 'Functionally Separate Entity' approach that requires hypothesising the PE as a separate and independent enterprise in a first step and the pricing of the recognised dealings between the PE and another part of the enterprise on an arm's length basis in a second step.

Furthermore, the AOA not only brought the taxation of PEs closer in line with the taxation of subsidiaries, but also makes the TP Guidelines highly relevant for the taxation of PEs. Against this background, it was assessed whether the changes to the TP Guidelines 2017 as a result of BEPS Actions 8–10 have an impact on the taxation of PEs. The analysis revealed that the guidance developed under BEPS Actions 8–10 and implemented in the TP Guidelines 2017 undoubtedly influence and enlighten specific aspects of the two-step approach of the AOA. This influence is due to the fact that the PE Report 2010 either directly refers to certain aspects of the TP Guidelines that can be applied fairly directly in the PE context (e.g. guidance regarding the functional and factual analysis), or the limited guidance provided in the PE Report 2010 makes the TP Guidelines a valuable additional source of guidance to the extent examined (e.g. the guidance regarding the definition of intangibles and its remuneration if used by another group member of the MNE as well as the guidance regarding the attribution of risks and capital). Also, the enhanced guidance on the performance of the comparability analysis, such as the detailed guidance for comparability adjustments for group synergies, location savings and other local market features within MNEs as well as the enhanced guidance on the use of the TPSM certainly brings clarity on how to carry out the second step of the AOA.

On the other side, the analysis revealed that the implementation of the AOA not only imported the whole complexity associated with the application of the arm's length principle into the area of the taxation of PEs, but also raises a number of conceptual and practical problems. Some of these problems are caused by the very general and vague language used in the PE Report 2010 and the Commentary to Article 7 OECD MC, leaving a wide margin for interpretation and leeway with regard to the application of the AOA. This situation does not promote a uniform implementation of the principles into domestic tax law of the various jurisdictions and ultimately comes at the expense of tax certainty. Against this background, it was further elaborated that for the AOA to become fully applicable it is necessary to a) implement national provisions into the tax law of the respective jurisdictions, and b) include the new Article 7 OECD MC in the bilateral tax treaty network of the respective jurisdictions. Both of these dimensions were analysed and brought about the following results.

With regard to the first issue, the national implementation of the AOA principles, the analysis revealed that the AOA principles have only been implemented in domestic law by a few countries. Nevertheless, in Germany the AOA was implemented into domestic law in Section 1(5) ETRA as early as 2013. Despite the fact that the rapid implementation of the AOA principles into German domestic tax law is generally to be welcomed, as, in the long run, swift implementation promotes the earliest possible consistent application of the AOA principles, it was outlined that several aspects on how the AOA was implemented into German domestic law must be criticised.

First of all, the actual implementation of the AOA principles within Section 1 ETRA must be seen critical. This is due to the fact that Section 1 ETRA is a provision for one-sided income adjustment leading to the situation that an adjustment of income in the PE context is only possible if the transfer prices for the dealings between the PE and another part of the enterprise negatively impact the amount of taxable income in Germany. It follows that the principles of the AOA as set out by the OECD were only implemented partially for income adjustments that work in favour of the German tax administration which may result in double taxation for the taxpayer.

Besides this general issue of implementation, it was illustrated that further areas exist where the German AOA approach deviates from the OECD approach. These deviations are caused by the situation that the German tax administration provides for provisions in the BsGaV that are not in line with the principles as set out in the PE Report 2010. In this context, two categories of deviations were identified. The first category of deviations results from an unequal treatment of inbound and outbound PEs that is clearly fiscally motivated and intends to safeguard the German tax base. In this context, the approach for the attribution of free capital to inbound and outbound PEs was highlighted. While the BsGaV determines the minimum capital approach—which is not an authorised OECD approach—as the general approach for the attribution of free capital to a foreign PE of a domestic enterprise, the capital allocation approach shall be the guiding principle for domestic PEs of foreign enterprises. The second category of deviations is caused by the fact that certain provisions in the BsGaV put forward attribution rules that are very prescriptive compared to the rather broad and flexible approach outlined by the OECD. In this context, it can be highlighted that in contrast to the OECD approach, the German approach does not allow for a pro rata attribution of tangible assets (Section 5 BsGaV), stakes, financial assets and similar assets (Section 7 BsGaV) as well as other assets (Section 8 BsGaV). Regardless of the kind of deviation, the hereby caused fundamental lack of consistency to the OECD approach may lead to double taxation if the foreign jurisdiction follows the concept of the AOA as outlined in the PE Report 2010.

With regard to the second issue, the implementation of the new Article 7 OECD MC in the bilateral tax treaty network, it was outlined that the lengthy adoption process requiring the implementation of this Article on a treaty-by-treaty basis has led to a very slow adoption rate of the AOA principles, even for those OECD member countries willing to take up the principles of the AOA. Ten OECD member countries have entered reservations on Article 7 OECD MC 2010 reserving the right to use the version of Article 7 OECD MC pre 2010. Outside the OECD, the adoption rate of the AOA is even lower. Even before the final version of Article 7 OECD MC 2010 and the PE Report 2010 were released, the UN Committee of Experts rejected the AOA approach since the principles were considered to be in direct conflict with Article 7(3) UN Model. Also, the vast majority of current German tax treaties are not yet based on the wording of the AOA version of Article 7 OECD MC. In fact, only five of the 96 tax treaties currently concluded and ratified are based on the wording of the AOA version of Article 7 OECD MC leading to the absence of a single standard for profit attribution to PEs. Nevertheless, the German AOA provisions are applicable regardless of whether or not the AOA has been implemented in the respective tax treaties. This situation often results in a different treatment of PE issues from a German national tax law perspective compared to a treaty perspective. As a consequence, double taxation or double non-taxation issues may arise.

In order to mitigate such a mismatch, the German legislator has enacted an 'escape clause' in Section 1(5) sentence 8 ETRA, which was analysed in further detail. In order to do so, a classification of the current tax treaty network was necessary. The analysis that followed revealed that the escape clause deserves, in principle, positive reception as a measure mitigating the risk of double taxation. Nevertheless, the fact that the escape clause can only be applied if the taxpayer succeeds in proving specific circumstances of the case does not only lead to high compliance and administration costs but also shows that the escape clause can merely mitigate the problems resulting from different treaty versions, but does not solve these problems. Given this background, the mismatch between the AOA provisions implemented under German domestic law and the wording of existing tax treaties remains a problem for cross-border PE taxation.

In chapter E, the focus was shifted to a very different set of challenges for the PE rules, namely the challenges resulting from the ongoing digitalisation of the economy. In this context, key characteristics frequently observed in digitalised business models were determined and the various challenges arising therefrom for the PE rules were elaborated. The following challenges were identified. First, digitalisation has enabled enterprises to be economically present in a market jurisdiction and generate substantial amount of profits in this jurisdiction without the need to establish a physical presence in the market jurisdiction (cross-jurisdictional scale without mass). Since the PE concept is predominantly rooted in physical presence requirements, this development challenges the market jurisdiction's ability to tax the corresponding profits generated within its borders. Second, data and user participation play a crucial role for many highly digitalised business models, especially multi-sided platforms. However, the presented case study of GoogCo illustrated that the current tax rules do not allow the market jurisdiction to tax the profits derived from the ultimate customer from whom the enterprise exploits user-generated content and data if the enterprise does not have a physical PE or a subsidiary established in the market jurisdiction.

Third, the increased importance of intangibles for business models challenges the market jurisdiction's capability to tax profits derived from the performance of such intangibles. This is mainly due to the mechanism of the AOA attributing profits derived from the performance of intangibles to the jurisdiction where the significant people function relevant for the creation or acquisition of such intangibles are performed, which is mostly the jurisdiction where the head office is located. The case study of AmazCo illustrated that even though the revisions to Article 5 OECD MC and its corresponding Commentary through BEPS Action 7 resulted in an increase of PEs in the market jurisdiction, mostly no significant profits can be attributed to these new PEs, as the activities carried out by these PEs are usually limited to service activities. The changes made to the OECD TP Guidelines through BEPS Actions 8–10 have not changed this situation either.

Against this background, the OECD's reform proposal to the tax challenges arising from the ongoing digitalisation of the economy under Pillar One, which provides for the introduction of a new taxing right that is no longer dependent on the actual physical presence of an enterprise in the market jurisdiction (Amount A) and new profit allocation rules, was analysed and assessed against the overarching principles of tax policy. The analysis produced the following results.

The fundamental idea of Amount A, which proposes a partial reallocation of taxable profits towards market jurisdictions using a formulaic approach deserves, in principle, positive reception. Given the diverse views of the members of the Inclusive Framework on how to overcome the challenges arising from the digitalisation of the economy, the approach provides a viable basis which could a) facilitate political compromise, and b) result in a more equitable allocation of taxation rights among jurisdictions. However, whether the benefits introduced through the new taxing right may outweigh the additional administrative and compliance costs largely depends on the final design of the approach. On the one side, the use of carve-outs, high revenue thresholds and a high residual profit threshold would ensure that additional compliance costs are only introduced for large and profitable businesses, as only such businesses would be affected by the new taxing right. On the other side, such limitations would negatively impact the neutrality and the effectiveness and fairness of the approach, as not only large enterprises with high residual profits are able to develop an active and sustained engagement in the market jurisdiction.

The analysis further revealed that the introduction of Amount A would introduce an additional layer of complexity raising a multitude of procedural and technical issues (e.g. how to prevent double taxation from the interaction of the current system and the Amount A regime). Insofar, the work on the introduction of legally binding and effective dispute prevention and resolution mechanisms appears to be an essential component for the success of the project and is certainly a step in the right direction. Also, the proposed fixed remuneration for baseline marketing and distribution activities as part of Amount B deserves, in principle, positive reception, as it could reduce the uncertainty that currently surrounds the computation of such transactions.

Overall it can be concluded that the international tax system will not become less complex, regardless of whether the ongoing work under Pillar One is brought to a successful conclusion. However, the alternative to the reform proposal under Pillar One would be a world where more and more countries implement uncoordinated unilateral measures to address the challenges arising from the digitalisation of the economy, resulting in an even more complex, fractured and distorted international tax system that would ultimately increase the risk of double taxation. Therefore, it seems worth to continue intensive work on Pillar One in order to reach a consensus-based solution among the members of the Inclusive Framework by mid-2021. Recommendations on how some of the technical and policy issues could be addressed were presented in chapter F.IV of this thesis. It is now time for each of the members of the Inclusive Framework to contribute their part to make the Pillar One approach work.

Annex

Table 1 Master File OECD

Organizational structure
• Chart illustrating the MNE's legal and ownership structure and geographical location of operating entities.
Description of MNE's business(es)
General written description of the MNE's business including: • Important drivers of business profit; • A description of the supply chain for the group's five largest products and/or service offerings by turnover plus any other products and/or services amounting to more than 5% of group turnover (*chart or diagram*); • A list and brief description of important service arrangements between members of the MNE group, other than research and development (R&D) services including a description of the capabilities of the principal locations providing important services and transfer pricing policies for allocating services costs and determining prices to be paid for intra-group services; • A description of the main geographic markets for the group's products and services (that are referred to on the third column); • A brief written functional analysis describing the principal contributions to value creation by individual entities within the group, i.e. key functions performed, important risks assumed, and important assets used; • A description of important business restructuring transactions, acquisitions and divestitures occurring during the fiscal year.

(continued)

S. Hentschel, *The Taxation of Permanent Establishments*, Hallesche Schriften zur Betriebswirtschaft 37, https://doi.org/10.1007/978-3-658-34000-1

Table 1 (continued)

MNE's intangibles
• A general description of the MNE's overall strategy for the development, ownership and exploitation of intangibles, including location of principal R&D facilities and location of R&D management. • A list of intangibles or groups of intangibles of the MNE group that are important for transfer pricing purposes and which entities legally own them. • A list of important agreements among identified associated enterprises related to intangibles, including cost contribution arrangements, principal research service agreements and license agreements. • A general description of the group's transfer pricing policies related to R&D and intangibles. • A general description of any important transfers of interests in intangibles among associated enterprises during the fiscal year concerned, including the entities, countries, and compensation involved.
MNE's intercompany financial activities
• A general description of how the group is financed, including important financing arrangements with unrelated lenders. • The identification of any members of the MNE group that provide a central financing function for the group, including the country under whose laws the entity is organised and the place of effective management of such entities. • A general description of the MNE's general transfer pricing policies related to financing arrangements between associated enterprises.
MNE's financial and tax positions
• The MNE's annual consolidated financial statement for the fiscal year concerned if otherwise prepared for financial reporting, regulatory, internal management, tax or other purposes. • A list and brief description of the MNE group's existing unilateral advance pricing agreements (APAs) and other tax rulings relating to the allocation of income among countries.

Source: Own illustration based on OECD, TP Guidelines 2017, Annex I to chapter V, pp. 501 et seqq.

Table 2 Local File OECD

Local entity
• A description of the management structure of the local entity, a local organization chart, and a description of the individuals to whom local management reports and the country(ies) in which such individuals maintain their principal offices. • A detailed description of the business and business strategy pursued by the local entity including an indication whether the local entity has been involved in or affected by business restructurings or intangibles transfers in the present or immediately past year and an explanation of those aspects of such transactions affecting the local entity.

(continued)

Table 2 (continued)

Controlled transactions
For each material category of controlled transactions in which the entity is involved, provide the following information: • A description of the material controlled transactions (e.g. procurement of manufacturing services, purchase of goods, provision of services, loans, financial and performance guarantees, licenses of intangibles, etc.) and the context in which such transactions take place. • The amount of intra-group payments and receipts for each category of controlled transactions involving the local entity (i.e. payments and receipts for products, services, royalties, interest, etc.) broken down by tax jurisdiction of the foreign payor or recipient. • An identification of associated enterprises involved in each category of controlled transactions, and the relationship amongst them. • Copies of all material intercompany agreements concluded by the local entity. • A detailed comparability and functional analysis of the taxpayer and relevant associated enterprises with respect to each documented category of controlled transactions, including any changes compared to prior years. • An indication of the most appropriate transfer pricing method with regard to the category of transaction and the reasons for selecting that method. • An indication of which associated enterprise is selected as the tested party, if applicable, and an explanation of the reasons for this selection. • A summary of the important assumptions made in applying the transfer pricing methodology. • If relevant, an explanation of the reasons for performing a multi-year analysis. • A list and description of selected comparable uncontrolled transactions (internal or external), if any, and information on relevant financial indicators for independent enterprises relied on in the transfer pricing analysis, including a description of the comparable search methodology and the source of such information. • A description of any comparability adjustments performed, and an indication of whether adjustments have been made to the results of the tested party, the comparable uncontrolled transactions, or both. • A description of the reasons for concluding that relevant transactions were priced on an arm's length basis based on the application of the selected transfer pricing method. • A summary of financial information used in applying the transfer pricing methodology. • A copy of existing unilateral and bilateral/multilateral APAs and other tax rulings to which the local tax jurisdiction is not a party and which are related to controlled transactions described above.
Financial information
• Annual local entity financial accounts for the fiscal year concerned. If audited statements exist they should be supplied and if not, existing unaudited statements should be supplied. • Information and allocation schedules showing how the financial data used in applying the transfer pricing method may be tied to the annual financial statements. • Summary schedules of relevant financial data for comparables used in the analysis and the sources from which that data was obtained.

Source: Own illustration based on OECD, TP Guidelines 2017, Annex II to chapter V, pp. 505 et seqq.

Table 3 Overview of the Allocation of Income, Taxes and Business Activities by Tax Jurisdictions (OECD Model Template for the CbC Report: Table 1/3)

Name of the MNE group: Fiscal year connected: Currency used:										
Tax Jurisdiction	Revenues			Profit (Loss) before Income Tax	Income Tax Paid (on Cash Basis)	Income Tax Accrued – Current Year	Stated Capital	Accumulated Earnings	Number of Employees	Tangible Assets other than Cash Equivalents
	Unrelated Party	Related Party	Total							

Source: Own illustration bssased on OECD, TP Guidelines 2017, Annex III to chapter V, p. 510.

Table 4 List of all the Constituent Entities of the MNE Group Included in Each Aggregation per Tax Jurisdiction (OECD Model Template for the CbC Report: Table 2/3)

Name of the MNE group: Fiscal year concerned:															
			Main business Activity(ies)												
Tax Jurisdiction	Constituent Entities Resident in the Tax Jurisdiction	Tax Jurisdiction of Organisation or Incorporation if Different from Tax Jurisdiction of Residence	Research and Development	Holding or Managing Intellectual Property	Purchasing or Procurement	Manufacturing or Production	Sales, Marketing or Distribution	Administrative, Management or Support Services	Provision of Services to Unrelated Parties	Internal Group Finance	Regulated Financial Services	Insurance	Holding Shares or Other Equity instruments	Dormant	Other
	1.														
	2.														
	3.														
	1.														
	2.														
	3.														

Source: Own illustration based on OECD, TP Guidelines 2017, Annex III to chapter V, p. 511.

Table 5 Additional Information (OECD Model Template for the CbC Report: Table 3/3)

Name of the MNE group: Fiscal year concerned:
Please include any further brief information or explanation you consider necessary or that would facilitate the understanding of the compulsory information provided in the Country-by-Country Report.

Source: Own illustration based on OECD, TP Guidelines 2017, Annex III to chapter V, p. 511.

Table 6 Local File—§ 4 GAufzV

Allgemeine Informationen über die Beteiligungsverhältnisse, den Geschäftsbetrieb und den Organisationsaufbau:
• die Darstellung der Beteiligungsverhältnisse zwischen dem Steuerpflichtigen und ihm nahestehenden Personen im Sinne des § 1(2) Nr.1, 2 AStG, mit denen der Steuerpflichtige unmittelbar oder über Zwischenpersonen Geschäftsbeziehungen unterhält, zu Beginn des Prüfungszeitraums und die Darstellung der Veränderungen dieser Beteiligungsverhältnisse innerhalb des Prüfungszeitraums; • die Darstellung der sonstigen Umstände, die das Nahestehen im Sinne des § 1(2) Nr. 3 AStG begründen können; • die Darstellung der organisatorischen und operativen Konzernstruktur, einschließlich Betriebsstätten und Beteiligungen an Personengesellschaften, zu Beginn des Prüfungszeitraums sowie die Darstellung der Veränderungen der Konzernstruktur innerhalb des Prüfungszeitraums; • die Beschreibung der Managementstruktur sowie der Organisationsstruktur des inländischen Unternehmens des Steuerpflichtigen; • die Beschreibung der Tätigkeitsbereiche des Steuerpflichtigen und der Geschäftsstrategie zu Beginn des Prüfungszeitraums sowie die Beschreibung der Veränderungen der Tätigkeitsbereiche und der Geschäftsstrategie innerhalb des Prüfungszeitraums.

(continued)

Table 6 (continued)

Aufzeichnungen über Geschäftsbeziehungen des Steuerpflichtigen:
• die Beschreibung der Tätigkeitsbereiche des Steuerpflichtigen und der Geschäftsstrategie zu Beginn des Prüfungszeitraums sowie die Beschreibung der Veränderungen der Tätigkeitsbereiche und der Geschäftsstrategie innerhalb des Prüfungszeitraums; • die Auflistung der wesentlichen immateriellen Werte, die dem Steuerpflichtigen gehören und die er im Rahmen seiner Geschäftsbeziehungen nutzt oder zur Nutzung überlässt.
Funktions- und Risikoanalyse:
• Informationen über die im Rahmen der Geschäftsbeziehungen ausgeübten Funktionen und übernommenen Risiken zu Beginn des Prüfungszeitraums sowie über die Veränderungen dieser Funktionen und Risiken innerhalb des Prüfungszeitraums; • Informationen über die eingesetzten wesentlichen Vermögenswerte; • Informationen über die vereinbarten Vertragsbedingungen; • Informationen über gewählte Geschäftsstrategien; • Informationen über die Markt- und Wettbewerbsverhältnisse, die für die Besteuerung von Bedeutung sind; • Beschreibung der Wertschöpfungskette und Darstellung der Wertschöpfungsbeiträge des Steuerpflichtigen; § 1 Absatz 3 Satz 4 GAufzV ist zu beachten.
Verrechnungspreisanalyse:
• Zeitpunkt der Verrechnungspreisbestimmung; • Aufzeichnung der im Zeitpunkt der Verrechnungspreisbestimmung verfügbaren und zur Preisbestimmung verwendeten Informationen, die für die Besteuerung von Bedeutung sind; • Darstellung der angewandten Verrechnungspreismethode; • Begründung der Auswahl und der Geeignetheit der angewandten Verrechnungspreismethode; • Unterlagen über die Berechnungen bei der Anwendung der gewählten Verrechnungspreismethode; • Auflistung und Beschreibung verwendeter vergleichbarer interner oder externer Geschäftsvorfälle.

(continued)

Table 6 (continued)

Weitere nach den Verhältnissen des Einzelfalls erforderliche Aufzeichnungen:
• Informationen über Sonderumstände wie Maßnahmen zum Vorteilsausgleich, soweit sie die Bestimmung der Verrechnungspreise des Steuerpflichtigen beeinflussen können; • bei Umlagen die Verträge, gegebenenfalls in Verbindung mit den Anhängen, den Anlagen und den Zusatzvereinbarungen, die Unterlagen über die Anwendung des Aufteilungsschlüssels und über den erwarteten Nutzen für alle Beteiligten sowie die Unterlagen über die Art und den Umfang der Rechnungskontrolle, über die Anpassung an veränderte Verhältnisse, über die Zugriffsberechtigung auf die Unterlagen des leistungserbringenden Unternehmens und über die Zuordnung von Nutzungsrechten; • Informationen über beantragte oder abgeschlossene Verständigungs- oder Schiedsstellenverfahren anderer Staaten sowie über unilaterale Verrechnungspreiszusagen und sonstige steuerliche Vorabzusagen ausländischer Steuerverwaltungen, die die Geschäftsbeziehungen des Steuerpflichtigen berühren; • Aufzeichnungen über Preisanpassungen beim Steuerpflichtigen, auch wenn diese die Folge von Verrechnungspreiskorrekturen oder Vorabzusagen ausländischer Finanzbehörden bei dem Steuerpflichtigen nahestehenden Personen sind; • Aufzeichnungen über die Ursachen von Verlusten und über Vorkehrungen des Steuerpflichtigen oder ihm nahestehender Personen zur Beseitigung der Verlustsituation, wenn der Steuerpflichtige in mehr als drei aufeinander folgenden Wirtschaftsjahren aus Geschäftsbeziehungen einen steuerlichen Verlust ausweist; • in Fällen von Funktions- und Risikoänderungen im Sinne des § 3(2) GAufzV Aufzeichnungen über Forschungsvorhaben und laufende Forschungstätigkeiten, die im Zusammenhang mit einer Funktionsänderung stehen können und in den drei Jahren vor Durchführung der Funktionsänderung stattfanden oder abgeschlossen worden sind; die Aufzeichnungen müssen mindestens Angaben über den genauen Gegenstand der Forschungen und die insgesamt jeweils zuzuordnenden Kosten enthalten. Dies gilt nur, soweit ein Steuerpflichtiger Forschung und Entwicklung betreibt und Unterlagen über seine Forschungs- und Entwicklungsarbeiten erstellt, aus denen die genannten Aufzeichnungen abgeleitet werden können. • Verwendet der Steuerpflichtige für die Bestimmung seiner Verrechnungspreise Datenbanken, muss er die von ihm dabei verwendete Suchstrategie, die dabei verwendeten Suchkriterien, das Suchergebnis und den außerhalb der Datenbank durchgeführten weiteren Selektionsprozess (Suchprozess) umfassend offenlegen. Der gesamte Suchprozess des Steuerpflichtigen muss nachvollziehbar und zum Zeitpunkt der Außenprüfung prüfbar sein. Die Konfiguration der Datenbank, mit der der konkrete Suchprozess durchgeführt wurde, ist vollständig zu dokumentieren. § 147(6) AO gilt sinngemäß.

Source: Own illustration based on Section 4 GAufzV.

Table 7 Local File—§ 4 GAufzV (English Translation)

General information about the ownership structure, the business operations and the organizational structure:
• a representation of the ownership structures between the taxpayer and related parties as referred to in Section 1(2) no. 1, 2 ETRA with whom the taxpayer maintains direct business relations or business relations via intermediaries at the beginning of the audit period and a representation of changes to these ownership structures during the audit period; • a representation of other circumstances that may justify classification as a related party as referred to in Section 1(2) no. 3 ETRA; • a representation of the organizational and operational structure of the group, including permanent establishments and holdings in partnerships, at the beginning of the audit period and a representation of changes to the group structure during the audit period, • a description of the management structure and the organizational structure of the taxpayer's domestic company; • a description of the taxpayer's areas of activity and the business strategy at the beginning of the audit period and a description of changes to the areas of activity and the business strategy during the audit period.
Records on the taxpayer's business relations:
• a representation of the taxpayer's business relations, overview of the type and scope of these business relations, for example goods purchases, services, loan arrangements and other transfers of usage rights, and cost contribution arrangements, and an overview of the contracts upon which the business relations are based and any changes to these contracts during the audit period; • a list of the main intangible assets that belong to the taxpayer and that the taxpayer uses, or transfers for the purpose of being used, in the context of the taxpayer's business relations.
Functional analysis and risk analysis:
• information about the functions performed within the scope of the business relations and the risks assumed at the beginning of the audit period, as well as any changes to these functions and risks during the audit period; • information about the main assets used; • information about the agreed contractual conditions; • the chosen business strategies; • information about any market and competition-related circumstances that are of relevance for taxation; • description of the value chain and representation of the taxpayer's contribution to the value chain; Section 1(3) sentence 4 GAufzV, must be observed.
Transfer pricing analysis:
• time of determination of transfer prices; • a record of any information that was available at the time of determination of transfer prices and was used to determine the prices, which is of relevance for taxation; • a representation of the transfer pricing method used; • justification for the choice of the transfer pricing method used and its suitability; • documentation about the calculations used when applying the chosen transfer pricing method; • a list and description of comparable internal or external business transactions that have been used.

(continued)

Table 7 (continued)

Additional records depending on the circumstances of the individual case:
• information about special circumstances such as measures to set-off benefits, insofar as they may influence the determination of the taxpayer's transfer prices; • where contribution arrangements are involved, the contracts, if necessary accompanied by the attachments, annexes, and additional agreements, documentation about the application of the allocation formula and about the expected benefits for all participants, as well as documentation about the type and scope of invoice verification, adjustments to changed circumstances, the right to access the documents of the company supplying the services and the allocation of usage rights; • information about applied-for or concluded mutual agreement procedures or arbitration procedures with other countries and about unilateral transfer pricing commitments and other tax rulings from foreign tax administrations that affect the taxpayer's business relations; • records on price adjustments on the part of the taxpayer, even if these adjustments are the result of transfer pricing corrections or rulings by foreign revenue administrations with regard to parties related to the taxpayer; • records on the causes of losses and on precautions by the taxpayer or parties related to the taxpayer to eliminate loss-making situations, if the taxpayer posts a tax loss from business relations in more than three consecutive fiscal years; • in cases involving changes of functions and risks as referred to in Section 3(2) GAufzV, records on research projects and ongoing research activities that could be related to a change in function and which took place or were concluded during the three years before the implementation of the change in function; the records must contain, as a minimum, details of the specific subject of the research and the total costs attributable to the research. This only applies if the taxpayer carries out research and development and keeps documentation on these research and development activities from which the above-mentioned records may be derived. • If taxpayers use databases to determine their transfer prices, they must provide comprehensive information on the search strategies used, the search criteria used, the search results and any additional selection processes used outside the scope of the database (search process). The taxpayer's entire search process must be transparent and verifiable at the time of the field audit. The configuration of the database which is used to perform the specific search process must be documented in full. Section 147(6) GFC applies mutatis mutandis.

Source: Own illustration based on Section 4 GAufV, english translation available at: https://www.bundesfinanzministerium.de/Content/EN/Downloads/Ordinance-on-the-documentation-of-profit-allocations.pdf?__blob=publicationFile&v=3.

Table 8 Master File—§ 5 GAufzV

Die Stammdokumentation umfasst Folgendes:
• grafische Darstellung des Organisationsaufbaus (Rechts- und Eigentümerstruktur) sowie der geografischen Verteilung der Gesellschaften und Betriebsstätten, die zur Unternehmensgruppe im Sinne des § 90(3) AO gehören; • Übersicht über bedeutende Faktoren für den Gesamtgewinn der Unternehmensgruppe; • Beschreibung der Lieferketten für die fünf Produkte oder Dienstleistungen der Unternehmensgruppe, die die höchsten Umsatzerlöse erzielen (eine aussagefähige Grafik oder ein entsprechendes Diagramm reicht aus); • Beschreibung der Lieferketten für alle weiteren Produkte oder Dienstleistungen, auf die jeweils mehr als 5 Prozent der Umsatzerlöse der Unternehmensgruppe entfallen (eine aussagefähige Grafik oder ein entsprechendes Diagramm reicht aus); • Auflistung und zusammenfassende Beschreibung wichtiger Dienstleistungsvereinbarungen zwischen Unternehmen der Unternehmensgruppe (ohne Forschungs- und Entwicklungsleistungen), einschließlich einer Beschreibung der Kapazitäten der Hauptstandorte, die bedeutende Dienstleistungen erbringen, sowie der Verrechnungspreispolitik für die Zuordnung der Dienstleistungskosten und für die Bestimmung der für konzerninterne Dienstleistungen zu zahlenden Preise; • Beschreibung der wichtigsten geografischen Märkte für die Produkte oder Dienstleistungen der Unternehmensgruppe (vgl. Punkt 3 und 4); • zusammenfassende Funktionsanalyse, die die Hauptbeiträge beschreibt, die die einzelnen Unternehmen der Unternehmensgruppe zur Wertschöpfung leisten, das heißt die ausgeübten Schlüsselfunktionen, die wichtigen übernommenen Risiken und die wichtigen genutzten Vermögenswerte; • zusammenfassende Beschreibung bedeutender, während des Wirtschaftsjahres erfolgter Umstrukturierungen der Geschäftstätigkeit der Unternehmensgruppe sowie eine Auflistung und zusammenfassende Beschreibung der von der Unternehmensgruppe während des Wirtschaftsjahres vorgenommenen bedeutender Unternehmenskäufe und -verkäufe; • allgemeine Beschreibung der Gesamtstrategie der Unternehmensgruppe für immaterielle Werte (Entwicklung, Eigentum, Schutz und Verwertung), einschließlich einer Auflistung der Standorte der wichtigsten Forschungs- und Entwicklungseinrichtungen und der Standorte des Forschungs- und Entwicklungsmanagements; • Auflistung der immateriellen Werte oder der Gruppen immaterieller Werte der Unternehmensgruppe, die für die Verrechnungspreisbestimmung von Bedeutung sind, sowie der Unternehmen, die rechtliche Eigentümer oder Inhaber dieser immateriellen Werte sind; • Auflistung wichtiger Vereinbarungen zwischen den Unternehmen der Unternehmensgruppe mit Bezug zu den immateriellen Werten, einschließlich Kostenumlagevereinbarungen sowie wesentlicher Forschungsdienstleistungsvereinbarungen und Lizenzvereinbarungen; • allgemeine Beschreibung der Verrechnungspreispolitik der Unternehmensgruppe in Bezug auf Forschung und Entwicklung sowie auf immaterielle Werte;

(continued)

Table 8 (continued)

• allgemeine Beschreibung aller wichtigen Übertragungen von Rechten an immateriellen Werten zwischen den Unternehmen der Unternehmensgruppe während des betreffenden Wirtschaftsjahres, einschließlich der entsprechenden Unternehmen, Staaten und Vergütungen; • allgemeine Beschreibung, wie die Unternehmensgruppe finanziert wird, einschließlich der Darstellung bedeutender Finanzierungsbeziehungen zu fremden Dritten; • Angabe derjenigen Unternehmen der Unternehmensgruppe, die eine zentrale Finanzierungs-, Cashmanagement- oder Assetmanagementfunktion ausüben, mit der Angabe, nach welchem Recht das jeweilige Unternehmen organisiert ist, und mit der Angabe des Orts der tatsächlichen Geschäftsleitung des jeweiligen Unternehmens; • allgemeine Beschreibung der Verrechnungspreisstrategie der Unternehmensgruppe in Bezug auf Finanzierungsbeziehungen innerhalb dieser Unternehmensgruppe; • Konzernabschluss der Unternehmensgruppe für das betreffende Wirtschaftsjahr, sofern ein solcher erstellt wurde; • Auflistung und kurze Beschreibung der bestehenden unilateralen Vorabverständigungen über die Verrechnungspreisgestaltung der Unternehmensgruppe sowie anderer Vorabzusagen im Zusammenhang mit der Aufteilung der Erträge zwischen den Staaten.

Source: Own illustration based on the Annex to Section 5 GAufzV.

Table 9 Master File—§ 5 GAufzV (English Translation)

The master file should contain the following information:
• a visual representation of the organisational structure (legal and ownership structure) as well as of the geographical distribution of the companies and permanent establishments that are part of the company group as referred to in Section 90(3) GFC; • an overview of the important drivers of the group's overall profit; • a description of the supply chains for the group's five products or services that generate the largest turnover (a meaningful chart or diagram is sufficient); • a description of the supply chains for any other products or services that individually account for more than 5 percent of group turnover (a meaningful chart or diagram is sufficient); • a list and brief description of important service arrangements between companies in the group (other than research and development services), including a description of the capabilities of the principal locations providing important services and transfer pricing policies for allocating services costs and determining prices to be paid for intra-group services; • a description of the main geographical markets for the group's products or services referred to under bullet point 3 and 4 above; • a brief functional analysis describing the principal contributions to value creation by individual entities within the group, i.e. key functions performed, important risks assumed, and important assets used;

(continued)

Table 9 (continued)

- a brief description of important restructurings of the group's business activities occurring during the fiscal year, and a list and brief description of important acquisitions and divestitures of companies carried out by the group during the fiscal year;
- a general description of the group's overall strategy for intangible assets (development, ownership, protection and exploitation), including a list of the locations of the principal research and development facilities and of the locations of research and development management;
- a list of the group's intangible assets or groups of intangible assets that are important for the determination of transfer prices and a list of the entities that are the legal owners or holders of these intangible assets;
- a list of important agreements between the group's companies with regard to intangible assets, including cost contribution arrangements, principal research service agreements and licence agreements;
- a general description of the group's transfer pricing policies with regard to research and development and intangible assets;
- a general description of any important transfers of interests in intangible assets among the companies of the group during the fiscal year concerned, including details on the entities, countries and compensation involved;
- a general description of how the group is financed, including a representation of important financing arrangements with unrelated third parties;
- details of any companies in the group that provide a central financing, cash management or asset management function, specifying under which country's law the entity is organised and specifying the place of effective management of the respective entity;
- a general description of the group's transfer pricing strategy with regard to financing arrangements within the group;
- the group's consolidated financial statement for the respective fiscal year, if one has been prepared;
- a list and brief description of any existing unilateral advance pricing agreements relating to the group's transfer pricing approach and any other tax rulings relating to the allocation of income among countries.

Source: Own illustration based on the Annex to Section 5 GAufzV, english translation available at: https://www.bundesfinanzministerium.de/Content/EN/Downloads/Ordinance-on-the-documentation-of-profit-allocations.pdf?__blob=publicationFile&v=3.

Table 10 Overview of the Allocation of Income, Taxes and Business Activities by Tax Jurisdiction According to Section 138a(2) No. 1 GFC (CbC Report: Table 1/3)

Name des multinationalen Konzerns: Betrachtetes Wirtschaftsjahr: Währung der angegebenen Beträge:										
Steuer-hoheitsgebiet	Umsatzerlöse und sonstige Erträge			Jahres-ergebnis vor Ertragsteuern	Im Wirtschaftsjahr gezahlte Ertragsteuern	Die im Wirt-schaftsjahr für dieses Wirtschafts-jahr gezahl-ten und zu-rückgestellten Ertragsteuern	Eigen-kapital	Einbe-haltener Gewinn	Zahl der Beschäftig-ten	Materielle Vermögens-werte
	Fremde Unterneh-men	Naheste-hende Un-terneh-men	Summe							

Source: Own illustration based on table 1 of the Annex to BMF, 11 July 2017, IV B 5—S 1300/16/10010:002, BStBl. I 2017, 974.

Table 11 Overview of the Allocation of Income, Taxes and Business Activities by Tax Jurisdiction According to Section 138a(2) No. 1 GFC (CbC Report: Table1/3—English Translation)

Name of the MNE group: Fiscal year connected: Currency used:											
Tax Jurisdiction	Revenue and other Income			Profit (Loss) before Income Tax	Income Tax Paid during the Fiscal Year	Income Taxes paid and accrued during the financial year for that financial year	Stated Capital	Accumulated Earnings	Number of Employees	Tangible Assets
	Unrelated Party	Related Party	Total							

Source: Own illustration and translation based on table 1 of the Annex to BMF, 11 July 2017, IV B 5—S 1300/16/10010:002, BStBl. I 2017, 974.

Table 12 List of All Enterprises and Permanent Establishments of the MNE Group per Tax Jurisdiction Together With the Most Important Business Activities They Perform According to Section 138a(2) No. 2 GFC (CbC Report: Table 2/3)

Name des multinationalen Konzerns: Betrachtetes Wirtschaftsjahr:														
Steuerhoheitsgebiet	In Steuerhoheitsgebiet ansässige Unternehmen und Betriebsstätten des Konzern	Wichtigste Geschäftstätigkeit(en)												
		Forschung und Entwicklung	Besitz oder Verwaltung von geistigem Eigentum	Einkauf oder Beschaffung	Verarbeitung oder Produktion	Verkauf, Marketing oder Vertrieb	Verwaltungs-, Management- oder Supportdienstleistungen	Erbringung von Dienstleistungen für unverbundene Dritte	Konzerninterne Finanzierung	Regulierte Finanzdienstleistung	Versicherungen	Besitz von Aktien oder anderen Wertpapieren mit Beteiligungscharakter	Ruhende Tätigkeit	Sonstige (Bitte geben Sie die Art der Tätigkeit der Geschäftseinheit in Tabelle 3 "Zusätzliche Informationen" an.)
	1.													
	2.													
	3.													
	1.													
	2.													
	3.													

Source: Own illustration based on table 2 of the Annex to BMF, 11 July 2017, IV B 5—S 1300/16/10010:002, BStBl. I 2017, 974.

Table 13 List of All the Constituent Entities of the MNE Group Included in Each Aggregation per Tax Jurisdiction According to Section 138a(2) No. 2 GFC (CbC Report: Table 2/3—English Translation)

Name of the MNE group: Financial year concerned:														
Tax Jurisdiction	Enterprises and Permanent Establishments Resident in the Tax Jurisdiction of the MNE group	Most Important business Activity(ies)												
		Research and Development	Holding or Managing Intellectual Property	Purchasing or Procurement	Manufacturing or Production	Sales, Marketing or Distribution	Administrative, Management or Support Services	Provision of Services to Unrelated Parties	Internal Group Finance	Regulated Financial Services	Insurance	Holding Shares or Securities of a Participating nature	Dormant Activities	Other (Please indicate the type of business activity under 'Additional Information' in table 3)
	1.													
	2.													
	3.													
	1.													
	2.													
	3.													

Source: Own illustration and translation based on table 2 of the Annex to BMF, 11 July 2017, IV B 5—S 1300/16/10010:002, BStBl. I 2017, 974.

Table 14 Additional Information According to Section 138a(2) No. 3 GFC (CbC Report: Table 3/3)

Name des multinationalen Konzerns: Betrachtetes Wirtschaftsjahr:
Bitte geben Sie hier kurz alle weiteren Angaben oder Erläuterungen an, die Sie für notwendig erachten oder die das Verständnis der vorgeschriebenen Informationen im länderbezogenen Bericht erleichtern können.

Source: Own illustration based on table 3 of the Annex to BMF, 11 July 2017, IV B 5—S 1300/16/10010:002, BStBl. I 2017, 974.

Table 15 Additional Information According to Section 138a(2) No. 3 GFC (CbC Report: Table 3/3- English Translation)

Name of the MNE group: Financial year concerned:
Please include any further brief information or explanation you consider necessary or that would facilitate the understanding of the compulsory information provided in the Country-by-Country Report.

Source: Own illustration and translation based on table 3 of the Annex to BMF, 11 July 2017, IV B 5—S 1300/16/10010:002, BStBl. I 2017, 974.

Table of Cases

Judgments of the German Fiscal Court of Justice (BFH)

Court	Date	File No.	Reference
RFH	4 Mar. 1927	B I 27	RStBl. 1927, 112
RFH	19 Dec. 1934	VI A 230/34	RStBl. 1935, 490
RFH	20 Feb.1935	I A 218/34	RStBl. 1935, 572
BFH	6 Aug. 1958	II 251/57 U	BStBl. III 1958, 379
BFH	10 May 1961	IV 155/60 U	BStBl. III 1961, 317
BFH	18 Oct. 1962	IV 319/60 U	BStBl. III 1963, 38
BFH	27 July 1965	I 110/63 S	BStBl. III 1966, 24
BFH	5 Oct. 1965	I B 387/62 U	BStBl. III 1965, 668
BFH	17 Aug. 1966	IV R 172/66	BStBl. II 1966, 548
BFH	1 Feb. 1967	I 220/64	BStBl. III 1967, 497
BFH	16 Dec. 1970	I R 44/67	BStBl. II 1971, 235
BFH	8 Dec. 1971	I R 3/69	BStBl. II 1972, 289
BFH	28 June 1972	I R 35/70	BStBl. II 1972, 785
BFH	15 June 1973	III R 118/70	BStBl. II 1973, 810
BFH	30 Oct. 1973	I R 50/71	BStBl. II 1974, 107
BFH	28 Oct. 1977	III R 77/75	BStBl. II 1978, 116
BFH	19 Mar. 1981	IV R 49/77	BStBl. II 1981, 583
BFH	23 Jan. 1985	I R 292/81	BStBl. II 1985, 417
BFH	21 Aug. 1985	I R 63/80	BStBl. II 1986, 4
BFH	25 June 1986	II R 213/83	BStBl. II 1986, 785
BFH	28 Aug. 1986	V R 20/79	BStBl. II 1987, 162
BFH	1 Apr. 1987	II R 186/80	BStBl. II 1987, 550
BFH	27 Jan. 1988	I R 241/83	BStBl. II 1988, 574
BFH	10 Feb. 1988	VIII R 159/84	BStBl. II 1988, 653
BFH	8 Mar. 1988	VIII R 270/81	BFH/NV 1988, 735
BFH	20 July 1988	I R 49/84	BStBl. II 1989, 140
BFH	23 Nov. 1988	II R 209/82	BStBl. II 1989, 82
BFH	3 Feb. 1993	I R 80–81/91	BStBl. II 1993, 462
BFH	19 May 1993	I R 80/92	BStBl. II 1993, 655
BFH	28 July 1993	I R 15/93	BStBl. II 1994, 148
BFH	30 Oct. 1996	II R 12/92	BStBl. II 1997, 12
BFH	21 Apr. 1999	I R 99/97	BStBl. II 1999, 694

Court	Date	File No.	Reference
BFH	17 Nov. 1999	I R 7/99	BStBl. II 2000, 605
BFH	25 May 2000	III R 20/97	BStBl. II 2001, 365
BFH	23 Aug. 2000	I R 98/96	BStBl. II 2002, 207
BFH	13 Sept. 2000	X R 174/96	BStBl. II 2001, 734
BFH	17 Oct. 2001	I R 103/00	BStBl. II 2004, 171
BFH	23 May 2002	III R 8/00	BStBl. II 2002, 513
BFH	13 Nov. 2002	I R 90/01	BStBl. II 2003, 249
BFH	17 Sept. 2003	I R 12/02	BStBl. II 2004, 396
BFH	14 July 2004	I R 106/03	BFH/NV 2005, 154
BFH	4 June 2008	I R 30/07	BStBl. II 2008, 922
BFH	18 Mar. 2009	III R 2/06	BFH/NV 2009, 1457
BFH	16 Dec. 2009	I R 56/08	BStBl. II 2010, 492
BFH	9 Feb. 2011	I R 54/10	BStBl. II 2012, 106
BFH	25 May 2011	I R 95/10	BFHE 234, 63
BFH	10 Jan. 2012	I R 66/09	BFHE 236, 304
BFH	25 May 2016	I R 64/13	BStBl. II 2017, 1185

Federal Constitutional Court (BVerfG)

Judgment	Date	File No.	Reference
BVerfG	15 Dec. 2015	2 BvL 1/12	BVerfGE 141, 1
BVerfG	9 Apr. 2003	1 BvL 1/01	BVerfGE 108, 52

Federal Supreme Court (BGH)

Judgment	Date	File No.	Reference
BGH	24 Oct. 1988	3 StR 533/87	HFR 1990, 150

Regional Tax Office (OFD)

Order	Date	File No.	Reference
OFD	16 Sep. 2014	S 130.1/316-St 222	IStR 2015, 887

Table of Statutes

Circulars of the German Federal Ministry of Finance (BMF)

BMF: 18 Feb. 2021, State of the Double Taxation Agreements and Other Agreements in the Field of Taxation and Negotiations on Agreements as of 1 January 2019 [DE: Stand der Doppelbesteuerungsabkommen und anderer Abkommen im Steuerbereich sowie der Abkommensverhandlungen am 1. January 2021], IV B 2—S 1301/07/10017-12, BStBl. I 2021, 265 (cited as: BMF, 18 Feb. 2021, IV B 2—S 1301/07/10017- 12, BStBl. I 2021, 265).

BMF: 17 Dec. 2019, Permanent Establishments without People Functions (so-called Non-Functional Permanent Establishments [DE: Betriebsstätten ohne Personalfunktion (sog. funktionslose Betriebsstätten], IV B 5—S 1341/19/10010 :003 03, BStBl. I 2020, 84 (cited as: BMF, 17 Dec. 2019, IV B 5—S 1341/19/10010 :003 03, BStBl. I 2020, 84).

BMF: 3 Apr. 2019, Withholding Tax under Section 50a paragraph 1 number 1 ITA with Respect to Income Derived from the Surrender of Use of Rights and of Commercial, Technical, Scientific and Similar Experience, Knowledge and Skills [DE: Steuerabzug nach § 50a Absatz 1 Nummer 3 EStG bei Einkünften aus der Überlassung von Rechten und von gewerblichen, technischen, wissenschaftlichen und ähnlichen Erfahrungen, Kenntnissen und Fertigkeiten], IV C 5—S 2411/11/10002, BStBl. I 2019, 256 (cited as: BMF, 3 Apr. 2019, IV C 5—S 2411/11/10002, BStBl. I 2019, 256).

BMF: 27 Oct. 2017, Limited Tax Liability and Tax Deduction as Regards to Cross-Border Surrender of Use of Software and Databanks [DE: Beschränkte Steuerpflicht und Steuerabzug bei grenzüberschreitender Überlassung von Software und Datenbanken], IV C 5—S 2300/12/10003 :004, BStBl. I 2017, 1448 (cited as: BMF, 27 Oct. 2017, IV C 5—S 2300/12/10003 :004, BStBl. I 2017, 1448).

BMF: 11 July 2017, Requirements for Country-by-Country Reports by Multinational Enterprise Groups [DE: Anforderungen an den länderbezogenen Bericht multinationaler Unternehmensgruppen (Country-by-Country Report)], IV B 5—S 1300/16/10010 :002, BStBl. I 2017, 974 (cited as: BMF, 11 July 2017, IV B 5—S 1300/16/10010 :002, BStBl. I 2017, 974).

BMF: 22 Dec. 2016, Administrative Principles on the Application of the Arm's Length Principle to Permanent Establishments under Section 1(5) of the

External Tax Relations Act (Administrative Principles on the Allocation of Profits of Permanent Establishments) [DE: Grundsätze für die Anwendung des Fremdvergleichsgrundsatzes auf die Aufteilung der Einkünfte zwischen einem inländischen Unternehmen und seiner ausländischen Betriebsstätte und auf die Ermittlung der Einkünfte der inländischen Betriebsstätte eines ausländischen Unternehmens nach § 1 Absatz 5 des Außensteuergesetzes und der Betriebsstättengewinnaufteilungsverordnung (Verwaltungsgrundsätze Betriebsstättengewinnaufteilung—VWG BsGa], IV B 5—S 1341/12/10001-03, BStBl. I 2017, 182 (cited as: BMF, 22 Dec. 2016, IV B 5—S 1341/12/10001-03, BStBl. I 2017, 182).

BMF: 22 Aug. 2013, Basis for the Agreement between the Federal Republic of Germany and ...—for the Avoidance of Double Taxation and the Prevention of Fiscal Evasion with Respect to Taxes on Income and on Capital, IVB2—S 1301/13/10009, available at: <https://www.bundesfinanzministerium.de/Content/DE/Standardartikel/Themen/Steuern/Internationales_Steuerrecht/Allgemeine_Informationen/2013-08-22-Verhandlungsgrundlage-DBA-englisch.pdf> (cited as: BMF, 22 Aug. 2013, IV B 2—S 1301/13/10009).

BMF: 12 Apr. 2005, Principles for the Examination of Income Allocation between Related Parties with Cross-Border Business Relationships as regards Duties of Investigation and Coordination, Adjustments as well as Mutual Agreement Procedures and EU Arbitration Procedures (Administrative Principles) [DE: Grundsätze für die Prüfung der Einkunftsabgrenzung zwischen nahestehenden Personen mit grenzüberschreitenden Geschäftsbeziehungen in Bezug auf Ermittlungs- und Mitwirkungspflichten, Berichtigungen sowie auf Verständigungs- und EU-Schiedsverfahren (Verwaltungsgrundsätze Verfahren], IV B 4—S 1341—1/05, BStBl. I 2005, 570 (cited as: BMF, 12 Apr. 2005, IV B 4—S 1341—1/05, BStBl. I 2005, 570).

BMF: 9 Nov. 2001, Principles Governing the Examination of Income Allocation between Internationally Related Companies in Cases where Employees are Temporarily Transferred (Administrative Principles—Secondment of Employees) [DE: Grundsätze für die Prüfung der Einkunftsabgrenzung zwischen international verbundenen Unternehmen in Fällen der Arbeitnehmerentsendung (Verwaltungsgrundsätze-Arbeitnehmerentsendung)], IV B 4—S 1341—20/01, BStBl. I 2001, 796 (cited as: BMF, 9 Nov. 2001, IV B 4—S 1341—20/01, BStBl. I 2001, 796).

BMF: 24 Dec. 1999, Administrative Principles Governing the Examination of Income Allocation to Permanent Establishments of Internationally Operating Enterprices (Permanent Establishments—Administrative Principles) [DE: Grundsätze der Verwaltung für die Prüfung der Aufteilung der Einkünfte bei Betriebsstätten international tätiger Unternehmen (Betriebsstätten-Verwaltungsgrundsätze)], IV B 4—S 1300—111/99, BStBl. I 1999, 1076 (cited as: BMF, 24 Dec. 1999, IV B 4—S 1300—111/99, BStBl. I 1999, 1076).

BMF: 23 Feb. 1983, Principles for the Examination of Income Allocation in the Case of Internationally Associated Enterprises (Administrative Principles) [DE: Schreiben betreffend Grundsätze für die Prüfung der Einkunftsabgrenzung bei international verbundenen Unternehmen (Verwaltungsgrundsätze)], IV C 5—S 1341—4/83, BStBl. I 1983, 218 (cited as: BMF, 23 Feb. 1983, IV C 5—S 1341—4/83, BStBl. I 1983, 218).

Ordinances and Decrees

Brazilian Federal Revenue Service, Advance Tax Ruling request No. 191/2017.

Ordinance on the Type, Content and Scope of Records as Referred to in Section 90 Subsection (3) of the Fiscal Code (Ordinance on the Documentation of Profit Allocation) [DE: Verordnung zu Art, Inhalt und Umfang von Aufzeichnungen im Sinne des § 90 Abs. 3 der Abgabenordnung (Gewinnabgrenzungsaufzeichnungs-Verordnung—GAufzV)], 12 July 2017 (cited as: GAufzV, 12 July 2017, BGBl. I 2017, 2367).

Ordinance on the Application of the Arm's Length Principle to Permanent Establishments under Section 1(5) of the External Tax Relations Act (Ordinance on the Allocation of Profits of Permanent Establishments) [DE: Verordnung zur Anwendung des Fremdvergleichsgrundsatzes auf Betriebsstätten nach § 1 Absatz 5 des Außensteuergesetzes (Betriebsstättengewinnaufteilungsverordnung—BsGaV)], 13 Oct. 2014 (cited as: BsGaV, 13 Oct. 2014, BGBl. I 2014, 1603).

Ordinance on the Type, Content and Scope of Records as Referred to in Section 90 Subsection (3) of the Fiscal Code (Ordinance on the Documentation of Profit Allocation) [DE: Verordnung zu Art, Inhalt und Umfang von Aufzeichnungen im Sinne des § 90 Abs. 3 der Abgabenordnung (Gewinnabgrenzungsaufzeichnungsverordnung—GAufzV)], 27 Nov. 2003 (cited as: GAufzV, 13 Nov. 2003, BGBl. I 2003, 2296).

Thailand's Ministry of Treasury and Finance, Communiqué No. 17 Amending the General Corporate Income Tax Communiqué No. 1 of 15 Feb. 2019.

Thailand's Presidential Decree No. 476, Official Gazette of 19 Dec. 2018.

Acts

Act on the Multilateral Convention of 24 Nov. 2016 on the Implementation of Tax Treaty Related Measures to Prevent Base Erosion and Profit Shifting [DE: Gesetz zu dem Mehrseitigen Übereinkommen vom 24. November 2016 zur Umsetzung steuerabkommensbezogener Maßnahmen zur Verhinderung der Gewinnverkürzung und Gewinnverlagerung], 22 Nov. 2020, BGBl. II 2020, 946 (cited as: MLI Implementation Act, 22 Nov. 2020, BGBl. II 2020, 946).

Act on Further Tax Incentives for Electromobility and on the Amendment of other Tax Provisions [DE: Gesetz zur weiteren steuerlichen Förderung der Elektromobilität und zur Änderung weiterer steuerlicher Vorschriften], 12 Dec. 2019, BGBl. I 2019, 2451 (cited as: Act on the Amendment of Tax Provisions, 12 Dec. 2019, BGBl. I 2019, 1451).

Act Implementing the Amendments of the Mutual Administrative Cooperation Directive and of Further Measures against Base Erosion and Profit Shifting [DE: Gesetz zur Umsetzung der Änderungen der EU-Amtshilferichtlinie und von weiteren Maßnahmen gegen Gewinnkürzungen und -verlagerungen], 20 Dec. 2016, BGBl. I 2016, 3000 (cited as: Mutual Administrative Cooperation Directive Implementation Act, 20 Dec. 2016, BGBl. I 2016, 3000).

Act on the Implementation of the Mutual Assistance Directive and the Change in Tax Provisions (Mutual Assistance Directive Implementation Act) [DE: Gesetz zur Umsetzung der Amtshilferichtlinie sowie zur Änderung steuerlicher Vorschriften (Amtshilferichtlinie-Umsetzungsgesetz—AmtshilfeRLUmsG)], 26 June 2013, BGBl. I 2013, 1809 (cited as: Mutual Assistance Directive Implementation Act, 26 June 2013, BGBl. I 2013, 1809).

Act on the Reduction of Tax Benefits and Exceptions (Tax Benefit Reduction Act) [DE: Gesetz zum Abbau von Steuervergünstigungen und Ausnahmeregelungen (Steuervergünstigungsabbaugesetz—StVergAbG], 20 Mai 2003, BGBl. I, 660 (cited as: Act on the Reduction of Tax Benefits and Exceptions, 20 Mai 2003, BGBl. I 2003, 660).

Act Amending the Imperial Act to Eliminate Double Taxation [DE: Gesetz zur Abänderung des Reichsgesetzes wegen Beseitigung der Doppelbesteuerung,

22 Mar. 1909, RGBl. I, 332 (cited as: German Double Taxation Act, 22 Mar. 1909, RGBl. 1909, 332).

Legislative Materials

Draft Legislation on the Modernisation of the Withholding Tax Relief and the Certification of the Withholding Tax (Withholding Tax Relief Modernisation Act) [DE: Entwurf eines Gesetzes zur Modernisierung der Entlastung von Abzugsteuern und der Bescheinigung der Kapitalertagsteuer (Abzugsteuer-entlastungsmodernisierungsgesetz—AbzStEntModG), 22 Jan. 2021, BR-Drs. 50/21 (cited as: BR-Drs. 50/21).

Draft Legislation on the Multilateral Convention of 24 Nov. 2016 on the Implementation of Tax Treaty Related Measures to Prevent Base Erosion and Profit Shifting [DE: Entwurf eines Gesetzes zu dem Mehrseitigen Übereinkommen vom 24. November 2016 zur Umsetzung steuerabkommensbezogener Maßnahmen zur Verhinderung der Gewinnverkürzung und Gewinnverlagerung], 27 May 2020, BT-Drs. 19/20979 (cited as: BT-Drs. 19/20979).

Draft Legislation of the Federal Government—Draft of an Act Governing the Implementation of the Amendments of the EU Mutual Assistance Directive and further Measures against Base Erosion and Profit Shifting [DE: Gesetzesentwurf der Bundesregierung—Entwurf eines Gesetzes zur Umsetzung der Änderungen der EU-Amtshilferichtlinie und von weiteren Maßnahmen gegen Gewinnverkürzungen und -verlagerungen], 5 Sep. 2016, BT-Drs. 18/9536 (cited as: BT-Drs. 18/9536).

Explanatory Statement to Ordinance on the Application of the Arm's Length Principle to Permanent Establishments under Section 1(5) of the External Tax Relations Act (Ordinance on the Allocation of Profits of Permanent Establishments) [DE: Erläuterungen zur Verordnung zur Anwendung des Fremdvergleichsgrundsatzes auf Betriebsstätten nach § 1 Absatz 5 des Außensteuergesetzes (Betriebsstättengewinnaufteilungsverordnung—BsGaV)], 28 Aug. 2014, BR-Drs. 401/14 (cited as: BR-Drs. 401/14, 63).

Draft Legislation of the Ordinance on the Application of the Arm's Length Principle to Permanent Establishments under Section 1(5) of the External Tax Relations Act (Ordinance on the Allocation of Profits of Permanent Establishments—Draft) [DE: Entwurf einer Verordnung zur Anwendung des Fremdvergleichsgrundsatzes auf Betriebsstätten nach § 1 Absatz 5 des Außensteuergesetzes (Betriebsstättengewinnaufteilungsverordnung—BsGaV-Entwurf)], 5 Aug. 2013 (cited as: BMF, 5 Aug. 2013, BsGaV-Draft).

Draft Legislation of the Federal Government—Draft of an Annual Tax Act [DE: Gesetzesentwurf der Bundesregierung—Entwurf eines Jahressteuergesetzes 2013], 19 June 2012, BT-Drs. 17/10000 (cited as: BT-Drs. 17/10000).

Industrial Code of Prussia [DE: Allgemeine Gewerbe-Ordnung], 17 Jan. 1845, Prussian statute book 41 (1845) (cited as: Industrial Code of Prussia, 17 Jan. 1845, Sec. 26, see Prussian statute book 41 (1845)),

Other Documentations and Internet Resources

OECD Documents:

OECD: Signatories and Parties to the Multilateral Convention to implement tax treaty related measures to prevent base erosion and profit shifting, Paris 2021, available at: <http://www.oecd.org/tax/treaties/beps-mli-signatories-and-parties.pdf> (cited as: OECD, BEPS Signatories and Parties to the Multilateral Convention).

OECD: Reports on the Pillar One and Pillar Two Blueprints—Public Consultation Document, OECD/G20 Base Erosion and Profit Shifting Project, Paris 2020, available at: <http://www.oecd.org/tax/beps/public-consultation-document-reports-on-pillar-one-and-pillar-two-blueprints-october-2020.pdf> (cited as: OECD, BEPS Action 1: Public Consultation Document 2020).

OECD: OECD/G20 Inclusive Framework on BEPS: Tax Challenges Arising from Digitalisation—Report on the Pillar One Blueprint, available at: <http://www.oecd.org/tax/beps/tax-challenges-arising-from-digitalisation-report-on-pillar-one-blueprint.pdf> (cited as: OECD, BEPS Action 1: Report on the Pillar One Blueprint 2020).

OECD: OECD/G20 Inclusive Framework on BEPS: Tax Challenges Arising from Digitalisation—Report on the Pillar Two Blueprint, available at: <http://www.oecd.org/tax/beps/tax-challenges-arising-from-digitalisation-report-on-pillar-two-blueprint.pdf> (cited as: OECD, BEPS Action 1: Report on the Pillar Two Blueprint 2020).

OECD: OECD/G20 Inclusive Framework on BEPS: Cover Statement by the Inclusive Framework on the Reports on the Blueprints of Pillar One and Pillar Two, available at: <http://www.oecd.org/tax/beps/cover-statement-by-the-oecd-g20-inclusive-framework-on-beps-on-the-reports-on-the-blueprints-of-pillar-one-and-pillar-two-october-2020.pdf>

(cited as: OECD, BEPS Action 1: Cover Statement on the Blueprints 2020).

OECD: OECD/G20 Inclusive Framework on BEPS: Tax Challenges Arising from Digitalisation—Economic Impact Assessment, available at: <https://doi.org/10.1787/0e3cc2d4-en> (cited as: OECD, BEPS Action 1: Economic Impact Assessment 2020).

OECD: Country-by-Country Reporting—Compilation of Peer Review Reports (Phase 3), BEPS Action 13, Paris 2020, available at: <https://doi.org/10.1787/fa6d31d7-en> (cited as: OECD, BEPS Action 13: CbC Reporting—Compilation of Peer Review Reports (Phase 3)).

OECD: OECD/G20 Inclusive Framework on BEPS: Progress Report July 2019-July 2020, Paris 2020, available at: <https://www.oecd.org/tax/beps/oecd-g20-inclusive-framework-on-beps-progress-report-july-2019-july-2020.pdf> (cited as: OECD, BEPS Progress Report 2020).

OECD: Update on Economic Analysis and Impact Assessment, Paris 2020, available at: <https://www.oecd.org/tax/beps/webcast-economic-analysis-impact-assessment-february-2020.htm> (cited as: OECD, Update on Economic Analysis and Impact Assessment 2020).

OECD: Statement by the OECD/G20 Inclusive Framework on BEPS on the Two-Pillar Approach to Address the Tax Challenges Arising from the Digitalisation of the Economy, Paris 2020, available at: <https://www.oecd.org/tax/beps/statement-by-the-oecd-g20-inclusive-framework-on-beps-january-2020.pdf> (cited as: OECD, BEPS Action 1: Statement on the Two-Pillar Approach 2020).

OECD: Guidance on the Implementation of Country-by-Country Reporting—BEPS Action 13, Paris 2019, available at: <http://www.oecd.org/tax/guidance-on-the-implementation-of-country-by-country-reporting-beps-action-13.pdf> (cited as: BEPS Action 13: Guidance on the Implementation of CbC Reporting).

OECD: Secretariat Proposal for a "Unified Approach" under Pillar One—Public consultation document, BEPS Action 1, Paris 2019, available at: <http://www.oecd.org/tax/beps/public-consultation-document-secretariat-proposal-unified-approach-pillar-one.pdf> (cited as: OECD, BEPS Action 1: Secretariat Proposal for a Unified Approach 2019).

OECD: Country-by-Country Reporting—Compilation of Peer Review Reports (Phase 2), BEPS Action 13, Paris 2019, available at: <https://doi.org/10.1787/f9bf1157-en> (cited as: OECD, BEPS Action 13: CbC Reporting—Compilation of Peer Review Reports (Phase 2)).

OECD: OECD/G20 Inclusive Framework on BEPS: Progress Report July 2018-May 2019, Paris 2019, available at: <http://www.oecd.org/tax/beps/inclusive-framework-on-beps-progress-report-july-2018-may-2019.pdf> (cited as: OECD, BEPS Progress Report 2019).

OECD: Programme of Work to Develop a Consensus Solution to the Tax Challenges Arising from the Digitalisation of the Economy, Paris 2019, available at: <https://www.oecd.org/tax/beps/programme-of-work-to-develop-a-consensus-solution-to-the-tax-challenges-arising-from-the-digitalisation-of-the-economy.pdf> (cited as: OECD, BEPS Action 1: Programme of Work 2019).

OECD: Addressing the Tax Challenges of the Digitalisation of the Economy—Public Consultation Document, OECD/G20 Base Erosion and Profit Shifting Project, Paris 2019, available at: <http://www.oecd.org/tax/beps/public-consultation-document-addressing-the-tax-challenges-of-the-digitalisation-of-the-economy.pdf> (cited as: OECD, BEPS Action 1: Public Consultation Document 2019).

OECD: Addressing the Tax Challenges of the Digitalisation of the Economy—Policy Note, OECD/G20 Base Erosion and Profit Shifting Project, Paris 2019, available at: <https://www.oecd.org/tax/beps/policy-note-beps-inclusive-framework-addressing-tax-challenges-digitalisation.pdf> (cited as: OECD, BEPS Action 1: Policy Note 2019).

OECD: Tax Challenges Arising from Digitalisation—Interim Report 2018: Inclusive Framework on BEPS, OECD/G20 Base Erosion and Profit Shifting Project, Paris 2018, available at: <http://www.oecd.org/tax/beps/tax-challenges-arising-from-digitalisation-interim-report-9789264293083-en.htm> (cited as: OECD, BEPS Action 1: Interim Report 2018).

OECD: Country-by-Country Reporting—Compilation of Peer Review Reports (Phase 1): Inclusive Framework on BEPS: Action 13, Paris 2018, available at: <https://doi.org/10.1787/9789264300057-en> (cited as: OECD, BEPS Action 13: CbC Reporting—Compilation of Peer Review Reports (Phase 1)).

OECD: Revised Guidance on the Application of the Transactional Profit Split Method: Inclusive Framework on BEPS: Action 10, OECD, Paris 2018, available at: <http://www.oecd.org/tax/beps/revised-guidance-on-the-application-of-the-transactional-profit-split-method-beps-action-10.pdf> (cited as: OECD, BEPS Action 10: Revised Guidance on TPSM 2018).

OECD: Milestone in BEPS implementation: Multilateral BEPS Convention will enter into force on 1 July following Slovenia's ratification, Press Release of 22 Mar. 2018, available at: <http://www.oecd.org/ctp/milestone-in-beps-implementation-multilateral-beps-convention-will-enter-into-force-on-1-july-following-slovenia-s-ratification.htm> (cited as: OECD, Milestone in BEPS implementation, Press Release of 22 Mar. 2018).

OECD: Additional Guidance on the Attribution of Profits to Permanent Establishments, BEPS Action 7, Paris 2018, available at: <http://www.oecd.org/tax/beps/additional-guidance-attribution-of-profits-to-a-permanent-establishment-under-beps-action7.htm> (cited as: OECD, BEPS Action 7: Additional Guidance 2018).

OECD: BEPS Action 13 on Country-by-Country Reporting—Guidance on the appropriate use of information contained in Country-by-Country reports, OECD/G20 Base Erosion and Profit Shifting Project, OECD, Paris 2017, available at: <http://www.oecd.org/tax/beps/beps-action-13-on-country-by-country-reporting-appropriate-use-of-information-in-CbC-reports.pdf> (cited as: OECD, BEPS Action 13: Guidance on the appropriate use of information contained in Country-by-Country Reports).

OECD: Country-by-Country Reporting XML Schema—User Guide for Tax Administrations, OECD, Paris 2017, available at: <http://www.oecd.org/tax/beps/country-by-country-reporting-xml-schema-user-guide-for-tax-administrations.pdf> (cited as: OECD, Country-by-Country Reporting XML Schema: User Guide for Tax Administrations).

OECD: Model Tax Convention on Income and on Capital: Condensed Version 2017, Paris 2017, available at: <https://doi.org/10.1787/mtc_cond-2017-en> (cited as: OECD MC Commentary 2017).

OECD: BEPS Action 10: Public Discussion Draft on the Revised Guidance on Profit Splits, 22 June—15 September 2017, available at: <https://www.oecd.org/ctp/transfer-pricing/Revised-guidance-on-profit-splits-2017.pdf> (cited as: OECD, BEPS Action 10: Revised Guidance on Profit Splits 2017).

OECD: Frequently Asked Questions on the Multilateral Instrument (MLI), Paris 2017, available at: <http://www.oecd.org/tax/treaties/MLI-frequently-asked-questions.pdf> (cited as: OECD, Frequently Asked Questions on the Multilateral Instrument (MLI)).

OECD: Federal Republic of Germany, Status of List of Reservation and Notification at the Time of Signature, Paris 2017, available at: <http://www.

oecd.org/tax/treaties/beps-mli-position-germany.pdf> (cited as: OECD, MLI Positions Germany).

OECD: OECD Transfer Pricing Guidelines for Multinational Enterprises and Tax Administrations 2017, Paris 2017, available at: <https://doi.org/10.1787/tpg-2017-en> (cited as: OECD, TP Guidelines 2017).

OECD: Inclusive Framework on BEPS: Progress Report July 2016-June 2017, Paris 2017, available at: <www.oecd.org/tax/beps/inclusive-framework-on-BEPS-progress-report-july-2016-june-2017.pdf> (cited as: OECD, Inclusive Framework on BEPS, Progress Report 2017).

OECD: Explanatory Statement to the Multilateral Convention to Implement Tax Treaty Related Measures to Prevent Base Erosion and Profit Shifting, Paris 2016, available at: <https://www.oecd.org/tax/treaties/explanatory-statement-multilateral-convention-to-implement-tax-treaty-related-measures-to-prevent-BEPS.pdf> (cited as: OECD, Explanatory Statement to the Multilateral Convention).

OECD: Public Discussion Draft on the Revised Guidance on Profit Splits, 4 July—5 September 2016, BEPS Actions 8–10, Paris 2016, available at: <http://www.oecd.org/tax/transfer-pricing/BEPS-discussion-draft-on-the-revised-guidance-on-profit-splits.pdf> (cited as: OECD, BEPS Actions 8–10: Revised Guidance on Profit Splits 2016).

OECD: Additional Guidance on the Attribution of Profits to Permanent Establishments (Part II), BEPS Action 7, Paris 2016, available at: <http://www.oecd.org/ctp/transfer-pricing/Comments-on-discussion-draft-beps-action-7-attribution-of-profits-to-permanent-establishments-part2.pdf> (cited as: OECD, BEPS Action 7: Comments on Discussion Draft (Part II)).

OECD: Explanatory Statement, OECD/G20 Base Erosion and Profit Shifting Project, Paris 2015, available at: <http://www.oecd.org/tax/beps-explanatory-statement-2015.pdf> (cited as: OECD, BEPS Project—Explanatory Statement).

OECD: BEPS Webcast #8—Launch of the 2015 Final Reports, Paris 2015, available at: <https://www.slideshare.net/OECDtax/beps-webcast-8-launch-of-the-2015-final-reports> (cited as: OECD, Launch of the 2015 Final Reports).

OECD: Addressing the Tax Challenges of the Digital Economy, BEPS Action 1—Final Report, Paris 2015, available at: <http://dx.doi.org/10.1787/9789264241046-en> (cited as: OECD, BEPS Action 1: Final Report 2015).

OECD: Designing Effective Controlled Foreign Company Rules, BEPS Action 3—Final Report, Paris 2015, available at: <http://dx.doi.org/10.1787/9789264241152-en> (cited as: OECD, BEPS Action 3: Final Report 2015).

OECD: Limiting Base Erosion Involving Interest Deductions and Other Financial Payments, BEPS Action 4—Final Report, Paris 2015, available at: <http://dx.doi.org/10.1787/9789264241176-en> (cited as: OECD, BEPS Action 4: Final Report 2015).

OECD: Countering Harmful Tax Practices More Effectively, Taking into Account Transparency and Substance, BEPS Action 5—Final Report, Paris 2015, available at: <http://dx.doi.org/10.1787/9789264241190-en> (cited as: OECD, BEPS Action 5: Final Report 2015).

OECD: Preventing the Granting of Treaty Benefits in Inappropriate Circumstances, BEPS Action 6—Final Report, Paris 2015, available at: <http://dx.doi.org/10.1787/9789264241695-en> (cited as: OECD, BEPS Action 6: Final Report 2015).

OECD: Preventing the Artificial Avoidance of Permanent Establishment Status, BEPS Action 7—Final Report, Paris 2015, available at: <http://dx.doi.org/10.1787/9789264241220-en> (cited as: OECD, BEPS Action 7: Final Report 2015).

OECD: Aligning Transfer Pricing Outcomes with Value Creation, BEPS Actions 8–10—Final Report, Paris 2015, available at: <http://dx.doi.org/10.1787/9789264241244-en> (cited as: OECD, BEPS Actions 8–10: Final Report 2015).

OECD: Transfer Pricing Documentation and Country-by-Country Reporting, Action 13—Final Report, Paris 2015, available at: <http://dx.doi.org/10.1787/9789264241480-en> (cited as: OECD, BEPS Action 13: Final Report 2015).

OECD: Developing a Multilateral Instrument to Modify Bilateral Tax Treaties, BEPS Action 15—Final Report, Paris 2015, available at: <http://dx.doi.org/10.1787/9789264241688-en> (cited as: OECD, BEPS Action 15: Final Report 2015).

OECD: Discussion Draft on the Use of Profit Splits in the Context of Global Value Chains, BEPS Action 10, Paris 2014, available at: <https://www.oecd.org/tax/transfer-pricing/discussion-draft-action-10-profit-splits-global-value-chains.pdf> (cited as: OECD, BEPS Action 10: Discussion Draft on the Use of Profit Split in the Context of Global Value Chains 2014).

OECD: Action Plan on Base Erosion and Profit Shifting, Paris 2013, available at: <http://dx.doi.org/10.1787/9789264202719-en> (cited as: OECD, Action Plan on Base Erosion and Profit Shifting 2013).

OECD: White Paper on Transfer Pricing Documentation, Paris 2013, available at: <http://www.oecd.org/ctp/transfer-pricing/white-paper-transfer-pricing-documentation.pdf> (cited as: OECD, White Paper on Transfer Pricing Documentation, 30 July 2013).

OECD: Keeping It Safe—The OECD Guide on the Protection of Confidentiality of Information Exchanged for Tax Purposes, Paris 2012, available at: <http://www.oecd.org/ctp/exchange-of-tax-information/keeping-it-safe-report.pdf> (cited as: OECD, Keeping It Safe—The OECD Guide on the Protection of Confidentiality of Information Exchanged for Tax Purposes).

OECD: Report on the Attribution of Profits to Permanent Establishments, Paris 2010, available at: <https://www.oecd.org/ctp/transfer-pricing/45689524.pdf> (cited as: OECD, PE Report 2010).

OECD: Articles on the OECD Model Tax Convention on Income and on Capital, Paris 2010, available at: <http://www.oecd.org/tax/treaties/47213736.pdf> (cited as: OECD, Model Tax Convention on Income and on Capital 2010).

OECD: Transfer Pricing Guidelines for Multinational Enterprises and Tax Administrations, Paris 2010, available at: <https://doi.org/10.1787/tpg-2010-en> (cited as: OECD, TP Guidelines 2010).

OECD: Report on the Attribution of Profits to Permanent Establishments, Paris 2008, available at: <http://www.oecd.org/ctp/transferpricing/41031455.pdf> (cited as: OECD, PE Report 2008).

OECD: Articles of the Model Tax Convention with Respect to Taxes on Income and on Capital, Paris 2008, available at: <http://www.oecd.org/tax/treaties/42219418.pdf> (cited as: OECD MC Commentary 2008).

OECD: E-Commerce: Transfer Pricing and Business Profits Taxation, OECD Tax Policy Studies, OECD Publishing, Paris 2005, available at: <https://doi.org/10.1787/9789264007222-en> (cited as: OECD, E-Commerce: Transfer Pricing and Business Profits Taxation).

OECD: Taxation and Electronic Commerce: Implementing the Ottawa Taxation Framework Conditions, Paris 2001, available at: <https://www.oecd.org/tax/consumption/Taxation%20and%20eCommerce%202001.pdf> (cited as: OECD, Taxation and Electronic Commerce 2001).

OECD: Clarification on the Application of the Permanent Establishment Definition in E-Commerce: Changes to the Commentary on the Model

Tax Convention on Article 5 of 22 Dec. 2000, Paris 2000 available at: <http://www.oecd.org/tax/treaties/1923380.pdf> (cited as: OECD Committee on Fiscal Affairs, Clarifications on the Application of the Permanent Establishment Definition in E-Commerce, 2000).

OECD: Electronic Commerce: Taxation Framework Conditions—A Report by the Committee on Fiscal Affairs, as presented to Ministers at the OECD Ministerial Conference, "A Borderless World: Realising the Potential of Electronic Commerce" on 8 Oct. 1998, Paris 1998, available at: <https://www.oecd.org/tax/consumption/1923256.pdf> (cited as: OECD, Electronic Commerce: Taxation Framework Conditions 1998).

OECD: Transfer Pricing Guidelines for Multinational Enterprises and Tax Administrations, Paris 1995 (cited as: OECD, TP Guidelines 1995).

OECD/Council of Europe: The Multilateral Convention on Mutual Administrative Assistance in Tax Matters: Amended by the 2010 Protocol, OECD Publishing, Paris 2011, available at: <http://dx.doi.org/10.1787/9789264115606-en> (cited as: OECD/Council of Europe, The Multilateral Convention on Mutual Administrative Assistance in Tax Matters).

IMF/OECD: The Tax Certainty—Report for the G20 Finance Ministers, Mar. 2017, available at: <https://www.oecd.org/tax/tax-policy/tax-certainty-report-oecd-imf-report-g20-finance-ministers-march-2017.pdf> (cited as: IMF/OECD, Report on tax certainty 2017).

European Commission Documents:

European Commission: Proposal for a Council Directive laying down rules relating to the corporate taxation of a significant digital presence, 21 Mar. 2018, COM(2018) 147 final, 2018/0072 (CNS), available at: <https://ec.europa.eu/taxation_customs/sites/default/files/e_proposal_significant_digital_presence_21032018_en.pdf> (cited as: EC, 21 Mar. 2018, COM(2018) 147 final).

European Commission: Proposal for a Council Directive on the common system of a digital services tax on revenue resulting from the provision of certain digital services, 21 Mar. 2018, Com(2018) 148 final, 2018/0073 (CNS), available at: <https://ec.europa.eu/taxation_customs/sites/default/files/proposal_common_system_digital_services_tax_21032018_en.pdf> (cited as: EC, 21 Mar. 2018, COM(2018) 148 final).

European Commission: Communication from the Commission to the European Parliament and the Council—A Fair and Efficient Tax System in the European Union for the Digital Single Market, 21 Sep. 2017, COM(2017)

547 final, available at: <https://ec.europa.eu/taxation_customs/sites/taxation/files/communication_taxation_digital_single_market_en.pdf> (cited as: EC, 21 Sep. 2017, COM(2017) 547 final).

European Commission: Proposal for a Council Directive on a Common Corporate Tax Base, 25 Oct. 2016, COM(2016) 685 final, 2016/0337 (CNS), available at: <https://ec.europa.eu/taxation_customs/sites/taxation/files/com_2016_685_en.pdf> (cited as: EC, 25 Oct. 2016, COM(2016) 685 final).

European Commission: Proposal for a Council Directive on a Common Consolidated Corporate Tax Base (CCCTB), 25 Oct. 2016, COM(2016) 683 final, 2016/0336 (CNS), available at: <https://ec.europa.eu/taxation_customs/sites/taxation/files/com_2016_683_en.pdf> (cited as: EC, 25 Oct. 2016, COM(2016) 683 final).

European Commission: Commission Expert Group on Taxation of the Digital Economy—Report, 28 May 2014, available at: <https://ec.europa.eu/taxation_customs/sites/taxation/files/resources/documents/taxation/gen_info/good_governance_matters/digital/report_digital_economy.pdf> (cited as: EC, 28 May 2014, Commission Expert Group on Taxation of the Digital Economy—Report).

European Commission: Communication from the Commission to the Council, the European Parliament and the Economic and Social Committee: Towards an Internal Market without tax obstacles—A strategy for providing companies with a consolidated corporate tax base for their EU-wide activities, 23 Oct. 2001, COM (2001), 582 final, available at: <https://eur-lex.europa.eu/LexUriServ/LexUriServ.do?uri=COM:2001:0582:FIN:EN:PDF> (cited as: EC, 23 Oct. 2001, COM(2001) 582 final).

European Council Documents:

European Council: Outcome of the Council Meeting, 12. Mar. 2019, 3678th Council meeting, Economic and Financial Affairs, available at: <https://www.consilium.europa.eu/media/38463/st07368-en19.pdf> (cited as: Council of the European Union, 12 Mar. 2019, Outcome of the Council Meeting).

European Council: Directive 2016/1164 of 12 July 2016 laying down rules against tax avoidance practices that directly affect the functioning of the internal market, available at: <https://eur-lex.europa.eu/legal-content/EN/TXT/PDF/?uri=CELEX:32016L1164&from=DE> (cited as: European Council, 12 July 2016, Directive 2016/1164).

European Council: Directive 2016/881 of 25 May 2016 amending Directive 2011/16/EU as regards mandatory automatic exchange of information in the field of taxation, available at: <https://eur-lex.europa.eu/legal-content/EN/

TXT/PDF/?uri=CELEX:32016L0881&from=DE> (cited as: European Council, 25 May 2016, Directive 2016/881).

European Council: Directive 2011/16/EU of 15 February 2011 on administrative cooperation in the field of taxation and repealing Directive 77/799/EEC, available at: <https://eur-lex.europa.eu/legal-content/EN/TXT/PDF/?uri=CELEX:32011L0016&from=de> (cited as: European Council, 15 Feb. 2011, Directive 2011/16/EU).

United Nations Documents:

United Nations: Practical Manual on Transfer Pricing for Developing Countries, New York 2017, available at: <https://www.un.org/esa/ffd/wp-content/uploads/2017/04/Manual-TP-2017.pdf> (cited as: UN, Practical Manual on Transfer Pricing for Developing Countries 2017).

United Nations: Model Double Taxation Convention on between Developed and Developing Countries, New York 2017, available at: <https://www.un.org/esa/ffd/wp-content/uploads/2018/05/MDT_2017.pdf> (cited as: UN, Model Double Taxation Convention 2017).

United Nations: Vienna Convention on the Law of Treaties, concluded at Vienna on 23 May 1969, Treaty Series 1155 (1969), 331, available at: <https://treaties.un.org/doc/publication/unts/volume%201155/volume-1155-i-18232-english.pdf> (cited as: UN, Vienna Convention on the Law of Treaties, Treaty Series 1155 (1969), 331).

League of Nations:

League of Nations: Double Taxation and Tax Evasion—Report Presented by the Committee of Technical Experts on Double Taxation and Tax Evasion, Document No. C.216.M.85.1927.II, Geneva 12. Apr. 1927, available at: <https://biblio-archive.unog.ch/Dateien/CouncilMSD/C-216-M-85-1927-II_EN.pdf> (cited as: League of Nations, 12 Apr. 1927, Double Taxation and Tax Evasion—Report).

League of Nations: Double Taxation and Fiscal Evasion, Collection of International Agreements and Internal Legal Provisions for the Prevention of Double Taxation and Fiscal Evasion, Vol. 1, Document No. C.345.M.102.1928.II, Geneva 1928 (cited as: League of Nations, Double Taxation and Fiscal Evasion, Collection of International Agreements 1928, Vol. 1, 249).

League of Nations: Fiscal Committee, London and Mexican Model Tax Conventions—Commentary and Text, Model Bilateral Convention for the Prevention of the Double Taxation of Income and Property (Mexico Draft),

Document No. C.88.M88.1946.II.A., Geneva 1946, Annex, pp. 58–85, available at: <https://biblio-archive.unog.ch/Dateien/CouncilMSD/C-88-M-88-1946-II-A_EN.pdf> (cited as: League of Nations, Mexico Draft 1943).

League of Nations: Fiscal Committee, London and Mexican Model Tax Conventions—Commentary and Text, Model Bilateral Convention for the Prevention of the Double Taxation of Income and Property (London Draft), Document No. C.88.M88.1946.II.A., Geneva 1946, Annex, pp. 59–85, available at: <https://biblio-archive.unog.ch/Dateien/CouncilMSD/C-88-M-88-1946-II-A_EN.pdf> (cited as: League of Nations, London Draft 1946).

Other Internet Documents:

Accountancy Europe: Public consultation OECD Secretariat Proposal for a "Unified Approach" under Pillar One, available at: <https://www.oecd.org/tax/beps/public-comments-received-on-the-secretariat-proposal-for-a-unified-approach-under-pillar-one.htm> (cited as: Accountancy Europe, Comments on Secretariat Proposal).

AICPA: Tax Policy Concept Statement 1: Guiding principles of good tax policy: A framework for evaluating tax proposals, available at: <https://www.aicpa.org/advocacy/tax/downloadabledocuments/tax-policy-concept-statement-no-1-global.pdf> (cited as: AICPA, Guiding principles of good tax policy).

Báez, Andrés/*Brauner*, Yariv: Taxing the Digital Economy Post BEPS … Seriously, University of Florida Levin College of Law Research Paper No. 19–16. Available at: <https://dx.doi.org/10.2139/ssrn.3347503> (cited as: *Báez/Brauner*, Taxing the Digital Economy Post BEPS … Seriously, University of Florida Levin College of Law Research Paper No. 19–16).

***Brauner*, Yariv/Báez, Andrés**: Withholding Taxes in the Service of BEPS Action 1: Address the Tax Challenges of the Digital Economy, IBFD Working Paper 2015, available at: <https://www.ibfd.org/sites/ibfd.org/files/content/WithholdingTaxesintheServiceofBEPSAction1-whitepaper.pdf> (cited as: *Brauner/Báez*, Withholding Taxes in the Service of BEPS Action 1, IBFD Working Paper 2015).

Business at OECD Tax Committee: OECD Secretariat Proposal for a "Unified Approach" under Pillar One, available at: <https://www.oecd.org/tax/beps/public-comments-received-on-the-secretariat-proposal-for-a-unified-approach-under-pillar-one.htm> (cited as: Business at OECD, Comments on Secretariat Proposal).

***Collier*, Richard/*Kari*, Seppo/*Ropponen*, Olli/*Simmler*, Martin/*Todtenhaupt*, Maximilian**: Dissecting the EU's Recent Anti-Tax Avoidance Measures: Merits and Problems, EconPol Policy Report, Munich 2018, available at: <https://

www.ifo.de/DocDL/EconPol_Policy_Report_08_2018.pdf> (cited as: *Collier/Kari/Ropponen/Simmler/Todtenhaupt*, Dissecting the EU's Recent Anti-Tax Avoidance Measures, EconPol Policy Report, Sept. 2018).

***Collin*, Pierre/*Colin*, Nicolas**: Task Force on Taxation of the Digital Economy: Report to the Ministry for the Economy and Finance, the Minister for Industrial Recovery, the Minister Delegate for the Budget and the Minister Delegate for Small and Medium-Sized Enterprises, Innovation and the Digital Economy, available at: <https://www.hldataprotection.com/files/2013/06/Taxation_Digital_Economy.pdf> (cited as: *Collin/Colin*, Task Force on Taxation of the Digital Economy).

Copenhagen Economics: The Unified Approach under Pillar One: Copenhagen Economics' response to the OECD consultation, available at: <https://www.oecd.org/tax/beps/public-comments-received-on-the-secretariat-proposal-for-a-unified-approach-under-pillar-one.htm> (cited as: Copenhagen Economics, Comments on Secretariat Proposal).

***Desai*, Mihir Arvind/*Hines*, James R. Jr.**: Economic Foundations of International Tax Rules, Washington 2003, available at: <https://citeseerx.ist.psu.edu/viewdoc/download?doi=10.1.1.169.1549&rep=rep1&type=pdf> (cited as: *Desai/Hines*, Economic Foundations of International Tax Rules).

***Devereux*, Michael P./*Auerbach*, Alan J./*Keen*, Michael/*Oosterhuis*, Paul/*Schön*, Wolfgang/*Vella*, John**: Residual profit allocation by income, A paper of the Oxford International Tax Group chaired by Michael P. Devereux, Working Paper 19/01, Mar. 2019, available at: <https://papers.ssrn.com/sol3/papers.cfm?abstract_id=3358291> (cited as: *Devereux/Auerbach/Keen/Oosterhuis/Schön/Vella*, Residual profit allocation by income, Working Paper 2019.).

Devereux: The OECD Pillar One Proposal, University of Oxford Saïd Business School Blog, 22 Oct. 2019, available at: <https://www.sbs.ox.ac.uk/oxford-answers/organisation-economic-co-operation-and-development-oecd-pillar-one-proposal> (cited as: *Devereux*, The OECD Pillar One Proposal, University of Oxford Saïd Business School Blog).

***Englisch*, Joachim**: OECD Public Consultation Document—Reports on the Pillar One and Pillar Two Blueprints, available at: <http://www.oecd.org/tax/beps/public-comments-received-on-the-reports-on-pillar-one-and-pillar-two-blueprints.htm> (cited as: *Englisch*, Comments on Pillar One Blueprint).

***Englisch*, Joachim**: OECD Public Consultation Document—Secretariat Proposal for a "Unified Approach" under Pillar One, available at: <https://www.oecd.org/tax/beps/public-comments-received-on-the-secretariat-proposal-for-a-unified-approach-under-pillar-one.htm> (cited as: *Englisch*, Comments on Secretariat Proposal).

European Union: Code of Conduct for Transfer Pricing Documentation for associated enterprises in the European Union (EU TPD), 2006/C 176/01, 28 July 2006, available at: <https://eur-lex.europa.eu/legal-content/EN/TXT/PDF/?uri=CELEX:42006X0728(01)&from=DE> (cited as: EU, Code of Conduct for Transfer Pricing Documentation, 2006/C 176/01, 28 July 2006, 1).

EY: Tax Insights, October 2015 available at: <https://assets.ey.com/content/dam/ey-sites/ey-com/en_in/topics/tax/india-tax-insights/ey-india-tax-insights-issue-6.pdf> (cited as: EY, Tax Insights, October 2015).

G20: G20 Leaders Declaration, Los Cabos, 18–19 June 2012, available at: <https://www.bundesregierung.de/resource/blob/975254/474794/4c6e936e58b252260ef6ffe9c2434396/g20-loscabos-leaders-declaration-data.pdf?download=1>(cited as: G20, Leaders Declaration, Los Cabos, 18–19 June 2012).

G-24 Working Group on tax policy and international tax cooperation: Proposal for Addressing Tax Challenges Arising from Digitalisation, 17 Jan. 2019, available at: <https://www.g24.org/wp-content/uploads/2019/03/G-24_proposal_for_Taxation_of_Digital_Economy_Jan17_Special_Session_2.pdf> (cited as: G-24 Working Group, Proposal for Addressing Tax Challenges, 17 Jan. 2019).

HM Revenue & Customs: Diverted Profits Tax: Guidance, 10 Dec. 2014, last updated 31 Dec. 2018, available at: <https://www.gov.uk/government/publications/diverted-profits-tax-guidance> (cited as: HM Revenue & Customs, Diverted Profits Tax: Guidance).

HM Revenue & Customs: Corporate Tax Reform: delivering a more competitive system, Nov. 2010, available at: <https://assets.publishing.service.gov.uk/government/uploads/system/uploads/attachment_data/file/81303/corporate_tax_reform_complete_document.pdf> (cited as: HM Revenue & Customs, Corporate Tax Reform).

***Johnson*, Stephanie Soong**: U.S. Pulls 'Safe Harbor' Idea Off Global Tax Reform Table, Tax Notes Today Federal 2021, available at: <https://www.taxnotes.com/tax-notes-today-federal/base-erosion-and-profit-shifting-beps/us-pulls-safe-harbor-idea-global-tax-reform-table/2021/03/01/38wcw> (cited as: *Johnson*, TNTF 2021, 39–7)

Karaboytcheva*, Miroslava**: Taxation of the digital economy: Latest developments Dec. 2020, available at: <https://www.europarl.europa.eu/RegData/etudes/ATAG/2020/659414/EPRS_ATA(2020)659414_EN.pdf> (cited as: ***Karaboytcheva, Taxation of the digital economy: Latest developments, Dec. 2020).

Keidanren: Tax Challenges Arising from Digitalization: Comments on Public Consultation Document concerning the Pillar One and Pillar Two Blueprint, available at: <http://www.oecd.org/tax/beps/public-comments-received-

on-the-reports-on-pillar-one-and-pillar-two-blueprints.htm> (cited as: Keidanren, Comments on Pillar One Blueprint).

Nestle: Public Consultation on the Secretariat Proposal for a "Unified Approach" under Pillar One: Comments by Nestlé Group Tax, available at: <https://www.oecd.org/tax/beps/public-comments-received-on-the-secretariat-proposal-for-a-unified-approach-under-pillar-one.htm> (cited as: Nestle, Comments on Secretariat Proposal).

Oxfam: Oxfam submission for the OECD public consultation on the Unified Approach, available at: <https://www.oecd.org/tax/beps/public-comments-received-on-the-secretariat-proposal-for-a-unified-approach-under-pillar-one.htm> (cited as: Oxfam, Comments on Secretariat Proposal).

***Pahlman*, Kari**: Comments on Secretariat Proposal for a "Unified Approach" under Pillar One, available at: <https://www.oecd.org/tax/beps/public-comments-received-on-the-secretariat-proposal-for-a-unified-approach-under-pillar-one.htm> (cited as: *Pahlman*, Comments on Secretariat Proposal).

***Petruzzi*, Raffaele/*Buriak*, Svitlana**: Comments to the Report on Pillar One Blueprint—Tax Challenges Arising from Digitalisation, available at: <http://www.oecd.org/tax/beps/public-comments-received-on-the-reports-on-pillar-one-and-pillar-two-blueprints.htm> (cited as: *Petruzzi/Buriak*, Comments on Pillar One Blueprint).

Ponemon Institute: 2019 Intangible Assets Financial Statement Impact Comparison Report, available at: <https://www.aon.com/getmedia/60fbb49a-c7a5-4027-ba98-0553b29dc89f/Ponemon-Report-V24.aspx> (cited as: Ponemon Institute LLC, 2019 Intangible Assets Financial Statement Impact Comparison Report)

PwC: PwC's comments in relation to the Reports on the Pillar One and Pillar Two Blueprints in light of the consultation document of 12 October 2020, available at: <http://www.oecd.org/tax/beps/public-comments-received-on-the-reports-on-pillar-one-and-pillar-two-blueprints.htm> (cited as: PwC, Comments on Pillar One Blueprint).

PwC: Comments on Secretariat Proposal for a "Unified Approach" under Pillar One, available at: <https://www.oecd.org/tax/beps/public-comments-received-on-the-secretariat-proposal-for-a-unified-approach-under-pillar-one.htm> (cited as: PwC, Comments on Secretariat Proposal).

PwC: Hungary: Corporate—Taxes on corporate income, available at: <http://taxsummaries.pwc.com/ID/Hungary-Corporate-Taxes-on-corporate-income> (cited as: PwC, Hungary: Corporate—Taxes on corporate income).

PwC: Israeli Tax Authority releases first guidance related to e-commerce, available at: <https://documen.site/download/israeli-tax-authority-releases-first-gui

dance-related-to-e-commerce-tax-insights_pdf> (cited as: PwC, Israeli Tax Authority releases first guidance related to e-commerce).

***Spengel*, Christoph/*Fischer*, Leonie/*Ludwig*, Christopher/*Müller*, Raphael**: Comments on the Public Consultation Document Concerning "Secretariat Proposal for a 'Unified Approach' under Pillar One", Mannheim 12. Nov. 2019, available at: <https://www.oecd.org/tax/beps/public-comments-received-on-the-secretariat-proposal-for-a-unified-approach-under-pillar-one.htm> (cited as: *Spengel/Fischer/Ludwig/Müller*, Comments on Secretariat Proposal).

Tax Foundation: Tax Foundation Response to OECD Public Consultation Document: Secretariat Proposal for a "Unified Approach" under Pillar One, available at: <https://www.oecd.org/tax/beps/public-comments-received-on-the-secretariat-proposal-for-a-unified-approach-under-pillar-one.htm> (cited as: Tax Foundation, Comments on Secretariat Proposal).

The Federal Constitutional Court: Treaty overrides by national statutory law are permissible under the Constitution, Press Release of 12 Feb. 2016, No. 9/2016, available at: <https://www.bundesverfassungsgericht.de/SharedDocs/Pressemitteilungen/EN/2016/bvg16-009.html> (cited as: The Federal Constitutional Court, Press Release of 12 Feb. 2016, No. 9/2016).

US Department of the Treasury: The Deferral of Income Earned Through U.S. Controlled Foreign Corporations: A Policy Study, Washington DC 2000, available at: <https://www.treasury.gov/resource-center/tax-policy/Documents/Report-SubpartF-2000.pdf> (cited as: US Department of the Treasury, A Policy Study).

Legal Status of the Cited Double Tax Agreements

Double Tax Agreement	Date of Signature	Reference
Commonwealth of Australia	12 Nov. 2015	BGBl. II 2016, 1114
Cyprus	19. Feb. 2021	amending protocol has not yet entered into force
Grand Duchy of Luxembourg	23 Apr. 2012	BGBl. II 2012, 1403
Hungary	28 Feb. 2011	BGBl. II 2011, 919
Ireland	3 Dec. 2014	BGBl. II 2015, 1323
Japan	18 July 2016	BGBl. II 2016, 1230
Kingdom of the Netherlands	12 Apr. 2012	BGBl. II 2012, 1414
Kingdom of Norway	24 June 2013	BGBl. II 2014, 906
Kingdom of Spain	3 Feb. 2011	BGBl. II 2012, 18
Malaysia	23 Feb. 2010	BGBl. II 2010, 1310
People's Republic of China	28 Mar. 2014	BGBl. II 2015, 1647
Principality of Liechtenstein	17 Nov. 2011	BGBl. II 2012, 1462
Republic of Albania	6 Apr. 2010	BGBl. II 2011, 1186
Republic of Armenia	29 June 2016	BGBl. II 2017, 1077
Republic of Austria	26 Mar. 2002	BGBl. II 2002, 734
Republic of Bulgaria	25 Jan. 2010	BGBl. II 2010, 1286
Republic of Costa Rica	13 Feb. 2014	BGBl. II 2014, 917
Republic of Finland	19 Feb. 2016	BGBl. II 2017, 466
Republic of India	19 June 1995	BGBl. II 1996, 706
Republic of Liberia	25 Nov. 1970	BGBl. II 1973, 1285
Republic of Mauritius	7 Oct. 2011	BGBl. II 2012, 1050
Republic of the Philippines	9 Sept. 2013	BGBl. II 2014, 822
Republic of South Africa	9 Aug. 2008	has not yet entered into force
Republic of Tunisia	8 Feb. 2018	BGBl. II 2020, 154
Republic of Turkey	19 Sept. 2011	BGBl. II 2012, 526
State of Israel	21 Aug. 2014	BGBl. II 2015, 1301
Syrian Arab Republic	17 Feb. 2010	BGBl. II 2010, 1359
United Arab Emirates	1 July 2010	BGBl. II 2011, 538
United Kingdom of Great Britain and Northern Ireland	17 Mar. 2014	BGBl. II 2015, 1297
United States of America	1 June 2006	BGBl. II 2006, 1184

References

***Ahmadov*, Jamil**: The "Most Appropriate Method" as the New OECD Transfer Pricing Standard: Has the Hierarchy of Methods Been Completely Eliminated?, International Transfer Pricing Journal 2011, pp. 184–202.

***Altshuler*, Rosanne/*Grubert*, Harry**: Formula Apportionment: Is it better than the current system and are there better alternatives?, National Tax Journal 2010, pp. 1145–1184.

***Andersson*, Krister**: Should We Use Value Creation or Destination as a Basis for Taxing Digital Businesses?—Kristen Andersson's Comments on the 2018 Klaus Vogel Lecture Given by Professor Michael Devereux, Bulletin for International Taxation 2018, pp. 684–689.

***Andersson*, Krister**: Taxation of the Digital Economy, Intertax 2017, pp. 590–592.

***Andresen*, Ulf**: Betriebsstättengewinnabgrenzung nach Abkommensrecht, in: Wassermeyer, Franz/Andresen, Ulf/Ditz, Xaver (Eds.), Betriebsstätten-Handbuch—Gewinnermittlung und Besteuerung in- und ausländischer Betriebsstätten, 2nd Edition, Cologne 2018, pp. 300–333.

***Andresen*, Ulf**: Regulations Provide Further Guidance on the Application of the Authorized OECD Approach to the Attribution of Profit to Permanent Establishments, International Transfer Pricing Journal 2015, pp. 77–84.

***Andresen*, Ulf**: Banken: Einkünfteabgrenzung für das Einlagengeschäft inländischer Bankbetriebsstätten unter Berücksichtigung des AOA, Internationale SteuerRundschau 2013, pp. 320–328.

***Andresen*, Ulf**: Missverstandener Authorised OECD Approach bei inländischer Bankbetriebsstätte mit mehrjährigen Verlusten, Der Betrieb 2012, pp. 879–885.

***Arndt*, Hans-Wolfgang/*Fetzer*, Thomas**: Der Internetserver im Ausland—ein Fall des § 42 AO?, Betriebs-Berater 2001, pp. 1175–1180.

***Auerbach*, Alan Jeffrey**: The Theory of Excess Burden and Optimal Taxation, in: Auerbach, Alan Jeffrey/Feldstein, Martin (Eds.), Handbook of Public Economics, Amsterdam 1985, pp. 61–127.

***Ault*, Hugh J./*Bradford*, David F.**: Taxing International Income: An Analysis of the U.S. System and Its Economic Premises, in: Razin, Assaf/Slemrod, Joel (Eds.), Taxation in the Global Economy, Chicago 1990, pp. 11–52.

***Aumayr*, Lisa/*Mayr*, Gunter**: CCTB—Is There a Chance of a Breakthrough, European Taxation 2019, pp. 153–160.

S. Hentschel, *The Taxation of Permanent Establishments*, Hallesche Schriften zur Betriebswirtschaft 37, https://doi.org/10.1007/978-3-658-34000-1

***Avi-Yonah*, Reuven S.**: Between Formulary Apportionment and the OECD Guidelines: A Proposal for Reconciliation, World Tax Journal 2010, pp. 3–18.

***Avi-Yonah*, Reuven S.**: International Tax as International Law: An Analysis of the International Tax Regime, Cambridge 2007.

***Baker*, Philip**: The Multilateral Convention to Implement Tax Treaty Related Measures to Prevent Base Erosion and Profit Shifting, British Tax Review 2017, pp. 281–284.

***Baker*, Philip/*Collier*, Richard**: 2008 OECD Model: Changes to the Commentary on Article 7 and the Attribution of Profits to Permanent Establishments, Bulletin for International Taxation 2009, pp. 199–203.

***Baker*, Philip/*Collier*, Richard**: General Report, in: Cahiers de droit fiscal international: The attribution of profits to permanent establishments, Amsterdam 2006, pp. 21–67.

***Bal*, Aleksandra**: Tax Implications of Cloud Computing—How Real Tax Fit into Virtual Clouds, Bulletin for International Taxation 2012, pp. 335–339.

***Baldamus*, Ernst-August**: Neues zur Betriebsstättengewinnermittlung, Internationales Steurrecht 2012, pp. 317–324.

***Baranowski*, Karl-Heinz**: Besteuerung von Auslandsbeziehungen, 2nd Edition, Herne 2000.

***Bärsch*, Sven-Eric**: Taxation of Hybrid Financial Instruments and the Remuneration Derived Therefrom in an International and Cross-border Context: Issues and Options for Reform, Berlin/Heidelberg 2012.

***Baumhoff*, Hubertus**: Verrechnungspreise und alternative Ansätze, in: Wassermeyer (Ed.), Doppelbesteuerung—Zum 75. Geburtstag von Franz Wassermeyer—75 Beiträge zum Recht der DBA—Eine Festgabe, Munich 2015, pp. 251–258.

***Baumhoff*, Hubertus**: Methoden zur Ermittlung des angemessenen Verrechnungspreises—B. Klassische Methoden, in: Wassermeyer, Franz/Baumhoff, Hubertus (Eds.): Verrechnungspreise international verbundener Unternehmen, Cologne 2014, pp. 317–351.

***Baumhoff*, Hubertus**: Aktuelle Entwicklungen bei den internationalen Verrechnungspreisen, Internationales Steurrecht 2003, pp. 1–6.

***Baumhoff*, Hubertus/*Liebchen*, Daniel**: Verrechnungspreise zwischen international verbundenen Unternehmen, in: Mössner, Jörg Manfred et al. (Eds.), Steuerrecht international tätiger Unternehmen: Handbuch der Besteuerung von Auslandsaktivitäten inländischer Unternehmen und von Inlandsaktivitäten ausländischer Unternehmen, 5th Edition, Cologne 2018, pp. 365–666.

***Baumhoff*, Hubertus/*Liebchen*, Daniel**: Methoden zur Ermittlung des angemessenen Verrechnungspreises—D. Rangfolge der Verrechnungspreismethoden, in: Wassermeyer, Franz/Baumhoff, Hubertus (Eds.): Verrechnungspreise international verbundener Unternehmen, Cologne 2014, pp. 389–414.

***Bayer*, Adebiola**: UN-Musterabkommen: Das neue Update zum UN-Musterabkommen, Steuer und Wirtschaft International 2011, pp. 539–542.

***Bähr*, Gottfried**: Gewinnermittlung ausländischer Zweigbetriebe, Munich 1971.

***Beck*, Diana**: Qualifikationskonflikte im Internationalen Steuerrecht: Ursachenanalyse, Systematisierung und Lösungskonzepte, Wiesbaden 2017.

***Becker*, Jan Dierk/*van der Ham*, Susann**: Paradigmenwechsel in der internationalen Unternehmensbesteuerung?—Die OECD unterbreitet vier Vorschläge zur Besteuerung grenzüberschreitend tätiger Unternehmen, Der Betrieb 2019, pp. 502–509.

***Becker*, Helmut**: Funktionsnutzen oder Erwirtschaftungsgrundsatz—Wege zur Ermittlung des zutreffenden Betriebsstättenergebnisses, Der Betrieb 1990, pp. 392–395.

***Becker*, Helmut**: Die Besteuerung von Betriebsstätten, Der Betrieb 1989, pp. 10–16.

***Becker*, Helmut**: Konzernumlagen und Konzernpreise bei Betriebsstätten, Europäische Steuer-Zeitung 1971, pp. 95–103.

***Beermann*, Albert/*Gosch*, Dietmar** (Eds.): Abgabenordnung, Finanzgerichtsordnung: mit Nebengesetzen, EuGH-Verfahrensrecht—Kommentar, loose-leaf collection, Bonn/Berlin (158th update, January 2021).

***Beiser*, Reinhold**: Das arm's length-Prinzip beim Güter- und Leistungstransfer zwischen Stammhaus und Betriebsstätten im Gemeinschaftsrecht, Der Betrieb 2008, pp. 2724–2728.

***Beiser*, Reinhold**: Das Leistungsfähigkeitsprinzip im Licht des Gemeinschaftsrechtes—„Rechtssicherheit ist Prinzipien- oder Regelsicherheit", Steuer und Wirtschaft 2005, pp. 295–305.

***Bendlinger*, Stefan**: „Additional Guidance" der OECD zur Gewinnabgrenzung neuer Betriebsstätten nach BEPS-Aktionspunkt 7, Transfer Pricing International 2018, pp. 53–62.

***Bendlinger*, Stefan**: Multilaterales Instrument zur automatischen Anpassung bestehender Doppelbesteuerungsabkommen, Steuer und Wirtschaft International 2017, pp. 2–10.

***Bendlinger*, Stefan**: Die Betriebsstätte in der Praxis des internationalen Steuerrechts, 3rd Edition, Vienna 2016.

***Bendlinger*, Stefan**: Zum Seminar A: Die Betriebsstätte—ein alternativer Betriebsstättentatbestand, Internationales Steuerrecht 2009, pp. 521–525.

***Bennett*, Mary/*Dunahoo*, Carol A.**: The Attribution of Profits to a Permanent Establishment: Issues and Recommendations, Intertax 2005, pp. 51–67.

***Bennett*, Mary/*Russo*, Raffaele**: Discussion Draft on a New Art. 7 of the OECD Model Convention, International Transfer Pricing Journal 2009, pp. 73–80.

***Benz*, Sebastian/*Böhmer*, Julian**: Besteuerung digitaler Unternehmen, Der Betrieb 2018, pp. 1233–1238.

***Benz*, Sebastian/*Böhmer*, Julian**: Die Änderungen der deutschen DBA durch das Multilaterale Übereinkommen, Der Betrieb 2017, pp. 2308–2312.

***Benz*, Sebastian/*Böhmer*, Julian**: BEPS: Das Multilaterale Instrument zur Umsetzung der abkommensrechtlichen Änderungsvorschläge der BEPS-Abschlussberichte, Internationale SteuerRundschau 2017, pp. 27–32.

***Bernales*, Roberto**: The Authorized OECD Approach: An Overview, in: Gutiérrez, Carlos/Perdelwitz, Andreas (Eds.): Taxation of Business Profits in the 21st Century—Selected Issues under Tax Treaties, Amsterdam 2013, pp. 135–181.

***Bernütz*, Stefan**: Ertragsbesteuerung grenzüberschreitender Internet-Transaktionen: Anknüpfung an eine deutsche Betriebsstätte?, Internationales Steuerrecht 1997, pp. 353–357.

***Bhogal*, Sandy/*Swanson*, Kitty**: A Review of the EU's Proposals for a Common (Consolidated) Corporate Tax Base, Tax Notes International, Vol. 84 (2016), pp. 1093–1096.

***Biergans*, Enno/*Wasmer*, Claudius**: Zum Tatbestand der Besteuerung und zum Leistungsfähigkeitsbegriff in der Einkommensteuer, FinanzRundschau 1985, pp. 57–63.

***Bierlaagh*, Huub**: Permanent establishments, the separate enterprise fiction: is it a fact?, Intertax 1992, pp. 156–160.

***Bilaney*, Sunny Kishore**: Revised OECD Draft Guidance on the Profit Split Method: The Need for Conceptual Refinements!, Bulletin for International Taxation 2017, pp. 239–242.

***Bird*, Richard M.**: Shaping a New International Tax Order, Bulletin for International Fiscal Documentation 1988, pp. 292–299.

***Bird*, Richard M.**: The Interjurisdictional Allocation of Income, Australian Tax Forum 1986, pp. 333–354.
***Birk*, Dieter**: Das Leistungsfähigkeitsprinzip in der Unternehmenssteuerreform, Steuer und Wirtschaft 2000, pp. 328–336.
***Birk*, Dieter**: Das Leistungsfähigkeitsprinzip als Maßstab der Steuernormen: Ein Beitrag zu den Grundfragen des Verhältnisses Steuerrecht und Verfassungsrecht, Cologne 1983.
***Birk*, Dieter**: Zum Stand der Theoriediskussion in der Steuerrechtswissenschaft—Erwiderung zu Walter Leisner, Von der Leistung zur Leistungsfähigkeit—die soziale Nivellierung, Steuer und Wirtschaft 1983, pp. 293–299.
***Blaufuß*, Kay/*Jacob*, Martin**: Tax-related implications of fair value accounting, in: Livne, Gilad/Markarian, Garen (Eds.), The Routledge Companion to Fair Value in Accounting, Abingdon, New York 2018, pp. 253–273.
***Blum*, Daniel W.**: Permanent Establishment and Action 1 on the Digital Economy of the OECD Base Erosion and Profit Shifting Initiative—The Nexus Criterion Redefined, Bulletin For International Taxation 2015, pp. 314–325.
***Böhmer*, Julian**: Base Erosion and Profit Shifting, in: Wassermeyer, Franz/Andresen, Ulf/Ditz, Xaver (Eds.), Betriebsstätten-Handbuch—Gewinnermittlung und Besteuerung in- und ausländischer Betriebsstätten, 2nd Edition, Cologne 2018, pp. 1038–1109.
***Bräutigam*, Rainer/*Kellermann*, Katharina/*Spengel*, Christoph**: Neuordnung der Besteuerungswelt durch den „OECD Pillar One": Bedeutungswandel der Kernbegriffe und (unlösbare?) Herausforderungen, Internationales Steuerrecht 2020, pp. 281–287.
***Brauner*, Yariv**: Taxing the Digital Economy Post-BEPS, Seriously, Intertax 2018, pp. 462–465.
***Brauner*, Yariv**: BEPS: An Interim Evaluation, World Tax Journal 2014, pp. 10–39.
***Brauner*, Yariv**: An International Tax Regime in Crystallization, 56 Tax Law Review 2003, pp. 259–328.
***Bron*, Jan**: Das Treaty Override im deutschen Steuerrecht vor dem Hintergrund aktueller Entwicklungen, Internationales Steuerrecht 2007, pp. 431–436.
***Brown*, Fred B.**: An Equity-Based, Multilateral Approach for Sourcing Income among Nations, Florida Tax Review 2011, pp. 565–641.
***Brülisauer*, Peter**: Gewinnabgrenzung zwischen Stammhaus und Betriebsstätte im internationalen Verhältnis: Neue Interpretation des «Dealing-at-arm's-length-Prinzips» durch die OECD, Der Schweizer Treuhänder 2005, pp. 720–729.
***Brüninghaus*, Dirk**: Kapitel K: Einkunftsabgrenzung bei Betriebsstätten, in: Vögele, Alexander/Borstell, Thomas/Engler, Gerhard (Eds.), Verrechnungspreise: Betriebswirtschaft—Steuerrecht, 5th Edition, Munich 2020, pp. 1225–1298.
***Brunsbach*, Stefan/*Endres*, Dieter/*Lüdicke*, Jürgen/*Schnitger*, Arne**: Deutsche Abkommenspolitik: Trends und Entwicklungen 2011/2012, Institut Finanzen und Steuern-Schrift Nr. 480, Berlin 2012.
***Buciek*, Klaus**: Aktuelle Entwicklungen zur Betriebsstättenbesteuerung, Deutsche Steuer-Zeitung 2003, pp. 139–147.
***Ceballos*, Alfredo Serna**: The Permanent Establishment Definition, in: Brugger, Florian/Plansky, Patrick (Eds.), Permanent Establishments in International and EU Tax Law, Vienna 2011, pp. 59–70.

***Chand*, Vikram**: Allocation of Taxing Rights in the Digitalized Economy: Assessment of Potential Policy Solutions and Recommendation for a Simplified Residual Profit Split Method, Intertax 2019, pp. 1023–1041.

***Chand*, Vikram/*Wagh*, Sagar**: The Profit Split Method: Status Quo and Outlook in Light of the BEPS Action Plan, International Transfer Pricing Journal 2014, pp. 402–408.

***Caillaud*, Bernard/*Jullien*, Bruno**: Chicken & egg: competition among intermediation service providers, The RAND Journal of Economics 2013, pp. 309–328.

***Collier*, Richard/*Andrus*, Joseph L.**: Transfer Pricing and the Arm's Length Principle after BEPS, Oxford 2017.

***Collier*, Richard/*Vella*, John**: Five Core Problems in the Attribution of Profits to Permanent Establishments, World Tax Journal 2019, pp. 159–187.

***Cousins*, Andrew**: Chapter 2: OECD Transfer Pricing Guidelines, in: Heimert, Michael A./Michaelson, T.J./Duff & Phelps (Eds.), Guide to International Transfer Pricing: Law, Tax Planning and Compliance Strategies, 8th Edition, Alphen aan den Rijn 2018, pp. 65–104.

***Das*, Rasmi Ranjan**: The Concept of Value Creation: Is It Relevant for the Allocation of Taxing Rights, Bulletin for International Taxation 2020, pp. 134–143.

***De Wilde*, Maarten Floris**: Comparing Tax Policy Responses for the Digitalizing Economy: Fold or All-in, Intertax 2018, pp. 466–475.

***De Wilde*, Maarten Floris**: Lowering the Permanent Establishment Threshold via the Anti-BEPS Convention: Much Ado About Nothing?, Intertax 2017, pp. 556–566.

***De Wilde*, Maarten Floris**: Sharing the Pie: Taxing Multinationals in a Global Market, Amsterdam 2017.

***De Wilde*, Maarten Floris**: Some Thoughts on a Fair Allocation of Corporate Tax in a Globalizing Economy, Intertax 2010, pp. 281–305.

***Debatin*, Helmut**: Doppelbesteuerungsabkommen und innerstaatliches Recht, insert to Deutsches Steuerrecht Issue 23 1992, pp. 1–8.

***Debatin*, Helmut**: Das Betriebsstättenprinzip der deutschen Doppelbesteuerungsabkommen: Teil II, Der Betrieb 1989, pp. 1739–1744.

***Debatin*, Helmut**: Das Betriebsstättenprinzip der deutschen Doppelbesteuerungsabkommen: Teil I, Der Betrieb 1989, pp. 1692–1697.

***Delarber*, Christian**: Steuerliche Einflüsse auf die grenzüberschreitende Betriebsstättenbesteuerung: Eine konzeptionelle Analyse und Fortentwicklungsansätze, Berlin 2015.

***Desai*, Mihir Arvind/*Hines*, James R. Jr.**: Evaluating International Tax Reform, National Tax Journal 2003, pp. 487–502.

***Devereux*, Michael P./*Vella*, John**: Taxing the Digitalized Economy: Targeted or System-Wide Reform?, British Tax Review 2018, pp. 387–406.

***Devereux*, Michael/*Vella*, John**: Implications of digitalization for international corporate tax reform, in: Gupta, Sanjeev/Keen, Michael/Shad, Alpa/Verdier, Genevieve (Eds.), Digital Revolutions in Public Finance, Washington 2017, pp. 91–112.

***Devereux*, Michael P./*Vella*, John**: Are We Heading towards a Corporate Tax System Fit for the 21st Century?, Fiscal Studies 2014, pp. 449–475.

***Diffring*, Philipp/*Saft*, Alexander**: Der Steuerabzug bei Online-Werbung am Beispiel Google Ads, Der Betrieb 2019, pp. 387–394.

***Dijkman*, Jeroen/*de Buck*, Sebastian/*Brouwers*, Dirk**: Guidance Issued on Profit Attribution to Permanent Establishments, International Transfer Pricing Journal 2011, pp. 207–210.

***Ditz*, Xaver**: Artikel 7 (2017) Unternehmensgewinne, in: Schönfeld, Jens/Ditz, Xaver (Eds.), Doppelbesteuerungsabkommen—Kommentar, 2nd Edition Cologne 2019, pp. 537–557.

***Ditz*, Xaver**: Artikel 7 (2008) Unternehmensgewinne, in: Schönfeld, Jens/Ditz, Xaver (Eds.), Doppelbesteuerungsabkommen—Kommentar, 2nd Edition, Cologne 2019, pp. 419–536.

***Ditz*, Xaver**: Der „Authorised OECD Approach" wird Wirklichkeit—Kritische Analyse des § 1 Abs. 5 AStG i.d.F. AmtshilfeRLUmsG, Internationale SteuerRundschau 2013, pp. 261–267.

***Ditz*, Xaver**: Betriebsstättengewinnabgrenzung nach dem „Authorized OECD Approach"—Eine kritische Analyse, Internationale SteuerRundschau 2012, pp. 48–55.

***Ditz*, Xaver**: Internationale Gewinnabgrenzung bei Betriebsstätten: Ableitung einer rechtsformneutralen Auslegung des Fremdvergleichsgrundsatzes im internationalen Steuerrecht, Berlin 2004.

***Ditz*, Xaver/*Bärsch*, Sven-Eric/*Engelen*, Christian**: Das neue Country-by-Country Reporting nach dem Regierungsentwurf des Anti-BEPS-Umsetzungsgesetzes v. 13.7.2016, Internationales Steuerrecht 2016, pp. 840–850.

***Ditz*, Xaver/*Bärsch*, Sven-Eric/*Engelen*, Christian**: Die neuen Pflichten zur Dokumentation von Verrechnungspreisen nach dem Regierungsentwurf des Anti-BEPS-Umsetzungsgesetzes v. 13.7.2016, Internationales Steuerrecht 2016, pp. 789–797.

***Ditz*, Xaver/*Heider*, Christian**: Austausch des Country-by-Country Reporting—Gemeinsame Erklärung Deutschland-USA gem. BMF v. 16.8.2018, Internationale SteuerRundschau 2018, pp. 399–403.

***Ditz*, Xaver/*Luckhaupt*, Hagen**: Betriebsstättengewinnaufteilungsverordnung—Neues Gewinnermittlungsrecht für Betriebsstätten, Internationale SteuerRundschau 2015, pp. 1–10.

***Ditz*, Xaver/*Pinkernell*, Reimar**: Die neue „Weltsteuerordnung" rückt näher: OECD veröffentlicht Blueprints zu den Säulen 1 und 2, Internationale SteuerRundschau 2020, pp. 417–429.

***Ditz*, Xaver/*Pinkernell*, Reimar**: BEPS Neudefinition internationaler Besteuerungsrechte durch das OECD Inclusive Framework on BEPS—Eine Würdigung aus deutscher Sicht, Internationale SteuerRundschau 2019, pp. 377–389.

***Ditz*, Xaver/*Pinkernell*, Reimar/*Quilitzsch*, Carsten**: BEPS-Reformvorschläge zu Lizenzgebühren und Verrechnungspreisen bei immateriellen Wirtschaftsgütern aus Sicht der Beratungspraxis, Internationales Steuerrecht 2014, pp. 45–51.

***Ditz*, Xaver/*Quilitzsch*, Carsten**: Erweiterung von Offenlegungspflichten durch Country by Country Reporting Steuerpolitischer Nutzen und verfahrensrechtliche Grenzen, Deutsches Steuerrecht 2014, pp. 127–131.

***Ditz*, Xaver/*Quilitzsch*, Carsten**: Aktuelle Entwicklungen im Hinblick auf die Definition der Betriebsstätte, FinanzRundschau 2012, pp. 493–501.

***Ditz*, Xaver/*Schneider*, Markus**: Änderungen des Betriebsstättenerlasses durch das BMF-Schreiben vom 25.8.2009, Deutsches Steuerrecht 2010, pp. 81–87.

***Ditz*, Xaver/*Tcherveniachki*, Vassil**: Gewinnzuordnung bei Betriebsstätten ohne Personal—Anmerkungen zum BMF-Schr. vom 17.12.2019, Internationale SteuerRundschau 2020, pp. 145–152.

***Dombrowski*, Martin**: Betriebsstättenbesteuerung vor und nach der Umsetzung des AOA: Eine Analyse unter besonderer Berücksichtigung von Vertreterbetriebsstätten, Berlin 2019.

Dorenkamp, **Christian**: Warum bei der sog. „OECD-Steuerrevolution" weniger mehr wäre—und wie man dahin kommen könnte, FinanzRundschau 2020, pp. 114–116.

Dourado, **Ana Paula**: Digital Taxation Opens the Pandora Box: The OECD Interim Report and the European Commission Proposals, Intertax 2018, pp. 565–572.

Dutriez, **Jean-François**: Attribution of Profits to a Permanent Establishment of a Company Engaged in Online Sales of Goods through a Local Warehouse, International Transfer Pricing Journal 2018, pp. 185–196.

Dziwiński, **Karol Adam**/*Peng*, **Claire (Xue)**: Introduction to the post-BEPS transfer-pricing aspects of intangibles, in: Lang, Michael/Storck, Alfred/Petruzzi, Raffaele/Risse, Robert (Eds.), Transfer Pricing and Intangibles—Current Developments, Relevant Issues and Possible Solutions, Vienna 2019, pp. 3–23.

Eicker, **Klaus**/*Scheifele*, **Matthias**: Die Betriebsstättenproblematik im Electronic Commerce, Internationale Wirtschafts-Briefe 1999, pp. 377–388.

Eigelshover, **Axel**/*Kratzer*, **Carsten**: Rechtsverordnung zu Aufzeichnungspflichten bei der Bestimmung angemessener Verrechnungspreise, Internationales Steuerrecht 2004, pp. 30–36.

Elschen, **Rainer**: Entscheidungsneutralität, Allokationseffizienz und Besteuerung nach der Leistungsfähigkeit: Gibt es ein gemeinsames Fundament der Steuerwissenschaften?, Steuer und Wirtschaft 1991, pp. 99–115.

Elschen, **Rainer**/*Hüchtebrock*, **Michael**: Steuerneutralität in Finanzwissenschaft und Betriebswirtschaftslehre—Diskrepanzen und Konsequenzen, FinanzArchiv 1983, pp. 253–280.

Endres, **Dieter**/*Freiling*, **Carla**: Musterfälle zu aktuellen Tendenzen in der deutschen Abkommenspolitik—Teil 2, Praxis Internationale Steuerberatung 2012, pp. 189–196.

Endres, **Dieter**/*Spengel*, **Christoph**: International Company Taxation and Tax Planning, Alphen aan den Rijn 2015.

Englisch, **Joachim**: Internationale Unternehmensteuerreform—mehr als kostspielige Symbolpolitik?, ifo Schnelldienst 3/2020, pp. 11–14.

Erdbrügger, **Andreas**: Änderungen der EU-Umsatzsteuervorschriften für den E-Commerce ab 2019 bzw. 2021, Deutsches Steuerrecht 2018, pp. 593–597.

Esterer, **Fritz**: Der Betriebsstättenbegriff im DBA und seine schleichende Auflösung, in: Beck'sche Steuerkommentare et al. (Eds.), Doppelbesteuerung—Zum 75. Geburtstag von Franz Wassermeyer: 75 Beiträge zum Recht der DBA—Eine Festgabe, Munich 2015, pp. 137–142.

Fehling, **Daniel**: Seminar I: Recent developments in international taxation, Internationales Steuerrecht 2019, pp. 656–659.

Fehling, **Daniel**/*Kampermann*, **Karoline**: Generalthema I: Assessing BEPS—origins, standards and responses, Internationales Steuerrecht 2017, pp. 638–644.

Fehling, **Daniel**/*Valta*, **Matthias**: Aktionspunkt 1: Besteuerung der digitalen Wirtschaft, in: Kofler, Georg/Schnitger, Arne (Eds.), BEPS-Handbuch: Maßnahmen gegen Gewinnverlagerung und Gewinnverkürzung internationaler Konzerne, Munich 2019, pp. 29–98.

Feuerstein, **David**: The Agency Permanent Establishment, in: Brugger, Florian/Plansky, Patrick (Eds.), Permanent Establishment in International and EU Tax Law, Vienna 2011, pp. 105–124.

Findeis, **Birgit**/*Eickmann*, **Marco**: Internet-Server als ertragsteuerliche Betriebsstätte nach dem Doppelbesteuerungsabkommen Deutschland—USA, Deutsche Steuer-Zeitung 2008, pp. 139–145.

Fink, **Jörn Ulrich**: Gewinnzurechnungsmethoden im Verhältnis zwischen inländischem Stammhaus und ausländischer Betriebsstätte, Recht der internationalen Wirtschaft 1988, pp. 43–51.

Fischer, **Lennart**/*Pitzer*, **Michaela**: Das MLI und die neuen allgemeinen Missbrauchsregelungen, Internationales Steuerrecht 2017, pp. 804–809.

Fleming, **J. Clifton Jr.**/*Peroni*, **Robert J.**/*Shay*, **Stephen E.**: Some Perspectives from the United States on the worldwide taxation vs. territorial taxation debate, Journal of the Australasian Tax Teachers Association 2008, pp. 35–86.

Fleming, **J. Clifton Jr.**/*Peroni*, **Robert J.**/*Shay*, **Stephen E.**: Fairness in International Taxation: The Ability-to-Pay Case for Taxing Worldwide Income, Florida Tax Review 2001, pp. 299–354.

Flick, **Hans**/*Wassermeyer*, **Franz**/*Baumhoff*, **Hubertus**/*Schönfeld*, **Jens** (Eds.): Außensteuerrecht—Kommentar, loose-leaf collection, Cologne (95th update, December 2020).

Förster, **Hartmut**: Die allgemeinen Verrechnungspreisgrundsätze des § 1 Abs. 3 AStG—Vergleich mit den aktualisierten Verrechnungspreisrichtlinien der OECD, Internationales Steuerrecht 2011, pp. 20–26.

Förster, **Hartmut**: Der Entwurf zur Aktualisierung der Kapitel I und III der OECD-Verrechnungspreisleitlinien, Internationales Steuerrecht 2009, pp. 720–727.

Förster, **Harmut**: Veröffentlichung der OECD zur Revision des Kommentars zu Artikel 7 OECD-Musterabkommen, Internationales Steuerrecht 2007, pp. 398–401.

Förster, **Hartmut**/*Greil*, **Stefan**/*Hilse*, **Armin**: Taxing the Digital Economy—The OECD Secretariat's new Transfer Pricing A-B-C and Alternative Courses of Action, International Transfer Pricing Journal 2020, pp. 3–18.

Franz, **Christoph**: Einkommensbegriffe im Steuer- und Sozialrecht, Steuer und Wirtschaft 1988, pp. 17–38.

Freedman, **Judith**: Financial and Tax Accounting: Transparency and "Truth", in: Schön, Wolfgang (Ed.), Tax and Corporate Governance, Berlin, Heidelberg 2008, pp. 71–92.

Fris, **Pim**/*Llinares*, **Emmanuel**/*Gonnet*, **Sébastien**: PEs and Transfer Pricing: The Playing Field in International Taxation Redefined, Tax Planning International Transfer Pricing 2008, pp. 1–6.

Frischmuth, **Markus**: UntStRefG 2008 und Verrechnungspreise nach § 1 AStG n.F., Internationales Steuerrecht 2007, pp. 485–489.

Frebel, **Maibrit**: Erfolgsaufteilung und -besteuerung im internationalen Konzern, Cologne 2006.

Froitzheim, **Aurelia**: Steuerliche Selbstständigkeitsfiktion der Betriebsstätte und deren Auswirkungen auf die Gewinnabgrenzung, Cologne 2015.

Froitzheim, **Aurelia**: Funktionsweise und Wirkung der AOA-Gewinnabgrenzung, Die Unternehmensbesteuerung 2015, pp. 354–359.

Frotscher, **Gerrit**: Internationales Steuerrecht, 5th Edition, Munich 2020.

Fuest, **Clemens**: Unternehmen am Ort der Wertschöpfung besteuern—eine neue Leitlinie für die internationale Besteuerung?, ifo Schnelldienst 3/2020, pp. 6–11.

Gassner, **Wolfgang**: Die Begründung von Betriebsstätten durch Bauausführungen, Montagen und ähnliche Tätigkeiten und Dienstleistungen (Art 5 Abs. 3 OECD-MA), in: Gassner,

Wolfgang/Lang, Michael/Lechner, Eduard (Eds.), Die Betriebstätte im Recht der Doppelbesteuerungsabkommen: Voraussetzungen der Besteuerung von Unternehmensgewinnen im Quellenstaat, Vienna 1998, pp. 57–76.

***Gebhardt,* Ronald**: Ist § 1 Abs. 5 S. 8 AStG-E i.d.F. des JStG 2013 ein Treaty Override?, Betriebs-Berater 2012, pp. 2353–2355.

***Gerlach*, Cosima/*Hagemann*, Tobias**: Hilfsbetriebsstätten unter BEPS-Aktionspunkt 7—Widersprüche zu gängigen Besteuerungsprinzipien und -zielen der OECD, FinanzRundschau 2017, pp. 1035–1042.

***Geurts*, Matthias**: Server as a permanent establishment?, Intertax 2000, pp. 173–175.

***Gonnet*, Sébastien**: Risks Redefined in Transfer Pricing Post-BEPS, in: Lang, Michael/Storck, Alfred/Petruzzi, Raffaele (Eds.), Transfer Pricing in a Post-BEPS World, Alphen aan den Rijn 2016, pp. 33–59.

***Görl*, Maximilian**: Art. 5 Betriebsstätte, in: Vogel, Klaus/Lehner, Moris (Eds.), Doppelbesteuerungsabkommen der Bundesrepublik Deutschland auf dem Gebiet der Steuern vom Einkommen und Vermögen—Kommentar auf der Grundlage der Musterabkommen, 6th Edition, Munich 2015, pp. 656–778.

***Gosch*, Dietmar**: Über die Zeit im Abkommensrecht, Internationales Steuerrecht 2015, pp. 709–717.

***Gosch*, Dietmar**: Über Entstrickung: Stand des unnötig komplexen „Entstrickungsbesteuerungsrechts“ und absehbare Entwicklungen, Internationale Wirtschafts-Briefe 2012, pp. 779–789.

***Gosch*, Dietmar/*Kroppen*, Heinz-Klaus/*Grotherr*, Siegfried/*Kraft*, Gerhard** (Eds.): DBA-Kommentar: Doppelbesteuerungsabkommen auf dem Gebiet der Steuern vom Einkommen und vom Vermögen, auf dem Gebiet der Erbschaftsteuer, loose-leaf collection, Herne (43th update, October 2020).

***Gradl*, Christoph/*Kiesewetter*, Michael**: Das Mehrseitige Übereinkommen (Multilateral Instrument) zur Umsetzung abkommensbezogener Maßnahmen aus dem OECD/G20-BEPS-Projekt und dessen voraussichtliche Auswirkungen auf die deutschen Doppelbesteuerungsabkommen, Internationales Steuerrecht 2018, pp. 1–11.

***Graetz*, Michael J.**: Taxing International Income: Inadequate Principles, Outdated Concepts, and Unsatisfactory Policies, Tax Law Review 2001, pp. 261–336.

***Graetz*, Michael J./*O'Hear*, Michael M.**: The "Original Intent" of U.S. International Taxation, Duke Law Journal 1997, pp. 1021–1110.

***Green*, Robert A.**: The Future of Sourced-Based Taxation of the Income of Multinational Enterprises, Cornell Law Review 1993–1994, pp. 18–86.

***Greil*, Stefan**: The Dealing at Arm's Length Fallacy: A Way Forward to a Formula-Based Transactional Profit Split?, Intertax 2017, pp. 624–630.

***Greinert*, Markus/*Metzner*, Susann**: Entwicklung des Fremdvergleichsgrundsatzes, Die Unternehmensbesteuerung 2014, pp. 307–316.

***Griffith*, Rachel/*Hines*, James/*Sørensen*, Peter Birch**: International Capital Taxation, in: Mirrlees, Sir James/Adam, Stuart/Besley, Timothy/Blundell, Richard/Bond, Stephen/Chote, Robert/Gammie, Malcolm/Johnson, Paul/Myles, Gareth/Poterba, James (Eds.), Dimensions of Tax Design: The Mirrlees Review, Oxford 2010, pp. 914–1027.

***Groß*, Bernhard**: Anpassung der Ergebnisse von Verrechnungspreisen an die Wertschöpfung: Der G20/OECD-Abschlussbericht zu den Maßnahmen 8–10 des BEPS-Aktionsplans, Internationales Steuerrecht 2016, pp. 233–241.

***Grotherr*, Siegfried**: Erschwerung von Gestaltungen zur Vermeidung des Betriebsstättenstatus durch das Multilaterale Instrument (Teil II), Die Unternehmensbesteuerung 2017, pp. 188–195.

***Grotherr*, Siegfried**: Erschwerung von Gestaltungen zur Vermeidung des Betriebsstättenstatus durch das Multilaterale Instrument (Teil I), Die Unternehmensbesteuerung 2017, pp. 125–133.

***Grotherr*, Siegfried**: Automatischer Informationsaustausch im Steuerrecht über länderbezogene Berichte von Konzernsteuerunternehmen—Rechtsgrundlagen, Inhalt, Datenschutz und Probleme beim CbC Reporting, Recht der Internationalen Wirtschaft 2017, pp. 1–17.

***Grotherr*, Siegfried**: Anwendungsfragen bei der länderbezogenen Berichterstattung—Country-by-Country Reporting, Internationales Steuerrecht 2016, pp. 991–1008.

***Grotherr*, Siegfried/*Endert*, Volker**: Neue steuerliche Risiken bei Outbound-Investitionen in Form von Betriebsstätten, in: Lüdicke, Jürgen/Mössner, Jörg Manfred/Hummel, Lars (Eds.), Das Steuerrecht der Unternehmen: Festschrift für Gerrit Frotscher zum 70. Geburtstag, Freiburg 2013, pp. 157–173.

***Gummert*, Heinke/*Trapp*, Stephan**: Der Internet-Server als ertragsteuerliche Betriebsstätte, MultiMedia und Recht 1998, pp. 350–354.

***Gutmann*, Daniel/*Raingeard de la Blétière*, Emmanuel**: CC(C)TB and International Taxation, EC Tax Review 2017, pp. 233–245.

***Guyton*, John L./*O'Hare*, John F./*Stavrianos*, Michael P./*Toder*, Eric J.**: Estimating the Compliance Cost of the U.S. Individual Income Tax, National Tax Journal 2003, pp. 673–688.

***Häck*, Nils**: Abkommensrechtliche Zuordnung von Beteiligungen zu Betriebsstätten nach BFH, OECD und Finanzverwaltung, Internationale SteuerRundschau 2015, pp. 113–121.

***Haarmann*, Wilhelm**: Die Vertreterbetriebsstätte und die faktische Verpflichtung (Kommissionärsmodell), in: Beck'sche Steuerkommentare et al. (Eds.), Doppelbesteuerung—Zum 75. Geburtstag von Franz Wassermeyer: 75 Beiträge zum Recht der DBA—Eine Festgabe, Munich 2015, pp. 161–170.

***Haase*, Florian**: Onlinewerbung im Fokus der Betriebsprüfung: Replik zu Hruschka DStR 2019, 88, Deutsches Steuerrecht 2019, pp. 761–766.

***Haase*, Florian**: Das sog. Multilaterale Instrument: Zukunft des Abkommensrechts, Internationale Wirtschafts-Briefe 2017, pp. 16–22.

***Haase*, Florian**: Art. 5 Betriebsstätte, in: Haase, Florian (Ed.), Außensteuergesetz/Doppelbesteuerungsabkommen, 3rd Edition, Heidelberg 2016, pp. 792–853.

***Haase*, Florian/*Dorn*, Katrin**: Eckpunkte der OECD Tax Agenda 2011: Die Zukunft des internationalen Steuerrechts aus Sicht der OECD, Internationale Wirtschafts-Briefe 2011, pp. 721–726.

***Hadzhieva*, Eli**: Impact of Digitalisation on International Tax Matters, Study for the Committee on Financial Crimes, Tax Evasion and Tax Avoidance, Policy Department for Economic, Scientific and Quality of Life Policies, European Parliament, Luxembourg 2019.

***Hagiu*, Andrei/*Wright*, Julian**: Marketplace or Reseller, Management Science 2015, pp. 184–203.

***Hagiu*, Andrei/*Wright*, Julian**: Multi-sided platforms, International Journal of Industrial Organization 2015, pp. 162–174.

***Hahn*, Hartmut**: Server als Betriebsstätte, Steuer und Wirtschaft International 2002, pp. 17–21.

***Haiß*, Uta**: Gewinnabgrenzung bei Betriebsstätten im Internationalen Steuerrecht: Vermögens-, Aufwands- und Ertragszuordnung nach OECD-Musterabkommen und neuem Betriebsstättenerlass, Neuwied 2000.

***Haller*, Heinz**: Die Steuern: Grundlinien eines rationalen Systems öffentlicher Abgaben, Tübingen 1964.

***Hanlon*, Michelle**: Country-by-Country Reporting and the International Allocation of Taxing Rights, Bulletin for International Taxation 2018, pp. 209–217.

***Harpaz*, Assaf**: The OECD's Unified Approach: Nexus, Scope, and Coexisting With DSRs, Tax Notes International, Vol. 96 (2019), pp. 909–913.

***Haun*, Jürgen/*Kahle*, Holger/*Goebel*, Sören/*Reiser*, Hagen** (Eds.): Außensteuergesetz, loose-leaf collection, Herne (44th update, December 2020).

***Haverkamp*, Lars H.**: Betriebsstättengewinnabgrenzung, in: Mössner, Jörg Manfred et al. (Eds.), Steuerrecht international tätiger Unternehmen: Handbuch der Besteuerung von Auslandsaktivitäten inländischer Unternehmen und von Inlandsaktivitäten ausländischer Unternehmen, 5th Edition, Cologne 2018, pp. 667–759.

***Heger*, Karin**: Das Verhältnis von Abkommensrecht und nationalem Steuerrecht, Steuer und Wirtschaft International 2011, pp. 95–104.

***Heggmair*, Maik/*Riedl*, Andreas/ *Wutschke*, Christopher**: Betriebsstätten von Unternehmen der Digital Economy—Eine kritische Analyse der zu erfüllenden Tatbestandsmerkmale für eine Betriebsstätte in der Digital Economy, Internationales Steuerrecht 2015, pp. 92–97.

***Heil*, Svetlana/*Pupeter*, Alexander**: Google-Tax: Gibt es sie schon? Zur Abzugsteuer auf Online-Werbung nach § 50a EStG, Betriebs-Berater 2019, pp. 604–611.

***Heinsen*, Oliver**: Betriebsstättenbegriff, in: Looks, Christian/Heinsen, Oliver (Eds.), Betriebsstättenbesteuerung: Inboundinvestitionen, Outboundinvestitionen, Steuergestaltungen, Branchenbesonderheiten, 3rd Edition, Munich 2017, pp. 45–102.

***Hemmelrath*, Alexander**: Art. 7 Unternehmensgewinne, in: Vogel, Klaus/Lehner, Moris (Eds.), Doppelbesteuerungsabkommen der Bundesrepublik Deutschland auf dem Gebiet der Steuern vom Einkommen und Vermögen—Kommentar auf Grundlage der Musterabkommen, 6th Edition, Munich 2015, pp. 858–994.

***Hemmelrath*, Alexander/*Kepper*, Philipp**: Die Bedeutung des „Authorized OECD Approach" (AOA) für die deutsche Abkommenspraxis, Internationales Steuerrecht 2013, pp. 37–42.

***Hentschel*, Sven**: Deutsche Regelungen zur internationalen Funktionsverlagerung: kritische Analyse unter besonderer Berücksichtigung der Transferpaketbewertung, Wiesbaden 2015.

***Hentschel*, Sven/*Hörnicke*, Gabriel/*Kraft*, Gerhard**: Von der Wertschöpfung zum „Unified Approach"—Die andauernde Suche nach einer Konsenslösung für BEPS-Aktionspunkt 1, Die Unternehmensbesteuerung 2019, pp. 673–683.

***Hentschel*, Sven/*Kraft*, Gerhard/*Moser*, Till**: Permanent Establishment Taxation in Germany in a Post-AOA-Implementation Era: A Primer on Exceptions and Problem Areas, European Taxation 2018, pp. 73–81.

***Hentschel*, Sven/*Kraft*, Gerhard/*Moser*, Till**: Klassifizierung uns Systematisierung von Abkommenstypen als Anwendungshilfe der Escape-Klausel des § 1 Abs. 5 Satz 8 AStG, Die Unternehmensbesteuerung 2016, pp. 144–151.

***Herzig*, Norbert**: Comment on Hieman and Reichelstein: "Transfer Pricing in Multinational Corporations: An Integrated Management- and Tax Perspective", in: Schön, Wolfgang/Konrad, Kai A. (Eds.), Fundamentals of International Transfer Pricing in Law and Economics, Wiesbaden 2012, pp. 19–24.

***Hey*, Johanna**: "Taxation Where Value is Created" and the OECD/G20 Base Erosion and Profit Shifting Initiative, Bulletin for International Taxation 2018, pp. 203–208.

***Hey*, Johanna**: § 3 Steuersystem und Steuerverfassungsrecht, in: Tipke, Klaus/Lang, Joachim (Eds.), Steuerrecht, 24th Edition, Cologne 2020, pp. 71–155.

***Hey*, Johanna**: Das Territorialitätsprinzip als theoretische Grundlage der beschränkten Steuerpflicht—isolierende Betrachtungsweise und Objektsteuercharakter als konkrete Ausprägungen, Internationale Wirtschafts-Briefe 2004, pp. 2003–2016.

***Hey*, Johanna**: Harmonisierung der Unternehmensbesteuerung in Europa: ein Vorschlag unter Auswertung des Ruding-Berichts und der US-amerikanischen "integration debate", Cologne 1997.

***Heyd*, Steffen**: Internationale Gewinnabgrenzung bei der Geschäftstätigkeit über Betriebsstättenstrukturen—Eine betriebswirtschaftliche Analyse im Kontext europäischer und internationaler Harmonisierungsbestrebungen, Berlin 2014.

***Hidien*, Jürgen W./*Rodenhäuser*, Veronika**: Der Rechtsbegriff der mehrgemeindlichen Betriebsstätte (§ 12 AO i.V.m. §§ 28, 30 GewStG) und seine Anwendung auf großtechnische Netzwerke am Beispiel der Telefonkabel des Telefonnetzes der Deutschen Telekom AG, Deutsche Steuer-Zeitung 2007, pp. 689–702.

***Higinbotham*, Harlow N.**: The Profit Split Method: Effective Application for Precision and Administrability, Tax Management Transfer Pricing Special Report 1996, pp. 1–27.

***Hilbert*, Lukas/*Engel*, Benjamin**: OECD Discussion around the Definition of Permanent Establishments: A German view on Proposed Amendments to the Model Commentary and Their Effect on Business Profit Allocation and International Assignments, Intertax 2012, pp. 462–476.

***Hildebrandt*, Mathias**: Was ist beim Thema Online-Werbung los?, Neue Wirtschafts-Briefe 2019, p. 625.

***Holler*, Guido/*Heerspink*, Frank**: Betriebsstättenbegründung durch Errichtung eines Verkaufsservers im Internet?, Betriebs-Berater 1998, pp. 771–773.

***Homburg*, Stefan**: Allgemeine Steuerlehre, 7th Edition, Munich 2015.

***Hongler*, Peter/*Pistone*, Pasquale**: Blueprint for a New PE Nexus to Tax Business Income in the Era of the Digital Economy, Working Paper, IBFD 2015.

***Hoogterp*,Pieter**: Internal Interest Dealings for Financial and Non-Financial Enterprises and Art. 7 of the OECD Model Tax Convention, International Transfer Pricing Journal 2009, pp. 396–400.

***Hruschka*, Franz**: Onlinewerbung im Fokus der Betriebsprüfung, Deutsches Steuerrecht 2019, pp. 88–92.

***Hruschka*, Franz**: Artikel 5 (2014) Betriebsstätte, in: Schönfeld, Jens/Ditz, Xaver (Eds.), Doppelbesteuerungsabkommen—Kommentar, Cologne 2019, pp. 271–347.

***Huibregtse*, Steef/ *Verdoner*, Louan/ *Valutyte*, Igne/ *Offermanns*, René**: Status of Implementation of the Authorized OECD Approach into Domestic Tax Law and Tax Treaties—Part 1, European Taxation 2015, pp. 363–373.

***Hunt*, Jonathan/*Educate*, Mike/ *Wentland*, Rob**: Another Front in the Brewing CbC Public Disclosure Battle, Tax Notes International, Vol. 85 (2017), pp. 835–840.

***Hübschmann*, Walter/*Hepp*, Ernst/*Spitaler*, Armin** (Eds.): Abgabenordnung, Finanzgerichtsordnung: Kommentar, loose-leave collection, Cologne (260th update, October 2020).

***Hüning*, Carsten/*Hennemann-Raschke*, Vera/*Kampes*, Richard**: Änderungen der Gewinnabgrenzungsaufzeichnungsverordung (GAufzV)—Welche Änderungen ergeben sich bei der Erstellung der Verrechnungpreisdokumentation, Internationale Wirtschafts-Briefe 2017, pp. 779–786.

***Hüning*, Carsten/*Hewera*, Daniel/*Geyik*, Dennis**: BEPS-Aktionspunkt 10: Dienstleistungen mit geringer Wertschöpfung—Werden diese bald nur noch durch den vereinfachten Ansatz vergütet?, Internationale Wirtschafts-Briefe 2016, pp. 298–301.

***Hutter*, Helga/*Schmidt*, Jürgen:** Aktueller Überblick zum Thema e-commerce—unter besonderer Berücksichtigung der Frage: Betriebsstätteneigenschaft eines Internetservers, Internationales Steuerrecht 2000, pp. 650–654.

Institut der Wirtschaftsprüfer: Determination of profits of permanent establishments, Intertax 1988, pp. 427–433.

***Jacobs*, Otto H.**: Internationale Unternehmensbesteuerung—Deutsche Investitionen im Ausland—Ausländische Investitionen im Inland, 8th Edition, Munich 2016.

***Jacobs*, Otto H./*Spengel*, Christoph/*Schäfer*, Anne**: ICT and Profit Allocation within Multinational Groups, Intertax 2004, pp. 268–283.

***Jacobs*, Otto H./*Spengel*, Christoph/*Schäfer*, Anne**: ICT and International Corporate Taxation: Tax Attributes and Scope of Taxation, Intertax 2003, pp. 214–231.

***Jeitler*, Matthias**: The Attribution of Functions, Assets and Risks to Permanent Establishments, in: Brugger, Florian/Plansky, Patrick (Eds.), Permanent Establishments in International and EU Tax Law, Vienna 2011, pp. 185–202.

***Jerabek*, Richard/*Kofler*, Georg/*Kroppen*, Heinz-Klaus/*Rasch*, Stephan**: Aktionspunkt 8–10: Verrechnungspreise im Einklang mit Wertschöpfung, in: Kofler, Georg/Schnitger, Arne (Eds.), BEPS-Handbuch: Maßnahmen gegen Gewinnverlagerung und Gewinnverkürzung internationaler Konzerne, Munich 2019, pp. 437–520.

***Jiménez*, Adolfo Martín**: BEPS, the Digital(ized) Economy and the Taxation of Services and Royalties, Intertax 2018, pp. 620–638.

***Junkers*, Lars**: Zur Missbräuchlichkeit der Entwicklung von Geschäftsmodellen, Internationales Steuerrecht 2019, pp. 850–854.

***Kadet*, Jeffrey M.**: Expansion of the Profit Split Method: The Wave of the Future, Tax Notes International, Vol. 77 (2015), pp. 1183–1188.

***Kaeser*, Christian**: Generalthema I: Besteuerung grenzüberschreitender Dienstleistungen, Internationales Steuerrecht 2012, pp. 674–677.

***Kaeser*, Christian/*Bremer*,Sven**: Transfer Pricing and Documentation Requirements, in: Lang, Michael/Storck, Alfred/Petruzzi, Raffaele (Eds.), Transfer Pricing in a Post-BEPS World, Alphen aan den Rijn 2016, pp. 187–208.

***Kaeser*, Christian/*Owens*, Jeffrey/*Sim*, Sam**: Going the Way of the Polaroid: Digital Taxation and the End of the Arm's-Length Principle?, Tax Notes International 2019, Vol. 95 (2019), pp. 211–219.

***Kahle*, Holger**: Steuergestaltung bei international tätigen Personengesellschaften, Steuer und Wirtschaft 2005, pp. 61–70.

***Kahle*, Holger/*Baschnagel*, Matthias/*Kindich*, Aaron**: Aktuelle Aspekte der Ertragsbesteuerung von Server-Betriebsstätten, FinanzRundschau 2016, pp. 193–203.

***Kahle*, Holger/*Kindich*, Aaron**: Begriff der Betriebsstätte nach nationalem Recht und DBA-Recht, in: Lübbehüsen, Thomas/Kahle, Holger (Eds.), Brennpunkte der Besteuerung von Betriebsstätten, 2nd Edition, Herne 2019, pp. 87–248.

***Kahle*, Holger/*Kindich*, Aaron**: Erfolgs- und Vermögensabgrenzung bei Betriebsstätten, in: Lübbehüsen, Thomas/Kahle, Holger (Eds.), Brennpunkte der Besteuerung von Betriebsstätten, 2nd Edition, Herne 2019, pp. 323–522.

***Kahle*, Holger/*Mödinger*, Jörg**: Erfolgs- und Vermögensabgrenzung bei ausländischen Betriebsstätten—Status Quo und aktuelle Entwicklungen, Der Betrieb 2011, pp. 2338–2343.

***Kahle*, Holger/*Mödinger*, Jörg**: Die Neufassung des Art. 7 OECD-MA im Rahmen der Aktualisierung des OECD-MA 2010, Internationales Steuerrecht 2010, pp. 757–763.

***Kahle*, Holger/*Schulz*, Sebastian**: Zum Einkünftekatalog des § 49 EStG nach den jüngsten Rechtsentwicklungen, Deutsche Steuer-Zeitung 2008, pp. 784–798.

***Kahle*, Holger/*Ziegler*, Steffen**: Betriebsstättenbegriff—Grundfragen und aktuelle Entwicklungen, Deutsche Steuer-Zeitung 2009, pp. 834–847.

***Kaminski*, Bert/*Strunk*, Günther**: BFH-Urteil zu Betriebsstätte und E-Commerce—Anmerkung zum Urteil vom 5.6.2002, I R 86/01, Internationale Wirtschafts-Briefe 2002, pp. 947–952.

***Kamphuis*, Eric**: Significant People Functions and Functional Ownership: The New Motto in Transfer Pricing, Tax Management Transfer Pricing Report 2008, pp. 300–313.

***Kaufman*, Nancy H.**: Fairness and the Taxation of International Income, Law and Policy in International Business 1998, pp. 145–203.

***Kempny*, Simon**: Die Leistungsfähigkeit des Steuerrechts—Bericht über das Abschiedssymposium für Dieter Birk am 8.7.2011 an der Westfälischen Wilhelms-Universität Münster, Steuer und Wirtschaft 2011, pp. 377–384.

***Kessler*, Wolfgang/*Förster*, Guido/*Watrin*, Christoph** (Eds.): Unternehmensbesteuerung: Festschrift für Norbert Herzig zum 65. Geburtstag, Munich 2010.

***Kessler*, Wolfgang/*Huck*, Friederike**: Grenzüberschreitender Transfer von Betriebsvermögen—Die Verlagerung von Einzelwirtschaftsgütern, Betriebsstätten und Betrieben ins Ausland, Steuer und Wirtschaft 2005, pp. 193–215.

***Kessler*, Wolfgang/*Peter*, Markus**: Weiterentwicklung des Betriebsstättenprinzips: Neuinterpretation eines traditionellen Besteuerungskonzepts durch die OECD vor dem Hintergrund des zunehmenden E-Commerce, Betriebs-Berater 2000, pp. 1545–1553.

***Kirchhof*, Paul**: Die Leistungsfähigkeit des Steuerrechts—Steuerrecht und Verfassungsrecht, Steuer und Wirtschaft 2011, pp. 365–371.

***Kirchhof*, Paul**: Der verfassungsrechtliche Auftrag zur Besteuerung nach der finanziellen Leistungsfähigkeit, Steuer und Wirtschaft 1985, pp. 319–329.

***Kirchhof*, Paul**: Steuergleichheit, Steuer und Wirtschaft 1984, pp. 297–314.

***Kleineidam*, Hans-Jochen**: Gerechtigkeits- und Kausalitätsgesichtspunkte bei der internationalen Einkünftezurechnung auf Betriebsstätten. Ein Plädoyer für eine modifizierte globale Einkünftezurechnungsmethode, in: Kleineidam, Hans-Jochen (Ed.), Unternehmenspolitik und internationale Besteuerung: Festschrift für Lutz Fischer zum 60. Geburtstag, Berlin 1999, pp. 691–712.

***Kleineidam*, Hans-Jochen**: Perspektiven der internationalen Einkunftsabgrenzung im Lichte globaler Unternehmensstrategien, in: Klein, Franz/Stihl, Hans Peter/Wassermeyer, Franz

(Eds.), Unternehmen—Steuern: Festschrift für Hans Flick zum 70. Geburtstag, Cologne 1997, pp. 857–872.

***Kleineidam*, Hans-Jochen**: Gewinnermittlung bei Auslandsbetriebsstätten (Teil II), Internationales Steuerrecht 1993, pp. 395–400.

***Kleineidam*, Hans-Jochen**: Gewinnermittlung bei Auslandsbetriebsstätten (Teil I), Internationales Steuerrecht 1993, pp. 349–352.

***Kluge*, Volker**: Zur unmittelbaren Anwendung von DBA-Vorschriften bei der Gewinnermittlung, Steuer und Wirtschaft 1975, pp. 294–305.

***Knödler*, Christoph**: Besteuerung von Ertrag und Umsatz im Electronic Commerce, Wiesbaden 2004.

***Kobetsky*, Michael**: International Taxation of Permanent Establishments: Principles and Policy, Cambridge 2011.

***Koenig*, Ulrich**: § 12 Betriebsstätte, in: Koenig, Ulrich (Ed.), Abgabenordnung: §§ 1 bis 368—Kommentar, 3rd Edition, Munich 2014, pp. 99–110.

***Kofler*, Georg**: Article 9 OECD Model Tax Convention: Associated Enterprises, in: Reimer, Ekkehard/Rust, Alexander (Eds.), Klaus Vogel on Double Taxation Conventions, 4th Edition, Alphen aan den Rijn 2015, pp. 577–704.

***Kofler*, Georg/*Mayr*, Gunter/*Schlager*, Christoph**: Digitalisierung und Betriebsstättenkonzept—Teil II: Lösungsvorschläge, Betriebs-Berater 2017, pp. 1815–1819.

***Kofler*, Georg/*Mayr*, Gunter/*Schlager*, Christoph**: Digitalisierung und Betriebsstättenkonzept—Teil I: Problemstellung und internationale Entwicklung, Betriebs-Berater 2017, pp. 1751–1757.

***Kofler*, Georg/*Mayr*, Gunter/*Schlager*, Christoph**: Taxation of the Digital Economy: „Quick Fixes" or Long-Term Solution, European Taxation 2017, pp. 523–532.

***Kolck*, Joachim Dietrich**: Der Betriebsstättenbegriff im nationalen und internationalen Steuerrecht, Münster 1974.

***Kopecek*, Valerie/*Zehetner*, Daniel**: Vergleichbarkeit von Comparables in Datenbankstudien, Transfer Pricing International 2017, p. 252.

***Kosch*, Florian**: Der OECD-Betriebsstättenbericht 2008 im Vergleich zum deutschen Recht, Internationales Steuerrecht 2010, pp. 42–45.

KPMG (Ed.): German International Taxation—Deutsches Außensteuerrecht: Statutes and Materials, Munich 2010.

***Kraft*, Gerhard**: § 1 Berichtigung von Einkünften, in Kraft, Gerhard (Ed.): Außensteuergesetz: AStG—Kommentar, 2nd Edition, Munich 2019, pp. 1–198.

***Kraft*, Gerhard**: Softwareüberlassung und Gestattung von Datenbanknutzung durch ausländische Digitalanbieter (Teil 2), Neue Wirtschafts-Briefe 2018, pp. 937–944.

***Kraft*, Gerhard**: Softwareüberlassung und Gestattung von Datenbanknutzung durch ausländische Digitalanbieter (Teil 1), Neue Wirtschafts-Briefe 2018, pp. 868–876.

***Kraft*, Gerhard/*Ditz*, Xaver/*Heider*, Christian**: Internationaler Informationsaustausch—Überblick über die Rechtsgrundlagen und aktuellen Entwicklungen, Der Betrieb 2017, pp. 2243–2253.

***Kraft*, Gerhard/*Dombrowski*, Martin**: Ein Fallstudien-gestützter Vergleich der Rechtslage vor und nach der Transformation des AOA, Die Unternehmensbesteuerung 2015, pp. 143–152.

Kraft, Gerhard/*Dombrowski*, **Martin**: Die Folgen der Einführung des AOA für den Steuerpflichtigen: Im Spannungsfeld zwischen internationaler Genese und nationaler Umsetzung, Internationale Wirtschafts-Briefe 2015, pp. 87–94.

Kraft, Gerhard/*Dombrowski*, **Martin**: Die praktische Umsetzung des „Authorized OECD Approach" vor dem Hintergrund der Betriebsstättengewinnaufteilungsverordnung, FinanzRundschau 2014, pp. 1105–1114.

Kraft, **Gerhard**/*Gebhardt*, **Ronald**: Das Postulat der Kapitalinhaberschaftsneutralität im Kontext der EuGH-Judikatur zu National Grid Indus, FinanzRundschau 2012, pp. 403–406.

Kraft, **Gerhard**/*Heider*, **Christian**: Das Country-by-Country Reporting und seine innerstaatliche Umsetzung im Rahmen des „Anti-BEPS-Umsetzungsgesetzes", Deutsches Steuerrecht 2017, pp. 1353–1361.

Kraft, **Gerhard**/*Hentschel*, **Sven**/*Apler*, **Marc**: Die Bedeutung der Gemeinsamen Konsolidierten Körperschaftsteuer-Bemessungsgrundlage für die Gewinnabgrenzung zwischen Stammhaus und Betriebsstätte, Recht der internationalen Wirtschaft 2017, pp. 473–480.

Kraft, **Gerhard**/*Hentschel*, **Sven**/*Apler*, **Marc**: Besteuerungsstrukturen von Auslieferungslagern im Kontext sich abzeichnender BEPS-Entwicklungen illustriert anhand ausgewählter Fallstudien, Die Unternehmensbesteuerung 2017, pp. 318–327.

Kramer, **Jörg-Dietrich**: Gewinnabgrenzung und Gewinnermittlung bei Verbringung von Wirtschaftsgütern zwischen Betriebsstätten im Internationalen Steuerrecht, Steuer und Wirtschaft 1991, pp. 151–164.

Kroppen, **Heinz-Klaus**: Behandlung immaterieller Wirtschaftsgüter unter BEPS, in: Lüdicke, Jürgen/Schnitger, Arne/Spengel, Christoph (Eds.), Besteuerung Internationaler Unternehmen: Festschrift für Dieter Endres zum 60. Geburtstag, Munich 2016, pp. 199–209.

Kroppen, **Heinz-Klaus**: Neues zur Betriebsstätte unter Berücksichtigung der Vorschläge der OECD vom 31.10.2014 und vom 15.5.2015, in: Lüdicke, Jürgen/Mellinghoff, Rudolf/Rödder, Thomas (Eds.), Nationale und Internationale Unternehmensbesteuerung in der Rechtsordnung: Festschrift für Dietmar Gosch zum Ausscheiden auf dem Richteramt, Munich 2016, pp. 221–233.

Kroppen, **Heinz-Klaus**: Aufteilung zwischen Stammhaus und Betriebsstätte auf Basis von Personalfunktionen?, Der Betrieb 2014, pp. 2134–2135.

Kroppen, **Heinz-Klaus**: Der „Authorized OECD Approach" zur Gewinnaufteilung zwischen Stammhaus und Betriebsstätte, in: Kessler, Wolfgang/Förster, Guido/Watrin, Christoph (Eds.), Unternehmensbesteuerung—Festschrift für Norbert Herzig zum 65. Geburtstag, Munich 2010, pp. 1071–1094.

Kroppen, **Heinz-Klaus**: Betriebsstätte—Quo vadis?, Internationale Wirtschafts-Briefe 2005, pp. 727–740.

Kroppen, **Heinz-Klaus**: Betriebsstättengewinnermittlung, Internationales Steuerrecht 2005, pp. 74–75.

Kroppen, **Heinz-Klaus**/*Dawid*, **Roman**/*Keil*, **Viktoria**: Die Zukunft der internationalen Verrechnungspreise—Vortrag im Zuge der Wolfgang Gassner Gedächnisvorlesung 2019 an der WU Wien, Transfer Pricing International 2019, pp. 98–115.

Kroppen, **Heinz-Klaus**/*Eigelshoven*, **Axel**: Verrechnungspreise im Wandel, Transfer Pricing International 2019, pp. 2–5.

Kroppen, **Heinz-Klaus**/*Rasch*, **Stephan** (Eds.): Handbuch Internationale Verrechnungspreise, loose-leaf collection, Cologne (32nd update, August 2020).

***Kroppen*, Heinz-Klaus/*Rasch*, Stephan**: Country-by-Country Reporting: Die neue Sichtweise der OECD zur Verrechnungspreisdokumentation, Internationale SteuerRundschau 2014, pp. 358–364.

***Kroppen*, Heinz-Klaus/*Rasch*, Stephan**: Zehn Jahre Aufzeichnungspflichten für Verrechnungspreise—Eine Bestandsaufnahme—Dokumentation von Verrechnungspreisen, Internationale Wirtschafts-Briefe 2013, pp. 830–845.

***Kruse*, Heinrich Wilhelm**: Die Abgabenordnung—ein perfekter Mantel? Praktische Probleme beim Wohnsitz- und Betriebsstättenbegriff, Steuer und Wirtschaft 2003, pp. 344–348.

***Kulcsár*, Tamás**: How Fiction Becomes Reality: Equal Treatment for Permanent Establishments and Resident Enterprises, in: Gutiérrez, Carlos/Perdelwitz, Andreas (Eds.), Taxation of Business Profits in the 21st Century—Selected Issues under Tax Treaties, Amsterdam 2013, pp. 231–250.

***Kumpf*, Wolfgang**: Betriebsstätte: Prinzip und Definition, in: Haarmann, Wilhelm (Ed.), Die beschränkte Steuerpflicht: aktuelle Schwerpunkte in der Diskussion: Betriebsstätte, grenzüberschreitende Betriebsaufspaltung, Diskriminierung, Treaty-Shopping, Künstler und Sportler, Zinsabschlagsteuer, Verfahrensprobleme, Cologne 1993, pp. 27–47.

***Kumpf*, Wolfgang**: Ergebnis- und Vermögenszuordnung bei Betriebsstätten, in: Herzig, Norbert/Curtius-Hartung, Rudolf/Niemann, Ursula (Eds.), Steuerberater-Jahrbuch 1988/89: Zugleich Bericht über den 40. Fachkongress der Steuerberater in Köln, 3. bis 5. Oktober 1988, Cologne 1989, pp. 399–422.

***Kumpf*, Wolfgang**: Besteuerung inländischer Betriebstätten von Steuerausländern, Cologne 1982.

***Kurzewitz*, Christina**: Aufgabe des strikten Anwendungsvorrangs der Standardmethoden zur Verrechnungspreisbestimmung?—Diskussionsentwurf zur Änderung der OECD-Verrechnungspreisleitlinien, Internationale Wirtschafts-Briefe 2010, pp. 95–106.

***Kußmaul*, Heinz/*Delarber*, Christian/*Müller*, Florian**: Betriebsstättengewinnaufteilungsverordnung-Entwurf—Ein allgemeiner Überblick, Internationales Steuerrecht 2014, pp. 466–473.

***Kußmaul*, Heinz/*Müller*, Florian**: Das sogenannte Stufenmodell zur angemessenen Fremdvergleichspreisermittlung nach § 1 Abs. 3 AStG, Der Steuerberater 2013, pp. 187–193.

***Kußmaul*, Heinz/*Ruiner*, Christoph**: Zur Umsetzung des OECD functionally separate entity approach in nationales Recht—Anmerkungen zu Art. 5 des Regierungsentwurfes eines Jahressteuergesetzes (JStG) 2013 –, Betriebs-Berater 2012, pp. 2025–2029.

***Kußmaul*, Heinz/*Ruiner*, Christoph/*Delarber*, Christian**: Leistungsbeziehungen in internationalen Einheitsunternehmen mit Blick auf die Änderung des Art. 7 OECD-MA und die geplante Änderung des § 1 AStG, Die Unternehmensbesteuerung 2011, pp. 837–845.

***Kuźniacki*, Błażej**: The Principal Purpose Test (PPT) in BEPS Action 6 and the MLI: Exploring Challenges Arising from Its Legal Implementation and Practical Application, World Tax Journal 2018, pp. 233–294.

***Lampert*, Steffen**: Doppelbesteuerung und deren Beseitigung, in: Mössner, Jörg Manfred et al. (Eds.), Steuerrecht international tätiger Unternehmen: Handbuch der Besteuerung von Auslandsaktivitäten inländischer Unternehmen und von Inlandsaktivitäten ausländischer Unternehmen, 5th Edition, Cologne 2018, pp. 130–238.

***Lang*, Joachim**: Unternehmensbesteuerung im internationalen Wettbewerb, Steuer und Wirtschaft 2011, pp. 144–158.

Lang, **Joachim**: Verfassungsrechtliche Gewährleistung des Familienexistenzminimums im Steuer- und Kindergeldrecht: Zu den Beschlüssen des Bundesverfassungsgerichts vom 29.5.1990 und vom 12.6.1990, Steuer und Wirtschaft 1990, pp. 331–348.

Lang, **Michael**: Die Auslegung des multilateralen Instruments, Steuer und Wirtschaft International 2017, pp. 11–24.

Lang, **Michael**: Art. 3 Abs. 2 OECD-MA und die Auslegung von Doppelbesteuerungsabkommen: Auslegungsgrundsätze für DBA, Internationale Wirtschafts-Briefe 2011, pp. 281–294.

Lang, **Michael**: Wer hat das Sagen im Steuerrecht?—Die Bedeutung des OECD-Steuerausschusses und seiner Working Parties, Österreichische Steuerzeitung 2006, pp. 203–210.

Lang, **Michael**/*Brugger*, **Florian**: The role of the OECD Commentary in tax treaty interpretation, Australian Tax Forum 2008, pp. 95–108.

Lappé, **Silke**/*Schmidtke*, **Richard**: Praxisrelevante Fragestellungen im Zusammenhang mit der Einführung des Country-by-Country Reportings, Internationales Steuerrecht 2015, pp. 693–697.

Lehner, **Moris**: Grundlagen, in: Vogel, Klaus/Lehner, Moris (Eds.), Doppelbesteuerungsabkommen der Bundesrepublik Deutschland auf dem Gebiet der Steuer vom Einkommen und Vermögen, 6th Edition, Munich 2015, pp. 111–296.

Lehner, **Moris**/*Reimer*, **Ekkehart**: Generalthema I: Quelle versus Ansässigkeit—Wie sind die grundlegenden Verteilungsprinzipien des Internationalen Steuerrechts austariert? Internationales Steuerrecht 2005, pp. 542–551.

Leisner-Egensperger, **Anna**: DBA-Auslegung unter Rückgriff auf nationales Recht—zu Art. 3 Abs. 2 des OECD-MA, Internationales Steuerrecht 2014, pp. 10–15.

Lewis, **Alexander**/*Athanasiou*, **Amanda**: OECD Releases PE Discussion Draft, Revised Profit Split Guidance, Tax Notes International, Vol. 86 (2016), pp. 1175–1177.

Li, **Jinyan**: Global Profit Split: An Evolutionary Approach to International Income Allocation, Canadian Tax Journal 2002, pp. 823–883.

Linn, **Alexander**: Keine Steuerabzugsverpflichtung für Aufwendungen für Online-Werbung: Replik auf Hruschka, Deutsches Steuerrecht 2019, pp. 418–422.

Linn, **Alexander**: Die US-Steuerreform und Ihre Auswirkungen auf das deutsche Unternehmensteuerrecht, Deutsches Steuerrecht 2018, pp. 321–328.

Looks, **Christian**: Aufteilung der Unternehmensgewinne zwischen Stammhaus und Betriebsstätten, in: Looks, Christian/Heinsen, Oliver (Eds.), Betriebsstättenbesteuerung: Inboundinvestitionen, Outboundinvestitionen, Steuergestaltungen, Branchenbesonderheiten, 3rd Edition, Munich 2017, pp. 247–390.

Loschelder, **Friedrich**: § 49 EStG—Besteuerung beschränkt Steuerpflichtiger, in: Weber-Grellet (Ed.), Schmidt—EStG: Einkommensteuergesetz—Kommentar, 39th Edition, Munich 2019, pp. 2312–2346.

Luckhaupt, **Hagen**: Bestimmung von Verrechnungspreisen gemäß den OECD-TPG 2010 und § 1 Abs. 3 AStG, Die Unternehmensbesteuerung 2010, pp. 646–650.

Luckhaupt, **Hagen**/*Overesch*, **Michael**/*Schreiber*, **Ulrich**: The OECD Approach to Transfer Pricing: A Critical Assessment and Proposal, in: Schön, Wolfgang/Konrad, Kai A. (Eds.), Fundamentals of International Transfer Pricing in Law and Economics, Berlin 2012, pp. 91–121.

Lüdicke, **Jürgen**: Überlegungen zur deutschen DBA-Politik, Baden-Baden 2008.

Lüdicke, **Jürgen**: Recent Commentary Changes concerning the Definition of Permanent Establishment, Bulletin—Tax Treaty Monitor 2004, pp. 190–194.

Majdowski, **Filip/*Bronzewska*, Katarzyna**: Revolutionary Changes to the Arm's Length Principle under the OECD BEPS Project: Have CFC Rules Become Redundant, Intertax 2018, pp. 210–224.

Malherbe, **Jaques/*Daenen*, Philip**: Permanent Establishments Claim Their Share of Profits: Does the Taxman Agree?, Bulletin for International Taxation 2010, pp. 359–366.

Mank, **Katharina/*Salihu*, Pajtesa**: Praktische Fragen des Country-by-Country Reportings: Erfahrungen aus dem ersten Jahr Praxis, Internationale Wirtschafts-Briefe 2017, pp. 902–911.

Mank, **Katharina/*Totzek*, Alexander**: Die globale Verrechnungspreisdokumentation nach BEPS—ein kurzer Erfahrungsbericht nach einem Jahr, Internationale Wirtschafts-Briefe 2017, pp. 922–924.

Margerie, **Sophie**: Gewinnermittlung und Gewinnabgrenzung bei Betriebsstätten: eine Analyse des AOA und seiner Umsetzung in nationales deutsches Steuerrecht, Lohmar 2016.

McLure, **Charles E. Jr.**: Replacing Separate Entity Accounting and the Arm's Length Principle with Formulary Apportionment, Bulletin for International Taxation 2002, pp. 586–599.

McLure, **Charles E. Jr.**: Alternatives to the Concept of Permanent Establishment, CESifo Forum 2000, pp. 10–16.

McLure, **Charles E. Jr.**: Source-Based Taxation and Alternatives to the concept of the Permanent Establishment, in: Canadian Tax Foundation (Ed.), World Tax Conference 2000, pp. 6:1–6:15.

Melicher, **Mathias**: The Methods for the Attribution of Profits to Permanent Establishments, in: Brugger, Florian/Plansky, Patrick (Eds.), Permanent Establishments in International and EU Tax Law, Vienna 2011, pp. 219–234.

Merkert, **Hubert**: Die steuerliche Problematik der Bauausführung als Betriebsstätte, Der Betrieb 1968, pp. 1238–1240.

Meyer-Sandberg, **Nils/*Hecht*, Arne**: Der Vertreter im nationalen und internationalen Steuerrecht, in: Lübbehüsen, Thomas/Kahle, Holger (Eds.), Brennpunkte der Besteuerung von Betriebsstätten, 2nd Edition, Herne 2019, pp. 249–322.

Mock, **Oliver**: Proposal for a Common Corporate Tax Base (CCTB): The Case for Foundational Principles, European Taxation 2019, pp. 209–218.

Mödinger, **Jörg**: Internationale Erfolgs- und Vermögensabgrenzung zwischen Stammhaus und Betriebsstätte nach der Neufassung des Art. 7 OECD-MA, Lohmar 2012.

Möller, **Ralf**: Der Begriff der Betriebsstätte im deutschen Steuerrecht, Unternehmensteuern und Bilanzen 2005, pp. 350–356.

Monsenego, **Jérôme**: May a Server Create a Permanent Establishment? Reflections on Certain Questions of Principle in Light of a Swedish Case, International Transfer Pricing Journal 2014, pp. 247–257.

Moreno, **Andrés Báez**: A Note on Some Radical Alternatives to the Existing International Corporate Tax and Their Implications for the Digital(ized) Economy, Intertax 2018, pp. 560–564.

Morse, **Susan C.**: Revisiting Global Formulary Apportionment, Virginia Tax Review 2010, pp. 593–644.

***Moser*, Till**: Die Hinzurechnungsbesteuerung nach den §§ 7–14 AStG und die Besteuerung ausländischer Familienstiftungen nach § 15 AStG: systematischer Vergleich, Gestaltungspotential und Reformüberlegungen, Lohmar 2015.

***Moser*, Till/*Hentschel*, Sven**: The Provisions of the EU Anti-Tax Avoidance Directive Regarding Controlled Foreign Company Rules: A Critical Review Based on the Experience with the German CFC Legislation, Intertax 2017, pp. 606–623.

***Mössner*, Jörg Manfred**: Neuere Entwicklungen beim Betriebsstättenbegriff, in: Kirchhof, Paul/Lehner, Moris/Raupach, Arndt/Rodi, Michael (Eds.), Staaten und Steuern, Festschrift für Klaus Vogel zum 70. Geburtstag, Heidelberg 2000, pp. 945–962.

***Müller*, Katja**: Verwirklichung von Gerechtigkeit und Entscheidungsneutralität in den Einkommen- und Körperschaftsteuersystemen der EU-Mitgliedstaaten, Lohmar 2001.

***Musgrave*, Peggy B.**: Sovereignty, Entitlement, and Cooperation in International Taxation, Brooklyn Journal of International Law 2001, pp. 1335–1356.

***Musgrave*, Peggy B.**: Interjurisdictional equity in company taxation: principles and applications to the European Union, in: Cnossen, Sijbren (Ed.), Taxing Capital Income in the European Union: Issues and Options for Reform, New York 2000, pp. 46–77.

***Musgrave*, Peggy B.**: Interjurisdictional coordination of taxes on capital income, in: Cnossen, Sijbren (Ed.), Tax Coordination in the European Community, Deventer 1987, pp. 197–225.

***Musgrave*, Peggy B.**: Principles for Dividing the State Corporate Tax Base, in: McLure, Charles E. (Ed.), The State Corporation Income Tax: Issues in Worldwide Unitary Combination, Stanford 1984, pp. 228–252.

***Musgrave*, Peggy B.**: International Tax Base Division and The Multinational Corporation, Public Finance 1972, pp. 394–413.

***Musgrave*, Peggy B.**: United States Taxation of Foreign Investment Income: Issues and Arguments, Cambridge 1969.

***Musgrave*, Richard A.**: Criteria for Foreign Tax Credit, in: Taxation and Operations Abroad, Symposium conducted by the Tax Institute, Princeton 1960, pp. 83–93.

***Musgrave*, Richard A./*Musgrave*, Peggy B.**: Public Finance in Theory and Practice, 5th Edition, New York 1989.

***Musgrave*, Richard A./*Musgrave*, Peggy B.**: Inter-Nation Equity, in: Bird, Richard M./Head, John G. (Eds.), Modern Fiscal Issues: Essays in Honor of Carl S. Shoup, Toronto 1972, pp. 63–85.

***Naumann*, Manfred/*Groß*, Bernhard**: Die Dokumentation von Verrechnungspreisen—Der OECD Bericht zu Maßnahme 13 des BEPS Action Plan, Internationales Steuerrecht 2014, pp. 792–798.

***Neumark*, Fritz**: Grundsätze gerechter und ökonomisch rationaler Steuerpolitik, Thübingen 1970.

***Nientimp*, Axel/*Ludwig*, Christoph/*Stein*, Stefan**: Die finale Betriebsstättengewinnaufteilungsverordnung, Internationale Wirtschafts-Briefe 2014, pp. 815–826.

***Nientimp*, Axel/*Stein*, Stefan/*Schwarz*, Christian/*Holinski*, Nils**: Zuordnung und Vergütung immaterieller Werte in Betriebsstättenstrukturen, Betriebs-Berater 2017, pp. 407–414.

***Nikolakakis*, Angelo/*Austry*, Stephane/*Jones*, John Avery/*Baker*, Philip/*Blessing*, Peter/*Danon*, Robert/*Goradia*, Shefali/*Hattingh*, Johann/*Inoue*, Koichi/*Luedicke*, Juergen/*Maisto*, Guglielmo/*Miyatake*, Toshio/*van Raad*, Kees/*Vann*, Richard/*Wiman*,

Bertil: Some Reflections on the Proposed Revisions to the OECD Model and Commentaries, and on the Multilateral Instrument, With Respect to Fiscally Transparent Entities, British Tax Review 2017, pp. 295–373.

***Nitikman*, Joel**: The Painter and the PE, Canadian Tax Journal 2009, pp. 213–258.

***Nouel*, Luis**: Capital Structure and Financing of Permanent Establishments, in: Gutiérrez, Carlos/Perdelwitz, Andreas (Eds.), Taxation of Business Profits in the 21st Century—Selected Issues under Tax Treaties, Amsterdam 2013, pp. 183–208.

***Nürnberg*, Philip**: "Digitalsteuer" über § 49 i.V.m. § 50a EStG?, Die Unternehmensbesteuerung 2019, pp. 219–224.

***Oestreicher*, Andreas**: Die Vorschläge der OECD zur Reform der Besteuerungsrechte und Ihre Bedeutung für multinationale Unternehmen, ifo Schnelldienst 3/2020, pp. 18–21.

***Oestreicher*, Andreas**: Konzern-Gewinnabgrenzung: Gewinnabgrenzung—Gewinnermittlung—Gewinnaufteilung, Munich 2000.

***Oestreicher*, Andreas/*Duensing*, Matthias**: Eignung von Unternehmensdatenbanken zur Bestimmung der Verrechnungspreise an deutsche Vertriebsunternehmen, Internationales Steurrecht 2005, pp. 134–144.

***Oestreicher*, Andreas/*van der Ham*, Susann/*Andresen*, Ulf**: Die Neuregelung der Betriebsstättengewinnaufteilung in zwölf Fällen—zugleich eine Stellungnahme zum Entwurf der Betriebsstättengewinnaufteilungsverordnung, Internationales Steuerrecht 2014, pp. 1–32.

***Oestreicher*, Andreas/*Vormoor*, Christoph**: Verrechnungspreisanalyse mit Hilfe von Unternehmensdatenbanken—Vergleichbarkeit und Datenlage, insert to Internationales Steuerrecht 2014, pp. 95–106.

***Olbert*, Marcel/*Spengel*, Christoph**: International Taxation in the Digital Economy: Challenge Accepted, World Tax Journal 2017, pp. 3–46.

***Oppel*, Florian**: Die neue diverted profit tax in Großbritanien—Unilaterale Alternative zu BEPS oder wahlkampfbedingter Schnellschuss?, Internationales Steuerrecht 2015, pp. 333–341.

***Parada*, Leopoldo**: The Unified Approach Under Pillar 1: An Early Analysis, Tax Notes International 2019, pp. 983–989.

***Pěchota*, František**: The Interrelation between the Attribution of Profits under Tax Treaty Law and the Realization of Profits under Domestic Law, in: Brugger, Florian/Plansky, Patrick (Eds.), Permanent Establishments in International and EU Tax Law, Vienna 2011, pp. 171–184.

Peng, Claire (Xue): The Application of the Arm's Length Principle to the Allocation of Joint Efficiencies within MNEs, International Transfer Pricing Journal 2016, pp. 378–392.

***Perdelwitz*, Andreas**: A Certain Degree of Permanence—Between Temporary and Everlasting Business Activities, in: Gutiérrez, Carlos/Perdelwitz, Andreas (Eds.), Taxation of Business Profits in the 21st Century—Selected Issues under Tax Treaties, Amsterdam 2013, pp. 27–55.

***Peter*, Markus**: Fortentwicklung des Betriebsstättenprinzips, Frankfurt am Main 2002.

***Petruzzi*, Raffaele**: Global Transfer Pricing Developments, in: Lang, Michael/Storck, Alfred/Petruzzi, Raffaele (Eds.), Transfer Pricing Developments Around the World 2017, Alphen aan den Rijn 2017, pp. 1–46.

***Petruzzi*, Raffaele**: The Arm's Length Principle: Between Legal Fiction and Economic Reality, in: Lang, Michael/Storck, Alfred/Petruzzi, Raffaele (Eds.), Transfer Pricing in a Post-BEPS World, Alphen aan den Rijn 2016, pp. 1–32.

***Petruzzi*, Raffaele/*Buriak*, Svitlana**: Addressing the Tax Challenges of the Digitalization of the Economy—A Possible Answer in the Proper Application of the Transfer Pricing Rules?, Tax Notes International, Vol. 90 (2018), pp. 91–116.

***Petruzzi*, Raffaele/*Holzinger*, Raphael/*Screpante*, Mirna Solange/*Buriak*, Svitlana/*Capristano Cardoso*, Gabriela**: The OECD "Unified Approach"—Have the Cards Been Reshuffled?, Transfer Pricing International 2019, pp. 312–323.

***Petruzzi*, Raffaele/*Peng*, Claire (Xue)**: The Profit Split Method: Insights from BEPS Follow-Ups, Transfer Pricing International 2017, pp. 168–171.

***Petruzzi*, Raffaele/*Peng*, Claire (Xue)**: The Profit Split Method: A Holistic View of BEPS in Transfer Pricing, Transfer Pricing International 2017, pp. 110–120.

***Petruzzi*, Raffaele/*Peng*, Claire (Xue)**: The Profit Split Method: Historical Evolution and BEPS Insights, Transfer Pricing International 2017, pp. 44–54.

***Pfister*, Elisabetta**: Die Besteuerung der digitalen Wirtschaft: Implikationen auf die Steuersouveränität und auf die Steuerverteilungsnormen, Bern 2019.

***Pijl*, Hans**: The Relationship Between Article 5, Paragraphs 1 and 3 of the OECD Model Convention, Intertax 2005, pp. 189–193.

***Pinkernell*, Reimar**: Internationale Steuergestaltung im Electronic Commerce, Institut Finanzen und Steuern-Schrift 494, Berlin 2014.

***Pinkernell*, Reimar**: Neue OECD-Grundsätze zu Verrechnungspreisdokumentation und Country-by-Country Reporting (Maßnahme 13 des BEPS-Aktionsplans), FinanzRundschau 2014, pp. 964–971.

***Pinkernell*, Reimar/*Ditz*, Xaver**: Betriebsstättenbegriff, Einkünftequalifikation und Gewinnabgrenzung beim Online-Vertrieb elektronischer Produkte (Teil II), FinanzRundschau 2001, pp. 1271–1279.

***Pinkernell*, Reimar/*Ditz*, Xaver**: Betriebsstättenbegriff, Einkünftequalifikation und Gewinnabgrenzung beim Online-Vertrieb elektronischer Produkte (Teil I), FinanzRundschau 2001, pp. 1193–1206.

***Pinto*, Dale**: Options to Address the Direct Tax Challenges Raised by the Digital Economy—A Critical Analysis, Canadian Tax Journal 2017, pp. 291–331.

***Pinto*, Dale**: E-Commerce and Source-Based Income Taxation, Amsterdam 2003.

***Pistone*, Pasquale/*Pinto Nogueira*, João Félix/*Andrade*, Betty/*Turina*, Alessandro**: The OECD Public Consultation Document "Secretariat Proposal for a 'Unified Approach' under Pillar One": An Assessment, Bulletin for International Taxation 2020, pp. 14–27.

***Pistone*, Pasquale/*Pinto Nogueira*, João Félix/*Andrade*, Betty**: The 2019 OECD Proposals for addressing the tax challenges of the digitalization of the economy: an assessment, International Tax Studies 2019, Issue 2 pp. 1–44.

***Plansky*, Patrick**: Die Gewinnzurechnung zu Betriebsstätten im Recht der Doppelbesteuerungsabkommen, Vienna 2010.

***Porter*, Michael**: Competitive Advantage: Creating and Sustaining Superior Performance, New York 1985.

***Portner*, Rosemarie**: Ertragsteuerliche Aspekte des E-Commerce, Institut Finanzen und Steuern-Schrift 390, Bonn 2001.

***Portner*, Rosemarie**: Steuerliche Aspekte des elektronischen Handels aus deutscher Sicht: Betriebsstättenbegründung durch einen Internet-Server/Besteuerung im Quellenstaat, Internationales Steuerrecht 1999, pp. 641–647.

***Portner*, Rosemarie**: Betriebsstätte durch grenzüberschreitende Internet-Transaktionen?—Insbesondere vor dem Hintergrund der Entscheidung des BFH vom 30.10.1996, Internationales Steuerrecht 1998, pp. 553–557.

***Puls*, Michael R.**: Der Begriff der Betriebsstätte, in: Wassermeyer, Franz/Andresen, Ulf/Ditz, Xaver (Eds.), Betriebsstätten-Handbuch—Gewinnermittlung und Besteuerung in- und ausländischer Betriebsstätten, 2nd Edition, Cologne 2018, pp. 27–119.

***Puls*, Michael R.**: Funktions- und Risikoanalyse als Ausgangspunkt der Verrechnungspreisbestimmung, in: Wassermeyer, Franz/Baumhoff, Hubertus (Eds.), Verrechnungspreise international verbundener Unternehmen, Cologne 2014, pp. 279–305.

***Puls*, Michael R.**: Die Betriebsstätte im Abgaben- und Abkommensrecht, Cologne/Berlin/Munich 2005.

***Rasch*, Stephan/*Feistle*, Anja**: OECD-Entwurf der überarbeiteten Verrechnungspreisrichtlinien, Internationale Wirtschafts-Briefe 2009, pp. 982–984.

***Rasch*, Stephan/*Mank*, Katharina/*Tomson*, Susanne**: Die finale Fassung des neuen OECD Kapitels zur Dokumentation und zum „Country-by-Country Reporting"—Neue Herausforderungen für Unternehmen, Internationales Steuerrecht 2015, pp. 424–429.

***Rasch*, Stephan/*Wenzel*, Benedikt**: Die Entstrickungsbesteuerung in der BsGaV und ihre europarechtliche Würdigung, Internationale SteuerRundschau 2015, pp. 128–135.

***Rayport*, Jeffrey/*Sviokla*, John**: Exploiting the virtual value chain, Harvard Business Review 1995, pp. 75–85.

***Rehkugler*, Heinz/*Vögele*, Alexander**: Quantitative Verfahren bei der Prüfung von Verrechnungspreisen—Perspektiven und offene Fragen, Betriebs-Berater 2002, pp. 1937–1945.

***Reimer*, Ekkehart**: Permanent Establishment in the OECD Model Tax Convention, in: Reimer, Ekkehart/Schmid, Stefan/Orell, Marianne (Eds.), Permanent Establishments: a domestic taxation, bilateral tax treaty and OECD perspectives, 6th Edition Alphen aan den Rijn 2018, pp. 3–209.

***Reimer*, Ekkehart**: Meilenstein des BEPS-Programms: Das Multilaterale Übereinkommen zur Umsetzung der DBA-relevanten Maßnahmen, Internationales Steuerrecht 2017, pp. 1–6.

***Reimer*, Ekkehart**: Article 5. Permanent Establishment, in: Reimer, Ekkehart/Rust, Alexander (Eds.): Klaus Vogel on Double Taxation Conventions, 4th Edition, Alphen aan den Rijn 2014, pp. 293–409.

***Reiser*, Hagen/*Cortez*, Benjamin**: Betriebsstättenbegriff im Wandel—Zur veränderten Bedeutung des Kriteriums der Verfügungsmacht, Internationales Steuerrecht 2013, pp. 6–15.

***Richman*, Peggy B.**: Taxation of Foreign Investment Income: An Economic Analysis, Baltimore 1963.

***Richter*, Lutz/*Heyd*, Steffen**: Neujustierung der Betriebstätten-Gewinnabgrenzung durch die Implementierung des Authorized OECD-Approach, Die Unternehmensbesteuerung 2013, pp. 418–424.

***Ritter*, Wolfgang**: Grenzüberschreitende Gewinnabgrenzung bei Betriebsstätten—Ein systematischer Versuch, in: Jahrbuch der Fachanwälte für Steuerrecht 1976/1977, Institut für Steuerrecht der Rechtsanwaltschaft e.V., Herne 1977, pp. 288–311.

***Roeder*, Achim/*Friedrich*, Jürgen**: Regelungsmängel der Betriebsstättengewinnaufteilungsverordnung, Betriebs-Berater 2015, pp. 1053–1057.

***Roin*, Julie**: Taxation without Coordination, The Journal of Legal Studies 2002, pp. 61–94.

***Rosenblat*, Alex/*Stark*, Luke**: Algorithmic Labor and Information Asymmetries: A Case Study of Uber's Drivers, International Journal of Communication 2016, pp. 3758–3784.
***Roser*, Frank**: Überführung von Wirtschaftsgütern ins Ausland—eine Grundsatzentscheidung mit vielen Fragen, Deutsches Steuerrecht 2008, pp. 2389–2397.
***Sadiq*, Kerrie**: Unitary Taxation—The Case for Global Formulary Apportionment, Bulletin for International Taxation 2001, pp. 275–286.
***Saint-Amans*, Pascal/*Russo*, Raffaele**: The BEPS Package: Promise Kept, Bulletin for International Taxation 2016, pp. 236–241.
***Sasseville*, Jacques/*Skaar*, Arvid A.** : General Report, in: International Fiscal Association, Cahiers de Droit Fiscal International—Studies on International Fiscal Law 2009, Volume 94a, Subject I: Is there a permanent establishment?, pp. 17–66.
***Schäfer*, Anne**: International Company Taxation in the Era of Information and Communication Technologies: Issues and Options for Reform, Wiesbaden 2006.
***Schaffner*, Jean**: How fixed is a permanent establishment?, Alphen aan den Rijn 2013.
***Schanz*, Deborah**: An den Details kann die weltweite Neuordnung des Steuersystems noch scheitern, ifo Schnelldienst 3/2020, pp. 14–17.
***Schaumburg*, Harald** (Ed.): Internationales Steuerrecht: Außensteuerrecht, Doppelbesteuerungsrecht, 4th Edition, Cologne 2017.
***Schaumburg*, Harald**: Grenzüberschreitende Einkünftekorrektur bei Betriebsstätten, Internationale SteuerRundschau 2013, pp. 197–228.
***Schaumburg*, Heide/*Schaumburg*, Harald**: Steuergerechtigkeit in der Zeit, Steuer und Wirtschaft 2013, pp. 61–71.
***Scheffler*, Wolfram**: Internationale betriebswirtschaftliche Steuerlehre, 3rd Edition, Munich 2009.
***Schmidt-Heß*, Ole**: Die Verhinderung der künstlichen Vermeidung einer Betriebsstätte—Der OECD-Bericht zu Maßnahme 7 des BEPS-Aktionsplans, Internationales Steuerrecht 2016, pp. 165–170.
***Schmidtke*, Richard**: Maßnahme 8 des BEPS-Aktionsplans—Der Fremdvergleichsgrundsatz und BEPS, Internationales Steuerrecht 2015, pp. 120–126.
***Schmitz*, R. C. Albert**: Kommentar zum internationalen Steuerrecht der Bundesrepublik Deutschland, Düsseldorf 1957.
***Schneider*, Dieter**: Leistungsfähigkeitsprinzip und Abzug von der Bemessungsgrundlage, Steuer und Wirtschaft 1984, pp. 356–367.
***Schnitger*, Arne**: Änderungen des § 1 AStG und Umsetzung des AOA durch das JStG 2013, Internationales Steuerrecht 2012, pp. 633–645.
***Schnitger*, Arne/*Bildstein*, Christoph**: Praxisfragen der Betriebsstättenbesteuerung, Die Unternehmensbesteuerung 2008, pp. 444–451.
***Schnorberger*, Stephan**: Verrechnungspreis-Dokumentation und StVergAbG—Offene Fragen und Probleme, Der Betrieb 2003, pp. 1241–1247.
***Schön*, Wolfgang**: Die neue Weltsteuerordnung—politische Eile oder konzeptionelle Weile?, ifo Schnelldienst 3/2020, pp. 26–29.
***Schön*, Wolfgang**: One Answer to Why and How to Tax the Digitalized Economy, Intertax 2019, pp. 1003–1022.
***Schön*, Wolfgang**: Seminar F (IFA/OECD): Internationale Besteuerung der digitalisierten Wirtschaft, Internationales Steuerrecht 2019, pp. 647–650.

***Schön*, Wolfgang**: Ten Questions about Why and How to Tax the Digitalized Economy, Bulletin for International Taxation 2018, pp. 278–292.
***Schön*, Wolfgang**: Transfer Pricing Issues of BEPS in the Light of EU Law, British Tax Review 2015, pp. 417–428.
***Schön*, Wolfgang**: Neutrality and Territoriality—Competing or Converging Concepts in European Tax Law?, Bulletin for International Taxation 2015, pp. 271–293.
***Schön*, Wolfgang**: Konzerninterne Risikoallokation und internationales Steuerrecht, Steuer und Wirtschaft 2015, pp. 69–89.
***Schön*, Wolfgang**: International Taxation of Risk, Bulletin for International Taxation 2014, pp. 280—294.
***Schön*, Wolfgang**: Zur Zukunft des Internationalen Steuerrechts, Steuer und Wirtschaft 2012, pp. 213–224.
***Schön*, Wolfgang**: International Tax Coordination for a Second-Best World (Part I), World Tax Journal 2009, pp. 67–114.
***Schön*, Wolfgang**: Legal fictions, profit attribution, CCCTB and European tax law, in: Maisto, Guglielmo (Ed.): International and EC Tax Aspects of Groups and Companies, Amsterdam 2008, pp. 542–546.
***Schön*, Wolfgang**: Attribution of Profits to PEs and the OECD 2006 Report, Tax Notes International, Vol. 46 (2007), pp. 1059–1072.
***Schön*, Wolfgang**: Gewinnabgrenzung bei Betriebsstätten, in: Lüdicke, Jürgen (Ed.), Besteuerung von Unternehmen im Wandel: internationale Umwandlungen, Funktionsverlagerungen, Betriebsstätten, Cologne 2007, pp. 71–113.
***Schönfeld*, Jens/*Häck*, Nils/*Ellenrieder*, Nils**: Systematik der Doppelbesteuerungsabkommen in: Schönfeld, Jens/Ditz, Xaver (Eds.), Doppelbesteuerungsabkommen—Kommentar, 2nd Edition, Cologne 2019, pp. 1–90.
***Schönfeld*, Jens/*Zinowsky*, Tim/*Rieck*, Jan**: Die US-Steuerreform—Überblick über die wichtigsten Neuregelungen für Unternehmen, Internationales Steuerrecht 2018, pp. 127–134.
***Schoppe*, Christian/*Popat*, Neeraj:** Lagerung, Einkauf und Ausstellung als Betriebsstätten ab 2017, Betriebs-Berater 2016, pp. 1113–1118.
***Schoppe*, Christian/*Reichel*, Carolin**: Vertreterbetriebsstätten ab 2017, Betriebs-Berater 2016, pp. 1245–1252.
***Schoueri*, Luis Eduardo**: Arm's Length: Beyond the Guidelines of the OECD, Bulletin for International Taxation 2015, pp. 690–716.
***Schreiber*, Ulrich**: Sales-Based Apportionment of Profits, Bulletin for International Taxation 2018, pp. 259–272.
***Schreiber*, Ulrich**: Besteuerung der Unternehmen: Eine Einführung in Steuerrecht und Steuerwirkung, 4th Edition, Berlin 2017.
***Schreiber*, Ulrich**: Evaluating the Common Consolidated Corporate Tax Base, in: Schön, Wolfgang/Schreiber, Ulrich/Spengel, Christoph (Eds.), A Common Consolidated Corporate Tax Base for Europe, Berlin 2008, pp. 113–127.
***Schreiber*, Ulrich**: Unternehmensbesteuerung im Binnenmarkt. Angleichung der Gewinnermittlung und des Satzes der Körperschaftsteuer?, Steuer und Wirtschaft 2004, pp. 212–226.
***Schreiber*, Ulrich/*Fell*, Lisa Maria**: International Profit Allocation, Intangibles and Sales-Based Transactional Profit Split, World Tax Journal 2017, pp. 99–115.

Schreiber, **Ulrich**/*Greil*, **Stefan**: Das „Anti-BEPS-Umsetzungsgesetz", Der Betrieb 2017, pp. 10–18.

Schuch, **Josef**: Die Anti-Fragmentierungs-Regel des BEPS-Aktionspunktes 7 und ihre mögliche Auswirkung für die Substanzbeurteilung von internationalen Holdingstrukturen, Steuer und Wirtschaft International 2017, pp. 654–659.

Schwarz, **Bernhard**/*Pahlke*, **Armin** (Eds.), AO/FGO—Kommentar zur Abgabenordnung, Finanzgerichtsordnung, loose-leave collection, Freiburg (198th update, October 2020).

Sennewald, **Daniel**/*Geberth*, **Georg**: BMF veröffentlicht Verwaltungsgrundsätze zur Betriebsstättengewinnaufteilung, Der Betrieb 2017, pp. 31–33.

Shaw, **Jonathan**/*Slemrod*, **Joel**/*Whiting*, **John**: Administration and Compliance, in: Mirrlees, James/Adam, Stuart/Besley, Timothy/Blundell, Richard/Bond, Stephen/Chote, Robert/Gammie, Malcolm/Johnson, Paul/Myles, Gareth/Poterba, James (Eds.), Dimensions of Tax Design: The Mirrlees Review, Oxford 2010, pp. 1100–1162.

Sieker, **Klaus**: Betriebsstättengewinn und Fremdvergleichsgrundsatz, Der Betrieb 1996, pp. 110–113.

Silberztein, **Caroline**/*Naourès*, **Océane Le**: Country-by-Country Reporting: Handbook on Effective Tax Risk Assessment, International Transfer Pricing Journal 2018, pp. 3–10.

Skaar, **Arvid Aage**: Permanent Establishment—Erosion of a Tax Treaty Principle, 2nd Edition, Deventer/Boston 2020.

Slemrod, **Joel B.**: Which is the Simplest Tax System of Them All?, in: Aaron, Henry Jacob/Gale, William G. (Eds.), Economic Effects of Fundamental Tax Reform, Washington D.C. 1996, pp. 355–391.

Smith, **Adam**: An Inquiry into the Nature and Causes of the Wealth of the Nations, Oxford 1976.

Sokolov, **Timur**: The History of Article 5 OECD Model Convention, in: Brugger, Florian/Plansky, Patrick (Eds.), Permanent Establishments in International and EU Tax Law, Vienna 2011, pp. 13–29.

Spengel, **Christoph**: Internationale Unternehmensbesteuerung in der Europäischen Union: Steuerwirkungsanalyse, Empirische Befunde, Reformüberlegungen, Düsseldorf 2003.

Spinosa, **Lisa**/*Chand*, **Vikram**: A Long-Term Solution for Taxing Digitalized Business Models: Should the Permanent Establishment Definition Be Modified to Resolve the Issue or Should the Focus Be on a Shared Taxing Rights Mechanism?, Intertax 2018, pp. 476–494.

Stabell, **Charles B.**/*Fjeldstad*, **Øystein D.**: Configuring Value for Competitive Advantage: On Chains, Shops, and Networks, Strategic Management Journal 1998, pp. 413–437.

Stähli, **Lukas**: The Use of the Profit Split Method in Highly Integrated Transactions, International Transfer Pricing Journal 2018, pp. 280–288.

Steimel, **Frank**: Seminar A: Das OECD-Musterabkommen—2000 und darüber hinaus: Electronic Commerce und die Abkommensentwicklung in die New Economy, Internationales Steuerrecht 2000, pp. 490–499.

Stein, **Stefan**/*Schwarz*, **Christian**/*Holinski*, **Nils**: Funktionales Eigentum und Wertschöpfungsbeitragsanalysen: Steuerliche Erfolgsermittlung bei immateriellen Werten mithilfe betriebswirtschaftlicher Konzepte, Deutsches Steuerrecht 2017, pp. 118–125.

Storck, **Alfred**: Ausländische Betriebsstätten im Ertrag- und Vermögensteuerrecht, Frankfurt 1980.

***Storck*, Alfred/*Mechtler*, Lukas**: Permanent Establishments: Proposals Related to Article 5(3) and (4) of the OECD Model Convention, in: Lang, Michael/Pistone, Pasquale/Rust, Alexander/Schuch, Josef/Staringer, Claus/Storck, Alfred (Eds.), Base Erosion and Profit Shifting (BEPS): The Proposals to Revise the OECD Model Convention, Vienna 2016, pp. 51–82.

***Storck*, Alfred/*Petruzzi*, Raffaele**: Permanent Establishments: Proposals Related to Agency Permanent Establishments—Article 5(5) and (6) of the OECD Model Convention, in: Lang, Michael/Pistone, Pasquale/Rust, Alexander/Schuch, Josef/Staringer, Claus (Eds.), Base Erosion and Profit Shifting (BEPS): The Proposals to Revise the OECD Model Convention, Vienna 2016, pp. 83–106.

***Strothenke*,Stephan/*Holtrichter*, Thore**: Zuordnungsregeln im Entwurf einer Betriebsstättengewinnaufteilungsverordnung (BsGaV), Steuer- und Bilanzpraxis 2013, pp. 730–735.

***Strunk*, Günther**: OECD-Stellungnahme: Internet-Server als Betriebsstätte, Internationale Wirtschafts-Briefe 2001, pp. 151–152.

***Strunk*, Günther**: Ist es wirklich wichtig, ob der Internet-Server eine Betriebsstätte begründet?—Zugleich eine Ergänzung zum Beitrag von Holler und Heerspink, Betriebs-Berater 1998, pp. 1824–1826.

***Thiele*, Philipp J./*König*, Isabelle**: Die steuerliche Behandlung von Serverbetriebsstätten—Wertungen im Lichte der BEPS-Aktionspunkte 1 und 7, Internationale Wirtschafts-Briefe 2018, pp. 376–385.

***Thies*, Angelika**: chapter 10: Germany, in: Heimert, Michael A./Michaelson, T.J./Duff & Phelps (Eds.), Guide to International Transfer Pricing: Law, Tax Planning and Compliance Strategies, 8th Edition, Alphen aan den Rijn 2018, pp. 501–550.

***Tipke*, Klaus**: Die Steuerrechtsordnung: Steuerrechtfertigungstheorie, Anwendung auf alle Steuerarten, sachgerechtes Steuersystem, Vol. II, 2nd Edition, Cologne 2003.

***Tipke*, Klaus**: Die Steuerrechtsordnung: Wissenschaftsorganisatorische, systematische und grundrechtliche-rechtsstaatliche Grundlagen, Vol. I, 2nd Edition, Cologne 2000.

***Tipke*, Klaus**: Über "richtiges Steuerrecht", Steuer und Wirtschaft 1988, pp. 262–282.

***Tipke*, Klaus/*Kruse*, Heinrich Wilhelm** (Eds.): Abgabenordnung—Finanzgerichtsordnung: Kommentar, loose-leaf collection, Cologne (163rd update, October 2020).

***Tracana*, Dinis**: The Impact of BEPS Actions 8–10 on Comparability Analysis in the Context of Attribution of Profits to Permanent Establishments, Intertax 2017, pp. 411–416.

***Treidler*, Oliver**: Profit-Split Method Remains the Ugly Duckling of Transfer Pricing, Tax Notes International, Vol. 84 (2016), pp. 277–279.

***Treidler*, Oliver/*Grothe*, Bettina/*Paprotny*, Aleksandra**: Comparability—Moving to the Top Of the EU's Transfer Pricing Agenda, Tax Notes International, Vol. 85 (2017), pp. 921–925.

***Tresch*, Richard W.**: Public Finance: A Normative Theory, 3rd Edition, London/San Diego/Waltham/Oxford 2015.

***Truffer*, Ildiko**: The Attribution of Capital to Permanent Establishments, in: Brugger, Florian/Plansky, Patrick (Eds.), Permanent Establishments in International and EU Tax Law, Vienna 2011, pp. 203–217.

***Turina*, Alessandro**: Which 'Source Taxation' for the Digital Economy? Intertax 2018, pp. 495–519.

***Uckmar*, Victor**: Double Taxation Conventions, in: Amatucci, Andreas (Ed.), International Tax Law, 2nd Edition, Alphen aan den Rijn 2012, pp. 161–193.

Valta, **Matthias**: Die deutsche Verhandlungsgrundlage für Doppelbesteuerungsabkommen und Entwicklungsländer, Internationale SteuerRundschau 2013, pp. 186–190.

van der Ham, **Susann/*Retzer*, Daniel**: BMF, Schreiben v. 17.12.2019 zu Betriebsstätten ohne Personalfunktionen, Internationale Wirtschafts-Briefe 2020, pp. 86–92

van Raad, **Kees**: Deemed Expenses of a Permanent Establishment under Article 7 of the OECD Model, Intertax 2000, pp. 162–167.

van Wanrooij, **Josine S.A.**: Comments on the Proposed Article 7 of the OECD Model Convention, Intertax 2009, pp. 298–306.

Vogel, **Klaus**: Über „Besteuerungsrechte" und über das Leistungsfähigkeitsprinzip im Internationalen Steuerrecht, in: Kirchhof, Paul/Offenhaus, Klaus/Schöberle, Horst (Eds.), Steuerrecht, Verfassungsrecht, Finanzpolitik—Festschrift für Franz Klein, Cologne 1994, pp. 361–376.

Vogel, **Klaus**: Worldwide vs. source taxation of income—A review and re-evaluation of arguments (Part III), Intertax 1988, pp. 393–402.

Vogel, **Klaus**: Worldwide vs. source taxation of income—A review and re-evaluation of arguments (Part II), Intertax 1988, pp. 310–320.

Vogel, **Klaus**: Worldwide vs. source taxation of income—A review and re-evaluation of arguments (Part I), Intertax 1988, pp. 216–229.

Vogel, **Klaus**: Die Besteuerung von Auslandseinkünften, in: Vogel, Klaus (Ed.), Grundfragen des Internationalen Steuerrechts, DStJG 8, Cologne 1985, pp. 3–31.

Vogel, **Klaus/*Rust*, Alexander**: Introduction, in: Reimer, Ekkehart/Rust, Alexander (Eds.), Klaus Vogel on Double Taxation Conventions, 4th Edition, Alphen aan den Rijn 2015, pp. 1–72.

Wagemann, **Thorsten**: Verschärfungen des Betriebsstättenbegriffs nach OECD-MA: Der finale BEPS Aktionsplan 7, Internationale Wirtschafts-Briefe 2016, pp. 14–24.

Wagh, **Sagar**: The Taxation of Digital Transactions in India: The New Equalization Levy, Bulletin for International Taxation 2016, pp. 538–552.

Wagner, **Franz W.**: Kann die Besteuerung vereinfacht werden, wenn die Rechnungslegung komplexer wird?, Betriebswirtschaftliche Forschung und Praxis 2005, pp. 528–545.

Wagner, **Franz W.**: Steuervereinfachung und Entscheidungsneutralität—konkurrierende oder komplementäre Leitbilder für Steuerreformen?, Steuer und Wirtschaft 2005, pp. 93–108.

Wagner, **Franz W.**: Neutralität und Gleichmäßigkeit als ökonomische und rechtliche Kriterien steuerlicher Normkritik, Steuer und Wirtschaft 1992, pp. 2–13.

Waldhoff, **Christian/*Grefrath*, Holger**: Normenklarheit und Bestimmtheit der Vorschriften über die Hinzurechnungsbesteuerung als Problem des Steuervollzugs, Internationales Steuerrecht 2013, pp. 477–484.

Waltrich, **Andreas**: Cross-Border Taxation of Permanent Establishments: An International Comparison, Alphen aan den Rijn 2016.

Wang, **Huili/*Schreiber*, Mathias**: Country Perspectives—Germany, in: Reimer, Ekkehart/Schmid, Stefan/Orell, Marianne (Eds.), Permanent Establishments: A Domestic Taxation, Bilateral Tax Treaty and OECD Perspective, 6th Edition, Alphen aan den Rijn 2018, pp. 1–30.

Wassermeyer, **Franz**: Die abkommensrechtliche Aufteilung von Unternehmensgewinnen zwischen den beteiligten Vertragsstaaten, Internationales Steuerrecht 2012, pp. 277–282.

Wassermeyer, **Franz**: Kritische Anmerkungen zur Vertreterbetriebsstätte, Steuer und Wirtschaft International 2010, pp. 505–512.

***Wassermeyer*, Franz**: Modernes Gesetzgebungsniveau am Beispiel des Entwurfs zu § 1 AStG, Der Betrieb 2007, pp. 535–539.

***Wassermeyer*, Franz**: Diskriminierungsfreie Betriebsstättengewinnermittlung, Internationales Steuerrecht 2004, pp. 733–735.

***Wassermeyer*, Franz**: Dokumentationspflichten bei internationalen Verrechnungspreisen—Zum zweiten Entwurf einer Verordnung zu § 90 Abs. 3 AO, Der Betrieb 2003, pp. 1535–1539.

***Wassermeyer*, Franz**: Die Betriebsstätte—ein in vieler Hinsicht unbekanntes Wesen, in: Drenseck, Walter/Seer, Roman (Eds.), Festschrift für Heinrich Wilhelm Kruse zum 70. Geburtstag, Cologne 2001, pp. 589–603.

***Wassermeyer*, Franz**: Die Auslegung von Doppelbesteuerungsabkommen durch den Bundesfinanzhof, Steuer und Wirtschaft 1990, pp. 404–412.

***Wassermeyer*, Franz/*Kaeser*, Christian/*Schwenke*, Michael/*Drüen*, Klaus-Dieter** (Eds.): Doppelbesteuerung: Kommentar zu allen deutschen Doppelbesteuerungsabkommen, loose-leaf collection, Munich (151st update, October 2020).

***Wehnert*, Oliver**: Recent Developments on Transfer Pricing Documentation and Country-by-Country Reporting, in: Lang, Michael/Storck, Alfred/Petruzzi, Raffaele (Eds.), Transfer Pricing Developments Around the World 2017, Alphen aan den Rijn 2018, pp. 141–158.

***Weisbach*, David A.** : Formalism in the Tax Law, The University of Chicago Law Review 1999, pp. 860–886.

***Wellisch*, Dietmar**: Internationale Verrechnungspreismethoden, Neutralität und die Gewinne multinationaler Unternehmen, Jahrbücher für Nationalökonomie und Statistik 2003, pp. 332–359.

***Wendt*, Carsten**: A Common Tax Base for Multinational Enterprises in the European Union, Wiesbaden 2009.

***Wichmann*, Michael**: Aufteilung der Einkünfte und des Vermögens auf rechtlich selbstständige und unselbstständige Unternehmensteile, in: Fischer, Lutz/Strunk, Günther (Eds.), Steuerliche Aspekte des Electronic Commerce, Cologne 1998, pp. 65–80.

***Willmanns*, Jobst**: Verrechnungspreisdokumentation—Quo Vadis, in: Oestreicher, Andreas (Ed.), BEPS konkret und weitere Entwicklungen im deutschen Steuerrecht, Herne 2018, pp. 7–22.

***Williams*, Robert Lee**: Fundamentals of Permanent Establishments, The Hague 2014.

***Wittendorff*, Jens**: BEPS Actions 8–10: Birth of a New Arm's-Length Principle, Tax Notes International, Vol. 81 (2016), pp. 331–358.

***Wittendorff*, Jens**: Transfer Pricing and the Arm's Length Principle in International Tax Law, Alphen aan den Rijn 2010.

***Wuermli*, Richard J.**: Begründet der Kommissionär bald eine Betriebsstätte?, in: Beck'sche Steuerkommentare et al. (Eds.), Doppelbesteuerung—Zum 75. Geburtstag von Franz Wassermeyer: 75 Beiträge zum Recht der DBA—Eine Festgabe, Munich 2015, pp. 171–178.

***Wulf*, Martin**: Änderungen im Außensteuerrecht und Sonderregelungen zu Funktionsverlagerungen nach dem Unternehmensteuerreformgesetz 2008, Der Betrieb 2007, pp. 2280–2285.

***Ziehr*, Ulrich**: Einkünftezurechnung im internationalen Einheitsunternehmen: Veranlassungsprinzip und Selbstständigkeitsfiktion als Maßstäbe der Einkünftezurechnung zu Stammhaus und Betriebsstätte, Lohmar 2008.

***Zuber*, Barbara**: Anknüpfungsmerkmale und Reichweite der internationalen Besteuerung: eine normative Analyse unter Berücksichtigung der Personensteuern in der BRD und in den USA, Hamburg 1991.

The manufacturer's authorised representative in the EU is Springer Nature Customer Service Centre GmbH, Europaplatz 3, 69115 Heidelberg, Germany. If you have any concerns regarding our products, please contact ProductSafety@springernature.com

Printed and bound by CPI Group (UK) Ltd, Croydon, CR0 4YY
02/10/2026
02227135-0002